Brittany
Normandy

THE ROUGH GUIDE

There are more than one hundred Rough Guide titles
covering destinations from Amsterdam to Zimbabwe

Forthcoming titles include

Dominican Republic • Jerusalem • Laos • Melbourne • Sydney

Rough Guide Reference Series

Classical Music • European Football • The Internet • Jazz
Opera • Reggae • Rock Music • World Music

Rough Guide Phrasebooks

Czech • Egyptian Arabic • French • German • Greek • Hindi & Urdu
Hungarian • Indonesian • Italian • Japanese • Mandarin Chinese
Mexican Spanish • Polish • Portuguese • Russian • Spanish
Swahili • Thai • Turkish • Vietnamese

Rough Guides on the Internet
www.roughguides.com

ROUGH GUIDE CREDITS

Text editors: Olivia Eccleshall
Series editor: Mark Ellingham
Editorial: Martin Dunford, Jonathan Buckley, Jo Mead, Amanda Tomlin, Kate Berens, Ann-Marie Shaw, Paul Gray, Chris Schüler, Helena Smith, Judith Bamber, Kieran Falconer, Orla Duane, Ruth Blackmore, Sophie Martin, Geoff Howard, Claire Saunders, Anna Sutton, Gavin Thomas, Alexander Mark Rogers (UK); Andrew Rosenberg (US)
Production: Susanne Hillen, Andy Hilliard, Link Hall, Helen Ostick, James Morris, Julia Bovis, Michelle Draycott, Cathy McElhinney

Cartography: Melissa Flack, Maxine Burke, Nichola Goodliffe, Ed Wright
Picture research: Eleanor Hill, Louise Boulton
Online editors: Alan Spicer, Kate Hands
Finance: John Fisher, Katy Miesiaczek
Marketing & Publicity: Richard Trillo, Simon Carloss, Niki Smith, David Wearn (UK); Jean-Marie Kelly (US)
Administration: Tania Hummel, Alexander Mark Rogers, Charlotte Marriott

....

ACKNOWLEDGEMENTS

Thanks above all to Samantha Cook, for her constant support and encouragement, and many happy times in London and New Orleans. I also want to thank my parents and family, plus Rob and Jules, John and Nat, and Olivia Eccleshall for her great work, and great patience, in the office.

I owe a great deal to the many people who have contributed to this book over the years, especially Kate Baillie, who made extensive contributions to the original manuscript back in 1986; Mark Ellingham, who had the whole idea in the first place; and Susanne Hillen, who has been masterminding production since we were but children. For the production of this edition, thanks to Helen Ostick for typesetting, Maxine Burke and Jenny Booth for maps, Eleanor Hill for picture research, and Nikky Twyman for proofreading.

....

PUBLISHING INFORMATION

This sixth edition published June 1999 by Rough Guides Ltd, 62–70 Shorts Gardens, London WC2H 9AB
Distributed by the Penguin Group:
Penguin Books Ltd, 27 Wrights Lane, London W8 5TZ
Penguin Books USA Inc., 375 Hudson Street, New York 10014, USA
Penguin Books Australia Ltd, 487 Maroondah Highway, PO Box 257, Ringwood, Victoria 3134, Australia
Penguin Books Canada Ltd, 10 Alcorn Avenue, Toronto, Ontario, Canada M4V 1E4
Penguin Books (NZ) Ltd, 182–190 Wairau Road, Auckland 10, New Zealand
Typeset in Linotron Univers and Century Old Style to an original design by Andrew Oliver.
Printed in England by Clays Ltd, St Ives PLC
Illustrations in Part One and Part Three by Edward Briant

....

Brittany &
Normandy

THE ROUGH GUIDE

written and researched by

Greg Ward

THE ROUGH GUIDES

THE ROUGH GUIDES

TRAVEL GUIDES • PHRASEBOOKS • MUSIC AND REFERENCE GUIDES

 We set out to do something different when the first Rough Guide was published in 1982. Mark Ellingham, just out of university, was travelling in Greece. He brought along the popular guides of the day, but found they were all lacking in some way. They were either strong on ruins and museums but went on for pages without mentioning a beach or taverna. Or they were so conscious of the need to save money that they lost sight of Greece's cultural and historical significance. Also, none of the books told him anything about Greece's contemporary life – its politics, its culture, its people, and how they lived.

So, with no job in prospect, Mark decided to write his own guidebook, one which aimed to provide practical information that was second to none, detailing the best beaches and the hottest clubs and restaurants, while also giving hard-hitting accounts of every sight, both famous and obscure, and providing up-to-the-minute information on contemporary culture. It was a guide that encouraged independent travellers to find the best of Greece, and was a great success, getting shortlisted for the Thomas Cook travel guide award,

and encouraging Mark, along with three friends, to expand the series.

The Rough Guide list grew rapidly and the letters flooded in, indicating a much broader readership than had been anticipated, but one which uniformly appreciated the Rough Guide mix of practical detail and humour, irreverence and enthusiasm. Things haven't changed. The same four friends who began the series are still the caretakers of the Rough Guide mission today: to provide the most reliable, up-to-date and entertaining information to independent-minded travellers of all ages, on all budgets.

We now publish more than 100 titles and have offices in London and New York. The travel guides are written and researched by a dedicated team of more than 100 authors, based in Britain, Europe, the USA and Australia. We have also created a unique series of phrasebooks to accompany the travel series, along with an acclaimed series of music guides, and a best-selling pocket guide to the Internet and World Wide Web. We also publish comprehensive travel information on our Web site:

www.roughguides.com

HELP US UPDATE

We've gone to a lot of effort to ensure that this new edition of *The Rough Guide to Brittany & Normandy* is accurate and up to date. However, things change – places get "discovered", opening hours are notoriously fickle, restaurants and rooms raise prices or lower standards, extra buses are laid on or off. If you feel we've got it wrong or left something out, we'd like to know, and if you can remember the address, the price, the time, the phone number, so much the better.

We'll credit all contributions, and send a copy of the next edition (or any other Rough Guide if you prefer) for the best letters. Please mark letters: "Rough Guide Brittany & Normandy Update" and send to:
Rough Guides, 62–70 Shorts Gardens, London WC2H 9AB or Rough Guides, 375 Hudson St, 9th floor, New York, NY 10014.
Or send email to: mail@roughguides.co.uk
Online updates about this book can be found on Rough Guides' Web site at www.roughguides.com

THE AUTHOR

Greg Ward first visited Brittany as a seven-year-old, and twenty years later managed to convince Mark Ellingham that this experience made him the ideal choice to write the *Rough Guide to Brittany & Normandy*. He continues to visit the region several times per year, touring sometimes by car and sometimes, with increasing levels of both difficulty and self-satisfaction, by bicycle. After working for several years in the Rough Guides offices as both editor and DTP specialist, he reverted in 1994 to a life of full-time writing. He has written six other Rough Guides, including the USA, the Southwest USA, and Hawaii, and contributed to several more, including China, Mexico and Spain, and has also worked for several other travel publishers.

READERS' LETTERS

Readers whose letters have provided valuable and much-appreciated input to this sixth edition include Wendy Alderton, Robert Boutwood, Lucy Briggs, Dr A R Brown, Deborah Burke, Roger Clarke, J Davies, Ruth Deyermond, John and Brenda Field, Joe and Margaret Anne Fitzgerald, J D Hill, Peter T Holgate, Tim Howe, Donald McEwan, Anna Murray, M S T Price, Harriet Smith, Charles Stuart, Commander A T Welch, Matthew Zawadski, and Dr David McDonald, whose experiences in Questembert so uncannily matched my own.

CONTENTS

Introduction x

PART THREE   BRITTANY   183

PART FOUR CONTEXTS   353

LIST OF MAPS

MAP SYMBOLS

▨▨▨	Motorway	♜	Castle
═══	Road	♦	Point of interest
───	Minor road	⚠	Campsite
▬▬▬	Pedestrianized street	◓	Cave
⊞⊞⊞	Steps	▲	Peak
-----	Path	⵶	Lighthouse
────	Wall	⸺	Marshland
━●━	Railway	ⓘ	Tourist Office
─ ─ ─	Ferry route	⊠	Post Office
⌇⌇⌇	Waterway	▰	Building
━ ━ ━	Chapter division boundary	✛	Church
▰-▰-▰	Regional border	†₊†	Cemetery
▸━◂	Gate	▨	Park
✈	Airport	⠂⠂⠂	Beach

INTRODUCTION

Of all the strongly individual components of the French nation, **Brittany** and **Normandy** are among the most distinct. That sense of a separate identity – in cultures and peoples, landscapes and histories – is undoubtedly a major aspect of their appeal to visitors. A journey through the two regions enables you to experience much of the best that France has to offer: wild coast and sheltered white-sand beaches; sparse heathland and dense forests; medieval ports and evidence of the prehistoric past; and, every bit as important, abundant seafood and (especially in Normandy) a compelling and exuberant cuisine.

Brittany

Brittany is the more popular of the two regions, with both French and foreign tourists. Its attractions lie most obviously along the **coast**, which, speckled with offshore islands and islets, makes up over a third of the seaboard of France. In parts of the north, and in the western region of Finistère, the shoreline can be nothing but rocks and cliffs, its exposed headlands buffeted by the full force of the Atlantic and swept by dangerous currents. But elsewhere, especially in the sheltered southern resorts around the Morbihan and La Baule, it is caressed by the gentlest of seas, the sands rambling for kilometres or nestled into coves between steep cliffs.

Thanks to the sheer extent of the Breton coastline, it's always possible to find a spot where you can walk alone with the elements. Although in high season it can be hard to find solitude on the sandy beaches or in the small bays with their sun-struck swimmers, there could never be enough visitors to cover all the twists of Finistère's coast. As well as exploring the mainland resorts and seaside villages – each of which, from ports the size of **St-Malo** or **Vannes** down to little-known harbour communities such as Erquy, Le Pouldu, L'Aber-W'rach or Piriac-sur-mer, can be relied upon to offer at least one welcoming, characterful little hotel or restaurant – it's worth making the time to take in at least one of **the islands**. Boat trips out to these sea-encircled microcosms can be among the most enjoyable highlights of a trip to Brittany. The magical Île de Bréhat is just a ten-minute crossing from the north coast near Paimpol, while historic Belle-Île, to the south, is under an hour from Quiberon. Certain other islands are set aside as bird sanctuaries, while, off Finistère, the Îles d'Ouessant and Molène are as remote and strange as Orkney or the Shetland Isles.

The **Celtic** elements in Brittany are inextricably linked with its seafaring past. Anciently the land was known as *Armorica* (from the Breton for "the land of the sea", *ar-mor*), and it was from fishing and shipbuilding, along with occasional bouts of piracy and smuggling, that its people made their living. The harshness of the Breton coast and the poor communications with its interior and with "mainland" France enforced isolation. Christianity took time to establish itself, strongly but idiosyncratically, in a region where Druids survived on the Île de Sein until Roman times. Only in 1532 did the territory lose its independence and become a province of France. Even then it was a reluctant partner, treated virtually as a colony by the national government, which until well into the twentieth century felt it necessary to suppress the Breton language and traditions. In recent years there has been something of a reversal, with the **language** and **culture** being rediscovered and reasserted. If you are a Celt – Welsh, Scots or Irish – you will find shared vocabulary, and great appreciation in their use. For everyone, though, the traditions are active, accessible and enjoyable at the various Inter-Celtic **festivals**, the largest of which takes place at Lorient in early August.

Times even before the Celts are evoked by the vast wealth of **megalithic remains** scattered across Brittany. The single most famous site is Carnac, whose spectacular alignments of menhirs may have been erected as part of a prehistoric observatory. Lesser-known but equally compelling remains include the extraordinary burial tumuli on the island of Gavrinis, in the gulf of Morbihan, and at Barnenez outside Morlaix in the north. Not all such relics are found near the sea; the moors and woodlands of **inland Brittany**, too, conceal unexpected ancient treasures. This is the realm of legend, with the **forests** of Huelgoat and Paimpont in particular – left-overs from Brittany's mythic dark ages – identified with the tales of Merlin, the Fisher King and the Holy Grail. In the Little Britain of King Arthur's domain, an other-worldly element still seems entrenched in the land and people.

Normandy

Normandy has a less harsh appearance and a more mainstream – and more prosperous – history than its neighbour. It too is a seaboard province, colonized by Norsemen from Scandinavia, and colonizing in turn; first of all, in the eleventh and twelfth centuries, England, Sicily and parts of the Near East, and later on Canada. It has always had large-scale **ports**: Rouen, on the Seine, is as near as ships can get to Paris, while Dieppe, Cherbourg and Le Havre have important transatlantic trade. **Inland**, it is overwhelmingly agricultural – a wonderfully fertile belt of tranquil pastureland, where most visitors head straight for the restaurants of towns such as Vire and Conches.

The pleasures of Normandy are perhaps less intense and unique than those of Brittany. Many of its better-known areas of **seaside** are a little overdeveloped. Towards the end of the nineteenth century, the last of the Napoleons created a "Norman Riviera" around Trouville and Deauville, and a somewhat pretentious air still hangs about their elegant promenades. However, the ancient ports – **Honfleur** and **Barfleur** especially – are visual delights, and numerous seaside villages remain unspoilt by crowds or affectations. Even if you just plan to visit for a weekend break from England, delightful little towns are tucked away within 20km of each of the major Channel ports – the Cotentin peninsula around Cherbourg is one of the best, and least explored, areas – while the banks of the Seine, too, hold several idyllic resorts.

Normandy also boasts extraordinary **architectural** treasures, although only the much-restored capital, **Rouen**, has preserved a complete medieval centre. The attractions are more often single buildings than entire towns. Most famous of all is the spectacular *merveille* on the island of **Mont-St-Michel**, but there are also the monasteries at Jumièges and Caen; the cathedrals of Bayeux and Coutances; and Richard the Lionheart's castle above the Seine at Les Andelys. Bayeux can in addition offer its vivid and astonishing **Tapestry**. Many other great Norman buildings survived into this century, only to be destroyed during the Allied landings in 1944 and the subsequent **Battle of Normandy**, which has its own legacy in a series of war museums, memorials and cemeteries. These are hardly conventional sights, though as part of the fabric of the province they are moving and enlightening.

Routes

Individual **highlights** in each region are detailed in the chapter introductions throughout this book. Although hard-and-fast itineraries aren't given – much of the fun in both provinces is in rambling off on side roads – the text is structured as logically as possible in continuous routes or definable areas.

Ways to get around are set out on p.24 onwards. If you read this before you decide how to travel, consider **cycling**; both provinces are ideal, with short distances between each town and the next. Otherwise, a car is probably the best alternative. Unless you plan to stay within a limited area, public transport can be frustrating.

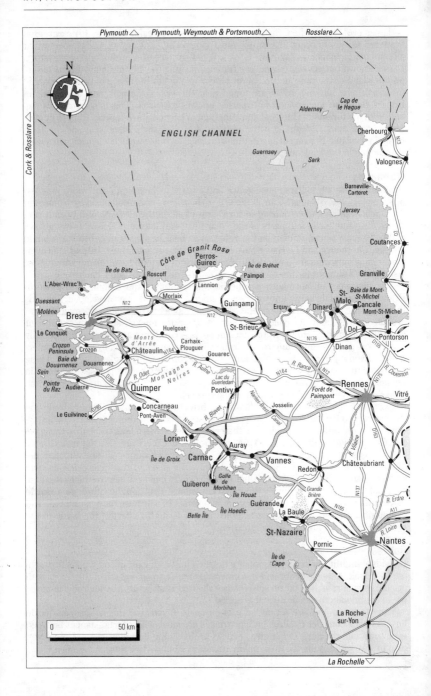

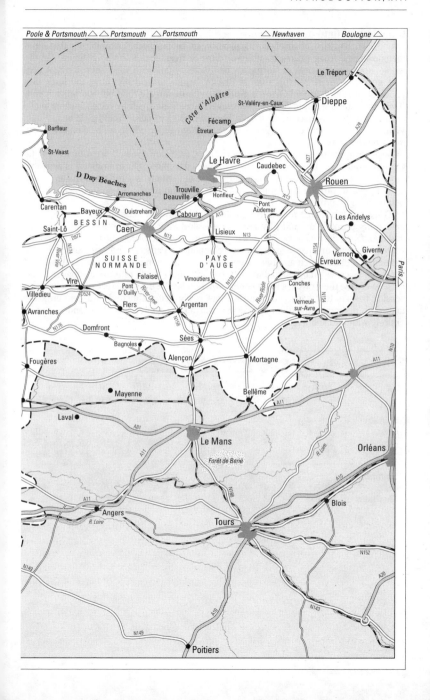

Climate and time of year

Every French town or district eagerly promotes a *"micro-climat"*, maintaining that some meteorological freak makes it milder or drier or balmier than its neighbours. On the whole, however, the bulk of Normandy and Brittany follows a fairly set pattern. A genuine **summer**, more reliable than in Britain, begins around mid-June and lasts, in a good year, through to mid-October. **Spring** and **autumn** are mild but sporadically wet. If you come for a week in April or November, it could be spoilt by rain; the rainy spells seldom last more than a couple of days, however, so a fortnight should yield better luck. **Winter** is not too severe, though in western Brittany especially it can be damp and very misty on the coast.

Sea temperatures are not Mediterranean, and any greater warmth felt in the Channel waters off the Norman coast as opposed to the south of England is probably more psychological than real. The south coast of Brittany is a different matter – consistently warm through the summer months, with no need for you to brace yourself before going into the sea.

The other factor that may affect planning is the **tourist season**. On the coast, this gets going properly around July, reaches a peak during the first two weeks of August and then fades quite swiftly – but try to avoid the great *rentrée* at the end of the month, when the roads are jammed with cars returning to Paris. Inland, the season is less defined; highlights such as Monet's gardens at Giverny and parts of the Nantes–Brest canal can be crowded out in midsummer but, in August at any rate, some smaller hotels close to enable their owners to take their own holidays at the seaside. Conversely, those seaside resorts that have grown up without really being attached to a genuine town take on a distinctly ghostlike appearance during the winter months – and are often entirely without facilities.

	April		May		June		July		Aug		Sept		Oct	
	Max °C	Hrs Sun	Max °C	Hrs Sun	Max °C	Hrs Sun	Max °C	Hrs Sun	Max °C	Hrs Sun	Max °C	Hrs Sun	Max °C	Hrs Sun
Brittany														
Brest	13	6.3	16	6.9	19	7.0	20	7.0	21	6.7	19	5.2	16	3.9
Carnac	13	7.3	15	7.8	18	8.5	19	8.5	20	8.1	18	6.6	15	4.7
St Brieuc	13	6.7	15	7.2	18	7.2	20	7.3	20	7.2	19	5.8	16	4.0
Normandy														
Caen	13	6.1	17	7.4	20	7.5	22	7.4	22	7.5	20	5.7	15	4.2
Cherbourg	12	6.0	15	7.3	18	7.1	19	7.2	20	7.2	18	5.5	15	3.7

CLIMATE CHART

PART ONE

THE
BASICS

GETTING THERE FROM BRITAIN

With the Channel Tunnel and the long-established ferry companies engaged in an all-out price war, there has never been a better time for British holiday-makers to visit Brittany and Normandy.

The tunnel itself crosses the Channel well to the east of Normandy – at the Pas de Calais, the narrowest point – but it is transforming tourism in the region. There are more English travellers in northern France than ever before, especially in such accessible Norman cities as Rouen, as well as increasing numbers of long-distance commuters.

FERRIES

The most direct route to Normandy or Brittany, for motorists, cyclists and pedestrians, is still to take the cross-Channel **ferry** to any of four Norman and two Breton ports; it is, however, slightly cheaper to travel via Calais, Boulogne or Dunkerque. All these services are detailed in the box on p.5.

Thanks to the tunnel, ferry **fares** have come down in the last few years, with the various operators moving away from their previous emphasis on one-way fares to suggest all sorts of bargain return deals. So many special offers, seasonal and off-peak discounts and all-inclusive packages are now on offer that it is all but impossible to predict what you will actually be asked to pay; each individual sailing has its own price code. Thus return fares for a **car** and two adults on Brittany Ferries sailings to Caen, Cherbourg, Roscoff or St-Malo range from £76 for five days in low season up to £314 for a month-long trip in midsummer, while equivalent trips with P&O European Ferries vary between £89 and £274. The return fare for a **foot passenger** with either company varies from as little as £20 in winter up to £60 in summer; **bicycles** are typically carried free in low season or for around £5 in summer. **Children** under 4 travel free, while those aged up to 13 are charged half the adult fare. Note, in addition, that **cabin**

COACHES TO FRANCE

The coach services listed below are marketed as **Eurolines** by National Express, who also operate coaches to London from all over Britain. Schedules, tickets and further information are available from National Express offices at regional coach terminals, or you can contact Eurolines direct on ☎0990/143219 (*www.eurolines.co.uk*).

From	To	Via	Frequency		Journey	Return fares	
			Summer	Winter		Adult	Youth
London	**Caen**	Portsmouth	1–2 daily	–*	12hr	£36	£32
London	**Cherbourg**	Portsmouth	2–3 daily	2–3 daily	11hr	£28	£23
London	**Cherbourg**	Poole	1 daily	–	11hr	£39	£34
London	**Le Havre**	Portsmouth	2 daily	2 daily	12hr	£28	£23
London	**Nantes**	Dover, Calais, Tours	5 weekly	4 weekly	14hr	£88	£79
London	**Roscoff**	Heathrow, Exeter, Plymouth	1 daily	–*	13hr	£56	£47
London	**St-Malo**	Portsmouth	1 daily	–*	13hr	£43	£39

* Service operates April to mid-November only.
Some fares are subject to a surcharge during peak seasons.

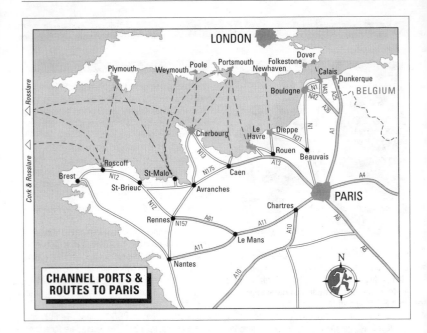

CHANNEL PORTS & ROUTES TO PARIS

accommodation on overnight crossings tends to cost £14–20 per person, and may be obligatory in high season. Probably the best deal of all is on P&O's Superstar Express service, which uses a high-speed catamaran to cross between Portsmouth and Cherbourg in less than three hours, while charging the same fare as the much slower traditional boats.

Booking ahead is strongly recommended for motorists, certainly in high season; foot passengers and cyclists can normally just turn up and board, at any time of year. Any **travel agent** will have a variety of fares and brochures on offer, so it's well worth shopping around for the most competitive deals. AA members who buy ferry tickets through a high-street AA shop can get extra discounts on brochure prices.

THE CHANNEL TUNNEL

The **Eurostar** rail service, via the **Channel Tunnel**, takes a mere three hours to get from London Waterloo International to Paris Gare du Nord. Around fifteen trains make the journey each day. Eurostar's original intention not to compete with ferry prices has long since been abandoned, so once again exact **fares** are unpredictable. The standard adult return fare to Paris tends to be around £119, but special offers are frequently available that can cost as little as £69.

By catching either the 8.53am (Mon–Sat) or the 12.27pm (daily) departure from London, and changing at Lille, two hours out, travellers heading for Brittany and Normandy can use connecting TGV services to bring the total journey time to **Rennes** or **Nantes** down to around six or seven hours.

Tickets can be bought directly over the phone from Eurostar (☎0990/186186), through SNCF (179 Piccadilly, London W1; ☎0990/848848), from most travel agents, or from all main train stations in Britain including Waterloo International. You can get through-ticketing – including the tube journey to Waterloo International – if you travel on GNER or Virgin train services from Manchester and Edinburgh, or on the Alphaline Rail Service from South Wales, Avon and West Wiltshire for around an extra £30. There is still no sign of the promised direct high-speed Eurostar services from the north of England, Scotland and the Midlands.

EUROTUNNEL

The Channel Tunnel also provides the fastest and most convenient way to take your **car** to France. For

FERRIES FROM BRITAIN: ROUTES AND FREQUENCIES

	Operator	Crossing time	Frequency
BRITTANY			
Portsmouth–St-Malo	Brittany Ferries	8hr 45min	mid-March to mid-Nov 1 nightly at 8.30pm; mid-Nov to mid-March daily except Sat 8.30pm
Plymouth–Roscoff	Brittany Ferries	6hr	mid-March to Oct 1–3 daily Oct to mid-Nov 1 daily at 11.30pm mid-Nov to mid-March Fri 10pm
Plymouth–St-Malo	Brittany Ferries	8hr	mid-Nov to mid-March only, Sun 11am
Weymouth–St Malo	Condor Ferries	4hr 20min	May to mid-Oct, 1 daily
NORMANDY			
Portsmouth–Cherbourg	P&O European Ferries	5hr–7hr 15min	Ship; 2–4 daily all year
Portsmouth–Cherbourg	P&O European Ferries	2hr 45min	Catamaran; 2–3 daily mid-May to Oct
Poole–Cherbourg	Brittany Ferries	4hr 15min	1–2 daily all year
Portsmouth–Caen	Brittany Ferries	6hr	2–3 daily all year
Portsmouth–Le Havre	P&O European Ferries	5hr 30min–8hr	3 daily all year
Newhaven–Dieppe	P&O Stena Line	4hr	Ship; 2 daily all year
Newhaven–Dieppe	P&O Stena Line	2hr 15min	Catamaran; 2–3 daily all year
PAS-DE-CALAIS			
Folkestone–Boulogne	Hoverspeed	55min	Seacat catamaran; 4 daily all year
Dover–Calais	Hoverspeed	35–50min	Hovercraft and Seacat; 11–17 daily all year
Dover–Calais	P&O Stena Line	1hr 30min	30 daily all year
Dover–Calais	Sea France	1hr 30min	15 daily all year

Brittany Ferries	☎0990/360360	**P&O Stena Line**	☎0990/980980
Condor Ferries	☎01305/761551	**P&O European Ferries**	☎0990/980855
Hoverspeed	☎0990/240241	**Sea France**	☎0990/711711

motorists, the tunnel entrance is less than two hours' drive from London, off the M20 at Junction 11A, just outside Folkestone. Once there, you drive your car onto a two-tier railway carriage; you're then free to get out and stretch your legs during the 35 minutes before you emerge from the darkness at Sangatte, just outside Calais. The sole operator, **Eurotunnel**, offers a continuous service with up to four departures per hour (only 1 per hour midnight–6am; 24hr recorded departure info ☎0891/555566, 50p per min). Because of the frequency of the service, you don't have to buy a ticket in advance (though this might be advisable in midsummer or during school holidays). You must, however, arrive at least 25 minutes before departure.

Tickets are available through Eurotunnel's Customer Service Centre or from your local travel agent. Fares are calculated per car, regardless of the number of passengers. Rates depend on the time of year, time of day and length of stay (the cheapest ticket is for a day-trip, followed by a five-day return); it's cheaper to travel between 10pm and 6am, while the highest fares are reserved for weekend departures and returns in July and August. By way of example, a five-day trip at an off-peak time starts at £95 (passengers included) in the low season and goes up to £135 in the peak period.

While the speed and efficiency of the tunnel journey itself is superb, however, drivers heading for Brittany or Normandy should not underestimate the length of time it takes to drive across northern France from the tunnel exit. Just to reach le Tréport, the eastern extremity of Normandy, takes a good two hours.

SPECIALIST AGENCIES IN BRITAIN

Campus Travel

52 Grosvenor Gdns, London	☎0171/730 3402
541 Bristol Rd, Birmingham	☎0121/414 1848
39 Queens Rd, Clifton, Bristol	☎0117/929 2494
5 Emmanuel St, Cambridge	☎01223/324283
61 Ditchling Rd, Brighton	☎01273/570226
53 Forrest Rd, Edinburgh	☎0131/668 3303
105–106 Aldates Rd, Oxford	☎01865/242067

Branches at YHA shops and university campuses.

STA Travel

86 Old Brompton Rd, London	☎0171/361 6161
117 Euston Rd, London	☎0171/361 6161
75 Deansgate, Manchester	☎0161/834 0668
88 Vicar Lane, Leeds	☎0113/244 9212
25 Queens Rd, Bristol	☎0117/929 4399
38 Sidney St, Cambridge	☎01223/366966
36 George St, Oxford	☎01865/792800

Also on various university campuses.

Council Travel

28a Poland St, London	☎0171/437 7767

Masterfare

19–21 Connaught St, London	☎0171/262 0599

Nouvelles Frontières

2–3 Woodstock St, London	☎0171/629 7772

Trailfinders

42–50 Earl's Court Rd, London	☎0171/938 3366
215 Kensington High St, London	☎0171/937 5400
22–24 The Priory, Birmingham	☎0121/236 1234
48 Corn St, Bristol	☎0117/929 9000
58 Deansgate, Manchester	☎0161/839 6969
254–285 Sauchiehall St, Glasgow	☎0141/353 2224

COMBINED TRAIN/FERRY ROUTES

You can buy **connecting tickets** from any British station to any French station, via any of the ferry routes. Details and prices (again with various special and seasonal offers) are obtainable from any British Rail **travel centre**. In London, the main international booking office is at Victoria Station (☎0171/834 2345).

Students and anyone under 26 can buy heavily **discounted tickets** from Eurotrain outlets such as Campus Travel (see above) and most student travel agents. For details of **rail passes** valid in Brittany and Normandy, including EuroDomino and InterRail passes, see the "Getting around" section, which starts on p.24.

Rail travellers catching ferries from **Portsmouth** should be warned that "Portsmouth Harbour" station is nowhere near the cross-Channel ferry terminals; there is a connecting bus service, but allow plenty of time.

BRIT AIR

Under franchise from Air France, **Brit Air** fly from London to three destinations in Brittany and three in Normandy; they also operate two daily flights between Bristol and Southampton and Paris, year round. For details and reservations, contact the Air France office in London (☎0181/742 6600). Apex return **fares** between Caen, Deauville or Le Havre and London are in the region of £160, with weekend returns costing around £120; the figures for Brest, Nantes and Rennes are more like £200 and £160 respectively.

All the flights listed below are from **London Gatwick**.

Destination	Phone	Via	Frequency	Journey time
Brest	☎02.98.32.01.10	Direct	1–2 daily	1hr 15min
Caen	☎02.31.26.58.00	Direct	1 daily	50min
Deauville	☎02.31.65.17.17	Direct	1 daily	50min
Le Havre	☎02.35.54.65.00	Direct	Mon–Fri	45min
Nantes	☎02.40.84.84.45	Direct	2–3 daily	1hr 25min
Rennes	☎02.99.29.60.10	Le Havre or Deauville	1–2 daily	1hr 40min

* No service in winter.

SPECIALIST TOUR OPERATORS FROM THE UK

Any travel agent can provide details of **package holidays** in Brittany and/or Normandy. The **French Holiday Service** at the French Travel Centre, 178 Piccadilly, London W1V 0AL (☎0171/355 4747) can book an especially large range, including most of those listed below. Most packages include ferry crossings, or occasionally flights, in the deal, which means they can work out very good value.

In addition to this (necessarily abbreviated) listing of some of the main operators, most of the ferry companies (see p.5) offer their own accommodation packages. More complete lists are available from the **French Government Tourist Office**, 178 Piccadilly, London (☎0891/244 123).

Blakes Holidays   ☎01603/784131
Wroxham, Norwich NR12 8DH
Self-catering canal trips in Brittany, starting from Messac, between Rennes and Redon. High-season rental rates range from around £700 per week for a two-berth boat to around £2000 for a twelve-berth vessel.

Brittany Direct Holidays   ☎0181/641 6060
362–364 Sutton Common Rd, Sutton,
Surrey SM3 9PL
Holidays throughout Brittany and Normandy. Self-catering accommodation, mostly in large houses, costs from £150 up to £400 each for two weeks in a group of four adults; or short city breaks, staying in hotels. They also operate less expensive summer-only mobile-home sites near Douarnenez and La Baule, guided walking (£450 for seven nights) and cycling (£400 for six nights) tours, and offer barge rental.

French Country Cruises   ☎01572/821330
54 High St East, Uppingham, Leics LE15 9PZ
Self-drive canal-boat rental from Redon, mid-March to mid-November only. In summer the weekly cost for the boat alone ranges from £819 for two people up to almost £2000 for eight.

Holiday in France   ☎01449/737664
Model Farm, Rattlesden, Suffolk IP30 0SY
Off-the-beaten-track specialists, with a variety of villas and some very attractive chambres d'hôte in châteaux and farmhouses. Also golf, horse-riding, skiing and boating holidays.

Holt's Battlefield Tours   ☎01304/612248
15 Market St, Sandwich, Kent CT13 9DA
Definitive guided tours to famous battlefields, including five-day tours of the D-Day landing beaches and associated sites for around £500, and three-day Dieppe trips for half that.

LSG Theme Holidays   ☎01509/231713
201 Main St, Thornton, Coalville, Leics LE67 1AH
Painting and art-appreciation courses, including a Monet tour to Giverny.

Martin Randall Travel   ☎0181/742 3355
10 Barley Mow Passage, London W4 4PH
Art-history tours from around £655 for a five-day Monet tour, including flights to Paris and accommodation.

Morbihan Travel   ☎01920/412013
10 Little Acres, Ware, Herts SG12 9JW
Self-catering holidays throughout southern Brittany; weekly rental rates for four-person gîtes range from £320 to £480.

Normandie Vacances   ☎01922/721901
113 Sutton Rd, Walsall, West Midlands
WS5 3AG
Self-catering accommodation in rural gîtes all over Normandy, costing up to £500 per adult for two weeks in high season, including ferry. Children free.

Vacances en Campagne   ☎01798/869411
Bignor, nr Pulborough, West Sussex RH20 1QD
A wide selection of properties for rent, up to and including positively luxurious châteaux. High standards, and high prices, but good value for money.

Vacances Franco-   ☎01242/240310
 Brittaniques
Normandy House, High St, Cheltenham,
Glos GL50 3FB
Cottages all over Brittany and Normandy, especially southern Finistère. Prices, including ferry travel, for a two-week holiday for two range from at least £230 per person in the low season up to as much as £550 in summer.

CAMPING OPERATORS

Allez France	☎0903/742345	**French Life**	☎0113/239 0077
Four Seasons	☎0113/256 4374	**Keycamp**	☎0181/395 4000
French Country Camping	☎01923/261311	**Select France**	☎01865/331350

GETTING THERE FROM IRELAND

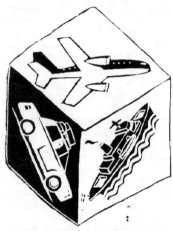

Much the cheapest way to get to Brittany or Normandy from Ireland – though unfortunately not available between January and March – is by ferry from Cork or Rosslare (outside Wexford) to either Roscoff in Brittany or Cherbourg in Normandy.

Ferry routes and operators are detailed in the box below. Exact **prices** vary according to the season and, for motorists, the size of car. Brittany Ferries is generally somewhat cheaper, with one-way fares for foot passengers ranging IR£30–60, and for a small car with two adults IR£95–260; the corresponding rates for Irish Ferries are IR£75 and IR£99–275.

Both companies offer reduced rates on fixed-period return tickets, as well as all-in **packages**, with a choice of accommodation in hotels, campsites, or self-catering *gîtes*. Irish Ferries sell combined **rail-and-ferry** tickets to French destinations from any station in Ireland.

You can either contact the companies direct to reserve space in advance (essential at peak season if you're driving), or any competent travel agent at home or in France can do it for you. Among those worth trying are Joe Walsh Tours (Dublin ☎01/876 3053, Belfast ☎01232/241144), Thomas Cook (Dublin ☎01/677 1721, Belfast ☎01232/554455) and USIT (Dublin ☎01/679 8833, Cork ☎021/270900, Derry ☎01504/371888, Waterford ☎051/872601, Belfast ☎01232/324073).

BY AIR

Only a very limited number of airlines **fly** direct between Ireland and France, and none to Brittany or Normandy. Aer Lingus (Dublin ☎01/844 4777, Cork ☎021/327155) fly direct from **Dublin and Cork** to Paris Charles de Gaulle, with a few seats at IR£129 return and a standard fare of IR£199. Ryanair (Dublin ☎01/609 7800) offer three daily flights from **Dublin** to Beauvais airport, outside Paris for £IR97.50 return. British Airways Lingus (Belfast ☎0345/222 111, Dublin ☎1800/626 747) fly directly from **Belfast** City Airport to Paris CDG. Otherwise, a routing through London or Amsterdam is the best option, while the Paris Travel Service (☎01992/456000) has package deals, including flights from Belfast.

FERRIES FROM IRELAND: ROUTES AND FREQUENCIES

	Operator	Crossing time	Frequency
Cork–Roscoff	Brittany Ferries	13–17hr	April–Oct 1 wkly
Rosslare–Roscoff	Irish Ferries	15hr	April–Dec 2–4 wkly
Rosslare–Cherbourg	Irish Ferries	18hr	May–Sept 1–2 wkly

| **Brittany Ferries** 42 Grand Parade, Cork | ☎021/277801 | **Irish Ferries** 2–4 Merrion Row, Dublin 2 Rosslare | ☎01/661 0511 ☎053/33158 |

GETTING THERE FROM NORTH AMERICA

Getting to France from the US or Canada is straightforward. Paris, the only French transatlantic gateway, has direct flights from over thirty major North American cities. From there, it's simple to continue to Brittany or Normandy by rail – Rouen is just over an hour away, while super-fast TGV trains get to either Rennes or Nantes in around two hours – or by air. A connecting flight on Air Inter, Air France's domestic arm, to Brest, the remotest Breton city, costs approximately US$150 extra.

ROUTES AND FARES

As detailed in the box on p.10, a dozen different scheduled airlines operate non-stop transatlantic flights to Paris, making it one of the cheapest destinations in Europe. In fact, only London can offer more discounted flights, and even then the price

difference is rarely sufficient to make a stopover in London a money-saving idea.

The least expensive way to take any of these scheduled flights is with a non-refundable **Apex** fare, which normally entails booking 21 days in advance of flying, travelling midweek, and staying for at least seven days. Apart from special offers, this is likely to be the best deal you'll get direct from an airline ticket counter.

The best guarantee of a cheap flight, however, is to contact a travel agent specializing in **discounted fares**. The travel sections of the *New York Times*, *Washington Post* and *Los Angeles Times* advertise them. Restrictions on such tickets are often not all that stringent; you need not assume that youth or student fares are the best bargain, nor worry if you're not eligible for them.

The **independent specialists** STA Travel and Council Travel are reliable, but (not surprisingly) the French group Nouvelles Frontières has some good offers. These firms, together with several others, act as "consolidators" for particular airlines with which they maintain contracts to sell seats on specific terms, invariably below the airlines' own fares, though sometimes less conveniently.

Estimating the cost of **round-trip economy-class fares** to Paris is tricky, especially as routes, carriers and the state of the market are in a constant state of flux. The round-trip fares shown in the box below are a general guide to what you might expect to pay; startling variations are owing to specific airlines engaging in price wars on specific routes. Fares are dependent on **season**, and are highest between early June and the end of August, when everyone wants to travel; they drop during

SAMPLE FARES TO PARIS

Typical lowest discounted fares in low season/high season, flying midweek. All prices are in US$ unless otherwise specified.

Atlanta	$500/810	**Montréal**	CDN$825/1249
Boston	$416/1140	**New York**	$550/800
Chicago	$473/900	**Philadelphia**	$560/750
Dallas	$409/914	**San Francisco**	$966/750
Halifax	CDN$1003/1353	**Toronto**	CDN$825/1249
Houston	$319/730	**Vancouver**	CDN$1115/1639
Los Angeles	$504/800	**Washington DC**	$490/767
Miami	$473/935		

AIRLINES IN NORTH AMERICA

All the flights listed below are to Paris. Only gateway cities in North America are listed for each airline; other routings are always possible using connecting flights.

Air Canada　　Canada: ☎1-800/555-1212
US: ☎1-800/776-3000
From Montréal, Toronto and Vancouver.

Air France　　US: ☎1-800/237-2747
Canada: ☎1-800/667-2747
From Atlanta, Boston, Chicago, Cincinnati, Houston, LA, Miami, Montréal, New York (JFK and Newark), San Francisco, Toronto and Washington DC.

American Airlines　　☎1-800/433-7300
From Chicago, Dallas-Fort Worth and Miami.

AOM French Airlines　　☎1-310/338-9613
From LA.

Continental Airlines　　☎1-800/231-0856
From Houston and New York.

Delta Airlines　　US: ☎1-800/241-4141
Canada: ☎1-800/555-1212
From Atlanta, Cincinnati and New York.

Northwest Airlines　　☎1-800/447-4747
From Detroit.

PIA　　☎1-800/221-2552
From New York.

Tower Air　　☎1-800/221-2500
From New York.

TWA　　☎1-800/982-4141
From New York and St Louis.

United Airlines　　☎1-800/538-2929
From Chicago, San Francisco and Washington DC.

US Air　　☎1-800/622-1015
From Philadelphia.

DISCOUNT AGENTS, CONSOLIDATORS AND TRAVEL CLUBS

Council Travel　　☎1-800/226-8624
Main office: 205 E 42nd St, New York, NY 10017
cts@ciee.org
Student travel organization with branches in forty US cities.

Flight Centre　　☎604/739-9539
S Granville St, Vancouver, BC
Discount air fares from Canadian cities.

High Adventure Travel Inc. ☎1-800/428-8375
253 Sacramento St #600, San Francisco, CA 94111
www.highadv.com
General travel agent.

Interworld Travel　　☎305/443-4929
800 Douglass Rd, Miami, FL 33134
Consolidator.

New Frontiers/Nouvelles Frontières
12 E 33rd St,　　☎1-800/366-6387
New York, NY 10016
1001 Sherbrook E,　　☎514/526-8444
Suite 720, Montréal, H2L 1L3
French discount-travel firm, which also markets charters to Paris and Lyon. Other branches in LA, San Francisco and Québec City.

STA Travel　　☎1-800/777-0112
Main office: 10 Downing St, New York, NY 10014

Worldwide specialist in independent travel, with branches in LA, San Francisco and Boston, as well as Paris and Grenoble.

Travac Tours　　☎1-800/872-8800
Main office: 989 Sixth Ave, New York NY 10018
Consolidator and charter broker.

Travel Cuts　　☎416/979-2406
Main office: 187 College St, Toronto, ON M5T 1P7
Canadian student-travel organization with branches all over the country.

Travel Savings Club　　☎1-800/444-9800
4501 Forbes Blvd, Lanham MD, 20706
Discount travel club.

Travelers Advantage　　☎1-800/548-1116
3033 S Parker Rd, Suite 900, Aurora, CO 80014
Discount travel club.

Unitravel　　☎1-800/325-2222
1177 N Warson Rd, St Louis, MO 63132
Consolidator.

Worldwide Discount Travel Club ☎305/534-2082
1674 Meridian Ave, Miami Beach, FL 33139
Discount travel club.

TOUR OPERATORS IN NORTH AMERICA

Abercrombie & Kent ☎1-800/323-7308
1520 Kensington Rd, Oak Brook, IL
Deluxe hiking, biking, rail and canal journeys, including Normandy.

American Airlines
Fly AAway Vacations ☎1-800/321-2121
Fly AAway Vacations offer a fourteen-day, twelve-night motorcoach "Best of France" package, with stops at Mont-St-Michel, D-Day beaches and Bayeux, for $1450 excluding airfare.

Backroads ☎1-800/462-2848
1516 Fifth St, Suite L101, Berkeley, CA 94710
Upmarket bike tours; an 8-night tour of Brittany and Normandy, staying in château accommodation, costs $3358 excluding airfare.

Euro-Bike Tours ☎1-800/321-6060
PO Box 990, DeKalb, IL 60115
Fourteen-day bike tours of Brittany, Normandy

and the Loire Valley, overnighting in luxury hotels, for $3095 excluding airfare.

The French Experience ☎1-800/28-FRANCE
370 Lexington Ave, # 812, New York, NY 10017
Four-day, three-night self-drive tours of Normandy ($339) or Brittany ($419), including good hotels and rental car pick-up anywhere in France.

Interhome ☎305/940-2299
1990 NE 163rd St, N Miami Beach, FL 33162
Short-term house and villa rentals in Normandy.

International Study Tours ☎1-800/833-2111
225 W 34th St, New York, NY 10122
Culture/art tours, including Normandy by barge.

Vacances en Campagne ☎1-800/327-6097
PO Box 299, Elkton, VA 22827
Châteaux and country houses for rent.

the "shoulder" seasons, September to October and April to May, while you'll get the best deals of all during the low season, November through March (excluding Christmas). Traveling on Friday, Saturday or Sunday tends to carry a premium. One-way fares are generally slightly more than half the round-trip.

CHARTER FLIGHTS

Charter flights (a flight chartered by a tour operator from an airline) can be even cheaper than discounted scheduled services, but to a much greater extent they hedge you in with restricted dates and major financial penalties if you cancel. They're worth considering if you're very organized and know exactly what you plan to do. Most agents sell them.

COURIER FLIGHTS

If you're prepared to travel light at short notice and for a short duration, it might be worth getting a **courier flight**. Return journeys to Paris are available for around $350, with last-minute specials (booked within three days of departure) as low as $150. Tickets are issued on a first-come, first-served basis, and there's no guarantee that the Paris route will be available at the specific time you want.

Now Voyager (☎212/431-1616) and Discount Travel International (☎212/362-3636) arrange such flights to Europe from JFK, Newark and Houston. For more information about what is available, get hold of a guide entitled *Courier Bargains: How to*

Travel Worldwide for Next to Nothing by Kelly Monaghan ($17.50 postpaid from the Intrepid Traveler, PO Box 438, New York, NY 10034).

FLYING VIA THE UK

Although **flying to London** is usually the cheapest way to reach Europe, price differences are so minimal that there's no point travelling to France via London unless you've specifically chosen to visit the UK as well. Major operators include Virgin Atlantic (☎1-800/862-8621) and British Airways (US ☎1-800/247-9297, Canada ☎1-800/668-1080).

PACKAGE TOURS

Dozens of tour operators specialize in travel to France. Many can put together very **flexible deals**, sometimes amounting to no more than a flight and accommodation. If you're planning to travel in moderate or luxury style, or if your trip is geared around special interests, such packages can work out cheaper than the same arrangements made on arrival.

Although a tour is almost certainly more confining than independent travel, it can help you make the most of your time if you're on a tight schedule.

The box above mentions a few of the possibilities, and a travel agent will be able to point out others (remember, bookings made through a travel agent cost no more than going through the tour operator).

GETTING THERE FROM AUSTRALIA & NEW ZEALAND

Airlines that fly to France from either Australia or New Zealand – all of which use Paris as their gateway – are listed in the box below. Intensive competition has brought prices to a lower level than ever, so there are plenty of bargains to be had.

Fares from both Australia and New Zealand fluctuate on the scale of A\$/NZ\$200–400 according to the time of year. Each airline defines its own seasons, but broadly speaking **low season** is mid-January to the end of February, plus all of October and the first week of November; **high**

season covers from mid-May to the end of August, and from the start of December until mid-January; the rest of the year counts as **shoulder season**.

FROM AUSTRALIA

The only direct flights to France from **Australia** are to Paris, but internal add-on flights are "common rated" to the same price. **Discount** agents should be able to get you at least ten percent off the following low-season published fares to Paris, some of which include conditions such as booking three months in advance: Alitalia/Qantas (via Milan) \$1395, KLM (Amsterdam), JAL (Tokyo), Lufthansa (Frankfurt), Olympic (Athens) \$1530, Thai International (Bangkok), Singapore Airlines, Qantas \$1670, Thai \$1792 (two stops), British Airways (via London) \$1885, Air France (on to 87 destinations within France) \$1903, Air France/Qantas \$1980 (three stops).

Airpasses, coupons and discounts on further flights within Europe vary with airlines, but the basic rules are that they must be prebooked with the main ticket, are valid for three months, and are available only with a return fare with the one airline – for example, you have to fly to France with British Airways alone to be eligible for their airpass deals. Air France offer a **Euroflyer** for use in France and Europe at A\$190 each flight (minimum three, maximum nine). KLM's **Passport to Europe** uses coupons for single

AIRLINES IN AUSTRALIA AND NEW ZEALAND		
	Australia	**New Zealand**
Aeroflot	☎02/9262 2233	
Air France/Qantas	☎02/9244 2100	☎09/303 3521
Alitalia/Quantas	☎1300/653 757	☎09/379 4457
British Airways	☎02/9258 3300	☎09/356 8690
Cathay Pacific	☎02/9931 5500	☎09/379 0861
Garuda	☎02/9334 9944	☎09/366 1855
JAL	☎02/9272 1111	☎09/379 9906
KLM	☎02/9231 6333	
Malaysian Airlines	☎02/9364 3500	☎09/373 2741
Qantas	☎02/9957 0011	☎09/357 8900
Singapore Airlines	☎02/9236 0044	☎09/350 0129
Thai Airways	☎1300/651 960	☎09/377 3886
United Airlines	☎13 1777	☎09/307 9500

SPECIALIST AGENTS IN AUSTRALIA AND NEW ZEALAND

AUSTRALIA

Adventure World
73 Walker St, North Sydney ☎02/9956 7766
333 Adelaide St, Brisbane ☎07/3229 0599
8 Victoria Ave, Perth ☎08/9221 2300
City mini-stays and active holidays throughout France.

Brisbane Flight Centre
260 Queen St, Brisbane ☎07/3229 9211

CIT
Level 2/263 Clarence St, Sydney ☎02/9267 1255
Offices in Melbourne, Brisbane, Adelaide and Perth. Accommodation, maps, bus and rail passes.

European Travel Office
122 Rosslyn St, W Melbourne ☎03/9329 8844
Level 20, 133 Castlereagh St,
  Sydney ☎02/9267 7727

Flight Centres
33 Berry St, North Sydney ☎02/9460 0555
19 Bourke St, Melbourne ☎03/9650 2899
Other branches nationwide.

France Unlimited
16 Goldsmith St, Melbourne ☎03/9531 8787
Walking and cycling holidays throughout France.

French Bike Tours
16 Goldsmith St, Melbourne ☎03/9531 8787
A varied selection of cycling holidays in France.

French Cottages and Travel
674 High St, E Kew, Melbourne ☎03/9859 4944

Passport Travel
401 St Kilda Rd, Melbourne ☎03/9824 7183

STA Travel
855 George St, Ultimo, Sydney ☎02/9212 1255
256 Flinders St, Melbourne ☎03/9654 7266
Other offices in state capitals and universities.

Thomas Cook
321 Kent St, Sydney ☎02/9248 6100
257 Collins St, Melbourne ☎03/9282 0222
Branches in other state capitals.

Thor Travel
228 Rundle St, Adelaide ☎08/8232 3155
A wide selection of walking holidays in France.

Top Deck Travel
Level 1/62 Clarence St, Sydney ☎02/9299 8844
Overland expeditions through France.

Tymtro Travel
428 George St, Sydney ☎02/9223 2211

YHA Travel
422 Kent St, Sydney ☎02/9261 1111
205 King St, Melbourne ☎03/9670 9611
38 Stuart St, Adelaide ☎08/8231 5583
Also offices in Brisbane, Perth, Darwin and Hobart. Accommodation and adventure tours.

NEW ZEALAND

Adventure Travel Shop
50 High St, Auckland ☎09/303 1805
Outdoor active tours in Normandy, Brittany and the rest of France.

Adventure World
101 Great South Rd, Auckland ☎09/524 5118
City mini-stays and active holidays throughout France.

Budget Travel toll-free ☎0800/808 040
16 Fort St, Auckland ☎09/366 0061
Other branches around the city.

European Travel Office
407 Great South Rd, Auckland ☎09/525 3074

Flight Centres
205–225 Queen St, Auckland ☎09/206 6171
152 Hereford St, Christchurch ☎03/379 7145
50–52 Willis St, Wellington ☎04/472 8101

STA Travel
10 High St, Auckland ☎09/309 0458
233 Cuba St, Wellington ☎04/385 0561
90 Castel St, Christchurch ☎03/379 9098
Other offices in Dunedin, Palmerston North and major universities.

Thomas Cook
St Luke's Square, Auckland ☎09/849 2071

---

flights within Europe: three coupons for A$476, up to six for A$841 in the low season, US$330 and US$590 in the shoulder period, US$390 and US$710 in the peak period; Lufthansa charge A$595 for three coupons, plus A$166 for each additional coupon (maximum nine). British Airways have a zone system: around A$135 for each flight within France, A$200 each for single flights to and around Germany, Italy and Belgium, although you may have to travel via London.

FROM NEW ZEALAND

The best deals to France **from New Zealand** – again, assuming you get a discount through one of the operators on p.12 – are Japanese Airlines (NZ$2200, overnight stop in Tokyo), Garuda (NZ$2249), Thai International (NZ$2265) and Malaysian Airlines (NZ$2295). For **stopovers** in Europe, British Airways charge NZ$2399 via London; Qantas/Alitalia are slightly less at NZ$2295 via Rome and London. If you want to make **side-trips** within Europe, Qantas/Lufthansa have a four-coupon deal on a six-month fare for NZ$2600.

RED TAPE AND VISAS

Citizens of EU countries and thirty other countries, including Australia, Canada, the United States, New Zealand, Malaysia and Singapore, do not need any sort of visa to enter France for a tourist stay of up to ninety days. All visitors must have full passports.

All other passport holders (including Australians and South Africans) must obtain a visa **before arrival in France**. Obtaining a visa from your nearest French consulate is fairly automatic, but check their hours before turning up, and leave plenty of time, as there are often queues (which can get particularly long in London in the summer).

Three types of **visa** are issued: a transit visa, valid for two months; a short-stay (*court séjour*) visa, valid for ninety days from the date of issue and good for multiple entries; and a long-stay (*long séjour*) visa, which allows for multiple stays of ninety days over three years, but is issued only after an examination of individual circumstances. Your passport must be valid for at least six months from your date of arrival in France.

EU citizens (or other non-visa citizens) who stay **longer than three months** are officially supposed to apply for a *Carte de Séjour*, for which you'll have to show proof of income at least equal to the minimum wage (6700F per month). However, EU passports are rarely stamped, so there is no evidence of how long you've been in the country. If your passport does get stamped, you can cross the border to a neighbouring country, and re-enter for another ninety days legitimately.

CUSTOMS

Customs and duty-free restrictions vary throughout Europe, with subtle variations even within the European Union.

However, since the inauguration of the EU Single Market, travellers entering Britain from another EU country do not have to make a declaration to Customs at their place of entry. You can effectively bring as much duty-paid wine or beer from France into Britain as you can carry – the legal limits are 90 litres of wine or 110 litres of beer, which has to be for your own use and not for resale. The volume of tax- or duty-free goods you can bring into Britain is still restricted. The current duty-free allowance for EU citizens is 200 cigarettes, one litre of spirits and five litres of wine; for non-EU residents the allowances are usually 200 cigarettes, one litre of spirits and two litres of wine.

Residents of the USA and Canada can take up to 200 cigarettes, 100 cigars and one litre of alcohol home, as can **Australian** citizens, while **New Zealanders** can take 200 cigarettes, 4.5 litres of beer or wine, and just over one litre of spirits.

FRENCH EMBASSIES AND CONSULATES ABROAD

AUSTRALIA
492 St Kilda Rd, Melbourne,
VIC 3001   ☎03/9820 0921

31 Market St, Sydney,
NSW 2000   ☎02/9261 5779

6 Perth Ave, Canberra,
ACT 2600   ☎02/6216 0100

CANADA
Embassy:
42 Promenade, Sussex,
Ottawa, ON K1M 2C9   ☎613/789 1795

Consulates:
1 place Ville Marie Bureau 22601,
Montréal, Québec H3B 4S3   ☎514/878 4385

130 Bloor St W, Suite 400,
Toronto, OT M5S 1N5   ☎416/925 8044

1201-736 Granville St,
Vancouver, BC V6Z 1H9   ☎604/681 4345

IRELAND
36 Ailesbury Rd, Dublin 4   ☎01/260 1666

NEW ZEALAND
1–3 Williston St, PO Box 1695,
Wellington   ☎04/720 200

UK
French Consulate General (Visas Section),
6a Cromwell Place,
London SW7 7EN   ☎0171/838 2050
                    (premium rate line) ☎0891/887733
11 Randolph Crescent,
Edinburgh   ☎0131/220 6324
                    (premium rate line) ☎0891/600215

USA
Embassy: 4101/Reservoir Rd NW,
Washington, DC 20007   ☎202/944 6000

Consulates:
10990 Wilshire Blvd, Suite 300,
Los Angeles, CA 90024   ☎310/235 3200

934 Fifth Ave, New York,
NY 10021   ☎212/606 3689

540 Bush St, San Francisco,
CA 94108   ☎415/397 4330

HEALTH AND INSURANCE

No visitor to France requires vaccinations of any kind, and general health care in the country is of the highest standard. Citizens of all EU and Scandinavian countries are entitled to take advantage of French health services under the same terms as residents, provided that they are carrying the correct documentation. British citizens need form E111, which is available in Britain from post offices, or in France, from offices of the health authorities, the **Caisse Primaire d'Assurance Maladie (CPAM)**. North American and other non-EU citizens have to pay for most medical attention and are strongly advised to take out some form of travel insurance.

MEDICAL TREATMENT

Under the French Social Security system, every hospital visit, doctor's consultation and pre-scribed medicine is charged for (though not upfront in an emergency). Although all employed French people are entitled to a refund of 70–75 percent of their medical expenses, this can still leave a hefty shortfall, especially after a stay in

For more details of what to do in a medical or other emergency, see p.46.

hospital (accident victims have to pay even for the ambulance that takes them there).

To find a **doctor**, stop at any *pharmacie* and ask for an address. Consultation fees for a visit should be around 110–150F, and in any case you'll be given a *Feuille de Soins* (Statement of Treatment) for later documentation of insurance claims. Prescriptions should be taken to a *pharmacie* which is also equipped – and obliged – to give first aid (for a fee). The medicines you buy will have little stickers (*vignettes*) attached to them, which EU travellers should remove and stick to their *Feuille de Soins* together with the prescription itself. A refund of between forty and eighty percent, depending on the kind of medicines, is payable in due course.

As getting a refund entails a complicated bureaucratic procedure, a better idea is to take out ordinary **travel insurance**, which generally allows full reimbursement, less the first few pounds of every claim.

In serious **emergencies** you will always be admitted to the **local hospital** (*Centre Hospitalier*), whether you arrive under your own power or by ambulance.

TRAVEL INSURANCE

Travel insurance policies usually cover such expenses as the consequences of charter companies going bankrupt, delayed or lost baggage, as well as sundry illnesses and accidents. The major difference between the standard policies sold in Britain and in North America is that British ones usually include a significant element of protection against theft or damage, while North American policies apply only to items lost from, or damaged in, the custody of an identifiable, responsible third party – hotel porter, airline, luggage consignment, etc. Note that very few insurers will arrange on-the-spot payments in the event of a major expense or loss; you will usually be reimbursed only after going home.

Remember that claims can only be dealt with if a report is made to the local police within 24 hours and a copy of the report (*constat de vol*) sent with the claim; addresses of the Commisariats de police are given in the main towns and cities).

BRITISH AND IRISH INSURANCE

In **Britain** and **Ireland**, travel insurance schemes to cover medical expenses and theft or loss are sold by all travel agents and banks. Policies for Europe cost anything from £26.50 per month; frequent travellers can get better value by buying a twelve-month policy from Columbus (see box), covering as many trips of up to sixty days as you like for £48 (Europe) or £89 (worldwide). With any policy, read the small print to see what is covered, although most policies are broadly similar. It is common for money and credit cards to be covered only if they are stolen from your person. If you have any other insurance policies – house and contents insurance, for example – you'll find some of the optional extra cover in travel insurance only duplicates what you already have at home.

NORTH AMERICAN INSURANCE

Travel insurance policies sold in the **US and Canada** tend to be expensive, and often include medical cover only. In particular, ask whether the policy pays medical costs up front or reimburses you later, and whether it provides for medical

TRAVEL INSURANCE COMPANIES			
BRITAIN		**ISIS**	☎1-800/777-0112
Campus Travel	see p.6	**Travel Assistance Int'l**	☎1-800/821-2828
Columbus Travel Insurance	☎0171/375 0011	**Travel Guard**	☎1-800/826-1300
Endsleigh Insurance	☎0171/436 4451	**Travel Insurance Services**	☎1-800/937-1387
Frizzell Insurance	☎01202/292333		
STA Travel	see p.6	**AUSTRALIA AND NEW ZEALAND**	
		AFTA	☎02/9264 3299
US AND CANADA		**Cover More**	☎02/9202 8000
Access America	☎1-800/284-8300	**Ready Plan**	☎1-300/555 017
Carefree Travel Insurance	☎1-800/323-3149	**UTAG**	☎02/9956 8399

evacuation to your home country. For policies that include lost or stolen luggage, check exactly what is and isn't covered, and make sure the per-article limit will cover your most valuable possession.

Before buying a policy, check that you're not already covered by existing insurance plans. **Canadians** are usually covered by their provincial health plans; holders of official **student and youth cards** are entitled to accident coverage and hospital in-patient benefits for the period during which the card is valid. **Students** will often find that their student health coverage extends during the vacations and for one semester beyond the date of last enrolment. Bank and **credit cards** (particularly American Express) often include some insurance cover on items paid for with the card – travel facilities, accommodation, tours and so on – while **Homeowners' or renters'** insurance may cover theft or loss of documents, money and valuables while overseas.

The best **premiums** are usually to be had through student/youth travel agencies – ISIS policies, for example, cost $48–69 for fifteen days (depending on level of coverage), $80–105 for a month, $150–207 for two months, and $510–700 for a year. If you're planning to do any "dangerous sports", be sure to ask whether these activities are covered – some companies levy a surcharge.

INSURANCE IN AUSTRALIA AND NEW ZEALAND

The travel insurance packages generally available in **Australia and New Zealand** are put together by the airlines and travel agent groups such as UTAG, AFTA, Cover More and Ready Plan, in conjunction with insurance companies. All are similar in premium and coverage, but Ready Plan probably give the best value for money. Typical prices are around A$196/NZ$220 for one month, A$270/NZ$320 for two months, and A$335/NZ$400 for three months. As with all policies, make sure that you are covered for any activities you might be planning.

DISABLED TRAVELLERS

France has no exceptional record for providing facilities for disabled travellers. For people in wheelchairs, the haphazard parking habits and stepped village streets are serious obstacles, and public toilets with disabled access are rare. In the major cities and coastal resorts, however, ramps or other forms of access are gradually being added to hotels, museums and some theatres and concert halls. APF, the French paraplegic organization (see p.18), which has an office in each *département*, will be the most reliable source of information on accommodation with disabled access and other facilities.

Public transport is certainly not wheelchairfriendly, and although many train stations now have ramps to enable wheelchair users to board and descend from carriages, at others it is still up to the guards to carry the chair. The high-speed **TGVs** (including Eurostar) all have places for wheelchairs in the First Class saloon coach for which you must book in advance, though no higher fee is charged; on other trains, a wheelchair symbol within the timetable denotes whether that service offers special features, and you and your companion are again upgraded to First Class with no extra charge. The *Guide du Voyageur à Mobilité Réduite*, available free at main train stations, details all facilities. **Taxis** are obliged by law to carry you and to help you into the vehicle, also to carry your guide dog if you are blind. Specialist taxi services are available in some towns: these are detailed in the Ministry of Transport and Tourism's pamphlet *Guide des Transports à l'Usage des Personnes à Mobilité Réduite*, available at airports, main train stations and some tourist offices.

Most of the cross-Channel **ferry companies** offer good facilities, though up-to-date information about access is difficult to get hold of. Eurostar, having been established in the 1990s, offers an excellent deal for wheelchair users. There are two special spaces in the First Class carriages for wheelchairs, with an accompanying seat for a companion. Fares are a flat-rate £72 return from Paris and London (with fully flexible dates) for both wheelchair-bound person and companion and, though it's not absolutely guaranteed, you will normally get the First Class meal as well. No advance bookings are necessary, though the limited spaces might make it wise to reserve ahead of time and also to arrange the special assistance which Eurostar offers at either end. As far as **airlines** go, British Airways has a better-than-average record for treatment of disabled passengers; while, from North America, Virgin and Air Canada come out tops in terms of disability awareness (and seating arrangements) and might be worth contacting first for any information they can provide.

Up-to-date information is best obtained from organizations at home before you leave or from the French disability organizations. The publication *Touristes Quand Même!*, produced by the CNFLRH (see box below), lists facilities throughout France but is not updated regularly. Some tourist offices have information but, again, it is not always very reliable. The Holiday Care Service has an information sheet on accessible **accommodation** in France.

Read your travel **insurance** small print carefully to make sure that people with a pre-exisiting medical condition are not excluded. And use your

---

TRAVEL WITH DISABILITY: USEFUL CONTACTS

FRANCE
APF ☎01.40.78.69.00
(Association des Paralysés de France)
17 bd Auguste-Blanqui, 75013 Paris
A national organization with regional offices all over France; useful information and lists of new and accessible accommodation. Their guide Où Ferons-Nous Étape *is available at the office for 70F or by post to a French address for 100F.*

CNFLRH ☎01.53.80.66.66
(Comité National Français de Liaison pour la Réadaptation des Handicapés)
236bis rue de Tolbiac, 75013 Paris
Information service for disabled travellers; details of accessible accommodation, holiday centres, etc, and various useful guides including the Guide Touristique pour les Personnes à Mobilité Réduite, *available in English for 60F.*

BRITAIN
Access Travel ☎01942/888844
16 Haweswater Ave, Astley, Greater Manchester M29 7BL
Specialists in holidays for people in wheelchairs; self-catering in gîtes *in Normandy from around £185 per person per week, including ferry crossing.*

Guide Dogs Adventure Group ☎01539/735080
Shap Rd, Kendal, Cumbria LA9 6NZ
Activity holidays for the visually impaired and unsighted. A week's tandem touring in Normandy for around £360 per person, with half board.

Holiday Care Service ☎01293/774535
2nd Floor, Imperial Building, Victoria Rd, Horley, Surrey RH6 7PZ
Information on all aspects of travel, including lists of accessible accommodation abroad, and information on financial assistance for overseas holidays.

RADAR ☎0171/250 3222
12 City Forum, 250 City Rd,
London EC1V 8AF . Minicom ☎0171/250 4119
Information on travelling with a disability. Advice on holidays and travel abroad.

Tripscope ☎0181/994 9294
The Courtyard, Evelyn Rd, London W4 5JL
Charity providing phone-in travel information and advice.

NORTH AMERICA
Mobility International USA ☎503/343-1284
PO Box 10767, Eugene, OR 97440
Information, access guides, tours and exchanges.

Society for the Advancement of Travel for the Handicapped (SATH) ☎212/447-7288
347 Fifth Ave, New York, NY 10016
Non-profit travel-industry referral service.

Twin Peaks Press ☎1-800/637-2256
PO Box 129, Vancouver, WA 98666
Publisher of the Directory of Travel Agencies for the Disabled *($19.95), listing more than 370 agencies worldwide;* Travel for the Disabled *($19.95); the* Directory of Accessible Van Rentals *($9.95); and* Wheelchair Vagabond *($14.95), loaded with personal tips.*

AUSTRALIA
ACROD ☎02/6282 4333
PO Box 60, Curtin, ACT 2605
Lists of agencies and tour operators.

NEW ZEALAND
Disabled Persons Assembly ☎04/472 2626
PO Box 10, 138 The Terrace, Wellington
Organization that will provide details of tour operators and travel agencies for people with disabilities.

travel agent to make your journey simpler: airline or bus companies can cope better if they are expecting you, with a wheelchair provided at airports and staff primed to help. A **medical certificate** of your fitness to travel, provided by your doctor, is also extremely useful; some airlines or insurance companies may insist on it. Make sure that you have extra supplies of drugs – carried with you if you fly – and a prescription including the generic name in case of emergency. Carry spares of any clothing or equipment that might be hard to find; if there's an association representing people with your disability, contact them early in the planning process.

INFORMATION AND MAPS

French Government Tourist Offices in various major cities of the world give away large quantities of maps and glossy brochures covering Brittany and Normandy, including lists of hotels and campsites. Some of these, such as the maps of the inland waterways, and lists of festivals and campsites, can be quite useful; others use a lot of space to say very little.

In France itself you'll find a tourist information centre – known as the Syndicat d'Initiative (**SI**), or sometimes Office du Tourisme – in practically every town and many villages (addresses and opening hours are detailed throughout this book). These supply free town plans, and local information such as listings of hotels, restaurants, leisure activities, bike rental and laundries. Many SIs also publish car and walking itineraries for their areas, and some even conduct free town tours.

Specific information on **Normandy**, including lists of all hotels and campsites, can be obtained from the Comité Regional de Tourisme de Normandie (Le Doyenné, 14 rue Charles Courbeaux, 27000 Évreux; ☎02.32.33.79.00, fax 02.32.31.19.04) or the Normandy Tourist Board in Britain (44 Bath Hill, Keynsham, Bristol BS18 1HG; ☎0117/986 0036, fax 0117/986 0379). The equivalent source for material on **Brittany** is Bretagne

---

FRENCH GOVERNMENT TOURIST OFFICES

Australia ☎612/9231 5244
Level 22/25 Bligh St, Sydney, NSW 2000

Canada
1981 av McGill College, ☎514/288 4264
Suite 490 Montréal, PQ H3A 2W9

Ireland ☎01/679 0813
10 Suffolk St, Dublin 2

UK (premium rate line) ☎0891/244 123
178 Piccadilly, London W1V 0AL

USA
444 Madison Ave, 16th Floor,
New York, NY 10022 ☎212/838 7800
676 North Michigan Ave #3360,
Chicago, IL 60611-2819 ☎312/751 7800
9454 Wilshire Blvd #715,
Los Angeles, CA 90212-2967 ☎310/272 2661

Note that New Zealand does not have a French Government Tourist Office.

Info (1 rue Raoul Ponchon, 35069 Rennes; ☎02.99.36.15.15, fax 02.99.28.44.40).

On the **Internet**, the most useful starting point for general information on France is the English-language site run by the French Government Tourist Office in the US, at *www.fgtousa.org*. This has links to other official French sites, plus package-holiday operators and specialists of all kinds. Detailed information on **Normandy** can be found at *www.normandy-tourisme.org*, while similar sites for **Brittany** include *www.brittanytourism.com* and *www.bretagne.com/eng.htm*.

MAPS

Though their town maps are often very good, the SI handouts very rarely contain usable regional maps. To supplement them – and the maps in this guide – you will probably want a reasonable **road map**. For most purposes, certainly for driving, the **Michelin** 1:200,000 area maps of Brittany (230) and Normandy (231) are more than adequate. Virtually every road they show is passable by any car, and those that are tinged in green are usually reliable as "scenic routes". A useful free map for car drivers, obtainable from filling stations and traffic information kiosks in France, is the *Bison Futé*, showing alternative back routes to avoid the congested main roads, which are clearly signposted on the ground by special green *Bison Futé* road signs.

If you're planning to **walk or cycle**, check the *IGN* maps – their green (1:100,000 and 1:50,000) and purple (1:25,000) series. The *IGN* 1:100,000 is the smallest scale available with contours marked, though the bizarre colour scheme makes it hard to read. *Michelin* maps have little arrows to indicate steep slopes, which is all the information most cyclists will need.

Anyone planning to visit the **battlefields of northern France** will find Major and Mrs Holt's *Battle Map Series* invaluable (mail order from T. & V. Holt, Oak House, Woodnesborough, Sandwich CT13 0NJ, England; ☎ & fax 01304/614123).

MAP AND GUIDE SUPPLIERS

BRITAIN AND IRELAND

Daunt Books
83 Marylebone High St,
London W1 ☎0171/224 2295

Hodges Figgis Bookshop
56–58 Dawson St,
Dublin 2 ☎01/677 4754

National Map Centre
22–24 Caxton St,
London SW1 ☎0171/222 2466

John Smith and Sons
57–61 St Vincent St,
Glasgow G2 ☎0141/221 7472

Stanfords
12–14 Long Acre,
London WC2 ☎0171/836 1321

52 Grosvenor Gdns,
London SW1W ☎0171/730 1314

156 Regent St,
London W1R ☎0171/434 4744

The Travel Bookshop
13–15 Blenheim Crescent,
London W11 ☎0171/229 5260

Maps by mail or phone order are available from Stanfords in London; ☎0171/836 1321.

NORTH AMERICA

Adventurous Traveler Bookstore
PO Box 1468,
Williston, VT 05495 ☎1-800/282-3963

The Complete Traveler Bookstore
199 Madison Ave,
New York, NY 10016 ☎212/685-9007

3207 Fillmore St,
San Francisco, CA 92123 ☎415/923-1511

Map Link Inc.
3 S La Petera Lane, #5
Santa Barbara, CA 93117 ☎805/692-6777

Open Air Books and Maps
25 Toronto St,
Toronto, ON M5R 2C1 ☎416/363-0719

Phileas Fogg's Books & Maps
#87 Stanford Shopping Center,
Palo Alto, CA 94304 ☎1-800/233-FOGG

Rand McNally*
444 N Michigan Ave,
Chicago, IL 60611 ☎312/321-1751

150 E 52nd St,
New York, NY 10022 ☎212/758-7488

595 Market St,
San Francisco, CA 94105 ☎415/777-3131

1201 Connecticut Ave NW,
Washington, DC 20003 ☎202/223-6751

Sierra Club Bookstore
6014 College Ave,
Oakland, CA 94618 ☎510/658-7470

Traveler's Bookstore
22 W 52nd St,
New York, NY 10019 ☎212/664-0995

Ulysses Travel Bookshop
4176 St-Denis, Montréal, PQ ☎514/843-9447

World Wide Books and Maps
736 Granville St,
Vancouver, BC V6Z 1E4 ☎604/687-3320

*For other locations, or for maps by mail order, call ☎1-800/333 0136 ext 2111.

AUSTRALIA AND NEW ZEALAND

Map Land
372 Little Bourke St,
Melbourne, VIC ☎03/9670 4383

The Map Shop
16a Peel St, Adelaide ☎08/8231 2033

Specialty Maps
58 Albert St, Auckland ☎09/307 2217

Travel Bookshop
Shop 3, 175 Liverpool St,
Sydney, NSW 2000 ☎02/9261 8200

COSTS, MONEY AND BANKS

Brittany and Normandy are not, on the whole, expensive places to visit. Distances (and transport costs) are relatively small; the price of food and accommodation is consistently lower than in Britain and much of northern Europe; and access, at least just across the Channel, is straightforward.

On a **shoestring level**, camping and eating at least one picnic meal a day, taking buses or cycling, you could get by easily enough on 200F (£22/US$35) a day. Moving slightly **more upmarket**, staying in modest hotels, spending a bit on restaurants and driving, you should reckon on around 400F (£45/US$70) a day and up.

Accommodation is likely to represent the bulk of your expenditure. Hotels average around 200F for a double room, in the simpler places (note that in this book all hotel prices are coded with symbols, which are explained on p.30). If you're sharing, that works out at little more per person than the 60–120F per person charged by hostels. Camping, of course, can cut costs dramatically, so long as you avoid the plusher private sites; the local Camping Municipal rarely asks for more than 30F a head.

Eating out is the real bargain. You should always be able to find a good three-course meal for 85–110F, or a takeaway for a lot less (though *crêperies* seldom work out as cheap as they might appear). Fresh food from shops and markets is surprisingly dear in relation to low restaurant prices, but it's always possible to save money with a basic picnic of bread, cheese and fruit. More sophisticated meals – takeaway salads and ready-to-heat dishes – can be put together for

reasonable prices if you shop at *charcuteries* (delis) and the equivalent counters of many supermarkets. On the other hand, **drinks** in cafés and bars can make a severe hole in your pocket. Nowhere in the region matches Paris prices, but a cup of coffee can easily cost 20F, and a cognac double that; you have to accept that you're paying for somewhere to sit.

Transport costs obviously depend entirely on how (and how much) you travel. Bikes cost nothing if you bring them, and around 70F per day (more like 100F for a mountain bike) if you rent from the network of bike shops and SNCF station outlets (see p.27). Trains and buses normally operate on a fixed tariff of 50 centimes (half a franc) per kilometre. If you're driving, petrol prices are among the highest in Europe, at something between 6F and 7F per litre (that's about 30F/imperial gallon, 25F/US gallon) and most motorways have tolls, which mount up at about 25 centimes per kilometre.

As for **sites and museums**, you may find that regular charges make you quite selective about what you visit – even with an student card to soften the blow (many museums have reduced admission for all under-26s, and not just students). But this is no special hardship: the region's attractions lie as much in its towns and landscapes as in anything fenced off or put in a showcase.

MONEY

French currency is the **franc** (abbreviated as F or sometimes FF), divided into 100 centimes. Francs come in notes of 500, 200, 100, 50 and 20F, and there are coins of 20, 10, 5, 2 and 1F, and 50, 20, 10 and 5 centimes. The exchange rate in recent years seems to have stabilized at around 9F to the pound sterling, or around 5F 50 to the dollar.

Standard **banking hours** are 8.30am to 12.30pm and 1.30pm to 4pm; closed Sunday and either Monday or, less usually, Saturday. **Rates of exchange** and **commissions** vary from bank to bank; the Banque de France, which has offices in St-Malo, Caen, Quimper and other large towns, usually offers the best rates and takes the least commission. There are **money-exchange counters** at the train stations of all big cities, and usually one or two in the town centre as well. However, it would be a sensible precaution to buy some French francs before leaving.

The best way to **carry money** depends on your bank, and what facilities it offers.

CREDIT CARDS

Much the easiest way to pay for the bulk of your expenses in France is with a **credit** or **debit card**. Mastercard (Eurocard/Access), American Express, Carte Bleue (Visa/Barclaycard), and Diner's Card are almost universally accepted in hotels, restaurants and shops, for a minimum purchase of around 80F. Most foreign credit and debit cards can also be used in French **cash dispensing machines** (ATMs); check with your bank before you leave if you're in any doubt. However, it's not a wise idea to use ATMs as your sole source of money on a long trip far from home – a lost, stolen or malfunctioning card leaves you with nothing.

It's also worth noting that many French credit cards incorporate a microchip (*puce*) that contains security information. British, American, Australasian and other cards with no such strip are sometimes rejected by card-reading machines in French shops and restaurants. French tourist authorities recommend that travellers who experience difficulties should say (or show) the following words to the retailer: "*les cartes anglaises ne sont pas des cartes à puce, mais à*

> To report a **lost or stolen credit card**, call one of the hotlines listed on p.47.

bande magnétique. Ma carte est valable et je vous serais reconnaissant d'en demander la confirmation auprès de votre banque ou de votre centre de traitement."

TRAVELLERS' CHEQUES

Travellers' cheques, generally considered to be the safest way to carry ready cash, are available from almost any major bank (whether you have an account there or not), usually for a service charge of one percent on the amount purchased. Some banks may take 1.25 percent or even 1.5 percent, and your own bank may offer cheques free of charge provided you meet certain conditions – ask first, as you may easily save £10 to £15 (US$15–25). Thomas Cook, Visa and American Express are the most widely recognized brands.

Obtaining **French-franc travellers' cheques** can be worthwhile: they can often be used as cash, and French banks are obliged by law to give you the face value of the cheques when you change them, so commission is only paid on purchase.

> ### THE EURO
> France is one of eleven countries who have opted to join the European Monetary Union and, from January 1, 1999, is beginning to phase in the single European currency, the **euro**. Initially, however, it will only be possible to make paper transactions in the new currency (if you have, for example, a euro bank or credit-card account), and the franc will remain the normal unit of currency in France. Euro notes and coins are scheduled to be issued at the beginning of 2002, and to replace the franc entirely by the end of that year.

GETTING AROUND

The best way to travel around Brittany and Normandy is with a car or a bike. Public transport is not very impressive. SNCF trains are efficient, as ever in France, and the Atlantique TGV has reduced the Paris–Rennes journey to a mere two hours. However, the rail network circles the coast and, especially in Brittany, barely serves the inland areas. Where the train stops, an SNCF bus may continue the route, and local buses can eventually get you anywhere, so long as you're prepared to fit in with timetables geared principally to market, school or working hours.

Approximate journey times and frequencies can be found in the "Travel details" at the end of each chapter in this book, and local peculiarities are also pointed out in the text.

If you come without your own transport, the ideal solution is to make longer journeys by train or bus, then to **rent a bike** (never a problem) to explore a particular locality.

DRIVING

Travelling by car has its disadvantages: the expense, most obviously, but also the strong likelihood of reducing your contact with people. However, you do gain freedom of movement and, especially if you're camping, can be a lot more self-sufficient.

Few British travellers consider **car rental** in France, which costs upwards of 2000F per week (from around 290–520F a day), to be an economic alternative to bringing their own car across the Channel. However, the major international rental

CAR RENTAL AGENCIES

BRITAIN			Budget	☎1-800/527-0700
Avis	☎0990/900500		Dollar	☎1-800/421-6868
Budget	☎0800/181181		Europe by Car	☎1-800/223-1516
Europcar	☎0345/222525		Hertz	☎1-800/654-3001
Hertz	☎0990/996699		in Canada	☎1-800/263-0600
Holiday Autos	☎0990/300400		Holiday Autos	☎1-800/422-7737
National Car Rental	☎0990/365365		National	☎1-800/CAR-RENT
Thrifty	☎0990/168238		Thrifty	☎1-800/367-2277

IRELAND			AUSTRALIA AND NEW ZEALAND	
Avis	☎01/874 5844		Avis	☎1-800/225 533
Budget	☎0800/973159			in New Zealand ☎09/525 1982
Europcar	☎01/874 5844		Budget	local-call rate ☎13 2848
Hertz	☎01/676 7476			in New Zealand ☎09/275 2222
Holiday Autos	☎01/872 9366		Citroën	Peugeot Euro Lease 02/9949 1711
			Fly and Drive Holidays	
USA AND CANADA				in New Zealand ☎09/529 3790
Alamo	international ☎1-800/522-9696		Hertz	local-call rate ☎13 1918
Auto Europe	☎1-800/223-5555			in New Zealand ☎09/309 0989
Avis	☎1-800/331-1084		Renault Eurodrive	☎02/9299 3344

A MOTORING VOCABULARY

car	*voiture*	oil	*huile*
garage	*garage*	air line	*ligne à air*
service	*service*	inflate the tyres	*gonfler les pneus*
to park the car	*garer la voiture*	battery	*batterie*
car park/parking lot	*un parking*	the battery is dead	*la batterie est morte*
free parking	*parking gratuit*	plugs	*bougies*
paid parking	*parking payant*	to break down	*tomber en panne*
no parking	*défense de*	insurance	*assurance*
	stationner/stationnement	green card	*carte verte*
	interdit	traffic lights	*feux*
petrol/gas	*essence*	red light	*feu rouge*
(unleaded)	*(sans plomb)*	green light	*feu vert*
petrol/gas station	*poste d'essence*	slow down	*ralentir*
diesel fuel	*gasoil*	give way	*cédez le passage*
petrol/gas can	*bidon*	give way to	*priorité aux piétons*
fill the tank	*faire le plein*	pedestrians	

chains are represented throughout the region. North Americans and Australians in particular should be forewarned that it is very difficult to rent a car with **automatic transmission**; if you can't drive a stickshift, you should try to book an automatic well in advance, possibly before you leave home, and be prepared to pay a much higher price for it.

Petrol/gas (*essence*) or diesel fuel (*gasoil*) is least expensive at out-of-town superstores, and most expensive on the *autoroutes*. At around 6.59F a litre for unleaded (*sans plomb*), 6.79F for four-star (*Super*) and 4.79F for diesel, it costs roughly fifteen percent more than in Britain, so it's worth filling up in the UK if you have the option.

Autoroute driving, if fast, is boring when it's not hair-raising, and the tolls in Normandy are expensive. (It's also rather irrelevant to this book, as if you stay on the autoroute for any length of time you won't be in Brittany or Normandy any more.) For information on road conditions call Inter Service Route on ☎48.58.33.33 (24hr). The helpful *Bison Futé* map, free from service stations, details lesser-known routes to steer clear of the crowds – invaluable if you're trying to avoid the endless traffic jams over the weekends between July 15 and August 15. For full French driving regulations, see the *AA Traveller's Guide to Europe* (AA Publications, £6.95).

If you run into **mechanical difficulties**, all the major car manufacturers have garages and service stations in France. You can find them in the Yellow Pages (*Pages Jaunes*) of the phone book under "Garages d'automobiles". For breakdowns, look under "Dépannages". If you have an accident or break-in, you should make a report to the local police (and keep a copy) in order to make an insurance claim.

LEGAL REQUIREMENTS

British, EU and North American **driving licences** are valid, though an International Driver's Licence makes life easier if you get a police officer unwilling to peruse a document in English. The minimum driving age is 18, and provisional licences are not valid.

The vehicle registration document and the **insurance** papers must be carried; only the originals are acceptable. It's no longer essential for motorists from other EU countries to buy a **green card** to extend their usual insurance. If you have insurance at home then you have the minimal legal coverage in France; whether you have any more than that, and (if not) whether you want to buy more, is something to discuss with your own insurance company, so check to see what they recommend. Breakdown insurance costs around £37 for eight days; look into the RAC's European Motoring Assistance (☎0800/550055; www.rac.co.uk), or the AA's Five-Star Europe cover (☎0800/444500; www.theaa.co.uk).

If your car is right-hand drive, you must have your **headlight dip** adjusted to the right before you go – it's a legal requirement – and as a courtesy change or paint them to yellow or stick on black glare deflectors. Shops at the ferry terminals sell special headlight deflectors which achieve both aims – you basically pay £6 for two small pieces of sticky yellow plastic, but they do the job.

Similarly, you must also affix **GB plates** if you're driving a British car, and carry a red **warning triangle** and a spare set of **headlight bulbs** in your vehicle.

Seat belts are compulsory for the driver and all passengers, and children under 10 can only sit in the front seat if they're in approved rear-facing child seats.

RULES OF THE ROAD

The main **rule of the road** to remember in France is that the French drive on the right. Most drivers used to driving on the left find it easy to adjust. The biggest problem tends to be visibility when you want to overtake; it's possible to buy special forward-view mirrors that may help.

The law of **priorité à droite** – which says you have to give way to traffic coming from your right, even when it is coming from a minor road – is being phased out, having long been a major cause of accidents. It still applies in built-up areas, so you still have to be vigilant in towns, keeping a lookout along the roadside for the yellow diamond on a white background that gives you right of way – until you see the same sign with an oblique black slash, which indicates vehicles emerging from the right have right of way.

"*STOP*" signs mean stop completely – you can be fined for inching forward – while "*CEDEZ LE PASSAGE*" means "Give Way".

French national **speed limits**, which apply unless otherwise posted, are: 130km/hr (80mph) on the tolled *autoroutes*, dropping to 110km/hr if it's raining; 110km/hr (68mph) on two-lane highways, or 100km/hr when wet; 90km/hr (56mph) on other roads, or 80km/hr when wet; and 50km/hr (31mph) in towns. Fines for driving violations are exacted on the spot, and only cash or a French bank account cheque are accepted. Exceeding the speed limit by 1 to 30kph can cost as much as 5000F.

TRAINS

French **trains**, operated by the nationally owned SNCF (Société National des Chemins de Fer), are by and large clean, fast and frequent, and their staff both courteous and helpful. All but the smallest stations (gares SNCF) have an information

desk and *consignes automatiques* – coin-operated lockers big enough to take a rucksack. Many (indicated in the text of the guide) also rent out bicycles.

Fares are reasonable, at an average – off peak – of a little over 50 centimes per kilometre. Children under 12 travel half-price, and under-4s go free. The ultra-fast TGVs (Trains à Grande Vitesse) require a supplement at peak times and compulsory reservation costing around 20F. The slowest trains are those marked "*Autotrain*" in the timetable, stopping at all stations.

Try to use the counter service for buying tickets, rather than the complicated computerized system; the latter changes the price of TGV tickets depending on the demand, and you may find you've bought an expensive ticket without realizing that a later train is cheaper.

All **tickets** – but not passes – must be date-stamped in the orange machines at station platform entrances. It is an offence not to "*Compostez votre billet*". Rail journeys may be broken any time, anywhere, for as long as the ticket is valid (usually two months), but after a break of 24 hours you must "*composte*" your ticket again when you resume your journey. On night trains an extra 100F or so will buy you a **couchette** – well worth it if you're making a long haul and don't want to waste a day recovering from a sleepless night.

Regional **rail maps** and complete **timetables** are on sale at tobacconist shops. Leaflet timetables for a particular line are available free at stations. "*Autocar*" at the top of a column means it's an SNCF bus service, on which rail tickets and passes are valid.

For details on taking your bicycle by train – or renting one at an SNCF station – see opposite.

RAIL PASSES

Anyone intending simply to visit Brittany and Normandy – or even to explore all of France – is very unlikely to make enough train journeys for it to be it worth purchasing a Europe-wide **rail pass**. If you do intend to travel throughout Europe, ask a travel agent for details of the **InterRail** pass (in the case of British travellers) or the **Eurail** pass (for North Americans and Australasians).

However, within France, SNCF itself offers a whole range of **discount fares** on *Période Bleue* (blue period) and *Période Blanche* (white period) days – in effect, most of the year. A leaflet showing the blue, white (smaller discount) and red (peak) periods is given out at gares SNCF. In addition, certain France-specific train passes, valid for one year, can be purchased through French travel agents or from main gares SNCF. For over-60s, the **Carte Senior** costs 285F for unlimited travel. It offers up to fifty percent off tickets on TGVs, subject to availability, or other journeys starting in blue periods, a 25 percent reduction on white period journeys, as well as a 30 percent reduction on through international journeys involving most countries in western and central Europe. The same percentage reductions are available for under-26s with a **Carte 12–25** pass (270F), while under-12s can obtain the same advantages for themselves and up to four travelling companions of any age by purchasing the **Enfant Plus Carte** (350F).

For a further range of reductions, no pass is required. Any two people travelling together (à *deux*), or a small group of up to five people – whether a married couple, friends, family, whatever – are entitled to a 25 percent discount on return tickets on TGVs, subject to availability, or on other trains if they start their journey on a blue period day; the same reduction applies to a group of up to four people travelling with a child under 12, to under 26-year-olds, over-60s, and for anyone who books a return journey of at least 200km in distance, including a Saturday night away (this latter is called the *séjour*).

BUSES

Buses cover far more Breton and Norman routes than the trains – and, even when towns do have a rail link, they're often quicker, cheaper and more direct. They are almost always short distance, however, making you change if you're going further than one town to the next. And, as stressed, **timetables** tend to be constructed to suit working, market and school hours – often dauntingly early when they do run, and prone to stop just when tourists need them most.

Larger towns usually have a central gare routière (bus station), most often found next to the gare SNCF. However, the private bus companies (who provide most of the Breton services) don't always work together and you'll frequently find them leaving from an array of different points. The most convenient lines are those run as an extension of rail links by SNCF; these always run to/from the SNCF station (assuming there is one).

CYCLING

Bicycles have high status in France. The car ferries and SNCF trains carry them for a minimal charge, and the French (Parisians excepted) respect cyclists – both as traffic, and, when you stop off at a restaurant or hotel, as customers. French drivers normally go out of their way to make room for you – it's the great British caravan you might have to watch out for.

Most importantly, however, **distances** in Brittany and Normandy are not great, the hills are sporadic and not too steep, cities like Rennes and Nantes have useful networks of cycle lanes, and the scenery is nearly always a delight. Even if you're quite unused to it, cycling sixty kilometres per day soon becomes very easy – and it's a good way of keeping yourself fit enough to enjoy the rich regional food.

These days more and more cyclists use **mountain bikes**, which the French call VTTs (Vélos Touts Terrains), for touring holidays, although if you've ever made a direct comparison you'll know it's much less effort, and much quicker, to cycle long distances and carry luggage on a traditional touring or racing bike. Whichever you prefer, do use cycle panniers; a backpack in the sun is unbearable.

One word of warning: most cyclists have a habit of lifting their bicycles by gripping the saddle. If you keep on doing that when you're using panniers, even just to get over kerbs, the entire saddle will eventually snap off when you least expect it, to leave you to ride off in search of a bike shop, sitting on a long, sharp spike.

Restaurants and hotels along the way are nearly always obliging about looking after your bike, even to the point of allowing it into your room. Most large towns have well-stocked retail and **repair shops**, where parts are normally cheaper than in Britain or the US. However, if you're using a foreign-made bike, it's a good idea to carry spare tyres, as French sizes are different; neither is it easy to find parts for mountain bikes, the French enthusiasm being directed towards racers instead. Inner tubes are not a problem, as they adapt to either size, though you should always be sure that you get the right valves. The best places to find foreign parts are in Raleigh stockists – at Rouen, Rennes and scattered around both provinces.

SNCF run various schemes for cyclists, all of them covered in the free leaflet *Train et Vélo*,

A CYCLING VOCABULARY

to adjust	*ajuster*	loose	*dévissé*
axle	*l'axe*	to lower	*baisser*
ball bearing	*le roulement à billes*	mudguard	*le garde-boue*
battery	*la pile*	pannier	*le pannier*
bent	*tordu*	pedal	*le pédale*
bicycle	*le vélo*	pump	*la pompe*
bottom bracket	*le logement du pédalier*	puncture	*la crevaison*
brake cable	*le cable*	rack	*le porte-bagages*
brakes	*les freins*	to raise	*relever*
broken	*cassé*	to repair	*réparer*
bulb	*l'ampoule*	saddle	*la selle*
chain	*la chaîne*	to screw	*visser*
cotter pin	*la clavette*	spanner	*la clef (mécanique)*
to deflate	*dégonfler*	spoke	*le rayon*
dérailleur	*le dérailleur*	to straighten	*rédresser*
frame	*le cadre*	stuck	*coincé*
gears	*les vitesses*	tight	*serré*
grease	*la graisse*	toe clips	*les cale-pieds*
handlebars	*le guidon*	tyre	*le pneu*
to inflate	*gonfler*	wheel	*la roue*
inner tube	*la chambre à air*		

available from most stations. You can normally load your bike straight onto the train at the **ferry** port – as on the boat train at Dieppe – but remember that you must first go to the ticket office of the station to register it. Don't just try to climb on the train with it, as both you and your bike will end up left behind. In addition to the ferries, both British Airways and Air France take bikes free. You may have to box them, though, and you should contact the airlines first. You will also be required to leave a deposit of 1000–1500F (credit cards accepted).

At most SNCF stations bikes are also available for **rental** for around 70F per day, depending on the type of bike. You can also rent bikes from some tourist offices and a fair number of bike shops (which are much more likely to offer you a mountain bike), and, on islands such as Belle-Île and Ouessant, from numerous seasonal **stalls**. The bikes are often not insured, however, and you will be presented with the bill for its replacement if it's stolen or damaged. Check whether your travel insurance policy covers you for this if you intend to rent a bike.

For advice on which **maps** to take, see the "Maps" section on p.20. In the UK, the Cyclists' Touring Club, Cotterell House, 68 Meadrow, Godalming, Surrey GU7 3HS (☎01483/417217) will suggest routes and supply advice for a small fee, and they run a good insurance scheme.

MOPEDS AND SCOOTERS

Mopeds and **scooters** are relatively easy to find: everyone in France, from young kids to grandmas, rides one of these, and, although they're not built for any kind of long-distance travel, they're ideal for shooting around town and nearby. Places which rent out bicycles will often also rent out mopeds; you can expect to pay 200F a day for a 50cc Suzuki, for example, or 250F for an 80cc motorbike. **Crash helmets** are compulsory on all machines.

BOAT TRIPS AND INLAND WATERWAYS

Boat trips on many of Brittany and Normandy's rivers, as well as out to the islands, are detailed throughout this book. More excitingly, you can **rent a canoe**, **boat** or even **houseboat** and make your own way along sections of the **Nantes–Brest canal**. The route along the canal is the core of Chapter Six, *Inland Brittany*, the various towns where you can rent vessels are detailed on p.316, and some British operators are listed on p.7.

French Government Tourist Offices can also provide lists of French and foreign operators who

Cruises on the **River Seine** are detailed on p.78.

arrange boat rental, or for a full list write to the Syndicat National des Loueurs de Bateaux de Plaisance, Port de la Bourdonnais, 75007 Paris (☎45.55.10.49). Specifically for Brittany, contact the **Comité de Promotion Touristique des Canaux Bretons,** Office du Tourisme, place du Parlement, 35600 Rennes (☎99.71.06.04).

If you are adventurous enough to take your own boat, there is no charge for use of the waterways in Brittany or Normandy, and you can travel without a permit for up to six months in a year. For information on maximum dimensions, documentation, regulations, and so forth, ask at a French Government Tourist Office for the booklet *Boating on the Waterways*.

WALKING

Neither Brittany nor Normandy is serious hiking country. There are no mountains – or extensive areas of wilderness – and casual rambling along the clifftops and beside the waterways is the limit of most people's aims. However, if you're into **long-distance walking**, 21 of the French **GR trails** – the *sentiers de grande randonnée* – run through the area. The GRs are fully signposted and equipped with campsites and rest huts along the way. The most interesting are the *GR 2* (*Sentier de la Seine*), which runs from Le Havre to Les Andelys; the *GR 341* (*Sentier de Bretagne*) along the Granît-Rose coast between Lannion and St-Brieuc; and the *GR 347* (*Val d'Oust au pays Gallo*) between Josselin and Redon.

Each GR path is described in a **Topoguide**, which gives a detailed account of the route (in French), including maps, campsites, sources of provisions, and so on. These are produced by the principal French walkers' organization, the Comité National des Sentiers de Grande Randonnée, 8 av Marceau, 75008 Paris (☎47.23.62.32), and can be ordered through good map shops overseas, such as those listed on p.21.

In addition, many tourist information offices provide guides to their local footpaths.

ACCOMMODATION

Most of the year, accommodation is plentiful in both Brittany and Normandy, and visitors can just turn up at a town and find a room or a place on a campsite. Booking a couple of nights in advance can, however, be reassuring; it spares you the risk of having to trudge around to find a place and ensures that you know what you'll be paying.

Hotels, hostels and campsites are recommended throughout this book, and their phone numbers provided. The "Language" section at the back should help you make the necessary phone call if you're uncertain of your French, though many hoteliers and campsite managers, and almost all youth-hostel managers, speak some English.

Problems arise mainly **between July 15 and August 15**, when the French take their own vacations en masse. The first weekend of August is the busiest time of all. During this period, hotel and hostel accommodation can be hard to come by – particularly in the coastal resorts – and you may find yourself falling back on local tourist information offices for help and ideas. With campsites, you can be more relaxed, unless you're touring with a caravan or camper van.

The **tourist season** in Brittany and Normandy runs roughly from Easter until the end of September; while hotels in the cities remain open all year, those in smaller towns and, especially, seaside resorts often close for several months during the winter. It's quite possible to turn up

ACCOMMODATION PRICE CODES

All **hotel prices** in this book have been coded using the symbols below. The price shown is for the least expensive double room in high season, which for categories ① and ② usually means a room without private bath, shower or toilet, though there's usually a washbasin. Most hotels in those categories also have a number of rooms with en-suite facilities, which typically cost around 50F extra. In the ③ category and above, all rooms tend to be equipped with private facilities.

Although many hotels offer rooms at differing prices, ranges (such as ②–⑦) are only indicated when the spectrum is especially broad, or where there are relatively few rooms in the lowest category.

① up to 160 F	③ 220–300F	⑤ 400–500F	⑦ 600–700F
② 160–220F	④ 300–400F	⑥ 500–600F	⑧ 700F and over

somewhere in January or February to find that every hotel is closed; in addition, many family-run places close each year for two or three weeks sometime between May and September, and some hotels in smaller towns and villages close for one or two nights a week, usually Sunday or Monday. Opening dates for each establishment are indicated throughout the book, but it's worth checking ahead if you're in any doubt.

HOTELS

French **hotels** tend to be consistently better value than they are in Britain and much of northern Europe. Recommendations are given in the guide for almost every town or village mentioned, with their prices indicated by the symbols ①, ②, ③, etc, as explained in the box above. In most towns, you'll be able to get a double room for around 175–220F (£19–24/US$30–40), or a single for around 130–160F (£14–18/US$23–30), though often if you're prepared to pay a little extra you can get something really special.

Especially if you're travelling in peak season, try to pick up the full **accommodation lists** available from any French Government Tourist Office (see p.19) or local SI. Look out too for a handbook or free leaflet for the **Logis et Auberges de France**. These are independent hotels, promoted together for their consistently good food and reasonably priced rooms; they're recognizable on the spot by a green-and-yellow logo of a hearth.

One of the great pleasures of travelling in France is the sheer quality of **village hotels**. Not always in terms of fixtures and fittings – at the bottom of the range, you'll find corduroy carpets creeping up the walls, blotchy linoleum curling from buckled wooden floors, pillows hidden away in obscure cupboards, and clanking great brass

keys that won't quite turn in the ill-fitting doors – but the standards of service are consistently high, and it's rare indeed to stay in a hotel that doesn't take pride in maintaining a well-appointed and good-value restaurant serving traditional local food.

All French hotels are **graded** with from zero to five stars. The price more or less corresponds to the number of stars, though the system is a little haphazard, having more to do with ratios of bathrooms per guest than genuine quality; ungraded and single-star hotels are often very good.

At the cheapest level, what makes a difference in **cost** is whether a room contains a shower: if it does, the bill will be around 30–50F more. **Breakfast**, too, can add 25–35F per person to a bill, though there is no obligation to take it. The cost of eating **dinner** in a hotel's restaurant can be a more important factor to bear in mind when picking a place to stay. Officially hotels are not supposed to insist that you take meals, but they often do, and in busy resorts you may not find a room unless you agree to *démi-pension* (half board). If you are unsure, ask to see the menu before checking in; cheap rooms aren't so cheap if you have to eat a 100F meal.

Genuine **single rooms** are rare; lone travellers normally end up in an ordinary double let at a slightly reduced rate. On the other hand most hotels willingly equip rooms with **extra beds**, for three or more people, at a good discount.

In recent years, outlets of several French **motel chains** have begun to proliferate, usually located alongside major through-routes on the outskirts of larger towns. Other than close to the ferry ports, there are fewer of these in Brittany and Normandy than elsewhere in the country, but those that do exist make a good alternative option for motorists, especially late at night. Among the cheapest is the one-star **Formule 1** chain, which tends to be characterless, but provides rooms for up to three people from 120F. With a Visa, Mastercard, Eurocard or American Express credit card, you can let yourself into a room at any hour of the day or night. Other inexpensive chains include *1er Classe*, *Étap Hôtel* and *Balladins*; more comfortable equivalents such as *Campanile*, *Ibis*, *Climat de France* and *Clarine* offer en-suite rooms with cable TV and direct-dial phones from 270 to 320F.

In country areas, in addition to standard hotels, you will come across **chambres d'hôte**, bed-and-breakfast accommodation in someone's house or farm. These vary in standard, but are rarely an especially cheap option – usually costing the equivalent of a two-star hotel. However, if you strike lucky, they may be good sources of traditional home cooking. Brown leaflets available in SIs list most of them.

HOSTELS, FOYERS AND GÎTES D'ÉTAPE

At anything from 60F up to 120F per night for a dormitory bed, **Auberges de Jeunesse** – youth hostels – are invaluable for single budget travellers. For couples, however, and certainly for groups of three or more people (see above), they'll not necessarily work out less than the cheaper hotels – particularly if you've had to pay a bus fare out to the edge of town to reach them. However, many of the hostels in Normandy and Brittany are beautifully sited, and they do allow you to cut costs by preparing your own food in their kitchens, or eating in cheap canteens.

Slightly confusingly, there are three rival French youth hostel associations (see box below). The main two are the Fédération Unie des Auberges de Jeunesse (FUAJ; 180 hostels), whose hostels are detailed in the *International Handbook*, and the Ligue Française pour les Auberges de Jeunesse (LFAJ; 100 hostels). To stay at hostels run by either of these organizations, you must be a member of Hostelling International (HI)/the International Youth Hostel Federation (IYHF). Head offices and membership fees, which differ from country to country, are listed in the box below. If you don't join up before you leave home, a membership card can be purchased

---

YOUTH HOSTEL ASSOCIATIONS

FRANCE
Fédération Unie des Auberges de Jeunesse (FUAJ)
27 rue Pajol, 75018 Paris ☎01.44.89.87.27
Ligue Française pour les Auberges de Jeunesse (LFAJ)
38 bd Raspail, 75007 Paris ☎01.45.48.69.84
Union des Centres de Rencontres Internationales de France (UCRIF)
27 rue Turbigo, 75002 Paris ☎01.40.26.57.64

AUSTRALIA
Youth Hostel Association
422 Kent St,
Sydney NSW 2000 ☎02/9261 1111

CANADA
Hostelling International
Suite 400, 205 Catherine St,
Ottawa, ON K2P 1C3 ☎613/237 7884

ENGLAND AND WALES
Youth Hostel Association (YHA)
Trevelyan House, 8 St Stephen's Hill,
St Alban's, Herts AL1 ☎01727/855215

14 Southampton St,
London WC2 ☎0171/836 8541

IRELAND
An Oige
61 Mountjoy St, Dublin 7 ☎01/830 4555
Youth Hostels Association of Northern Ireland
22 Donegal Rd, Belfast BT12 ☎01232/324733

NEW ZEALAND
Youth Hostels Association of New Zealand
cnr Tce & Wakefield streets,
Wellington ☎04/801 7280

SCOTLAND
Scottish Youth Hostel Association
7 Glebe Crescent, Stirling FK8 2JA
☎01786/451181

USA
Hostelling International
733 15th St NW, Suite 840,
Washington, DC 20005 ☎202/783 6161

in relevant French hostels for 100F. The third organization is the Union des Centres de Rencontres Internationales de France (UCRIF) with 60 hostels in France; membership is not required.

A few large towns provide a more luxurious standard of hostel accommodation in **Foyers des Jeunes Travailleurs/euses**, residential hostels for young workers and students, where you can usually get a private room for around 65F. They normally have a good cafeteria or canteen.

A further hostel-type alternative exists in the countryside, especially in hiking or cycling areas, in the form of the **gîtes d'étape**. These are less formal than the youth hostels, often run by the local village or municipality (whose mayor may well hold the key), and provide basic hospital-style beds and simple kitchen facilities. They are marked on the large-scale *IGN* walkers' maps and listed in individual *GR Topoguides*. A complete list of French *gîtes*, refuges and hostels is included in the publication *Gîtes et Refuges en France* (110F; Guides La Cadole), sold in French bookshops.

RENTED ACCOMMODATION

If you are planning to stay a week or more in any one place it might be worth considering **renting a house**. British travellers can check the adverts from private and foreign owners in Sunday newspapers (the *Observer* and *Sunday Times*, mainly); the boxes on pages 7, 11 and 13 of this book list holiday firms across the world that market accommodation/travel packages.

The French Government letting service, the **Gîtes de France**, no longer has an office in the United Kingdom, but their properties can be booked through Vacances Franco-Brittaniques. It's also possible to deal directly with the head office in Paris: Gîtes de France, 59 rue St-Lazare, 75009 Paris (Mon–Sat 10am–6.30pm; ☎01.49.70.75.75).

CAMPING

Practically every village and town in the country has at least one **campsite**, to cater for the thousands of French people who spend their holiday under canvas. The tourist boards for both Brittany and Normandy produce full lists of sites in their regions.

The cheapest – at around 20–30F per person per night – is usually the **Camping Municipal**, run by the local municipality. In season or when they are officially open, they are always clean with plenty of hot water, and often situated in the prime local position. Out of season, many of them don't even bother to have someone around to collect the overnight charge.

On the coast especially, there are **superior categories** of campsite, where you'll pay prices similar to those of a hotel for the facilities – bars, restaurants, sometimes swimming pools. These have a rather less transitory population than the Camping Municipals, with people often spending a whole holiday in the one base. If you plan to do the same – particularly if you've a caravan, camper van or substantial tent – book ahead.

Inland, **camping à la ferme** – on somebody's farm – is another (generally facility-less) possibility. Lists of sites are detailed in the tourist board's *Accueil à la Campagne* booklet.

Lastly, a **word of caution**: never camp rough (*camping sauvage*, as the French call it) on anyone's land without first asking permission. If the dogs don't get you, the guns might – farmers have been known to shoot before asking any questions. In many parts of France *camping sauvage* on public land is not tolerated – Brittany is the notable exception. On beaches it's best to camp out where there are other people doing so.

EATING AND DRINKING

The superb range of food available has to be one of the principal reasons to visit Brittany and, especially, Normandy. Restaurant quality is consistently high, prices remain reasonable and, to be honest, there are towns and villages where just about the only excitement is the gastronomic output.

With no wine production in Normandy (and only the *Muscadet*-style whites coming from the southeast of Brittany), the most interesting local **alcohol** is that derived from the region's orchards. **Cider** is made everywhere, along with its pear equivalent, **poiré**; and there is of course Norman Calvados (apple brandy), as well as numerous local firewaters.

BRETON FOOD

Brittany's proudest addition to world cuisine has to be the (white-flour) **crêpe**, and its savoury (buckwheat) equivalent, the **galette**. *Crêperies* throughout the region attempt to pass them off as satisfying meals, served with every imaginable filling. However, few people seriously plan their holidays around eating pancakes, and gourmets are more likely to be enticed to Brittany by its magnificent array of **seafood**, shellfish above all – mussels, oysters, clams, scallops. Restaurants in resorts such as **St-Malo** and **Quiberon** jostle for the attention of fish fanatics, while smaller towns – such as **Cancale**, which specializes in oysters (*huîtres*), and **Erquy**, with its scallops (*Coquilles St-Jacques*) – go so far as to depend on a single specific mollusc for their livelihood.

Although they can't claim to be uniquely Breton, two appetizers feature on every self-respecting menu. These are **moules marinières**, giant bowls of succulent orange mussels steamed open in white wine, shallots and parsley (and perhaps enriched with cream or *crème fraîche* to become *moules à la crème*), and **soupe de poissons**, served with a pot of the garlicky mayonnaise known as *rouille* (coloured with pulverized sweet red pepper) and a bowl of *croutons*. Jars of *soupe de poissons* – or crab, or lobster – are always on sale in seaside *poissonneries*, and make an ideal way to take a taste of France home with you. Paying a little extra in a restaurant – typically on menus costing 140F or more – brings you into the realm of the **assiette de fruits de mer**, a mountainous heap of langoustines, crabs, oysters, mussels, clams, whelks and cockles, most of them raw and all (with certain obvious exceptions) delicious. **Main courses** tend to be plainer than in Normandy, with fresh local fish being prepared with relatively simple sauces. Skate served with capers, or salmon baked with a mustard or cheese sauce, are typical dishes, while even the **cotriade**, a stew containing such fish as sole, turbot or bass, as well as shellfish, is distinctly less rich than the Mediterranean *bouillabaisse*.

Brittany is also better than much of France in maintaining its respect for fresh green **vegetables**, thanks to the extensive local production of peas, cauliflowers, artichokes and the like. Only with the **desserts** can things get rather too heavy; **far Breton**, considered a great delicacy, is a stodgy baked concoction of sponge and custard which owes its gravitas to the addition of such ingredients as pig's blood, while *îles flottantes* are meringue icebergs adrift in a sea of *crème brûlée* or custard.

NORMAN FOOD

The food of **Normandy** owes its most distinctive characteristic – its gut-bursting, heart-pounding richness – to the lush orchards and dairy herds of the region's agricultural heartland, and most especially the area southeast of Caen known as the Pays d'Auge. Menus abound in meat such as veal (*veau*) cooked in *vallée d'Auge* style, which consists largely of the profligate addition of

WEEKLY MARKETS

The list below features the biggest and best of the **markets** of Brittany and Normandy, with a particular emphasis on those specializing in **fresh food** and local produce.

Bear in mind that in addition to the specific days listed here, most large cities – **Rennes**, **Rouen** and **Caen**, for example – tend to have markets every day (with the occasional exception of Mondays).

	NORMANDY	BRITTANY
Monday	Bricquebec, Carentan, Pont-Audemer, St-Pierre-sur-Dives	Auray, Combourg, Concarneau, Lesneven, Ploërmel, Questembert, Redon, Vitré
Tuesday	Argentan, Cherbourg, Lessay, Portbail, Sourdeval, St-Lô, Villedieu-les-Poêles	Le Conquet, Locmariaquer, Paimpol, Pont-Aven, St-Malo, La Trinité
Wednesday	Évreux, Falaise, La Bouille, Orbec, Pontorson, Sées, Yvetot	Carnac, Tréguier, Paramé, Vannes
Thursday	Cherbourg, Conches-en-Ouche, Coutances, Deauville, Étretat, Forges-les-Eaux, Putanges, Ste-Mère-Église	Binic, Hennebont, Lannion
Friday	Argentan, Caen, Cormeilles, Eu, Pont-Audemer, St-Valéry, Valognes, Vire	Concarneau, Guingamp, Jugon-les-Lacs, Quimperlé, St-Malo, La Trinité
Saturday	Avranches, Bagnoles de l'Orne, Bayeux, Caudebec, Dieppe, Domfront, Falaise, Granville, Honfleur, Le Tréport, Lisieux, Mortagne-au-Perche, Neufchâtel, Orbec, Ry, St-Lô	Dinard, Fougères, Guingamp, Josselin, Locmariaquer, Morlaix, Paramé, Quimper, St-Brieuc, Vannes
Sunday	Alençon, Argentan, Brionne, La Ferrière-sur-Risle, St-Valéry (summer only)	Cancale, Carnac

cream and butter. Many dishes also feature orchard fruit, either in its natural state or in successively more alcoholic forms – either as apple or pear cider, or perhaps further distilled to produce apple brandies (Calvados in the case of apples, *poiré* for pears).

Normans have a great propensity for blood and guts. In addition to game such as rabbit and duck (a speciality in Rouen, where the birds are strangled to ensure that all their blood gets into the sauce), they enjoy such intestinal preparations as *andouilles*, the blood sausages known in English as chitterlings, and *tripes*, stewed for hours *à la mode de Caen*, but rendered no less palatable.

A full blowout at country restaurants in the small towns of inland Normandy – places like Conches, Vire and the Suisse Normande – will also traditionally entail one or two pauses

between courses for the *trou normand* – a glass of Calvados while you catch your breath before struggling on with the feast.

Normandy's long coastline ensures that it too is a great place for **seafood**, serving up much the same range of shellfish as detailed for Brittany, on p.33. Many of the larger ports and resorts have long waterfront lines of competing restaurants, each with its "*copieuse*" *assiette de fruits de mer*. **Honfleur** is probably the most enjoyable of these, but **Dieppe**, **Cherbourg** and **Granville** also spring to mind as offering endless eating opportunities. The menus tend to be much the same as those on offer in Brittany, if perhaps slightly more expensive.

The most famous products of Normandy's meadow-munching cows are of course its **cheeses**; you'll find a history and overview of cheese-making in the Pays d'Auge on p.163.

CAFÉS AND SNACKS

The days when hotels gave you mounds of crois-sants or *brioches* for **breakfast** seem to be long gone; now it's virtually always bread, jam and a jug of coffee or tea for about 30F. It makes more sense to pick up a croissant, *pain au chocolat* (a chocolate-filled croissant) or sandwich in a bar or café, for a fraction of the price, and wash it down with hot chocolate or coffee.

For **midday meals and light snacks**, most bars and cafés – there's no real difference – advertise *les snacks*, or *un casse-croûte* (a bite), with pictures of omelettes, fried eggs, hot dogs, or various sandwiches. Even when they don't, they'll usually make you a half or third of a *baguette* (French bread stick), buttered (*tartine*) and filled. Likely ingredients include *jambon* (ham), *fromage* (cheese), *thon* (tuna), *saucisson* (sausage) or *poulet* (chicken). Toasted sandwiches – most commonly *croques-monsieur* (cheese and ham) or *croques-madame* (cheese and bacon or sausage) – are also invariably on offer. Especially in rural areas, small bars may serve a moderate-priced *plat du jour* (chef's daily special) or *formule* (a limited or no-choice menu).

Many people also recommend **crêpes** for lunch. However, they may taste nice enough, but unless you buy from a market stall *crêpes* are extraordinarily poor value compared to a restaurant meal; you need to eat at least three, normally at over 20F each, to feel even slightly full. That they seem to excite children – presum-ably because they can drench them in chocolate syrup – shouldn't fool parents into thinking of a *crêperie* as a cheap alternative.

For **picnic and takeaway food**, there's noth-ing to beat buying fresh ingredients in one of the numerous local **markets**, details of which are given in the box opposite. If there isn't a market around on the day you need it, you'll find *charcu-teries* (delicatessens) everywhere – even in small villages. These sell cooked meats, prepared snacks such as *bouchées de la reine* (seafood vol-au-vents), ready-made dishes and assorted sal-ads. You can buy by weight or ask for *une tranche* (a slice), *une barquette* (a carton) or *une part* (a portion). The cheapest, in towns, are the super-markets' *charcuterie* counters.

· **Salons de thé**, which open from mid-morning to late evening, serve brunches, salads, quiches, etc, as well as cake and ice cream and a wide selection of teas. They tend to be a good deal pricier than cafés or brasseries – you're paying for the ritzy surroundings.

Patisseries, of course, have impressive arrays of cakes and pastries, often using local cream to excess. In addition to standard French pastries, the Bretons specialize in heavy, pudding-like affairs, dripping with butter, such as *kouïgn-anann*, and in *gaufres*, cream-drenched waffles.

RESTAURANTS

Brittany and Normandy hold an abundance of **restaurants**, and in many towns **brasseries** add to the choice. There's no distinction between the two in terms of quality or price range, though brasseries, which resemble cafés, serve quicker meals at most hours of the day; restaurants tend to stick to the traditional meal times of noon until 2pm and 7pm to 9.30pm. After 9pm or so, restau-rants often serve only *à la carte* meals – invari-ably more expensive than eating the set *menu fixe*. For the more upmarket places it's wise to make reservations – easily done on the same day.

VEGETARIANS

On the whole, **vegetarians** can expect a somewhat lean time in Brittany and Normandy. One or two towns have specifically vegetarian restaurants (detailed in the text), but elsewhere you'll have to hope you find a sympathetic restaurant (*crêperies* can be good standbys). Sometimes they're willing to replace a meat dish on the *menu fixe* with an omelette; other times you'll have to pick your way through the *carte*. Remember the phrase *je suis végétarien(ne); il y a quelques plats sans viande?* (I'm a vegetarian; are there any non-meat dishes?).

Many vegetarians swallow a few principles and start eating fish and shellfish on holiday; that of course is a matter for your conscience. Vegans, however, should probably forget all about eating in French restaurants; cook your own food, or just stay at home.

For details of the *Maison du Vert*, a British-run all-vegetarian guesthouse in the Pays d'Auge in Normandy, see p.167.

A LIST OF DISHES

BASICS

Pain	Bread	*Poivre*	Pepper	*Fourchette*	Fork
Beurre	Butter	*Sel*	Salt	*Couteau*	Knife
Oeufs	Eggs	*Sucre*	Sugar	*Cuillère*	Spoon
Lait	Milk	*Bouteille*	Bottle	*Table*	Table
Huile	Oil	*Verre*	Glass	*L'addition*	Bill

SNACKS

Crêpe	Pancake (sweet)
au sucre	with sugar
au citron	with lemon
au miel	with honey
à la confiture	with jam
aux oeufs	with eggs
à la crème de marrons	with chestnut purée
Galette	Buckwheat (savoury) pancake
Un sandwich/ une baguette . . .	A sandwich
jambon	with ham
fromage	with cheese
saucisson	with sausage
à l'ail	with garlic
au poivre	with pepper
pâté (de campagne)	with pâté (country-style)
Croque-monsieur	Grilled cheese and ham sandwich
Croque-madame	Grilled cheese and bacon, sausage, chicken or an egg sandwich
Oeufs	Eggs
au plat	Fried eggs
à la coque	Boiled eggs
durs	Hard-boiled eggs
brouillés	Scrambled eggs

Omelette . . .	Omelette . . .
nature	plain
aux fines herbes	with herbs
au fromage	with cheese
Salade de . . .	Salad of . . .
tomates	tomatoes
betteraves	beetroot
concombres	cucumber
carottes râpées	grated carrots

Other fillings/salads

Anchois	Anchovy
Andouillette	Tripe sausage
Boudin	Black pudding
Coeurs de palmiers	Palm hearts
Fonds d'artichauts	Artichoke hearts
Hareng	Herring
Langue	Tongue
Poulet	Chicken
Thon	Tuna fish

And some terms

Chauffé	Heated
Cuit	Cooked
Cru	Raw
Emballé	Wrapped
À emporter	Takeaway
Fumé	Smoked
Salé	Salted/spicy
Sucré	Sweet

SOUPS (SOUPES) AND STARTERS (HORS D'OEUVRES)

Bisque	Shellfish soup
Bouillabaisse	Marseillais fish soup
Bouillon	Broth or stock
Bourride	Thick fish soup
Consommé	Clear soup
Pistou	Parmesan, basil and garlic paste added to soup
Potage	Thick vegetable soup
Rouille	Red pepper, garlic and saffron mayonnaise served with fish soup

Velouté	Thick soup, usually fish or poultry

Starters

Assiette anglaise	Plate of cold meats
Crudités	Raw vegetables with dressings
Hors d'oeuvres variés	Combination of the above plus smoked or marinated fish

FISH (POISSON), SEAFOOD (FRUITS DE MER) AND SHELLFISH (CRUSTACES OR COQUILLAGES)

Anchois	Anchovies	*Éperlan*	Smelt or whitebait	*Louvine, loubine*	Similar to sea bass
Anguilles	Eels				
Barbue	Brill	*Escargots*	Snails	*Maquereau*	Mackerel
Bigourneau	Periwinkle	*Flétan*	Halibut	*Merlan*	Whiting
Brème	Bream	*Friture*	Assorted fried fish	*Moules (marinière)*	Mussels (with shallots in white wine sauce)
Cabillaud	Cod				
Calmar	Squid	*Gambas*	King prawns		
Carrelet	Plaice	*Hareng*	Herring		
Claire	Type of oyster	*Homard*	Lobster	*Oursin*	Sea urchin
Colin	Hake	*Huîtres*	Oysters	*Palourdes*	Clams
Congre	Conger eel	*Langouste*	Spiny lobster	*Praires*	Small clams
Coques	Cockles	*Langoustines*	Saltwater crayfish (scampi)	*Raie*	Skate
Coquilles St-Jacques	Scallops			*Rouget*	Red mullet
		Limande	Lemon sole	*Saumon*	Salmon
Crabe	Crab	*Lotte*	Burbot	*Sole*	Sole
Crevettes grises	Shrimp	*Lotte de mer*	Monkfish	*Thon*	Tuna
Crevettes roses	Prawns	*Loup de mer*	Sea bass	*Truite*	Trout
Daurade	Sea bream			*Turbot*	Turbot

FISH: SOME TERMS

Aïoli	Garlic mayonnaise served with salt cod and other fish	*Fumet*	Fish stock
		Gigot de mer	Large fish baked whole
Béarnaise	Sauce made with egg yolks, white wine, shallots and vinegar	*Grillé*	Grilled
		Hollandaise	Butter and vinegar sauce
Beignets	Fritters	*À la meunière*	In a butter, lemon and parsley sauce
Darne	Fillet or steak		
La douzaine	A dozen	*Mousse, mousseline*	Mousse
Frit	Fried		
Friture	Deep-fried small fish	*Quenelles*	Light dumplings
Fumé	Smoked		

MEAT (VIANDE) AND POULTRY (VOLAILLE)

Agneau (de présalé)	Lamb (grazed on salt marshes)	*Langue*	Tongue
		Lapin, lapereau	Rabbit, young rabbit
Andouille, andouillette	Tripe sausage	*Lard, lardons*	Bacon, diced bacon
		Lièvre	Hare
Boeuf	Beef	*Merguez*	Spicy, red sausage
Bifteck	Steak	*Mouton*	Mutton
Boudin blanc	Sausage of white meats	*Museau de veau*	Calf's muzzle
Boudin noir	Black pudding	*Oie*	Goose
Caille	Quail	*Os*	Bone
Canard	Duck	*Porc*	Pork
Caneton	Duckling	*Poulet*	Chicken
Contrefilet	Sirloin roast	*Poussin*	Baby chicken
Coquelet	Cockerel	*Ris*	Sweetbreads
Dinde, dindon	Turkey	*Rognons*	Kidneys
Entrecôte	Ribsteak	*Rognons blancs*	Testicles
Faux filet	Sirloin steak	*Sanglier*	Wild boar
Foie	Liver	*Steack*	Steak
Foie gras	Fattened (duck/ goose) liver	*Tête de veau*	Calf's head (in jelly)
Gigot (d'agneau)	Leg (of lamb)	*Tournedos*	Thick slices of fillet
Grillade	Grilled meat	*Tripes*	Tripe
Hâchis	Chopped meat or mince hamburger	*Veau*	Veal
		Venaison	Venison

MEAT AND POULTRY: DISHES AND TERMS

Boeuf bourguignon	Beef stew with burgundy, onions and mushrooms
Canard à l'orange	Roast duck with an orange-and-wine sauce
Cassoulet	A casserole of beans and meat
Coq au vin	Chicken cooked until it falls off the bone with wine, onions and mushrooms
Steack au poivre (vert/rouge)	Steak in a black (green/red) peppercorn sauce
Steack tartare	Raw chopped beef, topped with a raw egg yolk

Terms

Blanquette, daube, estouffade, hochepôt, navarin and *ragoût*	All are types of stews
Aile	Wing
Carré	Best end of neck, chop or cutlet
Civit	Game stew
Confit	Meat preserve
Côte	Chop, cutlet or rib
Cou	Neck
Cuisse	Thigh or leg
Epaule	Shoulder
Médaillon	Round piece
Pavé	Thick slice
En croûte	In pastry
Farci	Stuffed
Au feu de bois	Cooked over wood fire

Au four	Baked
Garni	With vegetables
Gésier	Gizzard
Grillé	Grilled
Magret de canard	Duck breast
Marmite	Casserole
Mijoté	Stewed
Museau	Muzzle
Rôti	Roast
Sauté	Lightly cooked in butter

For steaks

Bleu	Almost raw
Saignant	Rare
A point	Medium
Bien cuit	Well done
Très bien cuit	Very well cooked
Brochette	Kebab

Garnishes and sauces

Beurre blanc	Sauce of white wine and shallots, with butter
Chasseur	White wine, mushrooms and shallots
Diable	Strong mustard seasoning
Forestière	With bacon and mushroom
Fricassée	Rich, creamy sauce
Mornay	Cheese sauce
Pays d'Auge	Cream and cider
Piquante	Gherkins or capers, vinegar and shallots
Provençale	Tomatoes, garlic, olive oil and herbs

VEGETABLES (LÉGUMES), HERBS (HERBES) AND SPICES (ÉPICES) ETC

Ail	Garlic	*Endive*	Chicory
Algue	Seaweed	*Épinards*	Spinach
Anis	Aniseed	*Estragon*	Tarragon
Artichaut	Artichoke	*Fenouil*	Fennel
Asperges	Asparagus	*Flageolets*	White beans
Avocat	Avocado	*Gingembre*	Ginger
Basilic	Basil	*Haricots*	Beans
Betterave	Beetroot	*verts*	string (French)
Carotte	Carrot	*rouges*	kidney
Céleri	Celery	*beurres*	butter
Champignons, cèpes, chanterelles	Mushrooms of various kinds	*Laurier*	Bay leaf
		Lentilles	Lentils
Chou (rouge)	(Red) cabbage	*Maïs*	Corn
Choufleur	Cauliflower	*Menthe*	Mint
Ciboulettes	Chives	*Moutarde*	Mustard
Concombre	Cucumber	*Oignon*	Onion
Cornichon	Gherkin	*Pâte*	Pasta, pastry
Échalotes	Shallots	*Persil*	Parsley
		Petits pois	Peas

Piment	Pimento
Pois chiches	Chick peas
Pois mange-touts	Snow peas
Pignons	Pine nuts
Poireau	Leek
Poivron (vert, rouge)	Sweet pepper (green, red)
Pommes (de terre)	Potatoes
Primeurs	Spring vegetables
Radis	Radishes
Riz	Rice
Safran	Saffron
Salade verte	Green salad
Sarrasin	Buckwheat
Tomate	Tomato
Truffes	Truffles

VEGETABLES: DISHES AND TERMS

Beignet	Fritter	*Parmentier*	With potatoes
Farci	Stuffed	*Sauté*	Lightly fried in butter
Gratiné	Browned with cheese or butter	*À la vapeur*	Steamed
Jardinière	With mixed diced vegetables	*Je suis végétarien(ne).*	I'm a vegetarian. Are
À la parisienne	Sautéed in butter (potatoes);	*Il y a quelques*	there any non-meat
	with white wine sauce	*plats sans viande?*	dishes?
	and shallots		

FRUITS (FRUITS) AND NUTS (NOIX)

Abricot	Apricot	*Fruit de*	Passion fruit	*Poire*	Pear
Amandes	Almonds	*la passion*		*Pomme*	Apple
Ananas	Pineapple	*Groseilles*	Redcurrants	*Prune*	Plum
Banane	Banana		and goose-	*Pruneau*	Prune
Brugnon,	Nectarine		berries	*Raisins*	Grapes
nectarine		*Mangue*	Mango		
Cacahouète	Peanut	*Marrons*	Chestnuts	**Terms**	
Cassis	Blackcurrants	*Melon*	Melon	*Beignets*	Fritter
Cérises	Cherries	*Myrtilles*	Bilberries	*Compôte de . . .*	Stewed . . .
Citron	Lemon	*Noisette*	Hazelnut	*Coulis*	Sauce
Citron vert	Lime	*Noix*	Nuts	*Flambé*	Set aflame in
Figues	Figs	*Orange*	Orange		alcohol
Fraises	Strawberries	*Pamplemousse*	Grapefruit	*Frappé*	Iced
(de bois)	(wild)	*Pêche (blanche)*	(White) peach		
Framboises	Raspberries	*Pistache*	Pistachio		

DESSERTS (DESSERTS OR ENTREMETS) AND PASTRIES (PÂTISSERIE)

Bombe	A moulded ice-cream dessert	*Parfait*	Frozen mousse, sometimes
Brioche	Sweet, high-yeast breakfast roll		ice cream
Charlotte	Custard and fruit in lining of	*Petit Suisse*	A smooth mixture of cream
	almond fingers		and curds
Crème Chantilly	Vanilla-flavoured and	*Petits fours*	Bite-sized cakes, pastries
	sweetened whipped cream	*Poires Belle*	Pears and ice cream
Crème fraîche	Sour cream	*Hélène*	in chocolate sauce
Crème pâtissière	Thick, eggy pastry-filling	*Yaourt, yogourt*	Yoghurt
Crêpes Suzettes	Thin pancakes with orange		
	juice and liqueur	**Terms**	
Fromage blanc	Cream cheese	*Barquette*	Small boat-shaped flan
Glace	Ice cream	*Bavarois*	Refers to the mould, could be a
Île flottante/	Soft meringues floating on		mousse or custard
oeufs à la neie	custard	*Coupe*	A serving of ice cream
Macarons	Macaroons	*Crêpes*	Pancakes
Madeleine	Small sponge cake	*Galettes*	Buckwheat pancakes
Marrons Mont	Chestnut purée and cream	*Gênoise*	Rich sponge cake
Blanc	on a rum-soaked sponge cake	*Sablé*	Shortbread biscuit
Mousse au	Chocolate mousse	*Savarin*	A filled, ring-shaped cake
chocolat		*Tarte*	Tart
Palmiers	Caramelized puff pastries	*Tartelette*	Small tart

CHEESE (FROMAGE)

There are over 400 types of French cheese, most of them named after their place of origin. *Chèvre* is goat's cheese. *Le plateau de fromages* is the cheeseboard, and bread (but not butter) is served with it. The best-known cheeses from the area covered by this book all come from the Pays d'Auge region of Normandy: *Pont l'Evêque, Livarot* and, most famous of all, *Camembert*, and are discussed in detail on p.163.

And one final note: always call the waiter or waitress *Monsieur* or *Madame* (*Mademoiselle* if a young woman), never *garçon*, no matter what you've been taught in school.

In small towns it may be impossible to get anything other than a bar sandwich after 10pm; in major cities, central brasseries will serve until 11pm or midnight and one or two may stay open all night. Don't forget that hotel restaurants are open to non-residents, and are often very good value; the green-and-yellow *Logis de France* symbol is always worth looking out for. On the road, keep an eye open too for the red-and-blue sign of the *Relais Routiers* – always reasonably priced and gastronomically sound.

Prices and what you get for them are posted outside. Normally there is a choice between one or more *menus fixes* (set menus), where the number of courses has already been determined and choice is limited, and the *carte*, the full menu. At the bottom price range, say below 75F, **menus fixes** revolve around standard dishes, such as steak and chips (*steack frites*), chicken and chips (*poulet frites*), or various offal concoctions, though it's always worth looking out for the *plat du jour*, which may be more appealing. For 85F to 140F, virtually any of the restaurants recommended in this guide will serve you a good three-course meal, while four-course blowouts, including a starter as well as separate meat and fish courses, cost from 140F to 250F. Most expensive of the lot are the special seafood menus, offering giant platters of assorted crustaceans; away from the big centres such as Cancale and St-Malo, it pays to be wary of these, as the stuff may have been waiting around for several days for someone foolhardy enough to order it.

Going **à la carte** offers greater flexibility and, in the better restaurants, access to the chef's specialities – though you can expect to pay heavily for the privilege. A simple and perfectly legitimate ploy is to have just one course instead of the expected three or four. You can share dishes or just have several starters – a useful strategy for vegetarians. There's no minimum charge.

North American visitors should bear in mind that in France, an *entrée* is an appetizer or starter; the main course of the meal is the *plat principal*. In the French sequence of courses, any salad (sometimes vegetables, too) comes separate from the main dish, and cheese precedes a dessert. You will be offered coffee, which is always extra, to finish off the meal.

Service compris (*s.c.*) means the **service charge** is included, which is usually the case on all set menus; *service non compris* (*s.n.c.*), or ser-

> If eating out seems expensive, bear in mind it's not all the fault of the restaurants. A 100F fixed-price menu includes over 20F in value-added tax, plus 15F to cover service.

vice en sus, means that it isn't, and you need to calculate an additional fifteen percent. **Wine** (*vin*) or a **drink** (*boisson*) is unlikely to be included, although a glass is occasionally thrown in with cheaper menus. When ordering wine, ask for *un quart* (quarter-litre), *un demi-litre* (half-litre) or *une carafe* (a litre). You'll normally be given the house wine unless you specify otherwise; if you're worried about the cost, ask for *vin ordinaire*.

The French follow the North American rather than the British line in their attitude towards **children** in restaurants, not simply by offering reduced-price children's menus but in creating an atmosphere, even in otherwise fairly snooty establishments, that positively welcomes kids. It is regarded as self-evident that large family groups should be able to eat out together. A rather murkier area is that of **dogs** in the dining room; it can be quite a shock in a provincial hotel to realize that the majority of your fellow diners are attempting to keep dogs concealed beneath their tables.

DRINKING

Where you can eat you can invariably **drink**, and vice versa. Drinking is done at a leisurely pace, whether as a prelude to food (*apéritif*), a sequel (*digestif*) or the accompaniment, and **cafés** are the standard venue.

Every bar or café is obliged to display a full **price list**, which will usually show progressively increasing prices for drinks at the bar (*au comptoir*), sitting down (*la salle*) and on the terrace (*la terrasse*).

Wine (*vin*) is the regular drink. Red is *rouge*, white is *blanc*, or there's *rosé*. Vin de table – plonk – is generally drinkable and always cheap; it may be disguised (and priced up) as the house wine, or *cuvée*. Restaurant mark-ups for quality wines can be outrageous, in a country where wine is so cheap in the shops. In bars, you normally buy by the glass, and just ask for *un rouge* or *un blanc*; *un pichet* gets you a quarter-litre jug.

Strictly speaking, no wine is produced in Brittany or Normandy. However, along the lower Loire Valley, the *département* of Loire-Atlantique, centred on Nantes, is still generally regarded as "belonging" to Brittany – and is treated as such in this book. Vineyards here are responsible for the dry white Muscadet – which is what normally goes into *moules marinières* – and the even drier Gros-Plant. You'll find a brief account of how to visit some of the vineyards where they are made on p.315.

Cider (*cidre*) is extremely popular. In Brittany it's a standard accompaniment to a meal of *crêpes* and may be offered on restaurant *menus fixes*. Normans more often consume it in bars. Most of the many varieties are very dry and very wonderful. *Poiré*, pear cider, is also produced, but on a small scale and is not commercially distributed.

The familiar Belgian and German brands account for most of the **beer** you'll find. Draught (*à la pression*, usually Kronenbourg) is the cheapest drink you can have next to coffee and wine – ask for *un demi* (defined as 25cl). Bottled beer is exceptionally cheap in supermarkets.

British-style ales and stouts are also popular. Every town seems to have some Celtic-affiliated bar that sells Guinness, and specialist beer-drinking establishments can be found in cities like Brest, Rennes and Quimper. There's even a home-grown Breton real ale, Coreff.

Strong alcohols are drunk from 5am as pre-work fortifiers, right through the day; Bretons have a reputation for commitment to this. Brandies and dozens of *eaux de vie* (spirits) and liqueurs are always available. The most famous of these in Normandy are **Calvados**, brandy distilled from apples and left to mature for anything upwards of ten years, and **Benedictine**, distilled

at Fécamp from an obscure mix of ingredients (see p.67). Measures are generous, but they don't come cheap, especially in restaurants (where Calvados is traditionally drunk as a *trou*, or hole, between courses). The same applies to imported spirits like whisky (*Scotch*).

On the **soft drink** front, you can buy cartons of unsweetened fruit juice in supermarkets, although in cafés the bottled nectars such as apricot (*jus d'abricot*) and blackcurrant (*cassis*) still hold sway. Some cafés serve tiny glasses of fresh orange and lemon juice (*orange/citron pressé*); otherwise it's the standard fizzy cans. Bottles of **mineral water** (*eau minérale*) and spring water (*eau de source*) – either sparkling (*pétillante*) or still (*eau plate*) – abound, from the best-seller Perrier to the obscurest spa product. But there's not much wrong with the tap water (*eau du robinet*).

Coffee in Normandy is invariably espresso and very strong; in Brittany, particularly in villages, it is sometimes made in jugs, very weakly. *Un café* or *un express* is black, *un crème* is white, *un café au lait* (served at breakfast) is espresso in a large cup or bowl filled up with hot milk. Most bars will also serve *un déca*, decaffeinated coffee. Ordinary **tea** (*thé*) is Lipton's, nine times out of ten; to have milk with it, ask for *un peu de lait frais*.

After overeating, **herb teas** (*infusions*), served in every café, can be soothing. The more common ones are *verveine* (verbena), *tilleul* (lime blossom) and *tisane* (camomile). **Chocolat chaud** (hot chocolate) unlike tea, lives up to the high standards of French food and drink, and can be had in any café.

COMMUNICATIONS: POST, PHONES AND MEDIA

MAIL SERVICES

As a rule, French **post offices** – **postes** or **PTTs** – are open from 9am until noon and 2pm to 5pm (Mon–Fri), and 9am until noon only on Saturday. However, in the larger towns you'll find a main office open through the day (8am–7pm), while in Breton and Norman villages, lunch hours and closing times can vary enormously.

You can have letters sent to you **poste restante** at any post office in the country. For whatever town you choose, always specify the main post office (Poste Centrale) to avoid possible confusion. The addresses of the two largest in the region covered by this book are:

Poste Restante, Poste Centrale, 76000 ROUEN.

Poste Restante, Poste Centrale, 44000 NANTES.

To collect mail you'll need a passport, and should expect to pay a charge of a couple of francs. If you're expecting mail, it's worth asking the clerk to check under your surname, and all possible Christian names as well – filing systems tend to be erratic.

Sending letters, the quickest international service is by *aérogramme*, sold at all post offices. You can buy ordinary stamps (*timbres*) at any *tabac* (tobacconist). When this book went to press, the current rates for **postcards** (*cartes postales*) were 3F for the UK and Europe, 4.40F for North America, and 5.20F for Australia and New Zealand. Letters (*lettres*), naturally, cost a little more. If you're sending **parcels** abroad, remem-ber that small *postes* don't often send foreign mail and may need reminding of, for example, the huge reductions for printed papers and books. **Faxes** can be sent from all main post offices: the official French word is *télécopie*, but everyone understands *fax*.

TELEPHONES

You can make domestic and international phone calls from any call box (or **cabine**), and can receive calls where there's a blue logo of a ringing bell. Most payphones only take **phone cards** (*télécartes*). These are sold in post offices, PTT boutiques, train stations and some *tabacs*, and come in two sizes: 40F for 50 units, and 97F for 120 units. In coin-only boxes, still common in cafés, bars and rural parts, put the money in (50 centimes, 1F, 5F, 10F pieces) after you lift the receiver and before you dial – you can add more once you are connected. Certain digital British **mobile phones** also work in France.

For **calls** within France – local or long distance – simply dial all ten digits of the number. Local calls cost 0,813F for three minutes (1F minimum); long-distance calls cost up to 2,44F for three minutes. **Off-peak charges** apply for all calls on weekdays between 7pm and 8am, and from noon on Saturday until 8am Monday. Numbers beginning with ☎08.00. are free numbers; those beginning with ☎08.36 are premium rate (from 2.23F per minute), and those beginning with ☎06 are mobile and therefore also expensive to call.

The major **international calling codes** are given in the box opposite. From a private phone, a call to the UK (*Royaume-Unis*) will cost between 1.64F to 2.47F per minute, from a public phone 2,17F to 2,57F; to Ireland 1.95F to 2.97F a minute or 2,85F to 3,52F; to US (*États-Unis*) and Canada 1.95–2.97F a minute or 2,85F to 3,52F; to Australia and New Zealand 4.31–6.55F a minute or 7,99F to 10,16F. To avoid payment altogether, make a reverse charge or **collect call** (*téléphoner en PCV*). You can also do this through the operator in the UK, by dialling the Home Direct number ☎0800.89.00.33; to get an English-speaking operator for North America, dial ☎00.00.11.

An alternative to dialling internationally from *cabines*, if you prefer to avoid wrestling with piles of loose change, is to use the numbered **booths**

INTERNATIONAL CALLS

To place an international call **to France**, dial the following access code followed by the last nine digits of the ten-digit French number (thus omitting the inital 0).

Britain ☎00 33   Ireland ☎00 33   USA & Canada ☎011 33
Australia ☎011 33   New Zealand ☎00 44 33

To make an international call **from France**, dial ☎00, wait for a tone, and then dial the relevant country code, and the number you want minus its initial 0.

Britain ☎00 44   Ireland ☎00 353   USA & Canada ☎00 1
Australia ☎00 61   New Zealand ☎00 64

at main post offices. You apply at the counter to be assigned a number and then dial as above. The disadvantage – odd, given the French obsession with technology – is that you can't tell how much you're spending.

To speak to the **operator** dial ☎13; **directory enquiries**, both national and international, are on ☎12; **medical emergencies**, ☎15; the **police**, ☎17; **fire** ☎18.

MINITEL AND THE INTERNET

In theory at least, every French phone subscriber has a **minitel**, an online computer allowing access through the phone lines to all kinds of directories, databases, chat lines, etc. You will also find them in post offices, libraries and so on. Most organizations, from sports federations to government institutions to gay groups, have a code consisting of numbers and letters to call up information, leave messages, make reservations, etc. You dial the number on the phone, wait for a fax-type tone, then type the letters on the keyboard and, finally, press *"Connexion Fin"* (the same key ends the connection). If you're at all computer-literate and can understand keyboard terms in French (*retour* – return, *envoi* – enter, etc) you shouldn't find them hard to use. Most services cost more than the equivalent phone rates.

Most analysts believe France will have to junk the minitel box altogether as it embraces the **Internet** revolution. So far, the nation has been slow to get online, thanks in part to a low level of ownership of personal computers, and the dominance of the English language on the Net. Nonetheless, many French towns and organizations now have sites on the World Wide Web. You can get into a list of all French servers via the Centre National de Recherche Scientifique on *www.urec.fr/* or visit the Ministry of Culture's site on *web.culture.fr/*. Some sites that specifically offer tourist information are listed on p.20.

NEWSPAPERS AND MAGAZINES

British and North American **newspapers** – at the very least, the *International Herald Tribune* – are intermittently available. In the larger resorts, and in cities such as Nantes and Rouen, you should find reasonable selections of foreign-language papers. Elsewhere, it's mostly down to the British *Times*, *Daily Mail* or *Sun*.

As for the **French press**, the widest circulations are enjoyed by the **regional dailies**. Throughout Normandy and Brittany, the most important and influential paper is *Ouest-France*. This is based in Rennes but has numerous local editions – worth picking up for their listings supplements, if nothing else. Of the **national dailies**, *Le Monde* is the most intellectual and respected, with no concessions to entertainment (such as pictures), but a correctly styled French that is probably the easiest to understand. *Libération* (*Libé* for short; daily except Mon), is moderately left-wing, independent and colloquial with good, if choosy, coverage.

Weeklies, on the *Newsweek/Time* model, include the wide-ranging left-leaning *Le Nouvel Observateur*, and its rightist counterweight, *L'Express*. The best, and funniest, investigative journalism is in the satirical *Canard Enchaîné*, unfortunately almost incomprehensible to non-native speakers. **Monthlies** include the young and trendy – and cheap – *Nova*, which has excellent listings of cultural events, and *Actuel*, which is good for current events.

TV AND RADIO

French TV broadcasts six channels, three of them public, along with a good many more cable and satellite channels, which include the BBC World Service. If you've got a **radio**, you can tune into English-language news on the BBC World Service on 648khz at intervals throughout the day and night. BBC Radio 4 from 5am to 11.45pm GMT, and the World Service from 11.45pm to 5am GMT on 198 kHz long wave, is usually quite clear through-

out Brittany and Normandy, while the Voice of America transmits on 90.5, 98.8 and 102.4 FM. Radio Classique (101.1 FM) is a classical music station with a minimum of chat and no commercials. For **news** in French, there's the state-run France Inter (87.8 FM), Europe 1 (104.7 FM) or round-the-clock news on France Infos (105.5 FM).

BUSINESS HOURS AND HOLIDAYS

The basic hours of business in France are from 8am or 9am until noon, and from 2pm to 6pm or 7pm. Almost everything – shops, museums, tourist offices, most banks – closes for a couple of hours at midday.

Food shops often don't reopen until halfway through the afternoon, closing around 7.30pm or 8pm just before the evening meal. If you're looking to buy a picnic lunch, you'll need to get into the habit of buying it before you're ready to think about eating.

The standard **closing days** are Sunday and Monday, Food shops tend to close on Monday rather than Sunday, but in smaller towns you may well find everything except the odd *boulangerie* (bakery) shut on both days. This includes **banks**. It's all too easy to find yourself dependent on hotels for money-changing – an alternative that invariably means low rates and high commission.

Museums are not very generous with their hours, tending to open at around 10am, close for lunch at noon until 2pm (sometimes 3pm) and then run through until only 5pm or 6pm. Summer opening times, usually applicable between from mid-May or early June and mid-September, but sometimes only during July and August, often differ from winter times; all variations are indicated in the listings given in this book. The closing days are usually Monday or Tuesday, sometimes both. Admission charges can be very offputting, though most state-owned museums have one or two days of the week when they're free, and you can get a big reduction at most places by showing a

student card (or passport if you're under 26 or over 60).

Churches and **cathedrals** are almost always open all day, with charges only for the crypt, treasuries or cloister, and little fuss about how you're dressed. Where they are closed you may have to go during Mass to take a look, on Sunday morning, or at other times which you'll see posted up on the door. In small towns and villages, however, getting the key is not difficult – ask anyone nearby or hunt out the priest, whose house is known as the *presbytère*.

PUBLIC HOLIDAYS

France celebrates thirteen national holidays (*jours fériés*), when most shops and businesses, though not museums or restaurants, are closed:

January 1
Easter Sunday
Easter Monday
Ascension Day (forty days after Easter)
Pentecost (seventh Sunday after Easter, plus the Monday)
May 1 (May Day/Labour Day)
May 8 (V-E Day)
July 14 (Bastille Day)
August 15 (Assumption of the Virgin Mary)
November 1 (All Saints' Day)
November 11 (1918 Armistice Day)
Christmas Day

FESTIVALS AND EVENTS

The most interesting Breton events are without doubt the region's cultural festivals. At the largest of these, the **Lorient Festival Inter-Celtique** (August), music, performance, food and drink of all seven Celtic nations are featured in a completely authentic gathering that pulls in cultural nationalists (and ethnic music fans) from Ireland to Spain. If you can't get to Lorient, there are two – smaller, and more particularly Breton – alternatives in the **Nantes Quinzaine Celtique** (June/July) and Quimper's **Festival de Cornouaille** (July).

Look out also for local **club events** put on by individual Celtic folklore groups – *Cercles, Bagadou* or, best of the lot, *Fests-Noz*. These are most prolific in Nantes, though wherever you are in the

CALENDAR OF EVENTS

Whitsun – **Honfleur** Seamen's Festival

Third Sun in May – **Tréguier** *St Yves Pardon*

Third week in May – **Coutances** Jazz Festival

Late May – **St-Malo** *Étonnants Voyageurs*

Last weekend in May – **St-Brieuc** Art Rock Festival

Early June – **Rouen** Joan of Arc Festival

June 6 – D-Day Ceremonies on Invasion Beaches

Third week in June – **Balleroy** Balloon Festival (alternate years)

End June/start July – **Nantes** *Quinzaine Celtique*

Early July – **Lamballe** Golden Broom Folk Festival

First ten days of July – **Rennes** *Tombées de la Nuit* theatre and music festival

Second Sun in July – **Locronan** *Troménie Pardon*

July 16 – **La Haye du Routot** *Fête de Ste-Claire*

July 26 – **Ste Anne d'Auray** *Pardon*

July – **St-Brieuc** Festival of Breton Music

Third week in July – **Vannes** Jazz Festival

Late July – **Quimper** *Festival de Cornouaille*

Last Sun in July – **Locquirec** Festival of the Sea

Last Sun in July – **Paimpol** *Fête des Terres-Neuvas*

Aug 2 – **Le Tréport** Blessing of the Sea

First full week in Aug – **Lorient** *Festival InterCeltique*

First fortnight in Aug – **Quimper** *Semaines Musicales*

First fortnight in Aug – **Île de Fedrun** *Fête de la Brière*

Early Aug – **Dives** Puppet Festival

Second Sun in Aug – **Lizio** *Festival Artisanal*

Mid-Aug – **Guingamp** *Saint Loup* Breton Dance Festival

Mid-Aug – **Lamballe** Horse Festival

Mid-Aug – **Le Roche-Jagu** Jazz Festival

First Sun in Sept – **Le Pin** Horse Show

First Sun in Sept – **Le Folgoet** *Pardon*

Early Sept – **Douarnenez** Film Festival of International Minorities

First week in Sept – **Deauville** American Film Festival

Second weekend in Sept – **Lessay** Holy Cross cattle and animal fair

Second weekend in Sept – **Dieppe** Kite-flying festival

Sun nearest Sept 29 – **Mont St-Michel** Archangel Michael Festival

Last Sun in Sept – **Caudebec** Cider Festival (even-numbered years only)

Late Sept – **Bellême** Mycology Festival

Mid-Oct – **Le Havre** Blues Festival

Late Oct – **Beuvron-en-Auge** Cider Festival

First week in Dec – **Rennes** *Les Transmusicales* international rock festival province, listings pages of the *Ouest-France* can be worth scrutiny. The "Breton music" section at the end of this book has detailed recommendations of clubs and venues to check out in the province.

The religious **pardons**, sometimes promoted as tourist attractions in Brittany, are rather different affairs. These are essentially church processions, organized by a particular community on the local saint's day. Though generally small-scale, some, like that at Sainte-Anne d'Auray, have over the centuries taken on more region-wide status as pilgrimages. Rather than being carnivals or fêtes, they are primarily very serious occasions, centred on lengthy and rather gloomy church services. If you're not interested by the religious aspects, only the food and drink stalls, and low-key accompaniments, hold any great appeal.

By and large, **Normandy** lacks any specific cultural traditions to celebrate, doing its best to make up with celebrations of related **historic events** – births and deaths of William the Conqueror, Sainte-Thérèse, etc. The **D-Day** (June 6) landings along the Invasion Beaches are always marked in some way.

In both Normandy and Brittany, avoid the **Spectacles**, camp and overpriced outdoor shows on some mythical theme or other, held most regularly (and most tackily) at Bagnoles and Elven.

On the more mainstream **cultural side**, the larger cities – Rouen, Rennes and Nantes – have active theatre, opera and classical music seasons, though little happens during the summer. **Cinema** is most interesting in these cities, too, and the region is host to one of the more accessible French film festivals – Deauville's American Film Festival (September). Almost all foreign films will be dubbed into French; *v.o.* in the listings signifies original language.

Both **Rennes** and **Rouen** have laid recent claim to be "the capital of French **rock**"; Rennes is increasingly the one to watch, with its December *Transmusicales* attracting international stars to share the stage with local groups. St-Brieuc's rival Art Rock Festival caters to more specialist tastes. A few large rock concerts also take place during the holiday season, at places like Brest and Concarneau, with the usual bland multinational billing of fading "rock giants".

TROUBLE AND THE POLICE

Compared to Paris or the south of France, crime is a low-key problem in Brittany and Normandy. However, you still need to take normal precautions against petty theft – keep your wallet in your front pocket or your handbag under your elbow.

If you should be attacked, hand over the money and start dialling the cancellation numbers for your travellers' cheques and credit cards (see below). For British travellers, Barclaycard offers a free "International Rescue" service (☎0181/667 1393), in which a replacement card or cash can be sent to you within 24 hours.

If you need to report a theft, go to the local *gendarmerie* (police station), and do your best to persuade them to give you the requisite piece of paper for a claim; the first thing they'll ask for is your passport. The two main types of French police, the **Police Nationale** and the **Gendarmerie Nationale**, are for all practical purposes indistinguishable; you can go to either.

Drivers are one of the most obviously vulnerable groups, with the ever-present risk of a break-in. Vehicles are rarely stolen, but tape decks as well as luggage left in cars make tempting targets, and foreign number plates are easy to spot. Good insurance is the only answer – see p.16 –

LOST OR STOLEN CARDS

Before leaving home, check with your bank or credit card company as to what number to call if your credit card is **lost or stolen**; you may have to call your home country. Otherwise, contact these numbers in France; they'll tell you the British or US numbers if necessary.

American Express	☎01.47.77.72.00
Barclaycard	☎01.47.62.75.00
Diners' Club	☎01.49.06.17.50
Mastercard/Eurocard	☎01.45.67.53.53
Visa/Carte Bleue	☎01.42.77.11.90

but, whether you have it or not, make sure you don't leave your valuables in sight.

If you have an **accident** while driving, you have to fill in and sign a *constat à l'aimable* (jointly agreed statement); car insurers are supposed to give you this with a policy, though in practice few seem to have heard of it.

For non-criminal **driving violations** such as speeding, the police can impose on-the-spot fines. Should you be arrested on any charge, you have the right to contact your nearest consulate. Although the police are not always as cooperative as they might be, it *is* their duty to assist you – likewise in the case of losing your passport or all your money.

As for offences of your own making, treatment by the police is little different from anywhere else in Europe. **Camping** outside authorized sites can bring you into contact with the authorities, though it's more likely to be the landowner who tells you to move off. **Topless sunbathing** is universally acceptable, but **nudity** is limited to a few specifically naturist beaches.

Officially, you're supposed to carry **identification documents** at all times, and the police are entitled to stop you and demand it. In practice this doesn't happen much to tourists, at least to whites. If you're black it can be a different matter; the French police have a reputation for racism. In fact, being black can make entering the country difficult, and immigration officers can be obstructive to black holidaymakers.

Sexual harassment is generally no worse than in North America or the UK, though cultural and linguistic differences can make it difficult to judge a situation correctly. Women who need help may prefer to contact women's organizations in the larger cities – Femmes Batues, Femmes en Détresse or SOS Femmes, all reachable through the Hôtel de Ville – before trying the police, while a consulate is likely to be of most immediate assistance.

Hitching is definitely not advisable.

EMERGENCIES

Ambulance ☎15
Police ☎17
Fire Service ☎18

It's common to call the fire brigade (*les sapeurs pompiers*) for medical problems; they all have paramedical training and equipment.

STAYING ON: WORK AND STUDY

Although EU citizens are in theory free to move to France and find jobs with exactly the same pay, conditions and trade union rights as French nationals, for anyone who isn't a specialist, casual work in Brittany or Normandy is hard to come by. Furthermore, while the French minimum wage (the SMIC) is currently around 40F per hour, employers are likely to pay lower wages to temporary foreign workers who don't have easy legal resources.

The region has just one wine harvest (around Nantes), almost wholly automated, and there is small chance of picking up any other kind of short-term employment. Visitors from North America or Australasia without a prearranged job offer would be foolish to imagine they have any chance of finding paid employment.

For EU citizens who arrange things in advance, however, there are work possibilities in au-pairing, teaching English as a foreign language, and in the holiday industry. And if you're just looking for an interesting way to fill the summer, assorted archeological schemes, mostly on Brittany's megalithic sites, sometimes have space for foreign volunteers.

FINDING WORK

Whatever you are looking for, it's important to plan well ahead. A few books which might be worth consulting are *Work Your Way Around the World* by Susan Griffiths and *Living and Working in France* by Victoria Pybus (both published by Vacation Work), or *A Year Between* and *Working*

Holidays (both Central Bureau). **In France**, check out the "*Offres d'Emploi*" "Job Offers" in *Le Monde*, *Le Figaro* and the *International Herald Tribune*. The national employment agency, ANPE (Agence Nationale pour l'Emploi), with offices all over France, advertises temporary jobs in all fields and, in theory, offers a whole range of services to job-seekers who are EU citizens, but is not renowned for its helpfulness to foreigners. Non-EU citizens have to show a work permit to apply for any of their jobs. Vac-Job, 46 av Réné-Coty, 17014 Paris (☎01.43.20.70.51) publishes the annual *Emplois d'Été en France* (Summer Jobs in France).

TEACHING ENGLISH

Teaching English is one of the easiest ways to find a job in France. Such posts are freqently advertised in Britain; check the *Guardian's* "Education" section (every Tuesday), or the weekly *Times Educational Supplement*. Late summer is usually the best time. You don't need fluent French to get a post, but a TEFL (Teaching English as a Foreign Language) qualification may well be required. If you apply from home, most schools will fix up the necessary papers for you. It's also quite feasible to find a teaching job when you're in France, but you may have to accept semi-official status and no job security. For the addresses of schools, look under "*Écoles de Langues*" in the "*Professions*" directory of the local phonebook.

Offering **private lessons** (via university notice boards or classified ads), you'll have lots of competition, and it's hard to reach the people who can afford it, but it's always worth a try. The best places to live and teach are probably St-Malo, Quimper, Rennes and Rouen.

BECOMING AN AU PAIR

Au pair work is usually arranged through one of a dozen agencies, all of which are listed in Vacation Work's *Living and Working in France*. In Britain, *The Lady* is the magazine for classified adverts for such jobs, arranged privately. As initial numbers to ring, try Avalon au Pairs (☎01344/788246) in Britain; Accueil Familiale des Jeunes Étrangers (☎01.42.22.50.34; 690F joining fee) in France; or the American Institute for Foreign Study (☎203/869 9090) in the US. All offer positions for female au pairs only, and will be able to fill you in on the general terms and conditions (never very generous), and the state of the market. Don't accept less than 1650F a month (on top of board and lodging), and make sure you have an escape route (such as a ticket home) in case you find the conditions intolerable – many people have had bad experiences.

TRAVEL INDUSTRY JOBS

Temporary jobs in the **travel industry** revolve around courier work – supervising and working on bus tours and summer campsites. You'll need good French (and maybe even another language) and should write to as many tour operators as you can, preferably in early spring. Ads occasionally appear in the *Guardian's* "Media" section (every Monday), while travel magazines like the very reliable *Wanderlust* (every two months; £2.80) have a "Job Shop" section which often advertises job opportunities with tour companies. Working on a campsite usually involves putting up tents at the start of the season, taking them down again at the end, and general maintenance and trouble-shooting work in the months between; experienced teachers are also in demand to provide child care. Canvas Holidays (☎01383/644018) are worth approaching.

ARCHEOLOGICAL DIGS

Volunteer work on **archeological sites** varies from year to year, according to available grants and priorities. Recently, there have been opportunities to work on a number of Breton Gallo-Roman and megalithic sites – including Locmariaquer – and on Neolithic sites in Normandy. Food and campsite or student-hall accommodation is generally provided, though there may be a small weekly charge; travel costs are not normally paid. It's best to write a number of letters to potential authorities asking for details of any projects. Excavations are regularly organized by the following:

Laboratoire d'Anthropologie Préhistorique: write c/o Dr Jean Laurent Monnier, Charge de Recherche au CNRS, Université de Rennes I, Campus de Beaulieu, 35042 Rennes.

Ministère de la Culture, Circonscription des Antiquités Historiques et Préhistoriques de Bretagne, 6 rue du Chapitre, BP 927, 35011 Rennes Cedex.

Musée d'Histoire Naturelle: write c/o Jean Pierre Watte, Archéologue Municipal, place du Vieux Marché, 76600 Le Havre.

ORGANIC FARMING

One final offbeat possibility if you want to discover green rural life is being a **working guest** on an organic farm. The period can be anything from a week to a couple of months and the work may involve cheese-making, market gardening, bee-keeping, wine producing or building. For details of the scheme and a list of French addresses, write to Willing Workers on Organic Farms (WWOOF), 19 Bradford Rd, Lewes, East Sussex BN7 1RB, UK.

CLAIMING BENEFIT

Any British or EU citizen who has been signing on for **unemployment benefit** for a minimum period of four to six weeks at home, and intends to continue doing so in France, needs a letter of introduction from their own Social Security office, plus an E303 certificate of authorization (be sure to give them plenty of warning to prepare this). You must register within seven days with the ANPE (Agence Nationale pour l'Emploi), whose offices are listed under "*Administration du Travail et de l'Emploi*" in the Yellow Pages or "*ANPE*" in the White Pages.

It's possible to claim benefit for up to three months while you look for work, but it can often take that length of time for the paperwork to be processed (also see warning opposite).

British and other EU **pensioners** can arrange for their pensions to be paid in France, but unfortunately not to receive French state pensions.

STUDYING IN FRANCE

It's relatively easy to be a **student** in France, and many foreign students perfect their fluency in the language while studying. Foreigners pay no more than French nationals to enrol for a course, and the only problem then is to support yourself. Your *carte de séjour* and – if you're an EU citizen – Social Security will be assured, and you'll be eligible for subsidized accommodation, meals and all the student reductions. In general, French universities are relatively informal; strict entry requirements, including an exam in French, apply only for undergraduate degrees, not for postgraduate courses. For full **details and prospectuses**, contact the Cultural Service of any French embassy or consulate (see p.15).

If you're a full-time non-EU student in France, you can get a non-EU **work permit** for the following summer so long as your visa is still valid.

LANGUAGE SCHOOLS

Language schools all along the coast provide intensive French courses for foreigners. Many of these are listed in the handout *Cours de Français pour Étudiants Étrangers*, also obtainable from embassy or consular cultural sections, with the most popular being those organized each summer at St-Malo by the University of Rennes.

The École des Roches, in Verneuil-sur-Avre in Normandy (see p.156), is a well-equipped institute that runs intensive short courses in French for pupils aged 11 to 18; contact BP 710, 27137 Verneuil-sur-Avre (☎02.32.23.40.00).

DIRECTORY

BEACHES are public property within 5m of the high-tide mark, so you can walk past the private villas, and set foot on islands. Another law, however, forbids you to camp.

CAMERAS AND FILM Film is considerably cheaper in North America than in France or Britain, so stock up if you're coming by that way. If you bring a camcorder, make sure any tapes you buy in France are compatible.

CHILDREN AND BABIES are generally welcome everywhere, including most bars and restaurants. **Hotels** charge by the room, with a small supplement for an additional bed or cot, and many family-run places will babysit or offer a listening service while you eat or go out. Especially in the seaside towns, most **restaurants** have children's menus or cook simpler food on request. You'll have no difficulty finding disposable nappies (*couches à jeter*), but nearly all baby foods have added sugar and salt, and French milk powders are very rich indeed. SNCF charge nothing on **trains and buses** for under-4s, and half-fare for 4–11s (see p.26 for other reductions). Most SIs have details of specific activities for children – in particular, many resorts supervise "clubs" for children on the beach. And almost every town has a **children's playground** with a good selection of activities. Something to beware of – not that you can do much about it – is the difficulty of negotiating a child's **buggy** over the large cobbles that cover many of the older streets in town centres.

ELECTRICITY is almost always 220V, using plugs with two round pins.

FISHING You get fishing rights by becoming a member of an authorized fishing club – SIs have details. The main areas for river fishing are in Brittany, in the Aulne around Châteaulin and in the Morbihan.

GAY AND LESBIAN TRAVELLERS France is more liberal on homosexuality than most European countries. The legal age of consent is 15, and gay communities thrive in Paris and many southern towns, though lesbian life is rather less upfront. Brittany and Normandy, however, have little conspicuous gay life; the best source for clubs and meeting places is the *Gai Pied Guide*, widely available in France.

LAUNDRY Laundries (laundromats) are not all that common in Breton or Norman towns, although some are listed in this guide. The alternative *blanchisserie* or *pressing* services are likely to be expensive, and hotels in particular charge very high rates. If you're staying in hotels, only wash a few items yourself as most places officially forbid doing any laundry in your room.

LEFT LUGGAGE Lockers of various sizes are available at all SNCF stations, as well as *consigne* for longer periods or larger items.

SMOKING is banned on public transport and in museums in France, while all restaurants and bars are obliged to have non-smoking areas.

SWIMMING POOLS (*piscines*) are well signposted in most French towns, and reasonably priced. SIs have addresses.

TAX-FREE SHOPPING Visitors to France from non-EU countries can claim tax refunds on any purchases in a single shop of over 2000F. Ask for the relevant forms when you buy, then present them to Customs officials as you leave the country.

TIME France is one hour ahead of Britain throughout the year, except for a short period during October, when it's the same. It is six hours ahead of Eastern Standard Time, and nine hours ahead of Pacific Standard Time. This also applies during daylight-saving seasons, observed in France (as in most of Europe) from the end of March through to the end of September.

TV AND VIDEO French TV broadcasts using a different system to the British; only black-and-white portable British TVs work in France. Make sure that any video tapes you buy in France, whether blank for use in a camcorder, or prerecorded, are compatible with your own system.

VACCINATIONS are neither required nor necessary.

WATER The tap water is always safe to drink; bottled mineral water, always available, may taste better.

PART TWO

NORMANDY

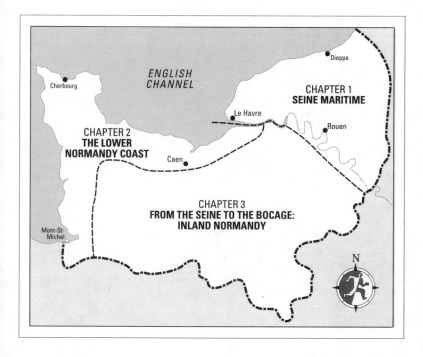

CHAPTER ONE

SEINE MARITIME

The *département* of **Seine Maritime** makes an atypical introduction to Normandy. Though scattered with characteristic Norman half-timbered houses and small farms, the landscape is stark along the coastline and often dull in the flatlands of the chalk Caux plateau behind. Only along the sheltered ribbon of the **Seine Valley** do you find the greenery, and profusion of flowers and fruit, that you might expect of the province.

This is not to say this is all territory to pass through or ignore. Arriving at **Dieppe** you can take advantage of the low-key resorts along the **Côte d'Albâtre**,

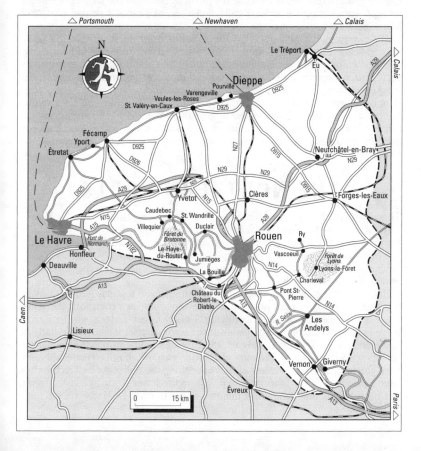

which hold occasional surprises behind their windswept and tide-chased walks. At **Fécamp**, you'll find an absurd Hammer House of Horror Benedictine distillery; at **Étretat**, spectacular stacks and arches of rock, to either side of one of the nicest little coastal towns in Normandy; at **Varengeville**, architect Edwin Lutyens' wonderful **Bois des Moutiers**. On the Seine estuary, while **Le Havre** may be less conventionally enticing, it's worth attention all the same, not only for its modern architecture and art collections but, as France's second port after Marseille, for its liveliness.

The extravagant meanders of the **River Seine**, however, determine most people's travels in this region. **Rouen**, scene of the trial and execution of Joan of Arc, is one of the major provincial capitals of France; the combination of contemporary verve with its heavily but effectively restored medieval centre makes it by far the most interesting city in Normandy. Along the valley and riverbanks there is plenty to delay your progress: tranquil villages such as **Villequier** and **La Bouille**; the evocatively ruined Romanesque abbeys of **St-Wandrille** and **Jumièges**; the English frontier-stronghold of **Château Gaillard** looming above **Les Andelys**; and, an unmissable last stop before Paris, **Monet's garden** and waterlilies at **Giverny**.

THE NORTHERN PORTS

There is no confusing the northern ports of Normandy, **Dieppe** and **Le Havre**, with their rivals to the east. Each has managed to retain a distinct individual identity in a way that Calais and Boulogne, which have to cope with ten times the number of passengers, simply do not; if you're using either port, you shouldn't feel obliged to rush on out as soon as you arrive, or dice with time to coincide to the minute with the ferries back.

Both offer the same obvious choice of **routes**: inland towards Rouen, or along the coast. If you're setting off from Dieppe with your own transport, the **coast road** is the most immediately gratifying. Until you get as far south as Rouen, there is little of interest on the plains of the Caux plateau inland, while harbour towns such as **Le Tréport** to the east, and **Étretat** and **Fécamp** to the west, make diverting overnight stops. Both are also within easy reach of Le Havre, although here you are poised at the start of the route along the Seine. As well as the river towns, places such as Honfleur (see p.103) on the lower Norman coast, covered in Chapter Two, only take a few minutes to get to from Le Havre via the huge Seine bridges.

Dieppe

Crowded between high cliff headlands, **DIEPPE** is an enjoyably small-scale port at which to arrive, very French but with a long and intimate association with England. As the nearest harbour and beach to Paris, 180km southeast, it has had an eventful history. Its existence was first recorded in 1030, when the abbey of Mont Ste-Catherine-de-Rouen acquired the area for an annual rent of 5000 smoked herrings. The port was regularly used by William the Conqueror when he was King of England, and passed into French hands in 1195 when Philippe Auguste burned Richard the Lionheart's fleet in the harbour. Having changed ownership several more times during the Hundred Years' War, Dieppe was finally taken for France by the future Louis XI in 1443.

It was from Dieppe, in 1524, that the Italian explorer Giovanni da Verrazano sailed to found the settlement that later became New York. Early emigrants to Canada used the port too, and the strong links established with the French colony there were to endure long after the French lost Canada to the British in 1759.

When the edict of Nantes was revoked in 1685, Dieppe was one of the main escape routes used by fleeing Protestants; similarly, during the French Revolution, three Brighton captains of the Channel Packet Service ran a regular – and profitable – service for aristocrats on the run. In 1848, the railway from Paris reached Dieppe and, from the 1850s, the Newhaven Packet operated a daily service. The town became a fashionable seaside resort, attracting French aristocracy and British royalty. The French would promenade along the seafront, while the English colony indulged in the peculiar pastime of bathing.

Modern Dieppe has a population of just under 36,000. It's not a place many travellers go out of their way to visit, but it's one of the nicer ferry ports in northern France, and you're unlikely to regret to spending an afternoon or evening here before or after a Channel crossing. With kids in tow, the aquariums of the **Cité de la Mer** are the obvious attraction; otherwise, you could settle for admiring the cliffs and the castle as you stroll the seafront lawns.

Arrival and information

Dieppe's **tourist office** is on the pont Ango, which separates the ferry harbour from the pleasure port; you can't miss it if you're arriving by ferry (July & Aug Mon–Sat 9am–1pm & 2–8pm, Sun 10am–1pm & 3–6pm; Easter–June & Sept, Mon–Sat 9am–1pm & 2–7pm, Sun 10am–1pm & 3–6pm; Oct–Easter Mon–Sat 9am–noon & 2–6pm; ☎02.35.84.11.77). A beach annexe where quai Duquesne reaches the oceanfront is open in summer only (mid-June to mid-Sept Sun–Thurs 10am–7.30pm, Fri & Sat 10am–8pm). The main **post office** is at 2 bd Maréchal-Joffre (Mon–Fri 8.30am–6pm, Sat 8.30am–noon; ☎02.35.04.70.14).

Between four and five P&O Stena Line **ferries** sail daily, all year round, between Newhaven in England and Dieppe's **gare maritime**; two sailings use conventional ships, taking four hours for the crossing, and the remainder use a catamaran, which takes just over half that; for information and reservations in Dieppe, call ☎02.35.06.39.03. Connecting trains for the ferries draw up on the quay, but the main **gare SNCF** (☎02.35.98.50.50) is 500m away on boulevard Clemenceau, 1km from the beach. Trains are much the quickest way to get to Rouen or Paris, but buses

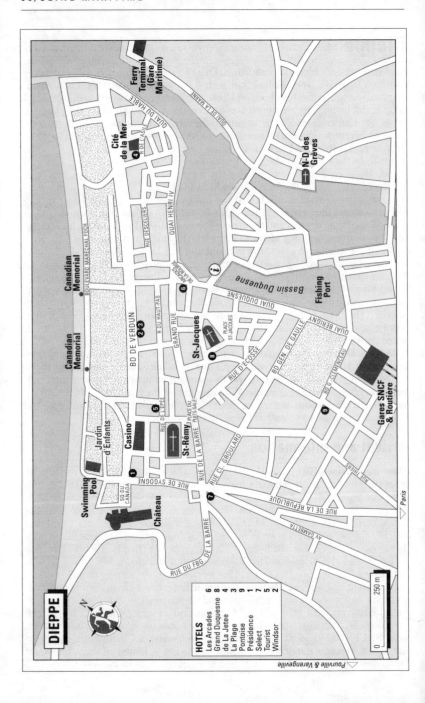

DIEPPE

Ferry Terminal (Gare Maritime)

Cité de la Mer ④

N-D des Grèves

Canadian Memorial

Canadian Memorial

QUAI DU HABLE

RUE DE L'ASILE

QUAI HENRI IV

RUE DESCELLERS

QUAI DE LA MARINE

BOULEVARD MARÉCHAL FOCH

BD DE VERDUN

R DU HAUT-PAS

GRAND RUE

RUE DE L'AGORGE

⑥

Bassin Duquesne

QUAI DUQUESNE

Fishing Port

②③

St-Jacques

PLACE ST-JACQUES

⑧

RUE D'ÉCOSSE

QUAI BÉRIGNY

BD GÉN DE GAULLE

BD G CLÉMENCEAU

⑨

Gares SNCF & Routière

RUE DES TISSERANDS

Jardin d'Enfants

Casino

⑤

RUE DE L'ÉPÉE

St-Rémy

PLACE DU PUITS SALÉ

RUE DE LA BARRE

RUE CL. GROULARD

RUE DE LA RÉPUBLIQUE

AV GAMBETTA

▷ Paris

Swimming Pool

SQ DU CANADA

①

RUE DE SYGOGNE

⑦

Château

RUE DU FBG DE LA BARRE

▷ Pourville & Varengeville

HOTELS
Les Arcades	6
Grand Duquesne	8
de La Jetée	4
La Plage	3
Pontoise	9
Présidence	1
Select	7
Tourist	5
Windsor	2

ⓘ

N

0   250 m

along the coast leave from the **gare routière** (☎02.35.84.21.97) alongside. In addition, free shuttle buses, timed to coincide with sailings, carry passengers between the ferry terminal and the town centre; the tourist office posts detailed schedules.

Dieppe is a small town, and **local buses** only serve three routes. All start at the gare SNCF, pass through the bus station and call at the tourist office. However, a **"petit train"** makes one-hour narrated tours of Dieppe, starting from the tourist office and heading first to the Cité de la Mer, then back along the full length of the beach and up to the Auchan hypermarket (8 daily 8am–5pm; adults 35F, under-10s 25F). **Bicycles** are available for rent from M.J.C. Plage, Rotonde de la Plage (☎02.35.40.05.15).

Accommodation

You're unlikely to experience much difficulty finding accommodation in Dieppe. There are plenty of **hotels**; on the whole, prices get progressively cheaper as you head further inland from the seafront, which is actually among the quietest areas of town, especially near the castle end, away from the car-ferry traffic.

The town's **youth hostel**, which offers beds in two-, four- and six-bed dorms only, is inconveniently located atop a hill at 48 rue Louis Fromager (mid-Feb to mid-Nov; ☎02.35.84.85.73, fax 02.35.84.89.62; 67F). Two kilometres southwest of the gare SNCF in the Quartier Janval, it's served by bus route #2 from the tourist office (direction Val Druel, get off at Château Michel). That same bus continues to a year-round **campsite**, the three-star *Camping Vitamin*, Chemin des Vertus (☎02.35.82.11.11).

Hotels

Many of the dearer hotels in Dieppe are at the western end of the boulevard de Verdun, facing the sea; they (and others with restaurants) are likely to insist on half board, or even full board, in the season, which can make them very expensive.

Hôtel Les Arcades, 1–3 Arcades de la Bourse (☎02.35.84.14.12, fax 02.35.40.22.29). Long-established hotel, under the eponymous arcades facing the port; particularly suitable for tired passengers arriving at midnight and not wanting to walk more than 200m to find a bed. Restaurant with full, good-value menus from 95F. ④.

Grand Duquesne, 15 place Saint Jacques (☎02.35.84.21.51, fax 02.35.84.29.83). Just off place du Puits Salé in view of the main door of the Cathedral, a small, well-refurbished pension, where every room has bath and phone. The simplest menu, at 72F, includes squid or salmon *choucroute*. ②.

Hôtel de la Jetée, 5 rue de l'Asile Thomas (☎02.35.84.89.98). Simple but very welcoming place overlooking the sea, near the Cité de la Mer, with ten plain but spacious rooms. ①.

Hôtel La Plage, 20 bd de Verdun (☎02.35.84.18.28, fax 02.35.82.36.82). Slightly upmarket rooms, all with English (satellite) TV, facing the sea but set back somewhat from the street, alongside the *Windsor*. No restaurant. ③.

Hôtel-Restaurant Pontoise, 10 rue Thiers (☎02.35.84.14.57). A basic, inexpensive option, not far from the gare SNCF and well away from the beach. ②.

Hôtel Présidence, bd de Verdun (☎02.35.84.31.31, fax 02.35.84.86.70). This ugly grey modern block, below the *château* at the far west end of the seafront, holds 89 spacious and well-equipped rooms, while menus at the rooftop *Panoramic* restaurant start at 85F. ④.

Hôtel Select, 1 rue Toustain (☎02.35.84.14.66, fax 02.35.84.28.78). Rather faded red-brick building at the western end of rue de la Baine, opposite the steps up to the *château*. There's a terrace bar serving afternoon teas, and live jazz on Fridays, but no restaurant. ③.

Hôtel Tourist, 16 rue de la Halle au Blé (☎02.35.06.10.10, fax 02.35.84.15.87). Plain rooms in converted town house, one block from the beach behind the Casino; an en-suite shower or toilet costs an additional 60F. No restaurant. ②.

Hôtel Windsor, 18 bd de Verdun (☎02.35.84.15.23, fax 02.35.84.74.52). You pay premium rates for sea-facing rooms in this *logis*, where the glass-fronted first-floor dining room – *Le Haut Gallion* – has menus from 105F. The rooms themselves can be quite shabby, but they do have satellite TV. ④.

The Town

Dieppe remains a busy **port**, and the sheer bustle and verve of the place cannot fail to strike passengers disembarking from the ferries. Vast quantities of **fruit** from all over the world – and forty percent of all **shellfish** eaten in France – are unloaded at its commercial docks, but the quayside **fish stalls** near the tourist office are what really grab the eyes. Every morning the previous night's catch is displayed with all the usual mouthwatering French flair, an appetizing profusion of sole, turbot, and the local speciality, scallops.

Modern Dieppe is still laid out along the three axes dictated by its eighteenth-century town planners, though these central streets have become a little run-down, and are in any case left in continual shadow. The **boulevard de Verdun** runs for over a kilometre along the seafront, from the fifteenth-century castle in the west to the port entrance, and passes the Casino, along with the grandest and oldest hotels. A short way inland, parallel to the seafront, is the **rue de la Barre** and its pedestrianized continuation, the **Grande Rue**. Along the harbour's edge, an extension of the Grande Rue, **quai Henry IV** has a colourful backdrop of cafés, brasseries and restaurants.

At the heart of the old town, the **place du Puits-Salé** is dominated by the huge half-timbered **Café des Tribunaux**, currently looking very spruce following a lavish restoration. The *Café* was built as an inn towards the end of the seventeenth century, and briefly became Dieppe's town hall after the previous one was bombarded by the British in 1694. In the late nineteenth century, it was favoured by painters and writers such as Renoir, Monet, Sickert, Whistler and Pissarro. It's now a cavernous café, with sombre wooden panels and dark-brown velveteen walls, the haunt of college students and open until after midnight. For English visitors, its most evocative association is that the exiled and unhappy Oscar Wilde drank here regularly. He lived (as M. Melmouth) at Berneval, 10km east of Dieppe, which was where he wrote *The Ballad of Reading Gaol*.

From the *Café*, rue St Jacques leads to the **church** of the same name, built in the twelfth century to greet English pilgrims embarking on the trail to Santiago de Compostella in Spain. The original church burned down a hundred years later, so its oldest part today is the fourteenth-century lantern tower. Inside, a chapel to the "Canadian Martyrs" neighbours the usual ones to Ste-Thérèse and the Sacred Heart. Dedicated in 1951, this has nothing to do with World War II; instead it's devoted to two Dieppe priests, shown in modern stained glass being hacked to death by "Mohawaks" in 1648. Nearby, the **Mur de Trésor** bears intricate and potentially fascinating carvings of Brazilian Indians dating from the seventeenth century. Unfortunately they're too high up to see clearly, and all but indecipherable.

Northwest of the place du Puits-Salé, **rue Bouchard** heads to the sixteenth-century church of St Rémy, which was partly destroyed when, used as an arms dump by the Germans, it was blown up the day before the town was liberated in August 1944. It is now being restored, but has yet to reopen to the public.

The beach

Dieppe's wide, steeply shelving **shingle beach** was deposited by a freak tide long after the rest of the town took shape. Hence the extravagant amount of clear space between the beach and the first buildings, taken up partly by the windswept grassy lawns that make an ideal venue for the town's annual kite festival (second week in September), and partly by car parks where departing ferry passengers munch last-minute picnics and drum their fingers.

The château

The most obvious and conspicuous sight in Dieppe is the medieval **castle** overlooking the seafront from the west, which is home to the **Musée de Dieppe** (June–Sept daily 10am–noon & 2–6pm; Oct–May daily except Tues; 15F). In addition to its exhibition on local history – and Dieppe's maritime past means that "local history" can stretch as far as including pre-Columbian pottery from Peru – this houses two showpiece collections. The first is a group of **Dieppe carved ivories** – virtuoso specimens of sawing, filing and chipping of the plundered riches of Africa. The ivory was shipped back to the town by early Dieppe "explorers", in such quantities that during the seventeenth century over three hundred craftsmen-carvers lived here.

The other permanent exhibition is made up of a hundred or so prints by the co-originator of Cubism, **Georges Braque**, who went to school in Le Havre, spent his summers in Dieppe, and is buried just west of the town at Varengeville-sur-mer (see p.65). Only a few prints are displayed at any one time – together with a small assortment of canvases by Pissarro, Renoir, Dufy and others – but in theory you can see the rest if you ask.

The square du Canada

A flight of steps leads down from the castle to the **square du Canada**, originally a commemoration of the role played by sailors from Dieppe in that country's colonization. After the last war, however, it acquired an additional significance, for it was at Dieppe in August 1942 that the Allied **commando raid**, Operation Jubilee, took place. The first large-scale assault on the continent after Dunkerque, the operation claimed over 3000 Canadian casualties in a near-suicidal series of landings and attacks up sheer and well-fortified cliff faces. Many were cut down as soon as they left their landing craft, before they even touched dry land, while some German defenders are reputed not to have bothered with firing their weapons – simply dropping projectiles over the edge.

The Allied Command later justified the carnage as having taught valuable lessons for the 1944 invasion; the Channel ports were seen to be too heavily defended to be vulnerable to frontal attack, and the invasion plan was changed to one that required the amphibious landing armies to bring their own harbour with them (see p.123).

The Cité de la Mer-L'Estran

37 rue de l'Asile-Thomas; Daily: May–Aug 10am–7pm; Sept–April 10am–noon & 2–6pm. Adults 28F, under-16s 16F.

Dieppe's most recent attempt to keep tourists in town for longer than it takes to get to or from the ferry terminal is the **Cité de la Mer-L'Estran**, housed in a featureless white concrete block in the tangle of streets just back from the harbour. Setting out simultaneously to entertain children and to serve as a centre for scientific research, this succeeds in both without being all that interesting for the casual adult visitor.

Kids are certain to enjoy learning the principles of navigation by operating radio-controlled boats (5F for 3min). Thereafter, the museum traces the history of seagoing vessels, leading from maps of the great Norman voyages of exploration and conquest, via a Viking *drakkar* under construction following methods depicted in the Bayeux Tapestry, right up to an oddly sketchy account of the insides of a nuclear-powered submarine. Next comes a very detailed geological exhibition covering the formation of the local cliffs, in which we learn how to go about converting shingle into sandpaper.

Visits culminate with the large **aquariums**, filled with the marine life of the Channel: flat fish with bulbous eyes and twisted faces, retiring octopuses, battling lobsters, and hermaphrodite scallops (a caption helpfully explains that the white part is male, and the orange, female). Thanks to a typical lack of sentimentality, jars of fish soup, whose exact provenance is not made explicit, are on sale at the exit.

Eating and shopping

The most promising area to look for **restaurants** in Dieppe is along the quai Henri IV, which, although it overlooks the port rather than the open sea, makes a lovely place to stroll and compare menus of a summer's evening. The beach itself holds no formal restaurants, but it does have a couple of open-air bistro-type cafés selling plates of mussels, salads, and so on, and plenty of *crêpe* stands. Further restaurants can be found all over town – and note that many of the hotels reviewed above also have good dining rooms. Competition for ferry passengers keeps prices relatively low, meaning that Dieppe is one of the few towns in Normandy where you can still find a good menu for under 80F.

As well as the daily spectacle of the fish on sale in the **port de pêche**, described above, there's an all-day open-air **market** in the place Nationale and Grande Rue on Saturday. Otherwise, the main shopping streets in Dieppe are rue de la Barre and the Grande Rue. The chain store Printemps, 7 Grande Rue, incorporates a duty-free shop, and there's a Shopi supermarket at 59 rue de la Barre. L'Épicier Oliver at 18 rue St-Jacques has more specialist items. The largest of several **hypermarkets** in the area is Mammouth (Mon–Sat 9am–9pm), out of town at the Centre Commercial du Belvédère on the route de Rouen (RN 27), and reached by free courtesy buses, as well as local bus #2, from the tourist office.

Restaurants

Les Écamias, 129 quai Henri IV (☎02.35.84.67.67). Small, friendly traditional French restaurant, at the quieter, seaward end of the main quay not far from the Cité de la Mer. Each of the two separate dining rooms (hence the plural) in neighbouring buildings serves the same menu, with a 70F option that includes *moules marinières* and stuffed shellfish; they also offer skate with capers. Closed Mon (except in Aug), and Sun pm in winter.

La Marmite Dieppoise, 8 rue St-Jean (☎02.35.84.24.26). Rustic, busy little restaurant, between St-Jacques church and the arcades de la Bourse. Lunch menu from 86F, dinners at 145F or 215F, with the latter featuring the local speciality *marmite Dieppoise* (seafood pot, with shellfish and white fish). Closed Sun pm and Mon, and also Thurs pm out of season.

Le Newhaven, 53 quai Henri IV (☎02.35.84.89.72). Reliable seafood specialist, at the slightly quieter end of the quayside, and serving good menus from 64F. The 100F menu of Dieppe specialities is fine if you hanker after fish livers and squid, while the 119F menu offers mussels followed by skate, and there are wonderful baked oysters on the 145F one. Closed Sun pm in winter.

Les P'tits Bateaux, 23 quai Henri IV (☎02.35.06.14.74). Menus 90F, 110F and up; pay 140F and you get a lobster to kick things off. Sixteenth-century cellar with live music until late; last orders midnight. Out front, there's a lavish display of seafood on ice, and a macaw; the brightyellow plastic tables are sheltered out of season.

Le St Jacques, 12 rue de l'Oranger (☎02.35.84.52.04). Busy, not to say peremptory bistro, in town near the St-Jacques church, with menus from 65F that include considerably more meat dishes than is normal in Dieppe, while still preparing the usual fishy delights. Closed Mon, and Thurs pm.

Les Tourelles, 43 rue du Commandant Fayolle (☎02.35.84.15.88). Welcoming little local restaurant, just behind the Casino, and renowned for its paellas, though it also serves the standard seafood dishes. Menus from 68F. Closed Mon.

The Côte d'Albâtre

The high white cliffs that characterize the Norman coast from Picardy in the east to Le Havre in the west have earned it the name of the **Côte d'Albâtre** – the Alabaster coast. All this shoreline is eroding at a ferocious rate, and it's conceivable that the small resorts here, tucked in at the mouths of a succession of valleys, may not last more than another century or so. For the moment, however, they are quietly prospering, with casinos, sports centres and yacht marinas ensuring a modest but steady summer trade.

Although to arrive at Dieppe and promptly head **east** along the coast towards Calais and Boulogne may not be instinctive behaviour for travellers embarking on a tour of Normandy, doing so gives the opportunity to see a couple of surprising little towns: venerable **Le Tréport**, and the village of **Eu** with its thick forest surround, just inland. Head **west**, on the other hand, and the coast road dips into a series of pretty little ports, with **Étretat** as the pick of the bunch.

Le Tréport

Thirty kilometres east of Dieppe, at the mouth of the River Bresle which serves as the border with Picardy, **LE TRÉPORT** is a seaside resort that has clearly seen better days. It was already something of a bathing station when the railways arrived in 1873, and promoted this as "the prettiest beach in Europe, just three hours from Paris". It remained the capital's favoured resort until the 1950s – and is still served by around five trains daily – but it can't ever have been that pretty, and these days its charms are definitely fading.

Le Tréport divides into three distinct sections: the flat wedge-shaped seafront area, bounded on one side by the Channel, on another by the harbour at the canalized rivermouth, and on the third by imposing 100-metre high white chalk cliffs; the old town, higher up the slopes on safer ground; and the modern town further inland. The **seafront** itself is entirely taken up by a hideous pink and orange concrete 1960s apartment block, with one or two snack bars but no other sign of life, facing the Casino and a drab grey shingle beach. It's the more sheltered harbourside **quai Francois 1ᵉʳ** around the corner that holds most of the action, lined with restaurants, souvenir shops and cafés. A venerable little brick fish market stands across the road by the water, alongside a turn-of-the-century carousel. The assorted stone jetties and wooden piers around the harbour are enjoyable to stroll around, watching the comings and goings of the fishing boats that still keep Le Tréport busy. In its heyday it was possible to ride up the cliffs on a *téléphérique*; the tunnel through which it pierced the cliff face is still open to the air at either end, but the cables have rusted away, and the facilities are abandoned.

Climbing up from the *quai*, you come to the heavily nautical **Église St-Jacques**, built in the fifteenth century to replace an eleventh-century original that crumbled into the sea, along with the cliff on which it stood. Nearby, next to the fortified former town hall that is now the local library, successive flights of steps, 365 of them in all, climb to the top of the cliffs. As well as views to either side of the decaying mansions of Le Tréport, you can see across to the longer beach of Mers-les-Bains, which, (being in Picardy), falls outside the scope of this book.

Practicalities

Both **trains** and **buses** arrive in Le Tréport on the far side of the harbour, a short walk from the main *quai*. Turning left as you hit the main drag will bring you to the town's **tourist office**, on quai Sadi-Carnot (Easter–Sept daily 10am–noon & 2–6pm; Oct–Easter Mon–Sat 10am–noon & 2–5pm; ☎02.35.86.05.69). That's the place to pick up a schedule of activities if you're lucky enough to be around for Le Tréport's major annual **festival**, the Blessing of the Sea on August 2.

Of the **hotels** in town, the best in terms of a sea view and good-quality food is the *Richelieu* at 50 quai Francois 1er (☎02.35.86.26.55; ③), which offers modernized rooms with showers on four floors, and a wide range of menus starting at 85F for a "bistrot" meal. The other seafood **restaurants** along the *quai* are too numerous to review in detail, each boasting of its fresh *assiette de fruits de mer* and serving similar meals from around 90F. The one with the highest gourmet reputation is the *Matelote*, 34 quai Francois 1er (☎02.35.86.01.13), where dining on the first floor gives you a panoramic overview of all the life of the port.

Eu

Queen Victoria twice visited Le Tréport with Albert. She didn't come to play on the beach, though, but to stay at the château at **EU**, a couple of kilometres inland. When she did so the first time, she became the first English monarch to visit France since Henry VIII arrived for the Field of the Cloth of Gold.

Today, Eu is something of a backwater, consisting of a few pedestrian streets at the top of a hill, and a straggle of newer districts reaching down the slopes. The **château** that stands at its heart has been heavily restored, and is now a rather routine museum (guided tours mid-March to Oct: daily 10am–noon & 2–6pm). This castle was constructed in the sixteenth century; of Eu's previous castle, deliberately burned in 1475 to forestall its capture by the English, only the tiny chapel remains, which was the site of William the Conqueror's marriage to Mathilda. Unlikely as it may sound, the town's Gothic church, **Notre-Dame et St-Laurent**, is dedicated to St Lawrence O'Toole, an Archbishop of Dublin who died here in 1181 while en route to visit Henry II in Rouen, to intercede on behalf of the Irish. His effigy still lies in the brightly lit and eerie crypt, along with various fourteenth-century members of the Artois family.

If you find yourself staying in Eu, you can spend an enjoyable afternoon by venturing into the **forest of Eu**, a mysterious and ancient tangled woodland dominated by tall beeches, with a lost Roman city supposedly hidden in its depths. A good way to explore it more thoroughly, though you'll need your own transport, is to follow the **River Bresle** upstream, along the border between Normandy and Picardy.

Practicalities

Eu is on the Lé Treport rail line, with its **gare SNCF** 500m down the hill from the centre, and its **tourist office** up in the pedestrianized section at 41 rue Bignon (May–Oct Mon 2–6.30pm, Tues–Sat 9.30am–12.30pm & 2–6.30pm, Sun 10am–1pm; Nov–April Tues–Sat 9.30am–noon & 2–5.30pm; ☎02.35.86.04.68). The *Hôtel de la Gare* at 20 place de la Gare (☎02.35.86.16.64; ④; closed second half of Aug) is a slightly dilapidated red-brick town house next to the gare SNCF, offering menus from 90F, and there's a **youth hostel** in the former royal kitchens, *Centre des Fontaines* (☎02.35.86.05.03; members 90F), which serves meals, and acts as a general resource for local youngsters. Eu is otherwise short of places to eat.

Pourville-sur-mer

Heading **west** from Dieppe along the coastal D75, which starts from rue Faubourg de la Barre, you come after 3km to the resort of **POURVILLE-SUR-MER**, an extremely tranquil last- or first-night stop for ferry passengers. It amounts to no more than a very simple curving bay which briefly interrupts the line of cliffs, with a few buildings along the road, most of them **hotels**. Among these is a *logis* confusingly named *Produits de la Mer* (☎02.35.84.38.34; ③), where all eight rooms have showers or baths, and the plainest seafood menu costs 85F. Next to it is a crazy golf course, and the *Le Marqueval* **campsite** (☎02.35.82.66.46; mid-March to Sept) is set in the fields further back from the sea.

Varengeville-sur-mer

If the museum in Dieppe has awakened your interest in **Georges Braque**, you may be interested in visiting **VARENGEVILLE-SUR-MER**, 8km west of Dieppe (afternoons only; 25min on bus #311 or #312). This small town has long been popular with artists, including at different times Monet, Dufy, Miró, and the parents of British Prime Minister Anthony Eden, who was born here. Braque (1882–1963), however, was its greatest devotee. His **grave** is situated outside a church perched spectacularly above the cliffs a couple of kilometres north of the centre, a smooth marble tomb topped by a sadly decaying mosaic of a white dove in flight. More impressive is his vivid-blue *Tree of Jesse* stained-glass window inside the church, through which the sun rises in summer.

Back along the road towards town from the church, the house at the **Bois des Moutiers**, built for Guillaume Mallet from 1898 onwards and un-French in almost every respect, was one of architect **Edwin Lutyens**' first commissions. Lutyens, then aged just 29 and heavily influenced by the "Arts and Crafts" ideas of William Morris, was at the start of a career that was to culminate during the 1920s when he laid out most of the city of New Delhi. The real reason to visit, however, is to enjoy the magnificent **gardens**, designed by Mallet in conjunction with Gertrude Jekyll, and at their most spectacular in the second half of May (mid-March to mid-Nov only: Sun–Fri 10am–noon & 2pm–sunset, Sat 2pm–sunset; admission 40F during May and June, otherwise 35F). Enthusiastic guides lead you through the highly innovative engineering of the house and grounds, replete with quirks and games. The colours of the Burne-Jones tapestry hanging in the stairwell were copied from Renaissance cloth in William Morris's studio; the rhododendrons were chosen from similar samples. Paths lead through vistas based on paintings by Poussin, Lorrain and other eighteenth-century artists; no modern roses, with their anachronistic colours, are allowed to spoil the effect.

Of **accommodation** possibilities in Varengeville, the *logis Hôtel de la Terrasse*, amid the pines on route de Vastérival on the cliffs west of town (☎02.35.85.12.54; ③; March to mid-Oct), stands out from the rest. Fishy menus in its panoramic dining room cost from 88F.

On from Varengeville

The coastal road immediately beyond Varengeville is not very interesting. **QUIBERVILLE**, the main name on the map, makes a popular target for windsurfers, but in itself is little more than an overgrown caravan park; at Veules, you pass a couple of ludicrous folk-sculptures, including a seashell snowman; **ANGIENS** is a pretty village but with nothing much to linger over.

St-Valéry-en-Caux

The first sizeable community west of Dieppe is **ST-VALÉRY-EN-CAUX**, a rebuilt but still attractive port where open-air stalls along the quayside of the narrow harbour sell fresh-caught fish daily. St-Valéry provides a clear reminder of the fighting – and massive destruction – of the Allied retreat of 1940. To either side of the shingle beach rise crumbling brown-stained cliffs. A monument on the western heights pays tribute to the French division who faced Rommel's tanks on horseback, brandishing their sabres with hopeless heroism, while beside the ruins of a German artillery emplacement on the opposite cliffs a second monument commemorates a Scottish division, the 51st Highlanders, rounded up while fighting their way back to the boats home.

There's now a characterless new Casino in the centre of the curve, and an even newer church in the streets a little way behind, which appears to be made almost entirely of stained glass.

Practicalities

Much the most attractive house to survive in St-Valéry is the Renaissance **Maison Henri IV** on the quai d'Aval, with its intricately carved wooden facade. It's now the **tourist office** (May to mid-Sept daily 10am–12.30pm & 3–7pm; mid-Sept to April Wed–Sat 10am–12.30pm & 3–7pm; Sun 10am–12.30pm; ☎02.35.97.00.63). Although no trains serve the town, from four to six SNCF **buses** connect each day with trains to and from Rouen at Motteville, 27km south.

The *Terrasses*, 22 rue le Perrey (☎02.35.97.11.22; ④; closed Xmas & Jan), is the only **hotel-restaurant** actually facing the sea; the other, much cheaper, *logis* in town, the seven-room *La Marine*, 113 rue St-Léger (☎02.35.97.05.09; ②; mid-Feb to mid-Nov), is tucked away in a backstreet on the west side of the harbour. There are also two year-round **municipal campsites**, the two-star *Falaise d'Amont* (☎02.35.97.05.07) on the eastern cliffs, and the larger four-star *d'Étennemare* (☎02.35.97.15.79), set back from the sea southwest of the harbour. The

Restaurant du Port, overlooking the harbour at 18 quai d'Amont (☎02.35.97.08.93; closed Sun pm & Mon in low season), has a delicious 118F menu, abounding in seafood. St-Valéry has a **market** on Fridays and summer Sundays, and plays host to a **herring festival** in mid-November.

Fécamp

FÉCAMP, roughly halfway between Dieppe and Le Havre, is, like Dieppe, a serious fishing port, albeit one with a more frivolous modern sideline as a holiday resort. Its name first features in a charter of 875 AD, as Fiscannum, from the Germanic *fisc* meaning "fish", and it has been a centre for shipbuilding ever since the Vikings set up a boatyard here in 911 AD. These days, it's a striking town, so much surrounded by high cliffs that, approaching from inland, you don't see the sea until you're right upon it. It was fortunate enough to sustain very little damage during the last war, though its reportedly magnificent Belle-Époque Casino was destroyed in 1945 by the Germans, who feared it could serve as a landmark for Allied invaders. The current, much uglier replacement was completed in 1958.

Fécamp still has its railway link, the tracks running right up to the small harbour, where fishing boats, yachts and *vedettes* jostle for position. The town's long promenade fronts a uniform steep beach of shingle, framed by crumbling and overhanging cliffs. As ever along this coast, windsurfing is more appealing than bathing. In the absence of any major attraction out to sea, the *vedettes* offer cruises to watch the sun set.

Arrival and information

Fécamp's main **tourist office** is opposite the distillery at 113 rue Alexandre-le-Grand (July & Aug Mon–Fri 10am–6pm; Sept–June Mon–Sat 9am–12.15pm & 1.45–6pm; ☎02.35.28.51.01); the peculiar hours are because there's another summer-only office alongside the Musée des Terres-Neuvas on the seafront (July & Aug daily 11am–1pm & 3–8pm; ☎02.35.29.16.34). Both can provide details of the regular programme of guided tours in and around Fécamp. The **gares SNCF** and **routière** are between the port and the town centre on avenue Gambetta.

Accommodation

Fécamp's **hotels** tend to be set back away from the sea, on odd side streets. It's a popular place, so you'll need to reserve a room in summer. The **youth hostel** (☎02.35.29.75.79, reservations ☎02.35.29.36.35; July to mid-Sept;) stands high up near the lighthouse on the Côte de la Vierge east of the port, along the route du Commandant Roquigny. A lovely **campsite**, the *Camping de Reneville* (☎02.35.28.20.97; March–Dec), is a short walk out of town on the western cliffs.

Hôtel d'Angleterre, 93 rue de la Plage (☎02.35.28.01.60, fax 02.35.28.62.95). Reasonable hotel just back from the sea, with its own restaurant and "English pub". ③.

Le Martin, 18 place St-Étienne (☎02.35.28.23.82). A handful of basic rooms above one of the better restaurants in the old town (see p.69). Closed first fortnight of both March & Sept. ①.

Hôtel de la Mer, 89 bd Albert 1er (☎02.35.28.24.64, fax 02.35.28.27.67). Simple but good-value hotel on the seafront that's nicer inside than it looks from the outside. Closed two weeks in Feb. ②.

Hôtel de la Plage, 87 rue de la Plage (☎02.35.29.76.51, fax 02.35.28.68.30). The smartest option close to the beach; no sea views, but a quiet location and good-quality refurbished rooms. ④.

Hôtel de l'Univers, 5 place St-Étienne (☎02.35.28.05.88, fax 02.35.27.82.58). Basic, inexpensive little hotel, facing St-Étienne church in the old town. ②.

The Benedictine Distillery

110 rue Alexandre-le-Grand. Admission on guided tours only, lasting 1hr 30min. Daily: June to mid-Sept, 10am–6pm; mid-March to May & mid-Sept to mid-Nov 10am–noon & 2–5.30pm; mid-Nov to mid-March 10.30am & 3.30pm. 27F.

Fécamp owes much of its popularity to an utterly bizarre tourist attraction – the **Benedictine Distillery**, amid the narrow streets that run parallel to the port towards the town centre. This mock-Gothic monstrosity may look like a decaying mansion that has survived nightmarish aeons, but was in fact built at the end of last century for the manufacture of the sweet liqueur known as Benedictine. To see inside you have to go round on a rather dismal guided **tour**, the first part of which treks through a museum of local antiquities and oddments. Most visitors are frantic to get to the alcohol at the end, but the tour does have its moments. These include headless bishops, serpentine musical instruments, carved wood and ivory, and – a kitsch treat – a stained-glass window in which Alexandre le Grand, former owner of the Benedictine company (Alexander the Great was no relation), is being treated to a bottle of his liqueur by a passing angel.

Eventually you pass on to the distillery section (although commercial operations have moved to a new factory outside town), where boxes of exotic herbs are thrown into great copper vats and alembics. There is then a massive surge drinkwards, for the (disappointingly modest) *dégustation* across the road; it must be said it's nice stuff, especially the "B&B", served either neat or on *crêpes*. Make sure you hang onto your admission ticket to get the free drink.

Église de la Trinité

If your aesthetic sensibilities need soothing after the distillery, head away from the sea to the **Église de la Trinité**. This medieval abbey church is light and almost frail with age, its bare nave echoing to the sound of birds flying free beneath the high roof. The wooden carvings are tremendous, in particular the dusty wooden bas-relief *Dormition of the Virgin*. The abbey also has a fine selection of saintly fingers and sacred hips, authenticated with wax seals, and even a drop of the Precious Blood itself, said to have floated all the way here in a fig tree dispatched by Joseph of Arimathea. Until Mont-St-Michel was built, this was the religious centre of Normandy; Edward the Confessor is more reliably known to have made extensive gifts to the abbey and may have lived here at some point before his coronation as king of England.

Opposite the main entrance, the few vestiges that remain of the palace of the early dukes of Normandy – both Richard I and Richard II are buried in the abbey – have been landscaped to create an attractive little public garden. William, bastard son of Duke Robert, was presented here at the age of 7 to the assembled lords and bishops of Normandy when his father left for the Crusades; and returned here as William the Conqueror to celebrate Easter 1067.

Musée des Terres-Neuvas et de la Pêche

27 bd Albert 1er. July & Aug daily 10am–noon & 2–6.30pm; Sept–June daily except Tues 10am–noon & 2–5.30pm. Adults 20F, under-18s free; same ticket gives admission to Musée Centre des Arts.

Just west of the rivermouth, though sealed from view of the Channel by the high sea wall, the modern Musée des Terres-Neuvas et de la Pêche commemorates

Fécamp's association with the sea from the Viking invasions onwards. Spreading across two floors, with lots of miniature model boats and amateur paintings, it focuses in particular on the long tradition whereby the fishermen of Fécamp decamp en masse each year to catch cod in the cold, foggy waters off Newfoundland. Life on board was both brutal and lonely, and the work was hard, with the fish being cleaned and salted on deck, and then sold in Spain or Portugal rather than being carried back to France. Sailing vessels continued to make the trek from the sixteenth century right up until 1931; today vast refrigerated container ships have taken their place.

Upstairs, there's a fascinating scale model of the port and town as it looked in 1830, shortly before Fécamp was transformed by the arrival of the first railway. At that point, it entirely lacked docks and warehouses; in fact nothing stood on the far side of the river, and the whole town was still surrounded by agricultural land.

Non-French speakers should ask at the front desk for their excellent folder of English translations of all the museum's captions.

Musée Centre des Arts

21 rue Alexandre-Legros. Daily except Tues 10am–noon & 2–5.30pm. Adults 20F, under-18s free; same ticket gives admission to Musée des Terres-Neuvas.

A splendid mansion in the small pedestrianized district at the heart of old Fécamp holds the town's fine arts museum. As usual for these parts, it's a haphazard assortment of carved ivories, painted porcelain, archeological nick-nacks and fading statues rescued from tumbledown churches. The most interesting section is up on the third floor, which holds an intriguing collection of everyday objects used in the Caux region during the eighteenth and nineteenth centuries.

Eating

In summer, Fécamp welcomes enough visitors to keep several very good **restaurants** in business – not surprisingly, the fish tends to be good – but things do get rather quieter in winter.

La Marée, 75 quai Bérigny (☎02.35.29.39.15). Very good fish restaurant, enjoying harbour views from a grand upstairs dining room above a wonderful fish shop. Menus from 100F, featuring all kinds of pescatorial pleasures plus a *tartellette Bénédictine* for dessert. Closed Sun pm & Mon.

Le Martin, 18 place St-Étienne (☎02.35.28.23.82). Small old-town restaurant where the cooking is rooted in the finest Norman tradition of adding strong alcohol to just about everything, whether it's gin with your scallops or brandy on your sole. Plenty of meat dishes too, and a 65F menu (not available on Saturday nights) that's a real bargain. Also has a few budget rooms. Closed Sun pm & Mon, plus first fortnight of both March & Sept.

Le Vicomté, 4 rue Coty (☎02.35.28.47.63). Cheery old-fashioned bistro near the distillery that serves just one 83F menu, which changes daily and includes hearty traditional meat and fish dishes. Closed Wed pm & Sun.

Le Viking, 63 bd Albert 1er (☎02.35.29.22.92). Brightly painted seafront restaurant offering top-quality menus from 98F, bursting with inventive specialities, such as their amazing salmon soufflé with scallops, and the roast lamb en croûte. Closed Sun pm & Mon in winter.

Yport

The tiny fishing port of **YPORT**, tucked into a narrow gap in the chalky cliffs 6km west of Fécamp, is something of a cross between Fécamp and Étretat. It's much smaller and more attractive than Fécamp, from which it's actually visible along the shoreline, without being nearly as photogenic (or crowded) as Étretat. Local legend has it that Yport was colonized over two thousand years ago by Greek fishermen from Asia Minor, who for some reason were not deterred by its complete lack of a harbour. Their descendants have remained ever since, meaning that Yport has a reputation for being an insular community. While it's not a place to spend your entire holiday, it would make an appealing and very peaceful overnight stop.

Practicalities

Yport's **tourist office**, just back from the sea in place J-P Laurens (July & Aug Mon–Sat 10am–noon & 3–7pm, Sun 10am–noon; Sept–June Mon–Fri 10am–noon & 3–5pm; ☎02.35.29.77.31), can provide details of clifftop hiking trails. Both the main **hotels** are painted to look as though they're half-timbered. The *Hôtel Normand*, also on place J-P Laurens (☎02.35.27.30.76; ③), is a *logis de France* with menus from 88F; *La Sirène*, 7 bd Alexandre-Dumont (☎02.35.27.31.87; ②), enjoys sweeping beachfront views, and serves the usual seafood menus at 75F, 98F and 140F. *La Falaise*, near the *Normand* at 32 rue Emmanuel Foy (☎02.35.29.35.07), is a traditional little French **restaurant**, with pale blue decor and no views, which offers good-value menus from 75F at lunchtime.

On to Étretat

The minor road **D28** runs from Fécamp through a thickly wooded and idyllic valley to **Benarville** – a good cycling route, even though it manages to lose the river somewhere along the way. The **D150** (covered by buses #261 and #311 from Fécamp) is less pastoral, but leads to the remains of the **Abbaye de Valmont** (April–Sept daily except Tues 10am–noon & 2–6pm). In its spacious grounds you can feast your eyes on a Renaissance chapel, grass-floored and open to the sky, and an intact Gothic Lady Chapel.

Étretat

ÉTRETAT, another 20km west towards Le Havre, is a very different kettle of fish to Fécamp. Here the alabaster cliffs are at their most spectacular – their arches, tunnels and the solitary "needle" out to sea will doubtless be familiar from tourist brochures long before you arrive – and the town itself has grown up simply as a pleasure resort. There isn't even a port of any kind; the seafront consists of a sweeping unbroken curve of concrete above the shingle beach. In summer, wooden boats hauled onto the promenade serve as seasonal bars.

Étretat is a very pretty little place, centring on the **place Foch** just back from the sea, where the old wooden market *halles* still stand; the ground floor is now converted into souvenir shops, but the beams of the balcony and roof are bare and ancient.

As soon as you step onto the beach you're confronted by the cliff formations to either side. To the west, on the **Falaise d'Aval**, a straightforward if precarious walk leads up the crumbing side of the cliff, with lush lawns and pastures to the inland side – much of them converted for use as a golf course – and German fortifications on the shore side extending to the point where the turf abruptly stops, occasionally ripped by the latest fall. From the windswept top you can see further rock formations and possibly even glimpse Le Havre, but the views back to the village sheltered in the valley, and the **Falaise d'Amont** on its eastern side – which Maupassant compared to an elephant dipping its trunk into the ocean – are what stick in the memory.

The cliff itself presents an idyllic rural scene, with a gentle footpath winding up the green hillside to the little chapel of Notre Dame. Just beyond that is the futuristic white arch erected to commemorate the French aviators Nungesser and Coli, who set out from Paris in the *Oiseau Blanc* in May 1927, hoping to make the first transatlantic flight, and were last seen over Étretat. What happened to them is not known – there are suggestions that they crashed somewhere in deepest Maine, New England – but a mere eighteen days later Charles Lindbergh arrived coming from the opposite direction (see p.139) and went into the history books. In the turf alongside the arch, a life-size aeroplane is set in concrete relief, and there's a museum nearby.

Practicalities

Étretat's **tourist office** is alongside the main through-road in the centre of town, on place M. Guillard (mid-June to mid-Sept daily 10am–7pm; mid-March to mid-June & mid-Sept to mid-Oct daily 10am–noon & 2–6pm; mid-Oct to mid-March Fri 2–6pm, Sat 10am–noon & 2–6pm, Sun 10am–noon; ☎02.35.27.05.21). **Mountain bikes** are available for rent from an informal stand alongside (daily from 10am; ☎02.35.27.47.84; 25F per hour, 80F per day).

Four **hotels** crowd onto the corners of place Foch, all significantly cheaper than the grand sea-view places. Much the most picturesque is the *Hôtel la Résidence*, 4 bd René-Coty (☎02.35.27.02.87; ②–④), a dramatic half-timbered old mansion that originally stood in Lisieux – it was moved here a century ago – and has beautiful wooden carvings decorating its every nook and cranny. The quality of rooms, however, is variable, and few are anything like as elegant as the facade. More dependable, and also without a restaurant, is the *Hôtel des Falaises*, opposite at 1 bd René-Coty (☎02.35.27.02.77; ②) – in fact from its modernized rooms you get a better view of the *Résidence* than if you're actually staying there. *L'Escale*, on place Foch itself (☎02.35.27.03.69; ③; closed Dec & Jan), has simple but pleasant rooms, and a snack restaurant downstairs specializing in *moules frites* and *crêpes*. **Campers** will find the *Camping Municipal* (☎02.35.27.07.67; April to mid-Oct) 1km out on rue Guy-de-Maupassant.

Much the best **restaurant** in Étretat is the *Galion*, distinct from the adjoining *Résidence* at 4 bd René-Coty (☎02.35.29.48.74; closed Wed & mid-Dec to mid-Jan), where the 115F menu makes a definitive introduction to all that's best in Norman cuisine. For an absolute blowout on seafood, however, you couldn't do better than the panoramic first-floor dining room of *La Huitrière*, in place de Gaulle at the foot of the steps up the Falaise d'Aval (☎02.35.27.02.82). As well as menus from 98F, it offers an enormous range of seafood platters, from 91F up to the four-person triple-decker 1112F *Abondance*, which comes with two lobsters and a scattering of caviar. There's also a row of reasonably good restaurants along the seafront, most of which offer terrace seating right on the promenade; *La Coquille Normand*, rue Général-Leclerc (☎02.35.27.02.12), is typical in offering a basic *assiette des fruits de mer* followed by *moules frites* on its 89F menu.

Le Havre

Most ferry passengers head straight out of the port of **LE HAVRE**, at the mouth of the Seine, as quickly as the traffic will allow, to escape a city that guidebooks tend to dismiss as dismal, disastrous and gargantuan. While it may not be the most picturesque or tranquil place in Normandy, neither is it the soulless urban sprawl the warnings suggest – even if the port, the second largest in France after Marseille, does take up half the Seine estuary, extending way beyond the town.

The city was originally built on the orders of François I in 1517. Its function was to replace the ancient ports of Harfleur and Honfleur, then already silting up, and its name was soon changed from Franciscopolis to Le Havre – "the Harbour". After serious flooding in 1540 it was redesigned, and rebuilt to a grid pattern, by Girolamo Bellarmato, an exiled Italian engineer who had experience of working in the unstable soil of Venice. It became the principal trading post of the northern French coast, prospering especially during the American War of Independence and thereafter, importing cotton, sugar and tobacco. In the years before the outbreak of war in 1939, it was the European home of the great luxury liners such as the *Normandie*, *Île de France* and *France*.

Le Havre suffered heavier damage than any other port in Europe during World War II. Following its all but total destruction, it was rebuilt to the specifications of a single architect, **Auguste Perret**, between 1946 and 1964 – which makes it a rather rare entity, and one visibly circumscribed by constraints of time and

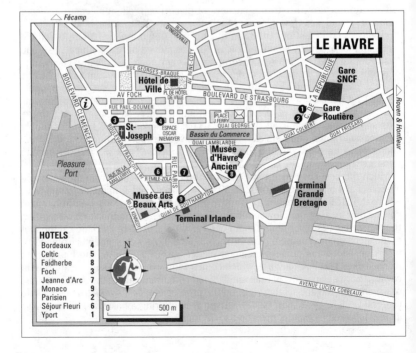

HOTELS
Bordeaux	4
Celtic	5
Faidherbe	8
Foch	3
Jeanne d'Arc	7
Monaco	9
Parisien	2
Séjour Fleuri	6
Yport	1

money. Nonetheless, the sheer sense of space can be exhilarating, the showpiece monuments have a dramatic and winning self-confidence, and the few churches and other relics of the old city to survive have been sensitively integrated into the whole. The skyline has been kept deliberately low – there are no tower blocks, and even the new mirrored World Trade Centre only manages five storeys – but the endless mundane residential blocks, which simply had to be erected as economically and swiftly as possible after the war, do get dispiriting after a while. However, with the sea visible at the end of almost every street, and open public space and expanses of water at every turn, even those visitors who ultimately fail to agree with Perret's famous dictum that "concrete is beautiful" may enjoy a stroll around his city.

Arrival and information

Le Havre's rather inconspicuous and not very central **tourist office** is on the main oceanfront drag, at 186 bd Clémenceau, near its intersection with avenue Foch (May–Sept Mon–Sat 8.45am–7pm, Sun 10am–12.30pm & 2.30–6pm; Oct–April Mon–Sat 8.45am–6.30pm, Sun 10am–1pm; ☎02.35.74.04.04), while the **post office** is at 62 rue Jules Siegfried (Mon–Fri 8am–7pm, Sat 8am–noon; ☎02.35.42.45.67).

Ferries
Three daily P&O **ferries** sail from Portsmouth to the **Terminal de Grande Bretagne**, not far from the train and bus stations in the Bassin de la Citadelle (☎02.35.19.78.78). The terminal has a tourist information kiosk, open in summer. There is no longer any service between Le Havre and Ireland.

Trains and buses
The **gare SNCF** (☎02.35.98.50.50) is 1.5km west of the Hôtel de Ville, on Cours de la République, right alongside the **gare routière** (☎02.35.26.67.23) across boulevard de Strasbourg. Fast **trains** (though not TGV) timed to connect with the ferries go to Rouen (1hr) and Paris (a further 1hr 15min). If you're travelling west, you have to change at Rouen – a very circuitous route. Commuter services run regularly to Harfleur in around five minutes.

Shuttle buses from the gare SNCF run to both ferry terminals. All the **buses** that pass the gare SNCF continue to the Hôtel de Ville. You can pick up timetables or make enquiries at the bus kiosk there or nearby at CGTE, 115 rue Jules Lecesne (☎02.35.41.72.22), which is where most buses park.

Express **buses** from the gare routière, run by Bus Verts du Calvados (☎02.31.44.77.44), take advantage of the new Pont du Normandie to connect Le Havre with Honfleur eight times daily, with two services continuing as far as Caen. Les Autos Cars Gris (☎02.35.28.19.88) run regular services to Fécamp and Étretat, while CNA (☎02.35.52.92.00) run down to Rouen.

Accommodation

It's hard to see why anyone would stay more than a single night in Le Havre. One consequence of the lack of idiosyncratic old buildings in the city is that its **hotels** tend to be faceless in the extreme, hidden away behind indistinguishable concrete facades. There are two main concentrations of hotels: one group faces the gare SNCF, and most of the rest lie within walking distance of the ferry terminal.

Although there's no **youth hostel** in Le Havre, it is usually possible to find a dorm room in the YMCA equivalent *Union Chrétienne des Jeunes Gens*, at 153 bd de Strasbourg (☎02.35.42.47.86).

The nearest **camping** is at the *Forêt de Montgeon* site (☎02.35.46.52.39; mid-April to Sept), north of the town centre in a 700-acre forest. Take bus #1 from the Hôtel de Ville or gare SNCF, direction *Jacques-Monod*, getting off at *Sainte-Cecile* or *Noisetriers*.

Hotels

Hôtel de Bordeaux, 147 rue Louis-Brindeau (☎02.35.22.69.44, fax 02.35.42.09.27). Smart, comfortable hotel, affiliated to the Best Western chain, on the north side of the Espace Oscar Niemeyer, facing the Volcano. ④.

Hôtel Celtic, 106 rue Voltaire (☎02.35.42.39.77, fax 02.35.21.67.75). Friendly and comfortable option, in the long buildings that flank the Espace Oscar Niemeyer, overlooking the Volcano. No restaurant. ②.

Hôtel Faidherbe, 21 rue Général-Faidherbe (☎02.35.42.20.27, fax 02.35.42.57.03). Simple rooms, some with sea views, in this welcoming family hotel very near the ferry port in the old town. ①.

Hôtel Foch, 4 rue de Caligny (☎02.35.42.50.69, fax 02.35.43.40.17). Plain cream-coloured cement building, beside the main entrance to the St-Joseph church. All rooms have TV plus bath or shower. ④.

Hôtel Jeanne d'Arc, 91 rue Émile-Zola (☎02.35.21.67.27, fax 02.35.41.26.83). Tiny little hotel, where the old-fashioned but clean rooms are given a personal touch by the owner's needlework. ①.

Hôtel Le Monaco, 16 rue de Paris (☎02.35.42.21.01, fax 02.35.42.01.01). Bright hotel on a busy corner overlooking the quay, handy for the ferries and with a good-value brasserie downstairs. Closed second fortnight in Feb, and Mon July–Oct. ②.

Grand Hôtel Parisien, 1 cours de la République (☎02.35.25.23.83, fax 02.35.25.05.06). A well-appointed place, with congenial management, facing the gare SNCF on a busy corner. All rooms have shower and TV. Twenty-five-percent reductions on Fri & Sat Dec–March. ②.

Hôtel Séjour Fleuri, 71 rue Émile-Zola (☎02.35.41.33.81, fax 02.35.42.26.44). On a sideroad off rue de Paris, close to the ferry terminal; not exactly *"fleuri"*, but cheered up by some bright red shutters and a couple of windowboxes. Two hotels knocked into one make for uneven corridors. No restaurant. ①.

Hôtel Yport, 27 cours de la République (☎02.35.25.21.08, fax 02.35.24.06.34). Another option opposite the SNCF station, this time slightly quieter, being set just back from the street, and unusually hospitable. Guests in the cheaper rooms are charged 25F to have a shower, so you might as well have en-suite facilities. No restaurant. ①–③.

The Town

One reason visitors tend to dismiss Le Havre out of hand is that it's easy, whether you're travelling by train, bus or your own vehicle, to get to and from the city without ever seeing its downtown area, and be left with an impression of an endless industrial sprawl.

The central **Hôtel de Ville**, a logical first port of call, is a low flat-roofed building that stretches for over 100m, topped by a seventeen-storey concrete tower. Surrounded by pergola walkways, flowerbeds and flowing water from several strata of fountains, it's an attractive, lively place with a hi-tech feel, and is often the venue for imaginative civic-minded exhibitions.

Perret's other major creation is the church of **St-Joseph**, the not dissimilar steeple of which is clearly visible some way northwest of the town hall. Instead of the traditional elongated cross shape, the church is built on a cross, whose four arms are equally short. From the outside it's a very plain mass of speckled concrete, the main doors thrown open to the street to hint at the dark interior spaces that resemble an underground car park. Once you get inside, it all makes sense. The altar is right in the centre, with the hundred-metre bell tower rising directly above it. Very simple patterns of stained glass, all around the church and right the way up the tower, produce a bright interplay of coloured light, all focusing on the altar to create the effect of a church "in the round". Its plain monolithic exterior has something almost Egyptian in its simplicity. A tight spiral concrete staircase winds its way up one corner of the shaft of the tower – not that visitors can climb it, or indeed would want to.

Le Havre's boldest specimen of modern architecture is considerably more recent – the cultural centre known as the **Volcano** (or less reverentially as the "yoghurt pot"), which stands at the end of the Bassin du Commerce dominating the **Espace Oscar Niemeyer**. The Brazilian architect for whom it is named designed this slightly asymmetrical smooth gleaming white cone, cut off abruptly just above the level of the surrounding buildings, so that its curving planes are undistributed by doors or windows; the entrance is concealed beneath a white walkway in the open plaza below. A large green copper hand emerges from the Volcano just above its base, slightly cupped and pouring out water as a fountain, inscribed with the sentiment that "One day, like this water, the land, beaches and mountains will belong to all." A smaller white building alongside also forms part of the centre.

The **Bassin du Commerce**, which stretches away from the complex, is in fact of minimal commercial significance; kayaks and rowing boats can be rented to explore its regular contours, and a couple of larger boats are moored permanently to serve as clubs or restaurants. It's all disconcertingly quiet, serving mainly as an appropriate stretch of water for the graceful white footbridge of the Passarelle du Commerce to cross.

The Musée des Beaux Arts André Malraux

Boulevard J.F. Kennedy. Daily except Tues 10am–noon & 2–6pm; 10F; all details currently subject to change.

Until recently, the modern **Musée des Beaux Arts André Malraux**, overlooking the harbour entrance, was renowned as one of the best-designed art galleries in France, using natural light to its full advantage to display an enjoyable assortment of nineteenth- and twentieth-century French paintings. However, at the time this book went to press the museum was closed for a thorough overhaul, with the aim of enabling it to show a much greater proportion of its permanent collection than was hitherto possible, and it remains to be seen whether the ambience will remain the same. The highlights will presumably still be over two hundred canvases by **Eugène Boudin**, including greyish landscapes produced all along the Norman coastline, with views of Trouville, Honfleur and Étretat, and a lovely set of works by **Raoul Dufy** (1877–1953), which make Le Havre seem positively radiant, whatever the weather outside. He depicts his native city at play, with drawings and paintings of festivals and parades, and even a panorama of the whole metropolis framed beneath an arching rainbow. Other treasures include a Gauguin from Tahiti, several Monets – including scenes of Westminster and Varengeville, plus a few waterlilies and a snowscape sunrise – as well as works by Corot, Courbet, Pissarro, Sisley, Léger, Braque and Lurçat.

Musée de l'Ancien Havre

1 rue Jerome Bellarmato. Wed–Sun 10am–noon & 2–6pm; 12F.

If you have the time, you might like to see what old Le Havre looked like in the prewar days when **Jean-Paul Sartre** wrote *La Nausée* here. He taught philosophy for five years during the 1930s in a local school, and his almost transcendent disgust with the place cannot obscure the fascination he felt in exploring the seedy dockside quarter of St François, in those spare moments when he wasn't visiting Simone de Beauvoir in Rouen. Little survives of the city Sartre knew, but pictures and bits gathered from the rubble are on display in one of the very few buildings that escaped, the **Musée de l'Ancien Havre**, somewhat incongruous amid the new concrete, just south of the Bassin du Commerce.

Harfleur

The once-great port of **Harfleur** is now no more than a suburb of Le Havre, 6km upstream from the centre. While visibly older than the modern city that engulfs it, it's no longer sufficiently distinctive to be worth visiting. It earned an undying place in history, however, as the landing place of Henry V's English army in 1415, en route to victory at Agincourt. During a month-long siege of the town, two thousand English soldiers died from eating contaminated seafood from the surrounding marshes. Harfleur surrendered in late September, following a final English onslaught spurred on – according to Shakespeare – by Henry's cry of "Once more unto the breach, dear friends . . ."

Eating and shopping

Few of the **restaurants** in Le Havre are worth making a fuss about, except perhaps for some in the suburb of **Ste-Adresse**, which is no longer quite as picturesque as you might imagine from Monet's depictions of it (and where the beachside bd Albert I commemorates the fact that this was the seat of the Belgian government in exile during World War I). There are, however, lots of bars, cafés and brasseries around the gare SNCF, and all sorts of crêperies and ethnic alternatives – couscous, South American, Caribbean – in the backstreets of the St-Francis district.

If you're **shopping** for food to take home, possibilities include the central market, just west of place Gambetta and ideal for fresh produce, and two hypermarkets: Mammouth at Montivilliers (signposted from the Tancarville road) or the larger Auchan at the Mont Gaillard Centre Commercial (Mon–Sat 8.30am–10pm; follow cours de la République beyond gare SNCF, through the tunnel, then look for signs). The *Flunch* (☎02.35.46.59.82) at Auchan is a good self-service cafeteria.

Restaurants

L'Huitrière, 12 quai Michel Féré (☎02.35.21.24.16). Seafood specialists in the St-Francis quarter, facing the rotating bridge between the English and Irish ferry ports. Even the simplest 91F *assiette* includes clams, shrimps and langoustines; the four-person 1112F *Abondance* has to be seen to be believed. They also have branches in Étretat and Dieppe.

Restaurant Palissandre, 33 rue de Bretagne (☎02.35.21.69.00). Old-fashioned wood-panelled bistro in the historic St-François district, where the conventional menus from 85F feature dishes such as fish stewed in cider, and an express menu guarantees service within 20min. Closed Wed pm, Sat am & Sun.

Le Petit Bedon, 37–39 rue Louis Brindeau (☎02.35.41.36.81). A relatively formal option near the Volcano, where menus from 120F include dishes such as monkfish cooked in squid ink. On the whole, the starters are more exciting than the main courses. Closed Sat am, Sun & first fortnight in Aug.

La Petite Auberge, 32 rue de Ste-Adresse (☎02.35.46.27.32). High-class traditional French cooking, aimed more at local businesspeople than at tourists, and offering few surprises but no disappointments. Menus at 118F, 155F and up. Closed Mon & Sun pm.

La Petite Brocante, 75 rue Louis Brindeau (☎02.35.21.42.20). Lively central bistro, where the set menus are a little pricey at 125F and up. but there's always a good-value *plat du jour*, as often as not fresh fish. Closed Sun & first three weeks in Aug.

Tilbury, 39 rue Jean-de-la-Fontaine (☎02.35.21.23.50). Attractive, unusual place in the old town – individual tables are kitted out like horse-drawn carriages – where the emphasis is on baked dishes (they even bake snail *brioches*) and low-priced lunches. Closed Sat am, Sun pm & Mon.

Entertainment and culture

If you're looking to pass an evening or two in Le Havre, the tourist office will be happy to provide information on cultural events in and around town. For all events sponsored by the municipality (a wide and impressive range), book at the Théâtre de l'Hôtel de Ville box office (☎02.35.41.45.74). The most likely venue has to be Le Volcan, in the Espace Oscar Niemeyer, described on p.75 (☎02.35.19.10.10), though you may also hear music performed in the cathedral and other churches. Among several **cinemas** in town are the Eden in the Espace Oscar Niemeyer (☎02.35.21.70.00), and the Sirius at 5 rue Duguesclin (☎02.35.26.52.15), which usually programmes V.O. films.

L'Audito, a FNAC-style shop selling records, CDs and videos at 104 rue Victor Hugo (☎35.42.13.38), is another useful source of information about local activities.

THE SEINE VALLEY

As far back as the Bronze Age, the **Seine** was a crucial part of the "Tin Road" linking Cornwall to Paris. Fortresses and monasteries lined its banks from the time of the Romans onwards. Now, with the threat of its tidal bore and treacherous sandbanks very much a thing of the past, heavy ships make their serene way up its sinuous course to the provincial capital of **Rouen**.

An enormous **new bridge** across the mouth of the Seine opened in 1995; the **Pont de Normandie** links Le Havre with Honfleur, and makes access between the coasts of Upper and Lower Normandy much more direct. Further inland, the immense **Tancarville** suspension bridge offers another choice of banks and routes. Scenically, the best way to go is along the **north (right) bank** – fortunately the route taken by Le Havre–Rouen buses (#191 and #192) – which incorporates such sights as the riverside towns of **Villequier** and **Caudebec**, and the

---

CRUISING ON THE SEINE

Le Cavelier de la Salle,
☎02.32.08.32.40. Trips around the port of Rouen, arranged by local tourist office.

Le Châteaubriand, ☎02.35.15.21.31. Gourmet excursions from Honfleur, Caudebec or Rouen, mid-Oct to April.

Le Château Gaillard,
☎02.43.78.28.28. Cruises between Paris and Rouen.

Le Guillaume le Conquérant,
☎02.35.78.31.70. Cruises between Rouen and Vernon.

Le Normandie, ☎01.45.75.52.60. Eight-day luxury cruises between Paris and Honfleur, with stops including Rouen and Caudebec.

Le River's King, ☎02.34.78.16.32. Cruises between Paris and Honfleur.

La Salamandre, ☎02.35.42.01.31. Cruises around the port of Le Havre, two hour trips from Caudebec, and a seven hour promenade between Rouen and Honfleur.

Le Winner, ☎06.80.10.34.84. Cruises between Paris and Rouen.

---

abbey of **Jumièges**. If you choose the **south bank** instead, you'll need your own transport in order to stray out and away from the motorway to Paris.

Between Tancarville and Rouen, just two **bridges** cross the river, both charging quite hefty tolls. However, there are also intermittent *bacs* (**ferries**) along the way; cheaper, these tend to leave on the hour (and to have long lunch breaks).

Towards Rouen

Le Havre and Rouen are such vast industrial conglomerates that the countryside in between the two might not seem to have any obvious promise. The refineries and cement works of Le Havre in particular feel as if they go on forever. However, just beyond them is the **Parc Naturel Régional de Brotonne**, an area that is surprisingly beautiful even if not entirely rural. The park shelters a wide range of conservation projects and traditional industry initiatives, run by local people, as well as its more obvious abbey and château sites.

If you have your own transport, it's worth taking time to cross the **Pont de Brotonne** to explore the less-frequented **southern side** – the edges of the Vernier marshes where Camargue horses and Scottish highland cattle graze, and the deep thick woods of the **Forêt de Brotonne**. Full details on all aspects of the park can be obtained from the very helpful Maison du Parc, next to the Pont de Brotonne in Nôtre Dame de Bliquetuit (May–Sept Mon–Fri 9am–6pm, Sat 2–6.30pm, Sun 11am–6.30pm; March, April & Oct Mon–Fri 9am–6pm, Sun 11am–6pm; Nov–Feb Mon–Fri 9am–6pm; ☎02.35.37.23.16).

Villequier

The first of the riverbank towns you come to on the **D81 along the north bank** is quite undeservedly one of the least known – **VILLEQUIER**. As a stop on the way to or from Le Havre it's ideal, having a quite exceptional **hotel**. The *Grand Sapin* (☎02.35.56.78.73; ③) is a gorgeous rambling old building, where most of the well-equipped rooms have rickety balconies overlooking the river. It's absolutely magical on a misty morning – and not bad in the evening, when the wood-panelled dining room is in full swing (menus start at 68F). Tables in the riverside garden are laid out under the shade of the eponymous *grand sapin* itself – a rather frail pine that's dwarfed by a giant blossoming lilac nearby.

There's no entertainment whatsoever in Villequier, and the only possible "sight" is a mournful statue of Victor Hugo peering out into the Seine, across a helpfully marked concrete arrow, to the spot where his daughter and her husband drowned in 1843, just six months after their marriage. That lies several hundred metres upstream of the centre, reached by an attractive waterfront promenade.

Caudebec-en-Caux

Just over 4km on from Villequier is the bigger and more popular **CAUDEBEC-EN-CAUX**. Few traces of this old town's past survived the firestorm devastation of the last war, but the local tourist authorities extend a rather sad invitation to visitors to join a "heritage trail" of places that used to be attractive. The damage – and previous local history – is chronicled in the museum at the thirteenth-century **Maison des Templiers**, one of the handful of buildings spared (July & Aug daily 2–6.30pm; Sept–June closed Tues; 15F). As well as enjoying "one of the most important collections of chimney plaques in France", you can take a look there at pictures of the Seine's regular tidal swell, which still threatens at this narrow point to swamp unwary promenaders. The magnificent flamboyant **Notre Dame church** still dominates the main square, which has been the site of a **market** every Saturday since 1390.

A little way south of town, a **stone aeroplane** propels itself out of the cliff face across the water – a memorial to another curious episode of aviation history, contemporary to that commemorated at Étretat. In 1928, a plane was being prepared here for an attempt at what would have been the first transatlantic flight. But shortly before it was due to set off, the Norwegian polar explorer Amundsen issued a worldwide appeal for help to rescue some Italian sailors who had been shipwrecked off Spitzbergen in the Arctic. The French government offered the plane, and its four crewmen left with Amundsen. Two days later they were lost.

Practicalities

Caudebec's **tourist office** is slightly south of the centre, in place Charles de Gaulle (April–Nov Mon–Sat 9.30am–1pm & 3–7pm, Sun 3–7pm; Dec–March daily 3–7pm; ☎02.35.96.20.65). Two absolutely indistinguishable *logis de France* stand side by side facing the river on quai Guilbaud, identical buildings with identical balconies, and all but identical prices and even phone numbers – the *Normotel La Marine* at no. 18 (☎02.35.96.20.11; ③; closed Jan), and the *Normandie* at no. 19 (☎02.35.96.25.11; ②; closed Feb); the restaurants in both are closed on Sunday evenings. Another *logis*, the slightly cheaper *Cheval Blanc*, is a little way back from the river at 4 place Réné-Coty (☎02.35.96.21.66; ②; closed first fortnight of Feb), and there's a riverside **campsite** to the north, the *Barre Y Va* (☎02.35.96.26.38; April–Sept). You can **rent bicycles** from Cycles Velhano at 10 rue de la Vicomte (☎02.35.96.24.77).

On the last Sunday in September of every even-numbered year (2000, 2002, etc), Caudebec comes alive with a large **Cider Festival**.

The Pont de Brotonne

Slightly upstream from Caudebec, the magnificent span of the **Pont de Brotonne**, completed in 1977 as the world's highest and steepest humpback bridge (charging a 12F toll for motorists), climbs out above the Seine. It has an unexpectedly appealing colour scheme – the suspension cables are custard yellow, the rails pastel green, the walkway maroon, and the vast concrete columns left bare. If you don't lose both heart and hat to the sickening drop and the seaborne winds, walking across it is one of the big treats of Normandy. From a distance, its stays refract into strange optical effects, while far below small tugs flounder in the wash of mighty cargo carriers.

Abbaye de St-Wandrille

Just beyond the Pont de Brotonne as you continue towards Rouen, the medieval **Abbaye de St-Wandrille** was founded, so legend has it, by a seventh-century count who, with his wife, renounced all earthly pleasures on the day of their wedding. The abbey's buildings make an attractive if curious collection: part ruin, part restoration and, in the case of the main buildings, part transplant – a fifteenth-century barn brought in just a few years ago from another Norman village miles away. Benedictine monks are on hand to show visitors around the abbey every afternoon at 3pm and 4pm, and also at 11.30am on Sunday (20F); you can hear their **Gregorian chanting** in their new church at morning (Mon–Sat 9.30am, Sun 10am) and evening (Mon–Wed, Fri & Sat 5.30pm, Thurs 6.45pm, Sun & hols 5pm) services.

There's a *crêperie* opposite the abbey, and the more upmarket *Deux Coronnes* restaurant (☎02.35.96.11.44; closed Sun pm, Mon & Sept), in the place de l'Église, is a seventeenth-century inn where delicious menus start at 130F.

Abbaye de Jumièges

In the next loop of the Seine, 12km upstream from St-Wandrille, squats the more famous **Abbaye de Jumiéges**. A haunting ruin, it was destroyed – as a deliberate act of policy – during the Revolution. Its main outline, as far as it can still be discerned, dates from the eleventh century; William the Conqueror himself attended its consecration in 1067. The towers, over 52m high, are still standing. So too is one arch of the roofless nave, while a one-sided yew tree stands in the centre of what were once the cloisters. How evocative you find these bleached stone ruins will depend on your mood. Visits consist of a 45-minute guided tour, though you can also take an unescorted ramble across the lawns (mid-June to mid-Sept daily 9am–6.30pm; mid-Sept to Oct & April to mid-June Mon–Fri 9am–noon & 2–5pm, Sat & Sun 9am–noon & 2–6pm; Nov–March Mon–Fri 10am–noon & 2–4pm, Sat & Sun 10am–noon & 2–5pm; 25F).

The *Auberge des Ruines* at no. 17 in the place de la Mairie (☎02.35.37.24.05; ②; closed Sun pm & Mon, plus all evenings except Fri & Sat Nov–Feb), a grand restaurant where dinner menus start at 130F, has a handful of simple rooms overlooking the abbey.

Hauville

On the opposite, southern, side of the river near **HAUVILLE** (off the road to La Mare-Guérard), it's possible to look round what's said to be the oldest still-functioning **windmill** in France, one of six owned by the monks of Jumièges, who farmed and forested all this area in the Middle Ages. Now restored by the *parc*, its outline – based on contemporary castle towers – looks like a kid's drawing (July & Aug daily 10 am–6.30pm; May, June & Sept Sat & Sun only same times; March, April & Oct to mid-Nov Sun only same times; 12F).

La Haye du Routot and Bourneville

If you've time, head 4km west of Hauville to the neighbouring village of **LA HAYE DU ROUTOT**. The churchyard is a novelty, featuring a pair of millennium-old yew trees that are still alive but have been sufficiently hollowed out to shelter a chapel and grotto. The feature for which the village is best known (at least in Normandy) is its annual **Fête de Ste-Claire**, held on St Claire's feast day, July 16. The centrepiece of this is a towering, conical bonfire, topped by a cross which must survive to ensure a good year. The smouldering logs are taken home to serve as protection against lightning. Should you miss the big day, a video recording of the goings-on is featured in the local crafts museum, which also displays a traditional functioning bread oven, adjacent to the church, and a clog-specialist shoemaker opposite (July & Aug daily; May, June & Sept Sat & Sun; March, April & Oct to mid-Nov Sun only; 10am–6.30pm; 10F).

The **Maison des Métiers** in **BOURNEVILLE** is a beautifully presented **museum** of traditional farming and building techniques (July & Aug daily 2–7pm; mid-Feb to June & Sept to mid-Oct Mon & Wed–Sat 2–6.30pm, Sun 2.30–6.30pm; 12F). For **accommodation** south of the river, there are *chambres de hôte* just outside Routot (c/o M. Vantornhout, ☎02.32.42.92.27; ②), while **La Mailleraye** has a nice little **campsite** (☎02.35.37.12.04; March to mid-Sept).

Duclair

If you want to **cycle** beside the river for any distance, the D982 tends to be forever climbing and descending, and in any event is a bit busy. However, the stretch from Le Mesnil (just beyond Jumièges) as far as Duclair is long, quiet and flat, and has a wonderful view of the lush riverside. **DUCLAIR** itself has a couple of nice **hotels**, with the *Hôtel de la Poste* opposite the landing stage for the town's little *bac*, at 286 quai de la Libération (☎02.35.37.50.04; ③), and *Le Tartarin* further up, at 125 place du Général-de-Gaulle (☎02.35.37.50.38; ①).

As you continue from here towards Rouen, you get a first panoramic prospect, from beside the church at Canteleu, of the docks, the island and the city. The road onwards coasts endlessly down into the maelstrom. (Don't attempt to cycle *out* of Rouen in this direction – the gradient, and the fumes, are unbearable.)

Rouen

ROUEN, the capital of Upper Normandy, is one of France's most ancient and historic cities. Standing on the site of Roman Rotomagus, which was the lowest point on the river then capable of being bridged, it was laid out by the Viking Rollo shortly after he became the first duke of Normandy in 911. Captured by the English in 1419, after a long siege, it became the stage in 1431 for the trial and execution of Joan of Arc, before returning to French control in 1449.

Over the centuries, Rouen has suffered repeated devastation; there were 45 major fires in the first half of the thirteenth century alone. It has had to be almost

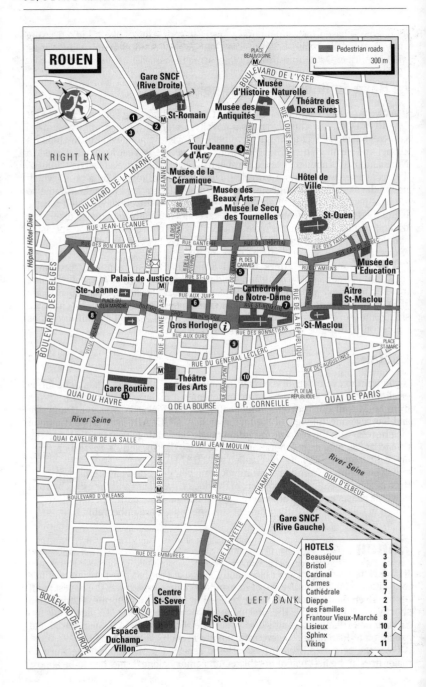

ROUEN

Gare SNCF (Rive Droite)
St-Romain
Musée d'Histoire Naturelle
Théâtre des Deux Rives
Musée des Antiquités
PLACE BEAUVOISINE
BOULEVARD DE L'YSER
RUE LOUIS RICARD
RUE BEAUVOISINE
Tour Jeanne d'Arc
RIGHT BANK
BOULEVARD DE LA MARNE
RUE JEANNE D'ARC
Musée de la Céramique
Musée des Beaux Arts
Musée le Secq des Tournelles
Hôtel de Ville
St-Ouen
SQ VERDREL
Hôpital Hôtel-Dieu
RUE JEAN-LECANUET
RUE DES BON ENFANTS
R DES BASNAGE
RUE GANTERIE
RUE DE L'HÔPITAL
RUE DES FAULX
RUE DE L'AUBETTE
Musée de l'Education
R ECUYERE
R DE LA
R DU CONTRAT
SOCIAL
PL DES CARMES
RUD D'AMIENS
Palais de Justice
Ste-Jeanne
BOULEVARD DES BELGES
PLACE DU VIEUX MARCHE
RUE DU GROS
RUE ST-LO
RUE AUX JUIFS
Cathédrale de Notre-Dame
Aître St-Maclou
RUE JEANNE D'ARC
VIEUX MARCHE
RUE DE L'HORLOGE
RUE ST-ROMAIN
RUE DE LA RÉPUBLIQUE
St-Maclou
Gros Horloge
RUE DES BONNETIERS
RUE AUX OURS
PLACE ST-MARC
RUE DU GENERAL LECLERC
RUE DES AUGUSTINES
Théâtre des Arts
Gare Routière
QUAI DU HAVRE
Q DE LA BOURSE
Q P. CORNEILLE
QUAI DE PARIS
RUE GRAND PONT
PL DE LA RÉPUBLIQUE
River Seine
QUAI CAVELIER DE LA SALLE
QUAI JEAN MOULIN
River Seine
QUAI D'ELBEUF
AV DE BRETAGNE
RUE ST-SEVER
CHAMPLAIN
BOULEVARD D'ORLEANS
COURS CLÉMENCEAU
Gare SNCF (Rive Gauche)
RUE DES EMMURÉES
RUE LAFAYETTE
Centre St-Sever
BOULEVARD DE L'EUROPE
St-Sever
LEFT BANK
Espace Duchamp-Villon

Pedestrian roads
0   300 m

HOTELS
Beauséjour   3
Bristol   6
Cardinal   9
Carmes   5
Cathédrale   7
Dieppe   2
des Familles   1
Frantour Vieux-Marché   8
Lisieux   10
Sphinx   4
Viking   11

entirely rebuilt during the last fifty years, and now you could spend a whole day wandering around the city without realizing that the Seine ran through its centre. Wartime bombs, specifically during the fierce onslaught that coincided with the D-Day landings, destroyed all its bridges, the area between the cathedral and the *quais*, and much of the left bank's industrial quarter. The immediate riverside area has never been adequately restored, and what you might expect to be the most beautiful part of this venerable city is in fact something of an abomination.

Enormous sums have, however, been lavished on an upmarket restoration job on the streets a few hundred metres north of the river, which turned the centre into the closest approximation to a medieval city that modern imaginations could come up with. The project was supervised by Louis Arretche, who redesigned postwar St-Malo so successfully (see p.188). The suggestion that for historical authenticity the houses should be painted in bright, clashing colours was not deemed appropriate by the city authorities, but, so far as it goes, the whole of this inner core can be very seductive, and its churches are extremely impressive by any standards.

Outside the renovated quarters, things are rather different. The city spreads deep into the loop of the Seine to the south, and increasingly into the hills to the north, while the riverbank itself is lined with a fume-filled, multi-laned motor way. As the nearest point that large container ships can get to Paris, the port remains the country's fourth largest – albeit in decline. Rouen's docks and industries stretch endlessly away to the south.

Arrival and information

Rouen's **tourist office**, opposite the cathedral at 25 place de la Cathédrale, stands in the early sixteenth-century "House of the Exchequer" (May–Sept Mon–Sat 9am–7pm, Sun 9.30am–12.30pm & 2.30–6pm; Oct–April Mon–Sat 9am–6.30pm, Sun 10am–1pm; ☎02.32.08.32.40). It serves each day as the starting point for two-hour **walking tours** of different areas of the city, each costing 35F. One departs at 10am to explore the area between the churches St-Romain and St-Ouen; another, at 3pm to head from the Cathedral to the place du Vieux-Marché. There's also a different themed tour at 12.30pm every Tuesday, and another at 2pm on Saturdays that covers the Jewish quarter. For more sedate visitors, a motorized **"petit train"** makes a forty-minute-loop tour from the tourist office at regular intervals (daily 10am, 11am, 2pm, 4pm & 5pm; 30F).

Rouen's **post office** is halfway down rue Jeanne-d'Arc, at no. 45, in the centre of town (post code 76000; ☎02.35.08.73.73; Mon–Fri 8am–7pm, Sat 8am–noon).

Trains

The main **gare SNCF** (☎02.35.98.50.50), high above the river at the top end of rue Jeanne-d'Arc, is Gare Rive Droite; Gare Rive Gauche on the south bank only handles goods traffic. The passenger station is not immediately conspicuous on most maps, because the train lines run underground, but on the ground you can't miss it. From the outside, its minaret makes it resemble a nineteenth-century confection, intended perhaps for Algiers or Istanbul; in fact it was completed in 1928. The main hall is decorated with garish murals.

Rouen is roughly halfway between Paris and the Channel ports; both **Le Havre** and **Dieppe** are one hour away on different train routes, while the journey to **Paris** takes an hour and a quarter. You can also get trains west to **Lisieux** (1hr 15min) and **Caen** (2hr).

Local transport

The city centre of Rouen, north of the Seine, is small enough to stroll around with ease, and there's also an efficient **bus** network. With an ever-expanding network of pedestrianized streets, it's not a city you can drive around with any ease; far better to park in one of the many underground car parks as soon as you arrive.

Rouen's pride and joy, its multibillion-franc new **métro** system, is on the whole more useful to commuters than tourists. From the Gare-Rue Verte, at the SNCF station, trains follow the line of the rue Jeanne-d'Arc, making two stops before they resurface to cross the river by bridge; thereafter the tracks dip below and above ground like a roller coaster. Individual journeys cost 8F; a book of tickets is 59F.

All **buses** except #2A from the gare SNCF take five minutes to run down rue Jeanne-d'Arc to the centre. From the fifth stop, the Théâtre des Arts by the river, the **gare routière** is one block west in rue des Charettes (☎02.35.71.81.71), tucked away behind the riverfront buildings. Out-of-town buses from here include services south to **Évreux** (1hr), #191 and #192 to **Le Havre** along the river, #193 to **Dieppe** via Tôtes, #150 to Dieppe and **Le Tréport**, and #261 to **St-Valéry**.

Cycle and car rental

You can rent **bicycles** from Rouen Cycles, 45 rue St-Éloi (☎02.35.71.34.30; Tues–Sat 8.30am–noon & 2–7pm), as well as at the gare SNCF. Among **car-rental** companies are Avis, at the gare SNCF (☎02.35.70.95.12), Budget, 14 rue de Lisbonne (☎02.35.98.64.38), and Hertz, 38 quai Gaston-Boulet (☎02.35.98.16.57).

Accommodation

With more than three thousand **hotel** rooms in town, there should be no difficulty in finding appropriate accommodation in Rouen, even at the busiest times. Few of the hotels have restaurants, chiefly because there's so wide a choice of places to eat all over town, and all those listed below remain open all year. Motorists who just want to spend a day or two looking at the sights of Rouen should seriously consider the possibility of staying at one of the delightful riverside hotels in **La Bouille** (see p.94), or in the woods at **Lyons-la-Forêt** (see p.95).

The city's **youth hostel** is south of the river at 118 bd de l'Europe (☎02.35.72.06.45; 59F; 11pm curfew). The easiest way to get there from the gare SNCF is to take the métro, direction *Hôtel de Ville* or *Technopôle*, as far as the *Europe* stop.

The surprisingly small **Camping Municipal**, intended more for caravanners than tent campers, is 4km northwest on rue Jules-Ferry in **Déville-lès-Rouen** (☎02.35.74.07.59), reached by taking bus #2 from the Théâtre des Arts, while the significantly less accessible *Camping L'Aubette* is 5km east at 23 Vert Buisson in **St-Léger du Bourg-Denis** (☎02.35.08.47.69).

Hotels

Hôtel Beauséjour, 9 rue Pouchet (☎02.35.71.93.47, fax 02.35.98.01.24). Good-value place near the station (turn right as you come out), though once you're past the attractive orange facade with its windowboxes, and the nice garden courtyard, the rooms themselves are on the plain side, even if they do all have shower and TV. ②.

Hôtel Bristol, 45 rue aux Juifs (☎02.35.71.54.21). Clean, pretty little nine-room hotel, in a half-timbered house overlooking the Palais de Justice. All rooms are en suite, and have TV. ②.

Hôtel le Cardinal, 1 place de la Cathédrale (☎02.35.70.24.42, fax 02.35.89.75.14). Very good-value hotel in a stunning location facing the cathedral; the rooms have excellent en-suite facilities. No restaurant. ③.

Hôtel des Carmes, 33 place des Carmes (☎02.35.71.92.31, fax 02.35.71.76.96). Twelve-room hotel in a beautifully decorated nineteenth-century house in a quiet central square, complete with blue shutters, a short walk north from the cathedral. Guests are not given keys to stay out late. No restaurant, but buffet breakfasts for 34F. ②.

Hôtel de la Cathédrale, 12 rue St-Romain (☎02.35.71.57.95, fax 02.35.70.15.54). One of the very nicest hotels in Rouen. Quiet, central rooms alongside the cathedral and archbishop's palace, with a quaint old courtyard with flowers. Set in a pedestrianized street – so parking is a problem – that's lined with fourteenth-century timber-framed houses. No restaurant. ④.

Hôtel de Dieppe, place Bernard Tissot (☎02.35.71.96.00, fax 02.35.89.65.21). Grand traditional hotel, immediately opposite the station, which is affiliated to the Best Western chain. Prices for the well-equipped rooms are greatly discounted at weekends. ⑤.

Hôtel des Familles, 4 rue Pouchet (☎02.35.71.88.51, fax 02.35.07.54.65). Very friendly and characterful place, set back beyond a small gravel yard and a short walk to the right as you come out from the gare Rive Droite. Incorporates the old *Hôtel de la Paix*; hence the two entrances. No restaurant. ②.

Hôtel Frantour Vieux Marché, 15 rue de la Pie (☎02.35.71.00.88, fax 02.35.70.75.94). Very modern place, set around a venerable old courtyard, just a toss of a match from the place du Vieux-Marché. A high standard of comfort has quickly made this the most popular upmarket hotel in town. ⑤.

Hôtel de Lisieux, 4 rue de la Savonnerie (☎02.35.71.87.73, fax 02.35.89.31.52). At the junction of rue de la Savonnerie and rue du Bec, between cathedral and river. Bishop Cauchon, who prosecuted Joan of Arc in 1431, is said to have stayed – and died – here in 1442. If so, it has been modernized since – every room now has en-suite facilities – losing much of the original character in the process. No restaurant. ③.

Hôtel Sphinx, 130 rue Beauvoisine (☎02.35.71.35.86). Very basic accommodation, at the north end of the street near the Musée des Antiquités. None of the rooms has a shower; there's a charge of 10F per shower, and an extra bed in the room costs 60F. No restaurant. ①.

Hôtel Viking, 21 quai du Havre (☎02.35.70.34.95, fax 02.35.89.97.12). Just in front of the gare routière, to the right at the bottom of rue Jeanne-d'Arc. Overlooking not only the river, but also the main roads, the noise of which is only partly dampened by the double glazing. No restaurant. ③.

The Town

Rouen spends a higher proportion of its budget on **monuments** than any other provincial town, which maddens many a Rouennais. As a tourist, your one complaint may be the lack of time to visit them all. Certainly there are some great sights to be seen – the **Cathédrale de Notre Dame**, the **Gros Horloge**, the **Aître St-Maclou**, all the delightful twisting streets of timbered houses – and the history too is there to be relished, most notably the links with **Joan of Arc**.

Place du Vieux-Marché

One obvious place to start exploring the city is the **place du Vieux-Marché**, where a small plaque and a huge cross, 20m high, adorn the public square in which Joan of Arc was burned to death on May 30, 1431. Louis Arretche was commissioned to design a memorial **church** to the saint in 1969, and the result was dedicated in 1979 (Mon–Thurs & Sat 10am–12.30pm & 2–6pm, Fri & Sun 2–6pm). A wacky, spiky-looking thing, said to represent either an upturned boat or the

JOAN OF ARC

Joan of Arc stands alone, and must continue to stand alone . . . There is no one to compare her with, none to measure her by . . There have been other young generals, but they were not girls; young generals, but they have been soldiers before they were generals; she began as a general; she commanded the first army she ever saw; she led it from victory to victory, and never lost a battle with it; there have been young commanders-in-chief, but none so young as she: she is the only soldier in history who has held the supreme command of a nation's armies at the age of seventeen.

Mark Twain, Joan of Arc

When the 17-year-old peasant girl known to history as **Joan of Arc** arrived at the French court in Chinon early in 1429, the Hundred Years' War had already dragged on for over ninety years. Most of northern France was in the grip of an Anglo–Burgundian alliance, whose major strongholds were the châteaux of the Loire. Since 1425, Joan had been hearing voices in her native village of Domrémy, in Lorraine near France's eastern frontiers. Convinced that she alone could save France, she came to Chinon to present her case to the as-yet-uncrowned Dauphin. Partly through recognizing him despite a simple disguise he wore to fool her at their first meeting, she convinced him of her divine guidance; and after a remarkable three-week examination by a tribunal of the French *parlement*, she went on to secure command of the armies of France. In a whirlwind campaign, which culminated in the raising of the siege of Orléans on May 8, 1429, she broke the English hold on the Loire Valley. She then escorted the Dauphin deep into enemy territory, with town after town rallying to her standard as they advanced, so that in accordance with ancient tradition he could be crowned King Charles VII of France in the cathedral at Reims, on July 17.

Within a year of her greatest triumph, Joan was captured by the Burgundian army at Compiègne in May 1430, and held to ransom. Chivalry dictated that any offer of payment from the vacillating Charles must be accepted, but in the absence of such an offer Joan was handed over to the English for 10,000 ducats. On Christmas Day 1430, she was imprisoned in the château of Philippe-Auguste at Rouen.

Charged with heresy, on account of her "false and diabolical" visions and refusal not to wear men's clothing, Joan was put on trial for her life on February 21, 1431. For three months, a changing panel of 131 assessors – only eight of whom were English-born – heard the evidence against her. Condemned, inevitably, to death, Joan recanted on the scaffold in St-Ouen cemetery on May 24, and her sentence was commuted to life imprisonment. The presiding judge, Bishop Pierre Cauchon of Beauvais, reassured disappointed English representatives that "we will get her yet". The next Sunday, Joan was tricked into breaking her vow and putting on male clothing, and taken to the archbishop's chapel in rue St-Romain to be condemned to death for the second time. On May 30, 1431, she was burned at the stake in the place du Vieux-Marché; her ashes, together with her unburned heart, were thrown into the Seine.

Charles VII finally reconquered Rouen in 1449. Seeing the verdict against Joan as reflecting on the legitimacy of his own claim to the French throne, he instigated a *Procés en Nullité*, which took evidence from all the surviving witnesses, and resulted in a papal declaration of Joan's innocence in 1456. Joan herself passed into legend, until the discovery and publication of the full transcript of her trial in the 1840s. The forbearance and devout humility she displayed throughout her ordeal added to her status as France's greatest religious heroine. She was canonized as recently as 1920, and soon afterwards became the country's patron saint.

flames that consumed Joan, it's indisputably an architectural triumph, part of an ensemble of buildings that manages to incorporate in similar style a covered food market, open daily except Monday, but designed more for show than practical shopping. The theme of the church's fish-shaped windows is continued in the scaly tiles that adorn its roof, which is hugely elongated to form a covered walkway across the square. Part of Arretche's brief was to incorporate some sixteenth-century stained glass, removed from the church of St-Vincent that stood on this site before it was destroyed in the war. It's now displayed beautifully, all on one facade of the new church, despite the fact that the windows that hold it are an utterly different shape. The outline of the foundations of the vanished old church is visible on the adjacent lawns, which also mark the precise spot of Joan's martyrdom. The square itself is surrounded by fine old brown and white half-timbered houses; many of those on the south side now serve as restaurants.

Also on the south side of the *place*, the privately owned **Musée Jeanne d'Arc**, in an ancient cellar in the back of a gift shop, draws large crowds to its collection of tawdry waxworks and facsimile manuscripts (daily except Mon: May to mid-Sept 9.30am–6.30pm; mid-Sept to April 10am–noon & 2–6.30pm; 24F). Among the bric-a-brac is a page from the records of the Paris *parlement*, dated May 10, 1429, which refers to reports reaching Paris that, on the previous Saturday, the French had trounced the British at Orléans. A sketch in the margin, possibly by a bored clerk, depicts a young woman, with her hair tied back, a banner in one hand and a sword in the other. The only contemporary portrait of the Maid of Orléans was not drawn from life, so there's no reason to think it any more authentic than the movie stills on display in the museum, showing Ingrid Bergman as Joan in both 1948 and 1954, and Jean Seberg in the role in 1957.

Gros Horloge

From place du Vieux-Marché, rue du Gros-Horloge leads east towards the cathedral. Just across rue Jeanne-d'Arc you come to the **Gros Horloge** itself. A colourful one-handed clock, it used to be on the adjacent Gothic belfry until it was moved down by popular demand in 1529, so that people could see it better. Assuming the restoration work that was in progress when this book went to press is now completed, you should be able to pay a small fee to climb up rather too many steps to see its workings and, if the sponginess of the lead roofing agrees with your nerves, totter around the top for a marvellous view of the old city, and the startling array of towers and spires around. The bell up there, cast in 1260, still rings what's known as the "Conqueror's Curfew" at 9pm daily. A block to the north are the Renaissance splendours of the former **Palais de Justice**.

Cathédrale de Notre Dame

The **Cathédrale de Notre Dame** (Mon–Sat 8am–7pm, Sun 8am–6pm) stands on the site of a Roman place of worship, erected some time in the third century AD at a major crossroads. Despite the addition of all sorts of different towers, spires and vertical extensions, it remains at heart the Gothic masterpiece that was built in the twelfth and thirteenth centuries. Later accretions include the Flamboyant **Tour du Beurre**, named for what was probably the erroneous belief that it was paid for by the granting of dispensations that allowed wealthy churchgoers to eat butter during Lent, and the nineteenth-century iron spire of the central lantern tower. Cast in the foundries of Conches, it was built to replace a tower that burned down in 1822, and was at the time, at 151m, the highest in France.

The **west façade** of the cathedral, which is intricately sculpted like the rest of the exterior, was Monet's subject for over thirty studies of changing light, which now hang in the Musée d'Orsay in Paris. Monet might not recognize it now, however – in the last few years, it's been scrubbed a gleaming white, free from the centuries of accreted dirt he so carefully recorded.

Inside, the carvings of the misericords in the choir depict fifteenth-century life, in secular scenes of work and habits, as well as the usual mythical beasts. The chapel dedicated to Joan of Arc, and paid for by an English commitee in 1956, contains a statue of Joan at the stake. The **ambulatory** and **crypt** – closed on Sundays and during services – hold the assorted tombs of various recumbent royalty, stretching back as far as **Duke Rollo**, who died "enfeebled by toil" in 933 AD. Rollo's effigy was destroyed by the bombs of 1944, and has now been replaced by a nineteenth-century copy of someone else's. Both he and **Richard the Lionheart** – whose eponymous heart reposes beneath a similar figure nearby – seem to be missing a foot.

Église St-Maclou and Aître St-Maclou

A short way east of the cathedral, the intricate wooden panelling in the porch of the fifteenth-century church of **St-Maclou** is the highlight of what is often cited as the most spectacular example of Gothic Flamboyant architecture in France (March–Oct Mon–Sat 10am–noon & 2–6pm, Sun 3–5.30pm; Nov–Feb Mon–Sat 10am–noon & 2–5.30pm, Sun 3–5.30pm). The whole building was so badly damaged by bombs on June 4, 1944 that it could only reopen in 1980, although the ornate stone stairway up to the organ inside is as ethereal as ever. That the interior is so light is in part because most of its stained glass was destroyed, and the windows are now clear. St Maclou himself – perhaps more familiar as St Malo – was a seventh-century missionary from Wales.

Nearby, with its entrance a little hard to find in between nos. 184 and 186 rue Martainville, is the **Aître St-Maclou** (daily 8am–8pm). This was built between 1526 and 1533, in an era of mass plague deaths, as a cemetery and charnel house. The ground floor was used as an open cloister and, in the rooms above, the bare bones of countless victims were exposed to view. At first sight it looks very picturesque – a tranquil garden courtyard of half-timbered houses – but look closely at the carvings on the beams of the one open lower storey of the surrounding buildings and you see traces of a macabre **Dance of Death**, while in the case to the right of the entrance is a mummified cat. The buildings are still in use, and still stimulating morbid imaginations, not as a morgue but as Rouen's Fine Arts school. In the square outside are several good antique bookshops and a few art shops.

St-Ouen

The last of Rouen's great churches is **St-Ouen**, next to the Hôtel de Ville in a large open square to the north (mid-March to Oct daily except Tues 10am–12.30pm & 2–6pm; Nov to mid-Dec and mid-Jan to mid-March Wed, Sat & Sun 10am–12.30pm & 2–4.30pm). It's larger than the cathedral and has far less decoration, with the result that its Gothic proportions and the purity of its lines have that instant impact with which nothing built since the Middle Ages can compete. Originally, it was an abbey church, founded in the seventh century before the Viking invasion. The present building was begun in 1318 and completed in the fifteenth century.

Immediately north of St-Ouen is the city's **Hôtel de Ville**, outside which parades an equestrian statue of Napoléon, weathered to an eerie green and looking like death incarnate.

Rue Eau de Robec

The **rue Eau de Robec**, which runs east from rue Damiette just south of St-Ouen, was described by one of Flaubert's characters in an earlier age as a "degraded little Venice". It's now a textbook example of how Rouen has been restored. Where once a shallow stream flowed beneath the raised doorsteps of venerable half-timbered houses, a thin trickle now makes its way along a stylized cement bed crossed by concrete walkways. It remains an attractive ensemble, if a rather ersatz one, and the houses themselves are now predominantly inhabited by antique dealers, interspersed with the odd café.

Tour Jeanne d'Arc

The pencil-thin **Tour Jeanne d'Arc** (daily except Tues 10am–noon & 2–5.30pm; 10F), a short way southeast of the gare SNCF at the junction of rue du Donjon and rue du Cordier, is all that remains of the castle of Philippe-Auguste, built in 1205 and scene of the imprisonment and trial of Joan of Arc. It served as the castle's keep and entranceway, and was itself fully surrounded by a moat. It was not, however, Joan's actual prison – that was the Tour de la Pucelle, demolished in 1809 – while the trial took place first of all in the castle's St-Romain chapel, and then later in its great central hall, both of which were destroyed in 1590.

Joan came to this building only once, on May 9, 1431, to be confronted with the fearsome torture chamber in its lowest level. Threatened by Bishop Cauchon with the words "There is the rack, and there are its ministers. You will reveall all, now, or be put to the torture", she responded: "I will tell you nothing more than I have told you; no, not even if you tear the limbs from my body. And even if in my pain I did say something otherwise, I would always say afterwards that it was the torture that spoke and not I."

The tall, sharp-pointed tower was bought by public subscription in 1860, and restored to its present state. After seeing a small collection of Joan-related memorabilia, visitors climb the steep spiral staircase to the very top, but you can't see out over the city, let alone step outside into the open air.

Musée des Beaux Arts

Rouen's imposing **Musée des Beaux Arts** commands the square Verdrel from just east of the central rue Jeanne-d'Arc (daily except Tues 10am–6pm; 20F). Even this grand edifice is not quite large enough to display some of its medieval tapestries, which dangle inelegantly from the ceilings to trail along the floor, but the collection as a whole is consistently absorbing. Unexpected highlights include dazzling Russian icons from the sixteenth century onwards, and an entertaining three-dimensional eighteenth-century Nativity from Naples.

Many of the biggest names among the **painters** – Caravaggio, Velázquez, Rubens – tend to be represented by a single minor work. However, there are several Monets, including a Rouen Cathedral from 1894, Paris's rue St-Denis aflutter with flags in 1894, and a recently acquired *Vue Générale de Rouen*, as well as canvases by Blanche Hoschedé-Monet, who was both the daughter of Claude Monet's mistress Alice and the wife of his son Jean. The central sculpture court, roofed over but very light, is dominated a wonderful three-part mural of the course of the Seine from Paris to Le Havre, prepared by Raoul Dufy in 1937 for the Palais de Chaillot in Paris.

Musée de la Céramique

Rouen's history as a centre for *faïencerie*, the manufacture of earthenware pottery, is recorded in the **Musée de la Céramique**, facing the Beaux Arts from rue Faucon to the north (daily except Tues 10am–1pm & 2–6pm; 13F). A series of beautiful rooms, some of which incorporate sixteenth-century wood panelling rescued from the demolished nunnery of St-Amand, display specimens from the seventeenth century onwards. Until polychrome appeared in 1698, everything was blue; at that time, Rouen's main rivals and influences were the cities of Delft and Nevers, well represented in this collection. Assorted tiles and plates reflect the eighteenth-century craze for chinoiserie, although the genuine Chinese and Japanese pieces nearby possess a sophistication contemporary French craftsmen could only dream of emulating. The mood changes abruptly in the Revolutionary era, as witnessed by a fascinating collection of plates bearing slogans from both sides of the political fence.

Musée Le Secq des Tournelles

Behind the Beaux Arts, housed in the old and barely altered church of St-Laurent on rue Jacques-Villon, stands an interesting and unusual museum of ironmongery, the **Musée Le Secq des Tournelles** (daily except Tues 10am–1pm & 2–6pm; 13F). It consists of a collection of wrought-iron objects of all dates and descriptions, among them nutcrackers and door knockers, locks and gates, nineteenth-century toys and jewellery, spiral staircases that lead nowhere, and hideous implements of torture.

Musée des Antiquités

The **Musée des Antiquités** (Mon & Wed–Sat 10am–12.30pm & 1.30–5.30pm, Sun 2–6pm; 20F), a short walk north of the town centre at the top of rue Beauvoisine, provides a dry but comprehensive run-through of ancient artefacts found in or near Rouen. Starting with an impressive pointed helmet from the Bronze Age and an assortment of early iron tools, it continues with some remarkably complete Roman mosaics from villas unearthed in Lillebonne and the Forêt de Brotonne. Then come a long gallery filled with wood carvings rescued from long-lost Rouen houses – including a lovely bas-relief of sheep that served as the sign for a medieval draper's shop – and some fine fifteenth-century tapestries.

> Note that the **Musée d'Histoire Naturelle, Ethnographie and Préhistoire**, next to the Musée des Antiquités, and the **Musée National de l'Éducation**, in rue Eau de Robec, were both closed for restoration as this book went to press.

The Pavillon Flaubert and the Musée Flaubert et de l'Histoire de la Médicine

For an insight into the Rouen that Flaubert knew, don't go to the **Pavillon Flaubert** at Croisset-Canteleu. Like Rouen's two other literary museums – the two homes of Pierre Corneille – it only proves the pointlessness of the genre. Visit, instead, the **Musée Flaubert et de l'Histoire de la Médicine**, at the Hôtel-Dieu Hospital (Tues–Sat 10am–noon & 2–6pm; free; ring several times). This stands on the corner of rue de Lecat and rue du Contrat-Social, walkable from the centre (or bus #2A), and it's infinitely more relevant to Flaubert's writings than the manuscript copies and personal mementos in the Pavillon museum.

Flaubert's father was chief surgeon and director of the medical school, living with his family in this house within the hospital. Even during the cholera epidemic when Gustave was 11, he and his sister were not stopped from running around the wards or climbing along the garden wall to look into the autopsy lab. Some of the medical exhibits would certainly have been familiar objects to him – a phrenology model, a childbirth demonstrator like a giant ragdoll, and the sets of encyclopedias. There's also one of his stuffed parrots, as featured in Julian Barnes' novel *Flaubert's Parrot*.

Eating

Rouen has a good reputation for **food**, with its most famous dish being *caneton* (duckling). Unlike the hotels, which sometimes have cheaper weekend rates, the city's upmarket restaurants tend to charge more over weekends, when families eat out. The greatest concentration of restaurants is in place du Vieux-Marché, an area in which, perversely, there are few hotels.

There's a daily **food market** in the square, while the area just north is full of Tunisian **takeaways, crêperies**, and so forth. There are, too, sumptuous **patisserie** shops everywhere.

Restaurants

Auberge St-Maclou, 224–226 rue Martainville (☎02.35.71.06.67). Half-timbered building in the shadow of St-Maclou church, with tables on the street outside and an old-style ambience inside. The pedestrian street gets crowded in summer, but the menus are far from overpriced – the 67F set lunch includes cocktail, wine and coffee. Prices to suit all budgets, and dishes including mussels and duck, as well as excellent desserts. Closed Sun pm & Mon.

Le Beffroy, 15 rue Beffroy (☎02.35.71.55.27). Intimate, very old-fashioned and very good Norman restaurant, with copper pans glowing in the flames of the venerable fireplace, and reliably hearty portions of delicious food. The fish, on menus that start at 100F, is especially good. Closed Sun pm & Tues pm.

Brasserie Paul, 1 place de la Cathédrale (☎02.35.71.86.07). The definitive address for Rouen's definitive bistro, an attractive Belle-Époque place with seating both indoors and on a terrace in full view of the cathedral. Daily lunch specials, such as the goats' cheese and smoked duck salad that was Simone de Beauvoir's regular favourite in 1937, cost around 60F.

Des Beaux Arts, 34 rue Damiette (☎02.35.70.17.15). On a pretty pedestrianized street north of St-Maclou church. Very-good-value Algerian cuisine: *couscous* from 50F or *tajine* from 68F, with all kinds of sausages and assorted meats. Closed Wed in winter.

Flunch, 60 rue des Carmes (☎02.35.71.81.81). Large and good self-service, with many fresh dishes and a 35F daily *formule*. On a street running north from the cathedral. Daily 11am–10pm.

Gill, 9 quai de la Bourse (☎02.35.71.16.14). Absolutely classic French restaurant, voted the best in the province by a local magazine on account of such Gilles Tournadre specialities as lobster grilled with asparagus and pigeon baked in puff pastry. The cheapest menu will set you back 199F. Closed Sun & Mon June–Sept, otherwise Sun pm & Mon.

Gill, Le Bistrot du Chef . . . en Gare, 1st Floor, Gare Rive Droite (☎02.35.71.48.66). The name may seem convoluted to outsiders, but to Rouennais it signals a true marvel; the bistro in the main train station is now run under the auspices of the city's top chef. There's an excellent self-service cafeteria downstairs, while the more formal dining room upstairs is open for lunch only, with set menus from 75F. Closed Mon pm, Sat am, Sun & all Aug.

Grill du Drugstore, 2 rue Beauvoisine (☎02.35.98.51.20). Not at all what the name might suggest; this is actually an elegant wood-panelled dining room, tucked away unexpectedly above a genuine pharmacy a short way north of the cathedral, and serving good-value lunches from 60F, including a drink. For a little extra, they also do top-quality steaks. Closed Sun.

Jumbo, 11 rue Guillaume-le-Conquerant (☎02.35.70.35.88). Another good self-service, off the northeast corner of place du Vieux-Marché. Put together your own large salad for under 25F, or choose from a variety of cooked dishes. Daily 11.15am–2.30 pm & 6.30–9.30pm.

Les Maraichers – Le Bistrot d'Adrien, 37 place du Vieux-Marché (☎02.35.71.57.73). Deservedly the most popular of the Vieux-Marché's many restaurants, with a streetside terrace right in front of the St-Jeanne church. Styled to resemble a *fin-de-siècle* Parisian bistro, serving varied set menus until 11pm nightly and *à la carte* until midnight. Menus start at 78F, with lots of *andouillettes*, snails and tongues, but plenty of wholesome possibilities too, and great desserts.

Les Nymphéas, 7–9 rue de la Pie (☎02.35.89.26.69). Beyond a half-timbered courtyard just west of place du Vieux-Marché. The chic-est restaurant in Rouen, if a little over-the-top for most tastes, with set menus at 165F, 195F and 250F; recommendations include the scallop salad, and the beef with truffles. Closed Sun pm & Mon.

Pascaline, 5 rue de la Poterne (☎02.35.89.67.44). North of Palais de Justice, near the flower market; classic bistro with a green wooden enclosure attached to the front of a half-timbered house. They do great-value buffets of salads (32F), main courses (45F) and desserts (37F) – you can have all three for 79F – as well as more formal set menus from 99F that provide a good opportunity to sample Rouennais *caneton* (duckling).

Le P'tit Bec, 182 rue Eau de Robec (☎02.35.07.63.33). Friendly brasserie-cum-tearoom that has become Rouen's most popular lunch spot, with a simple 75F menu holding such joys as salmon tagliatelle and chocolate fondants, with plenty of vegetarian options; also serves afternoon tea. There's seating both indoors and outside, on the pedestrianized street, beside the running water and in view of the gorgeous blue half-timbered mansion next door. The only evening it's open is Friday; closed all day Sun.

Au Temps des Cerises, 4–6 rue des Basnages (☎02.35.89.98.00). If you've come to Normandy for the cheeses, this is the place to get it all out of your system. Turkey breast in Camembert, goats'-cheese *crêpes*, and above all fondues of every description. Lunch menus from 60F, from 88F in the evening. Trendy if slightly overstyled. Closed Mon am & Sun.

Auberge du Vieux-Carré, 34 rue Ganterie (☎02.35.71.67.70). You have to be in the mood for a rich experience to come to this lovely little restaurant a few blocks north of the cathedral, where some seating is in a garden courtyard; counting your calories (or your pennies) is not really an option. The cheapest, 120F menu features a *marmite des pêcheurs* with three kinds of fish; on the 230F menu, that becomes a soufflé of three fishes, followed perhaps by pigeon stuffed with *foie gras* and a chocolate cake *à la crème d'orange*. Closed Sun pm & Mon.

Shopping

Most of the classier **shops** in Rouen are in the pedestrian streets near, and slightly north of, the cathedral. If you are looking for fancy foodstuffs, patisseries, chocolates and the like, there are shops on rue Jeanne-d'Arc around and just above rue du Gros-Horloge. For **hypermarkets** and cheap clothes, however – or just for a laugh on a rainy day – go south of the river to the modern multistorey St-Sever complex. There's an open-air antiques and bric-a-brac **market** nearby in the place des Émmurées.

For books, maps and guides, largely in French, visit l'Armitière, 5 rue des Basnages, or the more specialist Imprimateur, 34 rue St-Nicolas. English-language titles, as well as a wide range of CDs, videos and computer paraphernalia, can be found at the all-purpose FNAC, 39 rue Écuyère (Mon 2–7pm, Tues–Sat 10am–7pm), behind the post office near the place du Vieux-Marché, or the English specialist ABC Bookshop, 9–11 rue des Faulx (Tues–Sat 10am–6pm), near the St-Ouen church.

Nightlife and entertainment

As you would expect in a conurbation of 400,000, there's always plenty going on in Rouen, from classical concerts in churches to alternative events in community and commercial centres. An annual handbook, *Le P'tit Normand*, available in all newsagents, is helpful with addresses and telephone numbers. For current events, pick up the free *Cette Semaine à Rouen* from the tourist office. Tickets (and further information) can also be had from FNAC, on rue Écuyère.

Rouen has several **theatres**, which mainly work to winter seasons. The most highbrow and big-spectacle is the **Théâtre des Arts**, 22 place des Arts (☎02.35.98.50.98), which puts on opera, ballet and concerts. The more adventurous repertory company of the **Théâtre des Deux Rives** (☎02.35.70.22.82), based opposite the Antiquités museum at the top end of rue Louis-Ricard (no. 48; happily at the junction with rue de Joyeuse), presents work by playwrights such as Beaumarchais, Shakespeare, Beckett and Gorky.

Major **concerts** often take place in the **Théâtre Duchamp-Villon** in the St-Sever complex (☎02.35.62.31.31). Also south of the river, but a long way further out, are the **Théâtre Charles Dullin**, allée des Arcades, Grand Quévilly (☎02.35.68.48.91), and the **Théâtre Maxime-Gorki**, rue François-Mitterrand, Petit Quévilly (☎02.35.72.67.55), which specializes in contemporary and traditional music from around Europe. There are two multi-screen **cinemas** just north of the river, and another in the St-Sever complex.

Bars and music venues

Some of Rouen's most agreeable **bars** are in the maze of streets between rue Jean-Lecanuet and place du Vieux-Marché. Incoming sailors used to head straight for this area of the city, and the small bars are still there even if the sailors aren't.

Le Bateau Ivre, 17 rue des Sapins (☎02.35.70.09.05). Low-key but atmospheric hangout, with wooden tables, which puts on a mostly rock-oriented programme of music and performance, with an open-mike night on Thursdays that seems to attract lovers of traditional French *chansons*. Open Tuesday & Wednesday until 2am, Thursday–Saturday until 4am. Closed Sun, Mon & all Aug.

Big Ben Pub, 95 rue du Gros-Horloge (☎02.35.88.44.50). Right under the big clock – hence the name. A Mexican-themed restaurant which incorporates an always-packed bar, strictly speaking entered from a side street – 30 rue des Vergetiers. Usually as crowded inside as is the street outside. Open noon–2am. Closed Sun.

Exo 7, 13 place des Chartreux (☎02.35.03.32.30). Traditionally the centre of Rouen's heavy-rock scene, a long way south of the centre, the *Exo 7* (note the pun) is these days becoming a bit more eclectic, with the odd techno dance night as well. Open Wed–Sat 10.30pm–4am.

La Luna, 26 rue St-Étienne-des-Tonneliers (☎02.35.88.77.18). Glamorous late-night club that specializes in all things South American, with steamy salsa dancing most nights. Open Tues–Thurs until 2am, Fri & Sat until 4am.

Scottish Pub, 21 rue Verte (☎02.35.71.46.22). Bar and restaurant right next to the station, open until 2am, which puts on jazz groups from time to time. Closed Sat lunchtime & Sun.

La Taverne St-Amand, 11 rue St-Amand (☎02.35.88.51.34). Popular bar with draught Guinness, off rue de la République above the cathedral.

Le Traxx, 4 bd Ferdinand-de-Lesseps (☎02.32.10.12.02). Rouen's top gay club offers a regular diet of house and techno to a flamboyant clientele that loves to go wild on a special occasion. Open Wed–Sat 10pm–4am.

Around Rouen

Though it only takes a few minutes of travelling along the river from Rouen in either direction to reach pleasant small towns well worth an overnight stop – such as Villequier or Les Andelys, both described elsewhere in this chapter – a number of places only just outside the city proper make good day-trips while you are based in the city. Some are also worth considering as alternative bases for visits to the metropolis.

The Château du Robert-le-Diable
A long and very badly signposted haul southwest from central Rouen, past the docks and refineries of Petit and Grand Quévilly (where there are at least a few cycle lanes), suddenly climbs from Moulineaux up to the ruined **Château du Robert-le-Diable** (March to mid-Nov daily 9am–7pm; mid-Nov to Feb Sun 9am–6pm; 40F). Robert the Devil is a legendary figure who may or may not have been William the Conqueror's father, but certainly didn't build this early Norman castle. It's now privately run, with a crazy-golf course, a slightly clumsy reconstruction of a Viking *drakkar*, and tacky waxworks of the Battle of Hastings and other such scenes. But its strengths are the very damp and spooky passages underground, and then the magnificent view from the top of the tower down to the Seine, the port of Rouen and the châteaux on the other side. The only drawback is that the château is right next to an extremely busy motorway.

Just across the motorway is the **Forêt de la Londe**. Although dissected by a number of busy train lines, it survives in the gaps – and is used by local cyclists to race the pollution of Rouen out of their systems.

La Bouille
More or less immediately below the Château du Robert-le-Diable, 10km southwest from central Rouen along the southern riverbank, the small village of **LA BOUILLE** stands near a magnificent sweeping bend in the Seine. Little more than a couple of narrow twisting lanes lined with gnarled half-timbered houses, pressed hard against the steep hillside, it's an utter contrast to the noise and bustle of the city, and makes a perfect place to spend a couple of nights for anyone not dependent on public transport. Not far north, a little *bac* (ferry) crosses the river to the small Forêt de Roumare.

Two expensive but exquisite **hotels** overlook the main road through the village; both the *Bellevue* (☎02.35.18.05.05; ③) and the luxurious *St-Pierre* (☎02.35.18.01.01; river views ⑤, otherwise ④) have superb dining rooms.

Clères
Roughly 16km northeast of Rouen, and reachable on bus #161, the pretty village of **CLÈRES** has a large and popular **zoo** (Easter–Sept Mon–Fri 9am–6.30pm, Sat 9am–6.30pm, Sun 9am–7pm; March–Easter, Oct & Nov Mon–Sat 9am–noon &

1.30–5pm, Sun 9am–noon & 1.30–6pm; 30F), set in the grounds of an eleventh-century castle of which few traces remain. The more modern château which replaced it was in turn recently devastated by a fire, but the animals survived. One aviary is even housed in what was the château's main hall. Colette made the impenetrable but presumably complimentary remark that "At Clères, in the zoo park, it is easy to lose the melancholy feeling of inevitability."

The Forêt de Lyons

Around 25km east of Rouen, the **Forêt de Lyons** was a thousand years ago a favoured hunting ground of William the Conqueror and other dukes of Normandy. In 1135, Henry I of England died in the central village of Lyons-la-Forêt of a surfeit of lampreys consumed after a late-November hunting expedition.

Parts of the forest feel as though they can have changed little in the intervening millennium – remarkable considering its proximity not only to Rouen but also to Paris. Almost any of the little roads through these dense woods rewards exploration by cyclists or walkers; the oaks and beeches are consistently magnificent, with particularly vast specimens indicated by road signs.

Lyons-la-Forêt

At the heart of the forest, the little hill village of **LYONS-LA-FORÊT** was the site of William's now completely indiscernible castle, but has retained a superb ensemble of half-timbered Norman houses dating from around 1610. In the centre of the village stand the plain old wooden *halles*, often used as a film set, while the roads around abound in splendid rural mansions. One such, on rue d'Enfer, was much-used by the composer Ravel in the 1920s.

Lyons's central **tourist office** (June–Aug Mon 2–6pm, Tues–Sat 10am–noon & 2–6pm, Sun 10.30am–1pm & 2–6pm; Sept–May Sat 10am–noon & 2–6pm, Sun 10.30am–1pm & 2–6pm; ☎02.32.49.31.65) has information on the whole forest area. **Hotels** in the village include the brick-fronted *Grand Cerf*, right next to the *halles* on place Benserade (☎02.32.49.60.44; one room ③, the rest ④; closed Dec–March) – which has a secluded garden tucked away behind the archway and serves *moules marinières* for 50F and full menus from 85F – and the *Licorne* nearby (☎02.32.49.62.02; ④; closed mid-Dec to mid-Jan), where the cheapest dinner menu is 200F. There are also a couple of less expensive restaurants with outdoor seating in the main square.

Abbaye de Mortemer

Half a dozen kilometres south of Lyons, clearly signed off a main road, the ruins of the twelfth-century Cistercian **Abbaye de Mortemer** amount to little more than heaps of rubble scattered across gentle lawns, amid a landscape of rolling parklands (park daily 1–6pm; guided tours half-hourly Easter–Sept daily 2–6pm, Oct–Easter Sat & Sun 2–5.30pm; 20F admission, 35F with tour). Plenty of outbuildings survive, however, including a round stone *pigeonnier*, with a spider's-web tangle of wood inside, and little niches for hundreds of pigeons (reared by the monks for food); a cast-iron pigeon stands permanently on top. The highlight of the visit are tours of the museum in the eighteenth-century château that dominates the grounds, where you see models of the abbey as it is now, and an audio-visual show of life as it used to be, complete with plenty of tales of hauntings and bumps in the night.

Beyond the abbey, which was quarried after the Revolution to build the nearby village of Lisors, a couple of marshy lakes are populated by geese and swans and surrounded by woods and lawns that accommodate free-roaming deer.

Charleval

In **CHARLEVAL**, on the edge of the woods 7km west of the abbey, the *Auberge de l'Écurie* at 16 rue Grande (☎02.32.49.30.73; ①; closed Sun pm & Mon) has some of the forest's least expensive – if rather dilapidated – rooms. It also offers a very atmospheric low-ceilinged dining room, where the 90F menu includes salmon baked in foil, there's an open wood barbecue, and the desserts come flamboyantly decorated with coloured designs on custard.

Vascoeuil and Ry

The small but graceful **Château de Vascoeuil**, on the northwest edge of the forest 12km from Lyons, is renowned for having top-quality temporary art exhibitions (July & Aug daily 11am–7pm; mid-April to June, Sept & Oct Mon–Sat 2.30–6.30pm, Sun 11am–7pm; March to mid-April Sat & Sun 2.30–6.30pm; prices vary). However, the village of **RY**, 4km northwest, is of more dependable interest, as the real-life location of Flaubert's fictionalized Madame Bovary. A monument in its churchyard commemorates Delphine Couturier, who committed suicide in Ry in 1849 having married a local doctor ten years previously, at the age of 17.

Ry consists of one main street, with green hills visible rising at either end, and a church to one side with an unusual carved wooden porch. Delphine's husband is buried in the churchyard, and Madame Bovary is immortalized throughout the village, which seems to have had little else to celebrate for a century or so. The local florist is Emma's, the video shop is Bovary; the pharmacy was her real house.

An expensive museum of automata, of appeal largely to young children, though some of its mannequins jerkily act out the less explicit moments of Madame Bovary's career, stands next to a pretty bridge over the Crevon (Easter–June, Sept & Oct, Mon, Sat & Sun 11am–noon & 2–7pm; July & Aug Mon, Sat & Sun 11am–noon & 2–7pm, Tues–Fri 3–6pm; 25F). There are no hotels, but the *Rôtisserie Bovary* serves reasonable lunches (☎02.35.23.61.46; closed Mon pm & Tues) in the town's smartest building, near the church.

Upstream from Rouen

Upstream from Rouen towards Paris, high cliffs on the north bank of the Seine imitate the coast, looking down on waves of green and scattered river islands. By the time you reach **Les Andelys**, 25km out of Rouen, you're within 100km of the capital, meaning that accommodation and eating prices tend to be geared towards affluent weekend- and day-trippers.

Large country estates abound in this agreeable countryside, and public transport, too, is minimal – it's assumed any visitor has, if not a residence, then at least a car. However, infrequent buses run from Rouen to Les Andelys, while trains from Rouen call at Vernon.

Pont St-Pierre

The first point south of Rouen at which the Seine begins to be enticing again is **PONT ST-PIERRE**, where it's joined by the River Andelle. Any surplus money you may have could be enjoyably spent on a stay at the pink-and-brown *Hostellerie la Bonne Marmite* (☎02.32.49.70.24; ⑤; closed last week of July & first two weeks in Aug), set around a little courtyard a little way south of the eponymous bridge on the main road. Duck-and-lobster-loaded menus in the restaurant start at 140F.

At the junction of the two rivers you are confronted with the spectacularly sharp **Côte des Deux Amants**. This sheer escarpment, leading to a plateau high above the Seine, takes its name from a twelfth-century legend, in which a cruel king stipulated that the man who would marry his daughter must first run with her in his arms to the top of this hill. Noble Raoul sprinted up carrying the fair Caliste, but then dropped dead and out of sympathy, so did she. That story provides precious little incentive for anyone else to make the climb – but rumour has it that the view from the top does.

Les Andelys

The next town of any size is **LES ANDELYS**, which as the name implies consists in fact of two towns, overshadowed by the magnificent Château Gaillard. **Petit Andely**, which was the birthplace in 1594 of Nicolas Poussin, is a gorgeous little place. Its main street, parallel to the Seine, is lined with ancient half-timbered houses, while from the grassy riverbank behind you can see north to some imposing white bluffs as well as south to the castle. **Grand Andely**, at the end of a 1.5kilometre-long boulevard stretching inland, is the centre for shops, bars, and a **market** on Saturday.

Château Gaillard

The single most dramatic sight anywhere along the Seine short of Paris – especially awesome and magical by night – has to be **Château Gaillard**, perched high above Les Andelys. The castle was constructed in the space of a single year, 1196–97, under the auspices of Richard the Lionheart. A previous truce had expressly forbidden the construction of a castle here, but Richard went ahead and seized the rock on which it stands from Archbishop Walter of Rouen, and then bribed the pope for permission to build. His object was to deny the King of France access to Rouen by establishing total control of traffic along the Seine, by both road and river. That was successful until after Richard's death, when Philippe-Auguste managed to storm the castle in 1204 (his armies gaining access via the latrines). It might well have survived intact into this century, though, had Henry IV not ordered its destruction in 1603. Even then, it would have taken more recent devices to reduce Château Gaillard to rubble. The stout flint walls of its keep, roughly 4m thick, remain reasonably intact, and the outline of most of the rest is still clear, arranged over assorted green and chalky knolls. The castle was originally divided into two separate segments, linked by a bridge across a moat that was never intended to be filled with water – you can still explore the storage caves hidden in its depths.

Visits to the château are permitted between mid-March and mid-November only (Mon & Thurs–Sun 10am–noon & 2–6pm, Wed 2–6pm, closed Tues; 18F).

On foot, you can make the steep climb up via a path that leads off rue Richard Coeur-de-Lion in Petit Andely. The only route for motorists is extraordinarily convoluted, following a long-winded one-way system that starts opposite the church in Grand Andely.

Les Andelys Practicalities

The **tourist office** for Les Andelys is at 24 rue Philippe-Auguste in Petit Andely (June–Sept Mon–Sat 9.30am–noon & 2–6pm, Sun 9.30am–noon & 2–5.30pm; Oct–May daily 2–5.30pm; ☎02.32.54.41.93). The nicest places to **stay** have to be the two attractive Seine-side hotels in Petit Andely; the eighteenth-century *Chaîne d'Or*, opposite the thirteenth-century St-Sauveur church at 27 rue Grande (☎02.32.54.00.31; ⑤; closed Jan, Sun pm & Mon), and the *Normandie* at 1 rue Grande (☎02.32.54.10.52; ③; closed Dec; restaurant closed Wed pm & Thurs). Both have high-quality expensive restaurants – even breakfast at the *Chaîne d'Or* costs 70F. The food is cheaper at the *Soleil Levant* at 2 rue du Général-de-Gaulle in Grand Andely (☎02.32.54.23.55; ③; restaurant closed Sun pm, & Mon Oct–March), but it's a bit too far to walk back to the river for an evening stroll. There's also a lovely riverside **campsite**, far below the château, the *L'Île des Trois Rois* (☎02.32.54.23.79; April–Oct).

Giverny

Had it not caught the eye of Claude Monet from a passing train carriage, the little village of **GIVERNY** might by now have decayed into insignificance; instead it ranks among the most visited tourist attractions in Normandy. Standing a few hundred metres back from the right bank of the Seine, 20km south of the ancient fortifications of Les Andelys and a mere 40km from Paris, it welcomes a constant stream of traffic in summer. Between November and March, however, when Monet's house and gardens are closed to visitors, everything else seems to close down too.

The road south to Giverny from Les Andelys crosses a flat plain dotted with lovely little villages. **Port Mort** in particular, where the road is lined by an almost unbroken stone wall, is well worth a stop. The closest **trains** come to Giverny is **Vernon**, 4km north across the river (see p.100) and on the Rouen–Paris-St-Lazare line. Either rent a bike at the gare SNCF, or catch the connecting bus to Monet's gardens.

Musée Claude Monet

Gardens and house open April–Oct daily except Mon 10am–6pm; last ticket sold 5.30pm, no advance sales; 35F house and gardens, 25F gardens only. There's free parking opposite the house; don't be fooled by signs for private car parks elsewhere in Giverny.

If anything, art lovers who make the pilgrimage to the former home of Claude Monet are outnumbered by garden enthusiasts. None of Monet's original paintings are on display – most are in the Orangerie and Musée d'Orsay in Paris – whereas the **gardens** that many of his friends considered to be his masterpiece are still lovingly tended in all their glory.

Visits start in the huge **studio**, built in 1915, where Monet painted his last and largest canvases depicting waterlilies (in French, *nymphéas*). It now serves as a well-stocked book and gift shop, albeit disappointingly short of good-quality reproductions of the famous works. A gravel footpath leads from there to the **house** proper.

CLAUDE MONET AT GIVERNY

Claude Monet first rented the Giverny home that now houses the Musée Claude Monet in 1883. At the age of 43, he was exactly halfway through his life. Born in Paris in 1840, he had grown up in Le Havre, and spent the previous decade living in Argenteuil, Vétheuil and Poissy. Although his reputation as a painter was already established – the movement known as **Impressionism** had taken its name from a critic's somewhat contemptuous response to his work *Impression, Sunrise*, shown in Paris in April 1874 as part of the First Impressionist Exhibition – his personal and financial circumstances were far from settled.

The Monet ménage whose houseboat arrived in Giverny on April 29, 1883 consisted of ten people. As well as Claude's two sons by his wife Camille, who had died in 1879, he was now also responsible for the six children of his long-term mistress **Alice Hoschedé**. Her husband Ernest was a former patron of the Impressionists who had fallen on hard times; she finally married Monet after his death in 1891.

Monet was to find both artistic and commercial success in Giverny. In his early years, he continued to travel to paint landscapes not only throughout Normandy but also in Brittany, on the Riviera and in England. As time went by, however, his advancing physical frailty and failing eyesight made extended trips increasingly daunting, while his growing prosperity enabled him to tailor his immediate environment to meet his needs as a painter.

Monet began to produce sequences of reworkings and renditions of the same scene, shown at different times of the day or seasons of the year, in 1890. The first such series consisted of 25 views of the **haystacks** on a neighbouring farm; all were arranged side by side in his studio, to be worked on simultaneously. Designed to be seen en masse, they went on show in Paris early in 1891, and proved hugely popular. The individual paintings sold out quickly, and from then on visiting American collectors – and would-be students – were a constant feature of life at Giverny.

In 1891, Monet painted a sequence showing the poplar trees that stood along the banks of the River Epte, about 1.5km south of his home. By now he was rich enough to buy the trees, for as long as his work was in progress, from a local timber merchant who was due to fell them. Having purchased his house outright, for 22,000F, he went on to buy a further plot of land, across the main road. With permission from the local authorities, he dammed the stream known as the Ru to feed an artificial pond, which he planted with **waterlilies** and spanned with a Japanese footbridge.

A team of gardeners worked to keep different sections of his **flower gardens** in bloom as much of the year as possible, so he would always have a suitable subject on which to work. One man had the full-time responsibility of tending the waterlilies to Monet's specifications, depending, for example, on whether he planned to use square or rectangular canvases. Monet would work outdoors for around six hours each day, avoiding the midday sun, and went to paint over 250 versions of his waterlilies (*Nymphéas*), not to mention the canvases he destroyed in disgust. One set of 48 waterlily pictures is said to have hung in his studio for six years, being constantly reworked, before it was exhibited in 1909.

Photographs of Monet in his later years show him as very much the white-bearded patrician, not only presiding over his studio and household but also playing host to leading painters and politicians. Despite a series of operations on his eyes, he continued to work almost until his death, in December 1926. The house at Giverny passed to his son, Jean Monet, who left it in turn to the Académie des Beaux Arts in 1966. After restoration, it reopened as a museum in 1980.

Apart from the bedroom, hung with family photos and paintings by friends and family, and the *salon* with its washed-out reproductions, all the main rooms are crammed almost floor-to-ceiling with Monet's collection of Japanese prints, especially works by Hokusai and Hiroshige. Most of the original furnishings are gone, but you do get a real sense of how the kitchen used to be, with all its walls and fittings painted a glorious bright yellow; Monet designed his own yellow crockery to harmonize with the surroundings. By contrast, the stairs and upstairs rooms are a pale blue.

Colourful flower gardens, with trellised walkways and shady bowers, stretch down from the house. At the bottom, a dank underpass beneath the road leads to the *jardin d'eau*, focused around the narrow waterlily pond. Footpaths around the perimeter, as well of course as arching Japanese footbridges, offer differing views of the waterlilies themselves, cherished by gardeners in rowing boats. May and June, when the rhododendrons flower around the pond, and the wisteria that winds over the Japanese bridge is in bloom, are the best times to visit. Whenever you come, however, you'll have to contend with camera-happy crowds jostling to capture their own impressions of the waterlilies.

Musée d'Art Américain

A few minutes' walk up Giverny's village street, to the left as you leave Monet's house, stands the new **Musée d'Art Américain** (April–Oct daily except Mon 10am–6pm; 35F). The exterior is far from attractive, but inside you'll find a spacious and well-lit gallery devoted to American artists resident in France between 1865 and 1915, and in particular those who congregated in Giverny from 1887 onwards. Although Monet accepted no formal pupils, some, such as Theodore Robinson, joined his circle of intimates. Some took their admiration to a point that now seems embarrassing, painting many of the same scenes as Monet himself. As well as the waterlilies, for example, John Leslie Brech produced a series of twelve haystacks within a year of Monet's.

Mary Cassatt, who lived in a château at Le Mesnil-Thérebus, is represented by a far more interesting series of woodcuts, heavily influenced by *ukiyo-e* Japanese woodcuts, as well as canvases that focus on the domestic life of women while clearly belonging to the Impressionist movement. John Singer Sargent and Winslow Homer both contribute scenes of Brittany, especially Cancale, while James Henry Whistler paintings include views of Dieppe and Étretat.

Practicalities

Giverny's one **hotel**, the *Musardière*, stands not far beyond Monet's house at 123 rue Claude-Monet (☎02.32.21.03.18; ④); dinner menus in its restaurant start at 145F. A pleasant little tearoom and restaurant, *Les Nymphéas* (☎02.32.21.20.31), is located opposite the house itself, and there's another restaurant inside the Musée d'Art Américain. If you've brought a picnic, eating in the grounds of the house is forbidden, and the surrounding countryside is not particularly appealing.

Vernon

VERNON itself straddles the Seine just before it leaves Normandy altogether, with walks laid out along either bank. The central *Hôtel d'Évreux*, 11 place d'Évreux (☎02.32.21.16.12; ③), has rooms at assorted prices, and a good restaurant, and you can also eat well at the *Restaurant de la Poste*, 26 av Gambetta (☎02.32.51.10.63; closed Tues pm & Wed), where menus start at 85F. Elvis Presley's dad was called Vernon.

travel details

Buses

From Dieppe 5 daily to Paris (2hr 15min); 3 daily to Le Tréport (30min); 4 daily to St-Valéry (#312; 1hr).

From St-Valéry 4 daily to Fécamp (#311; 1hr 20min).

From Fécamp 8 daily to Étretat (30min).

From Le Havre 8 daily to Honfleur (30min); 2 daily express services continue to Caen (1hr 25min); 7 daily to Étretat (50min) and Fécamp (1hr 30min).

From Rouen hourly to Le Havre (2hr 45min), #191 or #192 via Jumièges and Caudebec; 2 daily to Dieppe (1hr 45min) #163, and #150 on to Le Tréport (2hr 30min), Fécamp (2hr 30min) and Lisieux (2hr 30min). Also to Clères (45min), #161 to Le Neubourg (45min), #337, and SNCF buses to Lyons-la-Forêt (1hr).

Trains

Through-trains to Paris connect with all ferries.

From Dieppe 8 daily to Rouen (1hr); 8 daily to Paris-St-Lazare (2hr 15min).

From Le Tréport 5 daily to Paris (2hr 45min) via Eu (4min) and Beauvais (1hr 40min).

From Le Havre 12 daily to Rouen (1hr) and Paris (2hr 15min).

From Rouen 8 daily to Caen (2hr 15min); 12 daily to Paris-St-Lazare (1hr 15min); at least hourly to Fécamp (1hr); 4–6 daily to Motteville (20min) with connecting bus to St-Valéry (total 1hr 20min).

From Fécamp 6 daily to Rouen (45min).

From St-Valéry 4 daily to Rouen (30min) via Motteville.

Ferries

From Dieppe P&O Stena Line (☎02.35.06.39.03) 4–5 daily to Newhaven (2hr 15min–4hr).

From Le Havre P&O (☎02.35.19.78.78) 3 daily to Portsmouth (5hr 30min); Irish Continental (☎02.35.53.28.83) to Rosslare (3 weekly; 21hr) and to Cork (June–Aug 1 weekly; 21hr).

For more details, see p.3 onwards.

CHAPTER TWO

THE LOWER NORMANDY COAST

he **coast of Lower Normandy** progressively changes its character as you move from east to west. Along the **Côte Fleurie**, from Honfleur to Cabourg, it is moneyed and elegant, a would-be northern counterpart to the Côte d'Azur. Then, through the **Côte de Nacre** and into the area known as the **Bessin**, around Caen and Bayeux, it drifts into anonymity: wide stretches of sand, backed by scrubland and still pervaded by the memories of 1944, when they served as the landing beaches for the Allied forces. West again, separated from the bulk of the mainland by a series of marshes, is the **Cotentin Peninsula**, with low-key harbour villages along its east front, cliffs across the north, and vast dunes and wild beaches to the west. And finally there is the **bay of Mont-St-Michel**, where the island abbey is swept by treacherous tides.

The most enjoyment along the Côte Fleurie is to be had from **Honfleur** – a real gem of a harbour town, familiar from the paintings of Eugène Boudin, Monet and other Impressionists. Elsewhere, the prevailing air is one of wealthy sterility. **Trouville**, **Deauville** and **Cabourg** preoccupy themselves with such events as Rolls Royce rallies, forever harking back to a nineteenth-century past of leisured aristocrats, albeit with futuristic prices.

The Côte de Nacre and the **Bessin**, despite the prominence of their war past, are much more likeable; in the small-scale traditional resorts here, the sea may be a little overexposed, but you can at least eat well and wander without crowds. The history of the D-Day landings – and the numerous cemeteries and memorials – draws its own kind of tourists, still with many veterans among them. A tour can be instructive and moving. For sites actually to enjoy, however, **Bayeux** must be the pre-eminent destination. It holds, of course, the famous **tapestry**, its drama remaining as vivid as its colours, and is a stylish and interesting town in its own right. Considerably more so, in fact, than war-ravaged **Caen**, though the infrastructure of the latter has received a hefty boost over the decade since the opening of the cross-channel ferry harbour at **Ouistreham**.

Cherbourg is even less of a ferry port to linger over. But if you arrive here you're just a short distance from the beaches, dunes and amazing windsurfing along the western coastline of the Cotentin Peninsula, between **Carteret** and **Coutainville**. These serve to delay progress towards the glorious island abbey of **Mont-St-Michel**, France's most visited and most distinctive monument (after Versailles), and visible across the bay from **Granville** onwards.

The beaches of the Baie du Mont-St-Michel, however, are no temptation – dangerous for the most part, and flanked by generally tacky resorts. Having come

ACCOMMODATION PRICE CODES

All **hotel prices** in this book have been coded using the symbols below. The price shown is for the least expensive double room in high season, which for category ①️ often means a room without shower, bath and toilet. Most hotels in that category have other rooms with en-suite facilities, which typically cost 30–50F extra.

For a full explanation see p.30.

①️ Under 160F	③ 220–300F	⑤ 400–500F	⑦ 600–700F
② 160–220F	④ 300–400F	⑥ 500–600F	⑧ 700F and over

this far, better to head straight on to the delights of the Breton **Côte d'Émeraude** (see Chapter Four).

The Côte Fleurie and the Norman Riviera

The only section of the Norman coast to have any serious delusions of grandeur is the stretch that lies immediately east of the mouth of the Seine. The new Pont de Normandie across from Le Havre is starting to make such places as Trouville and **Deauville** altogether too hectic for comfort, but only Honfleur could really be said to have much that it would be a shame to lose, with the appealing Côte Fleurie just west of town. The coastline between **Trouville** and **Cabourg** has earned the epithet of the **Norman Riviera**, with Trouville playing Nice to Deauville's Cannes.

There's an obvious distinction all along this stretch of the coast between old ports such as **Honfleur** and **Dives**, which have over the centuries been pushed further and further back from the sea by heavy deposits of silt from the Seine but retain their historic medieval buildings, and the new resorts that have sprung up alongside the resultant sandy beaches, most of them unimaginatively laid out during the nineteenth century and characterless in the extreme. The happiest balance is found at places such as **Houlgate**, where development has remained low-key and the rocky coastline has stood firm against the river – giving the added bonus of pleasant corniche drives.

Honfleur

HONFLEUR, the best preserved of the old ports of Normandy and the first you come to on the eastern Calvados coast, is a near-perfect seaside town which lacks only a beach. It used to have one, but with the accumulation of silt from the Seine the sea has steadily withdrawn, leaving the eighteenth-century waterfront houses of boulevard Charles V stranded and a little surreal. The ancient port, however, still functions – the channel to the beautiful "*Vieux Bassin*" is kept open by regular dredging – and though only pleasure craft now use the moorings in the harbour basin, fishing boats continue to tie up alongside the pier nearby. Fish is usually on sale either directly from the boats or from stands on the pier, still by right run by fishermen's wives.

Honfleur is highly picturesque, and has been moving upmarket at an ever greater rate since the vast new **Pont de Normandie** spanned the mouth of the Seine in 1995. Despite now being just a few minutes' drive from the giant metropolis of Le

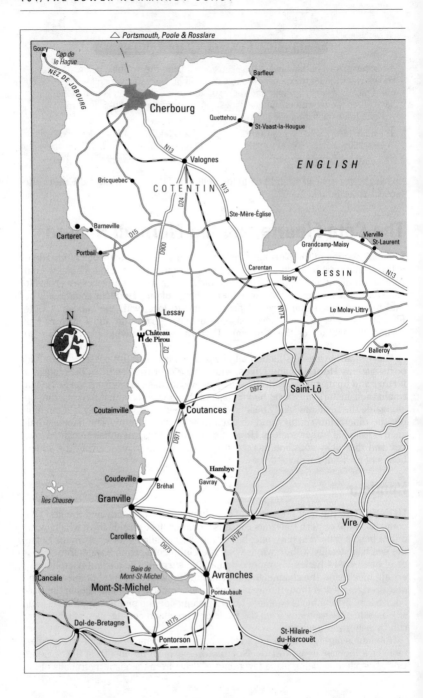

△ Portsmouth, Poole & Rosslare

Goury
Cap de
le Hague
NEZ DE JOBOURG
Cherbourg
Barfleur
Quettehou
St-Vaast-la-Hougue
N13
Valognes
ENGLISH
Bricquebec
COTENTIN
N13
D24
Ste-Mère-Église
D15
Barneville
Carteret
D900
Portbail
Grandcamp-Maisy
Vierville
St-Laurent
Carentan
BESSIN
N13
Isigny
D2
Lessay
N174
Le Molay-Littry
Château
de Pirou
Balleroy
D972
Saint-Lô
Coutainville
Coutances
D971
Hambye
Coudeville
Gavray
Îles Chausey
Bréhal
Granville
Vire
Carolles
N175
D973
Baie de
Mont-St-Michel
Cancale
Avranches
Mont-St-Michel
Pontaubault
Dol-de-Bretagne
N175
St-Hilaire-
du-Harcouët
Pontorson

N

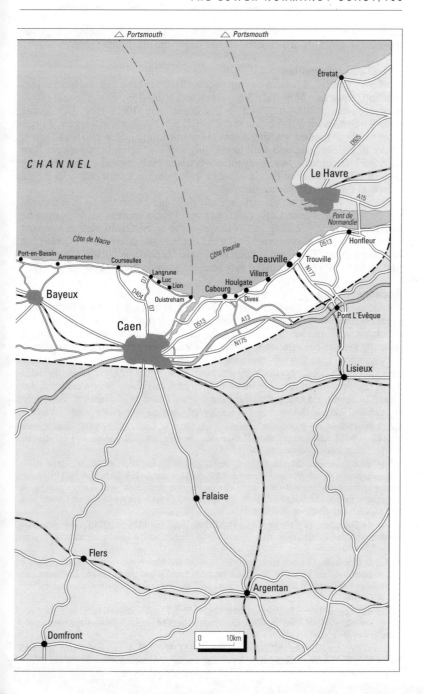

Havre, however, the old port still feels not so very different to the fishing village that appealed so greatly to artists in the second half of the nineteenth century.

Arrival and information

Honfleur's **tourist office** can be found across from the town hall on place Arthur-Boudin (July & Aug Mon–Sat 9.30am–7pm, Sun 10am–1pm; Easter to mid-July & Sept Mon–Sat 9.30am–12.30pm & 2–6.30pm, Sun 10am–1pm; Oct–Easter Mon–Sat 9am–noon & 2–5.30pm; ☎02.31.89.23.30). For much of the year, it organizes two-hour **guided walking tours** of the town (mid-July to mid-Sept Tues & Thurs 10pm, Sat 3pm; mid-April to mid-July and last fortnight of Sept Sat 3pm only; 28F). In summer, two ninety-minute **cruises** each day sail upriver from the eastern side of the Avant-Port, a minute's walk from the tourist office, for a closer look at the Pont de Normandie.

The **gare routière**, on place de la Porte-du-Rouen, is served by over a dozen direct daily **buses** from Caen (#20), and up to eight express services from Le Havre (Bus Verts; ☎02.31.89.28.41). However, the nearest **train station** is at Pont l'Évêque (see p.161), connected by the Lisieux bus, #50 (20min ride). **Cycles** can be rented from Town and Country, 12 quai Lepaulmier (daily 10am–10pm; ☎02.31.89.46.04), 100m from the gare routière towards the harbour.

Accommodation

It's not as easy to live the bohemian life in Honfleur as it used to be. If finding budget accommodation is one of your main priorities, it probably makes sense not to stay here at all, and simply to visit for the day. Especially on summer weekends, so many visitors come to what is after all a small town, that even the most ordinary hotel can get away with charging rates well above the average for Normandy. In addition, no hotels overlook the harbour itself, while motorists face the additional problem that it is all but impossible to park anywhere near a central hotel. There is however a **campsite**, the *Camping du Phare* (mid-March to Sept only; ☎02.31.89.10.26) at the west end of boulevard Charles V on place Jean-de-Vienne.

Hôtel Belvédère, 36 route Émile-Renouf (☎02.31.89.08.13, fax 02.31.89.51.40). Small, central nine-room hotel, with tranquil and tasteful rooms, an exquisite little garden, and a restaurant where dinner menus start at 98F. ④.

Hôtel des Cascades, 17 place Thiers (☎02.31.89.05.83, fax 02.31.89.32.13). Large hotel-restaurant open onto both place Thiers and the cobbled rue de la Ville behind. Slightly noisy rooms upstairs, and a good-value if not all that exciting restaurant with outdoor seating on both sides; menus climb upwards from 80F towards the expensive *fruits de mer*. Closed Mon pm, all Tues out of season, and Dec–Feb. ②.

Hôtel du Dauphin, 10 place Berthelot (☎02.31.89.15.53, fax 02.31.89.92.06). Grey-slate town house just around the corner from Ste-Catherine church, with a wide assortment of rooms. Closed Jan. ④–⑨.

Hôtel le Hamelin, 16 place Hamelin (☎02.31.89.16.25). Five basic rooms, some with showers, in plain building very near the Lieutenance in the liveliest part of town. The restaurant downstairs has standard seafood menus from 88F, and manages to squeeze a few tables onto the street. ②–④.

Hôtel des Loges, 18 rue Brûlée (☎02.31.89.38.26). Brightly refurbished hotel on a quiet side street just 100m inland from Ste-Catherine church, decked out with flowers and with a good standard of rooms. ④.

Tilbury, 30 place Hamelin (☎02.31.98.83.33, fax 02.31.89.85.06). Absolutely central, a stone's throw from the Lieutenance. Well-equipped and comfortable rooms above a *crêperie*. ③.

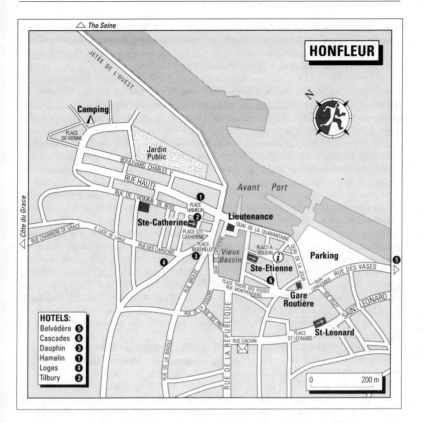

The Town

Visitors to Honfleur inevitably gravitate towards the old centre, around the **Vieux Bassin**. At the *bassin*, slate-fronted houses, each of them one or two storeys higher than seems possible, harmonize despite their tottering and ill-matched forms into a backdrop that is only excelled by the **Lieutenance** at the harbour entrance. This latter was the dwelling of the king's Lieutenant, and has been the gateway to the inner town ever since Samuel Champlain sailed from Honfleur to found Québec in 1608. The church of **St-Étienne** nearby is now the **Musée de la Marine**, which combines a collection of model ships with several rooms of antique Norman furnishings (July & Aug daily 10am–1pm & 2–6.30pm; April–June & Sept daily except Mon 10am–noon & 2–6pm; mid-Feb to March & Oct to mid-Nov Tues–Fri 2–5.30pm, Sat & Sun 10am–noon & 2–5.30pm; 15F). Just behind it, two seventeenth-century **salt stores**, used to contain the precious commodity during the days of the much-hated *gabelle*, or salt tax, now serve as the **Musée d'Ethnographie et d'Art Populaire Normand** (same hours; 15F, or combined with Musée de la Marine 25F), filling ten rooms with a fascinating assortment of everyday artefacts from old Honfleur.

Honfleur's artistic past – and its present concentration of galleries and painters – owes most to Eugène Boudin, forerunner of Impressionism. He was born and worked in the town, trained the 15-year-old Monet, and was joined for various periods by Pissarro, Renoir and Cézanne. At the same time, Baudelaire paid visits to the town, which was also home to the composer Érik Satie. There's a fair selection of Boudin's works in the **Musée Eugène Boudin**, west of the port on place Érik-Satie, and his crayon seascapes in particular are quite appealing here in context, though the Dufys, Marquets, Frieszes and (above all) the Monets are the most impressive paintings on show (mid-March to Sept daily except Tues 10am–noon & 2–6pm; Oct–Dec & mid-Feb to mid-March Mon & Wed–Fri 2.30–5pm, Sat & Sun 10am–noon & 2.30–5pm; 16F).

The church of **Ste-Catherine** (daily 9am–noon & 2–6pm), with its distinctive detached **belfry** – one of Monet's favourite subjects in his younger days – is the town's most remarkable building. It was built almost entirely of wood, during the Hundred Years' War; all stone was at that time reserved for military use, and so the town's shipbuilders, experienced in working with wood, took responsibility for its construction. All the timbers inside are now exposed to view, having been sheathed in white plaster during the nineteenth century, when an incongruous four-columned porch (long since removed) was added to the front. The changing patterns on its tiles, both along the main body and the belfry, delineate religious symbols. It all makes a change from the great stone Norman churches, and has the added peculiarity of being divided into twin naves, with one balcony running around both. The belfry itself is open the same hours as the Musée Eugène Boudin; admission is 10F, or 30F in conjunction with the Boudin museum. Nearby, along the rue de l'Homme-de-Bois, incongruous views combine the stately backs of what were once shipbuilders' houses with the industrial desert of Le Havre's docks in the distance.

A couple of blocks below, past the public gardens by the place Augustin-Normand, you can follow the **shipping channel** out towards the mouth of the Seine and the sea. A rusty old pipeline runs alongside, inside which you can hear rats and mice scampering to and from the sea. However, it would not occur even to the most hard-nosed mud-caked sewer rat to swim in the sea once it got there – the shore is a slimy grey wasteland, the water foul and sluggish. Nonetheless, it is possible to slip and squirm your way onto the shingle and then walk along the sea coast, with the beautiful wooded hills of the Côte du Grâce tantalizingly above you. Inland, the grand old houses of ancient aesthetes, and the **Chapelle Notre Dame de Grâce**, beloved of the Impressionists, nestle dry-footed in the forests.

Eating

With its abundance of day-trippers and hotel guests, Honfleur supports an astonishing number of **restaurants**, most naturally specializing in seafood and many of them very good at it indeed. Surprisingly few restaurants actually face onto the harbour itself; the narrow buildings around the edge seem to be better suited to being snack bars, *crêperies*, cafés and ice-cream parlours. Few of the town's hotels attempt to compete with the restaurants; the *Cascades* (see p.106) is probably the best of the few that do.

One local speciality, available in October and November, is *crevettes grises* – tiny shrimp eaten with an unsalty Spanish-style bread, *pain brié*. If you're buying your own food, look out for the excellent *Panatérie*, a *boulangerie* selling granary and wholemeal breads, on the corner of the rue des Prés and av de la République.

L'Absinthe, 10 quai de la Quarantaine (☎02.31.89.39.00). This lovely eighteenth-century mansion houses the most imaginative of the row of five restaurants that stand just around the corner from the *bassin*, with such dishes as scallop *carpaccio* or *foie gras* in ginger nestling on menus that range from 169F to 350F. Closed mid-Nov to Dec.

L'Assiette Gourmand, 2 quai des Passagers (☎02.31.89.24.88). One of the very finest restaurants in Normandy, in the heart of old Honfleur. It's possible to spend an absolute fortune, but the 165F menu, with its salmon *tartare* and irresistible desserts, gives you a pretty good idea of what chef Gérard Bonnefoy can achieve. Closed Sun pm & Mon out of season.

Auberge de la Lieutenance, 12 place Ste-Catherine (☎02.31.89.07.52). Not in fact by the Lieutenant, despite the name. Plenty of outdoor seating on the cobbled pedestrian square, facing both church and belfry and overshadowed for no obvious reason by a giant thumb. Gourmet dining with a heavy emphasis on oysters; menus start at 98F. Closed Sun pm & mid-Nov to Dec.

Bistro du Port, 14 quai de la Quarantaine (☎02.31.89.21.84). The middle of five adjacent and substantially similar restaurants, all with outdoor seating but in a not very picturesque setting beside the main road just east of the harbour. The *Bistro* has a slight competitive edge on prices for its conventional seafood menus, with the cheapest at 75F, and good ones at 95F and 135F (featuring a *tartare de poissons* and a *couscous de la mer*). Closed Mon pm & Tues out of season.

Au Gars Normand, 8 quai des Passagers (☎02.31.89.05.28). Right in the thick of things, two small dining rooms crammed into a little house all but next door to the Lieutenance. Menus from 85F, with clams and mussels, but very unadventurous main courses. Closed Mon & Dec.

Au P'tit Mareyeur, 4 rue Haute (☎02.31.98.84.23). No distance from the centre, but all the seating is indoors and there are no views. Very good fish dishes – red crab soup with garlic – plus plenty of creamy *pays d'Auge* sauces and superb desserts. The main menu, at 120F, includes warm oysters. Closed Mon pm & Tues.

Taverne de la Mer, 35 rue Haute (☎02.31.89.57.77). Small converted bar not far from place Hamelin, with no outdoor seating, but a magnificent selection of fresh seafood, including specialities grilled on an open wood fire. The only set menu, at 119F, consists entirely of fish, with main courses such as Basque-style tuna steaks; you can also get a large *assiette de fruits de mer* for a similar price. Closed Mon & Tues am.

La Tortue, 36 rue de l'Homme de Bois (☎02.31.98.87.91). A welcoming place near Ste-Catherine church, where 99F buys a great-value five-course meal, 230F brings you a seven-course feast over which you have no say whatsoever, and there's even a 75F vegetarian menu, consisting of vegetables followed by cheese or salad. Closed Tues, plus mid-Jan to mid-Feb.

Le Vieux Honfleur, 13 quai St-Étienne (☎02.31.89.15.31). The best of the restaurants around the harbour itself, with spacious alfresco dining – in shade at lunchtime – on the pedestrianized eastern side of the harbour. Very simple menus, but the seafood is very good, as befits prices starting at 160F. Closed Jan.

Along the Côte Fleurie

For the 15km **west along the corniche** from Honfleur to Trouville, green fields and fruit trees line the land's edge, and cliffs rise from sandy beaches. The resorts, **Villerville** most conspicuously, aren't cheap, but they're relatively undeveloped, and if you want to stop by the seaside this is the place to do it.

Trouville and Deauville

The adjacent towns of Trouville and Deauville lie within a stone's throw of each other to either side of the mouth of the River Touques, sharing many of their amenities, and also their rather exclusive reputations.

TROUVILLE retains at least some semblance of a real town, with a constant population and industries other than tourism. But it is primarily a resort, and has been ever since Napoléon III started bringing his court here for the summer in the 1860s (his empress, Eugénie, fled France from here in 1870 in the yacht of an English admirer). Spectacular villas such as *L'Hôtel des Roches Noires* line the beach, patterned with complex brickwork and topped by ornate turrets; several were painted by Monet during a visit in 1870.

One of Emperor Napoléon's dukes, looking across the river, saw not marshlands but money, and lots of it, in the form of a **racecourse**. His vision materialized, and villas appeared between the racecourse and the sea to become **DEAUVILLE**. Now you can lose money on the horses, cross five streets to lose more in the Casino, where Winston Churchill spent the summer of 1906 gambling every night until 5am, and finally lose yourself in the 200m of sports and "cure" facilities, and private bathing huts, that intervene before the *planches*. Beyond this 500m of duckwalk, rows of primary coloured parasols obscure the sea.

If you're tempted to **gamble** in Deauville's Casino, formal attire is compulsory, and you have to pay a temporary membership fee of around 100F to be allowed anywhere near the tables. One more congenial reason to visit is the **American Film Festival** held in Deauville in the first week of September – a festival that's the antithesis of Cannes, with public admission to a wide selection of previews.

Practicalities

Visits to the **tourist office** on place de la Mairie in Deauville (Mon–Sat 9am–12.30pm & 2–6.30pm, Sun 11am–4pm; ☎02.31.14.40.00), or the one at 32 quai F. Moureaux in Trouville (July & Aug Mon–Sat 9.30am–12.30pm & 2–7pm, Sun 10am–4pm; April–June, Sept & Oct Mon–Sat 9.30am–noon & 2–6.30pm, Sun 10.30am–12.30pm; Nov–March Mon–Sat 9.30am–noon & 2–6pm, Sun 10.30am–12.30pm; ☎02.31.14.60.70), are repaid with some spectacularly revolting brochures (in English).

Trouville and Deauville share their **gare SNCF** (served by trains from Paris via Lisieux) and **gare routière** (☎02.31.88.95.36), in between the two just south of the marina. Each day, seven of the hourly buses from Caen continue along the coast to Honfleur.

As you might imagine, **hotels** tend to be either luxurious or overpriced. The *Café-Hôtel des Sports*, 27 rue Gambetta (☎02.31.88.22.67; closed Sun in winter; ③), behind Deauville's fish market, is the least expensive, while the *Charmettes*, 22 rue de la Chapelle (☎02.31.88.11.67; closed Jan; ③), and *Le Trouville*, 1 rue Thiers (☎02.31.98.45.48; closed Jan; ③), are Trouville's closest equivalents. Trouville also has a couple of **campsites**, *Le Hamel* (April to mid-Sept; ☎02.31.88.15.56) and *Le Chant des Oiseaux* (April–Sept; ☎02.31.88.06.42).

Chez Henri at 44 rue Mirabeau in Deauville (☎02.31.87.18.17) is a top-quality **bistro** with prices that are high but not outrageous; good **fish restaurants** in Trouville include *Les Vapeurs* at 160 bd F.Moureaux (☎02.31.88.15.24), and *La Petite Auberge*, 7 rue Carnot (☎02.31.88.11.07; closed Tues & Wed in winter), though both get very crowded at weekends.

Villers-sur-mer

To the west of Deauville, the shoreline at first stays flat, and the main coast road passes through a succession of what are almost suburban resorts – significantly less snobbish than Trouville and Deauville, but equally crowded and equally short of inexpensive hotels. At the largest of these, **VILLERS-SUR-MER**, you're greeted by a true triumph of topiary; a giant **brontosaurus**, interrupting its browsing on the central seafront roundabout to raise its long neck skywards. Villers is also noteworthy for straddling the Greenwich Meridian, which runs right through the local **campsite**, *Camping Bellevue* (April–Oct; ☎02.31.87.05.21).

Houlgate

A hundred years ago, **HOULGATE**, 7km west of Villers-sur-mer, was every bit as glamorous and sophisticated a destination as its neighbours. What makes it different today is that it has barely changed since then. Its long straight beach remains lined by a stately procession of ornate Victorian villas, with what few commercial enterprises the town supports confined to the narrow parallel street, the **rue des Bains**, around 50m inland. As a result, Houlgate is the most relaxed of the local resorts, ideal if you're looking for a peaceful family break where the only stress is deciding whether to paddle or play mini-golf.

So long as you keep an eye on the tides, it's possible to walk between Villers and Houlgate along the foot of the **Vaches Noires** (Black Cows) cliffs, which force the main road at this point up and away from the sea. However, industrial Le Havre is a bit too visible across the water for it to be an especially picturesque stroll.

Practicalities

Houlgate's **tourist office** is by the main roundabout as you come into town from the east, on boulevard des Belges (mid-June to mid-Sept Mon–Sat 9am–7pm, Sun 9am–12.30pm & 2–7pm; mid-Sept to mid-June Mon–Sat 9am–12.30pm & 2–6.30pm; ☎02.31.24.34.79). The *Hostellerie Normandie*, just off the rue des Bains at 11 rue E.Deschanel (☎02.31.28.77.77; closed Oct–Feb, plus Mon pm & Tues in low season; ③), is a pretty little **hotel** covered with ivy and creeping flowers, with a 65F lunch menu on which you can follow half a dozen oysters with a plate of *moules frites*. Nearby, at 17 rue des Bains, the more formal red-brick *Le 1900* (☎02.31.28.77.77; closed Jan to mid-Feb, plus Mon pm & Tues in low season; ③), holds a glassed-in Belle-Époque bistro where dinner menus start at 98F. Above the cliffs on the corniche road east of town, *La Ferme Auberge des Aulnettes* (☎02.31.28.00.28; closed Jan, plus Tues pm & Wed in low season; ③), is a lovely country house set in pleasant gardens, with a good restaurant and room to sit outside in the evening. The best **campsite** in the area, *Les Falaises* (April–Oct; ☎02.31.24.81.09), is not far away, though technically in the separate community of **Gonneville-sur-Mer**.

Cabourg

At **CABOURG**, you are confronted by little more than an exercise in style – a pure creation for a certain aged class, contemporary with Deauville and seemingly stuck entirely in the nineteenth century. There's an awful lot of town planning, but not really any town.

At the centre of the straightest promenade in France, the **Grand Hôtel** looks out towards the sea, while behind it the crescent that defines the formal **Jardins du Casino** is the first of several concentric crescents, spreading out like ripples

---

PROUST IN CABOURG

As both child and adult, between 1881 and 1914, Marcel Proust stayed repeatedly at the *Grand Hôtel* in Cabourg. The town is the "Balbec" of *Du Côté de Chez Swann*, and the hotel itself – now officially located on the boulevard Marcel-Proust – thrives on its Proustian connection. All guests are served with a *madeleine* for breakfast, and Proust's own room is available at a cost of over 1200F per night (not the most expensive in the hotel by any means). The rock star Sting stayed in that very room in 1991, and drank from the same well of inspiration. The main dining room, which has a superb sea view, is now called *Le Balbec*. For the ambivalent Proust it was "the aquarium"; each night locals would press their faces to its window in wonder at the luxurious life within, "as extraordinary to the poor as the life of strange fishes or molluscs".

---

and lined with large, placid, undistinguished – and usually empty – houses. Cabourg makes an unlikely twin town for the raucous, downmarket gambling mecca of Atlantic City, New Jersey; notices for example request that you "avoid noise on the beach", and picnics are forbidden.

Practicalities

Trains run all the way from Paris Gare Ste-Lazare to the **gare SNCF** that Cabourg shares with Dives (see below) every day in July and August, and otherwise at weekends only. Arriving by **bus** – it's on the Caen–Honfleur route (#20) – you'll be dropped off at the gardens on avenue Pasteur; walk through them and turn right down avenue de la Mer to reach the Jardins du Casino.

The **tourist office** in the Casino gardens has full details on **hotels** (July & Aug daily 9.30am–7pm; Sept–June Mon–Sat 9.30am–12.30pm & 2–6.30pm, Sun 10am–12.30pm & 2.30–6pm; ☎02.31.91.01.09). The *Oie qui Fume*, at 18 av de la Brèche-Buhot (☎02.31.91.27.79; closed Sun pm, Mon & mid-Nov to mid-Feb; ③), is 100m back from the sea on a quiet road half a dozen streets west of the centre; menus at 134F and 190F both feature goose (*oie*). The similarly half-timbered *Hôtel de Paris*, 39 av de la Mer (☎02.31.91.31.34; ③), is more central, on Cabourg's only commercial (semi-pedestrianized) street. It has no restaurant, but *La Crémaillère*, two doors down at no. 41 (☎02.31.91.14.40), has menus at all prices, and there are plenty of pizzerias and snack bars nearby.

Dives

Just across the river from Cabourg is the somewhat more interesting – and much older – town of **DIVES**. This was the port from which William the Conqueror sailed for Hastings, by way of St-Valéry; contemporary chronicles tell of vast stockpiles of supplies accumulating on the beach in the days preceding the invasion. Now, like Honfleur, pushed well back from the sea, Dives has nothing in common with its aristocratic neighbour, other than its significance for Proust, whose dream vision "land's end church of Balbec" is the town's **Notre Dame** church.

A lively **Saturday market** focuses around the ancient wooden *halles*, tucked away south of the main through-road. The steep tiled roof of the *halles* must be five times the height of its walls, and its venerable weather-beaten timbers are held together by tight metal bands; on market days, it's crammed with mouth-watering delicacies and Norman specialities, while more mundane produce and imported jeans are sold in the square alongside and up and down the narrow streets. The town hosts a **puppet festival** in early August.

Dives has a reasonable **hotel**, the *de la Gare* (☎02.31.91.24.52; closed Dec & Jan; ②), and there's a **campsite** on the way to Cabourg (and two more off the Cabourg–Lisieux road).

Franceville

Continuing along the coast towards Caen, in **FRANCEVILLE** the main road passes a half-timbered *logis*, once again called the *Hôtel de la Gare*, at 8 rte du Cabourg (☎02.31.24.23.37; ③), with adequate rooms and good food, and the bizarre *Le Surfer*, a disco concealed in a German bunker.

A little further on, you can turn right, across what used to be Pegasus Bridge (see p.121), for direct access to Ouistreham and the Landing Beaches.

Caen

Appropriately enough for a city that has been fought over throughout its long history, the name of **CAEN**, capital and largest city of Basse Normandie, originally came from a Celtic word meaning "battlefield". This site was first fortified in 1060 by William the Conqueror, who preferred it to Rouen because it was further from the marauding Franks, and because the navigable river Orne afforded him safe access to the Channel. During the succeeding centuries, Caen repeatedly changed hands, and was twice sacked by the English: first by Edward III in 1246, and then by Henry V in 1417. In 1432, the English Henry VI founded the university, but Caen has been French since Charles VII took it back in 1450.

The modern city began to take shape when a canal to the sea was completed in 1850, running parallel to the heavily silted Orne. At the same time, the Bassin St-Pierre was built, creating a central marina that is now reminiscent of the "port" in Vannes (see p.337). The smaller River Odon was covered over, and the number of bridges across the Orne was doubled. **World War II**, however, devastated the city. It was the prime target of the Allied Invasion in June 1944, and historians still argue as to quite why it took so long to capture. The "Battle of Caen" lasted two full months – even after the Canadians entered the city four weeks after D-Day, the southern bank of the river remained in enemy hands. Three-quarters of the town had to be destroyed before they were finally dislodged.

Caen today is not a place where you're likely to spend much time, though in parts it remains highly impressive. The central feature is a ring of ramparts that no longer has a castle to protect, and, though there are the scattered spires and buttresses of two abbeys and eight old churches, roads and roundabouts fill the wide spaces where prewar houses stood. Approaches are along thunderous -

The Brittany Ferries service from Portsmouth, promoted as sailing to Caen, in fact docks at **Ouistreham**, 15km north; see p.120. Buses from Caen's gare routière connect with each sailing, and Bus Verts' express bus #1 runs the same route.

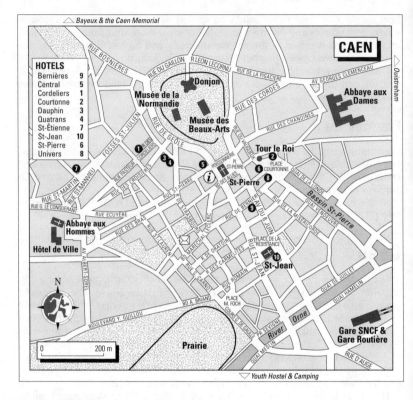

dual-carriageways through industrial suburbs – once an economic success story, currently hammered by unemployment.

Arrival and information

Caen's **tourist office** is in the central Hôtel d'Escoville, at 14 place St-Pierre (July & Aug Mon–Sat 10am–7pm, Sun 10am–1pm & 2–5pm; Sept–June Mon–Sat 10am–1pm & 2–6pm, Sun 10am–1pm; ☎02.31.27.14.14). This beautiful sixteenth-century house, across the street from the church of St-Pierre, is typical of the early Renaissance in Caen, with a strong Italian influence evident in its Florentine flourishes. For details of forthcoming events in the city, pick up a copy of their free weekly *Caen Scope*. On summer Sundays, when the banks are closed, the tourist office's currency-exchange service can be a life-saver. The main **post office** is on place Gambetta (Mon–Fri 8am–7pm, Sat 8am–noon; postcode 14000; ☎02.31.39.35.78).

The **gare SNCF** (☎02.31.83.50.50) is 1km south of the town centre across the river, with the **gare routière** so close at hand that you can walk directly to it from Platform 1. **Long-distance buses** from here include those run by Bus Verts, at 11 rue des Chanoines (☎02.31.44.77.44). Line #30 goes to Bayeux; #32 to Vire; #35 to Falaise; and #20 to Dives, Deauville, Trouville and Honfleur. Aurigny Air

Services (☎02.33.26.58.00) operate round-trip **flights** on Fridays and Sundays only to the Channel Island of Jersey, from the airport at Carpiquet, on the western outskirts of Caen; a weekend return costs 810F.

CTAC, the extensive **local bus** service (☎02.31.15.55.50), makes a one-way circuit through town between the Tour le Roi stop just north of the pleasure port and the gare SNCF, travelling north up avenue du 6 Juin and south down rue St-Jean. Digital displays at the main stops show when the next bus is due, and free timetables are available from CTAC, 11 bd Maréchal-Leclerc, and the tourist office.

Accommodation

Caen has a great number of **hotels**, though as ever in the bomb-damaged cities of Normandy, few could be called attractive; even those that advertise their antiquity tend to have been totally rebuilt. The main concentrations are near the gare SNCF, around the pleasure port, and just west of the castle and tourist office – the latter being particularly convenient for motorists heading to or or from the ferry. There are also a number of charmless motel-type places on the ring road around town. With plenty of dedicated restaurants in town, few hotels other than those specifically mentioned below bother to provide food.

Caen's summer-only, members-only **youth hostel** is in the *Foyer Robert-Remé* at 68bis rue E.Restout, Grâce-de-Dieu (June–Sept; ☎02.31.52.19.96), about 500m southwest of the gare SNCF. Beds in both four-bed dorms, or two-bed private rooms, cost 62F per person. Take bus #17 from the town centre (*Tour le Roi*) or gare SNCF, direction *Grâce-de-Dieu*, getting off at stop *Lycée Fresnil*. The municipal **campsite** (mid-May to Sept; ☎02.31.73.60.92) is nearby, beside the river Orne, on route de Louvigny (bus #13, direction *Louvigny*, stop *Camping*).

Hotels

Hôtel Bernières, 50 rue de Bernières (☎02.31.86.01.26, fax 02.31.86.51.76). Bright, central and very good-value hotel, halfway between the churches of St-Pierre and St-Jean. ①–③.

Central Hôtel, 23 place J.Letellier (☎02.31.86.18.52, fax 02.31.86.88.11). By Caen standards a budget hotel; not as quiet as it used to be, but very central. Good views of the château from the balconies of the higher rooms (but no lift to get up to them). ②.

Hôtel des Cordeliers, 4 rue des Cordeliers (☎02.31.86.37.14, fax 02.31.39.56.51). Smart, friendly hotel with a wide range of rooms, in small pedestrian street near the castle; bar but no restaurant. ②–④.

Hôtel Courtonne, place Courtonne (☎02.31.93.47.83, fax 02.31.93.50.50). Friendly, modernized hotel overlooking the pleasure port; all rooms have bath or shower, phone and TV. ③.

Hôtel-Restaurant le Dauphin, 29 rue Gémare (☎02.31.86.22.26, fax 02.31.86.35.14). Rather ugly but very central hotel, tucked away behind the tourist office. Part of it was a priory during the eighteenth century, not that you'd ever guess; the rooms are comfortable without being exciting in any way. Grand restaurant, with a 100F weekday menu; weekend menus 165F and 250F. Closed Sat, & mid-July to early Aug. ④–⑦.

Hôtel le Quatrans, 17 rue Gémare (☎02.31.86.25.57, fax 02.31.85.27.80). A little way behind the tourist office, but unmissable thanks to its garish neon-lit exterior. The pastel theme of the facade continues inside; some might find it all a bit cloying, but the service is friendly, and at least everything works. Cheaper rooms are without showers. ②.

Hôtel St-Étienne, 2 rue de l'Académie (☎02.31.86.35.82, fax 02.31.85.57.69). Friendly budget hotel in an old stone house in the characterful St-Martin district, not far from the Abbaye des Hommes. The cheapest rooms do not have showers. ①.

Hôtel St-Jean, 20 rue des Martyrs (☎02.31.86.23.35, fax 02.31.86.74.15). Simple but well-equipped rooms – all have shower or bath – facing St-Jean church near the *Petite Auberge*. No restaurant. ①.

Hôtel St-Pierre, 40 bd des Alliés (☎02.31.86.28.20, fax 02.31.79.89.44). In town, immediately opposite the Tour le Roi, alongside the eponymous bus stop and place Courtonne. Cheaper rooms do not have showers. No restaurant. ②.

Hôtel Univers, 12 quai Vendeuvre (☎02.31.85.46.14, fax 02.31.38.21.33). In town, near the port de Plaisance. All rooms have shower or bath. No restaurant. ②.

The City

A virtue has been made of the necessity of clearing away the rubble of Caen's medieval houses, which formerly pressed up against its ancient **château ramparts**. The resulting open green space means that those walls are now fully visible for the first time in centuries. In turn, walking the circuit of the ramparts gives a good overview of the city, with a particularly fine prospect of the reconstructed fourteenth-century facade of the nearby church of **St-Pierre**. Some magnificent Renaissance stonework has survived intact at the church's east end.

Within the castle walls, it's possible to visit the former **Exchequer**, which dates from shortly after the Norman Conquest of England, and to inspect a garden that has been replanted with the kind of herbs and medicinal plants that would have been cultivated here during the Middle Ages. Also inside the precinct, though not in original structures, are two **museums**. Much the best is the **Beaux Arts**, housed in a 1960s stone building (daily except Tues 10am–6pm; 20F, free on Wed). Its comprehensive displays – from fifteenth-century Italian and Flemish primitives to contemporary French artists – include masterpieces by Poussin, Géricault, Monet and Bonnard, as well as an exceptional collection of engravings by Dürer and Rembrandt. The other museum, the **Musée de Normandie** (April–Sept Wed–Fri 10am–12.30pm & 1.30–6pm, Mon, Sat & Sun 9.30am–12.30pm & 2–6pm; Oct–March daily except Tues 9.30am–12.30pm & 2–6pm; 10F, free on Wed), is devoted to Norman history, and ranges from archeological finds dating from Roman Rouen to the impact of the Industrial Revolution.

Just to the north of the château lies the complex of **university** buildings, originally founded in 1432 by Henry VI of England, and now the proud home of the largest nuclear particle accelerator in Europe. The only reason for tourists to pass this way is to see the large-scale **model of Ancient Rome**, as it stood around 300 AD, which has been laid out in the Maison de la Recherche en Sciences Humaines (Mon–Sat 7.30am–8pm; free).

When William the Conqueror married Matilda in Eu (see p.64), in 1051, both incurred excommunication. Historians argue as to the precise nature of their offence – they may have been distant cousins – but Pope Nicholas II only agreed to sanction their marriage and readmit them to the church in 1059, upon the solemn vow that each would build an abbey in Caen. William's, the **Abbaye aux Hommes** to the west of the city centre, was designed to hold his tomb, but his burial here, in 1087, was hopelessly undignified. The funeral procession first caught fire and was then held to ransom, as various factions squabbled over his rotting corpse for any spoils they could grab. A further interruption came when a man halted the service to object that the grave had been constructed without compensation on the site of his family house, and the assembled nobles had to pay him off before William could finally be laid to rest. During the Revolution the tomb was again ransacked, and it now holds at most a solitary thighbone rescued from the river. Still, the building itself is a wonderful Romanesque monument – although not enhanced by the latest desecration, "multilingual, computerized audiovisual visits" – and is also home to a fine collection of seventeenth- to nineteenth-century paintings. Guided tours take place daily at 9.30am, 11am, 2.30pm and 4pm. As you explore, look out for the huge wooden clock to the left of the altar.

The **Hôtel de Ville** alongside, which all but obscures the abbey, is housed in what used to be its convent buildings – hence the surprising harmony with which the two blend together.

William's queen, Mathilda, lies across the town in the **Abbaye aux Dames** at the end of rue des Chanoines. She had commissioned the building of the abbey church, La Trinité, well before the Conquest. It's starkly impressive, with a gloomy pillared crypt, superb stained glass behind the altar, and odd sculptural details like the fish curled up in the holy-water stoup (guided tours daily 2.30pm & 4pm; free).

The nineteenth-century **Bassin St-Pierre**, a short walk south of the Abbaye aux Dames, now serves as Caen's pleasure port, and marks the end of the canal that links the city to the sea. In summer, it's one of the liveliest areas in town, although, considering the crowds, it holds surprisingly few pavement cafés.

The Caen Memorial – a Museum for Peace

July & Aug daily 9am–9pm, last entry 8.15pm; Sept, Oct & mid-Feb to June daily 9am–7pm, last entry 5.45pm; Nov, Dec & mid-Jan to mid-Feb Mon–Sat 9am–6pm, Sun 9am–7pm. Closed first fortnight of Jan. ☎02.31.06.06.44 – note the significance. Adults 69F, students, ages 10–19 and over-65s 61F, under-10s and World War II veterans free. Served by buses #12 (Mon–Fri) and #14 (Sat & Sun) from Tour le Roi. See p.119 for details of tours of the Landing Beaches.

The **Caen Memorial** is a war museum with a big and very welcome difference, in that it proclaims itself to be a "Museum for Peace", and for the most part succeeds admirably in that intention. Located on a plateau named after General Eisenhower, just north of Caen at the end of avenue Marshal-Montgomery, it was funded by the governments of the US, Britain, Canada, Germany, Poland, Czechoslovakia and the former USSR, as well as France, and stands immediately above the headquarters used by the German army during June and July 1944.

All visitors have to follow a prescribed route through the ultra-modern building, which, with a slightly heavy-handed literalism, leads on a downwards spiral from World War I and the Treaty of Versailles towards the maelstrom of World War II. From the start you hear the voice of Hitler booming in the distance; his image recurs with increasing size and frequency on screens beside you as the events of the 1920s and 1930s are recounted.

The war itself is superbly documented, with a greater emphasis on the minutiae of everyday life in occupied France than on military technology. Nothing is glossed over in the attempt to provide a fully rounded picture of the nation under occupation and at war. The collaborationist Vichy government is set in its context without being excused, with such statements as Pierre Laval's "I wish for the victory of Germany, because without it Bolshevism will spread everywhere" on prominent display alongside a book of the "99 most touching answers of French schoolchildren to the question 'Why do you love Maréchal Petain?'. Secret Nazi reports show how Resistance activity in Normandy grew as the war continued, and what reprisals were taken.

Every visit culminates with three films, each in a separate auditorium. The first is a harrowing account of D-Day itself; the second traces the course of the rest of the war; and the third looks at the winners of the Nobel peace prize in arguing for the need to establish lasting peace in the world.

All in all, this museum creates something new in a genre which can occasionally seem morally suspect, and the display cannot be recommended too highly for anyone with a serious interest in the war and its lasting legacy. Allow at least two hours for a visit, as the films alone occupy a whole hour.

Eating

The centre of Caen offers two major areas for **eating**. Cosmopolitan restaurants in the attractive pedestrianized **quartier Vaugueux** include the *Kouba*, specializing in couscous, the creole *Au Pommier des Îles*, and even *L'Age de Pierre*, which claims to prepare "stone age" food by cooking slabs of horse meat on superheated stones. The streets off **rue de Geôle**, near the western ramparts, particularly rue des Croisiers and rue Gémare, house rather more traditional French restaurants. There are also several restaurants and brasseries facing the gare SNCF, of which many are either in, or connected with, hotels.

Restaurants

L'Alcide, 1 place Courtonne (☎02.31.44.18.06). Very conspicuous but rather anonymous-looking bistro-style place, which turns out to be surprisingly good, serving classic French dishes cooked with great attention to detail. Menus from 78F up to 139F. Closed Sat.

Le Bouchon du Vaugueux, 12 rue du Graindorge (☎02.31.44.26.26). Intimate little brasserie in the Vaugueux quarter, offering a daily lunch menu at 69F, good-value salads from around 45F, and dinner menus from 89F. Closed Mon pm, Sun, & first three weeks of Aug.

Le Gastronome, 43 rue St-Sauveur (☎02.31.86.57.75). Smart, modern restaurant, between the château and the Abbaye aux Hommes, offering a changing but consistently good 120F menu of Norman specialities. Closed Sat am, Sun pm & first fortnight of Aug.

Restaurant Maître Corbeau, 94 rue du Geôle (☎02.31.86.33.97). Fondue is the speciality in this eccentric little place, and they won't let you forget it, festooning the whole place with cheesy iconography. A typical fondue costs around 80F, while set menus start from 88F. Closed Sat am & Sun.

La Petite Auberge, 17 rue des Équipes-d'Urgence (☎02.31.86.43.30). Plain and simple restaurant, with a nice view of the St-Jean church. Very-good-value Norman specialities – a daily 68F menu that doesn't force you to eat tripe. Closed Sun pm, Mon & Sept.

Les Quatres Épices, 25 rue Porte-au-Berger (☎02.31.85.10.10). Lively West African restaurant, just off rue du Vaugueux. Everything is *à la carte* – prawns with sweet potato for 85F, grilled fish with ginger for 75F, plus plantains and meat galore – and African music plays non-stop.

Tongasoa, 7 rue du Vaugueux (☎02.31.43.87.15). Midday menu 55F; evening menus from 85F. Dishes from Madagascar, Réunion and the Seychelles – especially fish, curried, cooked with ginger and tropical fruits, or just plain. Cocktails galore, in lurid colours. Closed Sun lunchtime.

Shopping

Most of the centre of Caen is taken up with busy new **shopping** developments and pedestrian precincts, where the cafés are distinguished by such names as *Fast Food Glamour Vault*. The shops are good, possibly the best in Normandy or

Brittany, if Parisian style is what you're after. Outlets of the big Parisian department stores – and of the aristocrats' grocers, Hédiard, in the Cours des Halles – are here, along with good local rivals. Rue Écuyère has a fine assortment of shops full of unusual and cheap oddments, antiques, stuff for collectors and jokes.

If you're looking for books, records or tickets for local events, call in at the branch of FNAC (☎02.31.39.41.00) in the Centre Paul-Doumer, on the corner of rue Doumer and rue Bras. The main city **market** takes place on Friday, spreading along both sides of Fosse St-Julien, and there's also a Sunday market in place Courtonne.

The Invasion Beaches

Despite the best efforts of Stephen Spielberg, it is all but impossible now to picture the scene at dawn on **D-Day**, June 6, 1944, when Allied troops landed at points along the Norman coast from the mouth of the Orne to Les Dunes de Varneville on the Cotentin Peninsula.* For the most part, these are innocuous beaches backed by gentle dunes, and yet this foothold in Europe was won at the cost of 100,000 lives. That the invasion happened here, and not nearer to Germany, was partly due to the failure of the Canadian raid on Dieppe (see p.61) in 1942. The ensuing **Battle of Normandy** killed thousands of civilians and reduced nearly 600 towns and villages to rubble, but within a week of its eventual conclusion Paris was liberated.

The **beaches** are still often referred to by their wartime code names. The British and Commonwealth forces landed on **Sword**, **Juno** and **Gold** beaches between Ouistreham and Arromanches; the Americans, further west on **Omaha** and **Utah** beaches. Bits of shrapnel can still be found in the sands, five decades later, but more substantial traces of the fighting are rare. At Arromanches the remains are visible of one of the prefabricated Mulberry harbours that made such large-scale landings possible, and at Pointe du Hoc the cliff heights are still deeply pitted with German bunkers and shell-holes. Elsewhere, the reminders are **cemeteries** – British and Commonwealth, American and German, each highly distinct in character – and **war museums**, examples of which you'll find in almost every coastal town.

The D-Day events provide a focus for most foreign visitors to this part of the coast; travelling through, you are bound to come across veterans, and their descendants, paying their respects. Taken simply as holiday territory, however, some of the villages and towns can offer rewards. They are traditional seaside resorts, without the inflated prices or flashiness of the Deauville area – old-fashioned seafront villages, with rows of boarding houses and little wooden bathing huts that must have been kept in storage somewhere during the war. And increasingly there is **windsurfing** on offer – better suited to these north-facing resorts than chilly bathing.

The Caen Memorial (see p.117) organizes bilingual **guided tours** of the landing beaches all year round. In summer, you can choose between the half-day **Montgomery** tour, which covers Sword, Juno and Gold beaches (June–Sept daily 9am & 2pm; 340F), and the full-day **Eisenhower** tour, which takes in Omaha and Utah beaches as well (June–Sept daily 9am; 480F). In winter, they run a four-hour

*The "D" in "D-Day" stands simply for "day"; hence it is known as *J-Jour* in France.

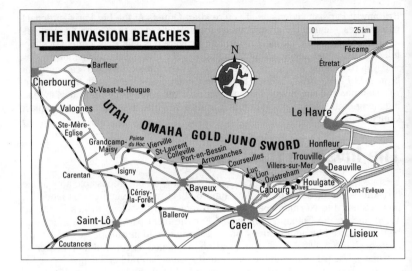

D-Day tour (Oct–March Sat & Sun 1pm; April & May daily 1pm; 340F). All ticket prices include admission to the Caen Memorial.

In addition, Bus Verts run all along this coast. **From Bayeux**, bus #74 goes to Arromanches and Courseulles, and bus #70 to Port-en-Bessin and Vierville. **From Caen**, bus #30 runs directly inland to Isigny via Bayeux, express bus #1 to Ouistreham, and express bus #3 to Courseulles.

Ouistreham-Riva Bella

The small community of **OUISTREHAM-RIVA BELLA**, on the coast 15km north of Caen and connected to it by a fast dual carriageway, still gives the impression that it can barely believe its luck at having become a major ferry port. Since Brittany Ferries started their regular service here from Portsmouth in 1986, the easternmost of the D-Day resorts has developed an extensive array of reasonable hotels and restaurants.

The town itself is not especially appealing, and most arriving passengers choose to press straight on out – this is one of the Channel's simpler ports to leave, as boats dock just a few hundred metres from the small central square, **place Courbonne**. Ouistreham's road system, at least in summer, is still not quite up to the task of coping with the volume of traffic, and motorists should allow plenty of time to catch their boats. All services are connected by bus with Caen.

If instead of setting off for Caen you head directly west along the coast from the ferry terminal, you come within a few hundred metres to the long straight main drag of **beach** – the **Riva Bella** itself. This is progressively shedding its somewhat run-down image; the large Casino has been remodelled as a 1930s passenger liner, housing an expensive restaurant and cocktail bar, and even the old-fashioned bathing huts have had a fresh lick of paint. Nearby, the **Musée du Mur de**

l'Atlantique (June–Sept daily 9am–7pm; mid-Feb to May & Oct to mid-Nov daily 10am–noon & 2–6pm; mid-Nov to mid-Feb Sat & Sun 10am–noon & 2–6pm; 25F) records the local Sword Beach landings.

The main road south passes close by **Pegasus Bridge**, where a museum and memorial mark the landing site of Allied gliders during the night before D-Day; their dangerous (and successful) mission was to secure the bridge a few hours in advance of the landings. Despite protests from veterans, the original bridge was removed in 1994. If you're **cycling**, the dedicated cycle path that follows the canal all the way to the centre of Caen makes a far more pleasant start to a holiday.

Practicalities

Ouistreham-Riva Bella's **tourist office** is in the place Alfred-Thomas, alongside the casino on the beach (mid-June to mid-Sept Mon–Sat 10am–7pm, Sun 10.30am–12.30pm & 3–7pm; mid-Sept to mid-June daily except Tues 11am–noon & 3–5pm; ☎02.31.97.18.63). For Brittany Ferries information, call the gare maritime (☎02.31.36.36.36). **Bikes** can be rented from Vérel, 77 av Foch (☎02.31.97.19.04).

Several cafés and brasseries in the place Courbonne, immediately outside the gare maritime, are eager to liberate passengers from their spare change, while *Le Channel*, just around the corner at 79 av Michel-Cabieu (☎02.31.96.51.69; ①–③), is just about the best value for both **eating and sleeping**. Menus in the restaurant start with the 55F *menu pêcheur*, which includes mussels, while the 88F and 144F options increase in splendour; the guest rooms are in a separate building across the street. The smart *Le Normandie et le Chalut*, a few doors down at 71 av Michel-Cabieu (☎02.31.97.19.57; closed mid-Dec to mid-Jan, plus Sun pm & Mon Nov–March; ③), has pleasant, quiet rooms, with one menu at 95F featuring a seafood quiche served with seaweed cream, and another at 165F that makes an excellent last-night blowout. Good-value hotels near the beach include the *Hôtel de la Plage* at 39–41 av Pasteur (☎02.31.96.85.16; closed Nov–Feb; ②), and the *St-Georges* at 51 av Andry (☎02.31.97.18.79; ④), while *Le Britania*, immediately across from the ferry terminal at 63 rue des Dunes (☎02.31.96.88.26; closed Jan), is a convenient top-quality restaurant.

Ouistreham to Arromanches: Sword and Juno beaches

The coast along Sword and Juno beaches is generally featureless, but the towns themselves are welcoming. A long promenade curves by the sea all the way from Ouistreham to Lion – it's built-up, though always in a low-key way, and makes a pleasant walk straight from the ferry.

Colleville-Montgomery, the first village after the port, is one of the few "Montgomeries" in the area really to be named after the British general rather than his Norman ancestors. It's not otherwise distinguished.

Luc-sur-mer

If you're looking for atmosphere – albeit sedate – **LUC-SUR-MER**, 11km from Ouistreham, has much to recommend it. It's a gentle resort with a small wooden pier, neon-lit *crêpe*-stands, and tearooms along the promenade, with the **hotel**

THE WAR CEMETERIES

The World War II **cemeteries** that dot the Norman countryside are filled with foreigners; most of the French dead are buried in the churchyards of their home towns. After the war, some felt that the soldiers should remain in the makeshift graves that were dug where they fell. Instead, commissions gathered the remains into purpose-built cemeteries devoted to the separate warring nations.

The **British** and **Commonwealth** cemeteries are magnificently maintained, and open in every sense. They tend not to be screened off with hedges or walls, or to be forbidding expanses of manicured lawn, but are instead intimate, punctuated with bright flowers. The family of each soldier was invited to suggest an inscription for his tomb, making each grave very personal, and yet part of a common attempt to bring meaning to the carnage. Some epitaphs are questioning – "One day we will understand"; some are accepting – "Our lad at rest"; some matter-of-fact, simply giving the home address; some patriotic, quoting the "corner of a foreign field that is forever England". And interspersed among them all is the chilling refrain of the anonymous: "A soldier . . . known unto God". Thus the cemetery at **Ryes**, where so many of the graves bear the date of D-Day, and so many of the victims are under 20, remains immediate and accessible – each grave clearly contains a unique individual. Even the monumental sculpture is subdued, a very British sort of fumbling for the decent thing to say. The understatement of the memorial at **Bayeux**, with its painfully contrived Latin epigram commemorating the return as liberators of "those whom William conquered", conveys an entirely appropriate humility and deep sadness.

An even more eloquent testimony to the futility of war is afforded by the **German** cemeteries, filled with soldiers who served a cause so despicable as to render any talk of "nobility" or "sacrifice" simply obscene. What such cemeteries might have been like had the Nazis won doesn't bear contemplation. As it is, they are sombre places, inconspicuous to minimize the bitterness they still arouse. At **Orglandes**, 10,000 are buried, three to each of the plain headstones set in the long flat lawn, almost hidden behind an anonymous wall. There are no noble slogans and the plain entrance is without a dedicatory monument. At the superb site of **Mont d'Huisnes** near Mont-St-Michel, the circular mausoleum holds another 10,000, filed away in cold concrete tiers. There is no attempt to defend the indefensible, and yet one feels an overpowering sense of sorrow – that there is nothing to be said in such a place bitterly underlines the sheer waste.

The largest **American** cemetery, at **St-Laurent-sur-mer** near the Pointe du Hoc, may already be familiar to you from the opening sequences of *Saving Private Ryan*. Here, by contrast, the atmosphere is one of certainty. The rows of crosses are as neat and clinical as graph paper. At one end, a muscular giant dominates a huge array of battlefield plans and diagrams, covered with surging arrows and pincer movements. Endless rows of impersonal graves stretch away into the distance; there are no individual epitaphs, just gold lettering for a few exceptional warriors. That the place is so much like a balance sheet or corporate report seems something more than a mere difference of emphasis: the American cemetery is the only one where placards tell visitors where to walk, what to wear and how to behave.

Beau Rivage, right on the seafront at 1 rue du Dr-Charcot (☎02.31.96.49.51; ③), as its most reasonable accommodation. Menus here start at 75F; options on the 150F one include a spectacular salad of smoked fish, *langoustines* and *foie gras*. *Le Marsouin*, across the road at no. 2 (☎02.31.97.32.08; ③), is similar in almost every respect. There's also a huge four-star **campsite** near the beach, *La Capricieuse* (April–Sept; ☎02.31.97.34.43).

Langrune and St-Aubin-sur-mer

Attractive individual seaside **hotels** are scattered all along the D-Day coast – typically with simple rooms upstairs above a large glass-fronted sea-view dining room – so ferry passengers have a choice of several *logis* for a first- or last-night stop. The *Hôtel de la Mer*, boulevard Aristide-Briand (☎02.31.96.03.37; ②), in **LANGRUNE** is particularly inexpensive for what you get, while further on, facing the beach across the pedestrian-only promenade at **SAINT-AUBIN-SUR-MER**, *Le Clos Normand* (☎02.31.97.30.47; closed Jan, Feb & Dec; ④) may be large, but it's extremely peaceful. Its restaurant has a seafront terrace, and offers a small lunch menu at 75F, plus a series of four-course *table d'hôte* menus, where the price, from 110F to 160F, depends on your choice of main course.

Courseulles

COURSEULLES is a bit more of a town, with an enjoyable Friday market in an old square set back from the sea, and, allegedly, the best oysters in Normandy. Briefly during the invasion it served as a crucial British beachhead; within ten days of D-Day it was visited by Winston Churchill and King George VI on morale-boosting excursions.

Courseulles' main activity these days is as a yachting port, and apart from an excellent *crêperie, du Moulin*, on the outskirts, there's not much choice of hotels and restaurants. The *Crémaillère-Le-Gytan*, boulevard de la Plage (☎02.31.37.46.73; ③), is probably the best option for both eating and sleeping, with menus from just under 100F.

Arromanches

At **ARROMANCHES**, 13km west of Courseulles and a total of 31km from Ouistreham, an artificial **Mulberry harbour**, "Port Winston", protected the landings of two and a half million men and half a million vehicles during the Invasion. Two of these prefab concrete constructions were built in segments in Britain, while "doodlebugs" blitzed overhead, then submerged in rivers away from the prying eyes of German aircraft, and finally towed across the Channel at 6km/h as the Invasion began. Meanwhile, the British 47 Royal Marine Commando were storming Arromanches itself to clear the way.

The seafront **Musée du Débarquement**, in Arromanches's main square (May–Aug daily 9am–6.30pm; Sept–April daily 9am–11.30am & 2–5.30pm; closed first three weeks of Jan; 35F), recounts the whole story by means of models, machinery and movies – and the evidence of your own eyes. A huge picture window runs the length of the museum, staring straight out to where the bulky remains of the harbour make a strange intrusion on the beach and shallow sea bed. Its sheer scale is impossible to appreciate at this distance; for the three months after D-Day, this was the largest port in the world. (The other Mulberry, slightly further west on Omaha Beach, broke up within two weeks, but this one was repairable; see p.124.)

There are war memorials throughout Arromanches, with Jesus and Mary high up on the cliffs above the invasion site and helicopter trips available to overlook the area.

Practicalities

Arromanches somehow manages to be quite a cheerful place to stay, with a lively pedestrian street of bars and brasseries, and a long expanse of sand where you can rent windsurf boards. Around a dozen daily Bus Verts services (#75) connect it with Bayeux. The local **tourist office** is just back from the sea at 2 rue Maréchal-Joffre (Mon–Wed 9am–7pm, Thurs–Sun 9am–noon & 1–7pm; ☎02.31.21.47.56).

La Marine, at 2 quai Canada (mid-Feb to mid-Nov; ☎02.31.22.34.19; ③), is a slightly expensive **hotel**, with an excellent sea-view restaurant that serves fishy menus from 95F. Across the main square, opposite the tourist office, stands the *Arromanches*, 2 rue du Colonel-Michel (☎02.31.22.36.26; closed Jan, plus Tues pm & Wed in winter; ③), which has menus from 72F up to 160F, while the cheaper *Normandie* is nearby at 5 place du 6-Juin (Feb to mid-Dec; ☎02.31.22.34.32; ②).

West to the Cotentin: Omaha Beach

PORT-EN-BESSIN, the nearest point on the coast to Bayeux (on the #70 bus route), has a thriving fishing industry and – rare on this coast – a sheltered, enclosed site. The fish, caught off Devon and Cornwall, are auctioned three times a week. It's not, however, desperately attractive, though the *de la Marine* (☎02.31.21.70.08; closed Dec & Jan; ③) is a classic seaside **hotel** on quai Letourner. The squalid *La Prairie* **campsite**, on the other hand, is definitely one to avoid.

The coastline west of Port-en-Bessin becomes steadily hillier, and as **Omaha Beach** it presented a stiff challenge to the American forces on D-Day. At **ST-LAURENT** is the larger of the two **American war cemeteries**; unlike the British and Commonwealth forces, the Americans repatriated most of their dead. It's a disturbing place, described on p.122. Just beyond St-Laurent, **VIERVILLE** was the site for the twin to Arromanches' Mulberry harbour, which lasted just thirteen days before breaking up in an unprecedented storm.

Further along, the most dramatic American landings took place along the cliff heights of the **POINTE DU HOC**, still today deeply pitted with German bunkers and shell-holes. Standing amid the scarred earth and rusty barbed wire, looking down to the rocks at the base of the cliff, it seems inconceivable that the first US sergeant was at the top five minutes after landing, and the whole complex taken within another quarter of an hour.

Grandcamp-Maisy and Isigny

GRANDCAMP-MAISY, centred on its fishing harbour and market, has a good **campsite**, the *Camping du Juncal* (Easter–Sept; ☎02.31.22.61.44), and the **hotels** *du Guesclin*, 4 quai Crampon (☎02.31.22.64.22; closed mid-Jan to mid-Feb; ②), and *Au Petit Marayeur*, place de la Mairie (☎02.31.22.65.91; closed mid-Dec to mid-Jan; ②). **Cruises** of the landing beaches to both the north and the east, on the sixty-passenger *Colonel Rudder*, cost from 70F for one hour and up to 200F for five hours; for a full schedule, contact the Tentations shop at 11 rue A.Briand (☎02.31.21.42.93).

ISIGNY nearby is renowned for its dairy products, butter in particular; though of no great beauty or interest, it does have a **hotel**, *de France*, 13 rue É.Demagny (☎02.31.22.00.33; closed mid-Nov to mid-Feb; ②), if you're stuck.

Bayeux

BAYEUX, with its perfectly preserved medieval ensemble, magnificent Cathedral and world-famous Tapestry, is 23km west of Caen – a twenty-minute

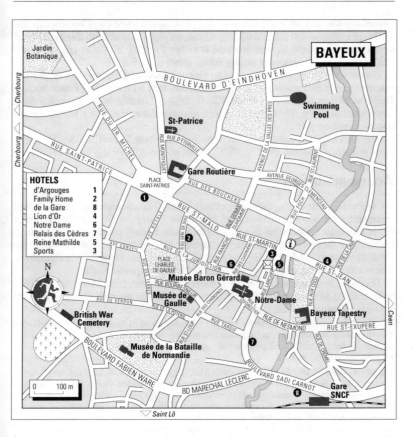

train ride. It's a smaller and much more intimate city, and a far more enjoyable place to visit despite the large crowds of summer tourists.

A mere 10km in from the coast, Bayeux was the first French city to be liberated in 1944, the day after the D-Day landings. It was occupied so quickly – before the Germans had got over their surprise – that it managed to escape any serious damage, and briefly became capital of Free France.

Arrival and information

Bayeux's **tourist office** stands in the very centre of town, in what used to be the fish market on the arched pont St-Jean (Mon–Fri 9am–6pm, Sat 9am–noon & 2–6pm, Sun 9.30am–noon & 2.30–6pm; ☎02.31.51.28.28). The **post office** is just around the corner at 14 rue Larcher (Mon–Fri 8am–7pm, Sat 8am–noon; ☎02.31.92.01.00).

The **gare SNCF** (☎02.31.92.80.50) is fifteen minutes' walk away to the west, just outside the "ring road", while the **gare routière** is on the other side of town on rue du Manche, alongside place St-Patrice (used as a car park, except during

Saturday's market), near the fire station. For information on **local buses**, call Bus Verts du Calvados (☎02.31.92.02.92), whose services stop at both the gare SNCF and the gare routière; tickets are sold at either the gare SNCF or Librairie 1000 Pages on place St-Patrice, or on the actual buses.

Travellers without cars who plan to visit the landing beaches and/or the war cemeteries are better advised to join a **minibus trip** with a local operator such as Bus Fly, 24 rue Montfiquet (☎02.31.22.00.08), or Normandy Tours, place de la Gare (☎02.31.92.10.70). Details of tours organized through the Caen Memorial can be found on p.117.

Bicycles can be rented from the Family Home (see below), Cycles-14, boulevard Winston-Churchill (☎02.31.92.27.75) or, as usual, from the gare SNCF.

Accommodation

As one of Normandy's most important tourist destinations, Bayeux is well equipped with accommodation. On the whole, however, the **hotels** are more expensive than usual; even the "unofficial youth hostel" listed below is far from cheap. The **hostel** in the municipal Centre d'Accueil at 21 rue des Marettes (☎02.31.92.08.19), 1.5km from the gare SNCF near the Musée de la Bataille de Normandie, is open all year, charging 92F for a tiny private room.

There's a large **campsite** on boulevard d'Eindhoven (mid-March to mid-Nov; ☎02.31.92.08.43), on the northern ring road (RN13) near the river – and the municipal sewage works.

Hôtel d'Argouges, 21 rue St-Patrice (☎02.31.92.88.86, fax 02.31.92.69.16). Very stylish eighteenth-century building, with an imposing courtyard entered via an archway on the west side of place St-Patrice, and a well-kept garden around the back. A quiet but expensive place to stay. No restaurant. ③–⑤.

Family Home, 39 rue Général-Dais (☎02.31.92.15.22, fax 02.31.92.55.72). Central seventeenth-century house which describes itself variously as a *maison d'hôtes* (guesthouse) and an *auberge de jeunesse* (youth hostel). Its prices are over the usual odds (hostel accommodation is 105F per person) and it's a bit self-consciously jolly – but it has its advocates, and people return again and again. Room prices include breakfast. Meals are taken communally, Madame Lefèvre presiding at the head of a long table in an old oak-beamed dining room. ①–③.

Hôtel de la Gare, 26 place de la Gare (☎02.31.92.10.70, fax 02.31.51.95.99). Old but perfectly adequate basic hotel, beside the station, on the ring road 15min walk from the cathedral. Tours of D-Day beaches arranged. No restaurant. ①.

Hôtel-Restaurant Lion d'Or, 71 rue St-Jean (☎02.31.92.06.90, fax 02.31.22.15.64). Grand old coaching inn set back behind a courtyard, just beyond the pedestrianized section of the rue St-Jean, outside Les Halles des Grains (now the assembly rooms). The rooms themselves are brighter and newer than the exterior might lead you to expect. Closed mid-Dec to mid-Jan. Menus from 150F. ⑤.

Hôtel-Restaurant Notre Dame, 44 rue des Cuisiniers (☎02.31.92.87.24, fax 02.31.92.67.11). Friendly and very pleasant *logis*, virtually in front of the cathedral, with a magnificent view. Menus from 90F, with a special Norman one at 125F. Closed mid-Nov to mid-Dec, plus Sun pm & Mon in winter. ②–③.

Hôtel Reine Mathilde, 23 rue Larcher (☎02.31.92.08.13, fax 02.31.92.09.93). Simple but well-equipped rooms – all have showers and TV – backing onto the canal, between the tapestry and the cathedral. No restaurant as such, but there's a really nice open-air brasserie downstairs that serves dinner between May and Sept, with the cheapest menu at 50F and a good four-course meal for 99F. ③.

Le Relais des Cèdres, 1 bd Sadi-Carnot (☎02.31.21.98.07). Pretty guesthouse, not far from the station but within sight of the cathedral. The rooms are fine, and good value, although the atmosphere is not all that welcoming. ①–③.

Hôtel Sports, 19 rue St-Martin (☎02.31.92.28.53, fax 02.31.92.35.40). Basic rooms not far from the river in the heart of town, with a brasserie downstairs. The management are very reluctant to turn the heating on, so this can be an icebox in winter. ②.

The Town

Within the confines of a busy ring road, the core of Bayeux is surprisingly small. It consists largely of one long street, which starts from the place St-Patrice in the west (scene of a Saturday market). As the rue St-Malo and rue St-Martin this is lined with the busy little shops of a typical Norman town; it then crosses the attractive canalized River Aure, passing the tourist office and the old **watermill**, Moulin Crocquevieille, to become the pedestrianized rue St-Jean on the east side, filled with cafés, brasseries, restaurants and souvenir shops (and itself the site of a market on Wednesdays).

Both Bayeux's principal attractions are south of this main thoroughfare. The **Cathedral** is in an attractive tangle of old streets, best reached along rue des Cuisiniers – the fourteenth-century half-timbered house that overhangs the street at 1 rue des Cuisiniers, on the corner with rue St-Malo, was until recently Bayeux's main tourist office. The **tapestry** is on the other side of the river, housed in an impressive eighteenth-century seminary, remodelled as the **Centre Guillaume le Conquérant**, and clearly signposted on rue de Nesmond.

The Bayeux Tapestry

Daily: May–Aug 9am–7pm; mid-March to April & Sept to mid-Oct 9am–6.30pm; mid-Oct to mid-March 9.30am–12.30pm & 2–6pm; last admission 1hr before closing. 38F.

The **Bayeux Tapestry** – also known to the French as the *Tapisserie de la Reine Mathilde* – is a seventy-metre strip of linen that recounts the story of the Norman Conquest of England. Although created over nine centuries ago, the brilliance of its coloured wools has barely faded, and the tale is enlivened throughout with scenes of medieval life, popular fables and mythical beasts. Technically it's not really a tapestry at all, but an embroidery; the skill of its draughtsmanship, and the sheer vigour and detail, are stunning. The work is thought to have been carried out by nuns in England, commissioned by Bishop Oddo, William's half-brother, in time for the inauguration of Bayeux Cathedral in 1077; recent suggestions by an English historian that the tapestry is considerably newer, in view for example of the "kebabs" being grilled in one beach scene, are discounted by most authorities.

The tapestry looks – and reads – like a modern comic strip. While it's generally considered to be historically accurate, William's justification for his invasion – his contention that during a visit to Normandy Harold had sworn to accept William as King of England – remains in dispute. In the tapestry itself, Harold is every inch the villain, with his dastardly little moustache and shifty eyes. At the point when he breaks his oath and takes the throne for himself, Harold looks extremely pleased with himself; however, his comeuppance swiftly follows, as William, the noble hero, crosses the Channel and defeats the English armies at Hastings.

Visits are well planned and highly atmospheric, if somewhat exhausting. You can't actually touch or linger over the tapestry itself, which is in any case kept for its preservation under very dim light. However, the display is excellent. First comes a slide show, projected onto billowing sheets of canvas hung as sails; you then pass along a photographic replica of the tapestry, with enlargements and detailed commentaries. Upstairs in the plush theatre, a film (French and English versions alternate) explains the general context and craft of the piece – which you can skip if you feel you know the 1066 story well enough by now. Beyond this – and the souvenirs table – you finally approach the real thing, which has a strong three-dimensional presence you might not expect from all the flat reproductions.

Although the tapestry makes such a bullish and effective piece of propaganda that Napoléon exhibited it in Paris – to show that a successful invasion of England was indeed possible – much of the pleasure of viewing it comes from the incidental vignettes of contemporary life that parallel the main story. The preparation of William's forces is shown in sufficient detail that museums such as those in Dieppe and Douarnanez (see pp.61 & 271) have constructed boats using the same methods, while the depiction of Halley's Comet blazing in the sky helped astronomers to establish its orbit. Only the faintest smattering of Latin is required to be able to follow the captions that accompany each major scene.

Cathédrale Notre Dame

Daily: July & Aug 9am–7pm; Sept–June 9am–6pm.

The **Cathédrale Notre Dame**, the first home of the tapestry, is a short and very obvious walk away from its latest resting place. Despite such eighteenth-century vandalism as the monstrous fungoid baldachin that flanks the pulpit, Bishop Oddo's original Romanesque plan is still intact, for the most part sensitively merged with Gothic additions. The crypt, entirely original, is particularly wonderful, with its frescoes of angels playing trumpets and bagpipes, looking exhausted by their eternal performance. Along the nave is some tremendous twelfth-century sculpture, and you shouldn't miss the beautifully carved wooden choir stalls. The tiled floor of the chapterhouse features a fifteenth-century maze depicting the road to Jerusalem. To get access to both crypt and chapterhouse, you may have to seek out the sacristan.

Musée Baron Gerard

Daily: June to mid-Sept 9am–7pm; mid-Sept to May 10am–12.30pm & 2–6pm. 38F.

The courtyard that adjoins the western facade of the cathedral is dominated by the **Liberty Tree**, a 200-year-old plane tree planted with much Revolutionary rejoicing in 1797. In its shadow to the north, the former palace of the archbishops of Bayeux has over the centuries received a considerable quantity of porcelain and lace donated by local families. Named the **Musée Baron Gerard** in honour of its most generous patron, it has recently been renovated to display its collection to far better advantage.

The General de Gaulle Memorial Museum

Mid-March to mid-Nov daily 9.30am–12.30pm & 2–6.30pm. 20F.

Although Bayeux's newest museum, the **General de Gaulle Memorial** at 10 rue de Bourbesneur, near place de Gaulle, is aimed squarely at French devotees of the great man, it makes an interesting detour for foreign visitors. The sheer obsession of the displays, which focus on the three separate day trips de Gaulle made to Bayeux during the course of his long life, somehow illuminates the extent to which he came to epitomize the very essence of a certain kind of Frenchness – which to foreigners seems scarcely removed from self-parody.

Over three floors, the life of the general is traced from his days as a dashing cadet, first seen in a magnificent plumed hat before he was united with his trademark flat-topped *képi*. He was wounded three times in World War I, including at both the Somme and Verdun. Having argued in vain that France should prepare for the new era of mechanized warfare, he became a general on the battlefield in 1940 just in time to be swept aside by the Nazi Blitzkrieg, and was in London by June 18 to launch his famous (but unrecorded) radio appeal to the "Free French"; the indecipherable manuscript is on display.

Then come his visits to Bayeux. The first and most significant was the day his exile ended; we see him addressing French sailors on the destroyer *Le Combattant*, then landing on French soil at Courseulles, with an incredible haunted look in his eyes, and finally declaiming before a delirious crowd in Bayeux, conducting them in the *Marseillaise*. De Gaulle is hailed throughout the museum as the embodiment of France, not least by the *sous-prefet* who welcomed him in 1944, narrates the closing video and who was still alive to chair the fiftieth-anniversary celebrations in 1994. The general returned in 1945 to welcome the first deportees to come home from Germany, and again on June 16, 1946, no longer in power, to proclaim his vision of a new constitution.

Place de Gaulle

A monument in **place de Gaulle**, just along from the museum, commemorates the spot where General de Gaulle made his first emotional speech after returning to French soil on June 14, 1944. That visit was a day-trip undertaken in the face of opposition from the Allied commanders; he was so unexpected that the first two civilians he encountered, two policemen wheeling their bicycles, failed to recognize him.

The Musée Mémorial 1944 de la Bataille de Normandie

Daily: May to mid-Sept 9.30am–6.30pm; mid-Sept to April 10am–12.30pm & 2–6pm. 31F.

Set behind massive guns, next to the ring road on the southwest side of town, Bayeux's **Musée Mémorial 1944 de la Bataille de Normandie** is one of the old school of war museums, with its emphasis firmly on hardware rather than humans. Much of its former heavy-handedness seems to have disappeared since the end of the Cold War, and it shows some evocative film footage of the landings, by both sea and air, but nonetheless the obsession with technical minutiae remains a little disconcerting.

By way of contrast, the understated and touching **British War Cemetery** stands immediately across the road (see box on p.122).

Eating

Several of the hotels, most notably the *Notre Dame*, have good restaurants, while the *Family Home* serves a filling and good-value dinner at 8pm each evening, for around 65F; non-guests should phone ahead to reserve a place. Otherwise, most of Bayeux's restaurants are in the rue St-Jean leading east from the river, or near the main door of the Cathedral. Watch out for Sundays: virtually everywhere is shut.

Le Petit Bistrot, 2 rue Bienvenue (☎02.31.51.85.40). Bright-yellow-painted restaurant opposite the cathedral, where the menus from 95F upwards boast a fine assortment of scallops. Closed Sun pm.

Le Petit Normand, 35 rue Larcher (☎02.31.22.88.66). Sixteenth-century house by the cathedral, offering good traditional cooking, with seafood specialities and local cider. Lunch menus from 60F, dinner from 95F. Closed Sept–June Sun pm.

Le Printanier, 2 rue des Bouchers (☎02.31.92.03.01). Good-value if garishly decorated bistro, slightly off the beaten track though very central, which serves inexpensive menus continuously from lunchtime until around 9pm. Closed Sun & Mon am.

La Rapière, 53 rue St-Jean (☎02.31.92.94.79). Probably the most popular traditional choice, housed in the fifteenth-century *Hôtel du Croissant*, down a clearly signed side alley. The cheapest menu is 79F; the next, at 145F, features oysters and skate. Closed mid-Dec to Jan, as well as Tues pm & Wed out of season.

La Table du Terroir, 42 rue St-Jean (☎02.31.92.05.53). A rendezvous for closet meat freaks, tucked away behind a butcher's shop and serving the freshest, bloodiest flesh on a well-judged trio of menus, at 55F, 95F and 135F. Closed Sun pm, & mid-Oct to mid-Nov.

Southwest from Bayeux

Travellers heading **southwest from Bayeux**, towards St-Lô (see p.176), pass close to two remarkable buildings: the Abbaye de Cerisy-la-Forêt and the Château de Balleroy. Neither is easy to get to without transport, but if you have a bike or car they shouldn't be missed.

Cerisy-la-Forêt
CERISY-LA-FORÊT is most pleasurably reached via Le Molay-Littry, which has a **mining museum** and a Raleigh cycle shop. The eleventh-century Romanesque **abbey** (Easter to mid-Nov daily 9am–6.30pm; free; guided tours: Easter–Sept Tues–Sun 10.30am–12.30pm & 2.30–6.30pm; Oct to mid-Nov Sat & Sun 10.30am–noon & 2–6pm; 8F) was founded by William the Conqueror's father on the site of an already venerable monastery. Set on a hill, overlooking an attractive pond just east of the little town, its triple tiers of windows and arches, lapping light onto its cream stone, make you sigh in wonder at the skills of medieval Norman masons.

Sitting in its own spacious grounds between town and abbey, the stately *Château de l'Abbaye* (☎02.33.55.71.73; closed Wed lunch in summer, all day Wed in winter; ⑤) offers luxurious country-house accommodation.

Balleroy
At **BALLEROY**, 8.5km south of Cerisy across the D572, you switch to an era when architects ruled over craftsmen. The main street of the village leads straight to the **château**, masterpiece of the celebrated seventeenth-century architect François Mansard. It stands like a faultlessly reasoned and dogmatic argument for the power of its owners and their class and, suitably enough, its most recent owner was the late American press magnate Malcolm S.Forbes, pal of presidents Nixon, Ford and Reagan, not to mention Elizabeth Taylor. You can tour the house to see its eclectic furnishings, pieces of modern sculpture and an original *salon* – with superb royal portraits by Mignard.

The focus, however, is on Forbes himself. Forbes was an acquisitor untrammelled by financial restraint – he owned the world's largest collection of Fabergé jewelled eggs (which were almost scrambled by a fire early in 1990), and his

Mont-St-Michel

Étretat

Rouen cathedral

Napoleon statue, Cherbourg

Monet's garden, Giverny

Caen

Mussel stall, Portbail

US cemetery, Omaha Beach

Villers-sur-mer

Beuvron-en-Auge

Norman farm

Mulberry harbour, Arromanches

palace in Tangier, containing 100,000 lead soldiers, was the scene of a notoriously extravagant seventieth birthday party. At Balleroy, he created a museum to his principal passion, **ballooning**. It's all a bit absurd, beginning with some interesting history, but degenerating into egomania: photos of Malcolm S.Forbes in various Forbes balloons winning various Forbes prizes (as seen, of course, in his own *Forbes Magazine*). Admission is expensive at 50F, and seems a poor substitute for indulging in the real thing, which unlike, say, running for the US Presidency – his son Steve's bid for world fame in 1996 – is more than a hobby for self-publicizing millionaires (both château and museum open mid-March to mid-Oct, daily except Wed 9am–noon & 2–6pm). Every two years, in the third week of June, Balleroy's magnificent grounds play host to Europe's largest **balloon festival**.

The Cotentin Peninsula

Until Brittany Ferries instigated its direct services to Brittany, the **Cotentin Peninsula**, in the far west of Normandy hard against the frontier with Brittany, provided many visitors with their first taste of western France. Now that Caen too has direct sailings, **Cherbourg** sees only a fraction of the traffic it had twenty years ago, but the rest of the largely rural peninsula remains well worth exploring.

Geographically, this is an area of transition. Little ports such as **Barfleur** on the indented northern headland presage the rocky Breton coast, while inland the meadows resemble the farmlands of the Bocage and the Bessin. The long western flank with its flat beaches serves as a prelude to **Mont-St-Michel**; hill towns such as **Coutances** and **Avranches** contain architectural and historical relics associated with the abbey.

Travelling by bus is not easy in northern Cotentin. Nor is hitching: the local *patois* has a special pejorative word for "stranger", applied indiscriminately to foreigners, Parisians and southern Cotentins alike.

Cherbourg

If the murky metropolis of **CHERBOURG** is your port of arrival in France, the best advice is probably to head straight out and on; the town itself is lacking in interest, and there are some much more appealing places within a very few kilometres to either side. Napoléon inaugurated the transformation of what had been a rather poor, but perfectly situated, natural harbour into a major transatlantic port, by means of massive artifical breakwaters. An equestrian statue commemorates his boast that in Cherbourg he would "recreate the wonders of Egypt". But there are, as yet, no pyramids nearer than the Louvre in Paris, and if you are waiting for a boat the best way to fill time is to settle into a café or restaurant or do some last-minute **shopping**, perhaps picking up some **wine** from the extensive selection at the British-run Maison du Vin, 71 av Carnot (☎02.33.43.39.79).

Cherbourg also boasts some appealing **markets**, held on Tuesday and Thursday around the rue des Halles, and on Wednesday next to the church of St-Pierre. Your best bets for large-scale shopping, however, are the Auchan hypermarket at the junction of RN13 and N13, south of town, or Le Continent, on the southeast corner of the Bassin du Commerce.

As for walking off lunch, the only area that really encourages a ramble is over by the Basilique de la Trinité and the town **beach** – an unexpected pleasure, even

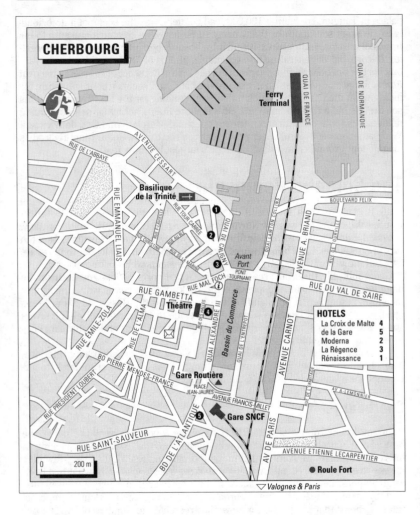

if you wouldn't dream of swimming from it. Over to the south, you could alternatively climb up to **Roule Fort** for a view of the whole port; the fort itself contains a museum of the war and liberation (April–Sept daily 10am–6pm; Oct–March daily except Mon 9.30am–noon & 2–5.30pm; 15F).

Arrival and information

The days of the great transatlantic liners may be over, but several cross-Channel ferry companies still sail into Cherbourg's gare maritime, just east of the town centre (daily 5.30am–11.30pm; ☎02.33.44.20.13). Services from **Portsmouth**, including the new Superstar Express, which takes a mere 2hr 45min for the crossing, are operated by P&O (5–6 daily; ☎02.33.85.65.70), and from **Poole** by Brittany Ferries (1–2 daily; ☎02.33.88.44.88) – Cherbourg is twinned with Poole, hence the British red telephone kiosk on quai de Caligny. Irish Ferries also sail to Cherbourg, from Rosslare (2–4 weekly; ☎02.33.44.28.96).

Cherbourg's **tourist office** is at 2 quai Alexandre III (June–Aug Mon–Sat 9am–6.30pm; Sept–May Mon 1.30–6pm, Tues–Fri 9am–noon & 1.30–6pm, Sat 9am–noon; ☎02.33.93.52.02). In summer there's also a tourist information kiosk at the ferry terminal, open to coincide with sailings (Mon–Fri 5–8.30am & 1.30–8.30pm, Sat 5–8.30am & 1.30–6.30pm, Sun 5–10am & 1.30–6pm). The **post office** is on rue d'Ancien Quai (Mon–Fri 8am–7pm, Sat 8am–noon; ☎02.33. 08.87.01).

The **gare SNCF** (☎02.33.57.50.50), on avenue François-Miller/place Jean-Jaurès, is served by regular trains to Paris, Bayeux and Caen. Buses to Coutances (☎02.33.98.13.38) and St-Lô, Valognes and Barfleur (☎02.33.44.32.22) run from the **gare routière** opposite, which is hidden from view by a building on avenue François-Miller.

Cycles can be rented from Cycles Peugeot-Kerhir, 31 bd Schumann (☎02.33.53.04.38), and Quai 34, 19 quai de l'Abbaye (☎02.33.93.08.98), while Europcar, 4 rue des Tanneries (☎02.33.44.53.85), offer weekend rates on **car rental**.

Accommodation

By the standards of the rest of Normandy, **room** rates in Cherbourg are very reasonable. There's no great reason for ferry passengers to avoid spending a night here – it's a lively enough place to pass an evening – though the crowds and traffic can get a bit much, and for motorists the lack of parking space during the day is a real problem. Few of the hotels, however, bother to maintain their own restaurants.

The local youth hostel has been closed for refurbishment for several years, but the *Foyer des Jeunes Travailleurs*, 33 rue de Maréchal-Leclerc (☎02.33.53.32.47; 70F), just over 1km east of the gare SNCF on bus #8, offers a reasonable equivalent.

The closest **campsite** to the ferry terminal is the *Camping de Collignon*, 3km east towards Barfleur at Tourlaville (May–Sept; ☎02.33.20.16.88).

Hôtel Croix de Malte, 5 rue des Halles (☎02.33.43.19.16, fax 02.33.43.65.66). Simple hotel without restaurant on three upstairs floors, one block back from the harbour and around the corner from the theatre. Clean and recently renovated rooms – all 24 have TV and at least a shower – with the cheapest rates being for the perfectly acceptable ones in the attic. ②.

Hôtel de la Gare, 10 place Jean-Jaurès (☎02.33.43.06.81, fax 02.33.43.12.20). Very convenient for the gares SNCF and routière, if not exactly stunning in itself. ①.

Hôtel Moderna, 28 rue de la Marine (☎02.33.43.05.30, fax 02.33.43.97.37). Rooms ranging from basic to lavish, slightly back from the harbour and tourist office; most have phones, showers and British TV. ①–③.

Hôtel La Régence, 42 quai de Caligny (☎02.33.43.05.16, fax 02.33.43.98.37). Small neat rooms with balconies overlooking the harbour, just around the corner from the tourist office. The restaurant downstairs kicks off with a reasonable 70F menu; it's not the best along the *quai*, but there's something to be said for eating where you sleep. ③.

Hôtel de la Renaissance, 4 rue de l'Église (☎02.33.43.23.90, fax 02.33.43.96.10). Rooms of all kinds, some with sea views, in friendly hotel, facing the port in the most appealing quarter of town – the *Église* of the address is the attractive Trinité. ①.

THE KEARSARGE AND THE ALABAMA

In June 1864, Cherbourg played host to one of the most extraordinary incidents of the **US Civil War** – a pitched **naval battle** between two rival warships, the Union *Kearsarge* and the Confederate *Alabama*.

The **Alabama** had been cruising the Atlantic for the previous year, harassing ships carrying supplies to the northern USA. By the time it docked at Cherbourg, to allow its crew a spell of shore leave and the boat itself a refit, it had captured, destroyed or held to ransom over eighty US merchant vessels. The **Kearsarge**, meanwhile, had been prowling the coasts of Europe in pursuit; **Captain John A. Winslow** heard of the *Alabama*'s arrival while in Amsterdam, and was anchored off Cherbourg within two days.

Both vessels then spent several days preparing for the inevitable duel. **Captain Raphael Semmes** of the *Alabama* – known as "Old Beeswax" on account of his huge pointed moustache – noted in his diary that "the combat will no doubt be contested and obstinate, but the two ships are so evenly matched that I do not feel at liberty to decline it". Cherbourg buzzed with excitement: its hotels filled with eager spectators brought by special trains from Paris, and hundreds more camped along the quaysides.

Sunday being Semmes' lucky day, he ordered the *Alabama* out of the harbour on the morning of Sunday June 12. At first, the *Kearsarge* seemed to retreat; then it turned, and charged the *Alabama* at full steam. The *Alabama* was the first to fire its guns. One shell lodged in the sternpost of the *Kearsarge*, but it failed to explode. Soon, however, a slow but steady barrage from the *Kearsarge* began to pound the *Alabama* to pieces.

To Captain Semmes' bewilderment, the *Alabama*'s shells kept bouncing off the *Kearsarge*. When it later transpired that the *Kearsarge* was lined below the water level with iron chains, he furiously expostulated that "It was the same thing as if two men were to go out and fight a duel, and one of them, unknown to the other, were to put on a suit of mail under his own garment."

Eventually, the doomed *Alabama* attempted to flee. Its escape was cut off, but Semmes himself managed to get away. As his ship went down, he whirled his sword above his head and flung it into the Channel, then leaped into the sea. Together with several members of his crew, he was picked up by a British holiday-maker who had watched the battle from his yacht, and taken to Southampton. Hailed by *The Times* as a "set of first-rate fellows", the defeated Confederates in due course managed to return home.

Captain Winslow – whose ship had suffered just three casualties, as opposed to the *Alabama*'s 43 – brought the *Kearsarge* into Cherbourg harbour after the battle. Their previous Confederate sympathies conveniently forgotten, the local citizens hailed him as a hero, before he made his way to a celebration banquet arranged by the American community in Paris.

Eating

Restaurant options in Cherbourg divide readily into the glass-fronted seafood places along the quai de Caligny, each with its copious *assiette de fruits de mer*, and the more varied, more adventurous and less expensive little places tucked away in the pedestrianized streets and alleyways of the old town.

Café de Paris, 40 quai de Caligny (☎02.33.43.12.36). Work your up through the ranks of *assiettes de fruits de mer*, from the 75F *Matelot* to the *Amiral* at 500F for two; there's also a quick 98F menu if you're in a hurry. Here it's the live lobsters in the fish tanks set into the windows that get the sea views, not you – but the food is excellent.

Café du Théâtre, 8 place de Gaulle (☎02.33.43.01.49). Attractive setup adjoining the theatre, with a café behind plate-glass windows on the ground floor and a full-scale brasserie upstairs, arranged on three sides of the central opening. Very varied menus – not just seafood – from 79F, and much more of a sense than usual of participating in the life of the town.

Le Faitout, 25 rue Tour-Carrée (☎02.33.04.25.04). Basement restaurant in the shopping district that offers traditional French cuisine at very reasonable prices; a bowl of mussels can be had for under 40F, and there's a daily special for 55F. Closed Sun, & Mon lunchtime.

Le Grandgousier, 21 rue de l'Abbaye (☎02.33.53.19.43). The definitive French fish restaurant; the rosy glow starts, but does not end, with the decor. Menus start at 99F, but this is a place to expect to spend a lot and dine well. The waiters share that expectation too – it's amiable enough, but they know their worth. Imagine any combination of fish, throw in a bit of caviar and a few crab claws, and you'll find it somewhere on the menu. Closed Sat lunchtime, Sun pm, and Mon lunchtime in winter.

La Moulerie, 73 rue au Blé (☎02.33.01.11.90). A restaurant solely devoted to the adoration of mussels, served in colossal ceramic bowls with a choice of a dozen wine-based sauces varying from sauerkraut through mustard to cumin, plus chips galore. Prices range from 45F to 60F, and there are set menus at 80F and 120F. You could if you want have a mussel salad to start, a *quiche aux moules*, or even snails for a change, but if you do you'll never finish the main course. Blue checked tablecloths, sailors' costumes, fishing nets . . . an absolute delight. Closed Sun, & Mon lunchtime.

Les Trois Capitaines, 16 quai de Caligny (☎02.33.20.11.66). One of the nicer of the quai de Caligny seafood specialists, with no outside seating but huge plate-glass windows. Two-course menus for 80F, four courses for 130F, with salmon *tartare* and changing daily specials. Closed Mon lunchtime.

East from Cherbourg

East from Cherbourg, the **D901**, which switchbacks through a series of pretty valleys, is the most direct route to the old ports of **Barfleur** and **St-Vaast**. Following the D116 along the coast, however, takes you past a succession of stunning viewpoints – particularly at the **pointe du Brulay** – and some really lovely quasi-fortified villages, shielded from the sea winds by stout stone walls.

Barfleur

The pleasant little harbour village of **BARFLEUR**, 25km east of Cherbourg, was the biggest port in Normandy seven centuries ago. The population has since dwindled from 9000 to 600, and fortunes have diminished alongside – most recently through the invasion of a strain of plankton which poisoned all the mussels. It's now a surprisingly low-key place, whose grey granite quayside and formal main street retain an appealing elegance. Although the sweeping crescent of the main harbour sees little tourist activity, clusters of tiny fishing vessels tie up alongside, and fresh fish is often had for sale.

Barfleur's small **tourist office** (☎02.33.54.02.48) is located near the church at the far left-hand end of the harbour. A lichen-covered rock on the shoreline nearby commemorates the fact that, when William the Conqueror embarked for southern England in 1066, it was in a ship constructed at Barfleur – the *Mora* – and piloted by a Barfleurais, Étienne. On November 25, 1120, his descendant, also called William, set out from here to return home after a visit to France. He was travelling in a separate vessel to his father, Henry I of England: according to a contemporary account, "she flew swifter than the winged arrow, sweeping the rippling surface of the deep; but the carelessness of the intoxicated crew drove her onto a rock, which rose above the waves not far from the shore". William (recently "outed" by historians as being gay) reached the safety of a small lifeboat, but turned back to sea upon hearing the cries of his sister, and was drowned together with 300 of his nobles. Since 1834, the rock upon which they came to grief has been guarded by the **Gatteville lighthouse**, the tallest in France and a pleasant thirty-minute walk north of Barfleur. It was joined in 1865 by France's first lifeboat station, at the start of the path from town.

Barfleur has a fine selection of **hotels**. *Le Conquérant* stands a short distance back from the sea at 16–18 rue St-Thomas-à Becket (☎02.33.54.00.82; closed mid-Nov to mid-March; ②); its nicest rooms face onto a lovely garden courtyard, and there's a summer-only *crêperie*. *Le Moderne* is tucked away south of the main road at 1 place de Gaulle (☎02.33.23.12.44; closed mid-Sept to mid-March; ①–③). Some of the rooms are very inexpensive, while the restaurant is quite superb, with the 150F menu including such treats as a grilled salmon trout stuffed with a salmon soufflé, a traditional blood-rich *coq au vin*, and goats'-cheese *millefeuille*.

St-Vaast

ST-VAAST-LA-HOUGUE, 11km south of Barfleur, is more of a resort, with lots of tiny Channel-crossing yachts moored in the bay where Edward III landed on his way to Crécy. The narrow spit of sand called **La Hougue**, south of the centre, holds various sporting facilities, such as tennis courts and a diving club, although the tip itself is a sealed-off military installation; the fortifications are graceful, courtesy (as ever) of Vauban. The whole area is at its best at high tide; low tide reveals, especially on the sheltered inland side, bleak muddy flats dotted with some of the country's best-loved oyster beds.

In 1692 a French and Irish army gathered at St-Vaast and set sail for Britain in an attempt to restore the deposed Stuart King James II to the English throne. The fleet was, however, destroyed by a combined Anglo-Dutch force, before it could get any further than La Hougue.

That battle took place just off the sandy flat island of **Tatihou**, which now doubles as a bird sanctuary and the location of an ecologically minded Musée Maritime. A limited number of visitors each day are carried across by amphibious mud-wallowing "**ferries**" from St-Vaast; the exact schedule is determined by the state of the tides (May–Sept daily 10am–12.30pm & 2–5pm; Oct–April Sat & Sun 10am–noon & 1.30–5pm; 30F return, or 50F including admission).

The **hotel** *de France et des Fuchsias*, just back from the sea in St-Vaast at 18 rue du Maréchal Foch (☎02.33.54.42.26; closed Mon in winter, & Jan to mid-Feb; ②–⑥), with its splendid gardens, is an ideal stopover for ferry passengers – in fact both it and the annexe at the end of the garden are packed throughout the season with British visitors. The restaurant, too, is excellent, with a 82F weekday menu that features *coquelet à l'orange*, and gourmet four-course dinners at the weekend for 125F. If you can't get a room there, *La Granitière*, down the road at 74 rue du Maréchal Foch (☎02.33.54.58.99; closed mid-Feb to March; ②–⑥), is a very acceptable alternative. It's also possible to stay overnight in some very comfortable rooms on Tatihou island; contact *Accueil Tatihou* (☎02.33.23.19.92; ③).

Valognes

VALOGNES, around 18km through the woods from St-Vaast on the main road south from Cherbourg, is somewhat ludicrously passed off in tourist handouts as "the Versailles of Normandy". The description might have had some meaning before the war, when the region was full of aristocratic mansions, but now only a scattering of fine old houses remain, along with the very scant ruins of a Gallo-Roman settlement called *Alauna*.

All Valognes has to show for itself are a **cider museum** housed in an old water-mill (April–Sept Mon, Tues & Thurs–Sat 10am–noon & 2–6pm, Sun 2–6pm; Oct–March groups by appointment; ☎02.33.40.22.73; 25F), crammed with bizarre old wooden implements and ancient warped barrels – including a particularly obscene example upstairs – a little public garden, and a big empty square, activated only for the Friday **market**. But it's a quiet, convenient alternative to waiting around in Cherbourg, and the country lanes around are enjoyable.

The rambling ivy-coated *Hôtel du Agriculture* at 16 rue L-Delisle (☎02.33.95.02.02; hotel closed Jan & Feb; ①) is the best of several inexpensive **hotels**, and serves top-quality food on menus that start at 75F (restaurant closed Sun pm & Mon).

Ste-Mère-Église

A short way inland from Utah Beach, the westernmost of the main Invasion Beaches, the church of the market town of **STE-MÈRE-ÉGLISE** featured in the film *The Longest Day* – with an unfortunate US paratrooper dangling from its steeple during the heavy fighting. The film was based on fact, and the man in question, John Steele, used to return occasionally to re-enact and commemorate his ordeal. He's now dead, but a uniformed mannequin is permanently entangled on the roof in his stead. The new stained glass above the main door of the church also depicts American parachutists, surrounding the Virgin with Child.

Just behind and to the right of the church, Ste-Mère's approximately parachute-shaped **Musée des Troupes Aéroportées** (Airborne Museum) tells the story of the landings, complete with tanks, jeeps, and even a troop-carrying plane (May to mid-Sept daily 9am–6.45pm; April & second half of Sept daily 9am–noon & 2–6.45pm; Feb, March, & Oct to mid-Nov daily 10am–noon & 2–6pm; mid-Nov to Dec Sat & Sun 10am–noon & 2–6pm; closed mid-Dec to Jan; 20F).

The only accommodation in Ste-Mère-Église is the ugly modern *logis Le Sainte-Mère*, south of the centre at the intersection of the main street with N13 (☎02.33.21.00.30; ③), which offers 75F buffet dinners and set menus from 90F. The small *Café Au Domino* is just outside the museum entrance, facing the church; its outdoor seating makes it a good spot for lunch.

West from Cherbourg

The stretch of coast immediately west of Cherbourg is similar to that to the east, although it holds no harbour town to compare with Barfleur or St-Vaast. The old villages of **Omonville-la-Petite** and **Omonville-la-Rogue**, 20km out of Cherbourg, are lovely places to stroll around, while all the way along you'll find wild and isolated countryside where you can lean against the wind, watch waves smashing against rocks or sunbathe in a spring profusion of wild flowers.

Cap de la Hague and Goury

The real drawback of this area is that the discharges of "low-level" radioactive wastes from the **Cap de la Hague nuclear reprocessing plant** may discourage you from swimming. In 1980, the Greenpeace vessel, *Rainbow Warrior*, chased a ship bringing spent Japanese fuel into Cherbourg harbour. The *Rainbow Warrior's* crew were arrested, but all charges were dropped when 3000 Cherbourg dockers threatened to strike in their support. In the spring of 1985 the French secret service finally took their revenge on the *Rainbow Warrior*, killing a member of the crew. The reprocessing plant would be delighted to welcome you to inspect their facilities (April–Sept Mon–Fri 9am–6pm; 3hr tours, free, minimum age 15; ☎02.33.02.61.04 for reservations). For a full update on the continuing controversies surrounding the plant, see p.366.

The main road, the D901, continues a couple of kilometres beyond the plant to **GOURY**, where the fields finally roll down to a craggy pebble coastline. Almost the only building amid the windswept splendour, the *Auberge de Goury* (☎02.33.52.77.01; closed Sun pm & Mon pm), is a really excellent **restaurant**, facing the octagonal lifeboat station and looking out towards a slate-grey lighthouse. It specializes in charcoal-grilled fish and meat, with a wide-ranging cheeseboard that includes the extraordinary *voluptueuse*, and is (not surprisingly) very popular at lunchtimes.

From the cape of **La Hague** itself, the northern tip of the peninsula, bracken-covered hills and narrow valleys run south to the cliffs of the Nez de Jobourg, claimed in wild local optimism to be the highest in Europe. **South of La Hague**, a great curve of sand – some of it military training ground – takes the land's edge to **FLAMANVILLE** and another nuclear installation.

On the other side, facing north, **PORT RACINE** declares itself rather ludicrously to be the smallest port in France – it consists of one little jetty, some way down a hillside from a tiny and extremely tranquil pension-only hotel, *L'Erguillère* (☎02.33.52.75.31; ④).

Barneville-Carteret

The next two sweeps of beach down to Carteret, with sand dunes like miniature mountain ranges, are among the best **beaches** in Normandy if you have transport and want solitude.

CARTERET itself, sheltered by a rocky headland, is the nearest harbour to **Jersey**, just 25km away across seas made somewhat treacherous by the fast Alderney current. The old port area is not especially attractive, but does have several seafront hotels, including a couple of *logis de France*, the *Hôtel de la Marine* at 11 rue de Paris in the little shopping street (☎02.33.53.83.31; closed mid-Nov to mid-Feb, plus Sun pm & Mon in Feb, March & Oct; ⑤), and the *Hôtel du Cap* on the quayside route de la Plage further out (☎02.33.53.85.59; closed Jan & Feb; ②).

Visitors who prefer to be beside a beach should head instead for the twin community of **BARNEVILLE**, directly across the mouth of the bay but a few kilometres away by road. Here an endless (and quite exposed) stretch of clean firm sand is backed by a long row of weather-beaten villas and the odd hotel, including the *Hôtel les Isles* near the northern end at 9 bd Maritime (☎02.33.04.90.76; closed mid-Nov to mid-Feb; ②), which has a superb restaurant that offers views clear to the Channel Islands on fine evenings.

There are two **campsites** in the dunes north of town, *Le Ranch* at Le Rozel (Easter–Sept; ☎02.33.52.40.09) and *Les Mielles* at Surtainville (☎02.33.04.31.04).

Portbail

Five kilometres further down the coast from Barneville, the dunes are interrupted once again by the broad estuary of the Ollonde River. Set slightly back from the sea, **PORTBAIL** is a delightful village with a sweet little Romanesque church. Its streets are thronged on summer Tuesdays with a bustling **market**, where as well as buying spit-roasted chickens and fresh oysters you can pick up a dining table or have your chairs re-upholstered. Access to two fine beaches is by way of an old stone bridge, beneath which crowds of fishermen wade thigh-deep in the river.

Portbail has a small year-round **hotel** in the main square – *La Galiche*, place E-Laquaine (☎02.33.04.84.18; ①), and a couple of good **restaurants**. Both *La Fringale*, near the start of the bridge (☎02.33.04.87.90), and *Au Rendezvous des Pêcheurs*, almost opposite but slightly closer to the square (☎02.33.04.81.37), specialize in seafood.

Bricquebec

Fifteen kilometres inland from Carteret, halfway to Valognes, the old market town of **BRICQUEBEC** is dominated by the well-preserved twelfth-century castle at its heart. Part of this attractive edifice, centred around a peaceful courtyard, is run as the upmarket *Hôtel-Restaurant du Vieux Château* (☎02.33.52.24.49; ②/④), which has one or two budget rooms. Queen Victoria once stayed here, but unfortunately while the tacky furnishings and slapdash service make it feel at first like a treasurable piece of kitsch, the restaurant is so bad that there's not much point in coming. Across the main square in front of the castle – scene of a busy Monday **market** – the unassuming *Donjon*, 2–4 place Ste-Anne (☎02.33.52.23.15; ②), is by contrast a very welcoming little hotel, with a good bistro restaurant.

Lessay

Heading south from Carteret, the road around the headland joins the main D900 at **LESSAY**, where an important Romanesque monastery stands right in the heart of town. Until the war it was one of the few early Norman churches still intact. When it had to be restored from scratch afterwards, guided by photographs, the job was done using not only the original stone but also the original tools and methods.

The square central tower of Lessay is similar to that which collapsed centuries ago on Mont-St-Michel (see p.147). Monks at the abbey sing Gregorian chants each Sunday, and are very much in evidence at the **Holy Cross Fair** in the first half of September, which also celebrates cattle and other animals (more information from the tourist office on ☎02.33.46.46.18). The town is served by buses en route between Cherbourg and Coutances.

Lessay's tiny aerodrome, south of town, was where **Charles Lindbergh** landed on completing the first transatlantic flight in 1927; the first beach he crossed is now called plage Lindbergh.

Château de Pirou

Off the main coastal road, the D650, roughly 2km south of the junction for Lessay, turns inland a few hundred metres to reach the **Château de Pirou** (July & Aug daily 9am–noon & 2–7pm; April–June & Sept daily 10am–noon & 2–6pm; Oct–March daily except Tues 10am–noon & 2–6pm; 20F). Although you see nothing from the road, once you've passed through its three successive fortified gateways you find yourself confronted by a ravishing little castle. Some historians have suggested that this is the oldest castle in Normandy, dating back to the earliest Viking raids; it's thought to have taken its current form around the twelfth century.

Considering that it was converted into a farm, and then for centuries forgotten and all but submerged in ivy, it remains remarkably complete. Originally built of wood, on the coast, it was later remodelled in stone and now stands encircled by a broad moat, its towers rising sheer from the water. At your own risk, you can pick your way up to the top of the keep and look out over the surrounding fields. In summer, a tapestry depicting the Norman invasion of Sicily is on display in a barn opposite the drawbridge.

Pirou-Plage

Heading towards the sea instead of inland at the turnoff for the Château de Pirou brings you to a dead end in a couple of hundred metres at the tiny community of **PIROU-PLAGE**. When the tide is low, you can see the "*buchôts*", poles used in the cultivation of shellfish, poking up from the six-kilometre strand of sand that stretches away to either side. To sample the local produce, call in at the seafront **restaurant** *de la Mer* (☎02.33.46.43.36).

Feugères and Le Mesnilbus

If you have time, it's worth straying east of the main roads towards Coutances, to spend a while on the **D57**, to enjoy the magnificent countryside. The village square of **FEUGÈRES** is completely taken up by an amazing tangle of warped wood, once some sort of cider press and mill. From there on to tiny **LE MESNILBUS** – where the delightfully rural *Auberge des Bonnes Gens* (☎02.33.07.66.85; closed Sun pm & Mon in low season; ②) offers menus to suit every palate and pocket, as well as arranging **horse-riding** expeditions – the undulating meadows are filled with rich flowers and sleek animals placidly waiting to be eaten.

Coutances

The old hill town of **COUTANCES**, 65km south of Cherbourg and confined by its site to just one main street, has on its summit a landmark for all the surrounding countryside – the **Cathédrale de Notre Dame**, whose twin towers stand in magnificent silhouette against the sky. Essentially Gothic, it is very Norman in its unconventional blending of architectural traditions; Louis XIV's master architect Vauban said the lantern tower must be "the work of a madman". The *sons et lumières*, on Sunday evenings and throughout the summer, are for once a true complement to the light stone building. Also illuminated on summer nights (and left open) are the fountained **Jardins Publiques**, highly formal gardens with smooth rolling lawns, a well of flowers, a fountain of obelisks and an odd ziggurat of hedges. They enclose a small **Musée Municipal** (daily except Tues 10am–noon & 2–6pm), which has a rather dull collection of paintings but a nice line in pretentious art exhibitions.

Practicalities

Coutances's **gare SNCF** (☎02.33.07.50.77), about 1.5km southeast of the town centre (at the bottom of the hill), also serves as the stop for buses heading both north and south. The local **tourist office** is housed in a new wing behind the Hôtel de Ville in place Georges-Léclerc (July & Aug Mon–Sat 10am–1pm & 2–7pm, Sun 3–7pm; Sept–June Mon–Fri 10am–12.30pm & 2–6pm; ☎02.33.45.17.79).

The cream-coloured *Hôtel du Normandie*, behind and below the cathedral at 2 place du Gaulle (☎02.33.45.01.40; closed Sun pm, Mon pm & Fri pm between Sept and mid-May; ①), has the usual assortment of **rooms**, and menus that range from the good-value 53F option (not Sun) to an excellent 95F spread. Not far to the south, the *Hôtel le Champ'bord*, 8 rue de Lycée (☎02.33.45.01.12; ①), offers simple rooms without showers, over a busy bar near St-Pierre church. A better alternative for motorists is the *Relais du Viaduc* (☎02.33.45.02.68; closed Fri pm, plus Sat in low season, and second fortnight of Feb; ②), at 25 av de Verdun – the junction of the D7 and D971, south of town – which can be a little noisy but serves some fine food.

The Manoir de Saussey

Roughly five steep kilometres south of Coutances, up the D7, the **Manoir de Saussey** is a slightly creepy old manor house containing a glass museum and an assortment of venerable furnishings (Easter–Sept daily 2–6.30pm; Oct, Nov & March Sat & Sun 2.30–5pm; 20F). Some of the fragile glassworks on show date back as far as the first century AD, when they were manufactured in the Near East; there are also pieces from sixteenth-century Venice. Outbuildings serve as antique shops, though not all of their bizarre bric-a-brac is for sale, and that which is tends to be very expensive. Visitors are welcome to walk around the lovely gardens without paying the admission fee.

Coutainville

COUTAINVILLE, the nearest resort to Coutances, is crammed in summer with bronzed and glamorous posers and their turbo-charged status symbols. This is an utterly nondescript stretch of coast, where the open sea batters against an endless, featureless beach. Huge tides expose massive sandflats, while behind the line of dunes dull holiday homes are punctuated by the occasional snack bar, campsite or motel.

A long walk south from town, fighting against the wind, brings you to the **Pointe d'Agon** after 3km or 4km, where a lighthouse commands a view of the dune environment at its most ecologically unspoiled.

Coutainville's tiny little centre, out of all proportion to the long strip of coast that comes under its sway, holds the *Hotel Hardy*, 23 av Tourville (☎02.33.47.04.11; closed mid-Jan to mid-Feb, plus Sun pm & Mon in low season; ③), a pleasant little *logis* with high-priced but very good food. Otherwise, there are several shorefront **campsites**, including *Le Martinet* (Easter–Oct; ☎02.33.47.05.20) and *Le Sémaphore* (July & Aug; ☎02.33.47.29.27).

Abbaye de Hambye

What's left of the **Abbaye de Hambye** stands in a very sylvan setting 20km southeast of Coutances (and 10km northwest of Villedieu, see p.180), with little lawns laid out in front, an orchard alongside, and cows grazing in the adjacent meadows (July & Aug daily 10am–noon & 2–6pm, Feb–June & Sept to mid-Dec daily except Tues 10am–noon & 2–6pm; 15F). The abbey, which is very reminiscent of such Yorkshire abbeys as Rievaulx, was constructed as a Cistercian monastery in the second half of the twelfth century, at a time when builders were trembling on the brink of abandoning the Romanesque tradition in favour of the new Gothic style. Much of the structure was quarried for stone and left in ruins after the Revolution; nineteenth-century prints show the walls drowning in rampant ivy. However, the central tower still stands foursquare above the high narrow walls of the nave, and a few delicate buttresses remain in place, the whole ensemble crammed in tight against a wooded hillside and inhabited mostly by crows. Beyond the little exhibition in the entrance room above the ancient gateway, visitors are left to wander around and among the ruins, with an optional pause to examine the rather dull displays of vestments in what was once the lay brothers' dormitory.

A luxurious rural hotel, the *Auberge de l'Abbaye*, is located 100m from the abbey at the turning off the D51 (☎02.33.61.42.19; closed Mon; ③). There being few alternative ways to pass an evening here, its restaurant is available to serve up extravagant gourmet dinners.

Granville

From Coutances, the D971 runs down to the coast at **GRANVILLE**, the Norman equivalent to Brittany's St-Malo, with a similar history of piracy and a severe citadel, the **haute ville**, guarding the approaches to the bay of Mont-St-Michel across from Cancale. Though the most lively town and most popular resort in the area, it simply doesn't match the appeal of its Breton rival, with its nightmarish traffic and hordes of tourists milling around in summer in the vain hope of finding some way of amusing themselves. The great difference between Granville and St-Malo is that here the fortified citadel contains virtually nothing of interest, just three or four long narrow parallel streets of forbidding grey-granite eighteenth-century houses. The views up and down the coast, across to Mont-St-Michel and out to the Îles Chausey, are dramatic, but no more so than in many other towns along the Cotentin coast.

Granville had an unexpected brush with destiny on March 9, 1945, when it was overrun for an hour and a half by German commandos from Jersey, long after the invading Allied forces had swept on to Germany.

Arrival and information

Granville's **tourist office** is down below the citadel at 4 cours Jonville (July & Aug Mon–Sat 9am–7.30pm, Sun 10.30am–12.30pm & 4–6pm; Sept–June Mon–Sat 9am–12.30pm & 2–7pm; ☎02.33.91.30.03). Trains between Paris and Cherbourg arrive well to the east at the **gare SNCF** (☎02.33.50.05.45) on avenue Maréchal-Leclerc, which doubles as the **gare routière** (☎02.33.50.77.89). Several **ferry** operators – listed on p.150 – sail to Jersey, Guernsey and Sark (all around 300F return), or to the Îles Chausey, while in summer Émeraude Lines also run daytrips to St-Malo in Brittany (3–4 weekly in July & Aug only; ☎02.33.50.16.36; 100F return).

Bikes can be rented from the station or Le Coulant on avenue de la Libération, and there's a covered **market** opposite the Mairie on Saturday mornings.

Accommodation

With so many visitors in summer, Granville is a place where it's well worth booking **accommodation** in advance. There are no hotels in the *haute ville*; most of the possibilities are concentrated in the new town, either beneath the walls near the Casino on the seaward side, or near the station. The modern, oceanfront *Centre Regional de Nautisme* (☎02.33.50.18.95; closed Sun in low season), 1km south of the station just south of the town centre, serves as Granville's **youth hostel**. Dorm beds cost 57F, while a private double is 98F; sailing lessons are easy to arrange.

Hotel de la Mer, 74 rue du Port (☎02.33.50.01.86, fax 02.33.50.67.56). Simple hotel in front of the piles of rusting ironmongery of the commercial port, a short walk from the town centre. The restaurant has a dull 85F menu but gets interesting at 110F; there's a small street-side terrace, but you have to sit upstairs to get a view. ③.

Hôtel Michelet, 5 rue Jules-Michelet (☎02.33.50.06.55, fax 02.33.50.12.25). White-fronted hotel, very near the sea and facing towards the high crags of the old town, which offers reasonably well-equipped but rather characterless rooms, and has no restaurant. ①.

Hôtel Normandy Chaumière, 20 rue Paul-Poirier (☎02.33.50.01.71, fax 02.33.50.15.34). Cheerful, very central hotel, set slightly back from (and, oddly, a bit below) a narrow little street in the thick of the new town, not far from the tourist office. Nice menus in the restaurant downstairs start at 99F. Closed Tues pm & Wed out of season. ③.

Hôtel Terminus, 5 place de la Gare (☎02.33.50.02.05). Simple, inexpensive hotel, immediately across from the station. ②.

Eating

Several of Granville's hotels have their own good restaurants, as described above, but where the town really excels is in its selection of waterfront **restaurants**, hard below the citadel walls.

L'Échauguette, 24 rue St-Jean (☎02.33.50.51.87). Cosy, stone-walled old-town *crêperie*, which serves good simple meals, grilled over an open fire. Closed Thurs.

Le Phare, 11 rue du Port (☎02.33.50.12.94). Seafront fish restaurant, facing the small-boat harbour towards the end of the peninsula, which has the standard mussels and *panaché de poissons* on its 86F menu, and an extraordinarily copious *assiette des fruits de mer* on the 138F one. Closed Jan, Tues pm & Wed Sept–June.

Restaurant du Port, 19 rue du Port (☎02.33.50.00.55). Top-quality seafood place, just along from the *Phare* at the small-boat harbour, with a mouthwatering assortment of very fishy menus, and an unbelievably garlicky fish soup as its speciality. Menus range from 69F ("except weekends and off days") up to 185F; 80F gets you six oysters and a plate of paella, while the good-value 125F menu features stuffed oysters and a delicious parcel of duck in Camembert sauce.

The Îles Chausey

Now an uninviting and virtually uninhabited wasteland – though equipped with long beaches of fine sand – the **Îles Chausey** were the site of the quarries which provided the granite that built Mont-St-Michel. They may once have been part of the ancient Forest of Scissy, the rest of which was submerged below the sea twelve centuries ago. There is just one (summer-only) **hotel**, the lonely *Hôtel du Fort et Îles* (☎02.33.50.25.02; closed Mon & Oct–April; ④), which insists on a minimum stay of three nights.

From one to three boats each day run out to the islands from Granville, operated by Jolie France II (March–Dec; ☎02.33.50.31.81) and Émeraude Lines (April–Sept; ☎02.33.50.16.36). The trip takes just under an hour each way, and day returns cost around 92F.

Around Granville

If you prefer to be out of town, the coastal countryside is best to the **north**, although the villages tend to be non-events. As well as the ubiquitous windsurfers, the huge flat sands attract hordes of sand-yachters. Among **accommodation** possibilities, **BRÉVILLE** has the small *Auberge des Quatre Routes*, 2 rue de l'Église (☎02.33.91.91.83; closed first fortnight of Oct; ②), while **COUDEVILLE** has a good campsite on its long beach, the *Dunes* (Easter–Sept; ☎02.33.51.06.07), and a large (and highly unrecommended) hotel in a converted sanatorium, the *Relais des Îles*.

To the south, **JULLOUVILLE** is younger, more upbeat and very tacky, with an endless drag of amusements, fast-food joints and soda bars, while **CAROLLES** has a good beach, but little more; its one hotel is uninviting. However, in the clifftop community of **CHAMPEAUX**, a short steep climb further on from Carolles, the *Hôtel les Hermelles* (☎02.33.61.85.94; closed Tues pm, Wed & all Jan; ④), enjoys a truly spectacular view out across the bay, and has a superb restaurant.

At **ST-JEAN-LE-THOMAS** – which promotes itself as "le Petit Nice de la Manche" but is remarkably *unlike* Nice in that it consists of a single street leading up to a beach – the bay becomes so narrow that at low tide it is possible to walk across to Mont-St-Michel. However, this is not a walk to take on a drunken, or any other, impulse; as the notices advise, "It's dangerous to risk you in the bay during the rising tide. This can surprise you at each time." A special telephone line provides details of the times of the tides, on ☎02.33.50.02.67.

Avranches

AVRANCHES, perched high above the bay on an abrupt granite outcrop, is the nearest large town to Mont-St-Michel. It has always had close connections with the abbey. The Mont's original church was founded by a bishop of Avranches, spurred on by the Archangel Michael, who supposedly became so impatient with the lack of progress that he prodded a hole in the bishop's skull (later gold-plated, it now forms part of the *trésor* of Avranches's St-Gervais basilica). Robert of Torigny, a subsequent abbot of St-Michel, played host in the town on several occasions to Henry II of England, the most memorable being when Henry was obliged, bare-footed and bare-headed, to escape excommunication by doing public penance for the murder of Thomas à Becket, on May 22, 1172.

The arena for Henry's act of contrition was **Avranches Cathedral**, designed by Robert himself, though without expertise; it eventually "crumbled and fell for want of proper support", and all that now marks the site of Henry's humbling is a fenced-off platform.

A more vivid evocation of the area's medieval splendours comes from the illuminated manuscripts, mostly from the Mont, on display in the town **museum** (July & Aug daily 9.30am–noon & 2–6pm; April–June & Sept closed Tues; 9.30am–noon & 2–6pm; 15F).

The ruins of the old **castle** stand high above the tourist office; the highest point of all is the former keep, which, together with the vestiges of a small section of ramparts, is now landscaped into a small garden. From the very top you get long views over Avranches itself, and the Mont away to the west. The terrace of Avranches's large formal public gardens, the **Jardin des Plantes** across town, is another good vantage point for the Mont.

A monument to General George Patton, southeast of the town centre, commemorates the spot where he stayed the night before his crucial Avranches breakthrough, at the end of July 1944. This small plot of land was ceded to the USA, so technically the statue stands on US soil – and literally it does, too, earth having been brought across the Atlantic to create a memorial garden.

Practicalities

In high summer, one **bus** per day runs to Mont-St-Michel from Avranches's **tourist office** at 2 place Général-de-Gaulle (July & Aug daily 9am–8pm; Sept–June Mon–Fri 10am–12.30pm & 2–7pm; ☎02.33.58.00.22). The **gare SNCF** is a long way below the town centre.

Reasonable **hotels** in town include *Le Jardin des Plantes*, 10 place Carnot (☎02.33.58.03.68; ①), which has a good-value basic restaurant, and the *Commerce*, opposite the tourist office at 5 rue du Général-de-Gaulle (☎02.33.58.07.66; ①), where the downstairs restaurant specializes in *choucroute*. The gloriously old-fashioned *Le Croix d'Or*, 83 rue de la Constitution (March–Nov; ☎02.33.58.04.88; ②–④), is significantly more expensive, but it boasts beautiful gardens and absolutely the best **restaurant** in town. There's a lively **market** on Thursdays.

If you're **camping**, a better base for the Mont than Avranches would be the English-owned *La Sélune* site (April–Oct; ☎02.33.60.39.00) at **PONTAUBAULT**, 7km to the south.

Mont-St-Michel

The island at the very frontier of Normandy and Brittany, which for over a millennium has housed – indeed, all but consisted of – the stupendous abbey of **MONT-ST-MICHEL**, was once known as "the Mount in Peril from the Sea". Many were the pilgrims in medieval times who were drowned or sucked under by

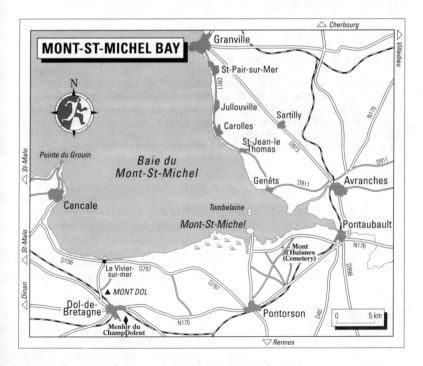

quicksand while trying to cross the bay to this eighty-metre-high rocky outcrop. The Archangel Michael was its vigorous protector, the most militant spirit of the Church Militant, with a marked tendency to leap from rock to rock in titanic struggles against Paganism and Evil.

The abbey dates back to the eighth century, when the Archangel appeared to a bishop of Avranches, Aubert, who duly founded a monastery on the island poking out of the Baie du Mont-St-Michel. Since the eleventh century – when work on the sturdy church at the peak commenced – new buildings have been grafted onto the island to produce a fortified hotchpotch of Romanesque and Gothic buildings, piled one on top of the other and clambering to the pinnacle of the graceful church, to form probably the most recognizable silhouette in France after the Eiffel Tower.

Over the course of its long history, the island has many times been besieged. However, unlike all the rest of northern France, it was never captured, not even when the English had a permanent fort on nearby Tombelaine; it took the Revolution to close it down (and convert it into a prison). Although the abbey was home to a large community – a fortress town – there were never more than forty monks, who said Mass for pilgrims and ran their own school of art. On its thousandth anniversary, in 1966, the Benedictines were invited to return; today, a handful of nuns and monks maintain a presence.

For many years now, the Mont has no longer, strictly speaking, been an island – the causeway (*digue*) that leads to it is never submerged, and is continuing to silt up to either side. Among plans that have recently been under consideration is a proposal that the causeway should be destroyed; tourist numbers would be far easier to control were the abbey to be accessible only by boat.

Arrival and information

Mont-St-Michel has its own **tourist office**, in the lowest gateway (mid-June to mid-Sept Mon–Sat 9am–7pm, Sun 9am–noon & 2–6pm; mid-Sept to mid-June, Mon, Tues & Thurs–Sat 9am–noon & 2–6pm; ☎02.33.60.14.30), and **post office**. In addition to the regular **bus** service from the nearest gare SNCF at Pontorson (see p.149), Les Courriers Bretons (☎02.99.56.79.09) run scheduled services from the gare SNCF in **Rennes** (connecting with the TGV from Paris, departing from Rennes Mon–Fri 9.45am, Sat & Sun 10.50am; last bus back daily 4.10pm), and from **St-Malo** (summer daily 9.30am; winter Wed & Sat 9.30am; last bus back summer Mon–Sat 5.30pm, Sun 4.30pm; winter Wed & Sat 5.30pm). Both cost around 100F return.

Tours

Walking tours across the bay to Mont-St-Michel set off from **Genêts** on a schedule that varies according to the tides. The basic half-day tour, as far as Tombelaine, costs 27F, while an eleven-hour trip, with a full day on the Mont, is 65F. The same operators also run horseback and carriage tours; call ☎02.33.70.83.49 for a full programme.

It's also possible to see the Mont by **helicopter**. Flash Helicoptère (☎02.33.48.51.62) takes off from the village of **Brée**, just west of Pontorson, charging 100F for virtually no time at all, 250F for five minutes, and 550F for a quarter of an hour.

The Island

The base of Mont-St-Michel rests on a primeval slime of sand and mud. Just above that, you pass through the heavily fortified **Porte du Roi** onto the narrow **Grande Rue**, climbing steadily around the base of the rock, and lined with medieval gabled houses and a jumble of overpriced postcard and souvenir shops, maintaining the ancient tradition of prising money out of pilgrims. A plaque near the main staircase records that Jacques Cartier was presented to King François I here on May 8, 1532 and charged with exploring the shores of Canada.

The rather dry **Musée Maritime** offers an insight into the island's ties with the sea, while the Archangel Michael manages in just fifteen minutes to lead visitors on a voyage through space and time in the **Archéoscope**, with the full majestic panoply of multimedia trickery. Further along the Grande Rue and up the steps towards the abbey church, next door to the eleventh-century **church of St-Pierre**, the absurd **Musée Grévin** contains such edifying specimens as a wax model of a woman drowning in a sea of mud (all open Feb to mid-Nov daily 9am–6pm; 75F for all, or 45F each one).

Large crowds gather each day at the **North Tower** to watch the tide sweep in across the bay. During the high tides of the equinoxes (March & Sept), the waters are alleged to rush in like a foaming galloping horse. Seagulls wheel away in alarm, and those foolish enough to be wandering too late on the sands toward Tombelaine have to sprint to safety.

From the **gardens** below the abbey (closed in winter), you can see the giant ramp up the side of the hill, up which prisoners used to haul supplies for the abbey by walking around a treadmill at the top.

The Abbey

The abbey, an architectural ensemble which incorporates the high-spired archangel-topped church and the magnificent Gothic buildings known since 1228 as the **Merveille** ("The Marvel") – incorporating the entire north face, with the cloister, Knights' Hall, Refectory, Guest Hall and cellars – is visible from all around the bay, but it becomes if anything more awe-inspiring the closer you approach. In Maupassant's words:

> I reached the huge pile of rocks which bears the little city dominated by the great church. Climbing the steep narrow street, I entered the most wonderful Gothic building ever made for God on this earth, a building as vast as a town, full of low rooms under oppressive ceilings and lofty galleries supported by frail pillars. I entered that gigantic granite jewel, which is as delicate as a piece of lacework, thronged with towers and slender belfries which thrust into the blue sky of day and the black sky of night their strange heads bristling with chimeras, devils, fantastic beasts and monstrous flowers, and which are linked together by carved arches of intricate design.

The Mont's rock comes to a sharp point just below what is now the transept of the **church**, a building where the transition from Romanesque to Gothic is only too evident in the vaulting of the nave. In order to lay out the church's ground plan in the traditional shape of the cross, supporting crypts had to be built up from the surrounding hillside, and in all construction work the Chausey granite has had to be sculpted to match the exact contours of the hill. Space was always limited, and yet the building has grown through the centuries, with an architectural ingenuity that constantly surprises in its geometry – witness the shock of emerging into the light of the cloisters from the sombre Great Hall.

Not surprisingly, the building of the monastery was no smooth progression; the original church, choir, nave and tower all had to be replaced after collapsing. The

---

VISITING MONT-ST-MICHEL

Access to the **island** of Mont-St-Michel is free and unrestricted, although there's a 15F fee to **park** on either the causeway or the sands below it (which are submerged by the tides). If you're visiting by car in summer, it's best to park on the mainland well short of the Mont, both to enjoy the walk across the causeway and to avoid the dense traffic jams. It also pays to **get there early**, before the tour parties arrive.

Between May and September, the **abbey** is open daily from 9am to 5.30pm; from October to April, it's open daily from 9.30am until 4.30pm. It's **closed** on Jan 1, May 1, Nov 1, Nov 11 and Dec 25. Paying the standard 40F **admission fee** – ages 12–25 25F, under-12s free – entitles you to wander the generally accessible areas, and to join an expert-led **guided tour** in the language of your choice. Tours last 45min between mid-June and mid-Sept, and a full hour the rest of the year; the daily schedule for each language is displayed at the entrance. There are also a number of more detailed **two-hour tours**, in French only, which take you both higher and deeper and cost 65F (ages 12–25 45F). **Mass** is said at 12.15pm every day, with a nursery provided below for children under eight years old.

In summer, the Mont reopens to visitors at **night** (mid-April to May Fri & Sat 10pm–1am; June–Aug daily except Mon 10pm–1am; last admission midnight; Sept daily except Mon 9.30pm–midnight; last admission 11pm; 60F, ages 12–25 50F). This experience is promoted as **Les Imaginaires**. Visitors are free to wander at their own pace through 24 rooms, each of which is illuminated and has music playing. Particularly after midnight, when most of the visitors have gone, it's an incredibly atmospheric way to explore the abbey, with sound echoing through its ancient chambers and a musty subterranean feel to the lower rooms that conjures up thousand-year-old ghosts. On a stormy night it's unforgettable.

---

style of decoration has varied, too, along with the architecture. That you now walk through halls of plain grey stones is a reflection of modern taste, specifically that of the director of the French Department of Antiquities. In the Middle Ages, the walls of public areas such as the refectory would have been festooned with tapestries and frescoes, while the original coloured tiles of the cloisters have long since been stripped away to reveal bare walls.

To get a clearer sense of the abbey's historical development, be sure to take a look at the intriguing scale models in the reception area, which depict it during four different epochs.

Accommodation and eating

The island holds a surprising number of **hotels** and **restaurants**, if nothing like enough to cope with the sheer number of visitors. Most are predictably expensive, though virtually all the hotels seem to keep a few cheaper rooms (presumably there just isn't the space to refit and expand them in order to put the prices up); all charge extra if you want to enjoy a view of the sea.

The most famous **hotel**, *La Mère Poulard* (☎02.33.60.14.01; ④–⑨), uses the time-honoured legend of its fluffy omelettes, as enjoyed by Leon Trotsky and Margaret Thatcher (not simultaneously), to justify extortionate charges. Higher up the Mont, however, prices fall to more realistic levels. The very cheapest options are the *Crêperie la Sirène* (☎02.33.60.08.60; ②), and the *Du Guesclin*

(☎02.33.60.14.10; closed mid-Nov to mid-March; ③), where all the rooms have TV, but the restaurant, without outdoor seating, is almost unique in Normandy in deserving to be called bad. Both the *Hôtel La Croix Blanche* (☎02.33.60.14.04; closed mid-Nov to mid-Dec; ⑤) and the *Mouton Blanc* (☎02.33.60.14.08; closed Jan; ④) serve much better food, in both cases with basic menus for around 76F and more attractive options for 100F and upwards. Every restaurant on the island seems to serve its own version of the *Mère Poulard* omelette as a budget alternative.

In addition, the main approach road to the island, the D976, is lined shortly before the causeway by around a dozen large and virtually indistinguishable hotels and motels, each with its own brasserie or restaurant. Typical among these are the *Motel Vert* (☎02.33.60.09.33; closed mid-Nov to mid-Feb; ③); the *Hôtel Formule Verte* (☎02.33.60.14.13; closed mid-Nov to mid-Feb; ③); and the *Hôtel de la Digue* (☎02.33.60.14.02; closed mid-Nov to mid-March; ④). The 350-pitch *Camping du Mont-St-Michel* (mid-Feb to mid-Nov; ☎02.33.60.09.33) is also on the mainland just short of the causeway.

Pontorson

Most visitors to Mont-St-Michel find themselves lodging either at Avranches or **PONTORSON**, 6km inland. The latter has the nearest **gare SNCF**, connected to the Mont by an overpriced bus service (35F day return), but also (as ever) renting out cycles. Nothing much about Pontorson itself is worth staying for, although the café attached to the station isn't bad.

The **hotels** are not especially interesting, but both the *Montgomery*, 13 rue du Couesnon (☎02.33.60.00.09; closed Nov–March; ③), and the *Le Bretagne*, 59 rue du Couesnon (☎02.33.60.10.55; closed Mon & mid-Jan to mid-Feb; ③), along the main road, have very distinguished restaurants. At the western end of the central drag, the *Tour Brette*, 8 rue de Couesnon (☎02.33.60.10.69; ②), is a friendly and inexpensive *logis* with good lunch menus from 59F. The cheapest budget alternative is the *Hôtel de France et Vauban*, 50 bd Clemenceau (☎02.33.60.03.84; ①), which oddly consists of two formerly separate hotels on either side of the level crossing beside the station; across from the *Vauban*, the *Relax* is a late-opening, youthful bar, with a pool table. An IYHF **youth hostel** stands near the cathedral, a kilometre west of the station, in the *Centre Duguesclin* on rue Général-Patton (Easter to mid-Sept; ☎02.33.60.00.18); dorm beds cost 43F per night.

Along the bay

The most direct **route from Pontorson to the Mont** runs alongside the River Couesnon, which marks the Normandy–Brittany border. The sands at the mouth of the Couesnon are those from which Harold can be seen rescuing two floundering soldiers in the Bayeux Tapestry, in the days when he and William were still getting on with each other. The sheep that graze on the scrubby pastures of the marshes at the sea's edge provide meat for the local delicacy, *mouton pré-salé*.

A more roundabout road to the abbey can take you to the **German war cemetery** at **MONT D'HUISNES**, a grim and unforgettable concrete mausoleum on a tiny hill (see p.122).

travel details

Trains

From Trouville-Deauville to Lisieux (20min) and Paris (2hr); about 6 daily out of season and much more frequently in summer; service extends to **Villers**, **Houlgate** and **Dives-Cabourg** (40min from Trouville) on Sundays and holidays throughout the year, and daily in July & Aug.

From Caen at least hourly to Paris-St-Lazare (2hr); 4 daily to Rennes (3hr) via Bayeux (20min), St-Lô (50min), Coutances (1hr 15min) and Pontorson (2hr); 9 daily to Le Mans (2hr) and Tours (2hr 30min), via Argentan (50min) and Alençon (1hr 15min); frequently to Tours (3hr) and Rouen (2hr); hourly to Lisieux (30min); hourly to Cherbourg (1hr 15min), via Bayeux (20min) and Valognes (1hr).

From Cherbourg 10 daily to Paris (3hr 10min) via Valognes (20min) and Caen (1hr 15min).

From Granville frequently to Paris (3hr 30min) and Cherbourg (1hr); 8 daily to Coutances (30min).

From Coutances 2 daily to Cherbourg (1hr).

Buses

Much the most useful network in Lower Normandy is **Bus Verts** *(11 rue des Chanoines, Caen;* ☎*02.31.44.77.44). Contact them for details of the* Carte Plus *and* Carte Liberté *discount passes for regular passengers; however, bear in mind that the frequencies which follow apply to school periods only, and fewer services tend to run in July & August (let alone on Sundays).*

From Caen to Le Havre (2 daily; 1hr 25min) via Honfleur (55min); bus #20 to Cabourg (14 daily; 40min), Deauville (1hr) and Honfleur (1hr 30min); bus #36 to Pont L'Évêque (3 daily; 45min); to Ouistreham (12 daily; 20min), Lion, Courseulles and Arromanches; bus #30 to Bayeux (3 daily; 50min) and Carentan (2 daily; 1hr 15min); bus #32 to Vire (connections for Brittany; 2–5 daily; 1hr 30min); bus #34 (3–5 daily) to Thury-Harcourt (40min) and Clécy (50min); bus #35 to Falaise (5–6 daily; 50min).

From Bayeux bus #70 (3 daily) to Port-en-Bessin (25min) and Grandcamp-Maisy (1hr); bus #74 (2 daily) to Arromanches (25min) and Courseulles (50min); to Balleroy (30min) and St-Lô (50min).

From Arromanches to Pointe du Hoc (1 daily; 1hr).

From Mont-St-Michel to St-Malo (1–2 daily; 1hr 15min); to Rennes (1–2 daily; 1hr 20min).

Ferries

From Caen (**Ouistreham**) Brittany Ferries to Portsmouth (2–3 daily; 6hr), ☎02.31.36.36.36. See details on p.3.

From Cherbourg Brittany Ferries to Poole (1–2 daily; 4hr 30min), ☎02.33.88.44.68; P&O to Portsmouth (5–6 daily; 2hr 45min to 4hr 45min), ☎02.33.85.65.70; Irish Continental to Rosslare (17hr), ☎02.33.44.28.96. Further details on all these services can be found on p.3 onwards.

From Granville to Jersey, Guernsey and the Îles Chausey. Jolie France, ☎02.33.50.31.81; Emeraude Lines, ☎02.33.50.16.36; Channiland, ☎02.33.51.77.45.

Planes

From Cherbourg Aurigny-Air-Service to Jersey, Guernsey and Aurigny; Air Camelot to Bournemouth, Bristol and Exeter. Both from Maupertus Airport, ☎02.33.22.91.32.

CHAPTER THREE

FROM THE SEINE TO THE BOCAGE: INLAND NORMANDY

I t's hard to pin down specific highlights in **inland Normandy**. The pleasures lie not so much in sights, or individual towns, as in the feel of the
landscapes – the lush meadows, orchards and forests of the Norman countryside. And, of course, in the **food**, always a major motivation in these rich
dairy regions. To the French, the **Pays d'Auge**, **Calvados** and the **Suisse
Normande** are synonymous with cheeses, creams, apple and pear brandies,
and ciders.

However, the territory is not exactly devoid of other sensory pursuits. There
are spas, forests, rivers and lakes for lazing or stretching the muscles in, and,
everywhere, classic half-timbered houses and farm buildings. If you are staying
on the Norman coast, trips inland – even just ten to twenty kilometres – will show
rewards, while if you arrive at a Norman port intending to head straight for
Brittany or southern France you may find yourself tempted to linger, or at least to
take a circuitous route.

Travelling from **east to west**, you pass through a succession of distinct
regions. **South of the Seine**, a natural target from Le Havre, Dieppe or Rouen,
are the **river valleys** of the **Eure**, **Risle** and **Charentonne**. While certain areas
– especially along the Charentonne – have been disfigured by industrial development, the valleys remain for the most part rural and verdant. The occasional

---

ACCOMMODATION PRICE CODES

All **hotel prices** in this book have been coded using the symbols below. The price
shown is for the least expensive double room in high season, which for categóry ①
often means a room without shower, bath and toilet. Most hotels in that category
have other rooms with en-suite facilities, which typically cost 30–50F extra.

For a full explanation see p.30.

① Under 160F	③ 220–300F	⑤ 400–500F	⑦ 600–700F
② 160–220F	④ 300–400F	⑥ 500–600F	⑧ 700F and over

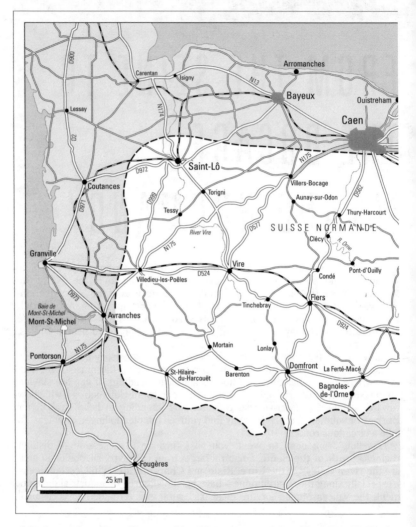

château, castle ruin or abbey provides a focus, most memorably at **Bec-Hellouin**, near Brionne, and at the country town of **Conches**. Further south lie the wooded hills and valleys of **the Perche**, home of the mighty Percheron horse and also of the original Trappists.

Following the rivers northwest, on the other hand, as they head towards the sea near Honfleur or Cabourg, brings you into the classic cheese and cider country of the **Pays d'Auge**, all rolling pastoral hills, grazing meadows and orchards, where **Livarot**, **Pont l'Évêque** and **Camembert** are renowned throughout the world for their cheeses, and **Lisieux**, as the home less than a century ago of Ste Thérèse, has become one of the major pilgrimage towns of France. To the **south**

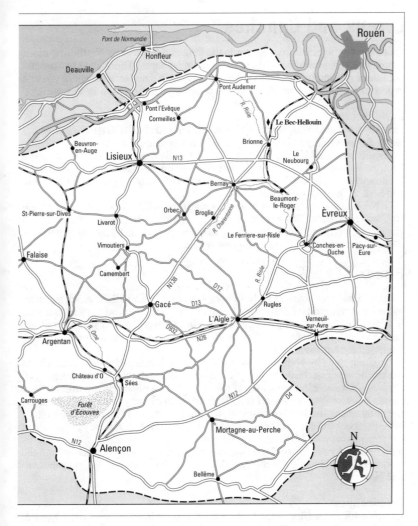

of the Pays d'Auge extend the forests of the **Parc Naturel Régional de Normandie-Maine**, with the sedate and famous spa at **Bagnoles** and the national stud at **Le Pin**.

Further west, on the routes inland from Caen or from Cherbourg and the Cotentin, there is something of a shift. Around Thury-Harcourt and stretching south to Pont d'Ouilly and Putanges is the area dubbed the **Suisse Normande**, for its "alpine" valleys and thick woods; fine walking country, if not genuinely mountainous. To its west is the **Bocage**, which begins with grim memories of war around **St-Lô** – this was the main 1944 invasion route – but subsides into a pastoral scene once more as you hit the gastronomic centres of the **Vire**.

Évreux and Conches

South across the Seine from Rouen is the long and featureless **Neubourg plain** – intensive agricultural land where the crumbling barns, Tudor-style houses and occasional grazing horses look oddly out of place. It's not an area where you can expect to find hidden charms; far better to press on to **Conches** or **Verneuil**.

Le Neubourg

The only town of any size on the Neubourg plain is **LE NEUBOURG** itself, which blows any possibility of being charming by festooning its streets with deafening loudspeakers. It holds little of interest to the traveller, but, 4km northwest on the D83, the seventeenth-century **Château du Champ-de-Bataille**, with its dramatic entrance arch, is worth a look (May to mid-Sept daily 2–6pm; March, April & mid-Sept to Dec Sat & Sun only).

Le Neubourg does hold a very good **restaurant** – the *Côté Jardin*, at 10 rue du Dr-Couderc(☎02.32.35.81.89; closed Sun pm & Mon) – but it's short on interesting hotels; **bed and breakfast** at *La Bergerie* (☎02.32.35.86.28; ③), a *chambre d'hôte* 6km away in Marbeuf, is the best option.

Évreux

Twenty kilometres south of Le Neubourg you come to **ÉVREUX**, which is capital of the Eure *département* despite not being on the Eure River itself. It's an extremely venerable place that throughout history has suffered violent reversals of fortune – as early as the fifth century its affluent Gaulish community made an inviting target for rampaging Vandals.

Bombing raids by both sides during World War II reduced much of the city to rubble, however, and Évreux today is almost disconcertingly lifeless. Even so, an afternoon's wander in the vicinity of the cathedral – a minor classic with its flamboyant exterior decoration and original fourteenth-century windows – and along the ramparts by the Iton riverbank is pleasant enough. In January 1995, Évreux's bishop, Jacques Gaillot, was dismissed by the pope for his advocacy of the use of condoms to prevent AIDS, and his statement that "homosexuals will precede us into the kingdom of heaven". Demonstrations on his behalf took place around the world, and he subsequently set himself up on the Internet as the world's first virtual bishop.

Practicalities

Évreux's **tourist office** is at 1 place de Gaulle (Mon–Sat 9.30am–12.30pm & 2–6.15pm; ☎02.32.24.04.43). Many of the cheaper hotels are shut during August, and in any case there is no great reason to stay. The old *Biche*, at 9 rue St-Joséphine on place St-Taurin at the edge of town (☎02.32.38.66.00; ①), is, however, a strange but splendid Belle-Époque structure that remains open all summer, with a lurid pink interior, a triangular dining room and even some triangular bedrooms. In its restaurant (closed Sun pm), 135F buys you a magnificent meal of oysters braised in cider and a garlicky seafood *pot au feu*, to the musical accompaniment of an unlikely assortment of funk and disco classics. In the heart of town, the *Français* on place Clemeceau (☎02.32.33.53.60) is a fine traditional brasserie.

Perhaps a more enticing prospect than a night in Évreux, however, would be to continue as far as **PACY-SUR-EURE**, 13km east, where the *Hôtel de l'Étape* (☎02.32.36.12.77; ③) nestles at the water's edge.

Conches-en-Ouche

Everybody you meet in Normandy seems to recommend **CONCHES-EN-OUCHE** – both for the town and for the forest around. The town stands above the Rouloir River on a spur so narrow and abrupt that the railway line is forced to tunnel right beneath its centre. Arriving, you're barely aware that the place exists at all; all you see is the cutting, deep into the hill.

On the highest point of the spur, in the middle of a row of medieval houses on the main rue Ste-Foy, is the **church of Ste-Foy**, its windows a sequence of Renaissance stained glass. Opposite is an interesting ironmongery shop, full of old-style metal jewellery; the town was once renowned for its foundries, which cast the iron spire of Rouen Cathedral in 1876. Behind, in the gardens of the **Hôtel de Ville**, a robust, if anatomically odd, stone boar gazes proudly out over a spectacular view, raising its eyes to the horizon far beyond the sewage works.

Next to the town hall, you can scramble up the slippery steps of the ruined twelfth-century **castle**, one of the many haunts of the ubiquitous Bertrand du Guesclin and twice captured by the English during the Hundred Years' War. Such sights ensure that Conches remains firmly rooted in the past, but the town is given an added contemporary flavour, too, by the pieces of modern sculpture that you come upon round seemingly every corner.

On the other side of the main road from the castle, you'll find a long and subtly formal **park**, with parallel avenues of trees, a large ornamental lake and fountain.

Practicalities

Full information on Conches's tourist facilities is available from the **tourist office** in the place Aristide-Briand (July & Aug Tues 2–6pm, Wed–Sat 10am–12.30pm & 2–6pm, Sun 10am–noon; ☎02.32.30.76.42). The **hotel** *Grand'Mare*, in a green and quiet location beside the park at 13 av Croix de Fer (☎02.32.30.23.30; ①), serves up enjoyable dinners in its restaurant, including a good 98F menu with oxtail braised in sherry and some fruit desserts; the *Bistro* in the same building is a less formal place to have lunch. Other accommodation options include the half-timbered *Donjon*, bulging out of the main street on the castle side, not far from the church (☎02.32.30.04.75; closed Tues pm & Wed; ②).

The finest **restaurant** in Conches is commonly acknowledged to be the *Toque Blanche*, towards the north end of town at 18 place Carnot (☎02.32.30.01.54), where 98F goes a very long way and they do good-value weekday lunches. There's also a **municipal campsite**, *La Forêt* (April–Sept; ☎02.32.30.22.49), and on Thursday the whole town is taken up by a **market**.

The Forêt de Conches

The **Forêt de Conches** is a wild and open woodland. If you feel the need for a direction in your wanderings, head for the village of **LA FERRIÈRE-SUR-RISLE**, where there's an especially beautiful church, with a garish altar but some fine wooden statues, and a restored fourteenth-century covered market hall. Paddocks and meadows lead down to the river, while on the single, very quiet, street you'll find a small and inviting **hotel**, the *Vieux-Marché* (☎02.32.30.70.69; ②), with a daily set menu at 56F.

Verneuil-sur-Avre

Southwest of Conches, the towns of Rugles and L'Aigle are both industrial and uninteresting. However, 25km due south on the D840 you come to the pretty little hilltop town of **VERNEUIL-SUR-AVRE**. This now marks nothing more significant than the transition from the Ouche to the Perche, but during the Hundred Years' War it was a crucial fortified outpost between (English-held) Normandy and France proper. Traces of its former ramparts and deep moat can still be seen along boulevard Casati on the west side of town, while the three main streets and numerous alleyways are lined with venerable half-timbered houses.

As you approach along the arrow-straight D840 from the north, the solid bell tower of **La Madeleine** is perfectly framed for several kilometres' distance by the avenue of trees. The actual church of La Madeleine to which it is somewhat inelegantly attached stands in the main square, completely dwarfed by the belfry. A walk down pedestrian lanes to the south brings you out at the Notre Dame church, built of crude red agglomerate stone in the twelfth century.

Practicalities

Verneuil's **gare SNCF**, five minutes' walk north of the centre, is served by four daily trains from Paris. At no. 89 on the main place de la Madeleine, the *Hôtel Le Saumon* (☎02.32.32.02.36; ②) is a cream-coloured *logis* where a tankful of live lobsters nervously await patrons of the more expensive menus; in midweek especially, the lower-priced menus are very good value, with a 65F option that consists of a buffet of *hors d'oeuvres*. The rooms in the main building are the most luxuriously appointed, and the breakfasts are consistently large. The *Hôtel Le Clos*, at 98 rue de la Ferté-Vidame (☎02.32.32.21.81; closed mid-Dec to mid-Jan; ⑨), is a bizarre little château near the Notre Dame church, and has an even better restaurant and phenomenally expensive rooms.

The **tourist office** (Mon 2–6pm, Tues–Fri 10am–noon & 2–6pm, Sat 10am–noon; ☎02.32.32.17.17), virtually next door to the *Saumon*, has details of occasional guided tours of the belfry. Nine kilometres southwest of Verneuil is the glass-covered dome of a family holiday complex run by Center Parcs (based in Paris: ☎02.42.18.12.12).

The Perche

All roads south of Verneuil start to undulate alarmingly as you enter the region known as the **Perche**. This holds some of Normandy's most bucolically appealing countryside, with green valleys nestled between heavily forested hills. Despite its apparent fertility, however, it has never been a particularly rich area: in the seventeenth century, times were hard enough for a large proportion of the population to emigrate to Canada. It is, however, well-known for the mighty **Percheron horses**, the strongest work horses in the world, while its remoteness and seclusion made it an ideal home for the first **Trappist** monks, who took their name from the Forêt de la Trappe.

THE TRAPPISTS

The **Abbaye de la Trappe** is set in open rolling fields on the fringes of the Forêt de la Trappe, just beyond a popular fishing lake and 10km north of Mortagne. This was the original home of one of the world's most famous – yet deliberately self-effacing, and consistently misunderstood – Christian monastic orders. Although the abbey was founded in the thirteenth century, and suffered the vicissitudes of the Hundred Years' War, it was not until the reforms instigated by the **Abbé Rancé** in 1664 that its monks began to follow the principles for which the Trappists are known today. The Abbé reacted against the excesses of his time by setting out to recreate the lives of the "**Desert Fathers**" of the first few centuries after Christ, who lived in contemplative isolation in the Sinai, and to follow St Benedict's precept that true monks should live by the labour of their own hands.

The monks were driven out by the Revolution, successively to Switzerland, Poland, Russia and as far as the United States, but succeeded in returning to their utterly devastated abbey in 1815, still under the leadership of Dom Augustin l'Estrange – which made them the only order of monks in France not to be wiped out.

The abbey as it exists today is entirely a nineteenth-century creation. The monks live communally – they don't have individual cells – and not literally in the absolute silence of popular myth, but speaking only for the necessities of work and community life and spending the rest of their time in quiet reflection. Not surprisingly, tourists are not encouraged to disturb them, but anyone with a genuine interest can watch a video in a reception room beside the main entrance. There's also an unusual **shop** (Mon–Sat 10am–noon & 2.30–6pm, Sun after 10am Mass until noon & 2.30–6.30pm) which sells all things monk-made: herbal teas, muesli, metal polish, shampoo, furniture wax; even local *boudin* and coffee grown in Cameroon.

Mortagne-au-Perche

The largest town of the Perche region stands on a hill set in the heart of the forests. **MORTAGNE-AU-PERCHE** has lost virtually all of its fortifications, but it remains an appealing country town, with a pleasant ensemble of stone town houses. The one part of the ramparts to survive is the **Porte St-Denis**, a fifteenth-century arch topped in the sixteenth century by two ordinary storeys of rooms that now contain an exhibition about Percheron horses.

Mortagne's liveliest square is the **place de Gaulle**, where the nineteenth-century market hall has been imaginatively converted into a cinema, with some post-modern spiral staircases attached to either side, and also holds the local tourist office. Nearby stands an unusual modern fountain, looking like an open mummy case made of copper, with bright starlight shining in its velvet-painted interior, standing on its end in a pool of turquoise water. Cross from here to the gardens of the Town Hall for fine views over the Perche hills.

Practicalities

Mortagne's former market hall, described above, is also the site of the local **tourist office** (Mon 10am–12.30pm & 2.30–6pm, Tues–Sat 9.30am–12.30pm & 2.30–6pm; ☎02.33.85.11.18). The nicest **hotel** in town has to be the *Hôtel du Tribunal*, a *logis* on the sleepy little tree-lined place du Palais (☎02.33.25.04.77; ③), which consists of two or three old stone buildings with a few exposed timbers, crammed together on the corner of an alleyway leading to Porte St-Denis. This is where Yves Montand chose to stay when filming locally; the comfortable bedrooms are in an annexe at the back, while the restaurant at the front has a reasonable 85F menu and gets exotic if you pay more, with such dishes as scallops in orange butter.

The *Genty-Home*, just off place de la République at 4 rue Notre-Dame (☎02.33.25.11.53; ②), has a handful of very plush rooms upstairs and a couple of restaurants downstairs; one serving formal menus from 100F, and the less formal *Grillade* alongside. Both serve Mortagne's speciality – the black *boudin noir*, a crumbly black pudding or blood sausage with a healthy dose of fat and tripe thrown in.

Bellême

Tiny **BELLÊME**, 17km due south of Mortagne on the switchback D938, is actually the capital of the Perche despite being very much smaller. In many ways it's more attractive, too, crammed so tightly onto the top of a sharp hill that the views are consistently superb. Here too hardly anything survives of the fortifications that once ringed the very crest of the hill. The one exception is the forbiddingly thick **Porche** – now the home of the local library, but still equipped to take a portcullis if things turn bad – reached by an alleyway leading off from a corner of the place de la République near the St-Sauveur church.

Practicalities

The grand white façade of Bellême's best **hotel**, the *Relais St-Louis*, 1 bd Bansard-des-Bois (☎02.33.73.12.21; closed Sun pm & Mon in low season; ③), may be in a slight state of disrepair, but it's elegant enough inside, with its light dining room looking out on one side to a flowery garden, and across the town's diminutive ring road on the other to a small vestige of moat overlooked by an imposing eighteenth-century mansion. There's also a tiny municipal **campsite** on the edge of town (mid-April to mid-Oct; ☎02.33.73.07.69).

The new **tourist office** (☎02.33.73.09.69), all but next door to the *Relais St-Louis* (as is a miniature golf course), can provide details of Bellême's annual five-day Mycology Festival, held late each September to celebrate the obscurer mushrooms of the surrounding forests.

The Charentonne and the Risle

The **River Risle** drains down from the Ouche region, north of the Perche, and passing at first through traditional and now very faded ironworking towns such as L'Aigle. Roughly 30km northwest of Conches, it's joined by a fast-flowing tributary, the **Charentonne**. In the area to either side of the confluence, and from then on northwards as the newly strengthened Risle heads towards the sea near Honfleur, several small riverside towns are worth visiting.

Broglie

The southernmost town of any size along the Charentonne is **BROGLIE**, 12km west of Orbec (see p.164). The impressive private **château** that stands on the brow of the hill above Broglie is the ancestral home of the de Broglie family. Its last but one owner, Prince Louis, won the Nobel Physics Prize for demonstrating that matter, like light, has wavelike properties. His work – to "seek the last hiding places of reality", as he put it – subsequently formed the foundation of the whole discipline of quantum mechanics. Originally a medieval historian, Louis was supposed to have been attracted to his great theory "purely on the grounds of intellectual beauty".

Downstream from Broglie

Immediately **downstream from Broglie**, the Charentonne sprawls between its banks on a wide flood plain. It is classic inland Normandy, uneventful and totally scenic; the one flaw in the whole thing is the unseemly preponderance of porcelain donkeys in people's front gardens.

At **ST-QUENTIN-DES-ISLES**, halfway along the valley, old houses are overshadowed by a derelict sawmill, which looms like a primordial swamp monster from among the riverside willows, in a dripping bulk of red ivy. A couple of kilometres north of St-Quentin on the D33, the sixteenth-century riverside windmill *Moulin Fouret* (☎02.32.43.19.95; closed Sun pm & Mon; ③), is primarily a restaurant, with menus from around 100F, but also has a few rooms, making it the nicest place to **stay** in the vicinity.

Bernay

As you approach **BERNAY**, 11km northeast of Broglie, more and more factories and warehouses line both sides of the river. The town itself, however, has a few humpback footbridges and picturesque half-timbered old streets interspersed between the more serious traffic routes, and one of those churches typical of the region with a spire that looks like a stack of inverted octagonal ice-cream cones. Work has been in progress to restore the ancient **abbey church** for years – it should look good when it is finished.

Bernay has few other claims to renown, though one of its bakers has found fame for *running* each stage of the Tour de France during the night before the cyclists race over it. The *Lion d'Or*, at 48 rue Général-de-Gaulle (☎02.32.43.12.06; closed Mon lunchtime, plus Sun pm in winter; ③), is a conventional, good-quality **hotel-restaurant** in the heart of town.

Beaumont-le-Roger and Serquigny

BEAUMONT-LE-ROGER is set beside the Risle 25km northwest of Conches and 17km east of Bernay, shortly before the Risle meets the Charentonne. Its ruined thirteenth-century priory church is gradually crumbling to the ground, the slow restoration of one or two arches unable to keep pace. Little happens in the village beyond the hourly hammering of the church bell – next door to the abbey – by a nodding musketeer; and with each passing hour, the ruins crumble a little more. Just across the Risle from here, on the D25 near Le Val-St-Martin, huge stables are spread across an absurdly sylvan setting, and horses are available for rent.

Beaumont-le-Roger is not exactly an exciting place to stay, but it is home to a sixteenth-century **coaching inn** with some quiet courtyard rooms – the *Lion d'Or*, 91 rue St-Nicolas (☎02.32.45.25.99; closed last two weeks July, first week Aug; ③) – and also a top-quality and very friendly **restaurant**, *La Calèche*, nearby at 54 rue St-Nicolas (☎02.32.45.25.99; closed Wed), which offers menus from 90F.

At **SERQUIGNY**, not only the two rivers but also several roads and rail lines converge, and the banks are once again briefly industrial, clogged with factories and fumes.

Brionne

The small town of **BRIONNE**, 10km north of Serquigny and the first stop on the rail line to Rouen, plays host to large regional **markets** on Thursday and Sunday. The fish hall is on the left bank; the rest, by the church on the right bank. Above them both, with panoramic views, is a **donjon**.

If you decide to stay in Brionne, it holds two good but pretty expensive **hotels** which also contain excellent restaurants – the *Auberge du Vieux Donjon*, facing the marketplace at 19 rue Soie (☎02.32.44.80.62; closed Mon, & Sun pm in low season, & last fortnight in Oct; ③), and the much more modern *Logis de Brionne*, 1 place St-Denis (☎02.32.44.81.73; closed Sun pm & Mon Oct–Easter; ③).

The Abbaye de Bec-Hellouin

Following the **Risle** on towards Honfleur and the sea, the **D39** is lined with perfect timbered farmhouses. Four kilometres from Brionne, the size and tranquil setting of the **ABBAYE DE BEC-HELLOUIN** give a monastic feel to the whole valley. Bells echo between the hills and white-robed monks go soberly about their business. From the eleventh century onwards, the abbey was one of the most important centres of intellectual learning in the Christian world; an intimate association with the court of William the Conqueror meant that two of its early abbots, first Lanfranc and then the philosopher Anselm, became archbishops of Canterbury.

Thanks to the Revolution, most of the monastery buildings are recent – the monks only returned in 1948 – but there are some survivals and appealing clusters of stone ruins. Recent archbishops of Canterbury have maintained tradition by coming here on retreat (tours: June–Sept Mon & Wed–Fri 10am, 11am, 3pm, 4pm & 5pm, Sat 10am, 11am, 3pm & 4pm, Sun & hols noon, 3pm, 3.30pm, 4pm & 6pm; Oct–May Mon & Wed–Sat 11am, 3.15pm & 4.30pm, Sun & hols noon, 3pm, & 4pm; 25F.)

In the rather twee adjacent town of **Bec-Hellouin** is a **vintage car museum** (mid-June to mid-Sept daily 9am–noon & 2–7pm; mid-Sept to mid-June Fri–Tues 9am–noon & 2–7pm; 25F), and a distinctly unascetic **restaurant**, the wonderful *Auberge de l'Abbaye* (☎02.32.44.86.02; closed Mon pm, all day Tues in winter, & all Jan; ⑤), which as well as offering gourmet dinner menus from 200F also has half a dozen expensive rooms. The *Restaurant de la Tour* on place Guillaume-le-Conquérant nearby (☎02.32.44.86.15; closed Dec, plus Tues pm & Wed in low season) is a more affordable place to eat, with some outdoor tables.

Pont-Audemer

Continuing north, the last major crossing point over the Risle is at **PONT-AUDEMER**, where medieval houses lean out at alarming angles over the crisscrossing roads, rivers and canals. It's an attractive little place, the scene of busy markets on Mondays and Fridays, while the *Auberge du Vieux Puits*, 6 rue Notre-Dame-du-Pré (☎02.32.41.01.48; closed Jan, plus Mon & Tues in winter; ④), makes an appealing old-fashioned place to stay. The more basic riverside *Hôtel de l'Agriculture*, 84 av de la République (☎02.32.41.01.23; closed Sun pm in winter; ①), is half the price.

From there you have the choice of making for the sea at Honfleur (see p.103), passing some tottering Giacometti-style barns on the way to St-Georges along the thickly wooded valleys of the D38, or going on towards the Seine. If you plan to cycle across the Forêt de Brotonne towards Caudebec (see p.79), be warned that, to discourage motorists from spoiling the nicest part of the forest, the road signs direct you the long way round via La Mailleraye.

Pont l'Évêque

There was little left after the war of the old **PONT L'ÉVÊQUE**, 35km west of Pont-Audemer and technically the northernmost town of the Pays d'Auge (see p.162). One or two ancient houses remain, most notably along rue St-Michel, but the town as a whole has become such a turmoil of major roads as to be a rather eccentric place to choose to stay. If you do end up in Pont l'Évêque, the *Lion d'Or*, 8 place du Calvaire (☎02.31.65.01.55; ②), offers reasonable rooms and excellent seafood dinners.

Cormeilles

The village of **CORMEILLES**, 17km southeast of Pont l'Évêque, makes a more appealing destination for a day out, having been left relatively unscathed by fighting. Each Friday sees a market in its tiny centre, and there are several half-timbered restaurants scattered around.

On the southern edge of town, the *Auberge du President*, 70 rue de l'Abbaye (☎02.32.57.80.37; closed Wed pm in low season; ③), is an efficient hybrid, featuring motel-style rooms around the back and a very traditional, formal and good plush-velvet restaurant in the old building facing the street, with menus from 75F.

Lisieux

LISIEUX is the main town of the Pays d'Auge, a regional capital successively under the Gauls, the Romans and the Franks. However, it was obliterated by barbarians in 275 AD, and again by the Allies in 1944, with the result that what had been a beautiful market town is now for the most part nondescript. Although it still boasts a Norman Gothic cathedral built in 1170, which holds a chapel erected by the judge who sentenced Joan of Arc to death, these days Lisieux's identity is thoroughly wrapped up in the life and death of **Ste Thérèse** – the most influential French spiritual figure of the last hundred years.

Pilgrims come to Lisieux in considerable numbers, and even a casual visitor will find the Thérèse cult inescapable. The garish and gigantic **Basilique de Ste-Thérèse**, on a slope to the southwest of the town centre, was modelled on the Sacré-Coeur in Paris. Completed in 1954, it was the last major religious building in France to be erected solely by public subscription. Thérèse is in fact buried in the chapel of the Carmelite convent, though her presence in the Basilica is ensured by selected bones from her right arm (in a reliquary given by Pope Pius XI) and by countless photographs (Thérèse being one of the very few saints to have lived since the invention of the camera). Huge mosaics of her face decorate the nave, and every night except Sunday between June and September, at 9.45pm, as part of a stunningly tasteless (and expensive) laser show, her beatific smile is simultaneously projected onto every column in the church.

In summer, a white, flag-bedecked funfair "train" runs fifty-minute tours around the holiest sites, chugging through the open, wide streets and squares, and past the delightful flower-filled park, raised above street level behind the restrained and sober Cathédrale St-Pierre (departures from the Basilica: July & Aug daily 11am, 2pm, 3pm, 4pm & 5pm; Sept Sat & Sun 11am, 2pm, 3pm, 4pm & 5pm; 30F).

SAINT THÉRÈSE

Born at Alençon in 1873, **Thérèse Martin** lived for the last nine years of her short life in the Carmelite convent in Lisieux, until she died of TB at 24. She had felt the call to take holy orders when only 9, but it took a pilgrimage to Rome and a special dispensation from the pope before she was allowed into the convent at the age of 15. The prioress said then that "a soul of such quality should not be treated as a child".

Thérèse owes her fame to her book *Story of a Soul*, in which she describes the approach to life she called her "Little Way" – a belief that all personal suffering, all thankless work and quiet faith, is made holy, and made worthwhile, as an offering to God. What to modern sensibilities might appear a meekness and lack of worldliness verging on the selfish proved astonishingly popular after her death, particularly in trying to make sense of the vast suffering of World War I, and Thérèse was rapidly beatified. In 1945, she joined her heroine Joan of Arc – she wrote several poems to Joan, and there are even photographs of her dressed as the imprisoned Joan (see p.86), chained to a wall – by being declared France's second patron saint. Her continuing contemporary relevance to Catholics is shown by the success of Alain Cavalier's film *Thérèse* (1986), and a pilgrimage to Lisieux by Pope John Paul II.

For an idea of Lisieux's former glories, take a look at the fading photos in the **Musée du Vieux-Lisieux**, 38 bd Pasteur (daily except Tues 2–6pm; 15F).

Practicalities

Lisieux is 35 minutes by train from Caen, en route to Paris or Rouen; the **gare SNCF** is on the south side of town, below the Basilica. Turn left out of the station, then right, to reach the **tourist office**, at 11 rue d'Alençon (June–Sept Mon–Sat 8.30am–6.30pm, Sun 10.30am–12.30pm & 2.30–5pm; Oct–May Mon–Sat 8.30am–noon & 1.30–6pm; ☎02.31.62.08.41), which can help with finding accommodation in Lisieux itself, and provides information on the rural areas further inland.

The quantity of pilgrims means that Lisieux is full of good-value places to stay – among its **hotels** are *de la Terrasse*, up on the hill near the Basilica at 25 av Ste-Thérèse (☎02.31.62.17.65; closed Jan, & Mon in winter; ②), the *de Lourdes*, 4 rue au Char near the cathedral (☎02.31.31.19.48; ②), and the *Hôtel des Arts*, backing onto the Bishop's Gardens at 26 rue Condorcet (☎02.31.62.00.02; ①). There is also a large **campsite**, *de la Vallée* (April to mid-Oct; ☎02.31.62.00.40), but campers would probably be better off somewhere more rural, such as Livarot or Orbec.

Most of the hotels are equipped with tempting restaurants, and you can also get a reasonable 60F lunch at *Au Vieux Normand*, in one of Lisieux's few surviving half-timbered houses at 14 rue H-Chéron (☎02.31.62.03.35; closed Mon). If Thérèse isn't your prime motivation, Saturday is the best day to visit, for the large **street market** – stacked with Pays d'Auge cheeses.

The Pays d'Auge

South of Lisieux, the rolling hills and green twisting valleys of the **Pays d'Auge** are scattered with magnificent half-timbered manor houses. The sprawling farms often consist of a succession of such "Tudor" (in fact the Norman tradition predates the English) treasures; each family house, as it becomes too dilapidated to live in, being converted for use as a barn, and replaced by a new one built alongside. The pastures here are the lushest in the province, producing the world-famous cheeses of Camembert, Livarot and Pont l'Évêque. And beside them are acres of orchards, yielding the best of Norman ciders, both apple and pear (*poiré*), as well as Calvados apple brandy.

The tourist authorities promote two main Pays d'Auge itineraries, the **Route de Fromage** and the **Route du Cidre**. It's not difficult to join either of these well-signposted routes, each of which serves as a welcome opportunity to get off the main highways. For the former, the best starting points are at St-Pierre-sur-Dives and Livarot; for the latter, head for Cambremer, just north of the N13 between Caen and Lisieux. In any event, it doesn't matter much if you stray off the routes – much of the appeal of this area lies in the scope just to wander, rather than to look for any specific sights, and to fill the days sampling the different ciders and cheeses. That said, the manor houses of **Beuvron-en-Auge** on the Cider Route, and **Montpinçon** and **Lisores** on the Cheese Route, are well worth finding, and at Lisores there's also the **Ferme-Musée Fernand Léger** (daily except Wed 10am–noon & 2–7pm), with its unlikely mosaics. **Cambremer** has a special crafts market on Sunday morning in July and August.

For fans of really good solid Norman cooking, this is the perfect area to look out for **Fermes Auberges**, working farms which welcome (paying) visitors to share their meals; lists are available from local tourist offices and from *Calvados Tourisme* (place du Canada, Caen; ☎02.31.86.53.30). The cider farms are signposted with the words "*Cru de Cambremer*" in green on white.

THE CHEESES OF THE PAYS D'AUGE

The tradition of cheesemaking in the Pays d'Auge is thought to have been started in the monasteries during the Dark Ages; the characteristics of the standard local product seem to have become fairly constant by the eleventh century. At first it was variously known as either *Augelot* or *Angelot*; the *Roman de la Rose* in 1236 referred to *Angelot* cheese, which was identified with a small coin depicting a young angel killing a dragon.

This cheese was the forerunner of the principal modern varieties, which began to emerge in the seventeenth century – **Pont l'Évêque**, which is square, with a washed crust, and is soft but not runny, and **Livarot**, which is round, thick and firm, with a stronger flavour.

Although Marie Herel is generally credited with having invented **Camembert** in the 1790s, a smaller and stodgier version of that cheese had already existed for some time. What seems to have happened is that a priest fleeing the Revolutionary Terror at Meaux (a certain Abbé Gobert) stayed in Mme Herel's farmhouse at Camembert and watched the methods she used for making cheese. He suggested modifications in line with the techniques he'd seen employed to manufacture Brie de Meaux – a slower process, gentler on the curd and with more thorough drainage. The rich full cheese thus created was an instant success in the market at Vimoutiers, and the development of the railways (and the invention of the chipboard cheesebox in 1880) helped to give it a worldwide popularity.

More details on all such matters are to be had from from the exhaustive *French Cheese Book*, by Patrick Rance (Macmillan, 1989).

Beuvron-en-Auge

No village has any right to be as pretty as **BEUVRON-EN-AUGE**, 7km north of the N13 halfway between Lisieux and Caen, which consists of an oval central *place*, ringed by a glorious ensemble of multicoloured half-timbered houses. The largest of these, the yellow and brown sixteenth-century **Vieux Manoir** at the south end of the village, backs onto a stream and open fields. The beams around its first storey bear weather-beaten carvings, including one of a Norman soldier. A map in the main square suggested details **walking routes** through the countryside nearby, while if you step off the square into the alleyway known as **rue de la Catouillette**, opposite the Vieux Manoir, you'll find another set of lovely half-timbered structures clustered around a tiny courtyard.

Beuvron-en-Auge stages its own **Cider Festival**, with a huge local market in the square, on about October 24 each year.

Practicalities
Immediately beside the Vieux Manoir stands the eighteenth-century *Auberge de la Boule d'Or* (☎02.31.79.78.78; closed Jan, plus Sun pm & Mon; ③), where you'd be lucky to find one of the three attractive bedrooms available; a former farmhouse opposite holds a *chambre d'hôte* (Mme Hamelin: ☎02.31.39.00.62; Easter–Oct; ③). The very centre of the *place* is taken up by the *Pavé d'Auge* **restaurant** (☎02.31.79.26.71; closed May–Aug Mon), where menus featuring chicken and *andouille* in cider or salmon start at 136F.

St-Germain-de-Livet

Around 7km south of Lisieux, and clearly signposted off the D579, the **château** of **ST-GERMAIN-DE-LIVET**(daily except Tues 10–11am & 2–6pm; 35F) is an appealing blend of fifteenth- and sixteenth-century architectural elements. From the main gate, its half-timbered older wing – home to some stirring military frescoes – is largely concealed by the more imposing later addition, with its cheerful checked facade of coloured stones and brick. The whole edifice is topped by classic pointed grey-slate turrets, circled by a moat, and surrounded by scrupulously maintained lawns. In summer, **carriage rides** leave from alongside the entrance to tour the grounds (June Sun 11am–6pm, July–Sept daily except Tues & Sat 11am–6pm; adult 35F, under-13s 20F); when not in use, the carriage is housed in an amazing tumbledown barn next door.

Orbec

The most attractive of the larger Pays d'Auge towns, **ORBEC**, lies just a few kilometres along a valley from the source of its river, the Orbiquet, 19km southeast of Lisieux. Consisting of little more than its main road, the Rue Grande, with the huge tower of Notre Dame church at its southern end, it epitomizes the simple pleasures of the region.

Along the Rue Grande, you'll see several houses in which the gaps between the timbers are filled with intricate patterns of coloured tiles and bricks. Debussy composed *Jardin sous la Pluie* in one of these, and the oldest and prettiest of the lot – a tanner's house dating back to 1568, and once again called the **Vieux**

Manoir – holds a museum of local history. On the whole, though, it's more fun just to walk down behind the church to the river, and its watermill and paddocks.

Practicalities

There's a good, slightly upmarket **hotel** at the top end of Rue Grande: *de France*, at no. 152 (☎02.31.32.74.02; closed mid-Dec to mid-Jan; ②). You can get a good meal there for 90F and upwards, or stroll down the street to its narrowest point, where *Le Caneton* in the half-timbered house at no. 32 serves gourmet menus from 98F. Orbec also has a municipal **campsite**, *Les Capucins* (June–Aug; ☎02.31.32.76.22).

Livarot

The centre of the cheese country is the old town of **LIVAROT**, 18km south of Lisieux. Set in a grand house near the Vie River on its western outskirts, the **Musée du Fromage** illustrates the history and manufacture of Livarot's eponymous cheese, and doles out free samples (April–Oct Mon–Fri 10am–noon & 2–6pm; 20F). For the best views of the valley, climb up to the thirteenth-century church of St-Michel de Livet, just above the town; to visit you contact a M Jean Fromage.

Practicalities

Livarot's **tourist office**, 1 place Georges-Bisson (July & Aug Mon–Sat 9.30am–noon & 2–6pm, Sun 10am–noon; Sept & Feb–June Mon–Sat 9.30am–noon & 2–6pm; Oct–Dec Mon–Sat 10am–noon & 2–5pm; ☎02.31.63.47.39), is almost next door to the (rather rundown and shabby) **hotel** and restaurant *du Vivier* (☎02.31.32.04.10; ②). The enjoyable *Café de la Paix* is further east, up from the central traffic lights, and there's also a tiny municipal **campsite** (May to mid-Sept; ☎02.31.63.53.19). The local **cheese fair** falls on the first weekend of each August.

St-Pierre-sur-Dives

The medieval wooden *halles* at **ST-PIERRE-SUR-DIVES**, burned to the ground in 1944, had been rebuilt by 1949. Only traditional techniques were used: there's not a single nail or screw in the place, whose timber frame rests on low stone walls and is held together by chestnut pegs alone. The buildings of the adjacent convent now house the local **tourist office**, along with a slightly academic annexe to the Livarot cheese museum (April–Oct daily except Tues 9.30am–12.30pm & 2–6.30pm; 25F).

The town's other focus of interest is its Gothic-Romanesque church (whose windows depict the history of the town). A large **market** still takes place every Monday in the open space next to the *halles*.

Practicalities

St-Pierre's best bet for **accommodation** is the *Renaissance*, a *logis de France* at 57 rue de Lisieux (☎02.31.20.81.23; closed Sun lunchtime; ②), which has a relatively ordinary restaurant. Its summer-only **campsite** (June–Sept; ☎02.31.20.97.90) is 1km south of town.

Falaise

William the Conqueror, or William the Bastard as he is more familiarly known to Normans, was born in **FALAISE**, 40km southwest of Lisieux. His mother, Arlette, a laundress, was spotted by his father, Duke Robert of Normandy, at the washing place below the château. She was a shrewd woman, who scorned secrecy in her eventual assignation by riding publicly through the main entrance to meet him. During her pregnancy, she is said to have dreamed of bearing a mighty tree that cast its shade over Normandy and England.

From a distance, the sheer wall of the **castle keep**, firmly planted on the massive rocks of the cliff (*falaise*) that gave the town its name, and towering over the **Fontaine d'Arlette** down by the river, is one of the most evocative historic sights imaginable. Both were, however, so heavily damaged during the war that they are still often closed for restoration, and are scarcely worth the ten-minute tour when they're not.

The whole of Falaise was devastated in the course of the struggle to close the "Falaise Gap" in August 1944 – the climax of the Battle of Normandy, as the Allied armies sought to encircle the Germans and cut off their retreat. By the time the Canadians entered the town on August 17, they could no longer tell where the roads had been and had to bulldoze a new four-metre strip straight through the middle. Set in almost derelict wilderness right next to the town centre (and opposite the tourist office) is an isolated survivor, the **Château de la Fresnaye**, housing a rather earnest local museum which is only open during the summer.

Practicalities

The **tourist office** can be found at 32 rue Georges-Clemenceau (May–Sept Mon–Sat 10am–6pm, Sun 10am–4pm; Oct–April Mon–Sat 10am–6pm; ☎02.31.90.17.26). As the main Caen–Argentan road, this is also the (rather noisy) location of most of Falaise's few **hotels**, such as the *Poste* at no. 38 (☎02.31.90.13.14; ③). The **campsite**, *Camping du Château* (Easter–Sept; ☎02.31.90.16.55), next to Arlette's fountain and the municipal swimming pool, is in a much better location.

Vimoutiers and Camembert

The war-ravaged and consequently rather ugly town of **VIMOUTIERS** contains yet another **cheese museum**, at 10 av Général-de-Gaulle (May–Oct Mon 2–6pm, Tues–Sat 9am–noon & 2–6pm, Sun 10am–noon & 2.30–6pm; Nov, Dec, March & April Mon 2–6pm, Tues–Fri 9am–noon & 2–6pm, Sat 9am–noon; 25F). This one features a glorious collection not to be missed by tyrosemiophiles – cheese-label collectors (they do exist) – who will find Camembert stickers ranging from remote Chilean dairies to Marks & Spencer. Most of the cheese on display, however, turns out to be polystyrene.

A statue in the main square honours Marie Harel, who, at the nearby village of **CAMEMBERT**, developed the original cheese early in the nineteenth century, promoting it with a skilful campaign that included sending free samples to Napoléon. There's a photo in the museum of the statue with its head blown off after a US air raid in June 1944; its replacement was donated by the cheesemakers of Ohio. Marie is confronted across the main street by what might be called the statue of the Unknown Cow.

Camembert itself, 3km southeast of Vimoutiers, is tiny, hilly and very rural, home to far more cows than humans. It has recently acquired its own **cheese museum** (April to mid-Nov daily 10am–12.30pm & 2–7pm; 15F), where the displays add little to those in Vimoutiers.

Even closer to Vimoutiers, in the same general direction, the beautifully sited lake known as the **Escale du Vitou** offers everything you need for windsurfing, swimming and horse-riding.

Practicalities

Vimoutiers is the venue of a **market** on Monday afternoons and Fridays. Its **tourist office**, in the cheese museum (same hours as museum; ☎02.33.39.30.29), has piles of information on local cheese-related attractions. Of its **hotels**, the very central but far from welcoming *Soleil d'Or*, 15 place Mackau (☎02.33.39.07.15; closed Feb; ①), has a good 65F menu and an even better 100F one, and there is also a superbly clean and very cheap year-round **campsite** near the lake, *La Campière*, 9 rue du 8-Mai (☎02.33.39.18.86).

Vegetarian travellers in particular – though not exclusively – should make a beeline for the little village of **Ticheville**, roughly 5km southeast on the D12. An unobtrusive house tucked away just north of the main street has been converted by its British owners into *La Maison du Vert* (☎02.33.36.95.84; ②), a friendly hotel that serves excellent vegetarian and vegan meals – dinner costs around 105F – and is set in lovely rolling gardens.

Ste-Foy de Montgommery

A couple of kilometres north of Vimoutiers, towards Livarot, the D579 passes through the village of **STE-FOY DE MONTGOMMERY**. Outside the *Café La Gosselinais* here, on the night of July 17, 1944, **Field-Marshal Rommel** was seriously injured when RAF Typhoons attacked his Mercedes. Rommel never returned to the battlefield, and committed suicide three months later. That his nemesis should overtake him in a place called "Holy Faith of Montgommery" became part of the legend surrounding the British field marshal.

South to Gacé

The **D26** runs along the **valley of the Vie** south of Vimoutiers – a route that is something of a microcosm of Norman vernacular architecture, lined along the way with ramshackle old barns, outhouses and farm buildings. Faded orange clay crumbles from between the weathered wooden beams of these flower-covered beauties.

GACÉ itself, 18km from Vimoutiers, is not wildly exciting, but it does have a handful of reasonable hotels. The *Normandie* on its main street (☎02.33.35.52.13; closed Jan, plus Sun pm & Mon; ①) has several well-priced menus.

Nonant-le-Pin, 12 km south of Gacé, was the birthplace in 1824 of Alphonsine Plessis, a celebrated courtesan who served as the inspiration for Dumas's *La Dame aux Camélias* and Verdi's *La Traviata*.

Argentan

ARGENTAN centres on a **castle ruin** – the site where Henry II of England received the news on New Year's Day 1171 that his knights had taken him at his word and murdered Thomas-à-Becket. In fact, the entire town was very comprehensively ruined during General Patton's bid to close the "Falaise pocket" in August 1944, and there's virtually nothing to see; the **church of St-Germain** which dominates all approaches has been under continuing restoration ever since, and remains closed to visitors. The castle ruin and the adjoining market square (active on Tues) make Argentan an enjoyable enough halt, and there are boat trips on the River Orne, but the main motivation for anyone to come here is not monuments but **horses**. Outside the town are numerous equestrian centres, with riding schools, stables, racetracks and studs.

Practicalities

Trains to Argentan pull in at the **gare SNCF**, across the Orne a short way southwest of the centre. Full information on the area is available from the **tourist office** at 1 place du Marché (July & Aug Mon 9am–noon & 2–7pm, Tues–Sat 9am–7pm, Sun 9am–1pm; Sept–June Tues–Sat 10am–noon & 2–6pm, Sat 10am–12.30pm & 1.30–5.30pm; ☎02.33.67.12.48). Of the **hotels** in town, the best budget option is the *Donjon*, above a brasserie at 1 place de l'Hôtel-de-Ville (☎02.33.67.03.76; ①), while the *France*, 8 bd Carnot (☎02.33.67.03.65; closed Sun pm; ②), has an excellent restaurant, with menus from 75F.

Le Pin-au-Haras

LE PIN-AU-HARAS, 15km east of Argentan on the N26, is an essential stop for horse lovers – it's the home of the **National Stud** (*Haras National*). The plan for the stud was originally conceived by Louis XIV's minister, Colbert, and the ground subsequently laid out by Le Nôtre from 1715 to 1730. It can be approached via a number of woodland avenues, but the most impressive is the D304, which climbs slowly from the hippodrome and is lined with jumps and hedges.

While the buildings are magnificent, they're nowhere near as sumptuous as the residents – around eighty of them – incalculable investments that include champions of Epsom and Longchamp, as well as prize specimens of the indigenous Norman Percheron.

Tours of the stud leave every thirty minutes from the main entrance (April to mid-Oct daily 9.30am–6pm; mid-Oct to March Mon & Wed–Sat 10am–noon & 2–5pm, Sun 2–4.30pm; 30F; arrive one hour before closing for the last tour). You are escorted by a groom through stables full of stomping, snorting, glistening stallions, rooms of polished harnesses and fine carriages, and great doorways labelled in stone, until eventually you come out to a pastoral vision of the horses grazing in endless sequences of gardens and paddocks. Each tour lasts for around an hour; if you find it hard to follow the rapid French-only commentary, you can amuse yourself by watching the way everybody scrupulously affects not to notice the rampant sexuality – which, of course, is the *raison d'être* of the whole place.

Between June and September, displays of horsemanship are held on Thursdays at 3pm, while there are also special events on the first Sunday in September, the second Sunday in October, and a few other summer weekends. Between February 15 and July 15, most of the horses are away; and the château itself is never open.

The Château d'O

Just outside Mortrée, 6.5km northwest of Sées on the N158, is the privately owned and postcard-perfect **Château d'O** (July & Aug daily 10.30am–noon &

2.30–6pm; April–June & Sept daily 2.30–6pm; Oct–March daily except Tues 2.30–5.30pm; 15F gardens, 25F house). This turreted château, whose grey-slate roof rises to a pencil-case-full of sharp points, is in perfect condition, with a full moat that widens out into a lake. The house dates from the end of the fifteenth century and, unusually, was designed purely as a domestic residence, with no military pretensions, while the lawns of the grounds hold a pitch-and-putt golf course.

Within the grounds, but with its own separate entrance, the *Ferme du Château d'O* (☎02.33.35.35.27; closed Sun pm & Mon) is a restaurant that boasts quite a gastronomic reputation. Lunch menus start at 95F, including ham cooked in cider, while on the 255F menu you get to sample crayfish *profiteroles*.

Sées

SÉES, midway between Argentan and Alençon, has long had an air of being lost in its own history. A succession of dusty and derelict squares, all with medieval buildings intact, surround the great Gothic, white-ceilinged **Cathedral**, which is the fifth to stand on the site and is magnificently illuminated every summer evening. One of its predecessors was burned down by its own bishop, attempting to smoke out a gang of thieves – much to the scorn of the pope.

However, Sées does hold several tasteful, long-established **hotels**. The *Cheval Blanc* overlooks the pretty little place St-Pierre on the main road south (☎02.33.27.80.48; closed Thurs pm & Fri in season, Fri & Sat out of season; ②), and offers menus from 69F, with a good 89F menu of regional specialities. The *Dauphin* is hidden away a little further west, in a quiet location at 31 place des Halles next to the old covered marketplace (☎02.33.27.80.07; closed Feb, Sun pm all year, & Mon pm in winter; ④), and has an equally good (if more expensive) restaurant, while the *Garden Hôtel* at 12 rue des Ardrillers (☎02.33.27.98.27; ②) is a peaceful, elegant refuge reached via an ivy-covered gatehouse in the northwest corner of another sleepy square, nearer the cathedral.

Le-Mêle-sur-Sarthe

LE-MÊLE-SUR-SARTHE, en route south from Sées, holds another *logis* worth stopping at. The *Hotel de la Poste,* 27 place de Gaulle (☎02.33.81.18.00; closed Sun pm all year, & Mon pm in winter; ②–④), has an acceptable 85F menu for guests who happen not to like eating, and a very good 110F one for those who do. They also serve some good-value menus where the price includes drinks and coffee.

Alençon

ALENÇON, a fair-sized and busy town, is best known for its traditional – and now pretty much defunct – **lacemaking** industry. The **Musée des Beaux Arts et de la Dentelle**, housed in a former Jesuit school (daily except Mon 10am–noon & 2–6pm; 20F), has all the best trappings of a modern museum. However, the highly informative history of lacemaking upstairs, with examples of numerous different techniques, can be rather deadly for anyone not already fascinated by the subject; if it does capture your imagination, time your visit to coincide with a guided tour and demonstration (July & Aug daily 2.30pm & 4.30pm; 10F extra). The temptation to leave without a visit to the "Minor Lace Exhibition Room" is almost overwhelming; but the room beyond it holds a collection of gruesome Cambodian artefacts, spears and lances, tiger skulls and elephants' feet, gathered by a "militant socialist" French governor at the turn of the century. The paintings in the Beaux Arts section downstairs are fairly nondescript, except for a touching Nativity by the Norman artist, Latouche, and a few works by Courbet and Géricault.

Stained glass in the **Notre Dame** church shows the medieval guilds of craftsmen who paid for each specific window, and the baptism of **Ste-Thérèse** is commemorated in the chapel in which it took place. If you haven't already had a surfeit of the saint at Lisieux, you can also wander over to her birthplace, on rue St-Blaise, just in front of the gare routière (daily except Tues: June–Oct 9am–noon & 2–6pm; Nov, Dec & Feb–May 9.30am–noon & 2.30–5pm; free).

The **Château des Ducs**, the old town castle, looks impressive but doesn't encourage visitors – it's a prison. People in Alençon have nightmare memories of its use during the war by the Gestapo.

Thanks to wartime bombardment, little is left of the buildings that once stood on the banks of the River Sarthe. Alençon was the first town in France to be liberated by French forces alone, and a monument right next to the Pont-Neuf honours their leader, the aristocratic **Général Leclerc** (whose headmaster at school was General de Gaulle's father). The movements of his army are chronicled through the deserts of North Africa, via Utah Beach, to Alençon, on August 12, 1944. Within two weeks he was in Paris; within a year, in Berlin; and by March 1946 he was in Hanoi – he died in a plane crash in North Africa in 1947.

Another **lace museum**, with a shop selling samples, stands opposite the monument (Mon–Sat 10am–noon & 2–6pm).

Practicalities

If you want to stay, Alençon has good shops and cafés in a few well-pedestrianized streets at the heart of its abysmal one-way traffic system. The **tourist office** is housed in the dramatic fifteenth-century Maison d'Ozé on place La Magdelaine (July & Aug Mon & Sat 9.30am–noon & 2–6.30pm, Tues–Fri 9.30am–6.30pm, Sun 10am–12.30pm & 2.30–5.30pm; Sept–June Mon–Sat 9.30am–noon & 2–6.30pm; ☎02.33.26.11.36). They also organize **guided tours** of town (July & Aug daily 2.30pm & 4.30pm, plus Fri 8.30pm; 25F).

The **gare routière** and the gare SNCF are both northeast of the centre, with the train station slightly the further out of the two. Its immediate environs hold Alençon's prime concentration of **hotels**. The two *logis*, *l'Industrie*, 20 place Général-de-Gaulle (☎02.33.27.19.30; closed Sun pm & Mon; ②), and the *Grand Hôtel de la Gare*, 50 av Wilson (☎02.33.29.03.93; ①), are decent and have fixed-price menus for around 70F. Back in the town centre, the *Jardin Gourmand*, 14 rue de Sarthe (☎02.33.32.22.56; closed Mon & Tues pm), is a romantic little restaurant with menus from 70F. The local **youth hostel**, 3km northwest of town on the D204 towards Colombiers at 1 rue de la Paix, Damigny (☎02.33.29.00.48; 40F), is not attractive in itself, but organizes lots of activities in the woods and on the river.

If you're interested in **horse-riding** – along the banks of the Orne – the Association Départementale de Tourisme Équestre et d'Équitation de Loisir de l'Orne has its headquarters in Alençon at 60 Grand-Rue. They can also tell you about the various local stud farms open to the public.

The Forêt d'Écouves

The **Forêt d'Écouves**, reached (under your own steam) from either Alençon or Sées, is the centrepiece of the Parc Régional Normandie-Maine, an amorphous area stretching from Mortain in the west to within a few kilometres of Mortagne-au-Perche in the east. A dense mixture of old spruce, pine, oak and beech, set on high hills a few kilometres north of Alençon, the Écouves forest is one of the most attractive in Normandy. These commanding heights were bitterly fought over during the war, and a Free French tank still guards the **Croix-de-Médavy** at their very apex.

Unfortunately, the forest is now a favoured spot of the military – and, in autumn, of deerhunters too. To avoid risking life and limb, check with the park's offices. You can usually ramble along the cool paths, happening on wild mushrooms and even the odd wild boar. The *gîte d'étape*, on the D26 near Les Ragotières on the edge nearest Alençon, is an ideal spot from which to explore the forest (contact the local *gîte* office at 60 rue St-Blaise in Alençon; ☎02.33.32.09.00).

Carrouges

One alternative base at the western end of the Forêt d'Écouves is the hill town of **CARROUGES**, which offers two appealing, very similar and almost adjacent small hotels. The *Hôtel du Nord* (☎02.33.27.20.14; closed mid-Dec to mid-Jan, plus Fri Sept–June; ①) offers delicious local cuisine on menus that start at 57F; all rooms at the tiny *St-Pierre* (☎02.33.27.20.02; ②) have showers, and the cheapest menu is 70F.

Carrouges's **château** (daily: mid-June to Aug 9.30–11.30am & 2–6.30pm; April to mid-June & Sept 10–11.30am & 2–6pm; Oct–March 10–11.30am & 2–4.30pm; 25F) is a fine old-style castle set in spacious grounds at the foot of the hill. Its two highlights are a superb restored brick staircase, and a room in which hang portraits of fourteen successive generations of the Le Veneur family, an extraordinary illustration of the processes of heredity. In the **Maison de Métiers**, the former castle chapel, local craftsmen sell their produce.

Heading onwards on the D908 towards Bagnoles, you come after a few kilometres to the delightful village of **JOUÉ-DU-BOIS**, with a diminutive château, lake and a cheap but delicious restaurant, the *Pomme d'Or* (☎02.33.37.08.97; closed Sun), where you can still get a four-course meal for under 70F.

Bagnoles de l'Orne

The spa town of **BAGNOLES DE L'ORNE** lies at the heart of a long, narrow wood, the Forêt des Andaines. Broad avenues radiate into the forest from the centre of the town. As you approach, you begin to encounter pale figures shuffling slowly outwards, blinking as if unused to the light of day, as though silently fleeing some nameless evil. In fact, the forbidding nineteenth-century building from which they emerge contains nothing more fearsome than **thermal baths**. Bagnoles is a mecca for the sick from all over France; its springs are such big business that they maintain a booking office next to the Pompidou Centre in Paris.

Although life in the town is conducted at a phenomenally slow pace, it is all surprisingly jolly – redolent with aged flirtations and gallantry. The lakeside gardens

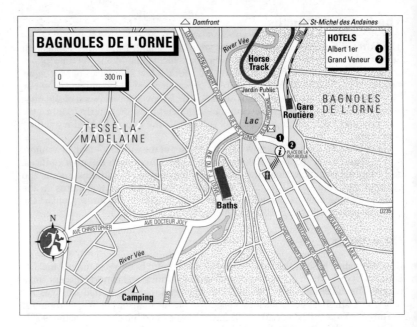

are the big scene, with pedalos, horse-drawn calèches and an enormous Casino. And with so many visitors to keep entertained, and spending money, there are innumerable cultural **events**, concerts and stage shows throughout the summer; the ostensible high spot, the annual *Spectacle* in July, is one of the less enthralling.

Away from its main roads, the **Forêt des Andaines** is pleasant, with scattered and unspoilt villages, such as Juvigny and St-Michel, and the secluded, private **Château de Couterne**, a visual delight even from the gates, with its lake and long grass-floored avenue approach.

Practicalities

Whether you'd actually want to spend time in Bagnoles depends on your disposable income as well as your health. Furthermore, the town as a whole operates to a season that lasts roughly from early April to the end of October; arrive in winter, and you may find everything shut. The numerous **hotels** are expensive and sedate places, in which it's possible to be too late for dinner at 7pm and locked out altogether at 9pm, and the **campsite**, *de la Vée* (April–Oct; ☎02.33.37.87.45), south of town, is rather forlorn.

Contact the **tourist office** on place du Marché (April–Oct daily 10am–noon & 2–6.30pm; Nov–March Mon–Fri 10am–noon & 2–6pm; ☎02.33.37.85.66) for details on accommodation in Bagnoles and its less exclusive sister town of **TESSE-MADELEINE**. Among the cheaper options in Bagnoles proper – all very near the central roundabout – are the *Albert 1er* at 7 av Dr-Poulain (Feb–Oct; ☎02.33.37.80.97; ②), which has excellent menus from 98F, and the *Grand Veneur* at 6 place République (April–Oct; ☎02.33.37.86.79; ②). **Restaurants**, in both towns, tend to be better value: the *de la Terrasse* (☎02.33.30.80.96) in Bagnoles is well tried and popular, with a traditional dining room offering six menus from 75F upwards, and a cheaper *crêperie*.

If you fancy **taking the waters**, a "complete cure" of 21 sessions costs around 1500F, with individual baths and showers for as little as 30F.

Domfront

The road **through the forest** from Bagnoles, the D335 and then the D908, climbs above the lush woodlands and progressively narrows to a hog's back before entering **DOMFRONT**. Less happens here than at Bagnoles, but it has the edge on countryside.

A public park, near the long-abandoned former train station, leads up to some redoubtable **castle ruins** perched on an isolated rock. Eleanor of Aquitaine was born in this castle in October 1162, and Thomas-à-Becket came to stay for Christmas 1166, saying Mass in the Notre-Dame-sur-l'Eau church down by the river, which has sadly been ruined by vandals. The views from the flower-filled gardens that surround the mangled keep are spectacular, including a very graphic panorama of the ascent you've made to get up.

A slender footbridge connects the castle with the narrow little **village** itself, which boasts an abundance of half-timbered houses. Near its sweet little central square, the modern **St-Julien** church, constructed out of concrete segments during the 1920s, is bursting with exciting mosaics. It's an odd-looking building, especially when its belfry is swathed in green netting, which it seems to be for much of the time.

Practicalities

On summer afternoons (July & Aug Mon–Sat 3pm), free **guided tours** of old Domfront leave from the **tourist office**, 21 rue St-Julien (Mon–Sat 10am–noon & 2.30–6.30pm; ☎02.33.38.53.97).

Domfront's **hotels**, clustered together at the foot of the hill below the old town, make useful and very pleasant stopovers. Two *logis de France* stand side by side; the *Relais St-Michel* (☎02.33.38.64.99; ②) has widely varied menus at under 100F, while the *Hôtel de France* (☎02.33.38.51.44; ①) is a little cheaper, and has a nice little bar and garden. Campers should take note that the local **campsite**, *du Champs Passais* (April to mid-Oct; ☎02.33.37.37.66), is exceptionally small.

The Suisse Normande

The area known as the **Suisse Normande** lies roughly 25km south of Caen, along the gorge of the River Orne, between Thury-Harcourt and Putanges. The name is a little far-fetched – there are certainly no mountains – but it is quite distinctive, with cliffs and crags and wooded hills at every turn. The energetic race along the Orne in canoes and kayaks, their lazier counterparts contenting themselves with pedalos or a bizarre species of inflatable rubber tractor, while high above them climbers dangle from thin ropes and claw desperately at the sheer rock face. For mere walkers, the Orne can be frustrating: footpaths along the river are few and far between, whatever maps may say, and often entirely overgrown with brambles. At least one road sign in the area warns of unexploded mines, so tread carefully.

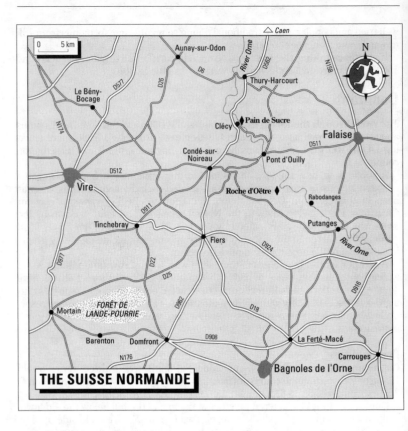

THE SUISSE NORMANDE

The Suisse Normande is most usually approached from Caen or Falaise, and contrasts dramatically with the prairie-like expanse of wheatfields en route.

Bus Verts #34 can take you to Thury-Harcourt or Clécy on its way to Flers, and SNCF run occasional special summer train excursions from Caen. If you're **cycling**, the least stressful approach is to follow the D212 from Caen, cruising across the flatlands to Thury-Harcourt; although swooping down the D23 from Bretteville, with thick woods to either side of you, is pretty exhilarating. To take the D235 from Caen, follow signs for Falaise, and head straight on through Ifs. Touring the Suisse Normande on a bike, however, is an exhausting business: the minor roads do not follow the gorge floor, but undulate endlessly over the surrounding slopes.

Thury-Harcourt
THURY-HARCOURT is really two separate towns: a little village around a bridge across the Orne, and a larger market town on the hill that overlooks it. The **tourist office**, 2 place St-Sauveur (Ascension to mid-Sept Tues–Sat 9.30am–noon & 2.30–6.30pm, Sun 10.30am–noon; mid-Sept to Ascension Tues & Thurs 9.30am–noon & 2.30–5pm, Fri 9.30am–noon; ☎02.31.79.70.45), can suggest walks,

rides and *gîtes d'étape* throughout the Suisse Normande; SIVOM at 15 rue de Condé rent out canoes. Between July and September, the grounds of the local manor house are open (for a 20F fee) between 2.30pm and 6.30pm every day, giving access to the immediate riverside.

Hotels in Thury-Harcourt are for the most part quite expensive, though the flowery *Hôtel du Val d'Orne*, 9 rte d'Aunay (☎02.31.79.70.81; closed Sat lunch in summer, Fri pm & all Sat in low season; ②), keeps its room rates down, and has a decent **restaurant**. There's also an attractive four-star **campsite**, the *Vallée du Traspy* (mid-April to mid-Sept; ☎02.31.79.61.80).

Clécy

The small village of **CLÉCY** stands on a hill about 1km up from the actual river at Pont du Vey. On the way down, in the Parc des Loisirs, is a **Musée du Chemin de Fer Miniature** (July & Aug daily 10am–noon & 2–6.30pm; Easter–June & Sept daily 10am–noon & 2–6pm; Oct–Nov Sun 2–5pm; March–Easter Sun 2–5.30pm; 25F), featuring a gigantic model railway layout certain to appeal to children.

For advice on accommodation and the wide variety of holiday activities available, the **tourist office** (☎02.31.69.79.95) is tucked in behind the church. Clécy is a slightly better bet than Thury-Harcourt for finding a **room**, although its visitors outnumber residents in high season and the whole area can get much too crowded for comfort. The *logis* facing the church, *Au Site Normand*, 1 rue des Châtelets (☎02.31.69.71.05; closed Tues pm & Wed out of season; ③), consists of an old-fashioned and good-value dining room in the main timber-framed building, and a cluster of newer units opening onto a courtyard around the back.

Down the hill, the *Moulin du Vey* (☎02.31.69.71.08; closed Dec & Jan; ⑤), set in spacious grounds on the far bank of the river, is a luxury hotel that takes its name from the restored watermill right by the bridge, which is itself, confusingly, now a restaurant. The western riverbank continues in a brief splurge of restaurants, takeaways and snack bars as far as the **campsite** (April–Sept; ☎02.31.69.70.36).

The Pain de Sucre

Across from Clécy, the opposite **east bank** of the Orne is is dominated by the exposed rock face of the giant **Pain de Sucre** or **Sugarloaf**, looming above the river. Small footpaths, and the tortuous Route des Crêtes, wind up to its flat top, making for some of the most enjoyable walks in Normandy. Picnic sites and parking places along the crest hold orientation maps so weather-beaten as to be almost abstract, but the views down to the flat fields of the Orne valley are stupendous. This is a prime site for **hang-gliders**; disconcertingly, at two points paved concrete ramps lead right to the edge of the precipice, built to facilitate launches.

Pont d'Ouilly

If you're planning on walking, or cycling, one good central spot in which to base yourself is **PONT D'OUILLY**, at the point where the main road from Vire to Falaise crosses the river. It's a small town, with a few basic shops, an old covered market hall and a promenade (with bar) slightly upstream alongside the weir; you can walk along the riverside down to **Le Mesnil Villement**. A *Grand Pardon du Ste-Roche* takes place along the river on the third Sunday in August.

As well as its **campsite**, overlooking the river (Easter–Sept; ☎02.31.69.46.12), Pont d'Ouilly can offer an attractive **hotel**, the *du Commerce* (☎02.31.69.80.16;

closed Sun pm & Mon Oct–May, plus all Jan; ②). This is the quintessential French village hotel, with a friendly welcome and attentive service. Its **restaurant** is very popular with local families, serving superb, definitive Norman cooking, with plenty of creamy *pays d'Auge* sauces, on menus that start at 65F; the dining room is appropriately filled with stuffed animals.

About 1km north of Pont d'Ouilly, the more upmarket *Auberge St-Christophe* (☎02.31.69.81.23; closed Sun pm, Mon & mid-Feb to mid-March; ③) stands in a beautiful setting on the right bank of the Orne, covered with ivy and geraniums and opposite a roofless and now overgrown Art Deco factory. The cheapest of its imaginative menus costs 95F.

The Roche d'Oëtre

A short distance south of Pont d'Ouilly is the **Roche d'Oëtre**, a high rock affording a tremendous view, not over the Orne but into the deep and totally wooded gorge of the Rouvre. The rock itself is private property, though you're under no obligation to visit the café there.

The river widens soon afterwards into the **Lac du Rabodanges**, formed by the many-arched Rabodanges Dam. It's a popular spot, with a multi-facility **campsite**, *Les Retours*, perfectly situated between the dam and the bridge on the D121. There's a play area for kids, and grassy picnic slopes lead down to the water's edge, where the occasional bather risks a swim among the waterskiers, speedboats, windsurfers, canoes and kayaks. The imposing Rabodanges château, higher up the hillside, is now a stud farm.

Putanges

Further climbing roads bring you to **PUTANGES**, another possible place to stay, with a small **campsite**, *le Val d'Orne* (Easter–Sept; ☎02.33.35.04.67). The town lies a bit beyond the main attractions of the region, but nevertheless it's a pleasant stop, with a few bars and pavement cafés and, just upstream from the bridge, the weirs over which the Orne appears from its source a short way south. The *Lion Verd* (☎02.33.35.01.86; closed Jan; ②), very near the river, is a well-priced **hotel**.

The Bocage

The region centring on **St-Lô**, west of Caen and just south of the Cotentin, is known as the **Bocage Normande**. The word *bocage* refers to a type of cultivated countryside common in the west of France, in which fields are cut by tight hedgerows rooted into walls of earth well over 1m high.

An effective form of smallhold farming, at least in pre-industrial days, it also proved to be a perfect system of anti-tank barricades. When the Allied troops tried to advance through the region in 1944, it was almost impenetrable – certainly bearing no resemblance to the East Anglian plains where they had trained. The war here was hand-to-hand, inch-by-inch slaughter; the destruction of villages often wholesale.

St-Lô

The city of **ST-LÔ**, a transport junction 60km south of Cherbourg and 36km southwest of Bayeux which was crucial in the war to the Allied breakout of the Cotentin, is still known as the "Capital of the Ruins". Black-and-white postcards of the wartime devastation are on sale everywhere and you keep coming on memorial sites as you wander about. In the main square, the gate of the old prison commemorates Resistance members executed by the Nazis, people deported east to the concentration camps and soldiers killed in action. When the bombardment of St-Lô was at its fiercest, the Germans refused to take any measures to protect the prisoners; the gate was all that survived. In similar vein, behind the cathedral, a monument to the dead of World War I is pitted with shrapnel from World War II. Less depressingly, at the foot of the rock under the castle you can see the entrance to caves where citizens sheltered from the onslaught, while somewhere far below are great vaults used by the German command. In Studs Terkel's book, *The Good War*, a GI reminisces about the huge party thrown there after the Americans found vast stockpiles of champagne; Thomas Pynchon's *Gravity's Rainbow* has a crazed drinking scene based on the tale. Samuel Beckett was here during the battle and after, working for the Irish Red Cross as interpreter, driver and provision-seeker – for such things as rat poison for the maternity hospitals. He said he took away with him a "time-honoured conception of humanity in ruins".

The newness of so much in St-Lô reveals the scale of fighting. Between the SNCF gare and the castle rock, for example, a walk leads along the canalized channel of the Vire – an attractive course but unmistakably an attempt to patch over the ravages. All the trees in the city are the same height, too, all planted to replace the battle's mutilated stumps. But the most visible – and brilliant – reconstruction is the **Cathédrale de Notre Dame**. The main body of this, with its strange southward-veering nave, has been conventionally repaired and rebuilt. Between the shattered west front and base of the collapsed north tower, however, a startling sheer wall of icy green stone makes no attempt to mask the destruction.

By way of contrast to such memories, a lighthouse-like 1950s folly spirals to nowhere on the main square. Should you feel the urge to climb its staircase, make your way into the brand-new and even more pointless labyrinth of glass at its feet, which now houses St-Lô's tourist office (for hours, see below), and pay the 10F admission fee. More compelling, around behind the Mairie, is a **Musée des Beaux Arts** (daily except Tues: April–Oct 10am–noon & 2–6pm; Nov–March 2–6pm; 10F). This is full of treasures: a Boudin sunset; a Lurçat tapestry of his dog Nadir and the Pirates; works by Corot, van Loo, Moreau; a Léger watercolour; a fine series of unfaded sixteenth-century Flemish tapestries on the lives of two peasants; and sad bombardment relics of the town.

Practicalities

St-Lô makes an interesting pause, but it's virtually abandoned at night. Full information on what it has to offer can be obtained from the **tourist office** in the central square, described above (mid-June to mid-Sept Mon–Fri 9am–noon & 2–6pm, Sat 9am–6pm, Sun 11am–4pm; mid-Sept to mid-June Mon 2–6pm, Tues–Fri 9am–noon & 2–6pm, Sat 9am–6pm; ☎02.33.05.02.09); the **gare routière** is on the rue des 80ᵉ and 136ᵉ, a short way south.

Most of the hotels, restaurants and bars, however, are just across the river, near the **gare SNCF**. Overlooking the river from the brow of a ridge beside the station, the upmarket *logis Hôtel des Voyageurs*, 5–7 av Briovère (☎02.33.05.08.63; ③), is home to the *Tocqueville* restaurant, which serves a delicious trout soufflé on its 96F menu. If you'd rather be up in town, try *La Cremaillère*, 27 rue Belle (☎02.33.57.14.68; closed Sat am & Sun; ②).

The Vire Valley

Once St-Lô was taken in the Battle of Normandy, the armies moved speedily on to their next confrontation. The **Vire Valley**, trailing south from St-Lô, saw little action – and indeed its towns and villages have rarely been touched by any historic or cultural mainstream. The motivation in coming to this landscape of rolling hills and occasional gorges is essentially to consume the region's cider, Calvados, and butter-rich fruit pastries.

Although the countryside is filled with orchards of apples and pears, the land is less fertile than elsewhere in Normandy – and has suffered heavily from the recent depression in the fruit market. A booming trade, however, has grown up around illicit Calvados, bolstering the faltering economy of many Vire farmers. Bootleggers smuggle hundreds of thousands of litres throughout France, using the hydraulic suspension of their Citröen cars to obscure the heavy loads they are carrying from the eyes of watching taxmen. One much-arrested smuggler has such James Bond accessories as automatically rotating licence plates, smoke screens and even oil jets for use against pursuing motorcycles.

Between St-Lô and Vire

The best section of the Vire is the valley that comes down from St-Lô through the Roches de Ham to Tessy-sur-Vire. The **Roches de Ham** are a pair of sheer rocky promontories high above the river. They are promoted as a "viewing table", though the pleasure lies as much in the walk up, through lanes lined with blackberries, hazelnuts and rich orchards.

La Chapelle-sur-Vire

Just downstream from the Roches, and a good place to stop over for a night, is **LA CHAPELLE-SUR-VIRE**. Its church, towering majestically above the river, has been an object of pilgrimage since the twelfth century. There's a weir nearby and a scattering of grassy islands. Next to the bridge on the lower road is the *Auberge de la Chapelle* (☎02.33.56.32.83; ①), a good but rather expensive restaurant that also offers a few cheap **rooms**. The cheapest menu on weekdays is 75F, at weekends it's over 100F; whenever you come, there'll be plenty of fresh river fish.

Torigni-sur-Vire

An alternative base for the Roches, over to the east, is **TORIGNI-SUR-VIRE**, which was the base of the Grimaldi family before they achieved quasi-royal status upon moving on to the principality of Monaco. A spacious country town, it boasts a few grand buildings and an attractive **campsite**, *Camping du Lac* (mid-March to Oct; ☎02.33.56.91.74), which offers more luxurious facilities in mid-summer. The *Auberge Orangerie* (☎02.33.56.70.64; closed Feb, Sun pm & Mon out of season; ②) is a good **restaurant**, with menus starting at 65F and half a dozen rooms.

Tessy-sur-Vire

At **TESSY-SUR-VIRE** there's little to see other than the river itself, banked by rolling meadows that make an ideal venue for a summer's day picnic, though the town again has a luxurious **campsite**, along with a couple of **hotels**, including the

Hôtel de France, a nice little *logis* on the main street (☎02.33.56.30.01; closed mid-Jan to mid-Feb; ①) and a Wednesday **market**.

Le Viaduc de la Souleuvre

At the eastern end of the sinuous Vire gorge, 6km west of Le Bény-Bocage, stands the former railway viaduct of **Le Viaduc de la Souleuvre**, designed by Gustave Eiffel. Only the six supporting granite pillars of Eiffel's original structure remain – the railway closed down in 1970 – but in 1990 a wooden boardwalk was relaid across half the span of the bridge, on which visitors can cross to the deepest part of the gorge. Once there, 61m up, they are seriously expected to **jump off** – this is A.J. Hackett's **bungy-jumping** centre (daily June to mid-Sept; Feb & mid-Dec Sat, Sun & hols, and other times on demand; closed mid-Dec to Jan; reservations essential ☎02.31.66.31.66). Jumpers have to be aged at least 13, and for one to three people to make a single jump each costs 400F; you also have to pay 15F for the privilege of parking in the adjacent field. Less intrepid souls can walk down to the meadows immediately beneath the viaduct and watch the plummeting from there.

Vire

The pride and joy of the people of **VIRE** are their *andouilles*, the blood sausages known in English as chitterlings. If you can avoid these hideous parcels of pigs' intestines, and the assortment of abattoirs that produce them, it's possible to have a good time; in fact Vire is a town worth visiting specifically for its food.

The only problem is what to do when you're not eating. You can look at the collection of minerals and fossils in the belfry that stands alone in the town centre (Mon–Sat 2.30–6.30pm; 10F). You can visit the museum of "How to Restore Old Norman Farmhouses". Or you can wander by the little scrap of **canal**, equipped with twee floating houses for the ducks, that lies just below the one stark finger that survives of the castle. The only action is at the Friday **market**, again obsessively dedicated to food.

For some exercise, head 6km south along the D76 to **Lac de la Dathée**. Set in open country, the lake is circled by footpaths; in summer it sometimes dries up completely, but when it's wet it can also be crossed by rented sailing boat or windsurf board – contact the Maison des Jeunes et de la Culture, 1 rue des Halles, Vire (☎02.31.68.08.04).

Practicalities

Vire's **tourist office** is in the square de la Résistance at the heart of town (Mon–Sat 10am–12.15pm & 1.45–7pm; ☎02.31.68.00.05). Choosing a **hotel**, it makes sense to go for one with a good dining room. At the central *Hôtel de France*, 4 rue d'Aignaux (☎02.31.68.00.35; ②), the 98F menu is packed with local specialities, including *andouille* for both starter and main course, but no one's going to make you eat it if you don't want to – there's always *tripes a là mode de Caen* instead. *Au Vrai Normand*, 14 rue Armand-Gasté (☎02.31.67.90.99), is the best **restaurant**.

West and south from Vire

Once past Vire, the roads towards Brittany present you with the choice either of heading southwest for the frontier towns of **Fougères** and **Vitré** (see pp.213–217), or directly to the coast and making the magnificent **Mont-St-Michel** (see p.145) your last port of call in Normandy.

West from Vire, the road to Villedieu passes through **ST-SEVER**, not in itself much to write home about but backed by a dark and magical **forest** in which there's a dolmen, an abbey and a scattering of pukka picnic spots marked by signs showing a champagne bottle in a hamper.

Villedieu-les-Poêles

VILLEDIEU-LES-POÊLES – literally "City of God the Frying Pans" – is a lively though touristy place, 28km west of Vire. Much of this ancient town still retains significant elements of its medieval appearance, especially in its backstreets where perfectly preserved old courtyards are tucked away behind unprepossessing wooden gateways. Ever since the twelfth century, Villedieu has been a centre for metalworking; copper souvenirs and kitchen utensils gleam from its rows of shops, and the tourist office can provide lists of dozens of local *ateliers* for more direct purchases. You can see examples illustrating the historical development of Villedieu's copperware in the **museum** at 54 rue Général-Huard (Easter–Oct Mon & Wed–Sun 10am–noon & 2–6.30pm, Tues 2–6.30pm; 15F).

All of this can seem a bit obsessive, though there is more authentic interest at the **Fonderie de Cloches** at 13 rue du Pont-Chignon, one of the twelve remaining bell foundries in Europe. Work here is only part time due to limited demand, but it's open to visits all year round, and you may find the forge lit (July & Aug daily 8am–6pm; Sept–June Tues–Sat 8am–noon & 2–5.30pm; 16F). Expert craftsmen will show you the moulds, composed of an unpleasant-looking combination of clay, goats' hair and horse shit.

Practicalities

Villedieu's **tourist office** is on place des Costils (June–Sept only; ☎02.33.61.05.69 – for the rest of the year, contact the Mairie, ☎02.33.61.00.16). If you're charmed into staying, the dining room of the comfortable *Fruitier* on place Gostils (☎02.33.90.51.00; closed Sat in winter; ③) has plate-glass windows to watch the goings-on in the square, there's a reasonable 69F menu, and the 115F menu is packed with regional delights. In the heart of the main street, the very welcoming *logis Hôtel St-Pierre et St-Michel*, 12 place de la République (☎02.33.61.00.11; closed Jan, plus Fri in low season; ③), houses the stylishly refurbished *Le Sourdin* restaurant, where the 115F menu features a fine *panaché de poissons*, and things get seriously gastronomic for 185F. There's also a **campsite** by the river, *Le Pré de la Rose* (Easter–Oct; ☎02.33.61.02.44).

Much the nicest **bar** in Villedieu – complete with tables in the cobbled square, Guinness, Rolling Rock and local cider, a good selection of music from around the world (especially the Celtic bits), and a youngish clientèle – is *Le Pussoir Fidèle*, 2 place du Pussoir Fidèle (☎02.33.51.94.58).

The Forêt de Lande-Pourrie

South from Vire, if you are heading for Fougères (see p.213) or Domfront (see p.173), you pass through the **Forêt de Mortain** and its continuation, the **Forêt**

de **Lande-Pourrie**. The **Fosse d'Arthur**, a remote spot in the forest to the east of Mortain, is one of the many unlikely claimants to King Arthur's death scene. A couple of waterfalls disappear into deep limestone caverns, but there's really very little to see.

Mortain

The war-ravaged town of **MORTAIN** perches high above the very deep gorge of the Cance, 24km south of Vire. It's not a place to linger very long, but the views, especially from the south end of the main street, are spectacular. A short walk west out of town leads into some lovely countryside, with two **waterfalls** – known as the Grande Cascade and the Petite Cascade – interrupting the river itself. Head up the high rocky bluff to the east, on the other hand, and from the tiny chapel at the top the neighbouring province of Maine spreads before you. On a clear day you can even see Mont-St-Michel.

If you want to spend a night in Mortain, the *Hôtel de la Poste*, 1 place des Arcades (☎02.33.59.00.05; closed Fri pm, Sat & Sun pm; ②), is the best option, with good menus from 90F.

Lonlay l'Abbaye and Barenton

On the far side of the Forêt de Lande-Pourrie – and just 9km out of Domfront (see p.173) on the D22 towards Tinchebray – **LONLAY L'ABBAYE** has a biscuit factory along with various vestiges of its eleventh-century Benedictine past.

At nearby **BARENTON** – an entirely rebuilt and unmemorable town – *Le Relais du Parc*, place Général-de-Gaulle, is a good cheap place for lunch that also has a couple of rooms (☎02.33.59.51.38; closed Mon; ①), and the **Maison de la Pomme et de la Poire** is a mildly diverting cider museum (April–Sept daily 10.30am–12.30pm & 2.30–7pm; 10F).

St-Hilaire-du-Harcoët

The thriving (Wednesday) market town of **ST-HILAIRE-DU-HARCOËT**, 28km north of Fougères, amounts to little more than a crossroads near the big market square. It does, however, hold a few restaurants and **hotels**, such as *Le Cygne* (☎02.33.49.11.84; closed Fri pm in winter; ③), a comfortable, newly modernized *logis* at 67 route de Fougères with an appealing set of somewhat pricey menus, and the cheaper *L'Agriculture* on rue Waldeck-Rousseau (☎02.33.49.10.60; ①), where the 60F menu includes fresh oysters in season.

St-Symphorien-des-Monts

As you head south from St-Hilaire towards Brittany, one last Norman stop, just off the N176 7km out of town, is the **wildlife sanctuary** at **ST-SYMPHORIEN-DES-MONTS**, set in the park of the now nonexistent château. Contented-looking beasts, like yaks and bisons and threatened domestic animals, graze in semi-liberty in fields and woods around a lake inhabited by swans and flamingos; wolves lurk somewhere in the undergrowth. Admission (Easter–Oct daily 10am–8pm; 35F) is a little more expensive than usual, but worth it.

travel details

Trains

From Évreux 5 daily to Conches (15min), Serquigny (30min), Bernay (45min), Lisieux (1hr) and Caen (1hr 30min); also 12 daily to Paris St-Lazare (1hr).

From Lisieux 6 daily to Rouen (1hr 30min) via Bernay (25min) and Serquigny (30min); regular service to Paris (2hr) via Bernay and Évreux (45min); 10 daily to Cherbourg (2hr 40min) via Caen (30min) and Bayeux (50min); to Trouville-Deauville (25min), about 6 daily out of season and more frequently in summer; service extends to Villers, Houlgate and Dives-Cabourg (40min from Trouville) on Sundays and holidays throughout the year, and daily in July & Aug.

From Alençon 6 daily to Caen (1hr 15min) via Sées (13min) and Argentan (30min); to Tours (2hr) via Le Mans.

From Bagnoles 5 daily to Briouze (30min) for Argentan (1hr 20min) and Paris (3hr 20min).

From St-Lô 4 daily to Caen (1hr) via Bayeux (30min); 4 daily to Rennes (2hr) via Coutances and Pontorson.

From Vire Regular service to Paris via Argentan (1hr) and L'Aigle (1hr 30min); to Villedieu (20min) and Granville (1hr).

Buses

The main inland bus networks are operated by **Bus Verts**, *who cover Calvados in particular from their base at 11 rue des Chanoines in Caen (☎02.31.44.77.44), and* **STAO**, *whose routes*

extend across most of the Orne region further south (Alençon ☎02.33.26.06.35; Argentan ☎02.33.67.04.66; Mortagne ☎02.33.25.19.11).

From Caen Bus Verts #32 to Vire (1–3 daily; 1hr 30min) via Villers-Bocage; Bus Verts #34 (5 daily, 2 on Sun) to Flers (1hr 20min) via Thury-Harcourt (36min) and Clécy (50min); Bus Verts #35 to Falaise (45min); to Lisieux (45min).

From Lisieux Bus Verts #50 to Pont l'Evêque (4 daily; 25min) and on to Honfleur (50min) or Deauville (45min); Bus Verts #52 to St-Pierre-sur-Dives (1–3 daily; 35min); Bus Verts #53 to Vimoutiers (4 daily; 1hr) via Livarot; Bus Verts #56 to Orbec (6 daily; 45min); to Le Havre (2 daily; 1hr 30min).

From L'Aigle to Gacé (1 daily; 45min); to Vimoutiers (1–2 daily; 1hr 10min); to Évreux (2–3 daily; 1hr 20min) via Conches (45min).

From Mortagne to Bellême (1–4 daily; 20min).

From Argentan to Carrouges (1–3 daily; 45min); to Domfront (1–3 daily; 1hr 50min) via Bagnoles (1hr).

From Alençon to Bagnoles (30min); to Évreux (1 daily; 2hr) via L'Aigle (1hr 40min); to Vimoutiers (1–3 daily; 1hr 30min) via Sées (30min) and Argentan (1hr 17min); to Mortagne (1–3 daily; 1hr); to Bellême (1–2 daily; 1hr).

From St-Lô to Bayeux (30min); to Cherbourg (1hr 30min); to Coutances (30min).

From Vire Bus Verts #81 to Condé-sur-Noireau (30min); to Fougères (1hr 30min); to Avranches (45min).

PART THREE

BRITTANY

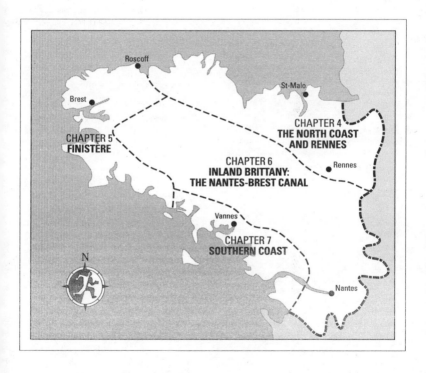

Roscoff

Brest

St-Malo

CHAPTER 4
THE NORTH COAST
AND RENNES

CHAPTER 5
FINISTÈRE

Rennes

CHAPTER 6
INLAND BRITTANY:
THE NANTES-BREST CANAL

Vannes

CHAPTER 7
SOUTHERN COAST

Nantes

N

CHAPTER FOUR

THE NORTH COAST AND RENNES

The **northern coast** of Brittany is varied in the extreme. Long sections, open to the full force of the Atlantic, are spectacular but much too dangerous for swimming; others shelter superb natural harbours and peaceful resorts. The old *citadelle* port of **St-Malo** makes an attractive point of arrival, from which you are well positioned for exploration, even if your main goals lie elsewhere, in the south or in Finistère.

The best of the **resorts** are concentrated along two separate stretches of coastline, the Côte d'Émeraude and the Côte de Granit Rose. As green as its name suggests, the **Côte d'Émeraude** remains largely unspoiled, at its wildest on the heather-covered headlands of Cap Fréhel. Thanks to gorgeous beaches, seaside towns such as **Le Val-André** and **Erquy** tend to be dominated by English visitors, but it's always possible to find a secluded campsite for a night or two's stopover.

Further west, beyond the placid **Baie de St-Brieuc** (the town of St-Brieuc itself is, for most holiday-makers, a nuisance to be avoided) the coastline erupts into a garish tangle of pink granite boulders, the famed **Côte de Granit Rose**. This harsher territory was once, at **Paimpol** and elsewhere, the home of cod and whaling fleets that ranged right across the Atlantic. Today it's reliant on tourism, especially at the twin resorts of **Perros-Guirec** and **Ploumanac'h**. These are attractive nonetheless, and there are plenty of smaller places where you can avoid the crowds, such as **Loguivy** on the mainland, and, just offshore, the **Île de Bréhat** – among the most beautiful of all northern French islands.

The first 20km of the route **inland** from St-Malo take you alongside the delightful **Rance estuary**. Frequent boats connect both St-Malo and Dinard with **Dinan**, a medieval fortress town *par excellence* that like most of this region owes its prosperity to an epic saga of trading and piracy on the high seas. Beyond it, to the

---

ACCOMMODATION PRICE CODES

All **hotel prices** in this book have been coded using the symbols below. The price shown is for the least expensive double room in high season, which for category ① often means a room without shower, bath and toilet. Most hotels in that category have other rooms with en-suite facilities, which typically cost 30–50F extra.

For a full explanation see p.30.

① Under 160F	③ 220–300F	⑤ 400–500F	⑦ 600–700F
② 160–220F	④ 300–400F	⑥ 500–600F	⑧ 700F and over

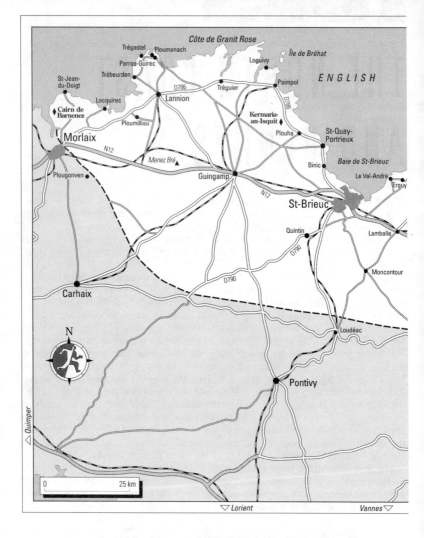

south of the far more ancient community of **Dol** – site of several fascinating prehistoric relics – lies a patchwork of waterways and woodlands, where rivers and canals cut through characteristic Breton **forests** like **Ville-Cartier**. Further **east**, the redoubtable **citadelles** of **Fougères** and **Vitré** still guard the frontier with Normandy.

At the heart of the *département* of Ille-et-Vilaine, just over 60km southeast of St-Malo, the city of **Rennes** has after centuries of rivalry with Nantes finally established itself as the indisputable capital of Brittany. Rennes may not be the prettiest town in the province, but it is without doubt the liveliest, hosting a considerable university

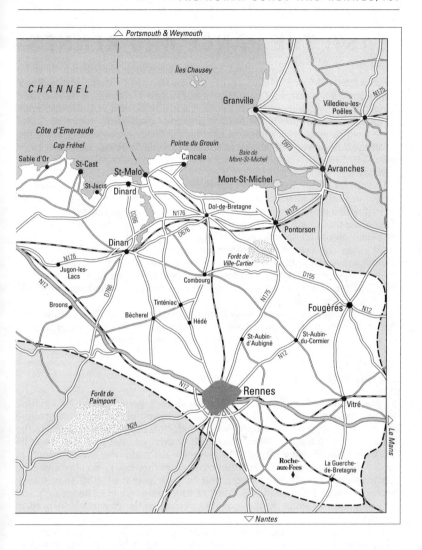

and most of the major Breton political and cultural organizations. It's also renowned for its **festivals**, devoting itself to ten days of theatre and music each July during the **Tombées de la Nuit**, and celebrating **Les Transmusicales**, one of the most important events in the calendar of French rock, in December.

Among numerous other annual events in northern Brittany, the biggest and most compelling is the **Breton Music** festival, held each July at **St-Brieuc**. That's also the venue of the ominous-sounding **Art Rock** festival in late May, while the region's largest traditional festival is the *pardon* of Saint-Yves in **Tréguier**, on the third Sunday in May.

EAST: THE RANCE AND RENNES

Whether you approach across the Channel by ferry from Portsmouth, or along the coast from Mont-St-Michel in Normandy, the wide estuary of the **River Rance** makes a spectacular introduction to Brittany. The towns of **St-Malo** and **Dinard** stand to either side of its mouth, each with its own very distinct ambience, while **Dinan** guards the head of the river itself 20km upstream. From those few places where it's possible to cross the Rance (most notably, along the top of the tidal power dam known as the **Barrage de la Rance**), you can enjoy magnificent views of its sheltered banks – rich, fertile and repeatedly pierced by tributaries.

To the east of the river spreads the **Baie du Mont-St-Michel**, dominated by the pinnacle of the Mont itself (see p.145; "Normandy"), and swept by extraordinary tides that render swimming out of the question. **Cancale**, the most sheltered point along the Breton side of the bay, is a good spot from which to appreciate it all, ideally as you fill up with the town's famed and acclaimed oysters. Inland, all roads either curl eventually to **Rennes**, or head out east towards Normandy. In addition to the medieval fortress towns of **Fougères** and **Vitré**, lesser-known and quieter pleasures are to be found beside the lake in **Combourg**, in the **Forêt de Ville-Cartier**, south of Dol, and along the **Ille-et-Vilaine canal**, around **Hédé** and **Tinténiac**.

Getting around anywhere away from the coast or off main routes to Rennes can be a problem. If you don't have your own transport, keep your sights low – even Fougères is served only by a scattering of market buses.

St-Malo

ST-MALO, walled and built with the same grey granite stone as Mont-St-Michel, was originally a fortified island at the mouth of the Rance, controlling not only the estuary but the open sea beyond. Now inseparably attached to the mainland, it is the most visited place in Brittany – and not just because of its ferry terminal. Walking through the *intra-muros* ("within the walls") streets of its **old citadelle** is a unique experience: at times they can be sombre and grim (particularly beneath grey skies), but in high summer or at sunset they become light and almost unreal. Most of what you see had to be lovingly and precisely rebuilt, stone by stone; eighty percent of the city was destroyed in August 1944.

Though the old city can, when busy, feel more than a little claustrophobic, St-Malo is a lively town, where there's always a lot going on. Having to spend a night here before or after a ferry crossing is a positive pleasure – so long as you take the trouble to reserve accommodation in advance.

Although it began as a monastic settlement, founded by SS Aaron and Brendan early in the sixth century and then from 550 AD onwards identified with the Celtic St Maclou (or possibly MacLow), St-Malo later became notorious as the home of a fierce breed of **pirate-mariners**. These adventurers were never quite under anybody's control but their own; for four years from 1590, St-Malo even declared itself to be an independent republic, under the

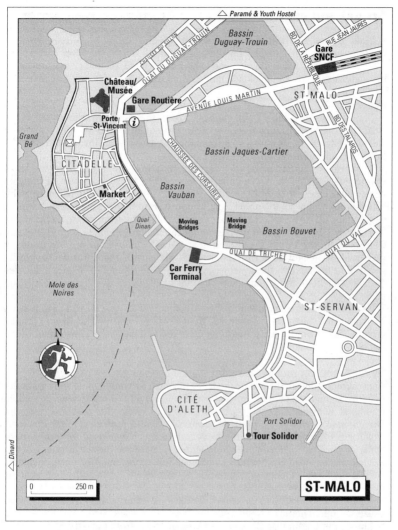

motto *"Ni Français, Ni Bretons, Malouins Suis"*. Over a period of centuries, the *corsaires* of St-Malo not only forced English ships passing up the Channel to pay tribute, but also brought wealth from further afield. Jacques Cartier, who colonized Canada, lived in and sailed from St-Malo, as did the first colonists to settle the Falklands – hence the islands' Argentinian name, Las Malvinas. Even when the duke of Marlborough landed 15,000 men just up the coast near Cancale in 1758, and attempted to take the city by land, St-Malo's defences proved too formidable.

Arrival and city transport

St-Malo presents its best face to the **sea**; if you don't arrive by Brittany Ferries, you may well want to consider the ten-minute shuttle across the River Rance from Dinard as an alternative. If you come in by **bus** or **train**, the old city is concealed by modern suburbs and dockside industry almost until you're in it.

Boats

St-Malo is always busy with **boats**. From the Gare Maritime du Naye (☎02.99.40.64.41), Brittany Ferries sail to Portsmouth (mid-March to mid-Nov daily at 10.45am, otherwise less frequently; 8hr 45min) and Plymouth (mid-Nov to mid-March Fri noon; 8hr).

In summer, regular passenger **ferries to Dinard** operate from the **quai Dinan**, just outside the westernmost point of the ramparts in front of the port (Émeraude Lines; ☎02.99.40.48.40; 20F single, 30F return). The trip across the estuary takes an all-too-short ten minutes. Émeraude Lines also conduct excursions up the river to Dinan (see p.200), day-trips from Granville in Normandy (see p.142), and cruises along the Brittany coast to Cap Fréhel and Cézembre, to the Pointe du Grouin near Cancale, and out to the Îles Chausey (see p.143). In addition, they connect St-Malo with the **Channel Islands**; you'll find details of their services, along with those of Condor Ferries (☎02.99.20.03.00) and Channiland (☎02.99.40.40.90), in the "Travel details" on p.238.

For a touch of luxury, in summer Le Chateaubriand (☎02.99.46.44.44) puts on gastronomic cruises in the Baie du Mont-St-Michel and up the Rance, costing around 250F, from the gare maritime de la Richardais, at the Dinard end of the Barrage de la Rance.

By road, and car and cycle rental

Approaching central St-Malo or the ferry terminal by **road** can be somewhat dismal; the signposts seem designed to confuse, and all the roads seem to end on tramlined docksides. Lost and bewildered cars circle the port like seagulls. Driving in to catch a ferry, keep the **Chaussée des Corsaires** in mind: this road, which links the old town with the ferry terminal, can be closed for long periods while its movable bridge is opened to let boats out of the Bassin Jacques-Cartier.

Most of the major **car-rental** companies are represented in town, including Avis at the ferry terminal and gare SNCF (☎02.99.40.58.68), and Hertz at 48 bd de la République (☎02.99.56.31.61).

If you prefer to enjoy more active pursuits, you can rent **bicycles** from Cycles Diazo, 47 quai Duguay-Trouin (☎02.99.40.31.63), Cycles Nicole, 11 rue Robert-Schumann in Paramé (☎02.99.56.11.06), or, as usual, from the gare SNCF.

Trains

St-Malo's **gare SNCF** (☎02.99.56.04.40) is 2km out from the *citadelle* on place Hermine, and convenient neither for the old town nor the ferry (take care if you're planning a tight connection). All trains to and from St-Malo pass through Dol. Most continue through to Rennes, so if you're heading west towards Dinan and St-Brieuc, or northeast into Normandy, you'll probably have to change at Dol.

Buses

Officially, the **gare routière** (☎02.99.40.83.33) – not a building, just an expanse of concrete – is right next to the tourist office (see below), but most buses, whether local or long-distance, coincide also with trains at the gare SNCF.

The Compagnie de Transport d'Ille et Vilaine (TIV; ☎02.99.40.82.67) run services to Dinard, Dinan, Cancale, Combourg and Rennes. Les Courriers Bretons, 13 rue d'Alsace (☎02.99.56.79.09), go to Cancale, Mont-St-Michel and Fougères, and also run day-trips to Mont-St-Michel (summer daily 9.30am; low season Wed & Sat only; 108F). Dinan buses are also operated by CAT (☎02.96.39.21.05).

Information

The helpful **tourist office** (July & Aug Mon–Sat 8.30am–8pm, Sun 10am–7pm; April–June & Sept Mon–Sat 9am–7pm, Sun 10am–noon & 2–6pm; Oct–March Mon–Sat 9am–noon & 2–6pm; ☎02.99.56.64.48) is housed in a single-storey building, right in front of the city walls, beside the Bassin Duguay-Trouin in the **Port des Yachts**. As well as good detailed city maps, they can provide information on annual festivals such as the **Étonnants Voyageurs** ("Amazing Travellers"), dedicated to the film and literature of travel and adventure, which takes place for three days in late May.

The main city **post office** is at 1 bd de la Tour d'Auvergne (July to mid-Sept Mon–Fri 8.30am–6.30pm, Sat 8.30am–12.30pm; otherwise Mon–Fri 8.30am–12.30pm & 1.30–5.30pm, Sat 8.30am–noon; ☎02.99.56.12.05), but for most travellers the branch office within the walls at 4 place des Frères Lamennais is more convenient (same hours; ☎02.99.40.89.90). If you want to arrange to pick up poste restante letters, make sure you distinguish between the two – specify either *35401 St-Malo Principal* or *35402 St-Malo intra-muros*.

Several shops and kiosks within the *citadelle* advertise that they handle **foreign-exchange** transactions without charging commission; the rates they offer are so abysmal that they don't need to.

Accommodation

St-Malo boasts of having over a hundred **hotels**, including the traditional seaside boarding houses just off the beach, and also has several **campsites** and a couple of **youth hostels**. In high season it needs every one of them: the demand is phenomenal. Motorists intending to stay the night before catching a summer ferry sailing should make reservations well in advance; if you don't have a reservation, don't demoralize yourself hunting around, and settle for spending the night somewhere else along the coast or nearby. Apart from the obvious alternatives of Dinard and Dinan, it's worth considering peaceful smaller towns such as Combourg, Cancale, Jugon-les-Lacs or Erquy.

Hotels in the citadelle

Hotel guests pay a premium for the privilege of staying **within the city walls**; that's where any nightlife takes place, and it's a fair walk in through the docks from any of the surrounding suburbs. *Intra-muros* hotels tend to take advantage of high summer demand by insisting that you eat in their own restaurants.

Hôtel-Restaurant aux Vieilles Pierres, 9 rue Thévenard (☎02.99.56.46.80). Six-room hotel that's one of the better bargains within the walls, near place aux Herbes. Open all year. Menus at 88F with fish soup and steak, or 125F for the full spread, in theory totalling six courses, but half of those are just intended to keep you ticking over until the next one arrives. ②.

Hôtel Bristol-Union, 4 place de la Poissonnerie (☎02.99.40.83.36, fax 02.99.40.35.51). Very correct rooms, in a nice little square facing the former fish market, just off the Grande Rue. No restaurant. Closed mid-Nov to Jan. ③.

Hôtel du Commerce, 11 rue St-Thomas (☎02.99.56.18.00, fax 02.99.56.04.68). Very cheap, very plain, but if you're on a tight budget you can't do better within the walls. Closed Jan to mid-Feb. ②.

Hôtel Le Croiseur, 2 place de la Poissonnerie (☎02.99.40.80.40, fax 02.99.56.83.76). Clean and relatively modern place, near the Grande Porte. No restaurant. Open all year. ②.

Hôtel du Louvre, 2 rue des Marins (☎02.99.40.86.62, fax 02.99.40.86.93). Pleasant family-run place just off Grande Rue, between the Grande Porte and Cathédrale St-Vincent. Closed Dec to mid-Feb, except Christmas and New Year. ③.

Hôtel-Restaurant Pomme d'Or, 4 place du Poids-du-Roi (☎02.99.40.90.24, fax 02.99.40.58.31). Seventeen modernized rooms in a venerable building, just inside the *citadelle* near the ramparts – take a sharp left after entering through the Grande Porte. Conventional menus start around 90F. The *patronne* has an eccentric predilection for animals. Closed Jan to mid-Feb. ③.

Hôtel-Restaurant Porte St-Pierre, 2 place du Guet (☎02.99.40.91.27, fax 02.99.56.09.94). Comfortable *logis de France*, peeping out to sea over the walls of the *citadelle*, near the small Porte St-Pierre and very handy for the plage de Bon Secours. Menus from 85F upwards. Closed Dec & Jan. ④.

Hôtel Quic en Groigne, 8 rue d'Estrées (☎02.99.20.22.20, fax 02.99.20.22.30). Friendly little hotel at the far end of the *citadelle*, with nicely styled en-suite rooms. ④.

Hôtel San Pédro, 1 rue Ste-Anne (☎02.99.40.88.57, fax 02.99.40.46.25). Small, twelve-room refurbished hotel in a nice quiet setting, just inside the walls in the north of the *citadelle*, near the porte des Bés. Rooms on the higher floors (reached using the world's smallest lift) enjoy sea views. ③.

Hôtel-Restaurant de l'Univers, 10 place Chateaubriand (☎02.99.40.89.52, fax 02.99.40.07.27). One of the grand hotels that face you immediately upon entering the porte St-Vincent. Some good-value rooms, and an excellent 75F menu in the restaurant downstairs, with tables out on the square opposite the château. Restaurant closed Wed. ③.

Hotels outside the walls

If cheaper rates are a high priority, a number of lower priced places can be found near the gare SNCF, or in suburban Paramé, but there's not all that much pleasure in staying outside the *citadelle* for the sake of saving a few francs.

Hôtel Arrivée, 52 bd de la République (☎02.99.56.30.78, fax 02.99.56.16.05). Budget hotel on a corner very near the gare SNCF. No restaurant. Open all year. ②.

Hôtel le Beaufort, 25 chaussée du Sillon, Paramé (☎02.99.40.99.99, fax 02.99.40.99.62). Sea-view hotel, 30min walk from the *citadelle*, with modernized rooms – some with lovely balconies – and a good restaurant. ④.

Hôtel les Charmettes, 64 bd Hébert, Paramé (☎02.99.56.07.31, fax 02.99.56.85.96). One of Paramé's cheaper options, not on the front itself (though a few rooms have sea views), but very near the beach and the imposing *Grand Hôtel*. No restaurant. Closed Jan. ②.

Hôtel de l'Europe, 44 bd de la République (☎02.99.56.13.42). Year-round cheap but clean rooms in a genuinely friendly (if noisy) hotel, near the gare SNCF. ②.

Hôtel la Rance, 15 quai Sebastopol, St-Servan (☎02.99.81.78.63, fax 02.99.81.44.80). Small, tasteful option in sight of the Tour Solidro, with eleven spacious rooms and no restaurant. ④.

Hôtel-Restaurant Terminus Gare, 8 bd des Talards (☎02.99.56.14.38). Reasonable hotel near the station (not to be confused with the other *Hôtel Terminus*, in distant Rothéneuf), with an inexpensive restaurant where menus start at 55F. Open all year. ②.

Hostel

St-Malo's year-round **youth hostel** – one of the busiest in France, although not formally part of the national network – is not within the walls, but in the suburb of Paramé. The *Centre Patrick Varangot*, also known as the *Centre des Rencontres International*, at 37 av du Père-Umbricht (☎02.99.40.29.80; dorm bed 69F, private doubles 164F; rates include breakfast), is 2km northeast of the gare SNCF on bus routes #1, #2 or #5, a short way back from the beach on Paramé's main street. It does not operate a curfew.

Camping

St-Malo's four municipal **campsites** tend to be full in July and August, and you may have to travel inland to find space; there are several private sites in the locality. If in difficulties, you could try ringing the Camping Department of the Mairie (☎02.99.40.71.11) for the up-to-date position.

La Cité d'Aleth, St-Servan (☎02.99.81.60.91). Much the nearest campsite to the *citadelle*, on the headland southwest of St-Malo. Open all year. Reachable in summer on bus #1.

Les Ilôts, avenue de la Guimorais, Rothéneuf (☎02.99.56.98.72). July & Aug only. Inland, to the northeast.

Le Nicet, av de la Varde, Rothéneuf (☎02.99.40.26.32). On the coast by Pointe de Nicet. Reservations essential. June–Aug only.

Les Nielles, avenue John Kennedy, Paramé (☎02.99.40.26.35). On the beach at the plage du Minhic. Mid-June to Aug only.

The Town

The **citadelle** of St-Malo, very much the prime destination for visitors, was for many years joined to the mainland only by a long causeway, before the original line of the coast was hidden forever by the construction of the harbour basin. Although its cobbled streets of restored seventeenth- and eighteenth-century houses can be crowded to the point of absurdity in summer (and the cobbles present quite a challenge to parents pushing buggies), away from the more popular thoroughfares random exploration is fun.

Thanks to the limitations on space on this tiny peninsula, the buildings tend to be a little more high-rise than you might expect. Stern and ancient as they may look, they are almost entirely reconstructed – photographs of the damage suffered in 1944, when General Patton bombarded the city for two weeks before the Germans surrendered, show barely a stone left in place. But you can surface to the sunlight on the **ramparts** – first erected in the fourteenth century, and redesigned by the master builder Vauban (see also p.327) four hundred years later – to enjoy wonderful views all round, especially to the west as the sun sets over the sea.

The main gate of the *citadelle* as you approach by road is the **Porte St-Vincent**. Until 1770, the whole town was sealed off by a 10pm curfew; as you walk through the gateway, you pass the small room where latecomers were obliged to spend the night. The **Musée de la Ville** in the castle to the right (Easter–Sept daily 10am–noon & 2–6pm; Oct–Easter daily except Mon same hours; 25F) is something

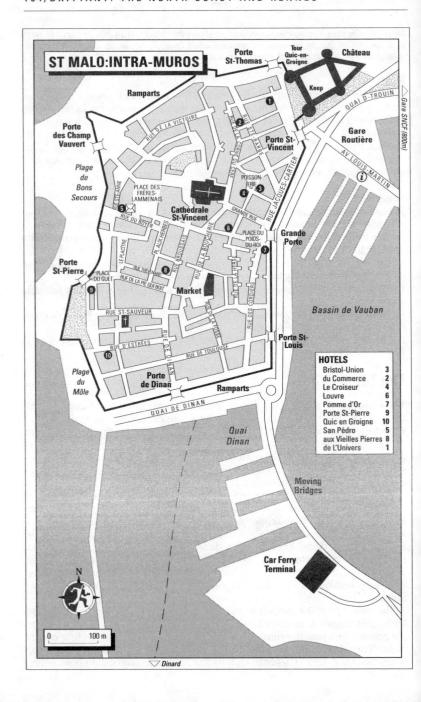

ST MALO:INTRA-MUROS

Porte St-Thomas
Tour Quic-en-Groigne
Château
Keep
Ramparts
Porte des Champ Vauvert
Plage de Bons Secours
RUE DE LA VICTOIRE
RUE ST-BARBE
Porte St-Vincent
Gare Routière
AV LOUIS-MARTIN
QUAI D-TROUIN
Gare SNCF (800m)
RUE JACQUES-CARTIER
POISSON-NERIE
PLACE DES FRÈRES-LAMMENAIS
Cathédrale St-Vincent
RUE ST-ANNE
RUE DU BOYER
GRANDE RUE
Grande Porte
PLACE DU POIDS-DU-ROI
LE PLACITRE
PL AUX HERBES
RUE BROUSSAIS
RUE DE LA BOUCHERIE
RUE DES HERBES
Porte St-Pierre
PLACE DU GUET
RUE THEVENARD
RUE DE LA PIE QUI BOIT
Market
RUE DES CORDIERS
Bassin de Vauban
RUE ST-SAUVEUR
RUE D'ESTRÉES
RUE DE DINAN
RUE DE TOULOUSE
Porte St-Louis
Plage du Môle
Porte de Dinan
Ramparts
QUAI DE DINAN

HOTELS

Bristol-Union	3
du Commerce	2
Le Croiseur	4
Louvre	6
Pomme d'Or	7
Porte St-Pierre	9
Quic en Groigne	10
San Pédro	5
aux Vieilles Pierres	8
de L'Univers	1

Quai Dinan

Moving Bridges

Car Ferry Terminal

N

0   100 m

▽ *Dinard*

of a paeaon of praise to the "prodigious prosperity" enjoyed by St-Malo during its days of piracy, colonialism and slave-trading. Climbing the 169 steps of the castle keep – whose walls are up to 7m thick – you pass a fascinating mixture of maps, diagrams and exhibits. Among them are chilling handbills from the Nazi Occupation, accounts of the "infernal machine" used by the English to blow up the port in 1693, and savage four-pronged *chaussetrappes*, thrown by pirates onto the decks of ships being boarded to immobilize their crews. At the top a gull's-eye prospect takes in the whole *citadelle*.

It is possible to pass **through the ramparts** at a couple of points on the western side of the peninsula. On the open shore beyond, a huge beach stretches away beyond the rather featureless resort-suburb of **Paramé**. Out to sea stand a procession of rocky islets, many of which still hold traces of medieval fortifications.

When the tide is low, an easy short walk across the sands leads to the small island of **Grand-Bé** – it's such a popular stroll that you may even need to queue to get onto the short causeway. Solemn warnings are posted of the dangers of attempting to return from the island when the tide has risen too far – if you're caught there, there you have to stay. The island "sight" is the tomb of the nineteenth-century writer-politician Chateaubriand (who was born in St-Malo on Sept 4, 1768, and died in 1848). Marx described him as "the most classic incarnation of French *vanité* . . . the false profundity, Byzantine exaggeration, emotional coquetry . . . a never-before-seen mishmash of lies". Suitably enough he features heavily on all the tourist brochures, which – with no apparent irony – extol his "modesty" in choosing so "isolated" a burial spot.

The coast along here is safer for paddlers than for swimmers, but it is very popular for **windsurfing**. Boards are available for rental from Surf School, 2 av de la Hoguette (☎02.99.40.07.47), or the Société Nautique de la Baie de St-Malo, quai du Bajoyer (☎02.99.40.84.42); most surfers make for the beaches further along the coast towards Cancale, the **plage du Verger** and the larger **Anse du Guesclin**.

St-Servan

St-Servan, within walking distance along the corniche to the south of the *citadelle*, is actually older than St-Malo itself. It was on the site of the Gallo-Roman city of *Aleth* that St Maclou established his church, and the seat of the bishopric only moved onto the impregnable island fortress when danger threatened in 1142.

St-Servan curves round several small inlets and beaches to face the tidal power dam across the river. It's dominated by the distinctive **Tour Solidor**, which consists of three linked towers built in 1382, and in cross-section looks just like the ace of clubs. Originally known in Breton as the *Steir Dor*, or "gate of the river", it now holds a museum of Cape Horn clipper ships, open all year for ninety-minute guided visits (Easter–Sept daily 10am–noon & 2–6pm; Oct–Easter daily except Mon same times; 20F). Most of the great European explorers of the Pacific are covered, from Magellan onwards, but naturally the emphasis is on French heroes such as Louis Antoine de Bougainville, who was responsible for spreading the brightly coloured bougainvillea plant around the globe. Tours culminate with a superb view from the topmost ramparts.

Follow the main road due south from St-Servan, ignoring signs for the Barrage de la Rance – or take bus #5 from the gare SNCF – and at a roundabout high above town you'll come to the new **Grand Aquarium** (daily: mid-June to mid-Sept 9am–9pm, 50F; mid-Sept to mid-June 9.30am–6pm, 44F). This postmodern structure can be a bit bewildering at first, but once you get the hang of it it's an entertaining place, where you can either learn interesting facts about slimy monsters of the deep or simply pull faces back at them. Its eight distinct fish tanks include one shaped like a Polo mint, where dizzy visitors stand in the hole in the middle as myriad fish whirl around them. There's actually another aquarium, logically enough named the **Petit Aquarium**, set into the walls of the old city, but this is far superior.

Rothéneuf

Just inside the eastern end of St-Malo's city limits, as the D201 winds towards Cancale, signs direct visitors away from the central streets of suburban **Rothéneuf** to the **Roches Sculptées**, or "sculpted rocks". The hermit priest Abbé Fouré spent 25 years, from the 1870s onwards, carving these jumbled boulders into the forms of dragons, giants and assorted sea monsters. Perched on a rocky promontory high above the water line, they're quite weathered now, and not all compelling in themselves, but with the town well out of sight this makes an appealing spot to stop and admire the coastline.

The gardens of the site also hold a small, sheltered café, and a shop that sells Breton pottery (daily: Easter–Sept 9am–9pm; Oct–Easter 10am–noon & 2–5.30pm; 15F).

Eating

Even more **restaurants** than hotels are crammed into *intra-muros* St-Malo, with a long crescent lining the inside of the ramparts between the porte St-Vincent and the Grande Porte. Prices are probably higher than anywhere else in Brittany, however, especially on the open café terraces – the demand is inflated by the numbers of day-trippers, from as far afield as the Channel Islands, and ferry passengers having last-night blowouts. Bear in mind that most of the *crêperies* also serve *moules* and similar quasi-snacks. If you just fancy an **ice cream**, call in at *Sanchez Glacier*, 9 rue de la Vieille-Boucherie.

All the restaurants listed below are in the *citadelle*.

Astrolabe, 8 rue des Cordiers (☎02.99.40.36.82). Quality cuisine, down a few steps just south of the Grande Porte. Lunch costs 80F, while in the evening you can compose your own menu from the extensive *carte*. 135F can buy a superb spread, with, for example, some sensational grilled *langoustines* and a *gratin du Granny-Smith* from the wide range of lush desserts. Serves until late. Open all year, but closed all day Mon & Tues lunchtime.

Borgnefesse, 10 rue du Puits-aux-Braies (☎02.99.40.05.05). Feels more like the tavern it once was, or a pub, than a restaurant. Heavily pirate-themed dining room with good solid French cooking. 62F lunch with steak, dinner menus from 85F. Closed for lunch on Mon & Sat, plus all day Sun.

Crêperie la Brigantine, 13 rue de Dinan (☎02.99.56.82.82). Sweet and savoury pancakes at very reasonable prices – the seafood fillings are exceptional. An individual *crêpe* can cost under 10F, and there's a 58F full menu. Closed Tues pm, Wed in low season, and mid-Jan to mid-Feb.

Le Chalut, 8 rue de la Corne du Cerf (☎02.99.56.71.58). Quite an exclusive dining room, in a stylish blue-painted bistro a short way in from the porte St-Vincent. A small 95F menu offers the catch of the day; otherwise you pay 175F or 300F for gourmet fish dinners, designed to be not quite as rich as the traditional norm. Reservations preferred; closed Mon, plus Sun pm between Sept and June.

Le Chasse Marée, 4 rue Grout de St-Georges (☎02.99.40.85.10). Nautical decor and *haute cuisine*, just round the corner from the post office, with a few tables out on the quiet street and more upstairs. The 87F menu, served until 9pm, has oysters followed by red mullet or coley; the 145F features a scallop and duck salad to start, and a mixed fish grill or fish couscous; for 190F you can pick at will from the *à la carte* menu, so half a lobster is a possibility. Closed Sun, plus Sat pm in low season.

Restaurant Chez Gilles, 2 rue de la Pie-qui-Boit (☎02.99.40.97.25). Bright, modern, good-value restaurant at the southern end of the pedestrian area, just off the central axis. The basic 89F menu is fine, while 130F brings you a duck-and-pistachio sausage and a rabbit *crêpe* with cider. Closed Wed lunchtime July & Aug, all day Wed Sept–June.

Delauney, 6 rue Ste-Barbe (☎02.99.40.92.46). Between porte St-Vincent and Cathédrale St-Vincent. Formerly owned by Jean-Paul Delauney, it has changed hands (albeit within the family) to Brigitte and Didier Delauney, but the traditional French cooking remains to the same high standard. The cheapest menu is 125F, served at lunchtime and 7–8pm only; otherwise menus start at 138F. Closed Sun.

Duchesse Anne, 5–7 place Guy-la-Chambre (☎02.99.40.85.33). Right next to the porte St-Vincent. The best known of St-Malo's upmarket restaurants, which continues to work hard to keep up its reputation – and its prices. There are no set menus; you might manage to get a lunch for under 100F, but dinner will be well over 200F. Whole baked fish is the main speciality. Closed Wed, plus Sun pm in low season, and all Jan & Dec.

Shopping

For last-minute **shopping** in St-Malo before you catch the ferry home, the *citadelle* contains a few specialists. Au Poids du Roy, for example, in the place du Poids-du-Roi, is a superb, if somewhat upmarket, *épicerie*. However, buying in any quantity is best done in Le Continent **hypermarket** on the southwest outskirts of the town (follow the signs to the barrage de la Rance if you're driving; thanks to the one-way systems it's a circuitous route, but you do get there).

There are **markets** in St-Malo (*intra-muros*) on Tuesdays and Fridays, in St-Servan on Mondays and Fridays, and in Paramé on Wednesdays and Saturdays.

Dinard

The former fishing village of **DINARD** sprawls around the western approaches to the Rance estuary, just across from St-Malo but a good twenty minutes' drive away. It's a town that might not feel out of place on the Côte d'Azur, with its Casino, spacious shaded villas and social calendar of regattas and ballet. Here in Brittany it's a little incongruous, though pleasant enough – and quite amusing in its uncanny resemblance to an enlarged mini-golf course.

The nineteenth-century metamorphosis of Dinard was largely thanks to the tastes of affluent English and Americans, though these days age rather than nationality seems to be the common factor uniting most of its summer influx of tourists. Although Dinard is a hilly town, undulating over a succession of pretty little coastal inlets, it attracts great numbers of older visitors; as a result, prices tend to be high, and pleasures sedate (literally so, with benches scattered in abundance where weary legs can rest while their indefatigable owners admire the views).

Arrival and information

Full information on Dinard's hotels, restaurants, local tours and transport facilities can be picked up from the **tourist office**, right in the centre at 2 bd Féart (July & Aug daily 9.30am–7.30pm; Easter–June & Sept Mon–Sat 9am–12.15pm & 2–7pm; Oct–Easter Mon–Sat 9am–12.15pm & 2–6pm; ☎02.99.46.94.12).

Many visitors, however, simply come over for the day on one of the regular Émeraude Lines **boats** from St-Malo; tickets can be bought in Dinard a couple of hundred metres east of the tourist office at 27 av Georges-V, directly above the pleasure port where the ferries actually come in (April to late Sept only; ☎02.99.46.10.45; 20F one-way, 30F round-trip, plus 15F for bicycles). If the ten-minute crossing only serves to whet your appetite, you can also take a trip down the Rance to Dinan.

Local **buses** run regularly between Dinard and St-Malo, across the dam, while long-distance buses go from the former gare SNCF and *Le Gallic* stop (near the tourist office) to Dinan and Rennes (run by both TIV, ☎02.99.46.13.13, and TAE, ☎02.99.50.64.17), as well as to St-Jacut, Cancale, Dol and Mont-St-Michel (in summer, TIV only). Dinan buses are also operated by CAT (☎02.96.39.21.05).

Cycles are available for rental from Cycles Duval, 53 rue Gardiner (☎02.99.46.19.63; closed Oct).

The Town

Central Dinard faces north to the open sea, across the curving bay that holds the attractive **plage de l'Écluse**. As so often in Breton resorts, the buildings that line the waterfront are, with the exception of the Casino in the middle, venerable Victorian villas rather than hotels or shops, and so the beach itself has a relatively low-key atmosphere, despite the summer crowds. An unexpected statue of Alfred Hitchcock dominates its main access point: standing on a giant egg, with a ferocious-looking bird perched on each shoulder, he was placed here to commemorate the town's annual festival of English-language films.

Enjoyable **coastal footpaths** lead off in either direction from the principal beach, enlivened by notice boards holding reproductions of various paintings produced at points along the way. It may well come as a surprise to see that Pablo Picasso's *Deux Femmes Courants sur la Plage* and *Baigneuses sur la Plage*, both of which look quintessentially Mediterranean with their blue skies and golden sands, were in fact painted here in Dinard, during his annual summer visits throughout the 1920s.

The path that heads east leads up to the Pointe du Moulinet for views over to St-Malo, and then (as the **Promenade du Clair du Lune**) continues past the tiny and now exclusive port, and down to the estuary beach, the plage du Prieuré. Between mid-June and mid-September, it is floodlit each evening. Setting off west, on the other hand, takes you around more rocky outcrops to the secluded strand at neighbouring St-Enogat.

The Barrage de la Rance

The road from St-Malo to Dinard crosses the Rance along the top of the world's first **tidal power dam**. Built in 1966, the Barrage de la Rance alas failed to set a non-nuclear example to the rest of the province, where less than a hundred years ago there were 5000 working windmills. You can see how the whole thing works in a half-hour visit (daily 8.30am–8pm; free) from the entrance on the west bank, just downstream from the lock. If you come here on foot or bicycle from St-Malo, try to make your way on the small roads through St-Servan, following the line of the estuary southwards rather than the signposted (circuitous) inland route used by motorists.

Accommodation and eating

On the whole, Dinard is an expensive place to stay, but it does at least have a wide selection of **hotels** to choose from. **Campsites** include the municipal *Port Blanc*, over 1km west of the centre near the plage du Port-Blanc on rue du Sergent-Boulanger (April–Sept; ☎02.99.46.10.74), and the grander *Ville Mauny* (mid-April to Sept; ☎02.99.46.94.73), in the woods southwest of the centre.

All the hotels listed below have reasonable **restaurants**. Good alternatives in town include the busy *Brasserie Le Cancaven*, whose outdoor tables take up most of place de la République (☎02.99.46.15.45); their 59F menu is not all that interesting, but for 110F they offer a real cornucopia of fish and shellfish, from spider crab to squid.

Hôtel-Restaurant Altair, 18 bd Féart (☎02.99.46.13.58, fax 02.99.88.20.49). Central and very English option, a little way inland from the tourist office, and boasting a nice garden. The cheapest menu, at 88F, offers the inevitable *moules marinières* or *soupe de poissons*. Closed Sun pm, plus Mon in low season, and second fortnight of Nov. ③.

Hôtel de la Gare, 28 rue de la Corbinais (☎02.99.46.10.84). Dinard doesn't have a gare SNCF these days, but that doesn't worry the *Hôtel de la Gare*, a basic inexpensive place 500m back from the beach in a rather dull part of town. Entrance is via the brasserie downstairs, *L'Épicurien*. ①.

Hôtel-Restaurant du Parc, 20 av Édouard-VII (☎02.99.46.11.39, fax 02.99.88.10.58). Friendly little hotel on a busy street a short way west of the place de la République. Simple restaurant offering menus from 60F. Closed Oct. ②.

Hôtel-Restaurant Printania, 5 av Georges-V (☎02.99.46.13.07, fax 02.99.46.26.32). Good-value place around 250m east of the centre, on a relatively quiet seafront street near the Port de Plaisance. Menus in the magnificent terrace restaurant, looking over to St-Malo, start at 95F, featuring stuffed clams and grilled salmon. Closed mid-Nov to mid-March. ②–⑤.

Hôtel-Restaurant de la Vallée, 6 av Georges-V (☎02.99.46.94.00, fax 02.99.88.22.47). Attractive *logis de France*, down at sea level in the pleasure port, but unfortunately facing the wrong way for views of St-Malo. The most basic rooms look straight onto a bare cliff face, but in principle this is a nice spot. Menus from 99F, featuring grilled sardines and skate. ③–⑥.

Dinan

The wonderful citadel of **DINAN** has preserved almost intact its three-kilometre encirclement of protective masonry, along with street upon colourful street of late medieval houses. However, for all its slightly unreal perfection (it would make the ideal film set for *The Three Musketeers*), it's seldom excessively overrun with tourists. There are no very vital museums; the most memorable architecture is vernacular rather than monumental, and time is most easily spent wandering from *crêperie* to café, admiring the overhanging half-timbered houses along the way.

Arrival and information

Dinan's **tourist office** is very central, almost opposite the Tour de l'Horloge, in the sixteenth-century *Hôtel Kératry* at 6 rue de l'Horloge (mid-June to Sept

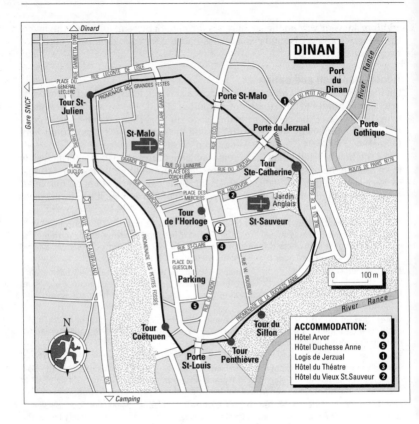

Mon–Sat 9am–7pm, Sun 10am–12.30pm & 3–5.30pm; Oct to mid-June Mon–Sat 9am–12.30pm & 2–6pm; ☎02.96.39.75.40), where the ground floor is built of stone with pillars, the first floor is lath and plaster, and the extensive garden is complete with a weeping willow. The **post office** is on place Duclos (☎02.96.39.25.07).

Both the Art Deco **gare SNCF** (☎02.96.39.22.39) and the **gare routière** (☎02.96.39.21.05) are in Dinan's modern quarter (a rather gloomy exile from the *enclos*), on place du 11-Novembre, ten minutes' walk west of the main (Grande Rue) entrance of the walled town. Armor Express **buses** (☎02.99.50.64.17) go direct to Dinard and to Rennes, which saves changing trains at Dol.

In summer, **boats** along the Rance take two and a half hours to sail between the port downstream and Dinard and St-Malo, with the exact schedule varying according to the tides (adults 95F, under-13s 60F). It's only possible to do a day return by boat (adults 130F, under-13s 75F) if you start from St-Malo or Dinard; starting from Dinan, you'd have to come back by bus or train. For details, contact Émeraude Lines in Dinan, on the quai de la Rance (☎02.96.39.18.04), Dinard (☎02.99.46.10.45) or St-Malo (☎02.99.40.48.40).

Accommodation

Unless you're prepared to pay upwards of 400F for a room, Dinan doesn't really have any of the welcoming good-value hotel-restaurants that characterize so many Breton towns. It's also not a very nice place to try to drive around, or to find a parking space in summer, so motorists might do best to visit only as a day-trip. If you're on foot, and don't mind climbing steep hills with heavy bags, there are, however, plenty of budget options around.

In addition, there is also an attractive year-round **youth hostel**, set amid green fields and trees far below the walls in the Moulin de Méen, Vallée de la Fontaine-des-Eaux (☎02.96.39.10.83; dorm bed 49F), 2km from the gare SNCF. Unfortunately it's not on any bus route; to walk there, follow the quay downstream from the port on the town side, and after a few hundred metres you'll see a small sign to the left. From there it's another 500m. **Camping** is permitted in the hostel grounds, and there's also a *Camping Municipal* at 103 rue Chateaubriand (June–Sept; ☎02.96.39.11.96), just outside the western ramparts.

Hôtel Arvor, 5 rue Pavie (☎02.96.39.21.22, fax 02.96.39.83.09). Renovated eighteenth-century town house, facing the tourist office, with some surviving flourishes of the convent that previously occupied the site. Smart, well-equipped rooms, and free parking. No restaurant. ③.

Bed & Breakfast, 55 rue de Coëtquen (☎02.96.85.23.49). Very friendly English-run B&B just southwest of the city walls, with one en-suite double bedroom. ③.

Hôtel-Restaurant Duchesse Anne, 10 place du Guesclin (☎02.96.39.09.43, fax 02.96.85.09.76). Comfortable if not luxurious rooms on the quieter side of the square, above a basic restaurant where set menus start at 62F. ②.

Logis de Jerzual, 25 rue du Petit Fort (☎02.96.85.46.54, fax 02.96.39.46.94). *Chambres d'hôte* on the exquisite little lane that leads from the port, halfway up to the porte du Jerzual. Garden terrace looking down on the street. Inaccessible by car, so deathly quiet in the mornings. ③.

Hôtel de l'Océan, 9 place du 11-Novembre (☎02.96.39.21.51). Extremely convenient and well-run (if rather basic) hotel, outside the walls opposite the gare SNCF. No restaurant. ①.

Hôtel de la Porte St-Malo, 35 rue St-Malo (☎02.96.39.19.76, fax 02.96.39.50.67). Very comfortable rooms in a tasteful small hotel just outside the walls, beyond the Porte St-Malo. No restaurant. ②.

Café-Hôtel du Théâtre, 2 rue Ste-Claire (☎02.96.39.06.91). Very simple rooms above a bar, right by the tourist office and Théâtre des Jacobins, and under the same efficient management as the nearby *Restaurant Cantorbery* (see p.202). ①.

Hôtel du Vieux St-Sauveur, 19 place St-Sauveur (☎02.96.85.30.20). Ancient edifice facing the St-Sauveur church, which has a slightly noisy bar downstairs, but four nicely equipped and very good-value en-suite rooms upstairs. No restaurant. ②.

The Town

Like St-Malo, Dinan is best seen when arriving by boat up the Rance. By the time the ferries get to the lovely **port du Dinan**, down below the thirteenth-century ramparts, the river has narrowed sufficiently to be spanned by a small but majestic old stone bridge. High above it towers the railway viaduct now used by the N176. The steep cobbled **rue du Petit-Fort** twists up from the artisans' shops and restaurants along the quay. Taking advantage of its many stone benches to catch your breath, it makes a wonderful climb, passing ancient flower-festooned edifices of wood and stone, as well as several *crêperies* and even a half-timbered poodle parlour, before it enters the city through the **porte du Jerzual**.

Above that imposing gateway, **St-Sauveur** church sends the skyline even higher. It's a real hotchpotch, with a Romanesque porch and an eighteenth-century steeple. Even its nine Gothic chapels feature five different patterns of vaulting in no symmetrical order; the most complex pair, in the centre, would make any spider proud. By contrast, a very plain cenotaph on the left contains the heart of Bertrand du Guesclin, the fourteenth-century Breton warrior (and later Constable of France) who fought and won a single combat with the English knight Thomas of Canterbury, in what is now place du Guesclin, to settle the outcome of the siege of Dinan in 1364. Relics of his life and battles are scattered all over Brittany and Normandy; in death, he spread himself between four separate burial places for four different parts of his body (the French kings restricted themselves to three burial sites).

At the heart of town, two small squares, the **place des Merciers** and the **place des Cordeliers**, hold the finest assortment of medieval wood-framed houses, painted in all sorts of lively hues, and with their upper storeys perching precariously on splintering wooden pillars that appear to buckle beneath the weight.

Unfortunately, you can only walk along one small stretch of the **ramparts**, from the Jardin Anglais behind St-Sauveur church to a point just short of Tour Sillon overlooking the river. You can, however, get a good general overview from the wooden balcony of the central **Tour de l'Horloge**, which dates from the end of the fifteenth century (April–Sept daily 10am–7pm; 14F). The original mechanism of the clock here was made in Nantes and put in place in 1498; in 1507, the ubiquitous Duchesse Anne presented the monumental bell. A small and not at all interesting shopping mall has recently been created around the foot of the belfry's stout stone walls.

As you might guess from its blending of two separate towers, the fourteenth-century keep that once protected the town's southern approach was built by Estienne Le Tour, architect of St-Malo's Tour Solidor (see p.195). It's now known as the **Château de Duchesse Anne**, with a small local-history museum housed in the ancient **Tour Coëtquen** (June to mid-Oct daily 10am–6.30pm mid-Oct to May daily except Tues 1.30–5.30pm; 20F). On the lower floor, a group of stone fifteenth-century notables looks for all the world like a medieval time capsule, about to depetrify at any moment.

During the first weekend in September (the date varies – check with the tourist office) the **Fête des Remparts** is celebrated with medieval-style jousting, banquets, fairs and processions, culminating in an immense fireworks display. There's a **market** every Thursday in the adjoining places du Champ and du Guesclin, which constituted the original fairground but are now for most of the week just a large open-air car park.

Eating and drinking

All sorts of specialist **restaurants**, including several ethnic alternatives, are tucked away in the old streets of Dinan. Stroll of an evening through the town and down to the port, and you'll pass at least twenty places to choose from, with the vast majority offering better value for money than Brittany's seaside resorts.

Once you've eaten, the area to head for **bars** is the series of tiny parallel alleyways between the place des Merciers and the rue de la Ferronnerie. Along rue de la Cordonnerie, the busiest of the lot, the various hangouts define themselves by their taste in music; *À la Truye qui File* at no. 14 is a contemporary folky Breton dive, while *Morgan's Tavern*, next door at no. 12, is considerably more raucous.

Le Cantorbery, 6 rue Ste-Claire (☎02.96.39.02.52). Reasonable food served in an old stone house with rafters, a spiral staircase and a real wood fire. Open every day in season. Lunch from 70F, traditional dinner menus from 98F, with a good 135F option. Closed Sun pm & Mon, plus all Feb.

Chez La Mère Pourcel, 3 place des Merciers (☎02.96.39.03.80). Beautiful half-timbered fifteenth-century house in the central square. The lunch menu, at 97F, is pretty minimal, but for 135F you can get stuffed clams and red mullet in olive cream, and you're up to gourmet class with the exquisitely simple fish on the 162F one. Closed Sun pm, and Mon in low season, and all Feb.

Crêperie Connetable, 1 rue de l'Apport (☎02.96.39.02.52). Magnificent old house opposite the *Mère Pourcel* beside the place des Merciers. Sit if you dare at the pavement tables, where all that prevents the upper storeys from crashing down around your ears are a couple of misshapen pillars. *Crêpes* and snacks in the perfect spot for people-watching.

Le Relais des Corsaires, 7 rue du Quai, port du Dinan (☎02.96.39.40.17). Just across the road from the waterfront. Restaurant menu from 98F, offering cockles and mussels followed by scallops or monkfish. The good-value *Grill* menu, in theory served in the adjacent *Petit Corsaire* but in low season served in the same building, costs 88F and is "grill" in name only, featuring dishes like leek *soufflé* and *îles flottantes*. Closed Sun pm & Wed in low season.

La Courtine, 6 rue de la Croix (☎02.96.39.74.41). Friendly little restaurant not far from from the St-Malo church, offering a 62F lunch menu during the week, and dinner menus from 85F featuring such delights as duck cooked with cherries. Closed Tues in low season.

Le St Louis, 9–11 rue de Léhon (☎02.96.39.89.50). Very-good-value restaurant just inside the porte St-Louis, specializing in buffets; a 75F menu entitles you to choose at will from extensive buffets of *hors d'oeuvres* and desserts, while the 89F option offers the same deal plus a conventional main course.

Around the Baie du Mont-St-Michel

The **coastal road** D201 runs east from St-Malo to Cancale, past a succession of coves and beaches, where lines of dunes attempt to hang on against the battering from the sea. At the **Pointe du Grouin** – a perilous and windy height that also overlooks the bird sanctuary of the **Îles des Landes**, to the east – the line of cliffs turns sharply back on itself, at one extremity of the **Baie du Mont-St-Michel**. This is a huge flat expanse of mud and sand, over which the tide – as just about every piece of literature on this region will tell you – can race faster than a galloping horse. It is dangerous to wander out too far, quite apart from the risk of quicksands, and, in the Breton part of the bay at least, the beaches have little appeal for bathers.

The course of the **River Couesnon**, which marks the border between Brittany and Normandy, has shifted repeatedly over the centuries. So too has the shoreline of the bay – in which traces of long-drowned villages can be seen when the tide is out. Bretons like to say that it is just an accident that the river now runs west of Mont-St-Michel; be that as it may, the Mont and Pontorson, the nearest town to it, are both in Normandy (see p.145). The pinnacle of *La Merveille*, however, remains clearly visible from every vantage point along the coast.

CRUISING THE BAY

Sightseeing cruises around the Baie du Mont-St-Michel, aboard the *Sirène de la Baie*, depart throughout the summer from Le Vivier-sur-Mer, 8km north of Dol (May–Oct daily at 10am, 1pm, 4pm & 7.30pm; ☎02.99.48.82.30). The standard fare is 99F for adults, 59F for children, while menus costing from 130F upwards are served on the slightly longer 1pm and 7.30pm trips.

Cancale

Just south of the Pointe du Grouin, and less than 15km east of St-Malo, **CANCALE** is not so much a one-horse as a one-mollusc town – the whole place is obsessed with the **oyster**, and with "*ostréiculture*". Its current population is, at 4600, less than it was a century ago, but the town looks much bigger than that would suggest – and the reason must be the visitors attracted by its edible hinged bivalves.

Cancale is divided into two distinct halves; the old town up on the hill, and the port area down below, now very pretty and very smart. Oysters may have been a cheap working-class staple in the past, but these days they're clasped to the bosoms and slurped by the lips of elegant *bourgeois* holiday-makers. In the old church of **St-Méen**, at the top of the hill, a small **Musée des Arts et Traditions Populaires** documents this obsession with meticulous precision (July–Aug Mon 2.30–6.30pm, Tues–Sun 10am–noon & 2.30–6.30pm; June & Sept Thurs–Sun 2.30–6.30pm, and groups by appointment on ☎02.99.89.79.26; 15F). Cancale oysters have been found in the camps of Julius Caesar; were taken daily to Versailles for Louis XIV; and even accompanied Napoléon on the march to Moscow. The most famous symbol of the town – and its oyster cultivation – is the stark **Rocher du Cancale** just offshore; the museum lists all the *Rochers du Cancale* restaurants that have ever existed, including ones in Shanghai and Phnom Penh, and one in Moscow which closed in the 1830s.

From the rue des Parcs, next to the jetty of the port, you can see at low tide the **parcs** where the oysters are grown. At one time there was an annual event, *La Caravanne*, when a huge flotilla of sailing vessels dragged nets along the bottom of the sea for wild oysters; now they are farmed like any other crop. The sea bed is divided into countless segments of different sizes, each segment having an individual owner who has the right to sell what it produces. The oysters are cultivated from year-old "spat" bought in from elsewhere. Behind, the rocks of the cliff are streaked and shiny like mother-of-pearl; underfoot the beach is littered with countless generations of empty shells.

Follow the corniche road out of Cancale to the southwest, and you'll soon come to the **Ferme Marine**, a working *parc* where the entire oyster-raising process is described on enjoyable guided tours (mid-June to mid-Sept daily at 11am, 3pm & 5pm; mid-Feb to mid-June & mid-Sept to Oct Mon–Fri at 3pm; 38F).

Practicalities

Cancale's main **tourist office** is up the hill at 44 rue du Port (July & Aug daily 9am–6pm; Sept–June Mon–Sat 9am–12.30pm & 2–6pm, Sun 10am–1pm; ☎02.99.89.63.72), but most visitors prefer to call in at the **information office** on the waterfront in the heart of the harbour, across from the upmarket glass-fronted hotels and restaurants that line quai Gambetta.

Most **hotels** insist that you eat if you want to stay, but that's no great problem considering that there's nothing much else to do in town. Among the best value are *Le Phare* (☎02.99.89.60.24; ③) and the *Émeraude* (☎02.99.89.61.76; ④) – both set above their own restaurants, at nos. 6 and 7 respectively on quai Thomas – and *La Houle*, 18 quai Gambetta (☎02.99.89.62.38; ②). By far the best **campsite** in the vicinity is the *Municipal Pointe du Grouin* (March–Oct; ☎02.99.89.63.79), where the views are quite sensational.

There's no great reason to recommend any one of Cancale's **restaurants** above the rest; all without exception serve enticing seafood spreads, and which of the twenty or so adjacent options you choose will depend on your mood and your particular favourite dish. If you're looking for scallops, *Le Phare* prepares a superb scallop kebab on its 152F menu. As a rule, **oysters** are no less expensive than on a Paris boulevard, but *Au Pied de Cheval*, 10 quai Gambetta (☎02.99.89.76.95), is an informal place to sample a few, with great baskets of them spread across its wooden quayside tables. A dozen raw oysters on a bed of seaweed cost from 26F.

Cancale has a **market** on Sunday in the streets behind the main church, the rue de la Marine and the rue Cocar.

Dol-de-Bretagne

During the Middle Ages, **DOL-DE-BRETAGNE**, 30km west of Mont-St-Michel, was an important bishopric; its first bishop was appointed by the Breton hero King Nominoë in the ninth century. It no longer has a bishop, but the fortified thirteenth-century **Cathédrale St-Samson** endures, with its strange, squat, tiled towers and ornate porches. Alongside is the **Musée Historique de Dol** (Easter–Sept daily 2.30–6pm), bloated by the usual array of posed waxworks but with two rooms of astonishing wooden bits and pieces rescued in assorted states of decay from churches, often equally rotten, all over Brittany. These carvings and statues, some still brightly polychromed with their crust of eggy paint, range from the thirteenth to the nineteenth centuries.

Dol still has a few streets packed with venerable buildings, most notably the pretty **Grande-Rue**, where one Romanesque edifice dates back as far as the eleventh century, an assortment of 500-year-old half-timbered houses look down on the bustle of shoppers below, and a laundry claims to have been visited by Victor Hugo in 1836.

Mont Dol

All approaches to Dol from the bay are watched over by the former island of **Mont Dol** – now eight rather marshy kilometres in from the sea. This abrupt granite outcrop, looking mountainous beyond its size on such a flat plain, was the legendary site of a battle between the Archangel Michael and the Devil. Various fancifully named indentations in the rock, such as "the Devil's Claw", testify to the savagery of their encounter, which was inevitably won by the saint. The site has been occupied since prehistoric times – flint implements (now housed in the Musée de Bretagne in Rennes) have been unearthed alongside the bones of mammoths, sabre-toothed tigers and even rhinoceroses. Later on, it appears to have been used for worship by the druids, before becoming, like Mont-St-Michel, an island monastery.

Traces of the abbey have long vanished, though the mythic battle may recall its foundation, with Christianity driving out the old religion. A plaque proclaims that visiting the small chapel on top earns a Papal Indulgence (presumably on the condition that you don't add to the copious graffiti on its walls). The climb is pleasant, too, a steep footpath winding up among the chestnuts and beeches to a solitary bar.

If you fancy an extended walk, Dol and Mont Dol are in fact located on the longdistance **GR34** trail, which leads east to Mont-St-Michel (reckoned as an 8hr stroll), and west along the coast way beyond St-Malo.

The Menhir du Champ-Dolent

A short way out of Dol to the south, a small picnic area fenced off among the fields contains the **Menhir du Champ-Dolent**. According to one legend, this 9.6-metre standing stone dropped from the sky to separate two brothers who were on the point of mutual fratricide. Another has it that the menhir is inching its way into the soil, and the world will end when it disappears altogether. It has to be said that this would not be a particularly interesting spot on which to experience the end of the world. The unadorned stone, big though it undoubtedly is in its banal setting, has little of the romance or mystery of the megalithic sites of the Morbihan and elsewhere.

Practicalities

There is not a great deal to keep casual visitors in Dol for very long. However, the **tourist office**, at 3 Grande-Rue (July & Aug daily 9.30am–12.30pm & 2.30–7.30pm; Easter–June & Sept daily 10.30am–noon & 3.30–7pm; Oct–Easter Thurs 2–4pm; ☎02.99.48.15.37), can direct you eastwards to a very reasonable **hotel**, the *Bretagne*, next to the market at 17 place Chateaubriand (☎02.99.48.02.03; closed Oct; ②). Rooms at the back look out across a small vestige of ramparts towards Mont Dol. Among good **campsites** nearby are the *Vieux Chêne* (April–Sept; ☎02.99.48.09.55), 3km east towards Baguer-Pican on RN176, and the phenomenally luxurious *Castel-Camping des Ormes* (May to mid-Sept; ☎02.99.73.49.59), set around a lake in the grounds of a château 6km south towards Combourg on the N795, which arranges **horse-riding** for its guests.

A couple of nice **fish restaurants** can be found in the ancient houses on rue Ceinte, as it winds its way from Grande-Rue to the Cathedral: *Le Porche au Pain* at no. 1, and *La Grabotais* at no. 4 (closed Mon; ☎02.99.48.19.89). After you eat, the *Katédral* bar, between the church and museum (☎02.99.48.05.40), is worth a brief pause.

The Forêt de Ville-Cartier

The *Circuit Touristique* signposted from Dol continues beyond the menhir and the village of Trans to the **Forêt de Ville-Cartier**. The pines and beech of the forest sweep thickly down to a lake in which it is possible – in fact almost irresistible – to swim. Keeping to the *circuit*, along the D155, would lead eventually to Fougères (see p.213).

Combourg

As well as being a pleasant little town in its own right, **COMBOURG**, 17km south of Dol and 24km southeast of Dinan, has two chief attractions. The first is a **château**, perched on a hill and dominating magnificent landscaped gardens, which was the childhood home of the writer Chateaubriand, now buried at St-Malo (see p.195). The Tour du Chat of the castle may be haunted, by a ghost taking the form of a cat. Chateaubriand himself claimed it was haunted by the ghost of the **wooden leg** of a former lord – and that the cat was merely an acquaintance of this phantasmal limb. The entrance to the château is not where you expect it to be: turn right at the end of Combourg's main square, instead of continuing straight towards the keep, and it's a short way up on the left (gardens July & Aug daily 9am–noon & 2–6pm, April–June & Sept–Nov daily except Tues same hours; château July & Aug daily 11am–noon & 2–5.30pm, April–June & Sept–Nov daily except Tues 2–5.30pm; 25F).

Down below both château and town, the tranquil cypress-lined **lake** is, if anything, more appealing than the château itself. Misty and quiet early in the morning, busy only with anglers, it provides a welcome opportunity for leisurely countryside walks, perhaps after a night of indulgence.

Practicalities

Two superb if somewhat expensive (and not very imaginatively named) **hotels** square off against each other across place Chateaubriand, which squeezes in between château and lake. While the *Hôtel du Château* at no. 1 (☎02.99.73.00.38; ③) is beyond reproach, the *Hôtel du Lac* at no. 2 (☎02.99.73.05.65; ③) just has the edge, with lake views from most of the rooms. Even its cheaper menus, which start at 62F, offer such delights as a cassoulet of mussels with wild mushrooms or half a dozen fresh oysters.

Beside the Canal: Hédé and Tinténiac

The main road **south to Rennes**, the N137, crosses a particularly pleasant stretch of the **Canal d'Ille-et-Vilaine**, between the two old towns of **HÉDÉ** and **TINTÉNIAC**. There are tempting places to collapse in the sun between the many locks and lock-keepers' cottages, although the towpath isn't consistent enough to follow for any distance on foot, let alone bike.

Both Hédé and Tinténiac are set on hills to the west of the canal, and have excellent **hotels**. At the southern end of Tinténiac – which is dominated by a truly bizarre multi-turreted church – the *Hôtel des Voyageurs* (☎02.99.68.02.21; ②) has menus from 82F. On the main road just north of Hédé, another *logis de France*, the *Hostellerie du Vieux Moulin* (☎02.99.45.45.70; closed Sun pm, Mon & Jan; ③) stands in a lovely rural setting below the ruined ramparts of the town castle; its restaurant is more expensive, with even lunch costing a minimum of 95F. In addition, a flower-festooned stone cottage just off the highway between Tinténiac and Hédé holds the inexpensive but high-quality *Restaurant le Genty-Home* (☎02.99.45.46.07), whose enthusiastic young chef prepares traditional meats and fishes on menus ranging 66F and up; 200F gets you a five-course feast including dressed crab, a mixed plate of shellfish, and pigeon or lamb.

St-Aubin d'Aubigné and St-Aubin du Cormier (see p.215) are other possible bases. The **Forêt du Paimpont** (see p.301), too, is well within reach and allows you to bypass Rennes.

Rennes

For a city that has been the capital and power centre of Brittany since the 1532 union with France, Rennes is – outwardly at least – uncharacteristic of the province, with its Neoclassical layout and pompous major buildings. What potential it had to be a picturesque tourist spot was destroyed in 1720, when a drunken carpenter managed to set light to virtually the whole city. Only sections of the area known as **Les Lices**, at the junction of the canalized Ille and the River Vilaine, were left undamaged; fortunately it was even then the oldest part of Rennes, so some traces of the medieval town do survive. The remodelling of the rest of the city was handed over to Parisian architects, not in deference to the capital but in an attempt to rival it.

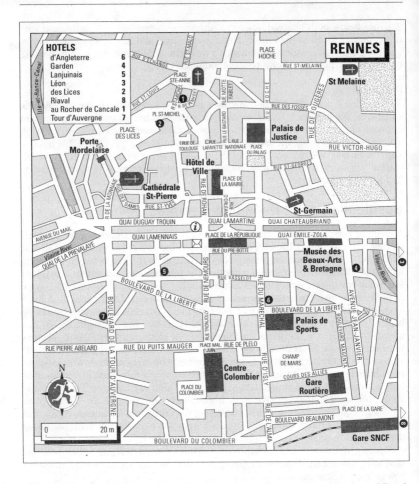

It was the successful siege of Rennes by Charles VIII in 1491 that obliged Duchess Anne to marry him, and led to the union of Brittany and France, sealed in 1532 in the Cohue in Vannes (see p.339). From 1561, the Breton parliament met in Rennes and helped to preserve a measure of autonomy for Brittany in the face of growing centralization. To "celebrate" four centuries of the union in 1932, Breton separatists blew up a statue outside the Hôtel de Ville which showed Brittany swearing allegiance to Louis XV. In 1994, during demonstrations staged by fishermen protesting against a visit by Prime Minister Édouard Balladur, a stray firework caused huge damage to the buildings of the Breton parliament.

The presence of so many students – over 40,000 all told – gives Rennes a rather more visible level of political and cultural activity than most places in Brittany (the Czech author Milan Kundera wrote *The Book of Laughter and Forgetting* while based at the university, which is on a huge campus to the east).

Arrival and information

Rennes's **tourist office** is in the very heart of town, on the Pont de Nemours, where the river briefly disappears (Mon 1–6pm, Tues–Sat 9am–6pm; ☎02.99.79.01.98). There's also an information office in the gare SNCF further south (Mon–Fri 8am–7pm, Sat & Sun 10am–1pm & 3–6pm; ☎02.99.53.23.23).

There are **post offices** in the Palais du Commerce in the heart of town on the place de la République (Mon–Fri 8am–7pm, Sat 8am–noon; ☎02.99.79.50.71), and at 27 bd du Colombier, just west of the gare SNCF (same hours; ☎02.99.31.42.72).

The town council runs a **bike-rental** kiosk in the central place de la République (daily 9am–7pm; ☎02.96.79.63.72); the first hour is free, while five hours cost just 10F.

Trains

The modern **gare SNCF** (☎02.99.65.50.50) is south of the Vilaine, around fifteen minutes' walk from the tourist office and considerably more from the medieval quarter. As well as direct TGV trains to and from Paris – which take only just over two hours – it also has connections east to Brest, north to Dol and south towards Nantes.

Buses

Rennes has a new **gare routière**, on boulevard Solferino just east of the gare SNCF, but most local buses start and finish on or near place de la République, alongside the tourist office. Rennes is a busy junction, with direct services to St-Malo (TIV; ☎02.99.79.23.44), Dinan and Dinard (Armor Express; ☎02.99.50.64.17), and Nantes (Société Transports Tourisme de l'Ouest; ☎02.40.20.45.20). Les Courriers Bretons (☎02.99.56.79.09) run day-trips to **Mont-St-Michel**, timed to connect with the morning TGV from Paris (departing Rennes gare SNCF Mon–Fri 9.45am, Sat & Sun 10.50am; 108F return).

Accommodation

There are surprisingly few **hotels** in the old part of Rennes – and those that there are can be very hard to find. If you've arrived by train or bus, it's easier to settle for staying near the gares SNCF and routière. All Rennes's hotels seem to stay open all year round.

The city also has a year-round **youth hostel**, attractively located beside the Canal d'Ille et Rance, 3km north from the centre – the *Centre International de Séjour*, 10–12 Canal St-Martin (☎02.99.33.22.33). Charging between 82F and 130F per person per night for a dorm bed in a small room, and 190F for a private double, it has a cafeteria and a laundry, and operates a midnight curfew. You can get there on bus routes #20 and #22 from the gare SNCF, direction St-Gregoire, stop Coëtlogon; neither bus runs over the weekend, when you have to catch bus #18 instead.

The **Camping Municipal des Gayeulles** is 1km east of central Rennes at rue de Professeur-Maurice-Audin (April to mid-Oct; ☎02.99.36.91.22), reached by taking bus #3, direction *St-Laurent*, and getting off at *Parc des Bois*.

Hotels

Hôtel d'Angleterre, 19 rue du Maréchal-Joffre (☎02.99.79.38.61, fax 02.99.79.43.85). Not brilliant, but scrupulously maintained and relatively cheap, a short way south of the river towards the station. No restaurant. ①.

Garden Hôtel, 3 rue Duhamel (☎02.99.65.45.06, fax 02.99.65.02.62). Comfortable, nicely decorated and very personal hotel, north of the gare SNCF not far from the river, with a pleasant little garden café but no restaurant. ④.

Hôtel Lanjuinais, 11 rue Lanjuinais (☎02.99.79.02.03, fax 02.99.79.03.97). Standard refurbished upmarket hotel, on a quiet little street just around the corner from the tourist office, less than 50m south of the river. No restaurant. ③.

Hôtel de Léon, 15 rue de Léon (☎02.99.30.55.28, fax 02.99.36.59.11). Quiet little eleven-room hotel, off the beaten track northeast of the gare SNCF, offering old-fashioned but adequate rooms at knockdown rates. ①.

Hôtel des Lices, 7 place des Lices (☎02.99.79.14.81, fax 02.99.79.35.44). Forty rooms, all with TV, in a very comfortable and friendly modern hotel on the edge of the prettiest part of old Rennes, very convenient for the place des Lices parking. No restaurant. ③.

Hôtel Riaval, 9 rue de Riaval (☎02.99.50.65.58, fax 02.99.41.85.30). Friendly hotel with neat budget rooms, well away from the centre, but only a few minutes walk east of the gare SNCF, on a quiet street. No restaurant. ①.

Hôtel-Restaurant au Rocher de Cancale, 10 rue St-Michel (☎02.99.79.20.83). Four-room hotel on a lively pedestrian street, between place Ste-Anne and place St-Michel, in the heart of medieval Rennes and ideally positioned for the city's nightlife. Beautifully restored frontage and ground floor, but with modern facilities upstairs. The restaurant, which is closed at weekends, has menus from 62F at lunchtime and 90F in the evening; the 134F exclusively fish menu is excellent. ②.

Hôtel Tour d'Auvergne, 20 bd de la Tour-d'Auvergne (☎02.99.30.84.16). A very simple but welcoming option, above a little brasserie 10min walk from the tourist office, between the gare SNCF and the river. Some low-priced rooms have en-suite shower facilities. No restaurant. ①.

The City

Rennes's original **medieval core** – the "ville rouge", bordered by the canal to the west and the river to the south – is known to have been enclosed by walls well before 1422. Those walls were enlarged in 1440, when the **Porte Mordelaise** was constructed to serve as the ceremonial entrance to the city. Thanks to recent building work, that gateway is now more prominently exposed. The old quarter remains the liveliest part of town and it stays up late, particularly in the area around St-Aubin church and along rue St-Michel and rue de Penhöet.

Today, the **place des Lices** is dominated by two empty market halls, but originally it was, as its name suggests, the venue for tournaments – that is, jousting "lists". It was here, in 1337, that the hitherto unknown Bertrand du Guesclin, then aged 17, fought and defeated several older opponents. This set him on his career as a soldier, during which he was later to save Rennes when it was under siege by the English. However, after the Bretons were defeated at Auray in 1364, he fought for the French and twice invaded Brittany. He may be a French hero but, for some Bretons, he is a knave and a traitor. In 1946, Breton separatists destroyed a memorial to him in the Thabor gardens.

Magnificent medieval-style town houses overlook the place des Lices, but they're not as old as they look: most were built in the late seventeenth century to house Brittany's parliamentarians. The streets immediately northeast offer a more genuine glimpse of ancient Rennes. Wander around the back of the excellent *crêperie* at 5 place Ste-Anne, through an archway off rue Motte-Fablet, and you'll find an extraordinary specimen of medieval high-rise housing.

The **south bank** of the river is every bit as busy, if not busier, than the north – should you feel upon arriving that Rennes seems oddly empty, the chances are that everyone's in the giant **Centre Colombier**, just west of the gare SNCF. This vast new mall is Rennes at its most modern, packed with shops of all kinds, plus cafés and snack bars, and featuring an amazing crystal model of itself in its main entrance hall. Slightly nearer the river, **rue Vasselot** has its own array of half-timbered old houses.

The one central building to escape the 1720 fire was the **Palais de Justice** on rue Hoche downtown. Ironically, however, the Palais was all but ruined by a major conflagration in 1994; the exact circumstances remain somewhat mysterious, but it's thought the blaze was sparked by a stray flare set off during a demonstration by Breton fishermen. The entire structure has been concealed ever since behind plastic screens, and reconstruction is not expected to finish any time soon.

Contrary to several official guides, the Palais de Justice was *not* the scene of the retrial of **Captain Alfred Dreyfus** in 1899. He had been wrongly convicted of treason in 1896 and it took three years (and Émile Zola's famous letter "J'accuse") to obtain a retrial. In fact, the retrial took place in what is now the **Lycée Émile Zola**, and is marked, on the corner of avenue Janvier and rue Toullier, with a modern steel statue, *La Dégradation de Dreyfus*, by Igael Tumurkin.

The Museums

The **Vilaine** flows through the centre of Rennes, narrowly confined into a steep-sided channel, and even forced underground at one point. Two major **museums** are housed in former university buildings at 20 quai Émile-Zola, on its south bank (both open daily except Tues 10am–noon & 2–6pm; 25F combined ticket).

The **Musée des Beaux Arts** (20F) reaches back several millennia, featuring Egyptian, Greek, Etruscan and Roman artefacts. Many of its finest artworks – which include drawings by Leonardo da Vinci, Botticelli, Fra Lippo Lippi and Dürer – are, however, not usually on public display. Instead you'll find a number of indifferent Impressionist views of Brittany by the likes of Boudin and Sisley, interspersed with the odd treasure such as Pieter Boel's startlingly modern-looking seventeenth-century animal studies, the *Virgin and Child* by Georges de la Tour, and Pierre-Paul Ruben's *Tiger Hunt*, enlivened by the occasional lion. Picasso makes a cameo appearance, with a simple *Baigneuse à Dinard* from 1928, and a very late and surprisingly Cubist canvas from 1970.

The **Musée de Bretagne** (15F), entered via the same lobby, started life a few years ago as a very hi-tech introduction to the history and culture of Brittany. Currently, however, its collection is being plundered piece by piece to go towards a new even higher-tech museum, due to open in 2003, and there's no saying what if anything will be left here by the time you visit. For what it's worth, in principle it kicks off with the bones of a woolly rhinoceros found at Dol, then ranges through a model of the Cairn du Barnenez (see p.237) and an extraordinary first-century bronze *Goddess of Ménéz-Hom* up to the marriage contract of Duchess Anne and Charles VIII of France, and an assortment of nineteenth-century costumes from all over Brittany.

At the **Ecomusée de la Bintinais** (Mon & Wed–Fri 9am–noon & 2–6pm, Sat 2–6pm, Sun 2–7pm; 30F), south of the centre on the route Chatillon sur Seiche (reached on city bus #14 from the place de la République, getting off at the *Le Gacet* stop, or bus #61 from the gare routière to *La Bintinais*), the Ferme de la Bintinais is being preserved as a monument to the rural history of the area.

State-of-the-art techniques have been used to recount the minutiae of five centuries of daily life, showing the vital role Rennes has played in the evolution of Breton agriculture; living exhibits range from dairy cattle to honey bees.

The **Musée Automobile** (daily 9am–noon & 2–7pm; 30F), northeast of the city on the route de Fougères, holds over eighty vintage cars. If you don't have your own much-prized vehicle, take bus #3, direction *St-Laurent*, and get off at the Gayeulles roundabout – where you're still left with quite a walk.

Eating

Most of Rennes's more interesting **bars**, **restaurants** and nightlife in general are to be found in the streets just south of the place Ste-Anne, towards the place des Lices. Rues St-Michel and Penhoët, each with a fine assemblage of ancient wooden buildings, are the epicentre at the moment. Interesting ethnic alternatives can be found along rue St-Malo just to the north, which has long been the more or less exclusive preserve of students but is now decaying fast.

Rue Vasselot is the nearest equivalent south of the river, though if you're just looking for a quick snack don't forget the various outlets in the Centre Colombier.

L'Auberge St-Sauveur, 6 rue St-Sauveur (☎02.99.79.32.56). Classy, romantic restaurant, in an attractive medieval house near the cathedral, with rich, meaty dinner menus at 110F and 165F and lighter lunches for 60F. Closed Sat lunchtime & Sun.

La Chope, 3 rue de la Chalotais (☎02.99.79.34.54). A little way below place de la République on the south side of the river. Classic, busy brasserie open until midnight every day except Sunday, serving meals from 85F upwards.

Le Chouin, 12 rue d'Isly (☎02.99.30.87.86). A fine fish restaurant, not far from the gare SNCF. Menu 99F midday, *à la carte* in the evening. Closed Sun & Mon.

La Gange, 34 place des Lices (☎02.99.30.18.37). Quality Indian restaurant with a vegetarian menu at 85F, and meat-based ones from 110F. Closed Sun lunchtime.

Le Khalifa, 20 haut de la place des Lices (☎02.99.30.87.30). Assorted Moroccan dishes, served outside or in an atmospheric dining room. Couscous and brochettes 59F and up, tajine 69F, as well as various set menus. Closed Sat lunchtime & Sun.

Le Parc à Moules, 8 rue Georges-Dattin (☎02.99.31.44.28). On a small street leading north from the river halfway between the tourist office and the place des Lices. Mussels from Mont-St-Michel Bay cooked in twelve different delicious ways for around 45F, and a weekday lunch menu offering *moules frites* for 49F, plus more expensive fishy dishes. Closed Sat lunch & Sun.

La Tourniole, 37 rue Vasselot (☎02.99.79.05.91). Lovely, very traditional small restaurant halfway between the gare SNCF and the river, offering a hearty 65F set lunch, and dinner menus that start at 85F. Fish, meat and even vegetarian specialities prepared to perfection. Closed Sun & Mon.

Entertainment and culture

Rennes is seen at its best in the first ten days of July, when the **Festival des Tombées de la Nuit** takes over the whole city to celebrate Breton culture with music, theatre, film, mime and poetry in joyful rejection of the influences of both Paris and Hollywood (advance information from 8 place du Maréchal-Juin, 35000 Rennes; ☎02.99.30.38.01).

In the first week of December, the **Transmusicales** rock festival attracts big-name acts from all over France and the world at large, though still with a Breton emphasis. Over the last decade it has helped to make Rennes an important centre for French rock (information on ☎02.99.31.12.10).

The varied season of the Théâtre National de Bretagne, 1 rue St-Helier (☎02.99.31.55.33), runs from mid-October to mid-June. All year round, in a different auditorium on the same premises, *Club Ubu* (☎02.99.30.31.68) puts on large-scale gigs. Live **jazz** gigs take place daily except Sundays at *Déjazey Jazz Club*, 54 rue St-Malo (☎02.99.38.70.72). The *Barantic*, 4 rue St-Michel, is currently one of the city's favourite **bars**, putting on occasional live music for a mixed crowd of Breton nationalists and boisterous students; if you don't like the look of it, or it's too full, there are half a dozen similar alternatives within spitting distance.

The friendly bookshop Co-op Breizh at 17 rue Penhoët (☎02.99.79.01.87) has cassettes of Breton and Celtic music along with books and posters. L'Arvor cinema at 29 rue d'Antrain (☎02.99.38.72.40) shows V.O. (original language) films, and there's a large selection of English books in the FNAC bookshop in the Colombier shopping centre.

Fougères

FOUGÈRES, 50km short of Rennes on the main road into Brittany from Caen, promotes itself as the *"ville au joli nom"*, *fougères* being the French for "fern". Name apart, however, it's not an especially pretty town, and it has a topography impossible to grasp from a map. Streets that look a few metres long turn out to be precipitous plunges down the escarpments of its split-levelled site, and lanes collapse into flights of steps. The only efficient way to get around, needless to say, is on foot.

Perhaps the oddest feature of the site is the positioning of the **castle**, built well below the main part of the town, on a low spit of land that separates, and is towered over by, two mighty rock faces. Massive and stunningly strong, it was laid out in 1166 to replace a wooden fort destroyed by English invaders. Protected by great curtain-walls, and circled by a hacked-out moat full of weirs and waterfalls, it was also shielded in its heyday by the River Nançon. None of this, however, prevented its repeated capture by such medieval adventurers as, of course, du Guesclin.

Within the castle keep, a romantic setting in *Les Chouans* (see box p.214), the focus is disappointingly prosaic. Footwear, to this day the main industry of the town, is presented in a **museum** included in the hourly **château tours** (castle daily mid-June to mid-Sept 9am–7pm, no tours noon or 1pm; April to mid-June & second fortnight of Sept 9.30am–noon & 2–6pm; Oct–March 10am–noon & 2–5pm; 30F). Literally the high spot of the tours, in summer only, is the view from top of its clock tower.

The best approach to the castle is from **place des Arbres** beside St-Léonard's church off the main street of the old fortified town. The formal terraces give way to the water meadows of the River Nançon, which you can cross beside a little cluster of medieval houses still standing on the riverbank – the sculpted doorway at 6 rue de Lusignan is particularly attractive.

If, on the other hand, you take the longer route down rue Nationale, you'll pass, at no. 51, the **Musée de la Villéon**, which commemorates the Impressionist Emmanuel de la Villéon. Born in Fougères in 1858, he painted numerous memorable Breton landscapes (mid-June to Aug Wed–Sun 10.30am–12.30pm & 2.30–6.30pm; Easter to mid-June & first fortnight of Sept Sat & Sun 11am–12.30pm & 2.30–5pm; free).

BALZAC'S FOUGÈRES

The flavour of eighteenth-century Fougères is evoked in Balzac's *Les Chouans* – a bit of a potboiler with its absurd twists but nonetheless an essentially historical account of the events surrounding the *Chouan* rebellion in Brittany, the attempt to restore the monarchy after the Revolution. Balzac makes great play of the town's unusual layout and of the various bloodthirsty survivors of the revolt that he met while doing his research: "In 1827, an old man accompanied by his wife was selling cattle at the Fougères market unremarked and unmolested, although he was the killer of more than one hundred persons."

Practicalities

Fougères's old gare SNCF, down below the modern town, is now inactive; the buses to and from Vitré and Rennes that use the square beside it are the only form of public transport to pass through. The **tourist office** at 1 place Aristide-Briand provides copious information on all aspects of the town and local countryside (July & Aug Mon–Sat 9am–7pm, Sun 10am–noon & 2–4pm; Sept–June Mon–Sat 9.30am–12.30pm & 2–6pm, Sun 10am–noon & 2–4pm; ☎02.99.94.12.20).

The *Grand Hôtel des Voyageurs* at 10 place Gambetta (☎02.99.99.08.20; closed second fortnight of Aug; ②) is a particularly nice place to stay, with TVs in all rooms. It's just round the corner from the tourist office, on the main road – ask for a room at the back. Selecting the cheapest, 95F menu in the excellent downstairs restaurant (run by a different management, and closed Sat) gives you the choice of *tournedos de thon*, and grants you access to a well-laden *chariot des desserts*; other menus cost 125F and upwards.

Hôtel Balzac at no. 15 in the semi-pedestrianized rue Nationale (☎02.99.99.42.46; ②) is central and a little less expensive, with rooms that have recently been refurbished, while the *Buffet* down the street at no. 53 (☎02.99.94.35.76; closed Wed pm & Sun) does more economical meals. Its 59F menu allows you to gorge yourself on full buffets of both *hors d'oeuvres* and desserts; there's no main course, but that won't be a problem.

There are no hotels in the immediate vicinity of the château, but the squares on all sides are crammed with an abundance of appealing bars and *crêperies*. At *La Table du Roy* (☎02.99.99.77.37), which has lots of outdoor seating beside the moat, 50F buys a plate of *moules frites* and a glass of wine, and there are dinner menus at 82F and 98F.

The Forêt de Fougères

The **Forêt de Fougères**, a short way out on the D177 towards Vire (see p.179), is one of the most enjoyable in the province. The beech woods are spacious and light, with various megaliths and trails of old stones scattered among the chestnut and spruce. It's quite a contrast to their normal bleak and windswept haunts to see dolmens sporting themselves in such verdant surroundings. If you have time, walk through the forest as far as **Le Chatellier**, a village set high in thick woods.

For a **horseback** tour of the Forêt de Fougères, contact the Centre d'Initiation aux Activités de Plein Air in Chennedet (☎02.99.99.18.98).

St-Aubin-du-Cormier

Halfway between Fougères and Rennes on the N12, **ST-AUBIN-DU-CORMIER** makes a peaceful overnight stop. It's a bit too peaceful perhaps; the kind of town where the only entertainment in the only bar open at ten o'clock on a Saturday night is to take it in turns to look at a pet white hamster.

There is, however, a major sight in St-Aubin – the keep of its old **castle**, which was demolished after the great battle here in 1488 in which the forces of Duke Francis were defeated by the French army. Many Breton soldiers were dressed in the English colours of a black cross on white silk, to scare the French into believing that the duke had extensive English reinforcements. The victorious French were told to spare all prisoners except the English; and so the hapless Bretons were massacred. Just one sheer wall of the castle survives, with a fireplace visible halfway up. A small monument in a field marks the actual site of the battle.

Practicalities

St-Aubin's very cheap *Hôtel du Bretagne*, 68 rue de l'Écu (☎02.99.39.10.22; ①), has to be recommended – a rambling old building, with lumpy lino corridors stretching off in random directions upstairs, and good food downstairs.

The municipal **campsite** (April–Oct; ☎02.99.39.18.22) sprawls immediately below the castle, next to a small lake.

Half a dozen kilometres north of St-Aubin, the **Ville Olivier** on the D102 between St-Ouen and Mezières is a château that organizes riding, canoeing and kayaking, and has its own *gîte d'étape* (☎02.99.39.34.72).

Vitré

VITRÉ, just north of the Le Mans–Rennes motorway, is a lesser rival to Dinan as the best-preserved **medieval town** in Brittany. Occupation of the site dates right back to the Romans, when a certain Vitrius is known to have owned a villa here. While its thirteenth-century walls are no longer quite complete, their effect is enhanced by the fact that what lies outside them has changed so little. To the north are stark wooded slopes, while into the western hillside beneath the castle burrow thickets of stone cottages that must once have been Vitré's medieval slums. This little suburb is called **Rachapt**, a corruption of the French for "repurchase", in memory of the time during the Hundred Years' War when the castle's defendants finally paid the English army, by whom they'd been besieged for several years, to go away. By 1589, when the castle successfully resisted a siege by the Catholic League, Vitré had become a Huguenot stronghold.

In best fairy-tale fashion, the towers of the **castle** itself – which was first erected in 1060, and remodelled to its present appearance two hundred years later – have pointed slate-grey roofs that look like freshly sharpened pencils. Unfortunately, however, the municipal offices and **museum** of shells, birds, bugs and local history inside are not exactly thrilling (July–Sept daily 10am–12.30pm & 2–6.15pm; April–June daily 10am–noon & 2–5.30pm; Oct–March Wed–Fri 10am–noon & 2–5.30pm, Mon, Sat & Sun 2–5.30pm; 26F).

The admission fee for the castle also includes entry to three other museums in the general vicinity, all of which are open for the same hours as the castle. The **Musée**

St-Nicholas, on the outskirts of town, occupies the huge former chapel of a fifteenth-century hospital with a collection of medieval reliquaries and religious paraphernalia. The **Musée Faucillonnaie**, 3km northwest of the centre in Montreuil-sous-Pérouse, is a general mishmash of secular artefacts, mostly of more recent origin, while the **Château des Rochers Sévigné**, 10km southeast, is a place of pilgrimage for French devotees of the seventeenth-century society letter-writer Madame de Sévigné, which holds little interest for anyone not familiar with her work.

Vitré is a market town rather than an industrial centre, with its principal **market** held on Mondays in the square in front of Notre Dame church. The old city is full of twisting streets of half-timbered houses, a good proportion of which are bars. The **rue de la Baudrairie**, formerly the town's leather-working quarter, is the most picturesque, but the **rue d'en Bas**, which climbs up from Rachapt to the castle, has the best selection of bars; the *Aston*, for example, at no. 7, is a nice place to spend an evening.

An unusual visual treat, if you happen to be using the **post office**, is its modern stained-glass window behind the counter.

Practicalities

Vitré's **gare SNCF** is a little way south of the centre, where the ramparts have disappeared and the town imperceptibly blends into its newer sectors. Nearby is the **tourist office**, on the promenade St-Yves (July & Aug daily 10am–7pm; Sept–June Mon–Fri 10am–noon & 1.30–6pm, Sat 10am–noon; ☎02.99.75.04.46), which runs guided tours of the town in summer (Mon, Wed & Fri at 3pm; Tues, Thurs & Sat at 10am).

Most of the **hotels**, too, are near the gare SNCF, and Vitré makes a cheap, as well as pleasant, place to stay. The *Petit-Billot*, 5bis place du Général-Leclerc (☎02.99.75.02.10; ②), is good value, while rooms on the higher floors of the *Hôtel du Château*, 5 rue Rallon (☎02.99.74.58.59; closed Sun out of season; ②), on a quiet road just below the castle, have views of the ramparts.

Of the **restaurants**, *Le St-Yves*, immediately below the castle at 1 place St-Yves (☎02.99.74.68.78), serves menus from 55F to 175F; the 75F one should suit most requirements. *La Soupe aux Choux*, at the top of rue de la Baudrairie at 32 rue Notre-Dame (☎02.99.75.10.86; closed Tues), prepares simple but classic French food, with 45F lunches.

Around Vitré

There are several interesting smaller towns in the area. **DOMPIERRE** is attractive in its own right and claims a tiny (and disputed) place in history as the town where Roland, Charlemagne's nephew, might have died, were one to accept that the *Chanson de Roland* got the story entirely wrong.

CHAMPEAUX, 8km west of Vitré, has – is – a central paved square, surrounded by stone houses, with an ornate well in the centre. Its fifteenth-century collegiate church contains a superb stained-glass *Crucifixion* by Gilles de la Croix-Vallée, the ornate tombs of its founding family, and some fine carved choir stalls.

CHATEAUBOURG, halfway to Rennes, has a wonderful but expensive hotel, the *Ar Milin* (☎02.99.00.30.91; restaurant closed Sun in winter; ⑤–⑧), straddling the River Vilaine in huge gardens at 30 rue de Paris. Breakfast, at 49F, consists of an enormous buffet of fresh pastries.

The Roche-aux-Fées

About 15km to the south, not far from the road just off the D341 near Retiers, the **ROCHE-AUX-FÉES** is the least visited of the major megalithic monuments of Brittany. The "fairy rock" is a twenty-metre-long covered alleyway of purplish stones, with no apparent funerary purpose or, indeed, any evidence that it was ever buried. It's set on a high and exposed spot, guarded by just a few venerable trees, and it's thought the slabs had to be dragged a good 45km to get here. There's no admission charge.

Tradition has it that engaged couples should come to the Roche-aux-Fées on the night of a full moon and separately count the stones; if they agree on the total, things are looking good.

WEST ALONG THE COAST

To the west of the Rance, beyond Dinard, stretches the green of the **Côte d'Émeraude**. While this region has its fair share of developed family resorts, such as **St-Jacut**, **Erquy** and **Le Val-André**, it also offers wonderful camping, at its best around the heather-surrounded beaches near **Cap Fréhel** – for once unencroached upon by the military.

Further west, the coast becomes wilder and harsher. Beyond **St-Brieuc** the seaside towns tend to be crammed into narrow rocky inlets or set well back in river estuaries, and only a few beaches manage to break out from the rocks. Once past **Paimpol**, the shoreline is known as the **Côte de Granit Rose** – no figure of speech, but a literal description of its primeval tangle of vast pink granite boulders. They certainly deserve to be seen, at the very least as a quick detour before catching the ferry at Pointe de l'Arcouest (near Paimpol) for **Bréhat**.

The Côte d'Émeraude

The coast immediately **west of Dinard** is one of Brittany's most traditional family resort areas, with old-fashioned holiday towns, safe sandy beaches and a plethora of well-organized campsites.

St-Jacut-de-la-Mer

ST-JACUT, which takes up most of the tip of a narrow peninsula roughly 16km west of St-Malo, looks today like a classic nineteenth-century bathing resort, but was in fact founded a thousand years earlier by an itinerant Irish monk. Though possibly not the most exciting of places, it has everything young children could want – good sand, rocky pools to clamber about, and woods to scramble in.

Practicalities

St-Jacut boasts one of Brittany's most distinctive **hotels**; as the *Hôtel le Vieux Moulin* centres on a fifteenth-century windmill, in the middle of the peninsula, two of its guest rooms are completely round (☎02.96.27.71.02; closed Nov–March; ③). It also serves good, if unadventurous, food. The summer-only *Camping Municipal* is beside the plage de la Manchette (April–Sept; ☎02.96.27.70.33).

Much the best **fish restaurant** in the area is the *Restaurant la Presqu'île*, at 164 Grande-Rue (☎02.96.27.76.47; closed Mon in low season), where the menus start at 95F.

St-Cast-le-Guildo

The pleasant seaside community of **ST-CAST**, on the next promontory along, is a thirty-kilometre drive from St-Malo, and connected by SNCF buses with the nearest station, at Lamballe (see p.221). Most of its commercial activity takes place in the rather uninspiring Bourg, set back from the water, but the port area down below is very nice, and there are good walks along the coast to the headland.

Practicalities

Among medium-price **hotels** in St-Cast are the attractive *Hôtel des Mielles*, 3 rue du Duc d'Auguillon (☎02.96.41.80.95; closed mid-Sept to March; ③), just a few metres from the beach, and the plainer *Chrisflo*, 19 rue du Port (☎02.96.41.88.08; closed Oct to mid-April; ②), much further back. The **tourist office** on place Charles-de-Gaulle (July & Aug daily 9am–12.30pm & 2–7.30pm; Sept–June Mon–Sat 9am–noon & 2–6pm; ☎02.96.41.81.52), can provide details of local **campsites**, such as the *Châtelet* beside the bay (Easter to mid-Sept; ☎02.96.41.96.33).

Cap Fréhel

The only really out-of-the-ordinary place on this stretch, however, is **Cap Fréhel**. This high, warm expanse of heath, cliffs and heather is over-visited, but camping is prohibited for 5km around the tip. The headland itself, 400m walk from the road, remains unspoilt; with no more than a few ruins of old buildings and a small "tearoom" nearby. Offshore, the heather-covered islands are grand to look at, although too tiny to visit; the view from the cape's lighthouse can extend as far as Jersey and the Île de Bréhat.

The **Fort la Latte**, to the east, is used regularly as a film set. Its tower (containing a cannonball factory) is accessible only over two drawbridges. To visit, you have to take guided tours (June–Sept daily 10am–12.30pm & 2.30–6.30pm; Oct–May Sun & hols only 2.30–5.30pm; 15F).

Practicalities

The nearest places to stay to the cap are the ideal, isolated **campsite** at Pléherel, the *Camping du Pont L'Étang* (May–Sept; ☎02.96.41.40.45), and a basic summer-only **youth hostel** on the D16 just outside Plévenon en route towards the cape – full address: Kérivet-en-Frehel, La Ville Hardrieux (mid-April to mid-Sept; ☎02.96.41.48.98; 48F).

Erquy

The perfect crescent beach at **ERQUY**, around 20km west of Cap Fréhel, curves through more than 180 degrees. At low tide, the sea disappears way beyond the harbour entrance, leaving gentle ripples of paddling sand. Adventurers equipped with suitable boots could walk right across its mouth, from the grassy wooded headland on the left side over to the picturesque little lighthouse at the end of the jetty on the right.

Practicalities

Erquy's **tourist office** on the boulevard de la Mer (mid-June to mid-Sept daily 9.30am–12.30pm & 2–7pm; mid-Sept to mid-June daily except Mon 9.30am–12.30pm & 2–5pm; ☎02.96.72.30.12) coordinates information for the surrounding area. The *Hôtel Beauséjour*, 21 rue de la Corniche (☎02.96.72.30.39; closed Sun pm & Mon in winter; ③), has a good view of the bay, and excellent fish dinners from 78F, while the more upmarket **restaurant** *l'Escurial* (☎02.96.72.31.56; closed Sun pm & Mon) by the seafront serves a five-course menu (for 200F) that consists entirely of **scallops**, the town's speciality.

There are several **campsites** on the promontory (dotted with tiny coves) that leads to the Cap d'Erquy north of town, including the *St-Pabu* (April–Oct; ☎02.96.72.24.65) right beside the sea.

Le Val-André

The beach in the broader bay of **LE VAL-ANDRÉ**, another 11km down the coast, is not only on a slightly larger scale to that of Erquy, but it's composed of finer and somehow sweeter-smelling sand. The endless pedestrian promenade that stretches along the seafront feels oddly Victorian, consisting solely of huge old houses undisturbed by shops or bars. However, Le Val-André is definitely more of a town than Erquy, and rue A-Charner, running parallel to the sea one street back, is busy with holiday-makers in summer.

Practicalities

Le Val-André's helpful **tourist office** (July & Aug Mon–Sat 9am–12.30pm & 2.30–6pm, Sept–June Mon–Fri 9am–noon & 2.30–5pm; ☎02.96.72.20.55) is located in the modern Casino at the very centre of the waterfront.

Of its **hotels**, the tastefully refurbished *Hotel de la Mer*, 63 rue A-Charner (☎02.96.72.20.44; closed Jan; ①), serves food that is utterly magnificent, using a fine muscadet to transport *moules marinières* onto a hitherto undreamed-of plane (available on their 99F menu along with rabbit or quail and a delicious raspberry mousse). However, with the success of the business many guests find themselves having to sleep in the characterless *Nuit et Jour* motel, run by the same management, and one group even reported having to sleep in their car after being locked out of the hotel after an evening drink. The similar-looking but slightly more imposing *Hôtel Regina*, slightly nearer the centre at 45 rue A-Charner (☎02.96.72.22.63; ②), is a more dependable if perhaps less exciting choice; a couple of its rooms have attractive balconies.

The *Restaurant au Biniou*, 121 rue Clémenceau (☎02.96.72.24.35; closed Wed, and all Jan), is the best of several adjacent seafood specialists just back from the Casino; in addition to the usual choices, its 92F menu features stuffed mussels and oysters.

Dahouët

A few kilometres west of Le Val-André – reachable by an enjoyable footpath around the headland – the small lagoon of **DAHOUËT** is more secluded, and has its own

campsite. Though it's known to have been used by Viking raiders over a thousand years ago, the construction of a large yachting marina has obliterated all significant traces of its past. In summer, Les Vedettes de Bréhat (☎02.96.55.86.99) operates boat trips every four or five days, depending on the tides, from Erquy (8.30am; ☎02.96.72.30.12; 175F) and/or Dahouët (8.30am or 9am; ☎02.96.72.20.55; 175F) out to the island of Bréhat (see p.228).

St-Brieuc

The major city on the Côte d'Émeraude, **ST-BRIEUC**, is far too busy being the industrial centre of the north to concern itself with entertaining tourists. It's an odd-looking city, with two very deep wooded valleys spanned by viaducts at its core, and it's almost impossible to bypass, however you're travelling. The streets are hectic, with the town centre cut in two by a virtual motorway, unrelieved by any public parks, and not much distinguished either by a mega-shopping complex. Motorists and cyclists, unfortunately, have little choice but to plough straight through rather than attempting to negotiate the back roads and steep hills around.

Every July, St-Brieuc makes a concession to summer visitors by organizing a **Festival of Breton Music**, while at the end of May comes the **Art Rock Festival** (☎02.96.33.77.50); if you're interested, the tourist office (see below) can supply relevant information on both. Worth looking in on, too, are the **Comité Départmentale de Tourisme** for the Côtes-du-Nord at 29 rue des Promenades (☎02.96.62.72.00). Throughout the summer they organize one-day tours in the area to visit craft workshops of every variety – taxidermists, bakers, farmers, makers of furniture and of cider.

Practicalities

Trains between Paris, Dol and Brest stop at the gare SNCF, around 1km south of the centre of St-Brieuc, and regular buses run to the nearby resorts. There's an information desk at the station in summer, though the official **tourist office** is in the town centre, right by the cathedral at 7 rue St-Gouéno (July & Aug Mon–Sat 9am–7pm, Sun 10am–1pm; Sept–June Mon–Sat 9am–noon & 2–6.30pm; ☎02.96.33.22.50).

One ordinary but economical place to **stay** is the *Hôtel du Parc*, 8 rue Jean-Mermoz (☎02.96.33.51.02; ①). You can get significantly more class and comfort at the central *Champ de Mars*, 13 rue de Général-Leclerc (☎02.96.33.60.99; ③), as well as mussels or fish soup for around 45F in the old-fashioned green-painted brasserie downstairs. St-Brieuc also has a **youth hostel**, 2km out, in the magnificent fifteenth-century Manoir de la Ville-Guyomard (☎02.96.78.70.70); dorm beds cost around 60F per night. It's roughly 3km on foot from the place du Champ-de-Mars, which is on bus route #1 from the station, and has bicycles and canoes for rent.

Some of the nicest **eating** options in town are in the old quarter, up the small hill behind the cathedral. The traditional French cooking at *Le Madure*, 14 rue Quinquaine (☎02.96.51.20.17; closed Sun & Mon), is served *à la carte*, with steaks around 87F and salads half that; the fondues at *Le Chaudron*, 19 rue Fardel (☎02.96.33.01.72; closed Sun & Wed lunchtime) start at 80F per person.

The Inland Route: West to Morlaix

While following the coast from Dinard and Dinan is much the most scenic route westwards across Brittany, it can also be pretty slow. Travellers in a hurry to reach Morlaix and Finistère can choose instead to head **inland**, either by branching onto the D768 just south of St-Jacut, or following the N176 west out of Dinan. Both routes pass through the occasional time-forgotten little town or village; few have much in the way of tourist facilities but all are potentially pleasant opportunities to stretch your legs.

Jugon-les-Lacs

Tiny old **JUGON-LES-LACS** lies 15km southwest of the market town of **Plancoët** (home of a popular brand of mineral water, obtainable here free). Jugon is poised at one end of its own artificial lake (the *grand étang*); peculiarly, the central place du Martray – scene of a market each Friday – is well below the water level, and you have to climb uphill to reach the massive cobblestone dyke that shields it from inundation. At the opposite end of town, the N176 crosses high above the valley on a viaduct. Jugon, nestled cosily between the two, has no room to expand even if it wanted to – it's a subdued but atmospheric place, whose few streets are almost deserted in the evenings.

For most of the way around **the lake**, there's no approach road or footpath, only meadows and trees sweeping down to the water. However, at *Le Bocage* **campsite** (May–Sept; ☎02.96.31.60.16), just out of town along the D52 towards Mégrit, there's a small beach from which you can go swimming. It's very much a family campsite, with a heated swimming pool as well, and the rental of boats and **windsurfers** available with tuition from its École de Voile (☎02.96.31.64.58).

Practicalities

Jugon has a handful of moderately priced **hotels**, including two a couple of hundred metres east of the centre on the main road towards Dinan: *La Grande Fontaine*, 7 rue Penthièvre (☎02.96.31.61.29; ③), and *La Vallée Verte*, 11 rue Penthièvre (☎02.96.31.64.86; ③), which has menus from 80F and a lively bar. The local **tourist office** is in the Hôtel de Ville on the main square (☎02.96.31.61.62).

Lamballe

The main N176 westwards from Jugon brings you after 20km to **LAMBALLE**, an old town crammed into a narrow valley beside a broad river, dominated by a church high up on battlement walls. Its most famous former citizen was the princess of Lamballe, a lady-in-waiting to Marie Antoinette, who was guillotined in 1792.

A branch of the **national stud** (the *haras national*) all but adjoins Lamballe's picturesque main square, the place du Martray. Though not quite on the same scale as Le Notre's dramatic park near Argentan (see p.168), and specializing in any case more in sturdy Breton workhorses than glossy thoroughbreds, it will still delight any horse-lover (July & Aug daily 10.30am–12.30pm & 2–6pm; Sept–June Mon–Sat 2–5pm; 25F). It's the focus of a big **horse festival** on the first weekend after August 15.

Practicalities

Central **hotel-restaurants** in Lamballe include the *de la Porte St-Martin*, 12 rue de la Porte St-Martin (☎02.96.34.71.61; ①), and the *Tour d'Argent*, at no. 2 on rue Dr-Lavagne, which becomes the D102 (☎02.96.31.01.37; ②), a slightly more upmarket *logis* where menus start at 55F. The **tourist office** is in the grandest of the half-timbered buildings on place du Martray (Easter hols & June–Sept Mon–Sat 10am–12.30pm & 2.30–6pm; otherwise Tues & Fri 2.30–6pm; ☎02.96.31.05.38), which also holds a couple of tiny local museums.

Moncontour

The attractive little hill town of **MONCONTOUR**, 18km southeast of Lamballe and 23km southwest of St-Brieuc, was (during the Middle Ages) one of the more prosperous towns of the region, thanks to its hemp industry. Having been under no pressure to grow since then, it remains largely enclosed by its medieval fortifications – not that you get much impression of them once you're actually in the town, as the houses all face inwards onto the narrow streets.

Moncontour centres on the pretty, triangular **place du Penthièvre**, where the Romanesque tower of the church of St-Mathurin was blessed in 1902 by the addition of a delightfully eccentric new belfry, a confection of wooden eaves and grey-slate domes that now constitutes the highest point on the hill.

Practicalities

Moncontour's **tourist office** at 4 place de la Carrière (daily: mid-July to Aug 10am–6.30pm; mid-June to mid-July & Sept 10am–12.30pm & 2.30–6.30pm; ☎02.96.73.50.50). The village lacks any hotels, but it can offer a beautifully situated **B&B** – the four-room *Chambres d'hôte à la Garde Ducale*, in a sixteenth-century house at 10 place Penthièvre (☎02.96.73.52.18; ③). Near the tourist office, the *Chaudron Magique* (☎02.96.73.40.34) is a medieval theme restaurant where costumed waiters can serve you a decent meal for 65F and upwards.

On the final Sunday of August, Moncontour echoes its days of glory by playing host to a hectic and atmospheric "medieval fair".

Quintin

QUINTIN, 20km southwest of St-Brieuc, is in the official jargon "a little city of character", which prospered as a weaving community in the seventeenth and eighteenth centuries, and remains pretty much intact. Work on its grand **château** began in 1640, and was never completed, but you can tour a few of the rooms and see displays on the area (mid-June to mid-Sept daily 10.30am–12.30pm & 1.30–6.30pm; April to mid-June & mid-Sept to Oct daily except Tues 2–6pm). It's at its most imposing, however, when seen from down by the River Gouët below.

A twenty-minute stroll up from the river can show you the best of what Quintin has to offer. Follow the rue du Vau-du-Gouët from the east, and a stone staircase leads up through the vestiges of the old town walls, overshadowed by the round **Tour des Archives**, covered with creeping wild flowers. At the top is the late nineteenth-century **Basilique Notre Dame**. Beyond that, you enter the central place 1830, with the rue Grande stretching ahead. Most of its houses are made of elegant grey stone, standing proudly to attention, but a few of their half-timbered predecessors still slouch here and there in the ranks.

Turn right at the Hôtel de Ville at the far end of the rue Grande, and you'll soon come to the walled **Parc de Roz Maria**. These attractive formal gardens were laid out in the eighteenth century, and still hold a large public washplace that's now overgrown with green algae.

Practicalities

Quintin's **tourist office** is at no. 6 on the main place 1830 (daily: July & Aug 10am–7pm; Sept–June 9.30am–12.30pm & 2.30–5.30pm; ☎02.96.74.01.51). The ivy-coated *Hôtel du Commerce*, on the western fringes of the centre at 2 rue Rochenen (☎02.96.74.94.67; closed mid-Dec to mid-Jan, plus Sun pm & Mon pm in low season; ②), is a classic little village hotel, tasteful if far from fancy. Its solemn but attractive dining room serves good meals from 59F upwards.

Guingamp

Should you choose to skip St-Brieuc and the Côte de Granit Rose (see p.230), the most direct route towards Finistère carries across the centre of the northern peninsula. The only town of any size here is the old weaving centre of **GUINGAMP** – its name possibly the source of the striped or checked fabric "gingham". It's an attractive place of cobbled streets, but there's not much to see beyond the main square, where a fountain bedecked in griffins and gargoyles is overlooked by a splendid pair of lopsided old timber-frame houses propping each other up, and the Black Virgin in the thirteenth-century **basilica**. A big *pardon*, featuring a night procession to the basilica, is held on the first Saturday in July.

Practicalities

Guingamp is the first rail stop west of St-Brieuc; its **gare SNCF** (☎02.96.94.50.50) is southeast of the place du Vally, where you'll find the **tourist office** (July & Aug Mon 2–7pm, Tues–Sat 10am–7pm; Sept–June Mon 2–6pm, Tues–Sat 10am–noon & 2–6pm; ☎02.96.43.73.89) and the **gare routière**.

Of its **hotels**, the white-painted *Hôtel d'Armor*, 44 bd Clémenceau (☎02.96.43.76.16; closed Sun; ③), is probably the best value, and has a nice garden around the back. The best **restaurant** in town, however, is in the expensive hotel *Le Relais du Roy*, 42 place du Centre (☎02.96.43.76.62; ⑦), where you can eat in the magnificent dining room for a minimum of 135F.

The Ménéz Bré

On the road out towards Morlaix is the "mountain" of the **Ménéz Bré**, a spectacular height amid these plains. In the mid-nineteenth century the local rector was often observed to climb, laden with books, to the mountain's peak on stormy nights, accompanied only by a donkey. For all his exemplary piety, his parishioners suspected him of sorcery and witchcraft; he was in fact doing early research into natural electrical forces.

The Baie de St-Brieuc

St-Brieuc itself may be more of an obstacle to be avoided than an appealing destination, but it serves as a gateway to the further series of attractive little resorts that dot its eponymous bay. It also marks the point at which visitors usually begin to become aware that Brittany really does amount to something more than just another indistinguishable corner of the French coastline, and has its own very distinct culture and traditions.

As you move northwest from St-Brieuc along the edge of the V-shaped bay towards Paimpol, the countryside becomes especially rich – it's called the **Goëlo** – while the coast itself grows wilder and harsher. The seaside towns tend to be crammed into narrow rocky inlets or set well back in river estuaries.

Binic

BINIC is probably the nicest place to stay on the Baie de St-Brieuc. The whole place is on a very small scale with a narrow port, a sandy beach, a tiny promenade around the town and to either side Devon-like meadows that roll down to the sea. In the mid-nineteenth century, Binic was said to be one of the busiest ports in all France; these days it's simply a minor but appealing tourist resort, with a lucrative sideline of selling mud from the River Ic for fertilizer.

Six kilometres west of Binic, just off the D47, the **Jardin Zoologique de Bretagne** is a leafy park that holds the likes of llamas, ostriches and zebras in deceptively natural surroundings, and fiercer creatures such as lions firmly behind bars (Easter–Sept daily 10am–7pm; Oct–Easter Wed & Sun 2–5pm; 45F).

Practicalities

The good if relatively pricey *Hôtel Benhuyc*, 1 quai Jean-Bart (☎02.96.73.39.00; ④), offers the only waterfront **accommodation** in town, but there are several nearby **campsites**, the best of them the secluded *Les Madières*, back from the sea off the main road south of the centre (June–Sept; ☎02.96.79.02.48). Les Vedettes de Bréhat (☎02.96.73.60.12) run occasional day-trips during the summer to the Île de Bréhat (see p.228), costing 175F and setting off at 8.30am.

St-Quay-Portrieux

ST-QUAY, a little to the north, is considerably more upmarket and a bit soulless, though there's certainly a lot of activity going on in its sister town of

---

INTO THE BRETON HEARTLAND

At **Plouha**, a short way along the D786 from St-Quay, you cross what was traditionally the boundary between the French-speaking and Breton-speaking areas of Brittany. As a general indication, you can tell which language used to be spoken in a particular area by its place names. Thus, from here on west there is a preponderance of names beginning with the Breton "PLOU" (meaning parish), "TREZ" (sand or beach), "KER" (town) or "PENN" (head). See Contexts for a comprehensive glossary of Breton words that you are likely to come across.

PORTRIEUX, where a new yachting marina has encouraged what used to be a slightly seedy waterfront – dating back to the days of the Newfoundland fishing fleets (see p.68) – to smarten itself up.

Practicalities

In St-Quay itself, the *Gerbot d'Avoine*, 2 bd de Littoral (☎02.96.70.40.09; closed Jan, restaurant closed Sun pm & Mon pm in low season; ③) beside the beach, is an entertaining *logis*, where the food is good, with menus from 85F upwards, but the decor upstairs is truly astonishing. Crimson carpets creeping up the corridor walls make it look hideously like the hotel in *The Shining*, while in the rooms themselves washbasins and even showers are discreetly hidden away in cupboards. The *Hôtel le Bretagne*, 36 quai de la République (☎02.96.70.40.91; ②), is an alternative if you'd rather stay by the seafront in Portrieux.

In summer, Les Vedettes de Bréhat (☎02.96.70.40.64) run a few sailings each week, according to an erratic schedule, to the Île de Bréhat (see p.228), for a return fare of 175F (departures 8.30am).

Kermaria-an-Isquit

You may well get your first exposure to spoken Breton (see box) in smaller villages such as **KERMARIA-AN-ISQUIT**. This is not an easy place to find, especially coming from Lanloup to the north; the best signposted of its approaches is along the D21 from Plouha. Nonetheless, a fairly constant trickle of visitors make their way here throughout the summer to see the village's **chapel** and its extraordinary *Dance of Death*, one of the most striking of all French medieval images. The caretaker, Mme Hervé Droniou, usually keeps the church open (daily 9am–noon & 2–6pm; donation); when it's closed, you have to find her in the house just up the road on the left to let you in.

The **Dance of Death** is no delicate miniature. This huge series of frescoes – depicting Ankou, the skeletal death-figure, leading representatives of all social classes in a *Danse Macabre* – covers the arcades all round the chapel. Painted at the end of the plague-fearing fifteenth century, they were subsequently white-washed over, not to be rediscovered until 1856. Much of the work has vanished altogether, especially on the ceiling, and even in what survives the original colours have faded, and the figures are often no more than silhouettes. However, the fresco has lost little of its power to shock.

In yellow, on a red background, the skeleton alternates with such living characters as a King, a Knight, a Bishop and a Peasant. Verses below, now mostly illegible though available in transcription, have each person pleading for life and lamenting death, while Ankou insists that all must in the end come to him. Elsewhere in the church is a representation of the classic medieval theme of the encounter between the *Trois Vifs*, three finely apparelled noblemen out hunting, with the *Trois Morts*, three corpses reflecting in a cemetery on the transience of all things human:

Nous avons bien este en chance
Autrefoys, comme estes a present
Mais vous viendrez a nostre dance
Comme nous sommes maintenant.

In other words, we were lucky enough once to be like you, but you'll have to come and join our dance in the end.

The chapel was originally the property of the lords of the manor of Noë Vert, and is said to be linked by a tunnel, long since flooded, to their manor house 5km away. It was known in Breton as *"Itron Varia An Iskuit"*, meaning "Our Lady Who Helps". A small display case behind the altar contains the skull of one of the lords, and a couple of grotesque heart-shaped boxes hold the hearts of another and his wife. A unique statue shows the infant Jesus refusing milk from the Virgin's proffered breast, symbolizing the choice of celestial over terrestrial food.

Abbaye de Beauport

Mid-June to mid-Sept daily 10am–7pm, with regular 1hr 30min guided tours, mid-Sept to mid-June daily except Tues 10am–noon & 2–5pm. 25F.

As the D786 north of Kermaria and Binic meanders back towards the shoreline, a couple of kilometres short of Paimpol, it passes the substantial ruins of the **Abbaye de Beauport**. The abbey of Bellus Portus was established in 1202 by Count Alain de Goëlo, in memory of his parents. Sited halfway between St-Brieuc and Tréguier, its primary function was as a way station for English pilgrims en route to Compostella. Much of its income was drawn from thirteen parishes in Lincolnshire, and it never really recovered after the Reformation in England threw the monks here back onto their own resources. A merchant from Paimpol bought the entire estate after the Revolution, and his family owned it until 1992, when they sold it to the State.

The abbey is currently being restored, but the main appeal for visitors is the sheer romance of its setting and semi-dilapidated condition. Its stone walls are covered with wild flowers and ivy, the central cloisters are engulfed by a huge tree, and birds fly everywhere. The Norman Gothic **chapterhouse** is the most noteworthy building to survive, but wandering through and over the roofless halls you may spot architectural relics from all periods of its history.

The monks' refectory looks out across the **salt meadows** where they raised their sheep, and planted orchards on land that they reclaimed from the sea with an intricate network of dams. Footpaths lead all the way down to the sea, offering the same superb views of the hilltop abbey that must have been appreciated by generations of arriving pilgrims.

Paimpol

Though still an attractive town, with a tangle of cobbled alleyways lined with fine grey-granite houses, **PAIMPOL** has lost something in its transition from working fishing port to pleasure harbour. It was once the centre of a cod and whaling fleet that sailed for the fisheries of Iceland each February, sent off with a ceremony marked by a famous *pardon*. From then until August or September, the town would be empty of all young men. Within a few years of the first expedition in 1852, the annual exodus consisted of as many as fifty vessels, with 25 men in each. A haunting glimpse of the way Paimpol used to look can be seen in the recently rereleased silent film of Pierre Loti's book *Pêcheur d'Islande*, made on location here by Jacques de Baroncelli in 1924. Loti, and the heroine of his book, lived in the **place du Martray** in the centre of town.

Thanks to naval shipyards and the like, the open sea is not visible from Paimpol; a maze of waterways leads to its two separate harbours. Both are usually filled with the high masts of yachts, but still also used by the fishing boats that keep a fish market and a plethora of *poissonneries* busy. This is doubtless a very pleasant place to arrive by yacht, threading through the rocks, but from close quarters the tiny port area is a little disappointing, very much rebuilt and quite plain. Even so, it is always lively in summer.

Arrival and information

Paimpol's **tourist office** is in the Hôtel de Ville on rue Pierre-Feutren, near the prominent Notre Dame church (June to mid-Sept Mon–Sat 9am–7.30pm, Sun 9.30am–1pm; mid-Sept to May Tues–Sat 10am–noon & 2.30–6pm; ☎02.96.20.83.16).

Between June and September, four or five daily trains take 45 minutes to connect the **gare SNCF** in Paimpol (☎02.96.20.81.22) with **Guingamp**; there are also regular **buses** to and from St-Brieuc and Lannion.

Accommodation

Most of Paimpol's nicest **hotels** are clustered together on the northern side of the port, either right on the waterfront or in the network of semi-pedestrianized little alleyways just behind. There's also a year-round **youth hostel** in the grand old *Château de Kerraoul*, 2km west (all year; ☎02.96.20.83.60), which offers dorm beds for around 65F and has facilities for camping.

Hôtel Berthelot, 1 rue du Port (☎02.96.20.88.66). Very hospitable place, set slightly back from the pleasure port. ②.

Le Goëlo, quai Duguay-Truin (☎02.96.20.82.74, fax 02.96.20.58.93). Bright-pink, modern hotel in the ugly new block that lines the inland side of the fishing harbour, and which houses the simple brasserie *La Chaumière*. ②.

Hôtel de la Marne, 30 rue de la Marne (☎02.96.20.82.16, fax 02.96.20.92.07). Smart, twelve-room *logis de France* a little way back from the port, with a formal restaurant offering menus from 99F. ④.

Hôtel Origano, 7bis rue du Quai (☎02.96.22.05.49). Somewhat plain, but very comfortable hotel, opposite the *Berthelot*. ③.

Le Repaire de Kerroc'h, 29 quai Morand (☎02.96.20.50.13, fax 02.96.22.07.46). The most luxurious option, in a grand old house overlooking the small-boat harbour, and serving gourmet meals from 115F (135F on Sun) up to 350F. Closed Tues & Wed lunchtimes in low season, plus mid-Jan to Feb. ④.

Eating

Appealing **restaurants** stand on all sides of the port, as well as in the backstreets of the town proper, near the marketplace. The *Corto Maltese* **bar**, at 11 rue du Quai very near the *Origano* hotel, serves a fine selection of British and other beers.

Crêperie-Restaurant Morel, 11 place du Martray (☎02.96.20.86.34). Cavernous place in the heart of town, popular with locals not only for its inexpensive *crêpes*, but also for its good-value daily bistro specials. Closed Sun in low season, plus mid-Nov to mid-Dec.

La Cotriade, quai Armand-Dayot (☎02.96.20.81.08). On the far side of the harbour to the town centre, but a great bet for authentic fish dishes, with a simple 88F menu and a 150F menu featuring a delicious crab mousse. They positively prefer diners to pay using credit cards. Closed Wed pm & Thurs.

Restaurant du Port, 17 quai Morand (☎02.96.20.82.76). Attractive-looking place near the pleasure harbour and hotels, although the ambience can be spoilt by rude service and meagre portions. The 75F menu is basic in the extreme, and you have to allow at least 100F for a reasonable meal, with sardines or poached salmon. Closed Sun pm, Mon, & Jan.

La Vieille Tour, 13 rue de l'Église (☎02.96.20.83.18). Cosy but sophisticated upstairs dining room, tucked away from the port in the cobbled pedestrian area, and offering top-quality seafood; go for the sea trout on the 106F menu. Closed Sun pm, plus Wed in low season.

Loguivy-sur-mer

If Paimpol is too crowded for you, it's well worth continuing a few kilometres further across the headland to reach the little fishing hamlet of **LOGUIVY**. All of the long river inlets along this northern coast tend to conceal tiny coves – at Loguivy a working harbour manages to squeeze into one such gap in the rocks. Lenin came here for his summer holidays in July 1902.

Loguivy's only hotel is right on the waterfront, looking out towards Bréhat: the six-room *Le Grand Large* (☎02.96.20.90.16; ④), which serves fine fishy dinners from 85F. There are also *chambres d'hôte* (which work out little cheaper) at **Kéréveur** (M Chaboud; ☎02.96.55.82.76; ②) and **Kerloury** (I.Le Goaster; ☎02.96.20.85.23; ②).

The Île de Bréhat

The **ÎLE DE BRÉHAT** – in reality two islands joined by a slip of a bridge – gives the appearance of spanning great latitudes. On the north side are windswept meadows of hemlock and yarrow, sloping down to chaotic erosions of rock; on the south, you're in the midst of palm trees, mimosa and eucalyptus. All around is a multitude of little islets – some accessible at low tide, others *propriété privée*, most just pink-orange rocks. All in all, this has to be one of the most beautiful places in Brittany, renowned as a sanctuary not only for rare species of **wild flowers**, but also for **birds** of all kinds.

As you might expect, this island paradise has attracted Parisians, among others looking for holiday homes. Over half the houses now have temporary residents and young Bréhatins leave in ever-increasing numbers for lack of a place of their own, let alone a job. In winter the remaining three hundred or so natives have the place to themselves, without even a *gendarme*; the summer sees two imported from the mainland, along with upwards of three thousand tourists. As a visitor, though, you should find the *Bréhatins* friendly enough – it's the holiday-home owners that they really resent.

The beach to swim from at low tide is the **Grève de Guerzido,** on the east side facing the mainland. Near **LE BOURG** – Bréhat's village, which is the centre of all activity on the island – the sea tends to be a bit murky, and the east coast generally is less accessible because of private property. But in the north, even when Le Bourg is blocked up with visitors, you can walk and laze about in near solitude. Bréhat no longer has a castle (blown up twice by the English), but it does have a lighthouse and a nineteenth-century **fort**, in the woods near the campsite (see p.230).

Getting there

Bréhat is connected regularly by **ferry** from the Pointe de l'Arcouest, 6km northwest of Paimpol, and served by regular buses in summer from the gare SNCF there. Sailings, with Vedettes de Bréhat (☎02.96.55.79.50), are roughly hourly in high summer, and every two hours for the rest of the year, with the first boat out to Bréhat at 8.30am in summer, and last boat back at 7.45pm; the return trip costs

ÎLE DE BRÉHAT

Paon Lighthouse

ROUTE DU PAON

Baie de la Corderie

N

D 104

Le Bourg

Port-Clos

Fort
Camping

Greve du Guerzido

0   500 m

▽ Point de l'Arcouest (Paimpol)

40F. The same company also operates boats in summer from Binic and St-Quay-Portrieux (both p.224).

In addition, up to three daily 45-minute guided **boat tours** circle the island (April–Sept; 70F).

Practicalities

No **cars** are permitted on the Île de Bréhat, and there's barely a road wide enough for its few light farm vehicles. You can rent **bikes** by the day at the ferry port (or take one with you for 50F; to do so in summer you have to catch a ferry before 10am), but it's easy enough to **walk** from one end to the other in thirty minutes.

The **tourist office**, in the old Mairie in the main square in Le Bourg (Mon–Sat 10am–1pm & 3–6pm; ☎02.96.20.04.15), has full details on **accommodation** available on the island. The three hotels are expensive and in any case tend to be permanently booked through the summer, while all close for at least part of the winter. Both the *Vieille Auberge* in Le Bourg (☎02.96.20.00.24; closed Nov–March; ④) and the *Bellevue* in Port-Clos (☎02.96.20.00.05; closed Jan to mid-Feb; ⑤) insist on *demi-pension* in high season. The tourist office can also provide **campers** with information on the wonderful campsite in the woods high above the sea west of the port (mid-June to mid-Sept; ☎02.96.20.00.36). When that's closed, you can pitch your tent almost anywhere.

Restaurants are neither numerous nor cheap on Bréhat – though *La Potinière* on the beach at Guerzido (May–Sept; ☎02.96.20.00.29) serves inexpensive *moules frites*. Therefore, many visitors prefer to buy picnic food at the small **market** that's held most days in Le Bourg.

The Côte de Granit Rose

The whole of the northernmost stretch of the Breton coast, from Bréhat to Trégastel, has loosely come to be known as the **Côte de Granit Rose**. Great granite boulders are indeed scattered in the sea around the island of Bréhat, and at the various headlands to the west, but the most memorable stretch of coast lies around **Perros-Guirec**, where the pink granite rocks are eroded into fantastic shapes.

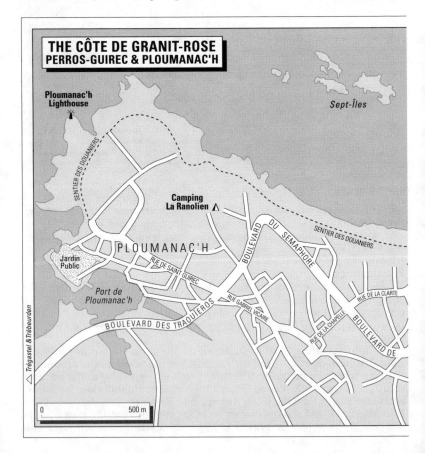

THE CÔTE DE GRANIT-ROSE
PERROS-GUIREC & PLOUMANAC'H

Ploumanac'h
Lighthouse

Sept-Îles

SENTIER DES DOUANIERS

Camping
La Ranolien

SENTIER DES DOUANIERS

Jardin
Public

PLOUMANAC'H

RUE DE SAINT GUIREC

BOULEVARD DU SEMAPHORE

RUE DE LA CLARTE

Port de
Ploumanac'h

RUE GABRIEL VICAIRE

RUE DE LA CHAPELLE

Trégastel & Trébeurden

BOULEVARD DES TRAOUÏEROS

BOULEVARD DE

0   500 m

Pink granite is an absolutely gorgeous stone, wearing smooth and soft but also glittering sharply. It's hard to tire of it – which is just as well, for everything in this area seems to be made of it: the houses are faced with granite blocks, and the streets paved with them; the breakwaters in the sea are granite, and the polished pillars of the banks are granite; the hotels even have overgrown granite mini-golfs with little pink granite megaliths as obstacles; and the markets claim to sell *granit-smith* apples.

Tréguier

The D786 turns west from Paimpol, passing over a green *ria* on the bridge outside Lézardrieux before arriving at **TRÉGUIER**. This is one of the very few hilltowns in Brittany, set at the junction of the Jaudy and Guindy rivers. It was rebuilt on this fortified elevation in 848 AD after an earlier monastery was destroyed by Norman raiders.

The central unmissable feature of Tréguier is the **Cathédrale de St-Tugdual**, whose geometric Gothic spire, dotted with holes, contrasts sharply with its earlier

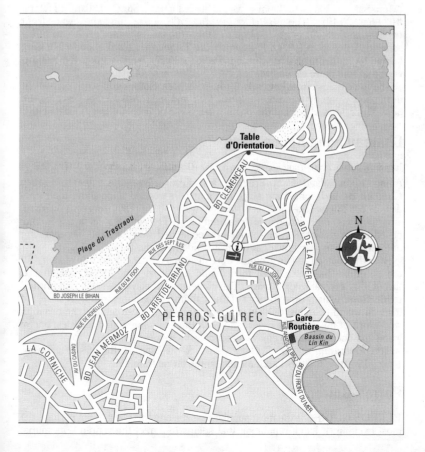

Romanesque "Hastings" tower. Inside, the masonry blocks are appealingly crude, and dripping with damp that has somehow spared the intricate carved animal on the wooden stalls. The cathedral contains the tomb of St Yves, a native of the town who died in 1303 and – for his incorruptibility – became the patron saint of lawyers. Attempts to bribe him continue to this day; his tomb is surrounded by marble plaques and an inferno of candles invoking his aid, including one special plea from a group of American lawyers. A *pardon* of St Yves is held each year on the Sunday closest to his feast day, May 19.

The half-timbered houses of the square outside look down on a statue of Ernest Renan, a local writer and philosopher whose work formed part of the great nineteenth-century attempt to reinterpret traditional religious faith in the light of scientific discoveries. Worthy Catholics were so incensed at the erection of this memorial in 1903 that they soon built their own "Calvary of Reparation" on the quayside.

Practicalities

Tréguier's **tourist office** is in the Hôtel de Ville, round the back of the cathedral (Mon–Sat 9.30am–12.30pm & 2.30–5.30pm, Sun 9.30am–12.30pm; ☎02.96.92.30.19). The *Hôtel-Restaurant d'Estuaire* on the waterfront (☎02.96.92.30.25; ③) is a nice place **to stay** – the sea views are great – with reasonable menus from 70F. *La Poissonnerie du Trégor* up in town, above a fish shop behind the cathedral at 2 rue Renan (☎02.96.92.30.27), is an excellent fish **restaurant** that's no more expensive.

The town holds a **market** each Wednesday, with clothes and so on spread out in the square up by the cathedral, and food and fresh fish further down by the port. The cafés and delis of the main square save their best displays for that day.

Château de la Roche-Jagu

July & Aug daily 10am–7pm, Easter–June & Sept–Oct daily 10.30am–noon & 2–6pm. 35F.

About 10km inland from Tréguier and Lézardrieux, the fifteenth-century **Château de la Roche-Jagu** stands on a heavily wooded slope above the meanders of the Trieux River, just as it starts to widen. It's a really gorgeous building, a harmonious combination of fortress and home. The central solid facade is composed of irregular red-granite boulders, cemented together, and incorporating one venerable turreted tower at the front and one at the back.

Both the château and its grounds were devastated by the hurricane of 1987, but the ensemble has since been turned into a modern landscaped park, traced through by several **hiking trails**. The château itself plays host to lavish **annual exhibitions**, usually on some sort of Celtic theme. The rooms within are bare, but it's well worth climbing right up to the top. Here you can admire the beautiful woodwork of the restored eaves, and walk the two long indoor galleries, one of wood and one of stone, to enjoy tremendous views over the river.

The *Restaurant de la Château de la Roche-Jagu*, in the castle gateway, (☎02.96.95.16.08), offers lunch menus on the lawns from 75F.

Perros-Guirec

PERROS-GUIREC is the most popular resort along this coast, if not perhaps the most exciting. It has a reputation that seems to attract the retired – its tourist brochures list "playing Scrabble" as an attraction – and an array of shops intended to match: antiques, bric-a-brac and pottery with a big line in granite guillemots and puffins. And Perros is, too, a lot less city-like than it looks on the maps: most of its network of roads turn out to be tree-lined avenues of suburban villas.

However, the commercial streets of the centre (up the hill from the port) hold little of interest, and are often jammed solid with traffic in summer. Much more enjoyable is to take a walk around the headland to see the magnificent view from the Table d'Orientation at the sharp curve of the boulevard Clémenceau.

The best beach is the **Plage de Trestraou**, on the opposite side of town to the port, a long curve of sand speckled with bars and restaurants. Between March and October, boats sail from here on round trips to the bird sanctuary of **Sept-Îles**. Both Vedettes Blanches (☎02.96.91.13.21) and Les Sept-Îles en Vedettes (☎02.96.91.10.00) offer the choice of a two-hour cruise that circles but doesn't actually land on the seven craggy islands for around 70F, and a two-and-a-half-hour trip that includes a brief landfall. Non-natives may well find it hard to keep up with the fast-flowing French commentary.

Practicalities

If you don't have your own transport, Perros-Guirec is surprisingly hard to reach. What buses there are arrive at and leave from the **Bassin du Lin Kin** in the port, a few hundred metres down from the town centre. If you arrive this way and plan to stay, a good first move is to rent a **bike**; Cycles Henry, near the *gendarmerie* on boulevard Aristide-Briand (☎02.96.91.03.33), can oblige.

The extremely efficient **tourist office** is at 21 place de l'Hôtel-de-Ville (July & Aug Mon–Sat 9am–7.30pm, Sun 10am–12.30pm & 4–6.30pm; Sept–June Mon–Sat 9am–12.30pm & 2–6.30pm; ☎02.96.23.21.15). If you'd rather stay here than in the smaller community of Ploumanac'h (see p.234), good **hotels** include the old-fashioned *les Violettes*, 19 rue du Calvaire (☎02.96.23.21.33; ②), which has a seriously cheap restaurant, and two with sea views, the *Gulf Stream*, high on the hillside at 26 rue des Sept-Îles (☎02.96.23.21.86; closed mid-Nov to March; ②), and the *Bon Accueil*, 11 rue de Landerval (☎02.96.23.25.77; ④), which has a gourmet restaurant.

Almost any of the glass-fronted sea-view **restaurants** that line boulevard Thalassa is worth trying, but it's hard to imagine any being able to top the *Flambert* (☎02.96.23.36.88) for a romantic sunset seafood extravaganza – a large spread here costs a mere 80F.

The nicest place to **camp** has to be *Le Ranolien* (March to mid-Nov; ☎02.96.91.43.58), which backs on to the Sentier des Douaniers (see below) near a little beach about halfway round, and is also directly accessible on the other side by road. However, the *Camping du Trestraou*, 89 av du Casino (May to mid-Sept; ☎02.96.23.08.11), right beside Trestraou beach, is almost equally attractive.

The Sentier des Douaniers

Perros-Guirec's Trestraou beach is made of ordinary sand; the pink-granite coast proper starts just beyond its western end. The long **Sentier des Douaniers** pathway winds round the clifftops to **Ploumanac'h** past an astonishing succession of deformed and water-sculpted rocks. Birds wheel overhead towards the sanctuary, and battered boats shelter in the narrow inlets or bob uncontrollably out on the waves. There are patches and brief causeways of grass, clumps of purple heather and yellow gorse. Occasionally the rocks have crumbled into a sort of granite grit to make up a tiny beach; one boulder is strapped down by bands of ivy that prevent it rolling into the sea.

The rocks, in good French cataloguing fashion, have all been given "names" based on supposed resemblances in their shapes. The more banal ones – such as the great big *Foot* and the *Pancake* – are in a way the best; you can't help wondering, though, what committee it was, and when, that went along labelling the *Torpedo*, the *Armchair*, the *Tortoise* and *Napoleon's Hat*.

Ploumanac'h

PLOUMANAC'H is a more active resort than Perros-Guirec, though again with a dominant and specific clientele – this time families with youngish children. In fact few places on earth can offer quite such enchantment for energetic kids, who love to scramble around the surreal sandscape that's revealed when the long tides draw out. Glinting pink-granite boulders, fringed with green seaweed, erupt from the depths, and rock pools bursting with crabs and other mysteries just wait to be explored. The most obvious focal point is the tiny **Château du Diable**, framing the horizon on one of the countless little islands in the bay – which was where the novel *Quo Vadis* was written around the turn of the century. When the tide is in, head instead for the pleasantly wild **municipal park** that separates Ploumanac'h's two halves, the Bourg and the Plage.

Practicalities

Slightly back from the beach, there's a small lively square of hotels, restaurants and snack bars. The unfortunately named *Coste Mor* has magnificent views but not desperately good food. A better bet is the *Mao*, at 147 rue St-Guirec nearby (☎02.96.91.40.92; no credit cards), a former snack bar that has expanded to take over several adjacent buildings, including a Polynesian-style thatched hut, and offers bargain menus from 55F (even less for *crêpes*). Like most places in Ploumanac'h, it has special cheap menus for children.

The emphasis on children does mean that Ploumanac'h goes to bed early – you can find yourself locked out of a slumbering hotel at 9.30pm. But prices at the *Hôtel du Parc* (☎02.96.91.40.80; closed mid-Jan to mid-Feb; ③) are at least reasonable, and it serves good seafood menus from 75F, while *Les Rochers* (☎02.96.91.44.49; closed Oct–Easter; ④) verges on the luxurious.

The Traouïéro Valleys

A very short distance west of Ploumanac'h, two dramatic little valleys, which bear a close resemblance to the forest at Huelgoat (see p.294), lead down to the sea. It was the devastation caused by the hurricane of 1987 that led to the **Grand Traouïéro** and the **Petit Traouïéro** becoming accessible to casual visitors – the process of clearing away ancient fallen trees, and disentangling them from centuries of ivy, resulted in the paths being sufficiently opened up so that now either valley makes a gorgeous and undemanding stroll of a few kilometres inland from the coast.

Each of the two is complete with its own gurgling creek, towered over by a huge tumble of pink granite rocks, cascading between old oaks and chestnut trees, with the occasional stand of Monterey cypresses. The Grand Traouïéro in particular is dwarfed beneath mighty boulders, reminiscent of gargantuan Henry

Moore sculptures; the Petit Traouïéro is less deep and more delicate. In spring, both are filled with bright bluebells, and the broom is in full blossom.

At the mouth of the Grand Traouïéro, you can visit a 400-year-old tidal mill, one of several in the area that were used to grind flour until the start of this century.

Trégastel and Trébeurden

Of the smaller villages further round the coast to the west, **TRÉGASTEL**, with a couple of **campsites**, including the *Tourony* by the beach (Easter–Sept; ☎02.96.23.86.61), and **TRÉBEURDEN**, with a **youth hostel**, (*Le Toëno*; open all year; ☎02.96.23.52.22; 46F), are functional stopovers. Trégastel has managed to squeeze in an **aquarium** under a massive pile of boulders, and has a couple of huge lumps of pink granite slap in the middle of its fine beach.

The strangest sight along this coast, however, outdoing anything the erosions can manage, is just south of Trégastel on the **route de Calvaire**, where an old stone saint halfway up a high calvary raises his arm to bless or harangue the gleaming white discs and puffball dome of the **Pleumier-Bodou Telecommunications Centre**. A new pink-granite "dolmen" commemorates its opening by de Gaulle in 1962, when it was the first receiving station to pick up signals from the American Telstar satellite. Now that the centre is no longer operational, it has been remodelled as a **Museum of Telecommunications**, which is also known as **Cosmopolis** (July & Aug daily 10am–7pm; May & June daily 10am–6pm; April daily except Sat 10am–6pm; Sept Sun–Fri 10am–6pm, Sat 2–6pm; otherwise peculiar hours which include being closed Sat Oct–March, & closed Sun in most of Nov & Jan; 43F). Inside the golf ball itself, the **Radôme**, frequent spectacular *son et lumiére* shows explain the history of the whole ensemble, and there's also a smaller **planetarium** alongside. One final incongruous note is struck by the reconstructed **Gaulish village** nearby (same hours; additional donation 15F), which is designed to raise money for a French charity working in Africa, and thus incorporates some traditional huts from Togo.

The Bay of Lannion

Despite being located significantly back from the sea on the estuary of the River Léguer, **Lannion** gives its name to the next bay west along the Breton coast – and it's the bay rather than the town that is most likely to impress visitors. One enormous beach stretches from **St-Michel-en-Grève**, which is little more than a bend in the road, as far as **Locquirec**; at low tide you can walk hundreds of metres out on the sands.

Lannion

LANNION, set amid plummeting hills and stairways, is a historic city with streets of medieval housing, and a couple of interesting old churches – but it's also a centre for a burgeoning and extremely hi-tech telecommunications industry, and as such one of modern Brittany's real success stories. Hence its rather self-satisfied nickname, *ville heureuse* or "happy town".

In addition to admiring the half-timbered houses around the place de Général-Leclerc and along rue des Chapeliers (look out for nos. 3 and 4), it's well worth climbing from the town up the 142 granite steps which lead to the twelfth-century Templar **Église de Brélévenez**. This church was remodelled three hundred years later to incorporate a granite bell tower, and the views from its terrace are quite stupendous.

Practicalities

Lannion's **gare SNCF** is across the river from town. Arriving passengers reach the centre across an attractive little bridge, from which you should spot the **tourist office**, next to the post office on the quai d'Aguillon (July & Aug Mon–Sat 9am–7pm, Sun 10am–1pm; Sept–June Mon–Sat 9am–12.30pm & 2–6pm; ☎02.96.46.41.00).

The *Hôtel le Bretagne*, opposite the station at 32 av de Général-de-Gaulle (☎02.96.37.00.33; closed Sat & Sun pm out of season; ③), is a *logis* with a good restaurant. The *Porte de France*, an eighteenth-century coaching inn in the heart of town at 5 rue Jean-Savidan (☎02.96.46.54.81; ③), is more luxurious but has no restaurant. There's also a year-round **youth hostel**, *Les Korrigans*, handily near the station and the town centre at 6 rue du 73ᵉ Territorial (☎02.96.37.91.28; 100F with breakfast). Its friendly management do not operate a curfew, and they arrange birdwatching and similar expeditions, and rent out bikes – not that you'll necessarily relish cycling around Lannion itself, with its ferocious hills.

Locquirec

LOCQUIREC, across the bay from Lannion and officially just within Finistère, manages to have beaches on both sides, without ever quite being thin enough to be a real peninsula. Around the main port, smart houses stand in sloping gardens, looking very southern English with their whitewashed stone panels, grey-slate roofs and jutting turreted windows.

On the last Sunday in July, Locquirec holds a combined *pardon de St-Jacques* and Festival of the Sea.

Practicalities

Locquirec veers dangerously close towards being over-twee, and none of its **hotels** is all that cheap, either – although the *Grand Hôtel des Bains*, 15 rue de l'Église (☎02.98.67.41.02; ⑦) has so gorgeous a setting that perhaps it doesn't matter. It became widely known in France when it was used as the location for *Hôtel de la Plage*, a coming-of-age movie about youngsters summering in Brittany.

Nearby, the *Hôtel du Port* (☎02.98.67.42.10; closed Dec–Easter; ②) also enjoys a sea view, and the municipal **campsite**, the *Toul ar Goue*, 1km south along the corniche (mid-April to mid-Sept; ☎02.98.67.40.85), is beautifully positioned, too.

St-Jean-du-Doigt

Locquirec is just across the border of the *département* of Finistère, and by the direct road it is only a few kilometres further to Morlaix (see p.246). Following the coast, however, you come to **ST-JEAN-DU-DOIGT**, where the parish church contains an object held in veneration as the finger of John the Baptist. This sanctified digit is dipped into the Sacred Fountain to produce holy water. It was brought here in 1437 and is the principal object of the *pardon* on June 23 and 24 each year. A more recent tradition of pilgrimage has made St-Jean the site of massive anti-nuclear demonstrations.

Ploumilliau

An alternative inland route – or a detour from Lannion – is to the trim little village of **PLOUMILLIAU** on the D30. Here the weathered granite parish church, surrounded by beds of colourful flowers, contains a unique white-painted wooden representation of **Ankou**, the skeletal symbol of death. The statue, carrying a scythe to catch the living and a spade to bury them, was once carried in local processions.

The Cairn du Barnenez

At the mouth of the Morlaix estuary, 6km north of Plouézoch, the prehistoric stone **Cairn du Barnenez** surveys the waters from the summit of a hill (daily: July & Aug 10am–1pm & 2–6.30pm; April–June & Sept 10am–12.30pm & 2–6.30pm; Oct–March 10am–noon & 2–5pm; 25F). As on the island of Gavrinis in the Morbihan (see p.343), its ancient masonry has been laid bare by recent excavations, and provides a stunning sense of the architectural prowess of the megalith builders. Radiocarbon testing has shown the work here to date back to around 4500 BC, which makes this one of the oldest large monuments in the world. In the words of André Malraux, it represents "the Breton Parthenon". There is evidence that it remained in continuous use for around 2500 years; it was probably used repeatedly as a place of burial, then sealed off and abandoned.

The ensemble consists of two distinct stepped pyramids, the older one constructed of local dolerite stone, and the other of grey granite from the nearby Île de Sterec. Each rises in successive tiers, built of large flat stones chinked with pebbles (but no mortar); the second was added onto the side of the first, and the two are encircled by a series of terraces and ramps. The whole thing measures roughly 70m long by 15m to 25m wide; the current height of 6m is thought to be smaller than that of the original structure. Both were long ago buried under an eighty-metre-long earthen mound. While the actual cairns are completely exposed to view, most of the passages and chambers that lie within them are sealed off. The two minor corridors that are open simply cut through the edifice from one side to the other, and were exposed by quarrying activities around thirty years ago – which inadvertently provided a good insight into the construction methods. Each is covered with great slabs of rock; in fact most of the familiar dolmens seen all over Brittany and elsewhere are thought to be the vestiges of similarly complex structures. Local tradition has it that one tunnel runs right through this "home of the fairies", and continues out deep under the sea.

travel details

Trains

From St-Malo to Rennes (12 daily; 1hr; connections for Paris on TGV); to Caen (8 daily; 3hr 30min); to Dinan (8 daily; 1hr). All trains pass through Dol (25min).

From Rennes 8 daily TGV trains to St Brieuc (45min), Morlaix (1hr 40min) and Brest (2hr 10min); 10 daily slower services also stop at Lamballe, Guingamp and Plouaret; 8 daily TGV trains to Paris-Montparnasse (2hr 10min), plus 5 ordinary services (3hr 15min); 4 daily to Caen (3hr) via Dol and Pontorson; to Vannes (4 daily; 1hr) and Quimper (2hr 30min); to Nantes (4 daily; 1hr 30min).

From Lannion to St-Brieuc via Plouaret and Guingamp (June–Sept only, 1–4 daily; 1hr).

From Paimpol to Guingamp (June–Sept only, 4–5 daily; 45min).

Buses

From St-Malo to Dinard (8 daily, 30min); to Dinan (4 daily; 45min); to Mont-St-Michel (4 daily; 1hr 30min); to Cancale (4 daily; 35min); to Fougères via Pontorson (3 daily; 2hr); to Combourg (2 daily; 1hr); to Rennes via Tinténic and Hédé (5 daily; 1hr 30min); to St-Cast via St-Jacut (3 daily; 1hr).

From Dinard to Mont-St-Michel via Dol (1 daily; 1hr 10min).

From Rennes to Fougères (7 daily; 1hr); to Dinan (6 daily, 1hr 20min); to Dinard (8 daily; 1hr 40min).

From Fougères to Vitré (2 daily;35min); to Vire in Normandy (2 daily; 1hr 30min).

From St-Brieuc to Lannion via Guingamp (4 daily; 1hr 40min); to St-Cast, via Lamballe, Le Val-André, Erquy and Cap Fréhel (4 daily; 1hr 50min); to Carhaix (1 daily; 3hr), more frequently to Rostrenen (2hr); to Paimpol (8 daily; 1hr 30min); to Dinan (4 daily; 1hr); to Moncontour (4 daily; 1hr).

From Lannion to Trégastel and Perros-Guirec (6 daily; 1hr); to Locquirec and Morlaix (4 daily; 1hr 20min).

Ferries

From St-Malo Brittany Ferries (St-Malo ☎02.99.40.64.01, Portsmouth ☎01705/827701) to Portsmouth (1 daily mid-March to mid-Nov, otherwise less frequently; 9hr daytime crossing) and Plymouth (1 weekly mid-Nov to mid-March; 8hr).

Regular ferries to Dinard (10min) in season, operated by Émeraude Lines (☎02.99.40.48.40), who also sail to Dinan up the River Rance, and along the Brittany coast to Cap Fréhel, Cézembre and Dinard (May–Sept). They also go to to Jersey, to Guernsey (mid-March to Oct), and Sark (April–Sept), and to the Îles Chausey in Normandy. Condor Ferries (☎02.99.20.03.00) run services to Jersey (4 daily April–Sept, 2 daily Oct, 1 daily second half of March and first half of Nov), Guernsey (2 daily April–Oct, 1 daily second half of March and first half of Nov) and Sark (daily April–Oct), and on from the Channel Islands to Weymouth. Channiland (☎02.99.40.40.90) go to Jersey (1–4 daily mid-March to mid-Nov), and slightly less frequently to Guernsey and Sark.

Bréhat Island is reached using Vedettes de Bréhat, who run regular 10min trips from Pointe de l'Arcouest (☎02.96.55.79.50), and excursions from Erquy and/or Dahouët (☎02.96.55.86.99), Binic (☎02.96.73.60.12), or St-Quay-Portrieux (☎02.96.70.40.64). Full details are given in each of the relevant accounts.

Barges

Boats for use on the River Rance and the Canal d'Ille-et-Vilaine can be rented from the following companies:

Chemins Nautiques Bretons, M et Mme Alan Gaze, La Vicomté-sur-Rance, 22690 Pleudihen-sur-Rance (☎02.96.83.28.71).

Diffusion Nautique R.M., M René Michel, La Vicomté-sur-Rance, 22690 Pleudihen-sur-Rance (☎02.96.83.35.40).

Les Chemins d'Eau, Roumoulin, 35190 La-Chapelle-aux-Filtzméens (☎02.99.45.34.16).

Breiz Marine, 5 Quai de la Donac, 35190 Tinténiac (☎02.99.68.10.15).

Argoat Nautic, BP 24 Port de Betton, 35830 Betton (☎02.99.55.70.36).

Base Nautique de Pont-Réan, M le Teinturier, Pont-Réan, 35580 Guichen (☎02.99.42.21.91).

Crown Blue Line, Port de Plaisance, 35480 Messac (☎02.99.34.60.11).

For **general information** *contact the* **Comité de Promotion Touristique des Canaux Bretons**, *Office du Tourisme, place du Parlement, 35600 Redon (☎02.99.71.06.04).*

CHAPTER FIVE

FINISTÈRE

Finistère – literally, "the End of the World" – has always been isolated from the French, even from the Breton, mainstream. This remote rural landscape was the last refuge of the Druids from encroaching Christianity, and its forests and elaborate parish closes testify to its role as the province's spiritual heartland. Today, although the port of Roscoff has reopened the old maritime links with England, high-speed TGV trains mean that Brest is just four hours from

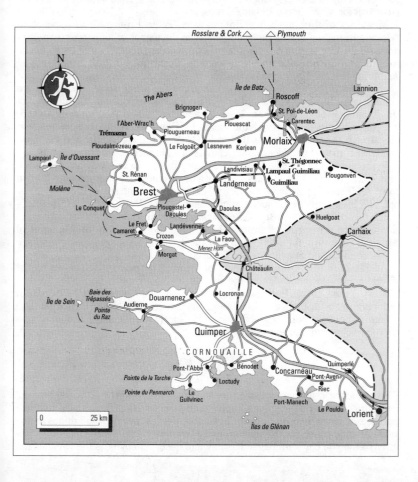

Paris, and the motorway now makes a complete loop around the end of the peninsula, it remains only sporadically touched by tourism and modern industry. Breton survives as a spoken language here more than anywhere else, and here too, especially in the "Bigouden country" in the south, traditional costumes are still worn for other than commercial reasons.

Memories of the days when Brittany was "Petite Bretagne", as opposed to "Grande Bretagne" across the water, linger in the names of Finistère's two main areas. Both the northern peninsula – **Léon**, once Lyonesse – and its southern neighbour – **Cornouaille**, the same word as "Cornwall" – feature prominently in Arthurian legend. The ragged **coastline**, indented with a succession of estuaries each of which shelters its own tiny harbour, is the prime attraction. Rarely are conditions as bleak as you might expect from a land exposed to the full force of the Atlantic; heading west from **Roscoff**, your most likely point of arrival, there are possible stopping places all the way to **Le Conquet**. What can be a treacherous stretch of ocean separates that from **Ouessant** and **Molène**; and yet those two islands have the mildest winter climate of all France.

In the south, Cornouaille boasts two classic resorts in **Loctudy** and **Bénodet**, either side of the Odet estuary, while if you'd rather stay in a genuine lived-in town, **Quimper** is just upriver – the liveliest place here and one of the most pleasant, and least-sung, in France. A short distance east, **Pont-Aven** was Gauguin's home before he made off to the South Seas, and still maintains its artistic traditions. There are surprises everywhere – take the **Museum of Mechanical Musical Instruments** near Combrit, or the perfectly preserved medieval village of **Locronan**, used as a film set for Polanski's *Tess*.

All Finistère offers the enticement of growing but not yet full-blown tourist development – facilities without the crowds. Its most popular region for holiday-makers is the **Crozon Peninsula**, jutting into the sea beneath the **Ménez-Hom** mountain as a distinct entity between the two ancient realms. **Morgat** and **Camaret** here are both ideal for long and leisurely seaside stays, and all around there are opportunities for secluded camping.

LÉON

The sequence of estuaries that score the coast in the north – the wildest and most dramatic in Brittany – are known both as *abers* (as in Welsh place names) and as *rias* (as in Spanish Galicia). In season, the vast beaches and dunes on the open Atlantic coast, for example around **Porspoder**, can be magnificent, while at any time you can stumble across tiny and deserted coves as the twisting and narrowing estuaries reach inland. One of the choicest spots is at **Trémazan**, where the ruins of an ancient castle look out across a great expanse of sand, while the working fishing village of **Le Conquet** is perhaps best of all. The one coastal place to avoid is the regional capital, and lone big city, of **Brest**, the base of the French Atlantic fleet.

Inland, the **parish closes** lie strung across the little villages that lie southwest of **Morlaix**, each ornate church and its associated ensemble still perpetuating a fierce medieval rivalry. Also deserving a detour from the coast are the Renaissance **château of Kerjean** and the **Menhir de Kerloas** (the highest stone monolith still standing).

Roscoff

ROSCOFF has long been a major port – Mary Queen of Scots, for example, landed here in 1548 on her way to Paris to be engaged to the son of Henri II of France, and so too did Bonnie Prince Charlie in 1746, after his defeat at Culloden – and the opening of its deep-water harbour in 1973 had especial significance in the general revitalization of the Breton economy. The town itself, however, has remained a small resort. It may not look so on the map, but almost all activity is confined to the **rue Gambetta** and the **old port** – the rest of the roads are residential backstreets full of retirement homes and stern institutions. The preservation of its old character is helped by the fact that both the ferry port and gare SNCF are some way from the town centre, which has recently been pedestrianized.

Arrival and information

Brittany Ferries **boats** from Plymouth (6hr) or Cork (19hr) dock at the Port de Bloscon (☎02.98.29.28.28), to the east (and just out of sight) of Roscoff. To get into the town, turn right from the terminal and follow the signs across a narrow promontory and down into the crescent of Roscoff's original natural harbour. Later than 9.15pm, it's difficult to find a restaurant still serving – if you're arriving on an evening ferry it's probably best to eat on the boat.

The helpful **tourist office** is at 46 rue Gambetta in town (July & Aug Mon–Sat 9am–12.30pm & 1.30–7pm, Sun 10am–12.30pm; April–June & Sept Mon–Sat 9am–noon & 2–6pm; Oct–March Mon–Fri 10am–noon & 2–5pm, Sat 10am–noon; ☎02.98.61.12.13), next to a *boulangerie* and the **post office** at 19 rue Gambetta (☎02.98.69.72.90). Regular trains run to Morlaix, with connections beyond from the **gare SNCF** (☎02.98.69.70.20), a few hundred metres south of the town proper. Most buses also go from here, including a direct service to Brest run by Les Cars du Kreisker (☎02.98.69.00.93). Another service to Morlaix leaves from the fish hall (known locally as *La Criée*) by the old harbour, with connections on Mondays, Thursdays and Saturdays to Quimper (CAT; ☎02.98.90.68.40).

Bikes can be rented from Desbordes François, 13 rue Brizeux (☎02.98.69.72.44), as well as from the gare SNCF.

Accommodation

For a small town, Roscoff is well equipped with **hotels**, which are accustomed to late-night arrivals from the ferries. Be warned, however, that most of them close for some or all of winter. There's also a **youth hostel** on the Île de Batz (see p.244), and two **campsites** – the *Municipal de Perharidy*, 2km west, just off the

ALEXIS GOURVENNEC AND BRITTANY FERRIES

Few British holiday-makers sailing to France with Brittany Ferries will realize the significance of ideology in the origins of that company. The ferry services from Roscoff to Plymouth and to Cork were started not simply to bring tourists, but also to revive the traditional trading links between the Celtic nations of Brittany, Ireland and southwest England – links which were suppressed for centuries as an act of French state policy after the union of Brittany with France in 1532.

Until the 1960s there were no direct ferries crossing the Channel to Brittany, and, until Brittany Ferries started up, all the cross-Channel operators were British-owned. Brittany Ferries is the creation of Alexis Gourvennec, who in 1961, at 24, was the militant leader of a Breton farmers' cooperative. Frustrated at the lack of French government support, the farmers decided to start their own shipping line to find new markets for their produce – the immediate region of Roscoff and Morlaix being particularly noted for its artichokes and cauliflowers.

The financial success of the company has been such that it has expanded to run services from Britain to the Norman ports of Cherbourg and Caen, as well as to Spain; but it has also been an important factor in a resurgence of Breton fortunes that has been as much cultural as commercial significance. Meanwhile Breton farmers have been campaigning for the expansion of Brest Airport (at Guipavas) so that it will be able to handle jumbo-jet loads of artichokes for same-day sale in New York!

See Contexts for more details.

route de Santec (May–Sept; ☎02.98.69.70.86), and the roomier *Manoir de Kérestat*, 2km south towards Saint-Pol (July & Aug; ☎02.98.69.71.92).

Hôtel-Restaurant des Arcades, 15 rue Amiral-Réveillère (☎02.98.69.70.45, fax 02.98.61.12.34). Sixteenth-century building with superb views from some of its modernized rooms and from the restaurant; menus 58F and upwards. Closed Oct–Easter. ②.

Hôtel-Restaurant le Bellevue, rue Jeanne d'Arc (☎02.98.61.23.38, fax 02.98.61.11.80). Seafront *logis de France*, on the opposite side of the pleasure harbour to the town centre and thus somewhat nearer the ferry terminal. It would in theory be quieter, were it not for the lively downstairs bar. Pleasant rooms, and fine views from the dining room, where the 110F menu offers salmon baked in cheese with mustard. Closed Dec to mid-March. ④.

Hôtel du Centre, 5 rue Gambetta (☎02.98.61.24.25). *Logis de France*, entered via the main street but looking out on the port. Very much a family hotel, also known as *Chez Janie*. Menus from 90F, with a squid salad to start. Closed Jan to mid-Feb. ③.

Hôtel les Chardons Bleus, 4 rue Amiral-Réveillère (☎02.98.69.72.03, fax 02.98.61.27.86). Very friendly and helpful hotel with a good restaurant (menus from 90F; closed Thurs in Sept–June, plus Sun in winter) but no sea views. Closed Feb. ③.

Hôtel le Gulf Stream, 7 rue Marquise de Kergariou (☎02.98.69.73.19, fax 02.98.61.11.89). Definitely one of the more expensive options, just south of the Institute of Oceanology, with a heated swimming pool and a quite superb seafood restaurant (where the cheapest menu is 145F). Closed mid-Oct to mid-March. ⑤.

Inter-Hôtel Regina, 1 rue Ropartz-Morvan (☎02.98.61.23.55, fax 02.98.61.10.89). Very comfortable rooms, but relatively expensive considering the location, near the gare SNCF. Menus from 90F upwards, and live jazz in the bar in what might otherwise be the quieter months. Closed Nov to mid-March. ③.

Hôtel les Tamaris, 49 rue É-Corbière (☎02.98.61.22.99, fax 02.98.69.74.36). Renovated, comfortably furnished rooms looking out towards the Île de Batz. No restaurant. Closed Oct–March. ③.

The Town

The old **harbour** is very much the liveliest part of Roscoff. Two long stone jetties enclose the fishing port – the local economy is still heavily based on the sea – while pleasure boats bob in the bay behind. Tourists gather all through the day to watch the fishermen at work, and to join the low-key pleasure trips to the **Île de Batz**. The island looks almost walkable; a narrow pier stretches over 400m metres towards it before abruptly plunging into deep rocky waters. The Pointe de Bloscon and the white fisherman's chapel, the Chapelle Ste-Barbe, make a good vantage point, particularly when the tide is in; the tide goes out a long way (and dictates the precise embarkation point for the boat trips). Below the headland are the *viviers*, where you can see trout, salmon, lobsters and crabs being reared for the pot.

In addition to the island ferries, detailed on p.244, Armein Excursions (☎02.98.61.77.75) also operate three-hour cruises from here around the **Bay of Morlaix** (July & Aug Mon–Sat 2.15pm; April–June & Sept–Oct, Wed & Sat 2.15pm; 55F), and excursions to the **Cairn du Barnenez** (see p.237), depending on the demand and the state of the tides.

Until the last couple of centuries, Roscoff made most of its money from piracy, like so many other ports along the Breton coast. There are a few reminders of that wealth along rue Gambetta, which becomes rue Amiral-Réveillère. Two of its ornate grey-granite houses, including no. 25 ("the House of Mary Stuart"), claim to be where Mary Queen of Scots spent her first night after eighteen stormy days at sea – despite the fact that both were built after she landed.

The sculpted ships and protruding stone cannons of the Renaissance belfry which tops the sixteenth-century town church, **Notre Dame de Croas Batz**, also recall the seafaring days. From the side, rows of bells can be seen hanging in galleries, one above the other, like a tall narrow wedding cake created by the young Walt Disney.

A short way past the church, on place Georges-Teissier, the **Charles Perez Aquarium** contains a well-displayed and comprehensive collection of marine fauna of the Channel (daily: July & Aug 10am–noon & 1–7pm; April–June & Sept 1–6pm; 25F). It's an interesting enough place, if a little disappointing for anyone expecting the exotic, and forms part of the Institute of Oceanology which undertakes oceanographic, and related biological, research.

Some way beyond the grand buildings of the Institute is the **Thalassotherapy Institute** of Rock Roum. Specializing in sea-water cures, it opened in 1899 as the first such establishment in France, and is still thriving a century on. A kilometre further on, you come to Roscoff's best **beach**, at Laber, surrounded by expensive hotels and apartments.

In the opposite direction from town, south along the coast from the ferry terminal, are the tropical gardens at **Rock Hievec** (daily: June–Sept 10am–7pm; Oct–May 10am–noon & 2–6pm). In this slightly surreal enclave, cacti, palm trees and flowers of South America and the Pacific flourish in the mild Gulf-Stream climate.

In 1828, Henri Ollivier took **onions** to England from Roscoff, thereby founding a trade which flourished until the 1930s. In the bar of the *Hôtel du Centre* (see opposite), you can see old photographs of "Johnnies", men in black berets with strings of onions hanging over the handlebars of their bicycles. Older people of the town remember travelling as children with their fathers as far afield as Glasgow.

Eating

Very much the obvious places to **eat** in Roscoff are the dining rooms of the hotels themselves – as detailed on p.242 – though it's seldom easy to get a meal much after 9pm. However, the town does hold a few specialist **restaurants** as well.

Crêperie de la Poste, 12 rue Gambetta (☎02.98.69.72.81). Central *crêperie*, where an *à la carte* meal of sweet and savoury pancakes can work out economical, so long as you don't get carried away by the exotic seafood options. Closed Wed Sept–April.

L'Écume des Jours, quai d'Auxerre (☎02.98.61.22.83). Cosy restaurant in a grand old house, which offers good-value set lunches for 55F on weekdays, plus dinner menus from 80F, featuring such delights as braised oysters or scallops with local pink onions. Closed Wed, plus Sat lunchtime in winter, and all of Dec & Jan.

Le Temps de Vivre, place de l'Église (☎02.98.61.27.28). Gourmet restaurant with sea views on the main church square, serving rich French cuisine with a modern twist on menus from 110F. Closed two weeks in both March & Oct.

The Île de Batz

The **ÎLE DE BATZ** (pronounced "Ba"), just off the coast at Roscoff and inhabited by just under a thousand hardy farmers and fishers, is a somewhat windswept spot, but well endowed with sandy beaches. For campers looking to have a stretch of coastline to themselves, it could be ideal.

The island's first recorded inhabitant was a "laidly worm", a dragon that infested the place in the sixth century. Such dragons normally symbolize pre-Christian religions, in this case perhaps a Druidic serpent cult. Allegorical or not, when St Pol arrived to found a monastery he wrapped a Byzantine stole around the unfortunate creature's neck and cast it into the sea. These days, there are no dragons; there aren't even any trees, just an awful lot of seaweed, which is collected and sold for fertilizer.

Ferries from Roscoff arrive at the quayside of the old island town. Walk uphill from there, past the youth hostel (see below), to reach the 44-metre lighthouse on the island's peak. All of 23m above sea level, it no longer welcomes visitors. Beyond that, it's just the sands and seaweed.

Practicalities

Two separate companies sail to the Île de Batz from Roscoff, for around 30F return. Armein Excursions run every half-hour on the half-hour, daily from 8am until 8pm between July and mid-September, and around eight trips daily for the rest of the year (☎02.98.61.77.75). In July and August, they also organize boat tours right around the island, with a visit to the Cairn du Barnenez if the tide permits (Mon–Sat 2.15pm; 55F). Vedettes de l'Île de Batz operate a similar timetable in summer, departing at quarter to and quarter past the hour, and nine trips daily at other times of the year (☎02.98.61.78.87). Both companies also run regular cruises from Morlaix, Plougasnou and Carantec.

The port is home to the basic *Hôtel-Restaurant Roch Ar Mor* (☎02.98.61.78.28; closed Oct–March; ②), but the **youth hostel**, at the evocatively named Creach ar Bolloc'h, provides a picturesque alternative (April–Sept; ☎02.98.61.77.69; 65F), and also runs sailing classes.

St-Pol-de-Léon

The main road **south from Roscoff** passes by fields of the famous Breton arti-chokes before arriving after 6km at **ST-POL-DE-LÉON**. Pleasantly sited amid rich gardens, this is not an exciting place but – assuming you've your own trans-port – has two churches that at least merit a pause.

The **Cathedral**, in the main town square, was rebuilt towards the end of the thirteenth century along the lines of Coutances (see p.140) – a quiet classic of uni-fied Norman architecture. The remains of St Pol are inside, alongside a large bell, rung over the heads of pilgrims during his *pardon* on March 12 in the unlikely hope of curing headaches and ear diseases.

Just downhill, the **Kreisker Chapel** is notable for its sharp-pointed soaring granite belfry, now coated in yellow moss. It was originally modelled on the Norman spire of St-Pierre at Caen, which was destroyed in the last war (see p.116), but as an elegant improvement on its Norman counterpart was itself much copied. Similar "Kreisker" spires are dotted all over rural Brittany. The dramatic view to be seen if you climb this spire (daily 10–11.30am & 2–6pm), out across the **Bay of Morlaix**, should be enough to persuade you to follow the road along the shore.

Practicalities

If you're looking for **accommodation** in St-Pol, you're likely to fetch up at either the *Hôtel de France*, 29 rue des Minimes (☎02.98.29.14.14; ③), or the *Hôtel-Restaurant le Passiflore*, near the station at 28 rue Pen-ar-Pont (☎02.98.69.00.52; closed Sun pm; ②). Both are open all year and have reasonable restaurants.

Carantec

From St-Pol, take the foliage-covered lane down to join the D58, where you can cross the **pont de la Corde** to reach the resort and peninsula of **CARANTEC**, studded with small coves and secluded beaches. The **Île de Callot**, an enticing hour's walk away from the slightly drab town itself at low tide, is the scene of a *pardon* and blessing of the sea on the Sunday after August 15 – a rather dour occa-sion, as are most of the religious festivals around Finistère.

The D78 runs on from Carantec beside the sea, the estuary narrowing until at Locquenolé it is just the width of the River Morlaix. From then on it is a beautiful deep valley, with promenades and gardens along the stone-reinforced banks, and views across to isolated villages such as Dourduff on the other side.

Practicalities

This stretch of coast comes alive in summer with a scattering of seasonal **camp-sites**, among them the excellent *Les Mouettes* (Easter to mid-Sept; ☎02.98.67.02.46), where you pay well over the usual odds for the benefit of having a supermarket, a swimming pool, a bar and a disco on site. For rooms in Carantec, the **hotels** *La Falaise* (mid-March to mid-Oct; ☎02.98.67.00.53; ③) and *Porspol* (Easter to mid-Sept; ☎02.98.67.00.52; ③) are both good value. Right on the water-front, the twin **restaurants** *La Cambuse* (☎02.98.67.08.92) and *Le Cabestan* (☎02.98.67.01.87) provide the focus of Carantec's nightlife, with the *Cabestan* hav-ing the edge on seafood, while the *Cambuse* concentrates on live music. Both close on Tuesdays, and also on Monday evenings in low season.

The Château de Taureau

A short way east of Carantec, the fortified **Château de Taureau**, off Pointe de Pen-al-Lann, guards the entrance to Morlaix Bay, 12km north of Morlaix itself. It was built after a succession of skirmishes that began in 1522, when Morlaix pirates raided and looted Bristol. Henry VIII's pride was hurt and, seeking revenge, he sent a sizeable fleet to storm Morlaix. The citizens were absent at a neighbouring festival when the English arrived. When they returned, they found the English drunk in their wine cellars. Once the Bretons had routed their enemies, they built the château to forestall further attacks from the sea.

In the seventeenth century, the Château de Taureau was used as a prison; now it's a sailing school. Meanwhile, Morlaix adopted the motto which it keeps to this day – "If they bite you, bite them back."

The only way to get a close-up view of the Château is from out on the water; if you don't have your own yacht, then take an organized boat trip from Roscoff or Morlaix. The best place from which to admire on the mainland is at the tip of the **Pointe de Pen-al-Lann**, 2km east of Carantec. Incidentally, a steep footpath from the car park here leads 300m down to one of the most delightful – and quiet – **beaches** in this region.

Morlaix

MORLAIX, one of the great old Breton ports, thrived off trade with England – in between wars – during the "Golden Period" of the late Middle Ages. Its sober stone houses were built up the slopes of the steep valley where the Queffleuth and Jarlot rivers join to flow together into Morlaix Bay, originally protected by an eleventh-century castle and a circuit of walls. Little is left of either, but the old centre remains in part medieval – cobbled streets and half-timbered houses. Later, the town grew still more prosperous on piracy and the tobacco trade (both legal and illegal), and spread north, down the valley, towards the port.

Arrival and information

The **tourist office** in Morlaix is in a solitary but central one-storey building, almost under the viaduct in place des Otages (mid-June to mid-Sept Mon–Sat 9.30am–12.30pm & 1.30–7pm, Sun 10am–12.30pm; mid-Sept to mid-June Tues–Sat 9am–noon & 2–6pm; ☎02.98.62.14.94). The **post office** is on rue de Brest (☎02.98.88.23.03).

The **gare SNCF** (☎02.98.63.56.24) is on rue Armand-Rousseau, high above the town at the western end of the viaduct. It was originally intended to connect the station with town by means of a funicular railway, but that was never built and you still have to reach it on foot, climbing the steep steps of the Venelle de la Roche. If you can't face the long trek up to the station to buy a ticket, you can make reservations at travel agencies down in the town proper.

All **buses** conveniently depart from place Cornic, right under the viaduct; long-distance routes include those south to Carhaix and on to Rosporden and Concarneau or Lorient (SCEATA; ☎02.98.93.06.98); and also those to Quimper and Vannes (CAT; ☎02.98.62.12.72).

Bicycles can be rented from Henri Le Gall, 1 rue de Callac (☎02.98.88.60.47).

Accommodation

In addition to the many (fairly uninspiring) **hotels** dotted around old Morlaix, there's a **youth hostel** at 3 route de Paris (open all year; ☎02.98.88.13.63; 48F), 1km from the town centre; take the *Kernégues* bus to either rue de Paris or place Traoulan, and then it's just off to the left. Morlaix no longer has a municipal campsite.

Hôtel de l'Europe, 1 rue d'Aiguillon (☎02.98.62.11.99, fax 02.98.88.83.38). Slightly eccentric but very central old place, near the Jacobin convent. While the rooms are modern and well equipped but not all that characterful, the public spaces, furnished in a variety of styles, are more flamboyant – and the restaurant is superb, with menus from 79F. ②.

Hôtel-Restaurant les Halles, 23 rue du Mur (☎02.98.88.03.86, fax 02.98.63.47.96). Friendly little hotel facing the attractive place des Halles, with a garage for motorbikes and bicycles. Slightly shabby rooms, but they're clean enough, and there's a very good cheap restaurant with menus at 55F and 75F. Closed Sun. ②.

Hôtel du Port, 3 quai de Léon (☎02.98.88.07.54). Bright, modern option, overlooking the port from the left bank. It doesn't have a restaurant, but each room has its own kitchenette – presumably for yacht owners who fancy a night on shore. ②.

Hôtel le Roy d'Ys, 8 place des Jacobins (☎02.98.63.30.55). Small central hotel, across the square from the town museum. The cheapest rooms do not have their own showers; guests have to pay 15F extra to use shared showers. No restaurant, but a downstairs bar. Closed Nov. ②.

Hôtel-Restaurant le St-Mélaine, 75–77 rue Ange-de-Guernisac (☎02.98.88.08.79). Self-styled family hotel, not easy to find, above place Cornic and all but under the viaduct. Value for money, but dull. The restaurant serves simple menus from 58F. Closed Sun & two weeks in May. ①.

The Town

Morlaix is dominated by its pink-granite **railway viaduct**, built high above the valley in the 1860s to carry trains en route between Paris and Brest. Despite all Allied attempts during World War II to destroy it with bombs, it still looms 60m above the central **place des Otages**, and as you enter the town today by road from the north your opening view is of shiny yacht masts in the pleasure harbour paralleling its slender pillars. The first level of the viaduct is intermittently open to visitors, usually (but not always) from 11am until 7pm each day.

There are few actual sights in town, but the pleasure anyway is more in roaming the length of the steep stairways that lead up from the places des Otages and Cornic, or in walking up to the viaduct from the top of Venelle aux Prêtres, along an almost rural overgrown path lined with brambles.

On her way from Roscoff to Paris, Mary Queen of Scots passed through Morlaix in 1548, and stayed at the **Jacobin convent** which fronts place des Jacobins. She was at the time just five years old, an aspect which may have contributed to local interest in the spectacle. A contemporary account records that the crush to catch a glimpse of the infant was so great that the inner town's "gates were thrown off their hinges and the chains from all the bridges were broken down".

The **Musée des Jacobins** (entrance on rue des Vignes), in what was once the convent church, contains a reasonably entertaining assortment of Roman wine jars, bits that have fallen off medieval churches, cannons and kitchen utensils, and a few modern paintings (July & Aug Sun, Mon & Wed–Fri 10am–12.30pm & 2–6.30pm, Sat 2–6.30pm; Easter–June & Sept–Oct Sun, Mon & Wed–Fri 10am–noon & 2–6pm, Sat 2–6pm; Nov–Easter Sun, Mon & Wed–Fri 10am–noon & 2–5pm, Sat 2–5pm; 25F).

COREFF – REAL ALE IN BRITTANY

1985 saw the inauguration of an unlikely new product in Morlaix – the first Breton real ale! Two young Frenchmen, Christian Blanchard and Jean-François Malgorn, set up their own brewery, with the ambition of emulating the beers they had enjoyed on visits to Wales.

You should be able to find the resultant brew, Coreff – logically enough, the name is an old Breton word meaning "beer" – both locally and throughout Brittany in those bars which take pride in all things Breton. It's also possible to visit the brewery, the Brasserie des Deux-Rivières at 1 place de la Madeleine, for a tour and a sample (tours Mon–Wed 10.30am, 2pm & 3.30pm; ☎02/98.63.41.92).

As for the beer itself, it's a sweet, rich brown ale – authentically "real" in that it isn't filtered or pasteurized – that can make a welcome change from the lagers everywhere on offer.

The austere church of **St-Mathieu**, off rue de Paris, contains a sombre and curious statue of the Madonna and Child, made in Cologne around 1400 AD. Mary's breast was apparently lopped off by a prudish former priest, to leave the babe suckling at nothing. The whole statue stands open down the middle, to reveal a separate figure of God the Father, clutching a crucifix; interior panels hold painted scenes from the life of the Virgin, including the Annunciation and the Assumption. In April 1993, the figure of Christ was stolen, but the thief, who preferred to pray at home, repented in October 1994 and returned it anonymously.

Duchess Anne of Brittany, who had by then become queen of France, visited Morlaix in 1506. She is reputed to have stayed at the **Maison de la Reine Anne**, 33 rue du Mur, which, although much restored, does indeed date from the sixteenth century. Its intricate external carvings, and the lantern roof and splendid Renaissance staircase inside, make it the most beautiful of the town's ancient houses, each of its storeys overhanging the square below by a few more centimetres. The house is open to the public in summer (April–Sept Mon–Sat 10.30am–6.30pm), and at other times by arrangement (☎02.98.88.23.26).

In the eighteenth century, Morlaix's wealth was sustained by boatbuilding, textiles and tobacco, and the **tobacco factory**, on quai de Léon by the port, remains active. It employs 500 people – who produce annually 300 million cigars, 50 tonnes of chewing tobacco and 15 tonnes of snuff, and can be visited on Wednesday afternoons (☎02.98.88.15.32).

Eating

The best hunting ground for **restaurants** in Morlaix is to be found between St-Mélaine church and place des Jacobins, but there are plenty of other options tucked away on the backstreets.

Les Bains Douches, 45 allée du Poan-Ben (☎02.98.63.83.83). Small bistro that doesn't quite live up to its unusual location – set in the former public baths, and reached via a little footbridge across a canal – but makes an attractive spot for a light 59F lunch. Closed lunchtime on Sat & Sun.

Brocéliande, 5 rue des Bouchers (☎02.98.88.73.78). In the southeast of town, beyond the place des Halles and St-Mathieu church. Elegant evening-only dining in a *fin-de-siècle* atmosphere; a typical main course from the choice *à la carte* menu costs around 75F, as does the cheapest set meal. Closed Tues.

La Dolce Vita, 3 rue Ange-de-Guernisac (☎02.98.63.37.67). Italian place in a pretty central alley, with pizzas mostly priced at 40–50F, plus pasta, salads, and a few conventional seafood and meat dishes. Closed Mon, plus three weeks in Feb and two weeks in Oct.

La Marée Bleue, 3 rampe Ste-Mélaine (☎02.98.63.24.21). Well-respected seafood restaurant, 1min walk up from the tourist office. The 78F menu is a bit limited, but 160F ensures you a superb *assiette de fruits de mer*, and 230F buys a five-course feast. Closed Sun pm & Mon Sept–June.

Le Passé Simple, 21bis place Charles-de-Gaulle (☎02.98.63.81.39). Lush and very pleasant restaurant, with some excellent seafood specialities on menus that start at 75F. Closed Sat lunchtime & Mon.

Nightlife and drinking

Among bars to look out for while you're in Morlaix are the venerable half-timbered *Ty Coz*, at 10 Venelle au Beurre (☎02.98.88.07.65; closed Thurs & all Sept), near the youth hostel, which has boisterous Bretons playing darts, and draught Coreff beer, and the lively and much more salubrious – or aseptic, depending on your perspective – *Tempo Piano Bar*, facing the port on quai de Tréguier (☎02.98.63.29.11), where there are regular jazz and blues concerts.

Onward routes from Morlaix

Moving on from Morlaix, you are strategically poised. To the **west** are the **parish closes** – described in the following section – and, beyond them, access to the best of the **Finistère coast** around Le Conquet and the Crozon peninsula. **South**, via the **Forêt de Huelgoat** (see p.294), is the direct route to **Quimper**; and **east** you can take in the remarkable **Cairn du Barnenez** (p.237) en route to the **Côte de Granit Rose**.

The parish closes

A few kilometres west of Morlaix, bounded by the valleys of the Elorn and the Penzé rivers, lies an area remarkable for the wealth and distinction of its **church architecture**. This is where the best-known examples of what the French call *enclos paroissiaux* are to be found. The phrase translates into English as "parish close", and is used to describe a walled churchyard which in addition to the church itself incorporates a trinity of further elements – a cemetery, a calvary and an ossuary.

The **ossuaries** – which now tend to contain nothing more alarming than a few rows of postcards – were previously charnel houses, used to store the exhumed bones of less recent burials. They are the most striking features of the closes, making explicit a peculiarly Breton proximity and continuity between the living and the dead. Parishioners would go to pray, with the informality of making a family visit, in the ossuary chapels where the dead bones of their families were on display. The relationship may have originated with the builders of the megalithic passage graves, which were believed to serve as doorways between our world and the netherworld.

The actual **cemeteries** tend to be small, and in many cases have disappeared altogether, while the **calvaries**, which complete the ensemble, are tenuously based on the hill of Calvary. Each is therefore in theory surmounted by a Crucifixion, but the definition is loose enough to take in any cluster of religious statuary, not necessarily even limited to biblical scenes, standing on a single base.

That there are so many and such fine *enclos* in this region is due to a period of intense inter-village rivalry during the sixteenth and seventeenth centuries, when parishes competed to outdo each other in complexity and ornament. It's no coincidence that most such Breton churches date from the two centuries to either side of the union with France in 1532 – Brittany's wealthiest period – and nothing is more telling of the decline in the province's fortunes than the contrast between the riches on show and the relative lack of prosperity of the present-day villages. An additional, more positive, layer is contributed, however, by the current revival of artisan traditions in the parishes. In several of the towns and villages, stonemasons are once more producing sculptures in granite.

A clearly signposted **route** leading past several of the most famous churches – St-Thégonnec, Guimiliau and Lampaul-Guimiliau – can be joined by leaving the N12 between Morlaix and Landivisiau at St-Thégonnec.

St-Thégonnec

At the **ST-THÉGONNEC** *enclos*, the church **pulpit**, carved by two brothers in 1683, is the acknowledged masterpiece, although it is covered so completely in detail – symbolic saints, sybils and arcane figures – that it is almost too ornate to appreciate. The painted oak **entombment** in the crypt under the ossuary has more immediate effect. Complete with a stunning life-size figure of Mary Magdalene, it was sculpted by Jacques Laispagnol of Morlaix in 1702, for a fee of 1550 pounds. The entire east wall of the church is a carved and painted retable, with saints in niches and a hundred different scenes depicted.

The upmarket *Auberge de St-Thégonnec*, 6 place de la Mairie (☎02.98.79.61.18; closed Jan & Feb, Sun pm, Mon pm in summer and all day Mon otherwise; ④), is a surprisingly smart hotel for such a small village. Its main building houses a superb restaurant, where menus start at 100F; the 220F gourmand option, which features lobster and spinach salad followed by scallop pancakes and roast sole, is out of this world. The *Restaurant du Commerce* at 1 rue de Paris (☎02.98.79.61.07; closed Sat, Sun & Aug), very near the church, serves more basic good-value meals, while the *Crêperie Steredden*, nearby at 6 rue de la Gare (☎02.98.79.43.34), is a friendly village *crêperie* that offers hundreds of speciality pancakes, on menus that range from 59F to 66F. Finally, in an almost absurdly pastoral riverside setting 2km west of St-Thégonnec, the *Moulin de Kerlaviou* (☎02.98.79.60.57; ③) is a ravishing farmhouse **B&B**, offering two well-equipped en-suite rooms.

Guimiliau

The showpiece at the pretty flower-filled village of **GUIMILIAU** is its calvary – an incredible ensemble of over two hundred granite figures, enacting scenes from the life of Christ and covered with what the brochure calls "secular lichen". A uniquely Breton illustration, just above the Last Supper, depicts the unfortunate Katell Gollet being torn to shreds by demons in punishment for stealing consecrated wafers to give to her lover (who of course turned out to be the Devil).

Inside the church, years of patient restoration have turned the seventeenth-century organ, until recently a tangle of mangled wood, back into its original harmonious condition.

Lampaul-Guimiliau

The third of the major parish closes, **LAMPAUL-GUIMILIAU**, is a few kilometres further on. Here the painted oak baptistry, the dragons on the beams and the appropriately wicked faces of the robbers on the calvary are the key components.

The *Hôtel de l'Enclos* (☎02.96.68.77.08; ③), 300m beyond the church on the left, is a new hotel with good rooms and a very reasonable restaurant.

Landivisiau

LANDIVISIAU, just south of the N12 20km west of Morlaix, makes a good alternative to Morlaix as a base from which to tour the nearby parish closes.

There's not much to the town itself, but the **tourist office** at 14 av Foch (July & Aug Mon 10am–noon & 2–7pm, Tues–Sat 9am–noon & 2–7pm; Sept–June Mon–Thurs 9am–noon & 2–6pm, Fri 9am–noon & 2–5pm; ☎02.98.68.03.50) provides details of recommended bike routes, and coach tours operate regularly from the main square. There's also a choice of cheap **hotels**, the best value of which are *Le Terminus*, 94 av Foch (☎02.98.68.02.00; closed Sun pm; ③), a *Routier* with excellent meals, and *de l'Avenue* (☎02.98.68.11.67; ②).

La Roche-Maurice

West of Landivisiau, the N12 autoroute races towards Brest, but the lesser D712 and the railway follow a far more pleasant route, along the banks of the pretty Elorn River. After about 12km – not far beyond the chapel of **Pont-Christ**, beside a broad waterfall – the village of **LA ROCHE-MAURICE** occupies a steep high bluff above a curve in the river.

Only the solemn ivy-covered keep now remains of the **castle** that has occupied this site since the eleventh century, and was once supposedly home to Katell Gollett. It was abandoned at the end of the seventeenth century, and its stones used to build the houses that now surround it. Visitors are free to climb the wooden stairway that's rather clumsily attached to the outside, but not to ascend any further inside the ruin itself.

Nearby stands another large **parish close**, notable mainly for its rendition of the death-figure **Ankou** (see box). This time he's carved above the holy-water stoup on the wall of the ossuary, facing the church, beneath the warning "I kill you all". The interior of the church is gorgeous, the nave divided in two by a lovely green and red rood screen, which shows the twelve apostles propped up by grotesque animals. Ringed by older carvings, the blue ceiling holds a celestial choir of angels. In summer, the ossuary houses local information, and an exhibition on the history of the town.

OTHER BRETON CHURCHES

Breton Catholicism has a very distinctive character, closer to the Celtic past than to Rome. There are hundreds of saints who've never been approved by the Vatican, but whose brightly painted wooden figures adorn every Breton church. Their stories merge imperceptibly with the tales of moving menhirs, ghosts and sorcery. Visions and miracles are still assumed; and death's workmate, Ankou, is a familiar figure, even if no one now would dread his manifestation.

If you're inspired by the parish closes to go in search of similar village churches elsewhere in Brittany, other notable closes and chapels include those at **Kermaria-an-Isquit**, **Ploumilliau**, **Grouannec**, **Pleyben**, **St-Fiacre** and **Guéhenno**.

In the square immediately below the castle, the *Auberge du Vieux Château* (☎02.98.20.40.52) offers excellent food, with menus starting at 74F. Alternatively, there's a lovely rural restaurant halfway between Landivisiau and La Roche-Maurice – the *Moulin de Brézal* (☎02.98.20.46.57), facing a little bridge that leads to the ruined 1533 chapel of Nôtre Dame de Bon Secours. All of its menus, priced at 90F, 110F and 160F, include a scallop kebab. This beautiful riverside spot would also make an ideal setting for a picnic.

La Martyre

The oldest parish close of all, built in 1460, stands at the heart of **LA MARTYRE**, 7km south of La Roche-Maurice on the road to Sizun (see p.293). This is the most attractive of all the local villages, with stones of its complete parish close seamlessly integrated into the walls of its main street. Ankou clutches a severed head above the stoup in the peculiarly lopsided entrance porch, watched over not only by a carved red-ochre Virgin, giving birth, but also a nestfull of house martins. Inside, the church is damp and somewhat faded, but it does have an attractive gilt altar.

Landerneau

If instead of detouring to La Martyre you continue west on the scenic D712 beyond La Roche-Maurice, you soon reach **LANDERNEAU**, at the mouth of the Elorn estuary. This too was once a major port; now it's more of a tourist showpiece. The **pont de Rohan** in the middle of town is said to be, along with the Ponte Vecchio in Florence, the last inhabited bridge in Europe, and is the site of the local **tourist office** (July & Aug Mon–Sat 9am–12.30pm & 1.30–7pm, Sun 10am–1pm; Sept–June Mon–Sat 9am–noon & 2–6pm, Sun 10am–1pm; ☎02.98.85.13.09).

Landerneau offers several **accommodation** possibilities. Either of *Le Clos du Pontic*, south of the river on rue du Pontic (☎02.98.21.50.91; closed Sat lunch & Mon, plus Sun pm in low season; ④), or *l'Amandier*, 55 rue de Brest (☎02.98.85.10.89; closed Sun pm & Mon; ③), would be a real treat, both being comfortable old-style hotels with excellent restaurants.

Plougastel-Daoulas

West of Landerneau, the Elorn broadens dramatically as it enters the Rade de Brest. The city of Brest (see p.260) sprawls along its northern banks at this point, but the southern side holds one final site associated with the parish closes. The church in the village of **PLOUGASTEL-DAOULAS** was built in 1870, and is far from interesting, but just outside it stands a **calvary** that ranks among the finest in Brittany.

This extraordinarily elaborate affair was completed in 1604, to celebrate the passing of an outbreak of the Plague – hence the bumps on the shaft of the main cross, designed to recall the sores on the bodies of the victims. Carvings on each of the four sides of the base depict scenes from the Life of Christ. Sadly, the rest of the village has not been restored so sensitively after the bombing of World War II. A weird shopping mall now overlooks the calvary, equipped with a giant Scrabble board for local senior citizens and a truly awful mural of the history of cinema.

Kerjean

July & Aug daily 10am–7pm; June & Sept daily except Tues 10am–6pm; at other times the opening hours are erratic – call ☎02.98.69.93.69 for details. Admission on tours only; the castle gates are shut while each tour is in progress; 25F, students 18F.

If not quite the "Versailles of Brittany", as it is promoted, **KERJEAN** is a surprisingly classic château for this remote corner of France. Though little more than 15km from Roscoff, it's not that easy to find – you need to be on the D30, running from Plouescat to Landivisiau, and to turn right shortly after St-Vougay. Roscoff–Brest buses stop at **Lanhouarneau**. What you're confronted by when you do arrive is a moated Renaissance **château**, set in its own park. It was built in the sixteenth century by the lords of Kerjean, with the express intention of overshadowing the mansion of their former feudal overlord, the Carman of Lanhouarneau. Under some archaic quirk of fealty the Kerjean lords had been obliged each year to take an egg, in a cart, and to cook it for the Carman (whatever a Carman may have been). The château must have made the memory a whole lot easier to bear.

The building, state property these days, is an odd jumble of the authentic, the restored and the imported. There is one original ceiling, one original floor and one original door; and the guide on the 45-minute tour has one original joke to match. Nevertheless it's an interesting place, and there's a certain amusement to be derived from the odd placing of objects and the lack of explanations. In the scullery are two thirteenth-century choirstalls from St-Pol cathedral, each seat carved with the head of its occupant; a statue of St Sebastian "run through with arrows" has not an arrow in sight; and it is unclear quite what St Anthony is doing "with the little pig". More standard Breton furnishings are the cupboard-like panelled box-beds which people used to climb inside to sleep – shut in tight for the night.

Kerjean is also used in summer for temporary exhibitions, and open-air theatrical performances have been scheduled in recent years for Friday nights in July and August.

Lesneven and Le Folgoët

Continuing inland, whether you are headed for southern Brittany or for Le Conquet and Ouessant island, **Le Folgoët** is another stop worth planning for. It is more easily accessible than Kerjean, though by bus you'll probably find yourself dropped a couple of kilometres out at the small town of **LESNEVEN**. The main features here are an abbey, on the main square, and some eccentric houses – slate-roofed and convex-panelled – in the narrow lanes. A visit to the **German war cemetery** a short distance southeast of the centre is a sobering experience (see p.122 for a general piece on war cemeteries).

Lesneven does not itself hold any great interest, though its ivy-coated café is an attractive place to break your journey, and the pretty *Hôtel Breizh-Izel*, 25 rue du Four (☎02.98.83.12.33; closed mid-Sept to mid-Oct; ①), provides cheap accommodation.

Le Folgoët
LE FOLGOËT is about half an hour's walk southwest of Lesneven. At first sight no more than a small village, with a well-kept and rather English-looking green, it owes its **Notre Dame** church – as well as its name, "Fool's Wood" – to a fourteenth-century simpleton called Solomon. After an unappreciated lifetime repeating the four Breton words for "O Lady Virgin Mary", he found fame in death by growing a white lily out of his mouth. The church was erected on the site of his

favourite spring, and holds a *pardon* on September 8 or the preceding Sunday. (On the fourth Sunday of July there is also a *pardon* of St Christopher, which involves a blessing of cars that non-motorists may find verging on the blasphemous.) In its quieter moments, however, it's a lovely church, colourfully garnished with orange moss and clinging verdure (a sign of the penetrating damp inside), and with a bumpy and stubbly approximation of a "Kreisker" spire. It has been restored bit by bit since the damage of the Revolution, and an unusual amount of statuary has been placed on the many low niches all around the outside. The most recent expenditure has been to put fresh white plaster noses on the apostles guarding its entrance, who in consequence look like hastily rounded-up and not quite well-scrubbed-enough choirboys.

Immediately opposite, a fifteenth-century manor house has arranged in the lush lawns by its front path a selection of decaying sculpture from the church – gargoyles and griffins and an armless Jesus.

The Abers of the northwest coast

The coast west from Roscoff is among the most dramatic in Brittany, a jagged series of **abers** – narrow estuaries, neither as deep nor as steep-sided as the fjords with which they are occasionally compared – in the midst of which are clustered small, isolated resorts. It's a little on the bracing side, especially if you're making use of the numerous **campsites**, but that just has to be counted as part of the appeal. In summer, at least, the temperatures are mild enough, and things get progressively more sheltered as you move around towards Le Conquet and Brest.

Plouescat
PLOUESCAT is the first real resort out of Roscoff. It is not quite on the sea itself, but there are **campsites** nearby on each of three adjacent beaches, with the nicest being *Poul Foën* (mid-June to Aug; ☎02.98.69.81.80). In the town, you'll find a high-roofed old wooden market hall, for picnic provisions, and a statue of a sea horse with a yin and yang symbol in its tail. Of the **hotels**, best value is the little *Roc'h-Ar-Mor*, right on the beach at Porsmeur (☎02.98.69.63.01; closed Oct–Easter; ①). Roscoff to Brest buses stop at Plouescat before turning inland.

At the village of **KEREMMA**, inland from the sea on the way between Plouescat and Brignogan, there's another lovely little **campsite** (mid-June to mid-Sept; ☎02.98.61.62.79), set along a green avenue lined with meadows of purple and yellow flowers.

> The council of **Plouescat** attained a certain notoriety in July 1987, when its members decided they could no longer live with the embarrassing presence of an exceptionally phallic rock on one of the local beaches and dynamited it to smithereens at dead of night. Local artists responded by creating several much more embarrassing substitutes which you might care to look out for.

Brignogan-Plage
BRIGNOGAN-PLAGE, on the next *aber*, has a small natural harbour, once the lair of wreckers, with beaches and weather-beaten rocks to either side, as well as its own menhir. Here once again the tide recedes way out towards the mouth of

the bay, leaving surreal clumps of seaweed-coated stone bulging up among the stranded boats. The **plage de Ménéham**, 2km west of town, is a gem of a beach.

The two high-season **campsites** are the central municipal site at Keravezan (June–Sept; ☎02.98.83.41.65) and the *du Phare*, east of town (April–Sept; ☎02.98.83.45.06), while the hotel *Castel Regis* (☎02.98.83.40.22; closed Oct–March; ③) is expensive but beautifully situated among the rocks, right at the headland. *Ar Reder Mor*, at 35 av de Gaulle in the centre of the little town (☎02.98.83.40.09; closed Nov–March; ②), is cheaper but fairly nondescript. There are also schools of both sailing and riding.

Plouguerneau, Lilia and Grouannec

Moving west again, along the D10, **PLOUGUERNEAU** is a village of just over 5000 inhabitants that was the unlikely recipient in 1990 of the **Prix de l'Europe**, awarded each year by the Council of Europe to the most exemplary European community. Previous winners include Istanbul, Avignon and The Hague; Plouguerneau was chosen largely on the basis of its vigorous and successful twinning with the German town of Edingen-Neckerhausen, near Heidelberg, which has so far produced twenty Franco-German marriages.

Five kilometres northwest of Plouguerneau, the dramatic waterfront community of **LILIA** makes a perfect setting for the **hotel** *Castel Ac'h* (☎02.98.04.70.11; ②), which has an excellent seafood **restaurant**. In summer, pleasure boats from here take a short cruise out to bob at the foot of the shaft of the **Vierge lighthouse** – at 78m, said to be the tallest in Europe (Easter–Sept; for schedules call ☎02.98.04.74.94).

Plouguerneau is also near to an unexpected pleasure, the church of **Notre Dame de Grouannec**, a small but complete parish close ensemble about 4km inland. It has been extensively restored, and looks all the better for it, with its fountain, ossuary, mini-cloister and profusion of gargoyles.

L'Aber-Wrac'h

The *aber* between Plouguerneau and the yachting port of **L'ABER-WRAC'H** has a stepping-stone crossing just upstream from the bridge at Lanillis, built in Gallo-Roman times, and its long cut stones still cross the three channels of water (access off the D28 signposted "Rascoll"), and continue past farm buildings to the right to "Pont du Diable".

L'Aber-Wrac'h itself is a promising place to spend a little time. It's an attractive, modest-sized resort, within easy reach of a whole range of sandy beaches and a couple of worthwhile excursions. Beyond the tiny fishing port, the Baie des Anges stretches away towards the Atlantic, with the only sound the cry of seagulls feasting on the oyster beds. The recently renovated *Hôtel la Baie des Anges* (☎02.98.04.90.04; closed Nov–Easter; ④) commands stunning views out to sea from the start of its vast curve; walk its full length to reach *Le Brennig* at the far end (☎02.98.04.81.12), a lovely restaurant with menus from 90F. A municipal **campsite**, *de Penn Enez* (mid-June to mid-Sept; ☎02.98.04.99.82), nestles among the dunes at the very tip of the headland.

Trémazan

Once past **PORTSALL**, the coast becomes a glorious succession of dunes and open spaces, with long beaches stretching at low tide way out towards tiny islands. A particularly romantic spot is where the crumbling walls of the *Sleeping Beauty*-style **castle** of **TRÉMAZAN** look down on a magnificent beach. This is where the fleeing Tristan and Iseult are said to have landed in Brittany, and the cracked ivy-covered keep still stands proud, pierced by a large heart-shaped hole. The castle is not formally open to the public; it's totally overgrown, and to reach it you have to scramble your way through the brambles that fill its former moat. Once you're there, however, it's a real haven for a summer afternoon.

In the immediate vicinity, the *logis* at **Kersaint Landunvez**, the *Hostellerie du Castel* (☎02.98.48.63.35; closed Oct–March; ③), is a good overnight stop. That's a little isolated, though, and you might prefer to stay either in L'Aber-Wrac'h or in Porspoder a few kilometres further on – pausing to look at the exquisite wooden seaside **chapel of St Samson** on the way.

Porspoder

PORSPODER is itself a pretty quiet place, but does serve as a centre for the many campers who set themselves up on the dunes of the **Presqu'île St-Laurent** which faces it. Most of the houses around are empty other than in summer – it must be pretty bleak in winter – but in season it's an attractive place to be, open to the ocean. There's a cheap **hotel**, the *Pen Ar Bed* (☎02.98.89.90.38; closed Oct–March; ①), on the long seafront rue de l'Europe.

Le Conquet

LE CONQUET, the southernmost of the *abers* resorts, at the far western tip of Brittany 24km beyond Brest, makes the best holiday base of all. A wonderful place, scarcely developed, it is flanked by a long beach of clean white sand, protected from the winds by the narrow spit of the Kermorvan peninsula, and has ferry access to the islands of Ouessant and Molène. It is very much a working fishing village, the grey-stone houses leading down to the stone jetties of a cramped harbour – which occasionally floods, to the intense amusement of the locals, the waves washing over the cars left by tourists making the trip to Ouessant.

The coast around Le Conquet is low-lying, not the rocky confrontation with a savage sea that one might expect, and Kermorvan, across the estuary, seems to glide into the sea – its shallow cliffs are topped by a strip of turf that looks as if you could peel it right off. Apart from the lighthouse at the end, the peninsula is just grassland, bare of buildings and a lovely place to walk in the evening across the footbridge from Le Conquet.

The most exciting trips out from Le Conquet are to the islands – detailed below. As a variation, though, a good walk 5km south brings you to the lighthouse at **Pointe St-Mathieu**, looking out to the islands from its site among the ruins of the Benedictine **Abbaye de St-Mathieu**. A small exhibition (July & Aug daily 11am–7pm; June & Sept daily 2.30–6.30pm; April & May Wed, Sat & Sun 2.30–6.30pm; Oct & Nov Wed, Sat & Sun 2–6pm; 10F) explains the abbey's history, including the legend that it holds the skull of St Matthew, brought here from Ethiopia by local seafarers.

Practicalities

The *Relais du Vieux Port*, quai Drellac (☎02.98.89.15.91; ②), offers three attractive but inexpensive **rooms** right by the jetty in Le Conquet, and has a simple *crêperie* downstairs. Nearby, the larger *Pointe Ste Barbe* (☎02.98.89.00.26; closed Mon out of season & mid-Nov to mid-Dec; ②–⑦) offers amazing sea views to guests in its more expensive rooms, and has a great restaurant, where menus start at 100F. There are also two well-equipped **campsites**, *Le Théven* (April–Sept; ☎02.98.89.06.90) and *Quère* (mid-June to mid-Sept; ☎02.98.89.11.71).

The *Hostellerie de la Pointe St-Mathieu*, housed in a thirteenth-century stone structure opposite the abbey entrance at Pointe St-Mathieu (☎02.98.89.00.19; closed Tues & Sun pm out of season; ③), is a top-quality restaurant that has recently added a new wing of tasteful ocean-view rooms. **Market** day in Le Conquet is Tuesday.

The Islands: Ouessant and Molène

The island of **Ouessant**, Ushant in English, lies 30km northwest of Le Conquet, and its lighthouse at Creac'h (said to be the strongest in the world) is regarded as the entrance to the English Channel. It's at the end of a chain of smaller islands and half-submerged granite rocks. Most are uninhabited, or, like Beniguet, the preserve only of rabbits, but **Molène**, midway, has a village and can be visited. Both Molène and Ouessant are served by at least one ferry each day from Le Conquet and Brest; however, it is not practicable to visit more than one in a single day. Note that the ferries can be very crowded in summer, and it's well worth booking your tickets in advance if at all possible.

Ouessant

The ride to **OUESSANT** is generally a tranquil affair – though the ferry has to pick its way from buoy to buoy, through a sea which is liable suddenly to blow up

---

GETTING TO OUESSANT AND MOLÈNE

Penn Ar Bed (☎02.98.80.24.68) sail to **Ouessant** and **Molène** all year, with up to five daily departures from **Le Conquet** (first sailing at 8am daily in summer; return fare adult 152F, under-17s 90F), and one daily at 8.30am from **Brest** (return fare adult 180F, under-17s 108F). They also depart from **Camaret** at 9am on Wednesday and Saturday from May until mid-July, and daily at 9am from mid-July until the end of August (return fare adult 164F, under-17s 98F).

Finist'Mer operate high-speed ferries to **Ouessant** in summer only, from **Camaret** (☎02.98.27.88.44; return fare adult 152F, under-17s 83F), **Le Conquet** (☎02.98.89.16.61; adult 140F, under-17s 72F) and **Lanildut**, 25km northwest of Brest (☎02.98.04.40.72; adult 145F, under-17s 77F). Bikes cost 65–70F extra. Between mid-May and early July, and in the first week of September, they offer a daily departure from **Camaret** at 8.30am, calling at **Le Conquet** at 9.30am, and another departure from **Le Conquet** at 11.15am. From early July until the end of August, they offer the same morning departure from **Camaret**, plus up to seven ferries from **Le Conquet**. Certain summer sailings call in at **Molène** as well. Between mid-July and late August they run an additional service from **Lanildut**, departing at 9.30am daily and taking just half an hour to reach **Ouessant**.

In addition, you can **fly** to Ouessant with **Finist'Air** (☎02.98.84.64.87). The fifteen-minute flights leave **Brest** daily at 8.30am and 5pm in summer, 8.30am and 4.45pm in winter. The adult fare is 350F, under-13s travel half-price, and groups of three or more adults go for 275F each.

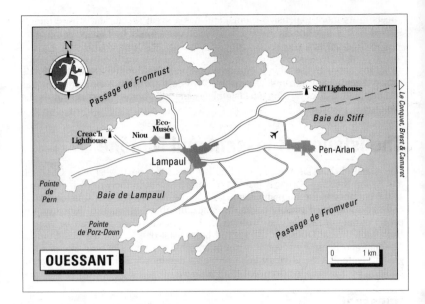

and become too dangerous to navigate. There have been many wrecks among the reefs, most famously the *Drummond Castle* which foundered as the finale to a concert celebrating the end of its voyage from Cape Town to England in June 1896. For all its storms, though, the climate is mild – Ouessant even records the highest mean temperatures in France in January and February.

You arrive on Ouessant at the new **harbour** in the ominous-sounding Baie du Stiff. There are a scattering of houses here, and dotted about the island, but the only town (with the only hotels and restaurants) is 4km distant at Lampaul. Everybody from the boat heads there, either by the bus that meets each arriving ferry, on bicycles rented for about 40F per day from one of the many waiting entrepreneurs, or in a long walking procession that straggles along the one road. Bicycle rental is the most convenient option, as the island is really too big to explore on foot.

LAMPAUL, as well as its more mundane facilities, has Ouessant's best beaches sprawled around its bay. There are few specific sights, and the whole place quickly becomes very familiar. But the town cemetery is worth visiting, with its war memorial listing all the ships in which the townsfolk were lost, and its graves of unknown sailors washed ashore. A unique Ouessant tradition is also on show in the cemetery chapel – an array of wax *proëlla* crosses, which were used during the funerals of those islanders who never returned from the sea, to symbolize their absent remains.

At nearby **NIOU**, the **Maison du Niou** is actually two houses, one of which is a museum of island history, and the other is a reconstruction of a traditional island house, complete with two massive "box-beds", one for the parents and the other for the children (June–Sept daily 10.30am–6.30pm; April & May daily except Mon 2–6.30pm; Oct–March daily except Mon 2–4pm; 15F). Officially, it forms half of the **Éco-Musée d'Ouessant**, in combination with the **Creac'h lighthouse** (May–Sept daily 10.30am–6.30pm; April daily except Mon 2–6.30pm; Oct–March

Saint-Malo

Côte de Granit Rose

Quimper

Ankou, La Roche-Maurice

Beach huts, Brittany

Thatched cottage, Grande-Brière

The château at Vitré

Dance of Death, Kermaria-an-Isquit

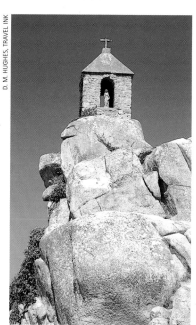

Côte de Granit Rose

Concarneau

Carnac

Rural Breton scene

daily except Mon 2–4pm). This contains a small museum about lighthouses, and makes a good point from which to set out along the barren and exposed rocks of the north coast. Particularly in September and other times of migration, it's a remarkable spot for birdwatching; puffins, storm petrels and cormorants can all be seen. The star-shaped formations of crumbling walls are not extraterrestrial relics, but built so that the sheep – peculiarly tame here – can shelter from the strong winds.

Practicalities

General information on Ouessant is available from the **tourist office** in the main square in Lampaul (April–Aug Mon–Sat 9.30am–12.30pm & 1.30–5pm, Sun 9.30am–12.30pm; Sept–March Mon–Sat 9.45am–noon & 2–4pm, Sun 10am–noon; ☎02.98.48.85.83).

In Lampaul, the adjacent **hotels** *Océan* (☎02.98.48.80.03; ②) and *Fromveur* (☎02.98.48.81.30; ②) both offer a fairly basic standard of accommodation; the *Fromveur* specializes in traditional island cooking, which consists of attempting to render seaweed and mutton as palatable as possible, while the *Océan* has a sideline in organizing musical evenings. The *Roch Ar Mor*, just down the street (☎02.98.48.80.19; closed Jan–March; ②), is a marginally more attractive alternative. There is a small official **campsite**, the *Penn ar Bed* (March–Nov; ☎02.98.48.84.65). You could, in fact, camp almost anywhere on the island, making arrangements with the nearest farmhouse (which may well let out rooms, too).

All the hotel **restaurants** serve menus for under 100F, but if you just come for a day it's a good idea to buy a picnic before you set out – the Lampaul shops have limited and rather pricey supplies.

Molène

MOLÈNE is quite well populated for a sparse strip of sand. The port itself is better protected than that of Ouessant, and so there are more fishermen based here. The island's inhabitants derive their income from seaweed collection and drying – and to an extent from crabbing and crayfish, which they gather on foot, canoe and even tractor at low tide. The tides are more than usually dramatic, halving or doubling the island's territory at a stroke. Hence the origin of the name Molène, which comes from the Breton for "the bald isle".

As for sights, there is even less of tangible note than on Ouessant. Walking the rocks and the coast is the basic activity. Once again, though, the island cemetery is poignant and interesting, redolent of small community life in its concentration of babies' graves from a typhoid epidemic in the last century; they are marked by silver crosses, repainted each November 1. Equally small-time is the island's main anecdote, told to anyone drinking an evening away, of the evening in 1967 when the whole population gathered to watch the oil tanker *Torrey Canyon* floundering offshore in the passage de Fromveur.

Practicalities

Few visitors do more than look around for an afternoon's excursion from Le Conquet, but it's quite possible to stay on Molène and to enjoy it. There are rooms – very chilly in winter – at *Kastell An Doal* (☎02.98.07.39.11; ②), one of the old buildings by the port, and it's also possible to arrange to stay in a private house (☎02.98.07.39.05 for details).

Brest

BREST is set in a magnificent natural harbour, known as the Rade de Brest, and sheltered doubly from the ocean storms – by the bulk of Léon to the north, and by the Crozon peninsula to the south. The Rade (or roadstead) is entered by the narrow deep-water channel of the Goulet de Brest, 5km long and 1.5km wide, with steep banks on both sides.

As one of the finest natural harbours in Europe, Brest has always played an important role in war and in trade whenever peace allowed. All the great names in French strategic planning – including Richelieu, Colbert, Vauban and Napoléon – have been instrumental in developing the port, which is today the base of the

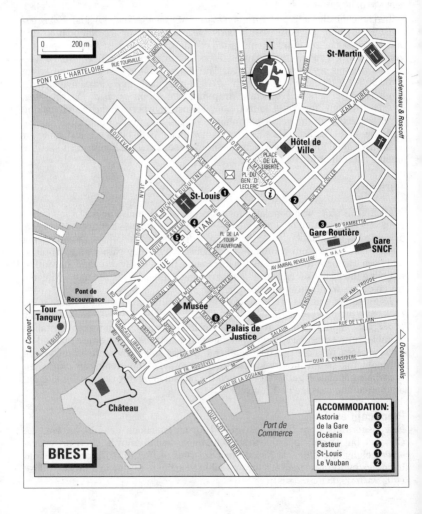

ACCOMMODATION:

Astoria	➏
de la Gare	➌
Océania	➍
Pasteur	➎
St-Louis	➊
Le Vauban	➋

French Atlantic Fleet. Its dry dock can accommodate ships of up to 500,000 tonnes and, as a ship-repair centre, it ranks sixth in the world.

During World War II, Brest was relentlessly bombed to prevent the Germans from using it as a submarine base. When the Americans liberated it on September 18, 1944, after a six-week siege, they found the town devastated beyond recognition. It was necessary for the city to resume normal life as soon as possible, which meant the rebuilding had to be rushed at the expense of restoration, and the architecture of the postwar town is raw and bleak. There have been attempts, as in Caen, to green the city, but despite the heaviest rainfall in France the site has proved too windswept to respond fully to these efforts.

From a distance, from across the bay, the city can look appealing. But closer in it takes a real effort of will to decide to stop longer than it takes to change buses or trains. The roads are racetracks; the suburbs, remorselessly industrial; and the last war comprehensively destroyed any historic interest that may once have existed. The most rational reason for an outsider to visit would probably be for the bagpipe festival, held here for three days in August.

Arrival and information

Brest's **tourist office** on avenue Clémenceau faces place de la Liberté (July & Aug Mon–Sat 9.30am–6.30pm, Sun 10am–noon & 2–4pm; Sept–June Mon–Sat 10am–12.30pm & 2–6pm; ☎02.98.44.24.96), while the main **post office** is on place Général-Leclerc.

The **gare SNCF** (☎02.98.80.50.50) and **gare routière** (☎02.98.44.46.73) are together in place du 19ème RI at the bottom of avenue Clémenceau. Brest is very much at the end of the railway system, though connected to Paris in just four hours, thanks to the TGV (which follows the northern route, via Morlaix and Rennes; the journey via Quimper takes much longer).

Bus services include those to Plouescat and Roscoff (Les Cars du Kreisker; ☎02.98.69.00.93); to the Crozon peninsula via Landevennec (Cars Douguet; ☎02.98.27.02.02); and to Le Conquet (Sarl St Mathieu Transports; ☎02.98.89.00.94).

Brest also has an **airport**, at Guipavas, 9km northeast of the centre, which is served by flights to **London** (Brit Air; ☎02.98.62.10.22) and **Ouessant** (Finist'Air; 2 daily in season; ☎02.98.84.64.87), as well as destinations throughout France. Should you need to rent a **car** on arrival, Avis have an office at 20bis rue de Siam (☎02.98.44.63.02).

Boats

As well as the sailings to Ouessant, detailed on p.257, in summer three or four **boats** per day make the 25-minute crossing from Brest's Port de Commerce to **Le Fret** on the Crozon peninsula (April–Sept; Société Azenor; ☎02.98.41.46.23). Sailings are met at the port in Le Fret by buses for Crozon (15min), Morgat (30min) and Camaret (40min). Société Azenor and other operators also do excursions around the harbour and the Rade de Brest (1hr 30min).

Accommodation

The vast majority of Brest's **hotels** remain open throughout the year; only a few, however, bother to maintain their own restaurants. Several lie within easy walking distance of the stations, in the vicinity of the central place de la Liberté.

The city also has a year-round **youth hostel**, near Océanopolis in a wooded setting on rue de Kerbriant, Port de Plaisance du Moulin-Blanc (☎02.98.41.90.41; 69F including breakfast). It's 3km east of the gares SNCF and routière, on bus #7, or the Bus Albatros.

The *Camping du Goulet* (☎02.98.45.86.84) is not easy to find, and not in any case warmly recommended – it's hard to see why campers would choose to stay in Brest. If you need to use it, it is on the outskirts of Brest, across the Pont de Recouvrance and then to the left of the Le Conquet road (D789) in Ste-Anne-Portzic – take bus #71.

Hotels

Hôtel Astoria, 9 rue Traverse (☎02.98.80.19.10, fax 02.98.80.52.41). Peaceful central hotel with a cheerful ambience and decor, not far up from the port. ③.

Hôtel Bellevue, 53 bd Victor-Hugo (☎02.98.80.51.78, fax 02.98.46.02.84). Six-storey sound-proofed building, equipped with a lift. Not easy to find, but not far from the gare SNCF and well on the way to the lively St-Martin area; look for St-Michel church. No restaurant. ②.

Hôtel de la Gare, 4 bd Gambetta (☎02.98.44.47.01, fax 02.98.43.34.07). Simple option opposite the stations, where you pay a little extra for an uninterrupted view of the Rade de Brest, from the upper storeys. No restaurant. ②.

Hôtel Océania, 82 rue de Siam (☎02.98.80.66.66, fax 02.98.80.65.50). Brest's finest upmarket hotel, offering large, attractively fitted rooms on the town's principal thoroughfare, plus a classy restaurant. ⑥.

Hôtel Pasteur, 29 rue Louis-Pasteur (☎02.98.46.08.73). Clean, good-value budget hotel near the St-Louis church. No restaurant. ②.

Hôtel St-Louis, 6 rue d'Algésiras (☎02.98.44.23.91, fax 02.98.46.07.94). Friendly, reasonably comfortable option, just off the main square near the tourist office. No restaurant. ①.

Hôtel-Restaurant Le Vauban, 17 av Clémenceau (☎02.98.46.06.88, fax 02.98.44.87.54). Very near the centre, between the gare SNCF and the Hôtel de Ville. Grand curving white edifice, with a surprisingly homely atmosphere. The simple restaurant, which serves couscous and so on from around 50F, is closed Sun pm & all day Mon. ①.

The Town

As a tourist centre, Brest has little to offer. Few relics of the past remain. The fifteenth-century **castle** looks impressive on its headland, and offers a superb panorama of the city, but once inside it is not especially interesting. Three of its towers house the **National Maritime Museum** (daily except Tues 9am–noon & 2–6pm; 30F).

The fourteenth-century **Tour Tanguy** on the opposite bank of the River Penfeld, with its conical slate roof, serves as the **Museum of Old Brest**. Dioramas convey a vivid impression of just how attractive a city Brest used to be, before World War II (June–Sept daily 10am–noon & 2–7pm; Oct–May Wed & Thurs 2–5pm, Sat & Sun 2–6pm; free).

The **Jardins Botaniques**, a short distance north of Océanopolis in the Parc du Vallon de Strangalard beyond the football stadium, claim to be second in Europe only to Kew Gardens (gardens daily summer 9am–8pm, winter 9am–6pm, free; greenhouses July & Aug Mon–Fri 2–5pm, 20F).

If all this fails to impress or excite you, you can always walk along the **Cours Dajot**, which displays the docklands in all their glory. It holds schools of various naval disciplines, arsenals, the marine records office and the **Pont de Recouvrance**, the largest drawbridge in Europe.

Océanopolis

June–Sept daily 9.30am–7pm; Oct–May Mon 2–6pm, Tues–Fri 9.30am–6pm, Sat, Sun & school hols 9.30am–7pm. 50F summer, 47F winter.

Brest's newest and largest attraction is **Océanopolis**, a couple of kilometres east of the city centre beside the Port de Plaisance du Moulin-Blanc. Beneath its futuristic white dome lies the largest **aquarium** in Europe, containing half a million gallons of water and all kinds of fish, seals, molluscs, seaweed and sea anemones. All is focused on the Breton littoral and Finistère's fishing industry, so the handful of tropical fish on display at the end provide a welcome splash of colour. In addition, the emphasis is very much on the edible, with the displays on the life-cycle of a scallop, for example, culminating in a detailed recipe.

The top floor of the complex is obsessively hi-tech, equipped with computers linked to the Internet to provide an up-to-the-minute report on the world's weather, and interactive quizzes for children. Some of it is quite playful – there's a bizarre kitchen in which the microwave, the fridge and each place setting on the table hold TV screens, all extolling the virtues of fish – and other parts seem to be purely aesthetic, such as a transparent cylinder filled with circling mackerel. The on-site **cafeteria** serves buffet lunches for 75F, as well as cheaper sandwiches.

For the moment, Océanopolis is not quite the fun palace you might expect from the advertisements on display all over Brittany, and it's not really worth going far out of your way to see it. However, shortly before this book went to press plans were announced to develop the complex into a "marine science theme park", with the addition of a 3-D cinema and two new pavilions, covering marine life in the polar and tropical regions. Watch this space.

Eating

As well as a concentration of low-priced places in the immediate area of the stations, Brest also offers a wider assortment of **restaurants**. Rue Jean-Jaurès, which climbs up east from the place de la Liberté, holds plenty of bistros and bars, while just off to the north, place Guérin is the centre of the student-dominated quartier St-Martin.

L'Amour de Pomme de Terre, 23 rue des Halles (☎02.98.43.48.51). The name says it all: this central restaurant specializes not merely in potatoes, but in one single kind of potato, the "samba". Most dishes are simply baked potatoes topped with cheese or sausage, but they're far better than any British equivalent, and there are also some tasty Breton stews.

L'Espérance, 6 place de la Liberté (☎02.98.44.25.29). Busy, inexpensive conventional restaurant in the lively square that faces the Hôtel de Ville, with a wide range of imaginative menus that start at 62F midweek. Closed Sun pm & Mon.

La Maison de l'Océan, 2 quai de la Douane (☎02.98.80.44.84). Blue-hued fish restaurant down by the port, open every day and serving wonderful assortments of seafood from 80F.

Ma Petite Folie, plage du Moulin-Blanc (☎02.98.42.44.42). Converted fishing boat, moored in the pleasure port, which serves a wonderfully fishy 110F set menu and also offers a wide range of *à la carte* dishes and daily specials. Closed Sun & two weeks in mid-Aug.

Le Ruffé, 1 rue Yves-Collet (☎02.98.46.07.70). An attractive place between the gare SNCF and the tourist office that prides itself on good, traditional French seafood dishes, served on menus costing 75F and upwards. Daily except Sun until 11.30pm.

La Taverne St-Martin, 92 rue Jean-Jaurès (☎02.98.80.48.17). A few hundred metres east (and up) from the tourist office. Warm and friendly brasserie/restaurant behind a wooden half-timbered facade. Lunch from 60F, dinner from 85F, plus lots of *à la carte* snacks. Steak tartare is the house speciality. Open daily 8am–1am.

Drinking

Brest is unusual by Breton standards in having plenty of lively **bars**. The basic choice lies between hanging out with the sailors and fishermen down by the port, with the business community around the place de la Liberté, or with the seriously trendy student population in the St-Martin quarter, high up on and around Jean-Jaurès. In July and August, Thursday night is party night, with a free open-air festival taking place along the quai de la Douane.

Bar Écossais, 241 rue Jean-Jaurès. An unlikely spectacle, way up at the top of the hill and positively festooned with Scottish memorabilia, which attracts an exuberant Celtic crowd. On November 11 each year (the anniversary of its opening), the owner hides a large Scottish shield in an unnamed pub somewhere in the city, and the regulars, dressed in full Highland costume and making passable attempts at reproducing the drone of the bagpipes by means of holding their noses and grunting, set off in a drunken stupor to try and locate it.

Pub Les Fauvettes, 27 rue Conseil (☎02.98.44.46.67). Large and extremely lively pub, with hundreds of bottled beers and deafening music, which also maintains another branch at 38 quai de la Douane.

Café de la Plage, 32 rue Massillon (☎02.98.43.03.30). Classic-looking open-fronted bar, on one corner of place Guérin. Heavy maroon decor and a transient population of citizens of all ages who share a common interest in talking at the tops of their voices.

Café le Triskel, 31 rue Massillon (☎02.98.44.56.65). Pub-style place with wooden tables, across the square from the *Plage*. Students and Breton activists come to drink and listen to the odd bit of music (literally).

Around Brest

Exploring Léon from a base in Brest, Le Conquet and Ouessant are very much the places to head for – ideally by boat from the Port du Commerce (see p.257 for timetable). Otherwise, the immediate area is far from bursting with interest.

Take **ST-RÉNAN** for example, 15km northwest of the city on the D5. French towns often set up signs along approach roads to advertise their splendours – "*son château*", "*sa charme*", and so on. St-Rénan can only find "*son Syndicat d'Initiative*" to boast about – but for all that it's quite a pleasant small town and there are two noteworthy prehistoric sites in the immediate area.

Lanrivoaré

Five kilometres northwest of St-Rénan is the **church** of **LANRIVOARÉ**, which has a tiny plot in its graveyard where, alongside eight round stones, the 7777 victims of a fifth-century massacre are supposed to lie buried. Legend records that the stones were transformed from loaves of bread by St Hervé – but they're in fact most likely to be "cursing-stones", which exist in several Irish chapels and were used for calling down disease or destruction on an enemy. The person invoking the curse, after a certain number of prayers, turned the stone round seven times.

The Menhir de Kerloas

To find the **Menhir de Kerloas** (also known as Kervéatous or Plouarzel), you need to walk or drive (there's no bus) about 5km west of St-Rénan on the *old* Plouarzel road, parallel to the more modern D5. The menhir stands in a small clearing hedged in by fields, and is the highest point for miles around in these flatlands. Although the tip was knocked off by lightning 200 years ago (and was subsequently used as a cattle-trough), it is (at 11m) the tallest menhir still standing in western Europe.

The stone is probably at its best looming out of a damp and ominous Breton mist, producing, in this isolated spot, a powerful effect on the imagination. A further aid to fantasy are the circular protuberances over a metre from the ground on either side, against which newly married couples would rub their naked bodies in the hope of begetting children.

Towards the Crozon peninsula

Heading south from Brest, cyclists and pedestrians can cut straight over to the Crozon peninsula by **ferry**. A regular service will shuttle you across the bay, for a few francs, to Le Fret (see p.286). The ferry doesn't, however, carry cars, so **drivers** have a longer and more circuitous route, crossing the Elorn River over the vast spans of the **Pont Albert-Louppe** (42m high and almost 1km long) and then skirting the estuaries of the **Plougastel peninsula**.

Plougastel-Daoulas, just across the bridge, is at the edge of the main parish closes region, and described on p.252.

Daoulas

Ten kilometres beyond Plougastel-Daoulas, the **abbey** at **DAOULAS** holds Brittany's only Romanesque cloister. It now stands beautiful and isolated at the edge of cool monastery gardens, since its surrounding buildings were destroyed during the Revolution. The abbey is a short walk above the town, and a welcome oasis on a hot summer's day. Since 1984 it has been used as a cultural centre for Finistère, which stages ambitious historical exhibitions lasting for around six months at a time (usual summer opening hours are daily 10am–7.30pm; current information on ☎02.98.25.84.39).

Le Faou

From Daoulas the motorway and railway cut down to Châteaulin (see p.289) and Quimper. For Crozon, you'll need to veer west at **LE FAOU**, a tiny medieval port, still with some of its sixteenth-century gabled houses and set on its own individual estuary. From beside the pretty little village church – whose porch holds some intriguing carved apostles – a sheltered corniche follows the river to the sea, where there are sailing and windsurfing facilities.

Le Faou holds two good and very similar **hotels**, each equipped with a top-class restaurant – the *Relais de la Place* (☎02.98.81.91.19; ③) and the *La Vieille Renommée* (☎02.98.81.90.31; closed Mon Sept–June, & all Nov; ④). The one snag is that they're not in the most attractive part of town, near the river, but a few hundred metres south in the newer and much noisier main square.

THE CROZON PENINSULA

The **Crozon peninsula** forms part of the **Parc Régional d'Armorique**, a haphazard area stretching from the forest of Huelgoat to the island of Ouessant that is, in principle at least, a protected natural landscape area. What this means in

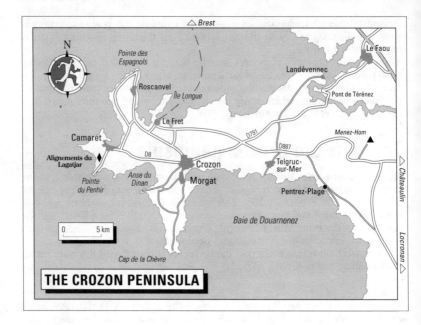

THE CROZON PENINSULA

reality is hard to fathom. Doubtless there are firm French bylaws against disturbing the wild flowers. However, for some reason these don't prevent nuclear submarines from lurking in the bay of Brest, nor low-flying helicopters from sporadically sweeping the skies above.

Nevertheless, military installations and operations notwithstanding, **Crozon**, with its wild beaches and craggy cliffs, is an attractive slice of countryside. A dramatic one, too, especially if you make the detour to climb up the **Menez-Hom** for an initial overview.

The Menez-Hom and around

At just 330m, the **Menez-Hom** is not really a mountain. But the summit stands sufficiently alone to command tremendous views across Crozon – a chaos of water, with lakes, rivers and bridges wherever you look, and usually a scattering of hang-gliders dangling in the sky. The exposed and windswept viewing table reveals it to be 300 miles (483km) from both London and Paris.

Landévennec
Nine kilometres west of Le Faou, by way of a beautiful shoreline road, the **Pont de Térénez** spans the Aulne – outlet for the Nantes–Brest canal – to the Crozon peninsula.

Doubling back to the right as soon as you cross the bridge brings you after a further 5km to **LANDÉVENNEC**, where archeologists are uncovering the outline of what may be Brittany's oldest **abbey** (June–Sept Mon–Sat 10am–7pm, Sun

2–7pm; Oct–May daily 2–6pm; 25F). Nothing survives above ground of the original thatched hut, constructed in a forest clearing by St Gwennolé around 485 AD. After the abbey had been pillaged by raiding Normans in 913 AD, however, it was rebuilt in stone. Those foundations can now be seen, together with displays on monastic history and facsimile manuscripts.

There's a small but attractive **hotel** in the heart of Landévennec, *Le St-Patrick* (☎02.98.27.70.83; ②).

The Musée de l'École Rurale

Still inland from the peninsula, roughly 3km north of the Menez-Hom and unfortunately not on any bus routes, is the village of **TRÉGARVAN**. At a solitary crossroads outside town, where the Argol–Dineault and Trégarven–Menez-Hom roads meet, you'll find the **Musée de l'École Rurale** (July & Aug daily 10.30am–7pm; Jan–March Mon–Fri 2–5pm; June & Sept daily 1.30–7pm; April & May daily 2–6pm; Oct–Nov Sun & hols 2–6pm; 20F). Housed in what used to be the local secondary school, it's one of those small, quirky French museums that sound slightly ludicrous on paper but are distinctly fascinating on the spot.

The school was closed down due to lack of numbers in 1974, then reopened a decade later as a recreation of a Breton classroom circa 1920. At that time, all the kids would have spoken Breton at home – but they were forbidden to speak it here. The teacher gave a little wooden cow to the first child to utter a word in the mother tongue, and they could get rid of the *vache* only by squealing on the next offender. The lesson, to parents and pupils alike, was obvious enough: that Breton was backward and a handicap. Breton was suppressed, with considerable efficiency, throughout the province, and only recently have things begun to change. As well as Breton-language nursery and primary schools, there's one secondary school and a fund-raising campaign for a lycée. While a few years back SNCF had to be taken to court before it would accept a cheque made out in Breton, there is now a Breton bank.

St-Nic Pentrez and Telgruc-sur-mer

Beyond the Menez-Hom, a magnificent road sweeps down across the heather on to the Crozon peninsula. At the foot of the hill, to the south, **ST-NIC PENTREZ** has excellent beaches – this is the sandy side of the peninsula – and several **campsites**, largest among them the *Menez Bichen* (June–Sept; ☎02.98.26.50.82).

There is another good beach and campsite, *Le Panoramic* (mid-May to mid-Sept; ☎02.98.27.78.41), further round towards Crozon at **TELGRUC-SUR-MER**, and some of the smaller towns inland have **hotels** and **gîtes d'étapes**. Among them are **PLOMODIERN** with the *Hôtel de Pors Morvan Cremaillère* (☎02.98.81.53.23; ④), and there is a *gîte* at the nearby Polébret Plage (c/o M Kervella; ☎02.98.26.50.14).

Morgat, Camaret and the beaches

The first town on the peninsula proper, **CROZON**, is not much more than a one-way traffic system to distribute tourists among the various resorts – though it does keep a market running most of the week.

Morgat

MORGAT, just down the hill from Crozon, makes a more realistic and enticing base. It has a long and very sandy crescent beach, much-loved by windsurfers, which ends beneath a pine slope, and a well-sheltered harbour that's filled with pleasure boats raced down from England and Ireland – and the leathery rich telling each other about their spinnakers.

The main plebeian attractions are **boat trips** around the various headlands, such as the Cap de la Chèvre (which is a good clifftop walk if you'd rather make your own way). The most popular is the 45-minute tour of the **Grottes**, multicoloured caves in the cliffs, accessible only by sea but with steep "chimneys" up to the clifftops, where in bygone days saints would lurk to rescue the shipwrecked. These cruises are organized by Vedettes Rosmeur on the quay (daily May–Sept; ☎02.98.27.10.71; 45F), and run as frequently as every quarter of an hour in high season. They often leave full, however, so it's worth booking a few hours in advance.

Practicalities

The **tourist office** for the whole peninsula is in what used to be the gare SNCF at Crozon (☎02.98.26.17.18); an information office for the Crozon–Morgat area stands at the start of Morgat's beach crescent on the boulevard du France (July & Aug Mon–Sat 9.30am–7pm, Sun 10am–1pm; May, June & Sept Mon–Sat 9.15am–noon & 2–6.30pm; ☎02.98.27.07.92).

All the **hotels** in Morgat are quite expensive. Appealing options include the grand *Hôtel-Restaurant de la Ville d'Ys*, which enjoys fabulous views from its perch just above the port (☎02.98.27.06.49; closed Oct–March; ③), and has a good dinner-only restaurant where menus start at 95F, and the quieter *Julia*, set 400m back from the beach at 43 rue de Tréflez (☎02.98.27.05.89; closed Nov to mid-Feb; ②). Immediately below the *Ville d'Ys* at the far end of the beach, *Les Échoppes*, 24 quai du Kador (☎02.98.26.12.63; closed Oct–Easter), is a flowery stone cottage with tiny little windows. Though there's no sign to tell you so, it's Morgat's best **restaurant**, serving good menus from 100F.

With a total of 865 pitches available, **campers** are spoilt for choice in Morgat; best are the three-star sites at *Plage de Goulien* (mid-June to mid-Sept; ☎02.98.27.17.10) and *Les Pins*, towards the Pointe de Dinan (mid-June to mid-Sept; ☎02.98.27.21.95).

Camaret

CAMARET is another sheltered port, at the very tip of the peninsula. Its most distinguishing feature is the pink-orange **château de Vauban**, standing foursquare at the end of the long jetty that runs back parallel to the main town waterfront. Walled, moated, and accessible via a little gatehouse reached by means of a drawbridge, it was built in 1689 to guard the approaches to Brest. These days it guards no more than a motley assortment of decaying half-submerged fishing boats, abandoned to rot beside the jetty. There are two **beaches** nearby – a small one to the north and another, larger and more attractive, in the low-lying (and rather marshy) *Anse de Dinan*.

Camaret also boasts one moment of historical significance. It was here in 1801 that an American, Robert Fulton, tested the first **submarine**. The *Nautilus* was a stuffy, leaking, oar-powered wooden craft, whose five-man crew spent some time scuttling about beneath the waves in the hope of sinking a British frigate. Fulton was denied his glory, though, when the frigate chose to sail away, ignorant of the heavy-breathing peril that was so frantically seeking it out.

In high season, Penn Ar Bed (☎02.98.70.02.37) operate an irregular **ferry** service from Camaret to the island of **Sein** (see p.273; 164F return), and also to **Ouessant** (see p.257; 164F return).

Practicalities

The town of Camaret is not large, though in season it offers all the shops and supplies you could need. A little walk away from the centre, around the port towards the protective jetty, the quai du Styvel contains a row of excellent **hotels**. Both the *Vauban* (☎02.98.27.91.36; ②) and *du Styvel* (☎02.98.27.92.74; ②) are exceptionally hospitable, but only the *Styvel* has a restaurant, with a 72F menu offering *moules à la Ouessane*, and crabs, oysters and scallops rearing their assorted heads on the 105F menu. Both have rooms that look right out across the bay, as does the more modern, upmarket *Thalassa* next door (☎02.98.27.86.44; ④), which has a heated sea-water swimming pool. There are also various **campsites** to fall back on, such as the four-star *Lambézen* (April to mid-Sept; ☎02.98.27.91.41) and the municipal *Lannic* (mid-June to mid-Sept; ☎02.98.27.91.31).

Back along the quayside in the centre of town, *La Voilerie*, 7 quai Toudouze (☎02.98.27.99.55), is an excellent **fish restaurant**. Lunch menus start at 65F, featuring a flavourful *soupe de poissons*, while four-course dinners, bursting with oysters and prawns, range 80F to 156F. *À la carte* options include poached skate, grilled sea bream, and game dishes such as roast guinea fowl.

From mid-June until September, Vedettes Sirènes (☎02.98.27.91.41) run boat trips that tour the offshore bird sanctuary of the Tas de Pois; their office is next to the **tourist office** on quai Toudouze in the port (Easter–Oct daily 9am–noon & 3–7pm; ☎02.98.27.93.60).

The Pointe du Penhir

A couple of worthwhile excursions can be made from the towns of the Crozon peninsula. At the **Pointe du Penhir**, footpaths lace around the various exposed and windy headlands, frequented mainly by binocular-toting twitchers eyeing up the guillemots and other sea birds that swoop on the Tas de Pois rock stacks, scattered out in the sea. Even crazier individuals abseil their way down similar rock stacks still attached to the mainland; here and there, a few paths pick their way down the sheer cliffs, but most peter out in the little natural amphitheatre that faces the Tas de Pois. A monument to the Breton Resistance stands nearby.

To one side of the road on the way out to the *pointe*, amid the brilliant purples and yellows of the heathland, are the megalithic **Alignements de Lagatjar**. Perhaps, though, you need to imagine that this heath is still blasted and empty, and that there's no "Dolmens" housing estate next to the stones, to appreciate this forlorn, unsignposted prehistoric ruin. The stones are little more than weather-beaten stumps, and it's hard to discern a pattern on the ground; the experts responsible for their restoration say there are four distinct lines rather than a circle.

The Pointe des Espagnols

The other popular trip is to the **Pointe des Espagnols**, where a viewing point signals the end of the peninsula. Brest is very close and very visible – without being any the more enticing. Around the cape are several forbidden military installations and abandoned wartime bunkers. You're not allowed to leave the road, and neither are you encouraged to turn the provided telescope towards Robert Fulton's modern counterparts at the nuclear submarine base on the Île Longue. Nearby **ROSCANVEL** offers a hotel, the *Kreis Ar Mor* (☎02.98.27.48.93; ②).

Locronan

LOCRONAN, a short way from the sea on the minor road that leads down to Quimper from the Crozon peninsula, is a prime example of a Breton town that has remained frozen in its ancient form by more recent economic decline.

From 1469 through to the seventeenth century, Locronan was a hugely successful centre for woven linen, supplying sails to the French, English and Spanish navies. It was first rivalled by Vitré and Rennes, before suffering the "agony and ruin" of the nineteenth century so graphically described in its small **museum** (daily 10am–7pm; 15F). The consequence of that ruin has been that the rich medieval houses of the town centre have never been superseded or surrounded by modern development. Film directors love its authenticity, even if Roman Polanski, to film *Tess*, deemed it necessary to change all the porches, put new windows on the Renaissance houses, and bury the main square in mud to make it all look a bit more English.

Today Locronan is once more prosperous, with its main source of income the tourists who buy wooden statues carved by local artisans, pottery brought up from the Midi, and handbags and leather jackets of less specified provenance. This commercialization shouldn't, however, put you off making at least a passing visit, for the town itself is genuinely remarkable, centred around the focal **Église St-Ronan**. Be sure to take the time to walk down the hill of the **rue Moal**, where there's a lovely little stone chapel, with surprising modern stained glass, and a wooden statue of a depressed-looking Jesus, sitting alone cross-legged.

Each year on the second Sunday in July the town hosts a **pardon** at St-Ronan church; the procession, known as the *petit Tromenie*, expands to a week-long festival, the *grand Tromenie*, every sixth year (the next is in 2001). The processions follow a time-hallowed route said by some to be St Ronan's favourite Sunday walk; by others, to be the outline of a long-vanished Benedictine abbey. It could even follow a pre-Christian circuit of megalithic sites.

Practicalities

If you decide you want to stay in Locronan, it can be an expensive business; contact the **tourist office**, in the main square, for details (daily: July & Aug 10am–7pm; Sept–June 10am–noon & 2–6pm; ☎02.98.91.70.14). One of the artisans suggested to the local authorities that the loft above his studio be converted to a *gîte d'étape* for young visitors, but that was felt not to be in keeping with the town's character – a character affording few opportunities of any kind for the young.

As it is, Locronan does have a **hotel**, *du Prieuré*, 11 rue du Prieuré (☎02.98.91.70.89; closed mid-Nov to mid-March; ③), which has a good restaurant with menus from 70F, but is normally reserved well in advance. In season, and probably out, you'll do a lot better heading on to the bay of Douarnenez.

The latest craze in Locronan is to follow the *Tromenie* route on a **mountain bike**, which you can rent from a garage in rue des Charettes (☎02.98.91.71.71).

CORNOUAILLE

Once past Locronan, you enter the ancient kingdom of **Cornouaille**. Its capital, **Quimper**, is a city as enticing as any in France, and along the south coast **Bénodet**, **Loctudy** and **Pont-Aven** (made famous by Gauguin) are thriving resorts. Roads radiate from Quimper in all directions, but the **western tip** of Finistère, if you follow the line of the Bay of Douarnenez, still feels isolated. With a few exceptions – most notably its "land's end" capes – it has kept out of the tourist mainstream.

The seaside village of **Ste-Anne-la-Palud**, north of **Douarnenez**, holds one of the best-known *pardons* in Brittany on the last Sunday in August.

Douarnenez

Sufficient quantities of tuna, sardines and assorted crustaceans are still landed at the port of **DOUARNENEZ**, in the superbly sheltered Baie du Douarnenez, south of the Crozon peninsula, to keep the largest fish canneries in Europe busy. However, the catch has been declining ever since 1923, when 800 fishing boats brought in 100 million sardines during the six-month season. Over the last fifteen years or so, Douarnenez has therefore set out – at phenomenal expense, the subject of considerable local controversy – to redefine itself as a living museum of all matters maritime.

The process of transformation culminated in 1993, when the whole area of **Port-Rhû**, on the west side of town, was officially declared open as the remarkable **Port-Musée** (daily: mid-June to Sept 10am–7pm; Oct to mid-June 10am–noon & 2–6pm; tickets sold in the Boat Museum June–Sept 60F, Oct–May 48F). The entire waterfront is taken up with fishing and other vessels gathered from all over northern Europe, which visitors are invited to roam in and out of, up and down ladders and all over the decks, through oily metallic-smelling engine rooms and sleeping quarters divided into separate wooden compartments. Rope- and sail-makers and net-menders work on the jetties, and children can operate a scaled-down eighteenth-century crane by walking inside a wooden treadmill. The far shore has been re-landscaped to reproduce a nineteenth-century environment populated by oystercatchers and the like (free ferries operate when the tide is high enough; otherwise you walk over a bridge).

Across the street, in the place de l'Enfer, the associated **Boat Museum** doubles as a working boatyard, where visitors can watch or even join in the construction of seagoing vessels, using techniques from all over the world and from all different periods. Once again, the emphasis is on fishing, and the craft on display include a *moliceiro* from Portugal and coracles from Wales and Ireland. With cafés and snack bars on site, there is easily enough here to spend a whole day without seeing it all, though even the most boat-hungry appetite may well be fully slaked after a couple of hours.

Of the three separate harbour areas still in operation in Douarnenez, much the most appealing is the rough-and-ready **port du Rosmeur**, on the east side, which is nominally the fishing port used by the smaller local craft. Its quayside – which is far from totally commercialized, but holds a reasonable number of cafés and restaurants – curves between a pristine wooded promontory to the right and the fish canneries to the left, which continue around the north of the headland. You can buy fresh fish at the waterfront, or go on a sea-fishing excursion yourself. The various **beaches** around town look pretty enough, but they are dangerous for swimming.

Practicalities

The **tourist office** in Douarnenez is at 2 rue du Dr-Mével (July & Aug Mon–Sat 9am–7pm, Sun 10am–1pm & 4–7pm; Sept–June Mon–Sat 9am–noon & 2–6pm; ☎02.98.92.13.35), a short walk up from the Port-Musée; they can inform you of the current status of plans to open a **youth hostel** in town.

Among good-value **hotels** are *de la Rade*, 31 quai du Grand-Port (☎02.98.92.01.81; closed Nov–Easter; ②), where behind the blue and white facade there's a bar downstairs and a restaurant on the first floor looking out on the port de Rosmeur, and *des Halles*, a little higher up alongside the still busy market *halles* (☎02.98.92.02.75; closed Sun & all Jan; ②), which has no restaurant.

Close by on the bay, there's a **campsite**, *Croas Men* (April to mid-Sept; ☎02.98.74.00.18), at Tréboul/Les Sables Blancs. Good seafood **restaurants** include *Le Tristan*, 25 rue du Rosmeur (☎02.98.92.20.17; closed Wed, plus Sun in winter), just above the port du Rosmeur, and the *Pourquoi Pas*, 15 quai de Port-Rhû (☎02.98.92.76.13), beside the museum, which does fine fishy lunches.

Audierne

Though on the whole the exposed southwestern extremities of Brittany are not areas you'd immediately associate with a classic summer sun-and-sand holiday, **AUDIERNE**, 25km west of Douarnenez on the Bay of Audierne, is something of an exception. An active fishing port, specializing in prawns and crayfish, it spreads along the northern shore of the Goyen estuary a short way back from the Atlantic. From the town centre, the road continues just over 1km to the long, curving and surprisingly sheltered **beach** of Ste-Evette, at the far end of which – at least 1km further on – is the departure point for boats to the Île de Sein (see opposite).

Practicalities

One of the few buildings on the seaward side of the road is the **hotel** *Au Roi Gradlon*, in a superb position at the very mouth of the estuary at 3 bd Manu-Brusq (☎02.98.70.04.51; closed Sun pm, Mon Oct–May, & all of Jan to mid-Feb; ④). Its unusual design means that the road-level dining room – where the 90F menu includes fresh tuna steaks – is in fact on the top storey, with several further floors, concealed from the road, dropping down below it to the beach. Rooms in the newer *L'Horizon*, slightly nearer the town proper at 40 rue J-J-Rousseau (☎02.98.70.09.91; closed mid-Nov to April; ③), are similarly priced, and it serves fish dinners from just 65F.

Plogoff

Most people take in Audierne en route to the Pointe du Raz, which is connected directly to Quimper by bus. Midway, signalled by fading graffiti on its walls and hoardings, is the tiny village of **PLOGOFF**, where ecologists, autonomists and local people fought riot police and paratroopers for six weeks in 1980, attempting to stop the opening move in a nuclear power station project. Although they lost the fight, abandonment of the project was part of François Mitterrand's manifesto for the 1980 presidential election – and he kept his promise.

The Pointe du Raz

The **Pointe du Raz** – the Land's End of both Finistère and France – has recently been designated as a "Grande Site Nationale", and with its former military installations now thankfully cleared away it makes a dramatic spectacle. You can walk out to the plummeting fissures of the *pointe*, filling and draining with a deafening surf-roar, and beyond, high above on precarious paths. (Shoes that can grip are not a bad idea.)

The Baie des Trépassés

The **Baie des Trépassés** (Bay of the Dead), just north of the Pointe du Raz, gets its grim name from the shipwrecked bodies that are washed up there, and is a possible site of sunken Ys (see p.274). However, it's actually a very attractive spot: green meadows, too exposed to support trees, end abruptly on the low cliffs to either side, there's a huge expanse of flat sand (in fact little else at low tide), and out in the crashing waves surfers and windsurfers get thrashed to within an inch of their lives. Beyond them, you can usually make out the white-painted houses along the harbour on the Île de Sein, while the various uninhabited rocks in between hold a veritable forest of lighthouses.

In total, less than half a dozen scattered buildings intrude upon the emptiness. There are no facilities for casual visitors on the beach, but the parking lot just back from the dunes is usually filled with camper vans from all over Europe, and there are also two **hotels**, both with tremendous views. Right in the middle is the pink *Hôtel de la Baie des Trépassés* (☎02.98.70.61.34; closed Jan to mid-Feb; ②–④), which has menus of wonderfully fresh seafood from 102F. The larger *Relais de la Pointe du Van* is slightly higher up, to the right (☎02.98.70.62.79; closed Oct–March; ③).

The Île de Sein

Just 8km out to sea, off the end of the Pointe du Raz, the little **Île de Sein** was made famous during World War II when the entire male population answered General de Gaulle's call to join him in exile in England. During his first muster of the French army in exile, de Gaulle observed that Sein appeared to constitute a quarter of France. The island was also reputed to have been the very last refuge of the Druids in Brittany, a misty and inaccessible spot where they held out long after the rest of the country was Christianized. Roman sources tell of a shrine served by nine virgin priestesses.

A popular saying has it that "Who sees Sein, sees his death"; but that's more because it happens to rhyme in French ("*qui voit Sein, voit sa fin*") than because of any particular evil there. The island is featureless enough to have been completely submerged by the sea on occasion, but a few hundred people still live on it, gathering rainwater and fishing for scallops, lobster and crayfish. Their houses are congregated in the tiny tightknit village where the island boats pull in; the rest of Sein, all 2km of it, is laid bare to view, and offers little beyond the prospect of a bracing walk.

Practicalities

Sein is hardly bursting with facilities for tourists, but can offer a **hotel**-cum-*crêperie*, the *Trois Dauphins* (☎02.98.70.92.09; closed Oct–May; ②), and a handful of more formal restaurants. For further information, contact the Mairie (☎02.98.70.90.35).

The principal departure point for **boats** to Sein is Ste-Evette beach, just outside **Audierne** (see p.272). Services are operated by Vedette-Biniou (June–early July, and first half of Sept daily at 10am; early July to end of Aug daily 10am, 1.30pm & 5pm; ☎02.98.70.21.15; adults 125F return, under-17s 65F), and Penn Ar Bed (April–Aug 1–3 departures daily, first at 9.30am; Sept–March daily except Wed 9.30am; adults 128F return, under-17s 65F; ☎02.98.70.02.37). Between mid-July and mid-August, Penn Ar Bed also run trips to Sein from **Brest** via **Camaret** on Saturdays and Sundays.

Quimper

QUIMPER, capital of the ancient diocese, kingdom and later duchy of Cornouaille, is the oldest Breton city. According to the only source – legend – the first bishop of Quimper, St Corentin, came with the first Bretons across the channel to the place they named Little Britain some time between the fourth and seventh centuries. He lived by eating a regenerating and immortal fish all his life, and was made bishop by one King Gradlon, whose life he later saved when the sea-bed city of Ys was destroyed (see box).

Modern Quimper is very relaxed, though active enough to have the bars – and the atmosphere – to make it worth going out café-crawling. Still "the charming little place" known to Flaubert, it takes at most half an hour to cross it on foot. The word *kemper* denotes the junction of the two rivers, the Steir and the Odet, around which are the cobbled streets (now mainly pedestrianized) of the medieval quarter, dominated by the cathedral towering nearby. As the Odet curves from east to southwest, it is crossed by numerous low flat bridges, bedecked with geraniums, and chrysanthemums in the autumn. You can stroll along the boulevards on both banks of the river, where several ultra-modern edifices blend in an oddly harmonious way with their ancient – and attractive – surroundings. Overlooking all is **Mont Frugy** (all of 87m above the river), once again green with trees after being denuded by the hurricane of 1987. There is no great pressure in Quimper to rush around monuments or museums, and the most enjoyable option may be to take a boat and drift down "the prettiest river in France" to the open sea at Bénodet.

THE DROWNED CITY OF YS

Legend has it that King Gradlon built Ys in the Baie de Douarnenez, protected from the water by gates and locks to which only he and his daughter had keys. She sounds like a pleasant sort, giving pet sea-dragons to all the citizens to do their errands, but St Corentin saw decadence and suspected evil. He was proved right: at the urging of the Devil, the princess used her key to open the floodgates, the city was flooded, and Gradlon escaped only by obeying St Corentin and throwing his daughter into the sea. Back on dry land, and in need of a new capital, Gradlon founded Quimper. Ys remains on the sea floor – it will rise again when Paris (*"Par-Ys"*, "equal to Ys") sinks – and, according to tradition, on feast days sailors can still hear church bells and hymns under the water.

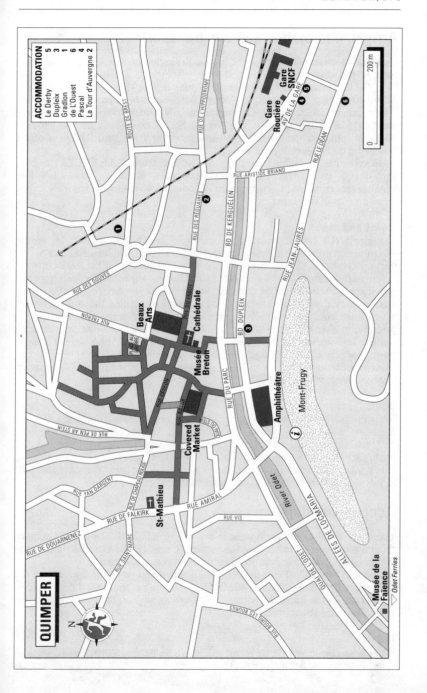

QUIMPER

N

ACCOMMODATION
Le Derby 5
Dupleix 3
Gradlon 1
de L'Ouest 6
Pascal 4
La Tour d'Auvergne 2

0   200 m

ROUTE DE BREST

RUE DE L'HIPPODROME

RUE DES REGUAIRES

RUE ARISTIDE BRIAND

BD DE KERGUÉLEN

Gare
Routière

Gare
SNCF

AV DE LA GARE

RUE LE DÉAN

RUE JEAN-JAURÈS

RUE DES DOUVES

RUE FRÉRON

Beaux
Arts

Cathédrale

Musée
Breton

BD DUPLEIX

RUE DU PARC

Amphithéâtre

Mont-Frugy

RUE DE PEN AR STEIR

RUE AU BEURRE

RUE KÉRÉON

RUE SAINT-FRANÇOIS

Covered
Market

RUE YAN DARGENT

RUE DE CHAPEAU ROUGE

St-Mathieu

RUE DE FALKIRK

RUE AMIRAL

RUE VIS

RUE DE DOUARNENEZ

RUE SAINT-MARC

River Odet

QUAI DE L'ODET

ALLÉES DE LOCMARIA

QUAI DE L'ODET

Musée de la
Faïence

Odet Ferries

RUE DE BOURG LES BOURGS

Arrival, information and city transport

Quimper's **tourist office** is housed in a small single-storey building on the south bank of the Odet at 7 rue de la Déesse, place de la Résistance (July & Aug Mon–Sat 9am–7pm, Sun 10am–1pm; April–June & Sept Mon–Sat 9am–12.30pm & 1.30–6.30pm, Sun 10am–1pm; Oct–March Mon–Sat 9am–noon & 1.30–6pm, Sun 10am–1pm; ☎02.98.53.04.05). They organize daily **guided tours** of the city in season (mid-March to mid-June & Sept Wed & Sat 2pm, Sun 3pm; mid-June to Aug Mon–Sat 2pm, Sun 3pm, plus English-language tour Tues 2pm). The **post office** is at 37 bd de Kérguelen (☎02.98.64.28.28).

Bicycles can be rented from the gare SNCF, or from Torch VTT, 58 rue de la Providence (☎02.98.53.84.41). The Fédération Bretonne des Clubs de Windsurfers (run by M Carn, route du Bénodet, 29000 Quimper) has information on all aspects of **windsurfing**.

Trains and buses

The **gare SNCF** (☎02.98.98.31.26) and **gare routière** (☎02.98.90.88.89) are next to each other on avenue de la Gare, 1km east of the centre. Local **buses** #1 and #6 connect with both, but all pass through place de la Résistance near the tourist office.

Although Quimper is well connected with the rest of Brittany by both train and bus, if you want to use public transport to get to the coast anywhere in the immediate vicinity the **bus** is your only option. Services include those to **Bénodet**, which leave from place de la Résistance (Compagnie Amoricaine de Transport, 5 bd de Kérguelen; ☎02.98.95.02.36); to **Audierne** and Pointe du Raz, from the gare routière or boulevard de Kérguelen (also CAT); to **Pont l'Abbé** and St-Guenolé, from place St-Corentin (Cariou Castric Lecoeur; ☎02.98.47.04.08); and to **Concarneau** and **Pont-Aven**, also from place St-Corentin (Sarl Transports Caoudal Réné; ☎02.98.56.96.72).

Boats

Between July and September you can **sail** from Quimper down the Odet to Bénodet, which takes about 1hr 15min, on Vedettes de l'Odet (Bénodet ☎02.98.57.00.58, Quimper ☎02.98.52.98.41; 110F return). Between two and four boats each day leave from the end of quai de l'Odet; times vary with the tides so check with the tourist office (who also sell tickets). The same company also sails in July and August to the Îles Glénan, for 200F return.

Accommodation

There are remarkably few **hotels** in the old streets in the centre of Quimper, though more can be found near the station. Rooms can be especially difficult to find in late July or early August, when reservations are advisable.

Quimper's municipal **campsite** is 2km downstream (west) of town at 6 av des Oiseaux in Bois de Seminaire (☎02.98.55.61.09), on bus route #1; there's a plusher alternative, the four-star *Orangerie de Lannion* site, on the route de Bénodet (mid-May to mid-Sept; ☎02.98.90.62.02).

Hotels

Hôtel le Derby, 13 av de la Gare (☎02.98.52.06.91, fax 02.98.53.39.04). Surprisingly quiet option above a bar facing the station. ②.

Hôtel le Dupleix, 34 bd Dupleix (☎02.98.90.53.35, fax 02.98.52.05.31). Quite expensive and modern hotel, overlooking the Odet with fine views across the river to the cathedral. No restaurant. ④.

Hôtel Gradlon, 30 rue du Brest (☎02.98.95.04.39, fax 02.98.95.61.25). Central but quiet, and exceptionally friendly. The rooms are not cheap, but they're very nicely decorated. No restaurant. ④.

Hôtel de l'Ouest, 63 rue le Déan (☎02.98.90.28.35). Small, unassuming, but very friendly hotel near the station. Closed Sun Sept–June. ①.

Hôtel-Restaurant Pascal, 19 av de la Gare (☎02.98.90.00.81, fax 02.98.53.21.81). Run-of-the-mill rooms, conveniently near the station; the unexciting restaurant has menus at 74F and 120F. ②.

Hôtel-Restaurant La Tour d'Auvergne, 13 rue des Réguaires (☎02.98.95.08.70, fax 02.98.95.17.31). Forty-one comfortable (if not exactly fancy) rooms in a refurbished *logis* tucked away in a quiet street just east of the cathedral, plus a good restaurant (see p.279). Closed Sun Oct–April. ③.

The Town

The enormous **Cathédrale St-Corentin** is said to be the most complete Gothic cathedral in Brittany, though its neo-Gothic spires date from 1856, and several years of elbow grease have now turned it a sparkling white. When the nave was being added to the old chancel in the fifteenth century, the extension would either have hit existing buildings or the swampy edge of the (then) unchannelled river. The masons eventually hit on a solution and placed the nave at a slight angle – a peculiarity which, once noticed, makes it hard to concentrate on the other Gothic splendours within.

The exterior, however, gives no hint of the deviation, with King Gradlon now mounted in perfect symmetry between the spires – though whether he would have advised a river-bed nave is another question. Before the Revolution, each St Cecilia's Day a climber would ascend to give the king a drink, and there was a prize of 100 *écus* for whoever could catch the glass, thrown down afterwards. During the sixteenth century, 1500 refugees died of plague inside the building.

Alongside the cathedral, the **Bishop's Palace** is quirky from the outside, nestling against one of the few remaining fragments of the old city walls, and has a wonderful staircase within, but its museum of Breton oddments is small and forgettable (June–Sept daily 9am–6pm, 25F; Oct–May Tues–Sat 9am–noon & 2–5pm, Sun 2–5pm, 20F). Much more compelling is the **Musée des Beaux Arts**, alongside the Hôtel de Ville at 40 place St-Corentin (July & Aug daily 9am–7pm; Sept & April–May daily except Tues 10am–noon & 2–6pm; Oct–March Mon & Wed–Sat 10am–noon & 2–6pm, Sun 2–6pm; 25F, July & Aug 30F), which holds amazing collections of drawings by Cocteau, Gustave Doré and Max Jacob (who was born in Quimper), nineteenth- and twentieth-century paintings of the Pont-Aven school, and Breton scenes by the likes of Eugène Boudin. Only the dull Dutch oils upstairs let the collection down.

The heart of **old Quimper** lies to the west of place St-Corentin, in front of the cathedral. This is where you'll find the liveliest shops and cafés, housed in the old half-timbered buildings, such as the Breton Keltia-Musique record shop at 1 place au Beurre, and the Celtic shop, Ar Bed Keltiek, nearby at 2 rue du Roi-Gradlon. The old market hall was burned down in 1976, but the light and spacious new **Halles St-Francis**, rue Astor, built to replace it is quite a delight, not just for the food, but for the view past the upturned boat rafters through the roof to the cathedral's twin spires. It's open from Monday to Saturday, with an extra-large market spreading into the surrounding streets on Saturdays.

The faïenceries of Quimper

Faïence – tin-glazed earthenware – was first popularized by the city of Faenza in Italy in the sixteenth century. Its production was subsequently taken up by Delft in Holland, Majolica in Spain – and in Quimper, from 1690 onwards. The whole story is told by the city's excellent pottery museum, the **Musée de la Faïence Jules Verlinque**, not far west of the tourist office, on the south bank of the Odet at 14 rue Jean-Baptiste-Bosquet (May–Oct Mon–Sat 10am–6pm; 26F).

As well as revealing the minerals used to create different colours, such as copper (green), cobalt (blue) and antimony (yellow), the museum demonstrates that little has changed in the Breton pottery business since some unknown artisan hit on the idea of painting ceramic ware with naive "folk" designs. That was in around 1875, just as the coming of the railways brought the first influx of tourists in search of authentic souvenirs. Highlights of the collection include pieces commemorating such events as World War I, the first automobile accident, and the death of Zola, but there are also some fascinating specimens produced by fine artists in the 1920s. In the age before plastics, they handled commissions like designing hood ornaments for Citroën cars.

As you walk through the town, it is impossible to ignore faïence – you are invited to look and to buy on every corner. On weekdays, it's also possible to visit the major atelier **H-B Henriot**, in the allées de Locmarion just behind the museum (Mon–Fri 9–11.30am & 1.30–4pm; 16F; ☎02.98.90.09.36). H-B Henriot maintain a bright, modern **gift shop** alongside; the prices, even for the seconds, are similar to those on offer everywhere else, but the selection is superb (Mon–Thurs 9.30am–7pm, Fri & Sat 9.30am–6pm).

Eating and drinking

Although the pedestrian streets west of the cathedral are unexpectedly short on places to eat, there are quite a few **restaurants** further east on the north side of the river, en route towards the gare SNCF. Rue Aristide-Briand here is a particularly promising area, and also contains a lively **Celtic bar**, the *Ceili* at no 4. For *crêperies*, the place au Beurre, a short walk northwest of the cathedral, is a good bet.

Restaurants

L'Ambroisie, 49 rue Élie-Fréron (☎02.98.95.00.02). Upmarket French restaurant on the main road north from the cathedral, with menus from 99F; closed Mon pm, except in summer.

L'Assiette, 5bis rue Jean-Jaurès (☎02.98.53.03.65). Relaxed and inexpensive red-painted bistro, south of the river, with imaginative menus that start at 60F. Closed Sun & Mon.

La Cambuse, 11 rue Déan (☎02.98.53.06.06). Lively place, south of the river, serving inexpensive *crêpes*, salads, and quiche-like savoury *tartes*. Behind the bright-orange facade there's more orange panelling, with wooden tables and a little garden as well. Closed Sun lunch and all day Mon.

Le Capucin Gourmand, 29 rue des Réguaires (☎02.98.95.43.12). Gourmet French cooking, not far east of the cathedral. Menus start at 80F and zoom on up to over 300F; most offer very little choice, though all those costing more than 100F feature at least some meat dishes. Closed Sun pm & Mon.

La Krampouzerie, 9 rue du Sallé, on the place au Beurre (☎02.98.95.13.08). One of the best of Quimper's many *crêperies.* Most *crêpes* cost under 20F, though you can get a wholewheat galette with scallops for 40F, or with seaweed for 28F. Closed Sun, & Mon in winter.

La Tour d'Auvergne, 13 rue des Réguaires (☎02.98.95.08.70). Formal hotel dining room that offers high-quality menus from 125F up to 270F, with an emphasis on fresh local seafood: the mussels and monkfish are recommended, the baked strawberries divine. Closed Sun Oct–April.

Trattoria Mario, 35 rue des Réguaires (☎02.98.95.42.15). Italian meals of pizza (from 33F) and fresh pasta, behind the post office. Closed Sun lunch and all day Mon.

Entertainment and culture

Quimper's **Festival de Cornouaille** started in 1923 and has gone from strength to strength since. This great jamboree of Breton music, costumes, theatre and dance is held in the week before the fourth Sunday in July, attracting guest performers from the other Celtic countries and a scattering of other, sometimes highly unusual, ethnic-cultural ensembles. The whole thing culminates in an incredible Sunday parade through the town. The official programme does not appear until July, but you can get provisional details in advance from the tourist office; it's well worth planning a little way ahead, as accommodation is at a premium in Quimper while the festival is on.

Not so widely known are the **Semaines Musicales,** which follow in the first three weeks of August. The music is predominantly classical, and tends to favour French composers such as Berlioz, Debussy, Bizet and Poulenc. Founded in 1978, the event serves to bring the rather stuffy nineteenth-century theatre on boulevard Dupleix alive each year.

Bénodet

Once out of its city channel, the Odet takes on the anarchic shape of most Breton inlets, spreading out to lake proportions then turning narrow corners between gorges. The resort of **BÉNODET** at the mouth of the river (reachable by boat from Quimper – see p.276) has a long sheltered beach on the ocean side. The town is a little overdeveloped but the beach is undeniably good, especially for kids, for whom there's a lot laid on – including horse-riding, windsurfing and "beach club" crèches. During its less busy periods, such as spring or autumn, Bénodet is a strong contender to be rated as the best spot for a family holiday in the whole of Brittany.

Across the rivermouth, the equally attractive **Ste-Marine** is served by regular pedestrian-only ferries. You can also drive there in a matter of minutes over the graceful **Pont de Cornouaille,** 1km upstream, which offers spectacular views of the estuary.

Arrival and information
Bénodet's **tourist office** is at 51 av de la Plage (June–Sept daily 9am–7pm; Oct–May Mon–Sat 9am–noon & 2–7pm, Sun 10am–noon; ☎02.98.57.00.14). During the school holidays, three **buses** a day run each way between Quimper and Bénodet; in school time, services are more frequent, but tend to run early in the morning. For details, contact CAT in Quimper (☎02.98.95.02.36). **Bicycles** can be rented from Cycletty, 20 rue Charcot (☎02.98.57.12.49).

Boat excursions from Bénodet or Quimper to the rather nondescript **Îles de Glénan** are less exciting than the river trips between the two towns. All these services, plus sailings west along the coast to Loctudy and east to Beg-Meil, La Forêt-Fouesnant and Concarneau – some of which operate in glass-bottomed boats – are run by Vedettes de l'Odet, 2 av de l'Odet (May–Sept; ☎02.98.57.00.58).

Accommodation and eating

Among the nicest **hotels in** Bénodet are the *Hôtel-Restaurant Le Minaret*, an odd-looking building in a superb position overlooking the sea on the corniche de l'Estuaire (☎02.98.57.03.13; closed Nov–March; ③), and the *Bains de Mer*, 11 rue du Kérguelen (☎02.98.57.03.41; closed mid-Nov to mid-March; ③). *Hôtel l'Hermitage*, 11 rue Laënnec (☎02.98.57.00.37; closed Oct to mid-May; ②), which is a few hundred metres up from the beach, and doesn't have its own restaurant, is a reasonable low-priced alternative.

For a good **meal**, the restaurants of the *Hôtel Gwel-Kaër*, 3 av de la Plage (☎02.98.57.04.38; ④), and the *Hôtel de Ste-Marine* at 19 rue Bac across the rivermouth (☎02.98.56.34.79; closed Wed in low season, & all Nov; ④), are also recommended, though neither offers a menu for under 100F, and in summer the *Ste-Marine* tends to be too full to feed non-guests.

Bénodet also has several large **campsites** – if anything, too many of them – including four-star ones such as the *Camping Port de Plaisance* (April–Sept; ☎02.98.57.02.38), which has a heated swimming pool, the enormous *du Letty*, southeast of the village next to the plage du Letty, on rue du Canvez (mid-June to mid-Sept; ☎02.98.57.04.69), and the *de la Pointe St-Gilles* (May–Sept; ☎02.98.57.05.37).

The Penmarch peninsula

At one time the **Penmarch peninsula** was one of the richest areas of Brittany. That was before it was plundered by the pirate La Fontenelle, who led three hundred ships in raids on the local peasantry from his base on the island of La Tristan in the Bay of Douarnenez; also before the cod, staple of the fishing industry, stopped coming.

Now, in the local tourist literature, the region is known as the **Pays de Bigouden**, after the elaborate lace *coiffes* you see worn in many of the villages. Often as much as a foot high, they are sometimes supported by half-tubes of cardboard; sometimes just very stiffly starched. The white of the *coiffes* swaying in the wind provides one of the memorable colours of the area, along with the red fields of poppies and verges of purple foxgloves.

Pont l'Abbé

PONT L'ABBÉ, the principal town of this corner, has a Bigouden museum, spread over three storeys of the keep of its fourteenth-century château (June–Sept Mon–Sat 9am–noon & 2–6.30pm; 15F) – though you'd need to be quite inspired by the costumes to find it of great interest. More accessible pleasures lie in a stroll through the woods along the banks of its estuary.

The *Hôtel de Bretagne*, in the main square at 24 place de la République (☎02.98.87.17.22; closed Sun pm & Mon out of season; ③), is the prettiest hotel in town.

Le Guilvinec

West of Pont L'Abbé, the world **windsurfing** championships are often held at **Pointe de la Torche**, and at any time there are likely to be aficionados of the sport twirling effortlessly about on the dangerous water. The coast only becomes swimmable, however, as you round the Pointe de Penmarch towards Loctudy. The first village you come to, **LE GUILVINEC**, is a not especially attractive (but surprisingly busy) fishing port, which is home to the fourth largest fish auction (*criée*) in France. The boats start to come home to the harbour, sheltered in the mouth of a little river, around 4pm most afternoons. A small but very pleasant beach faces onto the open sea.

The *Hôtel du Port*, at 53 av du Port in **Léchiagat**, on the far side of the estuary (☎02.98.58.10.10; ③), is thoroughly recommended – especially, of course, for its fish suppers, which start at 100F with a tasty array of scallops, skate and all sorts of dessert, and culminate in a lobster feast for 390F. Don't confuse the *Hôtel du Port* with the *Auberge du Port*, back in Le Guilvinec itself; if you do choose to stay in town, the very plain exterior of the *Hôtel du Centre* at 16 rue du Général-de-Gaulle conceals an attractive garden within (☎02.98.58.10.44; ②). The restaurant here isn't bad, so long as you ignore the cheapest menu and go for the 100F one instead.

Loctudy

LOCTUDY is a good target – an equally well-positioned but much less commercial version of Bénodet, which it faces across the mouth of the Odet. There are several **campsites** along its main beach, including the *Kergall* (mid-April to Sept; ☎02.98.87.45.93) and the *Mouettes* (April to mid-Sept; ☎02.98.87.43.51), and some good-value **hotels**, such as the *de Bretagne*, 19 rue du Port (☎02.98.87.40.21; ③).

Boats from Loctudy, too, sail up the Odet, as well as out to the Îles de Glénan (May–Sept; ☎02.98.87.45.63; 115F). The trips to Quimper should depart daily during the summer, but you need to make sure they are running on any particular day; services are cancelled in bad weather or simply if not enough people show up.

Along the South Coast

The coast that continues east of Bénodet is rocky and repeatedly cut by deep valleys. It suffered heavily in the hurricane of 1987, but the small resort of **BEGMEIL** survives, albeit with fewer trees to protect its vast expanse of dunes. With beaches every bit as nice as those of Bénodet, and far fewer visitors, Beg-Meil is ideal for **campers**. Just back from the seafront there's also the hotel *Thalamot* (☎02.98.94.97.38; closed Oct–April; ②).

Around **la Forêt-Fouesnant**, in particular, the hills are much too steep for cyclists to climb, and forbidden to heavy vehicles such as caravans. The Forêt-Fouesnant minor road may look good, but there are few beaches or places to stop. Motorists would do best to take the more direct D44, a few kilometres inland, followed by the D783, which leads close to the major towns along the route.

Concarneau

The first sizeable town you come to east of Bénodet, **CONCARNEAU**, ranks as the third most important fishing port in France. Nonetheless, it does a reasonable job of passing itself off as a holiday resort. Its greatest asset is its **Ville Close**, the small and very well-fortified old city located a few metres offshore on an irregular rocky island in the bay.

In the height of summer, the Ville Close can get too crowded for comfort, but otherwise it's a real delight. You reach it by crossing a narrow bridge and then passing through two successive gateways, marked by a little clock tower and a sundial. Like those of the *citadelle* at Le Palais on Belle-Île (see p.327), the ramparts were completed by Vauban in the seventeenth century. The island itself, however, had been inhabited for at least a thousand years before that, and is first recorded as the site of a priory founded by King Gradlon of Quimper.

Concarneau boasts that it is a *ville fleurie*, and the flowers are most in evidence inside the walls, where climbing roses and clematis swarm all over the various gift shops, restaurants and *crêperies*. Walk the central pedestrianized street to the far end, and you can pass through a gateway to the shoreline to watch the fishing boats go by. In summer, however, the best views of all come from the promenade on top of the ramparts (daily: July & Aug 9am–7pm; May, June & Sept 10am–6pm; 5F).

The **Musée de la Pêche**, immediately inside the Ville Close (daily: mid-June to mid-Sept 9.30am–7pm; mid-Sept to mid-June 9.30am–12.30pm & 2–6pm; 30F), provides an insight into the traditional life Concarneau shared with so many other Breton ports. The four rooms around the central quadrangle illuminate the history and practice of four specific aspects of fishing. The whaling room contains model boats and a genuine open boat from the Azores; the tuna room shows boats dragging nets the size of central Paris; a herring room; and a model of a sardine cannery – which this building once was. And there are oddities collected by fishermen in the past: the swords of swordfish and the saws of sawfish; a Japanese giant crab; photos of old lifeboatmen with fading beards; cases full of sardine and tuna cans; and a live aquarium, where the lobsters little realize they are in no immediate danger of being eaten. In addition, you can buy diagrams and models of ships, and even order a diorama of the stuffed fish of your choice.

Arrival and information

Concarneau's **tourist office** (July & Aug daily 9am–8pm; May & June Mon–Sat 9am–noon & 2–6.30pm, Sun 9.30am–12.30pm; Sept–April Mon–Sat 9am–noon & 2–6.30pm; ☎02.98.97.01.44) is on the quai d'Aiguillon, not far from the long-distance bus stop; there's no rail service, but SNCF buses connect with Quimper and Rosporden. It's also possible in summer to take **ferries** up the Odet to Quimper or out to the Îles de Glénan, with Vedettes Glénan (☎02.98.97.10.31) or Vedettes de l'Odet (☎02.98.50.72.12).

Accommodation

The Ville Close is almost completely devoid of **hotels**, so most of those that Concarneau has to offer skulk in the backstreets of the mainland and tend to be full most of the time. Probably the best bet of all is the **youth hostel** (open all year; ☎02.98.97.03.47; 46F); for once, very near the city centre but also enjoying magnificent ocean views. It's just around the tip of the headland on the quai de la Croix, with a good *crêperie* opposite and a windsurfing shop a little further along.

Hôtel de France et d'Europe, 9 av de la Gare (☎02.98.97.00.64, fax 02.98.97.00.89). Bright, modernized and very central hotel near the main bus stop. No restaurant. Closed Sat mid-Nov to mid-March. ④.

Le Galion, 15 rue St-Guénolé (☎02.98.97.30.16, fax 02.98.50.67.88). Upmarket restaurant at the far end of the Ville Close that offers a few expensive rooms, and is otherwise noteworthy only for the meagreness of the portions on its *nouvelle* menus, starting at 135F. Closed Sun pm, Mon, & all Feb. ④.

Hôtel-Restaurant les Océanides, 3 rue du Lin (☎02.98.97.08.61, fax 02.98.97.09.13). *Logis de France*, a couple of streets up from the sea above the fishing port, with a highly recommended and far from expensive restaurant. Closed Sun pm in May & June, all Sun Oct–April. ②.

Hôtel des Voyageurs, 9 place Jean-Jaurès (☎02.98.97.08.06). Cheap basic accommodation, right opposite the entrance to the Ville Close. ②.

Eating

For an atmospheric **meal** in Concarneau, your best bet is to choose from any of the restaurants along the main street that runs through the Ville Close, or explore the little lanes that lead off it. There are, however, plenty of cheaper places back in town.

The main **market** is held in front of the Ville Close on Friday, with a smaller one on Monday; the covered market *halles* on the far side of the square are open every morning, and hold plenty of snack stalls.

Chez Armande, 15 av du Dr-Nicholas (☎02.98.97.00.76). Excellent seafood not far south of the market on the mainland, on menus starting at 95F. Closed Wed, & Tues pm in winter.

L'Assiette de Pêcheur, 12 rue St-Guénolé (☎02.98.70.75.84). Smart seafood restaurant at the far end of the Ville Close, in the same square as *Le Galion*, with a good 92F menu. Closed Oct–Easter, plus Sun pm & Mon except July & Aug.

L'Écume, 3 place St-Guénolé (☎02.98.97.33.27). One of several good-value *crêperies* in the heart of the Ville Close. A great spot to watch the world go by, and menus to suit all tastes from 60F. Closed Wed, plus Nov–March.

L'Escale, 19 quai Carnot (☎02.98.97.03.31). Waterfront restaurant on the main road in town that's a favourite with local fishermen, with lunch menus for around 50F. Closed Sun.

Restaurant du Petit-Château, 12 rue Théophile-Louarn (☎02.98.97.49.98). Quiet little place hidden away in the Ville Close, pressed against the walls just off place St-Guénolé, and serving 48F lunches in a sweet little garden. Closed Fri.

Pont-Aven

PONT-AVEN, 14km east of Concarneau and just inland from the tip of the Aven estuary, is a small port packed with tourists and art galleries. This was where Gauguin came to paint in the 1880s, before he left for Tahiti in search of a South Seas idyll. By all accounts Gauguin was a rude and arrogant man who lorded it over the local population (who were already well used to posing in "peasant attire" for visiting artists). As a painter and printmaker, however, he produced some of his finest work in Pont-Aven, and his influence was such that the **Pont-Aven School** of fellow artists developed here. He spent some years working closely with these – the best known of whom was Émile Bernard – and they in turn helped to revitalize his own approach.

For all the local hype, however, the town has no permanent collection of Gauguin's work. The **Musée Municipal** (daily: mid-June to mid-Sept 10am–7pm; mid-Feb to mid-June & mid-Sept to Dec 10am–12.30pm & 2–6pm; 25F) in the Mairie holds changing exhibitions of the numerous members of the school, and other artists active in Brittany during the same period, but you can't count on paintings by the man himself.

Gauguin aside, Pont-Aven is pleasant in its own right, with countless galleries making it easy to while away an afternoon, and the small neat pleasure port boasting a watermill and the odd leaping salmon. Just upstream of the little granite bridge at the heart of town, the **promenade Xavier-Grall** crisscrosses the tiny river itself on landscaped walkways, offering glimpses of the backs of venerable mansions, dripping with red ivy, and a little "chaos" of rocks in the stream itself. A longer walk – allow an hour – leads into the **Bois d'Amour**, wooded gardens which have long provided inspiration to visiting painters – and a fair tally, too, of poets and musicians.

If you can't afford to take a souvenir canvas home with you, the town's other speciality is more affordable, and tastes better too. Pont-Aven is the home of two manufacturers of **galettes** – which here means "butter biscuits" rather than "pancakes" – and their products are on sale everywhere.

Throughout the summer, Les Vedettes Aven-Belon (☎02.98.71.14.59) run **cruises** from the pleasure port down to the sea at Port-Manech. Some continue around to **Port-Belon** near the mouth of the next estuary, where it's also possible to board the boats. The precise schedule is determined by the state of the tides (July & Aug 1–2 departures daily; April–June & Sept 1 departure virtually every day; short cruises 58F, long trips 79F).

Practicalities

Pont-Aven's **tourist office**, 5 place de l'Hôtel de Ville (July & Aug daily 9.30am–7.30pm; April–June & Sept–Oct daily 9.15am–12.30pm & 2–7pm; Nov–March Mon–Sat 10am–12.30pm & 2–6pm; ☎02.98.06.04.70), sells an excellent English-language guide booklet to the town, plus route maps of local walks, for a mere 2F.

Once the day-trippers have gone home, Pont-Aven makes a tranquil place to spend a night. Much the best of its three relatively expensive **hotels** is the central *Hôtel des Ajoncs d'Or*, 1 place de l'Hôtel de Ville (☎02.98.06.02.06; closed Jan; ④), where the gourmet menus start at 100F. The nicest of the local **campsites** is *Le Spinnaker* (May–Sept; ☎02.98.06.01.77), set in a large wooded park.

Riec-sur-Bélon

From the unremarkable village of **RIEC-SUR-BÉLON**, 5km southeast of Pont-Aven, back roads snake down for another 4km to reach a dead end at the **port du Bélon**, on the delightfully sinuous estuary of the Bélon River. The coastal footpath that leads away from here along the thickly wooded shoreline is clearly signposted to offer optional loop trails of 3km, 6km and 8km.

Some of the oyster beds visible at low tide in the sands off the port du Bélon belong to the private château de Bélon, and others to *Chez Jacky* (☎02.98.06.90.32), a deservedly popular seafood **restaurant**. Once past the well-stocked vivarium at its entrance, you'll find bare wooden benches and tables inside, and beyond that a lovely seafront terrace. The ambience is informal, but both the food and the prices are to be taken seriously. Local oysters are 80F a dozen and a huge platter of mostly raw shellfish costs 200F per person, while totally fishy menus range from the 105F *le Matelot* up to the gourmet 450F *l'Amiral*, which features a grilled lobster.

Quimperlé

The final town of any size in Finistère, **QUIMPERLÉ** straddles a hill and two rivers, the Isole and the Elle, cut by a sequence of bridges. It's an atmospheric place, particularly in the medieval muddle of streets around **Ste-Croix church**. This was copied in plan from schema of the Church of the Holy Sepulchre in Jerusalem, brought back by crusaders, and is notable for its original Romanesque apse. There are some good bars nearby and, on Fridays, a market on the square higher up on the hill.

The **hotels** *L'Europe* (☎02.98.96.00.02; ②) and *Auberge de Toulföen* (☎02.98.96.00.29; closed Oct; ④) both have reasonable rooms.

Le Pouldu

At the mouth of the River Laïta, which constitutes the eastern limit of Finistère, the community of **LE POULDU** was another of Paul Gauguin's favourite haunts. It is divided into two distinct sections. The tiny **port**, on one bank of the estuary – most of which has not even a road alongside, let alone any buildings – is shielded from the open sea by a curving spit of sand. The **beach**, more developed than in Gauguin's day but still very picturesque, is a couple of kilometres away, with the headland that separates the two indented with a succession of delightful little sandy coves.

The *Hôtel des Bains* (☎02.98.39.90.11; closed Sept–April; ③) drops down to the beach from the main road, with its large glass-fronted rooms commanding superb views, and menus starting at 85F, while the appealingly weather-beaten white *Hôtel du Pouldu* (☎02.98.39.90.66; closed Oct–March; ②) stands next to the port. Le Pouldu would also make an ideal spot to **camp** for a few days; among sites near the beach is the *Vieux Four* (June–Sept; ☎02.98.39.94.34).

travel details

Trains

From Brest 7 daily TGV services to Paris-Montparnasse (4hr), via Landerneau (12min), Landivisiau (20min), Morlaix (35min) and Rennes (1hr 10min); also 4 daily cheaper, slower services, taking 6hr. From Brest also to Quimper (6 daily; 1hr 30min), with connecting SNCF buses at Châteaulin for Crozon, and inland to Carhaix.

From Roscoff to Morlaix (6 daily; 30min).

From Quimper TGV services to Lorient (4 daily; 30min), Vannes (4 daily; 1hr) and Redon (2 daily; 1hr 40min), plus 6 slower services. Most continue to Rennes or Nantes, and on to Paris, Bordeaux or Toulouse.

Buses

From Roscoff to Morlaix (3–6 daily; 50min) and Vannes via Quimper (1 only, Mon, Thurs & Sat; 4hr).

From Morlaix to Roscoff (2–4 daily; 50min); Carantec (4 daily; 20min); Plougasnou and St-Jean-du-Doigt (5 daily; 30min); Lannion (2 daily; not Sun; 1hr); Huelgoat (3 daily; 45min) and Carhaix (3 daily; 1hr 30min); Quimper (2 daily; 1hr 50min); Vannes (1 daily 3hr 30min).

From Brest to Roscoff (5 daily; 1hr 30min), via Plouescat, Lanhouarneau, Lesneven and Gouesnou; to Le Conquet (4 daily; 30min); to Quimper (6 daily; 1hr 30min).

From Châteaulin to Crozon and Camaret (5 daily; 30min/50min); less often to Carhaix.

From Landévennec 3 daily to Camaret (45min) via Roscanvel and Crozon.

From Quimper 5 daily to Locronan (20min), Telgruc (1hr), Crozon (1hr 20min) and Camaret (1hr 30min); 3 daily to Audierne (1hr) and Pointe du Raz (1hr 15min); 6 daily to Concarneau (30min) and Quimperlé (1hr 30min); 6 daily to Fouesnant (1hr) and Beg-Meil (1hr 10min); 9 daily to the airport at Plugaffan; 8 daily to Bénodet (45min); also to Douarnenez (5 daily; 40min), Lorient (2hr) and Vannes (3hr).

Ferries

From Roscoff to **Plymouth** (6hr) and **Cork** (13–17hr). Both services Brittany Ferries, (Roscoff ☎02.98.29.28.28, Plymouth ☎01752/21321, Cork ☎215/07666). See p.3 onwards for more details.

From Roscoff to **Île de Batz** (very frequently; 15min), details of the two ferry operators are on p244; and in July and August, tours of the **Bay of Morlaix**.

From Le Conquet, **Lanildut**, **Brest** and **Camaret** to **Ouessant** and **Molène**; ferries run by two separate operators are detailed on p.257.

From Brest to **Le Fret** on the Crozon peninsula, (April–Sept; 3–4 daily, 25min; ☎02.98.41.46.23). Foot passengers and cyclists only, each trip is met by a minibus for **Crozon** and **Camaret**. Trips also run from Brest around the **Rade de Brest**.

From Morgat, trips to caves and headlands (☎02.98.27.10.71).

From Douarnenez, trips around **Bay of Douarnenez**, and occasional trips to Ouessant, run by Penn Ar Bed (☎02.98.80.24.68).

From Audierne to **Sein** island; see details on p.274.

From Quimper, down the Odet to **Bénodet**, and vice versa (May–Sept; ☎02.98.57.00.58).

You can also **tour the Odet**, daily from **Loctudy** (☎02.98.87.45.63), daily from **Concarneau** June 15 –Sept 15; (☎02.98.97.10.31), and thrice-weekly from **Port-la-Forêt** and **Beg-Meil** (☎02.98.94.97.94). All the Odet companies also do trips (average 1hr) to the **Glénan** islands.

Air

From Brest airport (Guipavas), 2 daily flights to **Ouessant**, subject to good weather (☎02.98.84.64.87; see p.257). For details of flights to **London** on Brit Air (Brest ☎02.98.32.01.10) see p.6.

From Quimper airport (Plugaffan), 2 daily flights to **Paris** (☎02.98.84.73.33).

CHAPTER SIX

INLAND BRITTANY: THE NANTES–BREST CANAL

The meandering chain of waterways known as the **Nantes–Brest canal**, which combines natural rivers with purpose-built stretches of canal, runs all the way from Finistère down to the Loire. En route it passes through medieval riverside towns, such as **Josselin** and **Malestroit**, which long predate its construction; commercial ports and junctions – **Pontivy**, most notably – that developed along its path during the nineteenth century; the old port of **Redon**, a checkerboard of water, where the canal crosses the River Vilaine; and a succession of scenic splendours, including the string of lakes around the **Barrage de Guerlédan** near Mur-de-Bretagne.

As a focus for exploring **inland Brittany**, perhaps cutting in to the towpaths along the more easily accessible stretches, and then detouring out to the towns and sights around, the canal is ideal. The detours can be picked almost at will – the **sculpture park** at Kerguéhennec, near Josselin, and the village of **La Gacilly** near Malestroit, are among the least known and most enjoyable.

All this area is supposed – in myth at any rate – to have been covered in the long-distant past by one vast forest, the *Argoat*. Though vestiges of ancient woodland do remain in several areas, natural and human forces seem to be conspiring to destroy them. The **forest of Huelgoat**, which, with its boulder-strewn waterfalls, bubbling streams and grottoes, was the most dramatic natural landscape in Brittany, has yet to recover from the devastating hurricane of 1987. **Paimpont** –

ACCOMMODATION PRICE CODES

All **hotel prices** in this book have been coded using the symbols below. The price shown is for the least expensive double room in high season, which for category ① often means a room without shower, bath and toilet. Most hotels in that category have other rooms with en-suite facilities, which typically cost 30–50F extra.

For a full explanation see p.30.

① Under 160F	③ 220–300F	⑤ 400–500F	⑦ 600–700F
② 160–220F	④ 300–400F	⑥ 500–600F	⑧ 700F and over

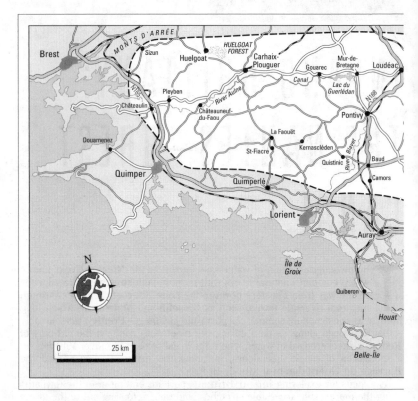

the legendary forest of Brocéliande which concealed the Holy Grail – survived that storm, only to be damaged by a serious fire in the autumn of 1990.

You cannot make the whole journey described in this chapter by literally keeping next to the canal. For much of the way there is no adjacent road, and even though the **towpath** is normally clear enough for walking it's not really practicable to cycle along for any great distance. However, it is certainly worth following the canal in short sections, which you can do quite easily by car, better by bike, or best of all by renting a **boat**, **barge** or even a **houseboat** along the navigable stretches. Full listings of **rental** outlets are given in the "Travel details" at the end of this chapter.

The canal in Finistère

The westernmost section of the canal, passing through Finistère, is now one of its least-used stretches. Those travellers who do set out to follow its course are far more likely to do so from the Crozon peninsula or the Menez-Hom – both covered in the previous chapter – than from Brest itself.

However, as recently as the 1920s, steamers made their way across the Rade de Brest and down the River Aulne to Châteaulin. The contemporary *Black's Guide*

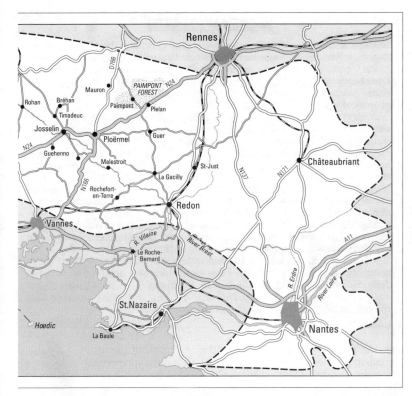

reckoned the six-hour journey "tedious [in a] boat often overcrowded with cattle"
– a judgement that seems a little churlish now that such pleasures are no longer
available.

Châteaulin

CHÂTEAULIN is the first real town on the canal route, though in actuality no
more than a brief, picturesque waterside strip, overlooked by the pretty little
chapel of Notre Dame. It's a quiet place, where the main reason to stay is the
River Aulne itself. Enticingly rural, it is renowned for its salmon and trout fishing;
if you're interested, most bars sell permits (as do angling shops, some of which
rent tackle). The only other factor that might draw you is cycling: regional championships are held each September on a circuit that races through the centre, and
on occasion it's used for the French professional championship, too.

Along the **riverbank**, a statue commemorates Jean Moulin, the Resistance
leader of whose murder SS man Klaus Barbie was found guilty in Lyon. Moulin
was *sous-préfet* in Châteaulin from 1930 to 1933; the inscription reads "mourir sans
parler".

Within a couple of minutes' walk upstream from the statue, and the town centre, you're on towpaths overhung by trees full of birds, with rabbits and squirrels

---

THE CANAL

The idea of joining together the inland waterways of Brittany dates back to 1627 – though, as ever, nothing was done to implement the scheme until it was seen as a military necessity. That point came during the Napoleonic wars, when English fleets began to threaten shipping circumnavigating the Breton coast. To relieve the virtual blockade of Brest in 1810, Napoléon authorized the construction of a canal network to link it with both Nantes and Lorient.

In the event, economic disasters held up its completion, but by 1836 a navigable path was cut and the canal officially opened. It was not an immediate success. Having cost sixty million francs to construct, the first years of operation, up to 1850, raised a mere 70,000 francs in tariffs. It survived, however, helped by a navy experiment of transporting coal cross-country to its ports. By the turn of the century the canal's business was booming. In the years between 1890 and the outbreak of World War I an annual average of 35,000 tonnes of cargo were carried. In addition to coal, the cargoes were mainly slate, from the quarries near Châteaulin, and fertilizer, which helped to develop agricultural production inland.

After the war, motor transport and more effective roads brought swift decline. The canal had always been used primarily for short journeys at either end – from Brest to Carhaix and Pontivy to Nantes – and in 1928 the building of a dam at Lac Guerlédan cut it forever into two sections, with the stretch from Carhaix to Pontivy becoming navigable only by canoe. Plans for the dam were approved on the basis that either a hydraulic lift, or a side channel, would enable barges to bypass it – but neither was ever built. In 1945 the last barge arrived at Châteaulin, and these days the only industry that has much use for the canal is tourism.

---

running ahead of you on the path. For the first couple of kilometres, diagrams of corpulent yet energetic figures incite you to join them in unspeakable exercises – if you can resist that temptation, you'll soon find yourself ambling in peace past the locks and weirs that climb towards the Montagnes Noires.

Practicalities

Unless a major cycling event is taking place, you should have little difficulty finding a room in any of Châteaulin's three or four modest **hotels**. The best value of them is *Le Chrismas* at 33 Grande-Rue, a *logis de France* a short walk up the road that climbs east of the town centre towards Pleyben (☎02.98.86.01.24; ②); meals in its restaurant start at 75F.

The municipal **campsite** – *Rodaven* (March–Oct; ☎02.98.86.32.93) – is very attractively situated beside the river, but is only open in high summer.

Pont Coblant

If you set out to walk the canal seriously from Châteaulin, **PONT COBLANT** and Pleyben may look just 10km distant on the map, but be warned: the meanders make it a hike of several hours (pick your side of the water, too; there are no bridges between Châteaulin and Pont Coblant).

It's possible to rent both **kayaks** and **houseboats** from this small village (contact Crabing-Loisirs, M. Mercier, 20 rue de Frout, 29000 Quimper; ☎02.98.95.14.02; or call ☎02.98.73.34.69). Pont Coblant also has a tiny **hotel**, the *Auberge du Poisson Blanc* (☎02.98.73.34.76; ③), and a **campsite** (mid-June to mid-Sept; ☎02.98.73.31.22).

Pleyben

PLEYBEN, 4km north of Pont Coblant, is renowned for its sixteenth-century **parish close** (see p.249). On its four sides the calvary traces the life of Jesus, combining great detail with an appealing naivety. The church of St-Germain itself, twin-towered, with a huge ornate spire dwarfing its domed Renaissance neighbour, features an altarpiece so blackened and buckled by age as to leave only two tiny "windows" decipherable, like an Advent calendar. Pleyben is more openly prosperous than the parish close villages further north: the church is well scrubbed, and currently undergoing major restoration (not this time due to hurricane damage).

There's a summer-only **tourist office** (mid-June to mid-Sept Mon–Sat 10am–12.30pm & 2.30–6pm; ☎02.98.26.71.05) in the spacious and grandiose main square, the place de Gaulle, as well as a **hotel**, *La Croix Blanche* (☎02.98.26.61.29; ②). On the N164 in between Châteaulin and Pleyben, the *Run Ar Puns* (☎02.98.86.27.95) is a **music club** and bar housed in old farm buildings.

Châteauneuf-du-Faou

CHÂTEAUNEUF-DU-FAOU, a little way south of the N164 25km east of Châteaulin, is in a similar sort of vein, sloping down to the tree-lined river. It's a little more developed, though, with a tourist complex, the *Penn ar Pont* (mid-May to Sept; ☎02.98.81.81.25), which boasts a swimming pool, *gîtes* and camping, as well as cycle and **boat rental**.

The **canal proper** separates off from the Aulne a few kilometres to the east at Pont Triffen, staking its own path on, past Carhaix, and out of Finistère.

Carhaix and onwards

CARHAIX, a further 25km east, is a road junction that dates back to the Romans, with cafés and shops to replenish supplies, but not much to recommend it. The most interesting building in town is the granite Renaissance **Maison de Sénéchal** on rue Brisieux, which houses the **tourist office** (July & Aug Mon–Sat 9am–12.30pm & 1.30–7pm, Sun 3–6pm; Sept–June Mon–Sat 10am–noon & 2–6pm; ☎02.98.93.04.42). The modern *Hôtel Gradlon* at 12 bd de la République (☎02.98.93.15.22; ③), near the church, makes a comfortable if rather pricey place to spend the night, and serves good food, with menus starting at 65F.

Beyond Carhaix, the canal – as far as Pontivy – is navigable only by canoe. If that's not how you're travelling, it probably makes more sense to loop round to the south, through the **Montaignes Noires**, Le Faouët and Kernascléden, before rejoining the canal at **Lac Guerlédan**. Alternatively, to the north – assuming you resisted the detour from Morlaix – there are the **Forêt de Huelgoat** and the **Monts d'Arrée**. These routes are covered in the next two sections.

South through the Montaignes Noires

The **Montaignes Noires** edge along the borders of Finistère, south of Châteauneuf. Despite the name, they are really no more than escarpments, though bleak and imposing nonetheless in a harsh, exposed landscape at odds with the gentle canal path. Their highest point is the stark slate **Roc de Toullaëron**, on the road between Pont Triffen and Gourin. From its 318-metre peak, you can look west and north over kilometres of what seems like totally deserted countryside.

Le Faouët and St-Fiacre

If you are driving, the D769 beyond Gourin offers access to the twin churches of St-Fiacre and Kernascléden, built simultaneously, according to legend, with the aid of an angelic bridge. En route is the secluded town of **LE FAOUËT**, served neither by buses nor trains, and distinguished mainly by its large old market hall. Above a floor of mud and straw, still used by local traders, rises an intricate latticework of ancient wood, propped on granite pillars and topped by a little clock tower.

The church at **ST-FIACRE**, just over 2km south, is notable for its rood screen, brightly polychromed and carved as intricately as lace. The original purpose of a rood screen was to separate the chancel from the congregation – the decorations of this 1480 masterpiece go rather further than that. They depict scenes from the Old and New Testaments as well as a dramatic series on the wages of sin. Drunkenness is demonstrated by a man somehow vomiting a fox; theft, by a peasant stealing apples; and so on.

Practicalities

Two similar and highly recommendable **hotels** in the immediate area of Le Faouët both offer good food. The *Croix d'Or*, opposite the old market in the heart of town at 9 place Bellanger (☎02.97.23.07.33; closed mid-Dec to mid-Jan, plus Sun pm & Mon in low season; ③), has a 125F menu that features snail ravioli and skate's wing with thyme. The *Cheval Blanc* (☎02.97.34.61.15; ③) stands by a lake a few kilometres east in **PRIZIAC**, reached along the pleasant (but steep) D132. Le Faouët also has its own riverside municipal **campsite**, the *Beg-er-Roch* (March to mid-Sept; ☎02.97.23.15.11).

Ste-Barbe

The fifteenth-century chapel of **Ste-Barbe** perches on a rocky outcrop a couple of kilometres east of Le Faouët. Accessible only along a very poor road that crosses a bridge over the main D769, it commands views of the deep wooded ravine of the Ellé River. Visitors ring a large bell in the crude bell tower on the hilltop, before descending a steep stone staircase to the chapel itself.

Kernascléden

At the ornate and gargoyle-coated church at **KERNASCLÉDEN**, 15km southeast of Le Faouët along the D782, the focus turns from carving to frescoes. The themes, however, contemporary with St-Fiacre, are equally gruesome. On the damp-infested wall of a side chapel, horned devils stoke the fires beneath a vast cauldron filled with the the souls of the damned, and you may be able to discern the outlines of a Dance of Death, a faded cousin to that at Kermaria (see p.225). The ceiling above the main altar holds better-preserved but less bloodthirsty scenes.

The Monts d'Arrée

A broad swath of the more desolate regions of Finistère, stretching east from the Crozon peninsula right to the edge of Finistère, is designated as the Parc Régional d'Armorique. The park, in theory at least, is an area of conservation and of rural regeneration along traditional lines; in reality, lack of funding creates rather less impact. The **Monts d'Arrée**, however, which cut northeast across Finistère from the Aulne estuary, are something of a nature sanctuary; kestrels circle high above the bleak hilltops, sharing the skies with pippits, curlews and great black crows.

Over to the east, the ancient woods of the **Forêt de Huelgoat** can offer an atmospheric afternoon's walking, with the lakeside village of Huelgoat itself making an attractive base if you have the time to linger.

East across the Monts d'Arrée

The administrative centre of the Parc d'Armorique is at **MENEZ-MEUR**, off the D342 near the Forêt de Cranou – just inland from the Brest–Quimper motorway. Menez is an official **animal reserve**, with wild boar and deer roaming free, and a museum of Breton horses (June–Sept daily 10am–7pm; May daily except Sat 1.30–5.30pm; Feb–April & Oct–Dec Sun, Wed & hols 10am–noon & 1–6pm). At the reserve gate you can pick up a wealth of detail on the park and all its various activities (☎02.98.68.81.71).

Ten kilometres north, at **SIZUN**, a research station, **aquarium** and fishing exhibition sets out to increase public awareness of the significance of Brittany's rivers and inland waterways (July & Aug daily 10.30am–7pm; June & Sept Mon–Sat 10.30am–12.30pm & 1.30–5.30pm, Sun 10.30am–12.30pm & 1.30–7pm; March–May & Oct Sun, Wed & hols 2–5.30pm; Nov–Feb Wed 2–5.30pm).

The Moulins de Kerouat

Another 3km east of Sizun, along the D764 to Commana, is the abandoned hamlet of **MOULINS DE KEROUAT** (*Milin-Kerroc'h* in Breton – and on the Michelin map), which has been restored as an **Eco-Musée** (July & Aug daily 11am–7pm; mid-May to June daily 2–6pm; mid-March to mid-May & Sept–Oct daily except Sat 2–6pm; otherwise by appointment on ☎02.98.68.87.76). Kerouat's last inhabitant died in 1967 and, like many a place in the Breton interior, it might have crumbled into indiscernible ruins. However, the idea of ecomuseums is big in France at present – they are usually excellent – and one of the hamlet's water mills has been restored to motion, and its houses repaired and refurnished. The largest belonged in the last century to the mayor of Commana, who also controlled the mills, and its furnishings are therefore those of a rich family.

Into the mountains

The highest point of the Monts d'Arrée is the **ridge** which curves from the **Réservoir de St-Michel** (also known as the Lac de Brennilis) to Menez Kaldor. It is visible as a stark silhouette from the underused **campsite** at **NESTAVEL-BRAZ** on the eastern shore of the lake. From this deceptively tranquil vantage point, the army's antennae near **Roc Trévezel** to the north are obscured, as are those of the navy at Menez-Meur to the west. Right behind you, however, is the Brennilis nuclear power station. In a rare manifestation of separatist terrorism, Breton nationalists attacked this in 1975 with a rocket-launcher; it survived. In 1987, the British SAS conducted an astonishingly offensive exercise in this area, when they were invited by the French government to subdue a simulated Breton uprising, and in the process managed to run over a local inhabitant.

Perhaps appropriately, across the lake where the tree-lined fields around the villages end, is **Yeun Elez** – a hole to hell, according to legend. You can walk around the lake – gorse and brambles permitting; be very careful not to stray from the paths into the surrounding peat bogs. The ridge itself is followed most of the way by a road, but in places it still feels as if miles from any habitation.

The Forêt de Huelgoat

The **FORÊT DE HUELGOAT** spreads out to the north and east of the village of Huelgoat, the halfway point between Morlaix and Carhaix on the minor road D769 and served by the four daily buses that connect the two towns.

While there may be doubt as to whether the *Argoat*, the great forest supposed to have stretched the length of prehistoric inland Brittany, ever existed, the antiquity of Huelgoat cannot be questioned. Until 1987, indeed, this was a staggering, almost impossible landscape, of trees, giant boulders and waterfalls tangled together in primeval chaos. Just how fragile it really was, just how miraculous had been its long survival, was demonstrated by the hurricane of that October, which smashed it to smithereens in the space of fifteen minutes.

After several years of cleaning up, the forest has now returned to a fairly close approximation of its former glories. You might be a little puzzled by some of the hyperbolic descriptions that survive from the old days in the local tourist literature and other sources, but it is (once again) possible to walk for several kilometres along the various paths that lead into the depths of the woods, and in spring and autumn in particular Huelgoat deserves a substantial detour.

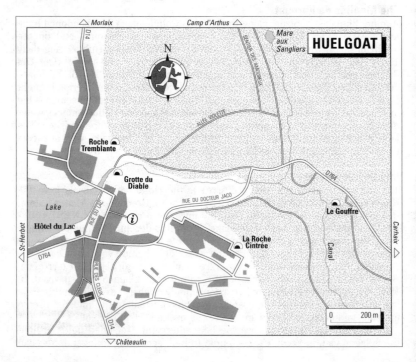

Granite being less delicate than timber, the strange rock formations of Huelgoat have survived better than the trees, and a half-hour stroll in the area close to the village enables you to scramble over, among, and even under a number of inconceivably large specimens. At the **Grotte du Diable**, you can make a somewhat perilous descent, between the rocks, to a subterranean stream. The local story is that a Revolutionary soldier, fleeing from the *Chouans* (see p.214), hid in the cave, lighting a fire to keep warm; when his pursuers saw him by the red glow, brandishing a pitchfork to defend himself, they thought they'd found the Devil. In summer, a "teahouse" and *crêperie* (☎02.98.99.93.00) serves snacks to walkers, a few metres from the disappointingly stable **Roche Tremblante**.

Further into the forest, beside the waterfall known as the **Mare aux Sangliers**, a solitary pine tree used to cling to a massive boulder, its exposed roots wrapped around the stone like tentacles. The hurricane brought it and all its neighbours down. New growth has now replaced it, but it's no longer such a compelling sight.

The **Camp d'Arthus** has been identified as a Gallo-Roman *oppidum*, or hillfort, large enough to be a settlement for a whole community rather than just a military encampment. Until the hurricane, it was also the spitting image of Astérix the Gaul's fictional village. It's now barely recognizable, although the obliteration of the tree cover enabled archeologists to get a clearer view of its history.

Practicalities

The village of **HUELGOAT** is still quite a pleasant overnight stop, next to its own small **lake** (on which they hold aquatic Citroën 2CV championships each July – and have the photographs to prove it).

The local **tourist office**, attached to the Hôtel de Ville, tucked in behind the central place Aristide-Briand (July & Aug daily 10am–12.30pm & 1.30–6pm; Sept–June Tues–Fri 2–5.30pm, Sat 10am–noon & 2–5.30pm; ☎02.98.99.72.32), supplies walking maps of the forest. One or two of the village's **hotels** were too hard hit by the post-hurricane decline in tourism to survive, but the *Hôtel du Lac*, beside the lake at 12 rue du Général-de-Gaulle (☎02.98.99.71.14; closed mid-Nov to mid-Dec; ③), is still there, offering well-refurbished **rooms** and good food. Also beside the lake, on the road towards Brest, the *Camping du Lac* (mid-June to mid-Sept; ☎02.98.99.78.80) is complete with swimming pool. **Bikes** are rented out at the garage at 1 rue du Lac.

Le Gouffre

A walk out from Huelgoat that avoids the heart of the forest is along the **canal** to the east. This stretch – not linked to any of the main Nantes–Brest waterways – was originally built to serve the old lead and silver mines, worked here from Roman times right up to this century. **LE GOUFFRE** is close by (at the junction where the road out from Huelgoat joins the D769 between Morlaix and Carhaix), worth the walk for its deep cave and, more so, for an exceptionally good (and cheap) *Routiers* **restaurant**.

Back to the canal

Although between Carhaix and Pontivy the **Nantes–Brest canal** is limited to canoeists, it's worth some effort to follow on land, particularly for the scenery along the middle stretch from Gouarec to Mur-de-Bretagne. At the centre trails the artificial **Lac de Guerlédan**, backed to the south by the **Forêt de Quénécan**.

Approaching by road, the canal path is easiest joined at Gouarec, covered by the five daily buses between Carhaix and Loudéac. En route, you pass the rather subdued (and unmemorable) **ROSTRENEN**, whose old facades are given a little life at the Tuesday market.

Gouarec

At **GOUAREC** the River Blavet and the canal meet in a confusing swirl of water that shoots off, edged by footpaths, in the most unlikely directions. The old schist houses of the town are barely disturbed by traffic or development, nor are there great numbers of tourists.

For a comfortable overnight stop, the two-star **hotel**, *du Blavet* (☎02.96.24.90.03; ②), is in an ideal waterside position; its restaurant is principally aimed at gourmets prepared to spend several hundred francs on a single bottle of wine, but they're quite happy to serve you with the same excellent food, such as a tasty leek flan or a fish terrine, on their cheapest menu (weekdays only; 89F) with no wine. The 160F menu features a *millefeuille* of *langoustines*.

There's also a well-positioned municipal **campsite**, the *Tost Aven* (April–Sept; ☎02.96.24.85.42), next to the canal and away from the main road.

Lac Guerlédan

For the 15km between Gouarec and Mur-de-Bretagne, the **N164** skirts the edge of the **Forêt de Quénécan**, within which is the series of artificial lakes created when the Barrage of Guerlédan was completed in 1928. Though the forest itself suffered severe damage in the hurricane, this remains a beautiful stretch of river, a little overpopular with British camper-caravanners, but peaceful enough nonetheless.

The best bases to stay are just off the road, past the villages of **ST-GELVEN** and **Caurel**. At the former, the ravishing *Hôtellerie de l'Abbaye Bon-Repos* (☎02.96.24.98.38; closed Tues pm & Wed in low season; ③) is an absolutely irresistible, amazingly inexpensive **hotel-restaurant**, nestling beside the water at the end of a venerable avenue of ancient trees, and housed in the intact outbuildings of a twelfth-century Cistercian abbey destroyed during the French Revolution. Porthole-like windows pierce the thick slate walls of its five cosy guest rooms, to look out across extensive riverfront grounds to the dramatic wooded slopes beyond. Even if you don't stay, it's worth pausing for a meal in the gorgeous medieval dining room, where menus start at 85F and a five-course seafood banquet costs 180F. A little further down the lane, a tiny stone bridge crosses the canal, and the towpath squeezes alongside meadows that are popular with picnickers.

From just before Caurel, the brief loop of the D111 leads to tiny sandy beaches – a bit too tiny in season – with **campsites** *Les Pins* (☎02.96.28.52.22) and *Les Pommiers* (☎02.96.28.52.35). At the spot known, justifiably, as **BEAU RIVAGE** is a complex containing a campsite, hotel, restaurant, snack bar and 140-seat glass-topped cruise boat.

Mur-de-Bretagne and Loudéac

MUR-DE-BRETAGNE, set back from the eastern end of the lake, is a lively place with a wide and colourful pedestrianized zone around its church. It's the nearest town to the barrage – just 2km distant – and has a **campsite**, the *Rond-Point du Lac* (mid-June to mid-Sept; ☎02.96.26.01.90), with facilities for windsurfing and horse-riding. There's also a pretty little **youth hostel**, a short way further along the N164 at **ST-GUEN** (April–Oct; ☎02.96.28.54.34; 49F) – take the Loudéac bus and get off at *Bourg de St-Guen*.

LOUDÉAC, useful for changing buses, is in itself unmemorable. Travelling on from Mur-de-Bretagne under your own steam, you'd do better to take the D767 instead and follow the River Blavet south.

The central canal

Beyond the barrage of Guerlédan, the historic town of **Pontivy** is the central junction of the Nantes–Brest canal, where the course of the canal breaks off once more from the Blavet and you can again take **barges** – all the way to the Loire.

Pontivy

PONTIVY owes much of its appearance, and its size, to the canal. When the waterway opened, the small medieval centre was expanded, redesigned and given broad avenues to fit its new role. It was even renamed Napoléonville for a time, in honour of the instigator of its new prosperity.

These days it is a bright market town, its twisting old streets contrasting with the stately riverside promenades. At the north end of the town, occupying a commanding hillside site, is the **Château de Rohan**, built by the lord of Josselin in the fifteenth century (June–Sept daily 10.30am–7pm; Oct–May Wed–Sun 10am–noon & 2–6pm; 20F). Used in summer for low-key cultural events and temporary exhibitions, the castle still belongs to the Josselin family, who are slowly restoring it. At the moment, one impressive facade, complete with deep moat and two forbidding towers, looks out over the river – behind that, the structure rather peters out.

Practicalities

Pontivy's helpful **tourist office** is just below the castle, in a former leprosy hospital on place de Gaulle (☎02.97.25.04.10). If you're looking for a place to stop over, the town also holds several **hotels**, among them the low-priced *Robic*, 2 rue Jean-Jaurès (☎02.97.25.11.80; closed Sun pm in winter; ②), which has a good restaurant with menus from 55F, and the smarter *Porhoët*, near the tourist office at 41 rue du Général-de-Gaulle (☎02.97.25.34.88; ③). In addition, the local **youth hostel**, 2km from the gare SNCF on the Île des Recollets (☎02.97.25.58.27; 49F), has undergone a long-overdue renovation, and is looking great.

Rohan and Bréhan

Immediately beyond Pontivy, the **course of the canal** veers north for a while, away from the Blavet. As it curves back, the stretch from St-Maudan to Rohan is wide and smooth-flowing, with picnic and play areas but without a road or towpath you can follow for any distance.

ROHAN looks prominent on the map but it's little more than a strip of houses by the canalside. To the northeast, the attractive village of **LA CHÈZE** has a tiny and private lake, with an equally diminutive **campsite**, *La Rivière* (mid-June to mid-Sept; ☎02.96.26.70.99). **LA TRINITÉ PORHOËT**, beyond, also has a **camp-site**, *St-Yves* (mid-June to mid-Sept; ☎02.97.93.92.00), on the long wooded slopes of the valley of the Ninian – otherwise scattered with stone farms and manor houses.

Southeast from Rohan, continuing along the canal towards Josselin, is the Cistercian **Abbaie de Timadeuc**, founded as recently as 1841. You can enter only to attend Mass, but it's beautiful anyway from the outside, with its front walls and main gate covered in flowers at the end of an avenue of old pines. The abbey also provides an excuse to stay at **BRÉHAN**, a couple of kilometres away – a quiet little village whose central **hotel**, the *Cremaillère* (☎02.97.38.80.93; ①), is among the best value in the province, with daily set menus at 50F and 65F.

West from Pontivy: along the Blavet

If you choose to follow the **River Blavet** west from Pontivy towards Lorient – rather than the canal – take the time to go by the smaller roads along the valley itself. The Blavet connects the canal with the sea, and once linked Lorient to the other two great ports of Brittany, Brest and Nantes.

Quistinic

The D159 to **QUISTINIC** passes through lush green countryside, its hedgerows full of flowers, where by June there's already been one harvest and grass is growing up around the fresh haystacks. The ivy-clad church of **St-Mathurin** in Quistinic is the scene of a *pardon* (in the second week of May) that dates from Roman times. The devotion to the saint is strongly evident on the village's war memorial, too – his name is that of almost half the victims.

You can **camp** on the edge of Quistinic, near the river at the *Île de Ménazen* (mid-June to mid-Sept; ☎02.97.39.70.99).

Baud: the Venus de Quinipily

The main reason to go on to **BAUD**, a major road junction just to the east of the river, is to see the **Venus de Quinipily** – signposted off the Hennebont road, 2km out of town. The Venus is a crude statue that at first glance looks Egyptian. Once known as the "Iron Lady", it is of unknown but ancient origin. It stands on, or rather nestles its ample buttocks against, a high plinth above a kind of sarcophagus, commanding the valley in the gardens of what was once a château. Behind its stiff pose and dress, the statue has an odd informality, a half-smile on the impassive face. It used to be the object of "impure rites" and was at least twice thrown into the Blavet by Christian authorities, only to be fished out by locals eager to reindulge. It may itself have been in some way "improper" before it was recarved, perhaps literally "dressed", some time in the eighteenth century.

The **gardens** around the statue, despite being next to a dry and dusty quarry, are luxuriantly fertile. To visit, you pay a small fee to a woman at the gatehouse, who matter-of-factly maintains that "pagans" still come to worship.

Meals in the wood-panelled dining room of the *Relais de la Forêt* (☎02.97.51.01.77; ②), opposite the town hall in Baud, start at 75F, and there are rooms to suit all price ranges. A a pricier *logis* stands nearby, the *Auberge du Cheval Blanc*, at 16 rue de Pontivy (☎02.97.51.00.85; ②).

Camors and Locminé

CAMORS, just south of Baud, has a smart square-towered church, with a weathercock on top and a little megalith set in the wall. The *Hôtel-Restaurant Ar Brug*, at 14 rue Principale opposite the church (☎02.97.39.20.10; ②), possesses an excellent restaurant (and one that doesn't scrimp on the portions), and the **campsite** *du Petit Bois* (mid-June to mid-Sept; ☎02.97.39.18.36) stands at one end of the series of forests that grow bleaker and harsher eastward to become the Lanvaux Moors.

Heading east from Baud, to rejoin the canal at Josselin, you pass through **LOCMINÉ**, another one of those towns reduced to piping rock music in its lifeless streets on summer afternoons in a desperate attempt to draw visitors. It, too, has a reasonable little hotel, the *Hôtel-Restaurant de Bretagne*, 10 rue Max-Jacob (☎02.97.60.00.44; ②), with a cheap good-value dining room.

Josselin

The three Rapunzel towers of the **Château de Rohan** at **JOSSELIN**, embedded in a vast sheet of stone above the water, constitute the most impressive sight along the Nantes–Brest canal. However, they turn out on close inspection to be no more than a facade. The building behind was built in the last century, the bulk of the original castle having been demolished by Richelieu in 1629 in punishment for Henri de Rohan's leadership of the Huguenots. The Rohan family, still in possession, used to own a third of Brittany, though the present incumbent contents himself with the position of local mayor.

Tours of the pompous apartments of the ducal residence are not very compelling, even if it does contain the table on which the Edict of Nantes was signed in 1598. But the duchess's collection of **dolls**, housed in the **Musée des Poupées**, behind the castle, is something quite special (château open July & Aug daily 10am–6pm; June & Sept daily 2–6pm; Feb–May & Oct to mid-Nov, Wed, Sun & hols 2–6pm; closed mid-Nov to Jan; doll museum same hours, but also open am June & Sept).

The **town** is full of medieval splendours, from the gargoyles of the basilica to the castle ramparts, as well as the half-timbered houses in between. It has a history to match. One of the most famous episodes of late chivalry, the **Battle of the Thirty**, took place nearby in 1351. Rivalry between the French garrison at Josselin and the English at Ploërmel led to a challenge being issued to settle differences in a combat of thirty unmounted knights from each side. The French won, killing the English leader Bemborough. The actual battle-site, marked by a small monument, is now isolated between the two carriageways of the N24 from Josselin to Ploërmel.

More accessible is the basilica of **Notre Dame du Roncier**, built on the spot where in the ninth century a peasant supposedly found a statue of the Virgin under a bramble bush. The statue was burned during the Revolution, but an important *pardon* is held each year on September 8. As ever, the religious procession and open-air services are solemn in the extreme, but there's a lot else going on to keep you entertained.

Practicalities

Josselin's **tourist office** is in a superb old house on the place de la Congrégation, up in town next to the castle entrance (☎02.97.22.36.43).

Just across from the basilica, the *Hôtel de France*, 6 place Notre Dame(☎02.97.22.23.06; closed Sun pm & Mon between Oct and March; ③), is an ivy-covered *logis* which is amazingly quiet considering its central location, where you can choose on the 81F menu between duck in cider or trout with almonds. The *Hôtel du Chateau*, 1 rue du Général-de-Gaulle (☎02.97.22.20.11; closed Feb; ③), is also a treat – it's a lovely medieval building by the river, facing the castle, with a gorgeous antique-filled banqueting hall. There's also a *gîte d'étape* nearby, right below the castle walls, where you can rent **canoes** (☎02.97.22.21.69). The nearest good **campsite** is at Bas de la Lande, half an hour's walk from the castle, south of the river and west of town (May–Sept; ☎02.97.22.22.20).

Much the best **restaurant** in town, a short walk east of the basilica as the road starts to drop towards the river, is the *Frères Blot*, at 9 rue Glatinier (☎02.97.22.22.08; closed Tues pm & Wed); lunch menus start at 80F.

Guéhenno

At **GUÉHENNO**, south of Josselin on the D123, is one of the largest and best of the Breton calvaries. Built in 1550, the figures include the cock that crowed to expose Peter's denials, Mary Magdalene with the shroud, and a recumbent Christ in the crypt. Its appeal is enhanced by the naivety of its amateur restoration. After damage caused by Revolutionary soldiers in 1794 – who amused themselves by playing *boules* with the heads of the statues – all the sculptors approached for the work demanded exorbitant fees, so the parish priest and his assistant decided to undertake the task themselves.

Kerguéhennec Sculpture Park

Another unusual sculptural endeavour, this time contemporary, is taking place at the **Domaine de Kerguéhennec**, which is signposted a short way off the D11 near St Jean-Brévelay. This innovatory **sculpture park** (April–Oct daily except Mon 10am–7pm; with guided tours mid-June to mid-Sept daily 4pm; mid-Sept to mid-June Sat & Sun 4pm; ☎02.97.60.57.78; 25F) is progressively building up a fascinating permanent international collection, under the auspices of the *département* of Morbihan.

Among the first pieces to be installed, back in 1986, were a massive railway sleeper painstakingly stripped down by Giuseppe Penone to reveal the young sapling within; since then the park has become an increasingly compelling stop. Its setting is the lawns, woods and lake of an early eighteenth-century château; studios and indoor workshops in the outbuildings are used by visiting artists.

Lizio

Over to the east, off the D151, the little village of **LIZIO** has also set itself up as a centre for arts and crafts, with ceramic and weaving workshops its speciality. For most of the year, you might pass along its single curving street of stone cottages without seeing a sign of life; on the second Sunday in August, however, it's the scene of a **Festival Artisanal**, featuring street theatre (and pancakes). Various farmers in the nearby countryside, who welcome visitors, are working to recreate traditional skills such as bee keeping and cider-making, and one is even rearing wild boars for food. For details of them all, and an overview of long-lost agricultural techniques and implements, call in at the **Eco-Musée des Vieux**

Métiers, 4km out of Lizio on the D174 towards Ploërmel (daily 10am–noon & 2–7pm).

Lizio has no hotels, but it does have a couple of restaurants. There are also several **gîtes** (information on ☎02.97.74.92.67) in the immediate area, and a municipal **campsite**, *Le Val Jouin* (mid-May to mid-Oct; ☎02.97.74.84.76).

Ploërmel

PLOËRMEL, defeated by Josselin in the fourteenth century, is still not quite a match for its rival. It's not on the canal, although it is on the railway line. Attractions are the artificial **Étang au Duc**, well stocked with fish, 2km to the north, and an interesting array of houses: James II is said to have spent a few days of his exile in one on rue Francs-Bourgeois, while the **Maison des Marmosets** on rue Beaumanoir has some elaborate carvings.

Both the good-value **hotels**, *St-Marc* (☎02.97.74.00.01; ①), near the station, and *Cobh*, 10 rue des Forges (☎02.97.74.00.49; ②), make suitable bases for venturing further away from the canal, up into Paimpont forest.

The Forêt de Paimpont

The **FORÊT DE PAIMPONT** has a definite magic about it. Though now just forty square kilometres in extent, it seems to retain the secrets of a forest once much larger, and everywhere recalls legends of the vanished *Argoat*, the great primeval forest of Brittany. The one French claimant to an Arthurian past that carries any real conviction, it is just as frequently known by its Arthurian name of Brocéliande.

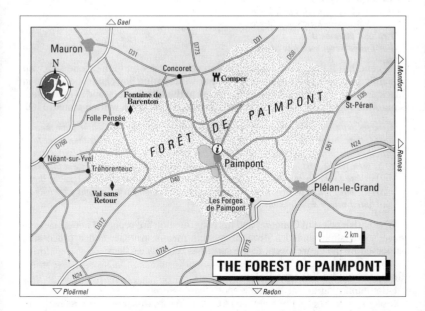

THE FOREST OF PAIMPONT

The Forest and its myths

Medieval Breton minstrels, like their Welsh counterparts, set the tales of King Arthur and the Holy Grail both in *Grande Bretagne* and here in *Petite Bretagne*. The particular significance of Brocéliande was as Merlin's forest – some say that he is still here, in "Merlin's stone", where he was imprisoned by the enchantress Viviane.

The stone is next to the **Fontaine de Barenton**, a lonely spot high in the woods that is far from easy to find. Turn off the main road into the forest from Concoret (a village notable for having once had the Devil as its rector) at La Saudrais, and you will come to the village of Folle Pensée. Go past the few farmhouses, rather than up the hill, and you arrive at a small car park. A footpath leads up to the right, running through pine and gorse. At a junction of forest tracks, continue straight ahead for about 200m, then veer left along an unobvious (and unmarked) path which leads into the woods, turning back to the north to the spring – walled in mossy stone in the roots of a mighty tree, and filled with the most delicious water imaginable.

Chrétien de Troyes sang of the fountain in the early Middle Ages:

> *You will see the spring which bubbles*
> *Though its water is colder than marble.*
> *It is shaded by the most beautiful tree*
> *That Nature ever made,*
> *For its foliage is evergreen*
> *And a basin of iron hangs from it,*
> *By a chain long enough*
> *To reach the spring;*
> *And beside the spring you will find*
> *A slab of stone which you will recognize -*
> *I cannot describe it*
> *For I have never seen one like it.*

Legend has it that, if after drinking, you splash water on to the stone slab, you instantly summon a mighty storm, together with roaring lions and a horseman in black armour. This story dates back at least to the fifth century and is recounted, somewhat sceptically, in Robert Wace's *Romance of the Rose*, written around 1160:

> *Hunters repair (to the fountain) in sultry weather; and drawing water with their horns, they sprinkle the stone for the purposes of having rain, which is then wont to fall, they say, throughout the forest around; but why I know not. There too fairies are to be seen (if the Bretons tell truth), and many other wonders happen. I went thither on purpose to see these marvels. I saw the forest and the land, and I sought for the marvels, but I found none. I went like a fool, and so I came back. I sought after folly, and found myself a fool for my pains.*

The parish priest of Concoret and his congregation are reported nonetheless to have successfully ended a drought by this means in 1835, and a procession endorsed by the church went to the spring as recently as 1925.

Comper and the Val sans Retour

At Barenton, you are at the very spot where Merlin first set eyes on Viviane, although you are not at the Fountain of Eternal Youth, which is hidden somewhere nearby and accessible only to the pure in heart. The enchantress is supposed to have been born at the château at **COMPER**, at the northern edge of the forest near Concoret. Today it serves as the **Centre de l'Imaginaire Arthurien**, which means that each summer it's the venue of different exhibitions and entertainments on Arthurian themes, and also organizes tours of the actual forest. Unless you're sure the theme of this year's temporary exhibition will interest you, don't bother paying to go in – the permanent displays of pointlessly posed mannequins are boring in the extreme (June–Aug daily except Tues 10am–7pm; April, May & Sept daily except Tues & Fri 10am–7pm; 25F).

Viviane's rival, Morgane le Fay, ruled over the **Val sans Retour** (Valley of No Return) on the western edge of the forest. The valley is situated just off the footpath GR37 from Tréhorenteuc to La Guette. Follow the path that leads out from the D141 south of Tréhorenteuc to a steep valley from which exits are barred by thickets of gorse and giant furze on the rocks above. At one point it skirts past an overgrown table of rock, the **Rocher des Faux Amants**, from which the seductress Morgane was wont to entice unwary and faithless youths.

Paimpont Village and other forest bases

PAIMPONT village is the most obvious and enjoyable base for exploring the forest. It's right at the centre of the woods, backs onto a marshy lake whose shores are thick with wild mushrooms (*cêpes*), and has some excellent accommodation. At the **hotel** *Relais de Brocéliande* in town (☎02.99.07.81.07; ②), a real flower-bedecked delight, you can stuff yourself for 120F in the restaurant under the gaze of stuffed animal heads. The food is hearty in the extreme, with menus packed with veal and guinea fowl; the owners raise their own pigs and even their own lobsters.

Information on local walking opportunities – the best megalithic site in the vicinity is undoubtedly the **Site des Pierres Droites**, a stone circle not far to the south – can be picked up from the summer-only **tourist office** next to the lakeside abbey (June–Sept Mon–Fri 10am–1pm & 2.30–6pm; ☎02.99.07.24.83). There are a couple of **campsites** in the heart of the forest, including the municipal one on the edge of the village (May–Sept; ☎02.97.07.89.16), a *gîte d'étape*-cum-*chambre d'hôte* in tiny Trudeau on the D40 (☎02.99.07.81.40; dorm beds 49F, B&B ③), and a lovely **youth hostel**, at Le Choucan-en-Brocéliande, a couple of kilometres out on the Concoret road (April to mid-Oct; ☎02.97.22.76.75; 49F).

Alternative places in which to base yourself include Les Forges and Plélan-le-Grand, at the southern edge of the forest, Mauron at the north, and, further out to the east, Montfort-sur-Meu.

Les Forges

The forges that gave **LES FORGES** its name, and once smelted iron from the surrounding forest, have long since disappeared. Now it's just a rural hamlet, set by a calm lake and disturbed only by the dogs in the hunting kennels. Among the houses coated with red ivy is a *gîte d'étape* (keys held by Mme Farcy; ☎02.97.06.93.46).

Plélan-le-Grand

The tiny village of **PLÉLAN-LE-GRAND**, at the other end of the lake, has an oddly dramatic history. In the ninth century it was the capital of one of Brittany's early kings, Solomon; its appeal presumably lay in its inaccessibity to Norse or other raiders. Later, in the sixteenth century, it was a part of the short-lived independent republic of Thélin, awarded to the local people after they had paid the ransom of their liegelord. And finally, after the Revolution, Plélan served as the headquarters of Puisaye, the Breton _Chouan_ leader.

Don't imagine from that that Plélan is in any sense an attractive place to stay. It does, however, have an affordable **hotel** in the _Bruyères_ (☎02.99.06.81.38; ②), while just outside the village is the _Manoir du Tertre_ (☎02.99.07.81.02; closed Tues & Feb; ④), a very grand old country house, preserved with all its furnishings and operating as a superb hotel-restaurant, with high but not outrageous prices (cheapest dinner menu 125F).

Bellevue and Guer

If you continue south you come to **BELLEVUE-COËTQUIDAN**, dominated by a large military camp; its hotels, full of the anxious relatives of soldiers, aren't the most attractive resting places.

Another 4km or 5km beyond is **GUER**, a gentle little town containing not much more than a rusty ideas box placed in the main square and a heated covered swimming pool. From here, the D776 rolls and tumbles through further woods until it reaches the canal at Malestroit.

Mauron

At the **northern** edge of the forest, the nearest rooms are at **MAURON**. A rambling country town, this has quite a charm – and a reasonable **hotel**, the _Brambily_ (☎02.97.22.61.67; ②), in the town centre. It also has a swimming pool; on the small side, but still more than welcome after a hot day in the forest.

Montfort-sur-Meu

If you've been seduced by the Paimpont forest, **MONTFORT-SUR-MEU**, east of the forest 25km short of Rennes, has an illuminating **Eco-Musée** which serves to provide some background information (Mon–Fri 8.30am–noon & 2–6pm, Sat 10am–noon & 2–6pm, Sun 2–6pm; 20F). Set in the one surviving tower of what in the fourteenth century was a complete walled town, it appears at first the usual small-town museum assortment – costumed dolls and the like. But don't be put off. Upstairs there is a detailed comparison between the forests of Paimpont and Trémelin, proving the shocking fact that the former is artificially planted (and therefore a poor candidate really to be Brocéliande). Of more tangible appeal, there's a remarkable display of the area's quarries – some of which can be seen from the top of the tower – and its stone, exhibited along with modern sculptures exploring their texture or building techniques. The museum also runs workshops, where children are taught traditional crafts with materials such as cow dung, and where sculptors explain their work to casual visitors.

Practicalities

Montfort is on the railway, with a reasonable **hotel**, the _Relais de la Cane_, 2 rue de la Gare (☎02.99.09.00.07; ③), close by the **gare SNCF**. Being only a few minutes away from Rennes by train, it is a possible point from which to set out if you're coming to Paimpont from the north. You can rent **bikes** at the station, as ever.

Malestroit and Rochefort

Should you choose to follow the course of the canal southwest from Josselin, as opposed to making the detour to the Forêt de Paimpont, the next significant town you come to is the small but appealing **Malestroit**. Beyond that, if you are not actually travelling on the canal, which at this stage is the **River Oust**, the D764 on the south bank, or the D147/149 on the north, will keep you parallel for much of its course towards Redon. Along the way there are two worthwhile detours: south of the canal to **Rochefort-en-Terre**, or north to **La Gacilly**.

Malestroit

Not a lot happens in **MALESTROIT**, which was a thousand years old in 1987. But the town is full of unexpected and enjoyable corners. As you come in to the main square, the **place du Bouffay** in front of the church, the houses are covered with unlikely carvings – an anxious bagpipe-playing hare looks over its shoulder at a dragon's head on one beam, while an oblivious sow in a blue buckled belt threads her distaff on another. The **church** itself is decorated with drunkards and acrobats outside, torturing demons and erupting towers within; each night the display is completed by the sullen parade of metal-festooned youth that weaves in and out of the *Vieille Auberge* bar opposite. The only ancient walls without adornment are the ruins of the **Chapelle de la Madeleine**, where one of the many temporary truces of the Hundred Years' War was signed.

Beside the grey canal, the matching grey-slate tiles on the turreted rooftops bulge and dip, while on its central island overgrown houses stand next to the stern walls of an old mill.

Practicalities

If you arrive in Malestroit by barge (this is a good stretch to travel), you'll moor very near the town centre. The helpful local **tourist office** stands on the boulevard du Pont-Neuf, right next to the main bridge over the river (daily 10am–noon & 2–6pm; ☎02.97.75.14.57); they can provide details of **boat rental**.

Nearby on the same road is the **gare routière**, served by buses from Vannes and Rennes, while across the river there's a **campsite**, *La Daufresne* (May–Oct; ☎02.97.75.13.33), down below the bridge in the Impasse d'Abattoir next to the swimming pool, and a **gîte d'étape** up at the canal lock (c/o M Hallier; ☎02.97.75.11.66).

However, what is now the only **hotel** in town is a few hundred metres away on the far side of the old centre. The unexciting *Hôtel St-Michel*, at 1 faubourg St-Michel (☎02.97.75.13.01; ①), is at the start of the D10 towards Serent, immediately as it leaves the main parking area and market square; it has a bar but no restaurant.

The Musée de la Résistance Bretonne

Two kilometres west of Malestroit (and with no bus connection), the village of **ST-MARCEL** hosts a **Musée de la Résistance Bretonne** (mid-June to mid-Sept daily 10am–7pm; mid-Sept to mid-June daily except Tues 10am–noon & 2–6pm; 25F). The museum stands on the site of a June 1944 battle in which the Breton *maquis*, joined by Free French forces parachuted in from England, successfully diverted the local German troops from the main Normandy invasion movements.

The museum's newest buildings house documents and artefacts highlighting the history of the Free French SAS. Its strongest feature, however, remains its presentation of the pressures that made so many French collaborate: the reconstructed street corner overwhelmed by the brooding presence of the occupiers; the big colourful propaganda posters offering work in Germany, announcing executions of *maquis*, equating resistance with aiding US and British big business; and, against these, the low-budget, flimsily printed Resistance pamphlets. All the labelling is in French, which non-speakers may find rather frustrating.

Rochefort-en-Terre

ROCHEFORT-EN-TERRE has a commanding site – the high end of a gorge that is followed by the D774 (and at its end by the connecting D777). Its most imposing face is occupied, predictably enough, by a **château**. Less expected, however, is the castle's appearance. Once the property of the American painter Alfred Klots, it is a jigsaw of a building, knocked together early this century from stone pieces of other local houses. Visits feature startling terrace views and a fairly standard collection of furniture, paintings and tapestries (July & Aug daily 10.30am–6.30pm; June & Sept daily 10.30am–noon & 2–6.30pm; April, May & Oct Sat, Sun & hols 10.30am–noon & 2–6.30pm; 25F).

The rest of the town is a prettified and polished version of Malestroit, something of a tourist trap with little antique shops and expensive restaurants. A curiosity is the Black Virgin in the church of **Notre Dame de Tronchaye**, which was found hidden from Norman invaders in a hollow tree in the twelfth century, and is the object of a pilgrimage on the first Sunday after August 15. More interesting, though, is the **Lac Bleu**, just south of the town, where there are ancient **slate quarries**, whose deep galleries are the home of blind butterflies and long-eared bats.

Practicalities

Unusually for Brittany, there are no hotels in Rochefort-en-Terre, although the **tourist office** (☎02.97.43.33.57 in summer ☎02.97.43.32.81 otherwise) in the main street displays a list of rather expensive *chambres d'hôte* in the neighbourhood, and operates the municipal **campsite**, *Le Moulin Neuf*, in the chemin de Bogeais (April–Sept; ☎02.97.43.37.52).

At the village of **ST-VINCENT-SUR-OUST**, on the D764 10km northwest of Redon, a **youth hostel**, *Ty Kendalc'h* (☎02.99.91.28.55; closed mid-Dec to Jan; 49F), serves as a centre for Breton music and dance.

The Parc de Préhistoire de Bretagne

Two kilometres southeast of Rochefort, outside the small community of Malansac, the very heavily publicized **Parc de Préhistoire de Bretagne** is a theme park aimed overwhelmingly at children (April to mid-Oct daily 10am–6pm; mid-Oct to Nov daily 2–6pm; 50F). Separate landscaped areas contain dioramas of gigantic (if stationary) dinosaurs, and human beings at various stages in their evolution; the story ends shortly after a bunch of deformed but enthusiastic Neanderthals hit on the idea of erecting a few megaliths.

La Gacilly

Fourteen kilometres north of the canal, **LA GACILLY** makes a good base for walking trips in search of megaliths, sleepy villages and countryside. The town itself has prospered recently thanks to the creation of a beauty-products industry based on the abundantly proliferating flowers in the Aff valley. It is, too, a centre for many active craftsworkers; a walk down the old stone steps of the cobbled street that runs parallel to the main road between town centre and river is both a pleasure in itself and an opportunity to look in on their workshops. The only real disappointment is that the riverfront is not accessible to walkers, though you can enjoy views of it from a couple of restaurants, and take two-hour **cruises** on it in summer (July & Aug daily 2.30pm & 4.30pm; ☎02.99.08.21.42; 55F).

Practicalities

Up in the town centre, the *Hôtel de France*, 15 rue Montauban (☎02.99.08.11.15; ②), is an extremely hospitable *logis*, with quiet and comfortable rooms in what used to be the separate *Hôtel du Square* reached through the long gardens at the back, and a good traditional restaurant. The *patron* is happy to provide detailed information on local walks and attractions for his guests.

Alternatively, the luxurious *chambres d'hôte* (☎02.99.70.04.79; ④) in the nearby château de Trégaret in **Sixt-sur-Aff** provide ideal countryside accommodation.

The Megaliths of St-Just

Around 10km east of La Gacilly, in the vicinity of the village of **ST-JUST**, the small windswept **Cojoux** moor is rich in ancient megalithic remains. Only in the last decade or so have they received any great public attention, as a programme of excavations has gradually uncovered all sorts of ancient tombs and sacred sites.

During the summer, you should find posters in local villages giving the times of explanatory Sunday **walking tours** of the various sites, many of them led by the archeologists responsible for the digs. In any case, it's a rewarding area to ramble around yourself; the larger menhirs and so on are signposted along dirt tracks and footpaths, and you'll probably stumble upon a few lesser ones by chance.

Redon

Thirty-four kilometres east of Malestroit, at the junction of the rivers Oust and Vilaine, on the Nantes–Brest canal, linked by rail to Rennes, Vannes and Nantes, and at the intersection of six major roads, **REDON** is not a place it's easy to avoid. And you shouldn't try to, either. A wonderful mess of water and locks – the canal manages to cross the Vilaine at right angles in one of the more complex links – the town has history, charm and life. It's among the best stops along the whole course of the canal.

The city was founded in 832 AD by St Conwoïon at the instigation of Nominoé, the first king of Brittany, and was a place of pilgrimage until the seventeenth century. Its Benedictine abbey is now the focus of the church of **St-Sauveur** – the rounded angles of the dumpy twelfth-century Romanesque lantern tower are unique in Brittany. All but obscured by later roofs and the high choir, the four-storey belfry is best seen from the adjacent cloisters. The later Gothic tower was entirely separated from the main building by a fire in

1780. Every Friday and Saturday from the end of June to the end of July, Redon puts on a large-scale *son et lumière* re-enactment of ten of the earliest years of its history, 835–845 AD.

Inside the church, you will find the tomb of the judge who condemned Gilles de Rais to be hanged in 1440 for satanism and the most infamous orgies. Gilles had fought alongside Joan of Arc, burned for heresy, witchcraft and sorcery in 1431, and in both cases the court procedures were irregular to say the least. Legends of the atrocities of Gilles de Rais served as the source for tales of the monstrous wife-murderer Bluebeard.

Until World War I Redon was the seaport for Rennes. Its industrial docks – or what remains of them – are therefore on the Vilaine, while the canal, even in the very centre of town, is almost totally rural, its towpaths shaded avenues. Ship-owners' homes from the seventeenth and eighteenth centuries can be seen in the port area – walk via quai Jean Bart next to the *bassin* as far as the **Croix des Marins**, returning along quai Duguay-Truin beside the river. A rusted wrought-iron workbridge, equipped with a crane rolling on tracks, still crosses the river, but the main users of the port now are **cruise ships**. These head 40km downstream, past La Roche-Bernard, to the Arzal dam, which is as close as they can get to the sea (see below for details).

Flowers abound throughout Redon, which achieves regular success in regional and national contests for the city with the best floral decorations (*villes fleuries*). In 1983, it won the national first prize. As late as October, swaths of chrysanthemums in autumn tints hang from balconies and the numerous iron bridges.

Arrival and information

A large and sprawling Monday **market** (at which you can buy superb *crêpes*) is centred on the modern *halles*, in the place du Parlement. The **tourist office** is based there too (July & Aug Mon–Sat 9am–7pm, Sun 10am–noon & 4–7pm; Sept–June Mon–Sat 9.30am–12.30pm & 3–6pm; ☎02.99.71.06.04); in summer they have an annexe in the port to serve the needs of what the notices in English call the "Pleasure People". There's a **post office** on rue St-Michel, north of the centre (☎02.99.71.02.30).

Redon's **gare SNCF** (☎02.99.71.74.10) is in the place de la Gare, five minutes' walk west of the town centre. Long-distance buses serve the town – it takes less than an hour to get to Rennes, Nantes or Vannes – also operate from here (details from Redon Transports, on ☎02.99.71.47.33).

Bicycles can be rented from Cycles Gicquel in the place St-Sauveur (☎02.99.71.02.82), and **canoes** and **barges** from the Comptoir Nautique at 2 quai Surcouf (☎02.99.71.46.03); further details of canal-boat rental are given in the "Travel details" at the end of this chapter.

On Thursday afternoons in July and August, **boat trips** run by Vedettes Jaunes (☎02.97.45.02.81; 100F) head downstream, past la Roche-Bernard to the Arzal dam (2hr 30min); passengers then return by coach via Lantierne, le Guerno, Beganne and Rieux (a further 2hr 30min). Tickets can be reserved at the tourist office, which also arranges cruises on summer Fridays as far as Malestroit.

Accommodation and eating

Redon's **hotels** are mostly concentrated in the town and near the gare SNCF rather than in the port area, but it's a small enough place that it makes little difference where you stay. The large white *Hôtel le France* looks down on the canal from 30 rue Duguesclin, at the corner with the quai de Brest (☎02.99.71.06.11; ①); its recently renovated rooms, all with en-suite bathrooms and TVs, offer a considerable degree of comfort for the price, but it lacks a restaurant. Not far from the main square and the tourist office, the *Hôtel Asther*, 14 rue des Douves (☎02.99.71.10.91; ②), has its own brasserie, *le Théâtre*. Nearer the station, the *Hôtel Chandouineau*, at 1 rue Thiers (☎02.99.71.02.04; ⑤), is a luxurious establishment with just seven bedrooms, where the restaurant serves gourmet menus from 95F.

La Bogue, 3 rue des États (☎02.99.71.12.95; closed Sun pm) in place du Parlement, is a friendly and good-value **fish restaurant** where menus start at 85F, while *L'Akene*, 10 rue de Jeu-de-Paume (☎02.99.71.25.15; closed Tues & Wed), is a *crêperie* very close to the port. Redon also has a modern **theatre**, near the main square – the season at Le Canal (☎02.99.71.09.50) runs from September to June.

Châteaubriant

Sixty kilometres east of Redon, and the same distance north of Nantes, the fortified town of **CHÂTEAUBRIANT** guards the border of Brittany and Anjou. While it's not a place to go out of your way to see, and the flat surrounding countryside holds precious little of interest, a couple of hours spent wandering in and around its venerable **château** makes a welcome interruption in a day spent travelling.

The castle walls still encircle the crest of a knoll just east of the town proper, although only the entrance keep (*donjon d'entrée*) remains of the original tenth-century structure. Visitors can simply stroll through that mighty gateway, to find a disparate assembly of buildings of different eras, in similarly assorted states of repair, interspersed with peaceful lawns and formal gardens. The most complete edifice is a self-contained Renaissance château, built from 1521 onwards, and equipped with a sort of secular cloisters. To see some of the apartments inside, join one of the regular **guided tours** (Mon, Tues & Sun 2–7pm, Wed–Sat 10am–noon & 2–7pm).

Practicalities

Châteaubriant's **tourist office** is in the centre of the old town, just north of the church, at 21 rue du Couéré (Mon 2–6pm, Tues–Sat 10am–noon & 2–6pm; ☎02.40.28.20.90). Immediately opposite the château, the *Hôtel au Vieux Château* (☎02.40.81.22.27; ①) has inexpensive rooms and serves pizzas from 35F.

Nantes

NANTES, the former capital of Brittany, is no longer officially part of the province: it was transferred to the Pays de la Loire in 1962 when the modern administrative regions were established. Nonetheless, such bureaucracy is not taken too seriously in the city, and its history is closely bound up with Breton fortunes. A considerable medieval centre, it later achieved great wealth from colonial expeditions, and by the end of the eighteenth century had become the principal port of France. Huge fortunes were made on the "ebony" (slave) trade, which brought in as much as 200 percent profit per ship. However, the abolition of

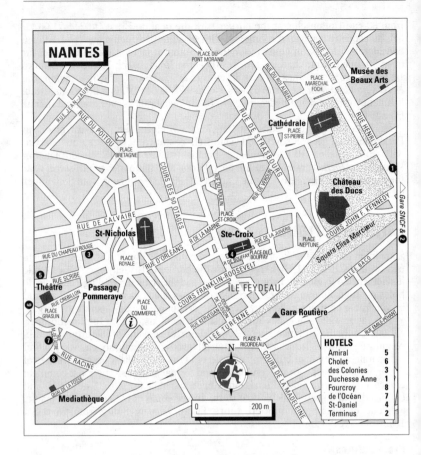

slavery coincided with an increased use of domestic French sugar beet as opposed to Caribbean sugar cane, the port began to silt up as it declined in significance, and heavy industry and wine production became more important.

Despite the tower blocks that mask the Loire and motorways that tear past the city, which mean that Nantes is not now an especially attractive place on first acquaintance, it remains to its inhabitants an integral part of Brittany. Although it's not a place to make a great priority on your travels, if you have the time and energy it holds plenty that is worth seeing – especially the **Château des Ducs** and the **Beaux Arts** museum – while the River Erdre, the vineyards of the Loire and the remarkable Italianate town of **Clisson** are all within reach.

Arrival and information

Nantes's **tourist office** is housed in a shack outside the colonnaded Palais de la Bourse, in place du Commerce (Mon–Fri 9am–7pm, Sat 10am–6pm, Sun

10am–1pm & 1.30–6pm; ☎02.40.47.04.51); the *palais* itself now houses a FNAC book store. The tourist office provides a free book-size guide, including an excellent town map, and runs various guided tours of the city. There's a subsidiary office alongside the château at 1 rue de la Château (Wed–Sun 10am–1pm & 1.30–6pm). The main **post office** is on place Bretagne (☎02.40.12.60.60).

The **gare SNCF** (☎02.40.08.50.50), a little way east of the château, is served by fast trains between Paris and Brittany (three or more TGVs daily reach Paris in as little as 2hr), as well as being the terminus for the local line westwards to St-Nazaire, La Baule and Croisic. The station has two exits; for most facilities (tramway, buses, hotels) use *Accès Nord*.

There are two central **bus** stations. Local buses use the Gare des Bus on cours Franklin, alongside place du Commerce, while the long-distance **gare routière** (☎02.40.47.62.70) is 400m away on allée Baco, near place Ricordeau. Modern rubber-wheeled **trams** run along the old riverfront, past the gare SNCF and the two bus stations. Flat-fare tickets are valid for one hour, rather than just a single journey, though one-day tickets are also available.

Bicycles can be rented from Seguir Bernard, 38 rue des Alouettes (☎02.40.46.56.32), as well as at the gare SNCF.

Accommodation

Although it holds plenty of **hotels** to suit all budgets, Nantes is one of those cities where you won't necessarily stumble upon a suitable place just by walking or driving around at whim. Instead, there are two main concentrations; one, as ever, in the immediate vicinity of the gare SNCF, and one in the narrow streets around the place Graslin. With the exception of the *St-Daniel* (see p.312), surprisingly few are to be found in the older part of town.

Nantes's summer-only **youth hostel**, *La Manu*, is easy to reach, being within 100m of the gare SNCF and also accessible by taking tramway #1 towards Malachère and getting off at stop *Manufacture*. It offers both dorms and individual rooms, using student accommodation in a postmodern former tobacco factory at 2 place de la Manu (July to mid-Sept; ☎02.40.20.57.25; 70F per night).

The nearest **campsite** is the well-managed and tree-shaded *Val du Cens*, 31 bd du Petit-Port (all year; ☎02.40.74.47.94).

Hotels

Hôtel Amiral, 26bis rue Scribe (☎02.40.69.20.21, fax 02.40.73.98.13). Well-maintained little hotel – even if it is above a porn cinema – on lively pedestrianized street just north of place Graslin, and perfect for young night owls. Room rates for Saturday and Sunday nights drop by up to 70F. ④.

Hôtel Duchesse Anne, 3–4 place de la Duchesse Anne (☎02.40.74.30.29, fax 02.40.74.60.20). Large and very grand hotel in a slightly noisy location, alongside the Château du Ducs less than 500m from the gare SNCF, with castle views from the most opulent of its consistently palatial rooms. ④.

Hôtel Cholet, 10 rue Gresset (☎02.40.73.31.04). Quiet, friendly option very close to place Graslin, where all the wide assortment of rooms have en-suite facilities. Rates drop at weekends. ③.

Hôtel des Colonies, 5 rue du Chapeau Rouge (☎02.40.48.79.76, fax 02.40.12.49.25). Neat, good-value little hotel a couple of blocks up from place Graslin, and in walking distance of everything. Discounts on weekends. No restaurant. ③.

Hôtel Fourcroy, 11 rue Fourcroy (☎02.40.44.68.00). Basic and economical rooms in a back-street just below place Graslin, near the Médiathèque. ②.

Hôtel l'Océan, 11 rue Maréchal-de-Lattre-de-Tassigny (☎02.40.69.73.51). A pleasant hotel, with helpful management, just below place Graslin near the Médiathèque. Parking space is available around the back. No restaurant, though there is a restaurant of the same name on the quai de la Fosse a few metres away at the bottom of the street. Closed last two weeks of Dec. ①.

Hôtel St-Daniel, 4 rue du Bouffay (☎02.40.47.41.25, fax 02.51.72.03.99). These simple but pleasant and well-lit rooms, on a cobbled street just off the place du Bouffay in the very heart of the old city, are much in demand in summer. Paying 20F extra gets you a TV in your room. ①.

Hôtel Terminus, 3 allée du Commandant-Charcot (☎02.40.74.24.51). Very near the gare SNCF, on the way towards the château. All rooms have double beds and TV. A reasonable restaurant, so long as you skip the very limited 50F menu and head for those at 80F and upwards. ②.

The City

The **Loire**, the source of Nantes's riches, has dwindled from the centre. As recently as the 1930s the river crossed the city in seven separate channels, but German labour as part of reparations for World War I filled in five of them. What are still called "islands" in the centre are now surrounded and isolated not by water, but by hectic dual carriageways. These thoroughfares are not easy to cross, but they do at least mean that Nantes is separated into a series of readily discernible districts, each of which can be experienced on its own terms.

The main distinction lies between the older medieval city, concentrated around the cathedral and with the château prominent in its southeast corner, and the elegant nineteenth-century town to the west, across the cours de 50-Ôtages (whose name commemorates a bloody incident during the Nazi Occupation in World War II). In a sense, that division has an additional political significance, for Nantes is not solely Breton. As trade along the Loire made the French influence on the city ever more significant, from the end of the eighteenth century onwards the newer area earned the nickname of "little Paris".

Place Royale was first laid out in the 1790s; damaged by bombing in 1943, it has now been restored. **Place Graslin**, with its theatre, dates from the same period; the theatre's Corinthian portico contrasts with the 1895 Art Nouveau of *La Cigale*, embellished with mosaics and mirrors and still a popular brasserie (see p.315).

A spectacular nineteenth-century multi-level indoor shopping centre, the **Passage Pommeraye**, drops down three flights of stairs towards the river on nearby rue Crebillon. The attention to detail lavished upon it by its architects is on a scale undreamed of in modern malls; each of the gas lamps that light the central area is held by an individually crafted marble cherub. While the building itself remains impressive, however, business is not exactly booming, and the place is starting to look run-down.

Many of the streets in the two principal regions of the city have been semi-pedestrianized, and they abound in pavement cafés, brasseries and shops. Just south of them both is the elongated **Île Feydeau**, a typical victim of the modern "development" of Nantes. Its eighteenth-century houses, seen at their best in rue Kervegan, retain some of their Baroque charm – but the road is bisected by cours Olivier-de-Clisson and the traffic jams of today.

RIVER CRUISES FROM NANTES

To explore the **last section of the Nantes–Brest canal**, you can take a river cruise from the **gare fluviale**, on quai de la Motte-Rouge a little way north of central Nantes. These cruises run up the **Erdre** as far as the point where it is joined by the canal coming from Redon. They thrive mainly because the Loire is not at present navigable by this sort of boat (although there are plans to change that), but the Erdre is itself beautiful and wide, with a fine selection of châteaux alongs its banks, chief among them **La Gascherie**. Boats operate between April and November, on weekends only in low season but with much greater frequency in midsummer. Typically, the choice is between a simple cruise (1hr 45min) costing a little over 50F, and setting off at around 3pm, or a three-hour trip on a floating restaurant for lunch (noon) or dinner (8pm), for something in the region of 250F. The tourist office in town is bursting with brochures and leaflets from rival companies, the best known of which is Bateaux Nantais (☎02.40.14.51.14), who also operate similar trips southwards along the **Sèvre**.

The Château des Ducs

Though no longer on the waterfront, and subjected to a certain amount of damage over the centuries, the **Château des Ducs** still preserves the form in which it was built by two of the last rulers of independent Brittany, François II, and his daughter Duchess Anne, born here in 1477. The list of famous people who have been guests or prisoners, defenders or belligerents, of the castle is impressive. It includes Gilles de Rais (Bluebeard), publicly executed in 1440; Machiavelli, a member of a Florentine delegation in 1498; John Knox as a galley slave in 1547–49; and Bonnie Prince Charlie preparing for Culloden in 1745. The most significant act in the castle, from the point of view of European history, was the signing of the **Edict of Nantes** in 1598 by Henri IV (who is said to have exclaimed, on first sight of the castle, "God's teeth, these Dukes of Brittany were no small beer"). The edict ended the Wars of Religion by granting a certain degree of toleration to the Protestants, but had far more crucial consequences when it was revoked, by Louis XIV in 1685. To their credit the people of Nantes took no part in the subsequent general massacres of the Huguenots.

The stout ramparts of the château remain pretty much intact, and most of the encircling moat is filled with water, surrounded by well-tended lawns that make a popular spot for lunchtime picnics. Within the walls stand a rather incongruous potpourri of buildings added in differing styles over the years. Until recently, these housed a number of museums, but all are currently closed while their contents are rationalized into one much larger mega-museum, which is unlikely to open much before 2005. Until then, visits will probably continue to consist of a brief walk into the courtyard and up onto the walls (July & Aug daily 10am–noon & 2–6pm; Sept–June daily except Tues same hours; 10F).

The Cathedral

In 1800 the Spaniards Tower, the castle's arsenal, exploded, shattering the stained glass of the fifteenth-century **Cathédrale de St-Pierre-et-St-Paul** over 200m away. This was just one of many disasters that have befallen the church. It was used as a barn during the Revolution; bombed during World War II; and damaged by a fire in 1971, just when things seemed sorted out again.

Restored and finally reopened, the building is made to seem especially light and soaring by the clean white stone. It contains the tomb of François II and his wife, Margaret, the parents of Duchess Anne – with somewhat grating symbols of Power, Strength and Justice for him and Fidelity, Prudence and Temperance for her. This imposing monument is illuminated by a superb modern stained-glass window devoted to Breton and Nantais saints.

The Mur des Cheminées

Five centuries of Nantais history can be seen written in stone, brick and mortar on the **Mur des Cheminées**, just off the place du Bouffay in the centre of the old city, where bomb damage during the war left exposed the huge wall of a venerable and much-reconstructed town house. Successive layers of masonry show the development of the building since it was erected in 1453; a fascinating diagram of this living cross-section illustrates exactly which pieces belong to which era.

The Museums

The **Musée des Beaux Arts**, east of the cathedral on rue Clémenceau, has a respectable collection of paintings displayed in excellent modern galleries, and plays host to a high standard of temporary exhibitions (Mon, Wed, Thurs & Sat 10am–6pm, Fri 10am–9pm, Sun 11am–6pm; 30F). Not all its Renaissance and contemporary works are on display at any one time, but you should be able to take in canvases ranging from a gorgeous *David Triumphant* by Delaunay to Chagall's *Le Cheval Rouge* and Monet's *Nymphéas*.

On rue Voltaire, west of place Graslin, the **Musée d'Histoire Naturelle** at no. 12 (Tues–Sat 10am–noon & 2–5pm, Sun 2–5pm; 30F) centres on a vivarium, whose miserable animals are not for the squeamish (the soft-shelled turtle in particular tugs at the heartstrings). But don't let this put you off the eccentric assortment of oddities of its museum collection: rhinoceros toenails, a coelacanth and an aepyornis egg, and slightly tatty stuffed specimens of virtually every bird and animal imaginable. There is an Egyptian mummy, too, as well as a shrunken Maori head and a complete tanned human skin – taken in 1793 from the body of a soldier whose dying wish was to be made into a drum.

Also in rue Voltaire you'll find the **Palais Dobrée** (daily except Mon 10am–noon & 1.30–5.30pm; 20F), a nineteenth-century mansion given over to two museums, one of which claims to feature Duchess Anne's heart in a box.

The **Musée Jules-Vernes**, on Île Feydeau at 3 rue de l'Hermitage (Mon & Wed–Sat 10am–noon & 2–5pm, Sun 2–5pm; 10F), commemorates the birthplace of the first serious writer of science fiction.

If you have time to kill, take the tram to the **Médiathèque** at 24 quai de la Fosse, where you'll find a superb modern library with bookshops and facilities to watch any of an eclectic selection of videos – *Sir Alf Ramsey* and the *Battle of Iwo Jima* side by side (Mon–Fri noon–7pm, Sat 10am–6pm). From there, you can walk along quai de la Fosse to the point where the two remaining branches of the Loire meet up, with a good view of the port.

Eating

Unlike hotels, **restaurants** fill the winding lanes of the old city in abundance. It shouldn't take you long to come up with something once you start wandering the pedestrian streets in the centre. Nantes is a big enough city to have all sorts of ethnic alternatives as well, with lots of Algerian, Italian, Chinese, Vietnamese and Indian places – especially in the rue de la Juiverie – in addition to those listed here.

La Cigale, 4 place Graslin (☎02.51.84.94.94). Famous late nineteenth-century brasserie, offering fine meals in opulent surroundings. Fish is a speciality. Menus 75F and 135F, served until midnight in keeping with the tradition of providing post-performance refreshments for patrons of the adjacent theatre.

Brasserie Côté Rive, 5 square Fleuriot-de-l'Angle (☎02.40.20.35.20). Bright, brisk brasserie a short walk west of the cours des 50-Ôtages and just east of place Royale. All-you-can-eat *moules frites* for 49F, seafood couscous at 82F, and a good fishy menu for 98F. Open daily until after midnight.

Le Carnivore, 7 allée des Tanneurs (☎02.40.47.87.00). The rendezvous of choice for incorrigible meat-eaters, offering not just the steaks you might expect, but even rarefied pleasures such as ostrich and buffalo. Menus start at 65F.

La Mangeoire, 16 rue des Petites-Écuries (☎02.40.48.70.83). Very good country food. The 58F lunch menu in particular is a real bargain, there's a solid 82F dinner menu, and the "Gourmet" for 142F is a delight; even if you can't stomach the dozen snails, there's a mixed fish grill to sate any appetite. Closed Sun & Mon.

Le Pescadou, 8 allée Baco (☎02.40.35.29.50). Despite being somewhat off the beaten track, near the gare routière, this is Nantes's most fashionable venue for fresh fish, with menus from 90F. Closed Sat lunch & Sun.

Le Petit Bacchus, 5 rue Beauregard (☎02.40.47.50.46). Red-painted half-timbered house, with the atmosphere and decor of a World War I *estaminet*, just off rue des 50-Ôtages in a little alley leading down to the cours F-Roosevelt. Lovely 80F menu featuring duck *à l'orange* or fish of the day. Closed Sun, plus first three weeks in Aug.

Le Sumo, 4 rue Thurot (☎02.40.48.57.20). Quite a rarity – a Japanese restaurant, just off the place du Commerce within a few metres of the tourist office. Sushi and sashimi menus at 90F, or entire set meals with skewered chicken, beef or salmon, plus soup and salad for around 60F. Closed Sun.

Within reach of Nantes

Immediately **upstream from Nantes** you are into the Loire wine-growing country that produces the two classic dry white wines, Gros-Plant and Muscadet. Any **vineyard** should be happy to give you a *dégustation*. Most operate on a very small scale. The largest, however, the **Chasseloir vineyard** (☎02.40.54.81.15) at **ST-FIACRE-SUR-MAINE**, is perhaps the most interesting. This occupies the grounds of a former château, with fifty acres of vines – some a century old. The vineyard sells mostly within the catering trade, but anyone is welcome to visit their cellars, which are decorated with painted Rabelaisian carvings and candelabras made from vine roots. Like so many of the vineyards in this region, the grapes are now picked and pressed by machines. The old tradition of employing seasonal migrant labour on the harvest is a thing of the past.

Clisson

To the south, at the point where the Sèvre meets the Maine, and the crossroads of the three ancient duchies of Brittany, Anjou and Poitou, is the town of **CLISSON**. This was remodelled by two French architects in the last century into a close approximation of an Italian hill town. The fact that they already had the raw material of a ruined fortress (daily except Tues 9.30am–noon & 2–6pm), a covered market hall and a magnificent situation makes it a sight not to be missed. The best **place to stay** is the *Hôtel de la Gare*, on place de la Gare (☎02.40.36.16.55; ②).

travel details

Trains

No railway line cuts across central Brittany; however, certain towns mentioned in this chapter can be reached by train.

Châteaulin is on the line from Brest to Quimper.

Carhaix is served by 4–6 trains daily from Guingamp (1hr); buses connect with the south coast.

Pontivy and **Loudéac** are served by 3–4 trains daily from St-Brieuc (1hr 30min/1hr), again with connecting buses running south.

Redon is on the main Rennes to Nantes line, and is the junction for trains coming from Brest, Quimper and Vannes.

Nantes connects directly with Paris (10 TGV daily; 2hr 15min), Rennes, Quimper, Brest and the south.

Buses

From Carhaix to Châteaulin (5 daily; 30min), Loudéac (5 daily; 1hr), Quimper (4 daily; 1hr) and Morlaix (hourly; 1hr).

From Vannes to Rennes (8 daily; 2hr) via Josselin (1hr) and St-Jean Brévelay (45min); to Pontivy; and 4 daily to Elven (25min), Malestroit (45min), and Ploërmel (1hr 25min).

Boats

For **general information** *on barges with accommodation, which can be available with bicycles and even caravans on board, contact the* **Comité de Promotion Touristique des Canaux Bretons**, *Office du Tourisme, place du Parlement, 35600 Rennes (☎02.99.71.06.04). Barges can also be rented from the following places:*

Les Bateaux de l'Aulne, Châteaulin (☎02.98.86.37.59).

Crabing-Loisirs, M Mercier, 20 rue de Frout, 29000 Quimper (☎02.98.95.14.02) – boats at Pont Coblant, near Pleyben.

Argoat Plaisance, BP41 Port de Plaisance, 29520 Châteauneuf-du-Faou (☎02.98.81.72.11).

Finistère Canal, Pleyben (☎02.98.73.35.20).

Rohan Plaisance, Écluse de Rohan, BP19, 56580 Rohan (☎02.97.38.98.66).

Nicols, route de St-Gouvry, 56580 Rohan (☎02.97.38.90.17).

Au File de l'Eau, Écluse de la Couard, St-Nicolas-des-Eaux, Plumeliau, 56150 Baud (on the Blavet).

Le Ray Loisirs, 14 rue Caradec, 56120 Josselin (☎02.97.75.60.98), and at 44000 Nantes (☎02.40.89.22.42).

Plasmor, M Bourçois, Z A 56460 Serent (☎02.97.75.95.70).

Heron Cruisers, M David Chin, La Daufresne, 56140 Malestroit (☎02.97.75.19.57).

Comptoir Nautique de Redon, 2 Quai Surcouf, 35605 Redon (☎02.99.71.46.03).

Bretagne Plaisance, 12 Quai Jean-Bart, 35600 Redon (☎02.99.72.15.80).

Gîtes Nautiques Bretons, La Cour, 44630 Plesse (☎02.40.51.90.77).

Bretagne Fluvial, Quai Cricklade, 44240 Suce-sur-Erdre (☎02.40.77.79.51).

Le Grand Large, M Bonami, Quai de Versailles, le Pont-Morand, 44000 Nantes (☎02.40.35.44.37), and 254 route de Vannes, 44000 Nantes-Orvault (☎02.40.63.37.87).

CHAPTER SEVEN

THE SOUTH COAST

B rittany's **southern coast** takes in the province's most famous sites and offers its warmest swimming. Not surprisingly, therefore, it's very popular with tourists. Around the **Gulf of Morbihan**, and especially to the south at **La Baule**, you can be hard pushed to find a room in summer – or to escape the crowds.

The whole coast is a succession of wonders, of both natural and human creation. If you have any interest in prehistory, or even if you just enjoy ruins, then the concentration of **megaliths** around the **Morbihan** should prove irresistible. **Carnac**, the most important site, may well be Europe's oldest settlement; the sun has risen more than two million times over its extraordinary and intriguing alignments of menhirs. **Locmariaquer**, too, has a gigantic ancient stone, which some theories hold to be the key to a prehistoric astronomical observatory. The most beautifully sited of all is the great tumulus on **Gavrinis**, one of the fifty or so islets scattered in chaos around the Morbihan's inland sea.

As for more hedonistic pastimes, in theory the best of the south's **beaches** are at La Baule. This, however, is also the one resort in Brittany to be conspicuously affected and overpriced, and almost entirely lacks the character of the rest of the region. Excellent, lower-keyed alternatives can be found all along the south coast: close by La Baule at **Le Croisic** and **Piriac-sur-mer**; at the megalith centres of Carnac and Locmariaquer; at **Quiberon**; and out on the **islands** of **Groix** and **Belle-Île**. The largest Breton island, Belle-Île is a perfect microcosm of the province – a beautiful place with grand countryside and a couple of lively towns.

The south coast is also host to Brittany's most compelling **festival**, the ten-day **Inter-Celtic** gathering at Lorient in August. The same month sees a **jazz festival** at the main Morbihan town, **Vannes**.

ACCOMMODATION PRICE CODES

All **hotel prices** in this book have been coded using the symbols below. The price shown is for the least expensive double room in high season, which for category ① often means a room without shower, bath and toilet. Most hotels in that category have other rooms with en-suite facilities, which typically cost 30–50F extra.

For a full explanation see p.30.

① Under 160F	③ 220–300F	⑤ 400–500F	⑦ 600–700F
② 160–220F	④ 300–400F	⑥ 500–600F	⑧ 700F and over

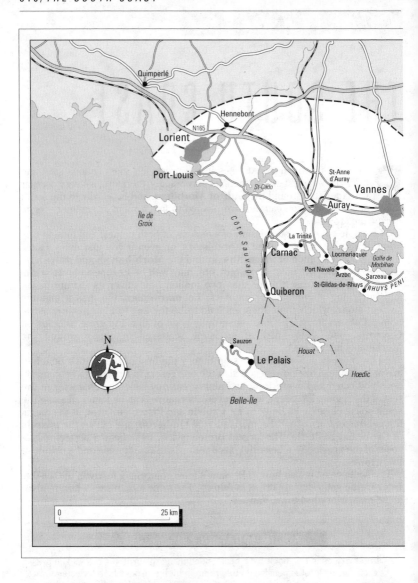

Lorient and its estuary

LORIENT, the fourth largest city in Brittany, is an immense natural harbour – protected from the ocean by the **Île de Groix** and strategically located at the junction of the rivers Scorff, Ter and Blavet. Though still the second most important fishing port in France, it's now a functional, rather depressing

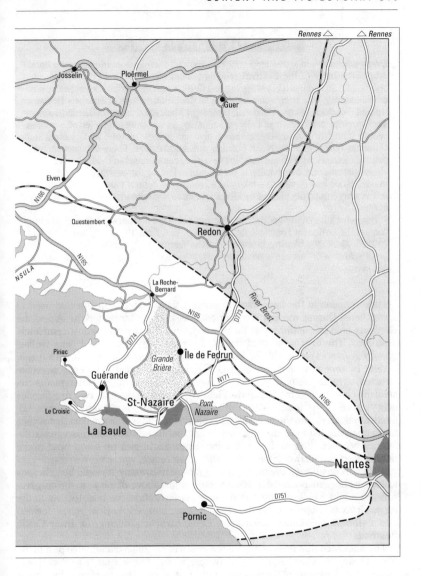

place. Once, however, it was a key base for French colonialism, founded in the mid-seventeenth century (in what its charter called a "vague, vain, and useless place") for trading operations by the Compagnie des Indes, the French equivalent of the Dutch and English East India Companies. The port's name was originally *L'Orient* ("The East"), and came from a mighty trading vessel, the *Soleil d'Orient*, which was the first ship to be built in its nascent dockyards.

THE INTER-CELTIC FESTIVAL

Every year, Lorient's shortcomings become quite irrelevant alongside the backdrop of the **Inter-Celtic Festival**, held for ten days from the first Friday to the second Sunday in August. This is the biggest Celtic event in Brittany, or anywhere else for that matter, with representation from all the Celtic nations of Europe – Brittany, Ireland, Scotland, Wales, Cornwall, the Isle of Man, Asturias and Galicia. In a genuine, popular celebration of cultural solidarity, as many as a quarter of a million people come to 150 different shows, five languages mingle, and Scotch and Guinness flow with French and Spanish wines and ciders. There is a certain competitive element, with championships in various categories, but the feeling of mutual enthusiasm and conviviality is paramount. Most of the activities – embracing music, dance and literature – take place around the central place Jules-Ferry, and this is where most people end up sleeping, too, as accommodation is pushed to the limit.

For schedules of the festival, and further details of temporary accommodation, contact the Office du Tourisme de Pays de Lorient, 2 rue Paul-Bart, 56100 Lorient (☎02.97.21.24.29), bearing in mind that the festival programme is not finalized before May. For certain specific events, you need to reserve tickets well in advance.

Little remains in the town itself to suggest the plundered wealth that used to arrive here. During the last war, Lorient was a major target for the Allies; the Germans held out until May 1945, by which time the city was almost completely destroyed. The only substantial traces to survive were the U-boat pens (subsequently greatly expanded by the French for their nuclear submarines). As a result, Lorient is somewhat reminiscent of Le Havre, in that it had to be entirely reconstructed, as rapidly as possible. Here, however, virtually nothing of interest was created; the church of **Notre Dame de Victoire** is typical of the drab concrete facades everywhere you look. Most of the waterfront is taken up by off-limits naval bases, and the one splash of colour is the little pleasure port that serves to separate the old town from the new – not that there's any very discernible difference between the two. If you imagine things might pick up if you head to the **fishing port**, a couple of kilometres south of the centre, you're very wrong.

All in all, considering the many joys elsewhere in Brittany, it would be ludicrous to suggest Lorient as a holiday destination. For just about all the year, the only reason you might feel it worthwhile to pause here is to take the boat trip out to the Île de Groix (see opposite). Briefly each August, however, Lorient is transformed into a vibrant, pulsating maelstrom of Celtic cavorting, during the **Inter-Celtic Festival**.

The one place that does contain a few relics of Lorient's exploitative past is the **Musée de la Compagnie des Indes**, across the estuary in Port Louis (June–Sept daily except Tues 10am–7pm; Oct & mid-Dec to May daily except Tues 1.30–6pm; closed Nov to mid-Dec; 30F). This is a good 20km by road, though you can get a ferry across from the Embarcadère des Rades, and it is in any case a somewhat dismal temple to imperialism.

Practicalities

Arriving in the main-line **gare SNCF**, you're faced with a 1km or so hike into the centre. Lorient's **tourist office**, beside the pleasure port on the quai de Rohan

(July & Aug Mon–Sat 9am–12.30pm & 2–6pm, Sun 10am–noon & 2–5pm; Sept–June Mon–Sat same hours; ☎02.97.21.07.84), can provide full details on local boat trips, and organizes some excursions itself.

Unless you arrive during the festival, there's a huge choice of **hotels**. Among reasonable, fairly central options are two on rue Lazare-Carnot as it curves away south of the tourist office. All the rooms in the *Victor Hugo Hôtel* at no. 36 (☎02.97.21.16.24; ②) have TV – which, not wishing to labour the point or anything, is something to be thankful for in Lorient – and there's an action-packed 99F menu offering *langoustines*, wild pheasant pâté and duck *à l'orange*, while the *Hôtel d'Arvor*, at no. 104 (☎02.97.21.07.55; ①), also has a good-value restaurant.

If you're desperate to find somewhere at festival time, there are a few more hotels along avenue de la Perrière, the main thoroughfare in the fishing port, such as the *Hôtel-Restaurant Gabriel* at no. 45 (☎02.97.37.60.76; closed Sun Oct–June; ①). Assuming you're not such a cheapskate as to get the hard-boiled egg and the intestine-packed *andouillette* on its 50F menu, sensible dinners here cost 68F and upwards. There's also an appealing (if noisy) year-round **youth hostel**, next to the River Ter at 41 rue Victor-Schoelcher, 3km out on bus line C from the gare SNCF (☎02.97.37.11.65; 70F), which has space for **camping** as well in summer. The *Oeuvres Sociales* hostel at 12 rue Colbert (☎02.97.21.42.80) was especially designed for the **physically handicapped**.

Le Pic, just south of the gare SNCF at 2 bd Maréchal-Franchet-d'Esperey (☎02.97.21.18.29; closed Sat lunchtime & Sun) is an imaginative little **restaurant**, with varied menus from 70F. One of the most congenial **bars** is the *Galway Inn*, near the train station, at 18 rue Belgique (☎02.97.64.50.77) – not that Jimmy the guard dog thinks of himself as particularly congenial. Plenty more bars can be found around place Aristide-Briand.

The Île de Groix

The coast immediately around Lorient is unenticing, plagued with thick drifts of weed, but straight out to sea is the eight-kilometre-long steep-sided rock of the **Île de Groix**, a sort of little sister to Belle-Île that's home to a few thousand nautically minded souls.

The island flourished during the seventeenth and eighteenth centuries with the soaring fortunes of Lorient, and then became a major centre for canning tuna in the nineteenth century. That industry has long since gone into decline, however, and Groix is now mainly of interest to geologists, who come to study its peculiar rock formations, and to birdwatchers. It also holds some appealing pocket beaches along the eroded southern shore, and even a few megaliths.

The boat from Lorient (see below) docks at Port-Tudy, about 500m downhill from the eponymous capital of **GROIX**. **Bicycles** are available for rent at the port – well worth it if you want to get away from the crowds – while the **Eco-Musée**, housed in a former tuna cannery nearby (June–Sept daily 9.30am–12.30pm & 3–7pm; mid-April to May daily 10am–12.30pm & 2–5pm; Oct to mid-April daily except Mon 10am–noon & 2–5pm; 25F), chronicles the island's history since the Bronze Age.

Practicalities

It takes 45 minutes to reach the Île de Groix by **boat** from the south quay of Lorient's new port (Compagnie Morbihannaise et Nantaise de Navigation; 4–8 sailings daily depending on the season; ☎02.97.64.77.64; adults 105F return, under-13s 64F, under-26s 64F on certain sailings only). On summer Saturdays, Vedettes Transrade (☎02.97.33.40.55) run afternoon tours that include a 45-minute stop on the island, departing Lorient at 2pm and Port-Louis at 2.30pm.

All the island's facilities are concentrated in and around Groix itself. In town, there's the **hotel-restaurant** *de la Marine* (☎02.97.86.80.05; closed Sun pm, all Jan, Mon in low season; ③), which serves large fish dinners for 70F and upwards, and the much more basic *Moulin d'Or* (☎02.97.86.82.16; ①). Not far away to the west, next to the sea and a small beach at the Pointe de la Croix, you'll find a summer-only **youth hostel** (April–Oct; ☎02.97.86.81.38; 45F), with a **campsite** alongside (☎02.97.86.53.08).

Hennebont

A few kilometres upstream from Lorient, at the point where the River Blavet first starts to widen into the estuary, is the old walled town of **HENNEBONT**. The fortifications, and especially the main gate, the Porte Broerec'h, are imposing, and walking around the top of the ramparts there are wide views of the river below. What you see of the old city within, however, is entirely residential – an assortment of washing-lines, budgies and garden sheds. All its public buildings were destroyed in the war and now not even a bar (or rented room) is to be found in the former centre.

The one time Hennebont comes alive is at the **Thursday market**, held below the ramparts and through the squares by the church. It's one of the largest in the region, with a heady mix of good fresh food, *crêpes* and Vietnamese delicacies, alongside livestock, flowers, carpets and clothes. On other days, the only places where you'll find any activity are along the **place Maréchal-Foch** (in front of the basilica) and the **quai du Pont-Neuf** beside the river.

Practicalities

If you decide to **stay** in Hennebont – and few people do – the renovated *Hôtel-Restaurant du Centre* at 44 rue du Maréchal-Joffre (☎02.97.36.21.44; ①) is good value, and as near the town centre as its name implies. The *Augerge de Toul-Douar* (☎02.97.36.24.04; closed Feb, plus Sun pm & Mon in low season; ①) – a *logis* which serves good meals from 80F in a grand dining room – takes a bit of finding, on the edge of town nearest Lorient across the river, but is closer to the **gare SNCF**. The **tourist office** is at 9 place Foch (mid-June to mid-Sept Mon–Sat 9am–12.30pm & 2–6.30pm, Sun 10am–noon; mid-Sept to mid-June Mon–Sat 9am–12.30pm & 2–6pm; ☎02.97.36.24.52).

The town's **campsite**, *Camping Municipal de St-Caradec* (June–Sept; ☎02.97.36.20.14), has a prime site on the riverbank opposite the fortifications. You can rent **bicycles** at 5 av de la République and at 87 rue du Maréchal-Joffre, and take **boat trips** either up the Blavet towards the Nantes–Brest canal (see Chapter Six) or out into the estuary around Lorient.

Lochrist

At **LOCHRIST**, just north of Hennebont, the great chimneys of the town's **iron-works** still stand, smokeless and silent, looking down on the Blavet. Strikes and demonstrations failed to prevent the foundry's closure in 1966, and the only work since then has been to convert it into the **Musée Forges d'Hennebont** (June–Sept Mon–Fri 10am–12.30pm & 2–6.30pm, Sat & Sun 2–6pm; Oct–May Mon–Fri 10am–noon & 2–6pm, Sun 2–6pm; 25F), which documents its hundred-year history from the workers' point of view. Some of the men put on the dole contributed their memories and tools; for others turning their workplace into a museum was adding insult to injury. It is in fact excellent, both in content and presentation, though in view of the joyful pictures of successful strikes in the 1930s its very existence seems a sad defeat. If it's on your route it's worth a stop; the bus station is just opposite on the other side of the river.

St-Cado

Fifteen kilometres southeast of Hennebont, or 12km east of Port-Louis, a large bridge spans the broad estuary of the **Etel** River. A short detour north of the village of **Belz** on the eastern shore brings you to the delightful islet of **ST-CADO**, a round speck on the water dotted with perhaps twenty white-painted houses.

From the mainland, you walk across a spindly little bridge to reach the island itself. Its main feature is a **twelfth-century chapel** that stands on the site of a Romanesque predecessor built by St Cado around the sixth century. Cado, who was a prince of "Glamorgant", returned in due course to his native Wales and was martyred, but Welsh pilgrims still make their way to this pretty little spot. As Cado is a patron saint of the deaf, it's said that hearing problems can be cured by lying on his stone "bed" inside the chapel. A little fountain behind the chapel only emerges from the sea at low tide.

Practicalities

There's nowhere to stay on St-Cado, but a couple of **restaurants** catering for day-trippers face it from the quayside on the mainland. *Les Asturies* (☎02.97.55.42.66), which specializes in seafood of all kinds, offers *moules marinières* for 45F.

The Quiberon peninsula

The **Presqu'île de Quiberon** is as close to being an island as any peninsula could conceivably be; the long causeway of sand that links it to the mainland narrows to as little as 50m in places. In the past this was always a strategic military location. The English held the peninsula for eight bloody days in 1746; *chouans* and royalists landed here in 1795 in the hope of destroying the Revolution, only to be sealed in and slaughtered; and part of the defoliation that threatens the dunes today is the result of German fortifications constructed during the last war. The peninsula is now, in the summer, packed with tourists. They come not so much to visit the towns, which, other than **Quiberon** itself, are generally featureless, but to use them as a base for trips out to **Belle-Île** or around the contrasting coastline.

The coast here has two quite distinct characters. The **Côte Sauvage**, facing the Atlantic to the west, is a bleak rocky heathland, lashed by heavy seas. It is the scene of innumerable drownings – the official tourist brochure contains a chilling description of just why it is absolutely impossible for *un imprudent* to swim back to land having once strayed beyond a certain distance. The sheltered eastern side, however, the **Baie de Quiberon**, contains safe sandy beaches, as well as yet another Thalassotherapy Institute.

On to the peninsula

As the D768 curves around the bay outside **PLOUHARNEL**, on its way to the start of the peninsula, you can't fail to notice a reconstructed **Spanish galleon**, standing in something less than 8cm of water. This is an obsessive shell museum and shop, with dioramas, created entirely from shells, of eighteenth-century street scenes in Venice and in China, of Donald Duck and his friends, Sioux Indians and flamenco dancers (daily: Easter–May 10am–noon & 2–6pm; June–Sept 9.30am–noon & 2–7pm; 25F). Across the road and the train line, there's a rather uninspiring **waxwork museum** (Easter to mid-Sept daily 10am–noon & 2–6pm; 25F), which focuses on the Chouan rebellion of 1795.

PORTIVY, tucked into the only real shelter along the Côte Sauvage just beyond the slender neck of the *presqu'île*, is a popular rendezvous point for **surfers** and **windsurfers**. If you want to join them, you can rent boards in Port Haliguen, near Quiberon town, at 16 rue des Corlis (☎02.97.50.25.03). There is a **campsite** just outside Portivy, *Camping de Port Blanc* on the route du Port Blanc (June–Sept; ☎02.97.30.91.30). Others nearby include the *Camping Municipal de Penthièvre* (April–Oct; ☎02.97.52.33.86) and the *Camping Municipal de Kerhostin* (May–Oct; ☎02.97.30.95.25).

Quiberon

The town of **QUIBERON** itself is a lively place, which centres on a miniature golf course surrounded by bars, pizzerias and some surprisingly good clothes and antique shops. The cafés by the long bathing beach are the most enjoyable, along with the old-fashioned *Café du Marché* next to the PTT.

Port-Maria, the fishing harbour and **gare maritime** for the islands of Belle-Île, Houat and Hoëdic, is the most active part of town and has the best concentration of **hotels** and **fish restaurants**. Port-Maria was once famous for its sardines, canned locally, but those days are long gone.

Port-Haliguen, the other port, is on the eastern coast. Today, it is an active marina, with a little commercial fishing. Boats from the islands occasionally shelter here, and use it for embarkation in rough weather. Captain Alfred Dreyfus disembarked here on his return from Devil's Island in 1899.

Arrival and information

Between July and September, the special Tire Bouchon train links Quiberon's **gare SNCF**, which is a short way above the town proper, with Auray. (The name, which means "corkscrew", refers to the bottleneck at the mouth of the peninsula rather than any circuitousness in the route.) There are also buses right to the gare maritime from Vannes (#23 and #24) and Auray (#24) via Carnac.

The **tourist office** at 14 rue de Verdun (July & Aug Mon–Sat 9am–8pm, Sun 9.30am–noon & 3–7pm; Sept–June Mon–Sat 9am–12.30pm & 2–6.30pm; ☎02.97.50.07.84), downhill and left from the gare SNCF, has an illuminated map outside which purports to monitor exactly which hotels are full, hour by hour. The **post office** is on rue Gambetta (☎02.97.50.09.16).

Bicycles can be rented from Cycl'omar, 47 place Hoche (☎02.97.50.26.00), and **horse-riding** can be arranged with the Centre Équestre l'Éperon, 38 rue Jean-Pierre-Callock, in Kerne (☎02.97.50.28.32).

Accommodation

For much the greater part of the year, it's hard to get a room in Quiberon. In July and August, the whole peninsula is packed, while in winter it gets very quiet indeed, with virtually all its facilities closed down. The nicest area in which to stay is along the seafront in Port-Maria, where several good hotel-cum-restaurants face the Belle-Île ferry terminal.

The local **youth hostel** is *Les Filets Bleus*, inland at 45 rue du Roc'h-Priol (May–Sept; ☎02.97.50.15.54; 46F), 1.5km southeast of the gare SNCF. **Campsites** on the sheltered east coast near Quiberon town include the *Do-Mi-Si-La-Mi*, St-Julien (April–Oct; ☎02.97.50.22.52), and *les Joncs du Roch*, rue de l'Aérodrome (Easter–Sept; ☎02.97.50.24.37). The Côte Sauvage has only one site, the *Camping Municipal* in the village of Kerne (July & Aug; ☎02.97.50.05.07).

Hôtel-Restaurant au Bon Accueil, 6 quai de Houat (☎ & fax 02.97.50.07.92). One of the best value of Port-Maria's seafront hotels. The rooms are basic but inexpensive, and the friendly dining room downstairs, with something of the atmosphere and decor of a village bar, serves good fish soup and seafood specialities on menus that start at 76F. Closed Jan. ②.

Hôtel-Restaurant de Kermorvan, 45 rue de Kermorvan (☎02.97.30.44.74). A good fallback in the busier seasons, away from the seafront up near Quiberon's gare SNCF. Reasonable meals, and an attractive garden. April–Oct only. ②.

Le Neptune, 4 quai de Houat (☎02.97.50.09.62, fax 02.97.50.41.44). Alongside *Au Bon Accueil* in Port-Maria, and offering a bit more luxury. Some rooms enjoy seafront balconies, and there are the usual seafood menus ranging from 89F to 195F. Closed Jan, & Mon in low season. ④.

L'Océan, 7 quai de l'Océan (☎02.97.50.07.58, fax 02.97.50.27.81). Seems to have given up the unequal struggle to keep a restaurant going, but still has reasonably priced rooms. Closed Oct–March. ②.

Eating

Once again, the most appealing area in which to go browsing the menus looking for a good **meal** is along the waterfront in Port-Maria, with its line of seafood restaurants competing to attract the ferry passengers. Hotel owners are very insistent on persuading guests to pay for half-board – and at the *Bon Accueil*, for example, that's no great hardship – but there are plenty of alternatives to choose from if you do manage to escape their clutches. To stock up on provisions, try the morning **markets** at Kerhostin on Wednesday, St-Pierre-Quiberon on Thursday and Quiberon on Saturday.

Ancienne Forge, 20 rue Verdun (☎02.97.50.18.64). Set back from the road that leads down to the port from the gare SNCF, with slightly unadventurous but good-value seafood-heavy menus from 82F. Closed Jan, & Wed in low season.

La Belle Époque, 42 rue de Port-Maria (☎02.97.50.17.68). Intimate little place as you come to the seafront in Port-Maria, with an adequate fishy menu at 80F, a better one at 90F, and an excellent one at 140F.

De la Criée, 11 quai de l'Océan (☎02.97.30.53.09). Changing fish specialities served every day, fresh from the morning's catch at the quayside. The 89F menu includes stuffed mussels, and fish smoked on the premises. Closed Jan, Sun pm, & Mon in low season.

Belle-Île

The island of **Belle-Île**, 15km offshore, due south of Quiberon, mirrors Brittany in its make-up. On the landward side it is rich and fertile, interrupted by deep estuaries with tiny ports; facing the ocean, along its own Côte Sauvage, sparse heather-covered cliffs trail rocky crags out into the sea.

You need to be able to cross and re-cross the island to appreciate these contrasts, so some kind of transport is essential – even if you just cross for a day-trip. This is no great problem: bicycles are available in profusion at the island port of **Le Palais**, and if you're happy to pay for the privilege, you can also take a small car over on the ferries.

The island once belonged to the monks of Redon; then to the ambitious Nicholas Fouquet, Louis XIV's minister; later to the English, who in 1761 swapped it for Minorca in an unrepeatable bargain deal. Along the way Belle-Île has seen a fair number of distinguished exiles. The citadel prison at Le Palais closed only in 1961, having numbered among its inmates an astonishing succession of state enemies and revolutionary heroes – including the son of Toussaint L'Ouverture of Haiti, Ben Bella of Algeria, and even, for a brief period after 1848, Karl Marx.

Less involuntarily, such celebrated figures as the painters Monet and Matisse, the writers Flaubert and Proust, and the actress Sarah Bernhardt all spent time on the island.

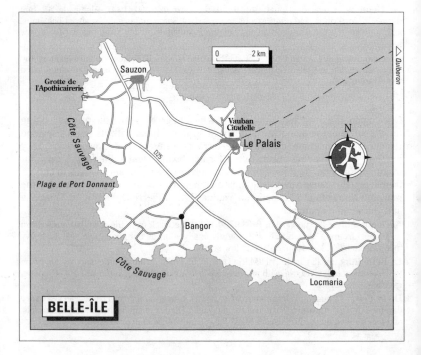

Getting to Belle-Île

Throughout the year, at least five **ferries** each day (up to 7 daily in high summer) sail from Port-Maria, at the southernmost tip of the Quiberon peninsula, to Belle-Île. They are operated by the Compagnie Morbihannaise et Nantaise de Navigation (Le Palais ☎02.97.31.80.01, Port-Maria ☎02.97.50.06.90; adults 105F return, under-13s 64F, under-26s 64F on certain sailings only, small car 404F return); the crossing takes 45 minutes. The usual port of call in Belle-Île is **Le Palais**, but in July and August the same company sends a few boats direct to **Sauzon**, which takes about half an hour, and also runs a limited service between Sauzon and **Lorient** (1hr 30min; Lorient ☎02.97.21.03.97).

Between July and September, and occasionally out of season as well, day-trips to the island, organized by Navix (☎02.97.46.60.00; 165F) set out regularly from Vannes, Port-Navalo and La Trinité, and slightly less frequently from Locmariaquer, Auray and Le Bono.

Le Palais

As you dock at the pleasant little harbour town of **LE PALAIS**, the abrupt star-shaped fortifications of the **Citadelle** are the first thing you see. Built along stylish and ordered lines by the great fortress builder Vauban early in the eighteenth century, it is startling in size – filled with doorways leading to mysterious cellars and underground passages, endless sequences of rooms and dungeons and deserted cells. Though derelict, the structure is quite sound: large signs – "DON'T BE AFRAID" – are scattered about the place, exhorting visitors to explore the abandoned shell. An informative, if over-literary **museum** (daily: July & Aug 9am–7pm; April–June 9am–6pm; Sept & Oct 9.30am–6pm; Nov–March 9.30am–noon & 2–5pm; 20F) documents the island's history, including its entanglement in Dumas's tales of *The Three Musketeers* (which feature an account of the death of Porthos on the island).

Practicalities

The **tourist office** for the whole island is right alongside the gare maritime in Le Palais (July to mid-Sept Mon–Sat 9am–7.30pm, Sun 9am–1pm; mid-Sept to June Mon–Sat 9.30am–6.30pm, Sun 10am–noon; ☎02.97.31.81.93).

Accommodation in Le Palais includes the reasonably priced *Hôtel du Commerce*, place Hôtel-de-Ville (☎02.97.31.81.71; ③), and the simple *Frégate* at the quayside (☎02.97.31.54.16; closed Nov–March; ①). The recently refitted *Hôtel-Restaurant de Bretagne* on quai Macé (☎02.97.31.80.14; ⑤) is a little more expensive and has an excellent sea-view restaurant.

There are also three **campsites**, including the year-round *Camping de l'Océan* (☎02.97.31.83.86), and a wildly oversubscribed **youth hostel** (☎02.97.31.81.33; closed Oct; 49F), a short way out of town along the clifftops from the Citadelle, at Haute-Boulogne.

Sauzon

SAUZON, Belle-Île's second town, is set at the mouth of a long estuary 6km to the west. If you're staying any length of time, and you've got your own transport, it's probably a better place to base yourself.

In addition to a good, inexpensive **hotel** in a magnificent setting, the *du Phare* (☎02.97.31.60.36; closed Nov–Easter; ③) – which insists that guests eat its delicious 85F fish dinners – Sauzon can also offer two **campsites**, *Pen Prad* (April–Sept; ☎02.97.31.64.82) and *La Source* (April–Sept; ☎02.97.31.60.95).

Around the island

The ideal way to explore the island is by walking the coastal footpath that runs on bare soil for the full length of the **Côte Sauvage**. Starting at the **Grand Lighthouse** (summer daily 10.30am–noon & 2–5.30pm), you can see the **Aiguilles de Port-Coton**, where a savage sea foams in the pinnacles of rock, and the delicate beach of **Port-Donnant**, where bathing (despite appearances) is dangerous. At the village of **BANGOR**, nearby, is an incongruous row of huge and very expensive hotels, including the *Castel Clara* (☎02.97.31.84.21; closed mid-Nov to mid-Feb; ⑨), where President Mitterrand was a guest in October 1994. Eventually you come to the **Grotte de l'Apothicairerie**, so called because it was once full of the nests of cormorants, arranged like the jars on a pharmacist's shelves. It's reached by descending a slippery flight of steps cut into the rock: take care, as most years at least one person falls – and drowns – from these stairs.

The **D30 inland** from the cave leads along a miniature tree-lined valley sheltered from the Atlantic winds. If you take the **D25** back towards Le Palais you pass the two **menhirs**, Jean and Jeanne, said to be lovers petrified as punishment for wanting to meet before their marriage. Another (larger) menhir used to lie near these two – it was broken up to help construct the road that separates them.

Houat and Hoëdic

The islands of **Houat** and **Hoëdic** can also be reached by ferry from Quiberon-Port-Maria with the Compagnie Morbihannaise et Nantaise de Navigation (☎02.97.50.06.90; adults 100F return, under-13s 50F). There is at least one sailing every day of the year, except for the first Thursday of each month in winter; the crossing to Houat takes forty minutes, and to Hoëdic another 25. Navix run day-trips to Houat only from Vannes and Port-Navalo on Thursdays in June and Sept, and daily in July and August (☎02.97.46.60.00; 115F).

You can't take your car (not that there would be any point in doing so) to these two very much smaller versions of Belle-Île. Both have a feeling of being left behind by the passing centuries, although the younger fishermen of Houat have revived the island's fortunes by establishing a successful fishing cooperative. There's a story that in the eighteenth century the rector of Hoëdic lost not only his sense of time but also his calendar, and ended up reducing Lent from forty days down to a more manageable three.

Houat, in particular, has excellent **beaches** – as ever on its sheltered (eastern) side – that fill up with campers in the summer.

Practicalities

Camping is not strictly legal on Houat; Hoëdic, on the other hand, has a large municipal **campsite** (☎02.97.30.63.32). There is a small and not particularly cheap **hotel** on each island – on Houat it's the *Hôtel-Restaurant des Îles* (☎02.97.30.68.02; closed Oct–March; ③) and on Hoëdic, *les Cardinaux* (☎02.97.52.37.27; closed Sun in winter; ③). Both accept visitors on a *pension* basis only. It's also possible to rent **gîtes** on Hoëdic – contact ☎02.97.30.68.32.

Carnac

CARNAC is the most important prehistoric site in Europe – in fact this spot is thought to have been continuously inhabited longer than anywhere else in the world. Its **alignments** of two thousand or so menhirs stretch over 4km, with great burial tumuli dotted amid them. The site, in use since at least 5700 BC, long predates Knossos, the Pyramids, Stonehenge or the great Egyptian temples of the same name at Karnak.

The town of Carnac is split into two distinct halves – the popular seaside resort of Carnac-Plage and, further inland, Carnac-Ville near the alignments. It's an amalgam that can verge on the ridiculous, with rows of shops named Supermarché des Druides and the like; but, for all that, Carnac is a relaxed and attractive place, and any commercialization doesn't intrude on the megaliths themselves. Fortunately, the ancient builders had the admirable foresight to construct their monuments well back from the sea.

Arrival and information

The main **tourist office** for Carnac is slightly back from the main beach at 74 av des Druides (July & Aug Mon–Sat 9am–7pm, Sun 3–7pm; Sept–June Mon–Sat 9am–noon & 2–6pm; ☎02.97.52.13.52). An annexe in the place de l'Église in town is open between Easter and September (Tues–Sat 9.30am–12.30pm & 2–6pm). Both provide fully comprehensive maps and details.

Buses to Auray, Quiberon and Vannes stop near the tourist office on avenue des Druides, and on rue St-Cornély in Carnac-Ville. The Tire Bouchon **rail** link with Auray and Quiberon runs between July and September; the nearest station to Carnac is at Plouharnel, 4km northwest. Pick up details from the gare SNCF there (☎02.97.52.11.87), or the SNCF bureau, 74 av des Druides (☎02.97.52.26.70) alongside the main tourist office. In addition, a motorized **Petit Train** chugs around a circuit between the town, the beach, the Archéoscope, La Trinité, and various alignments in summer (June–Sept, every 30min, roughly 10am–6pm; 30F).

Bicycles are available for rent from several of the town's campsites (see p.333), or from Le Randonneur, 20 av des Druides, Carnac-Plage (☎02.97.52.02.55), or Lorcy, 6 rue de Courdiec, Carnac-Ville (☎02.97.52.09.73). The *Grande Metairie* site also arranges tours on **horseback**.

Probably the best way of all to see the alignments is from the **air**, which, if you split the cost three or four ways, can cost not much more than a good meal. The year-round Quiberon Air Club (☎02.97.50.11.05) and the summer-only Thalass Air (☎02.97.30.40.00) both operate short flights over the Morbihan from the Aérodrome de Quiberon, near the tip of the Quiberon peninsula at Roc'h Priol (☎02.97.50.11.05).

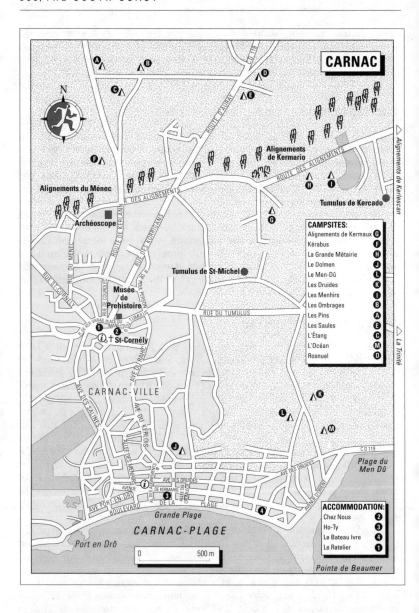

CARNAC

Alignements de Kermario

Alignements du Ménec

Archéoscope

Tumulus de Kercado

Tumulus de St-Michel

Musée de Prehistoire

St-Cornély

RUE DU TUMULUS

CARNAC-VILLE

Plage du Men Dû

Grande Plage

CARNAC-PLAGE

Port en Drô

Pointe de Beaumer

0   500 m

CAMPSITES:	
Alignements de Kermaux	**G**
Kérabus	**F**
La Grande Métairie	**H**
Le Dolmen	**J**
Le Men-Dû	**L**
Les Druides	**K**
Les Menhirs	**I**
Les Ombrages	**B**
Les Pins	**A**
Les Saules	**E**
L'Étang	**C**
L'Océan	**M**
Rosnual	**D**

ACCOMMODATION:	
Chez Nous	**2**
Ho-Ty	**3**
Le Bateau Ivre	**4**
Le Ratelier	**1**

The alignments

All sorts of conjectures have been advanced about the **Carnac megaliths**. One of the oldest stories was that they were Roman soldiers turned to stone as they pursued

Pope Cornély; one of the most recent, is the alleged belief of US soldiers in the last war that they were German anti-tank obstructions. The general consensus today is for a religious significance connected with their use as some sort of astronomical observatory. Professor Thom, whose popular theories have made him the best-known writer on the alignments, sees them – and most of the megaliths of the Morbihan – as part of a unified system for recording such phenomena as the extreme points of the lunar and solar cycles. According to this hypothesis, the Carnac stones provided a grid system – a kind of neolithic graph paper for plotting heavenly movements and hence to determine the siting of other stones (see the further account, together with map, in Contexts).

However, it's hard to see any real consistency in the size or the shape of the stones, or enough regularity in the lines to pinpoint their direction. Local tradition has it that new stones were added to the lines, illuminated by fire, each June. An annual ceremony in which willing participants set up one stone does sound more plausible than a vast programme of slave labour to erect them all at once. In any case, the physical aspect and orientation of the stones may have been subsidiary to their metaphysical significance. It's quite possible that no practical purpose was involved, nor a precise pattern, and that their importance was entirely symbolic.

The way you see them today cannot be said to be authentic. They were used for generations as a source of ready quarried stone, and then surreptitiously removed by farmers attempting to prevent the influx of academics and tourists damaging precious crops. Not only is it impossible to say how many of the stones have disappeared, but those that remain are not necessarily in their original positions – small holes filled with pink concrete at the base of the stones denote that they have been restored or re-erected.

The **menhirs** range in size from mere stumps to five-metre-high blocks; they stand alone, in circles known as cromlechs, or in approximate lines. In addition there are **dolmens**, groups of standing stones roofed with further stones laid across the top, that are generally assumed to be burial chambers. And there are tumuli – most notably the **Tumulus de St-Michel**, near the town centre, a vast artificial mound containing rudimentary graves. You can scramble through subterranean passages and tunnels beneath the mound to view little stone cairns and piles of charred bones; the tunnels are, however, again not authentic, being the recent creation of archeologists.

Taken all together, the stones make up three distinct major alignments, running roughly in the same northeast–southwest direction, but each with a slightly separate orientation. They are the **Alignements de Menec**, "the place of stones" or "place of remembrance", with 1169 stones in eleven rows; the **Alignements de Kermario**, "the place of the dead", with 1029 menhirs in ten rows; and the **Alignements de Kerlescan**, "the place of burning", with 555 menhirs in thirteen lines. All three are sited parallel to the sea alongside the "Route des Alignements", 1km or so to the north of Carnac-Ville.

Seeing the stones

Thanks to increasing numbers of visitors (and despite vehement local opposition), the principal alignments have recently been fenced off – you are no longer free to wander at will among them, as was possible until just a few years ago. The long-term plan is to allow the area to re-vegetate at a natural pace, but there's no predicting how long that process will take, and even when it's complete the chances are that access will still be restricted.

For the moment, a temporary **visitor centre** at the Alignements de Kermario (daily 9am–6pm) sells books and maps of the site, and holds an interesting scale model; a much larger facility is due to be constructed in the near future. The stones themselves are clearly visible on the far side of the fence, though from this (or, indeed almost any) distance they tend to look like no more than stumps in the heather.

The Archéoscope

Alignements de Menec mid-Feb to mid-Nov daily 10am–noon & 2–6.30pm. 45F. Call for the times of English-language performances ☎02.97.52.07.49.

The grandly named **Archéoscope** is presumably intended as some sort of substitute for a close-up inspection of the actual Alignements de Menec across the road. In fact, it's a terribly designed and uncomfortable building, containing a small theatre that puts on overpriced half-hour audiovisual presentations about the megaliths. Some of the effects are quite spectacular, but basically it takes a lot of portentous booming to manage to inform you that no one knows very much about them. Its roof – a vantage point perhaps 4m above ground level – offers inadequate views.

The Museum of Prehistory

10 place de la Chapelle, Carnac-Ville. July & Aug Mon–Fri 10am–6.30pm, Sat & Sun 10am–noon & 2–6.30pm, June & Sept daily except Tues 10am–noon & 2–6pm, Oct–May daily except Tues 10am–noon & 2–5pm. April–Sept 30F, Oct–March 25F.

Carnac's **Musée de Préhistoire** is a disappointingly dry museum of archeology that's likely to leave anyone whose command of French is less than perfect almost completely in the dark as to what all the fuss is about. It traces the history of the area from earliest times, starting with 450,000-year-old chipping tools and leading by way of the Neanderthals to the megalith builders and beyond. As well as authentic physical relics, such as the original "twisted dolmen" of Luffang, with a carving of an octopus-like divinity guaranteed to chill the blood of any devotee of H.P. Lovecraft, there are reproductions and casts of the carvings at Locmariaquer, a scale model of the Alignements de Menec, and diagrams of how the stones may have been moved into place. The captions are exclusively written in an impenetrable academic French, and the exhibits alone tend to be too mundane to hold the interest for long.

The Town and the Beaches

Carnac itself, divided between the original **Carnac-Ville** and the seaside resort of **Carnac-Plage**, is extremely popular and crowded, swarming with holiday-makers in July and August. For most of these, the alignments are, if anything, only a sideshow. But, as a holiday centre, it has its special charm, especially in late spring and early autumn, when it is less crowded – and cheaper. The town and seafront remain well wooded, and the tree-lined avenues and gardens are a delight – the climate is mild enough for the Mediterranean mimosa and ever-green oak to grow alongside the native stone pine and cypress.

Near the Museum of Prehistory (see above), in the centre of Carnac, the **church of St-Cornély** was built in the seventeenth century in honour of the patron saint of horned animals. Archeological discoveries suggest that the custom of bringing diseased cattle to Carnac to be cured, still honoured at least in theory at the saint's *pardon* on the second Sunday in September, dates back as far as the Romans. The Romans also had heated sea-water baths here; today the **Thalassotherapy Centre** is an ultramodern building where, among other things, they treat *maladies de civilisation*.

Carnac's five **beaches** extend for nearly 3km in total, with the largest of them – logically enough, the Grande Plage – running for the full length of the built-up area known as Carnac-Plage. For much of the way it's hidden from view by the slightly raised line of dunes that separates it from the boulevard de la Plage, which is in turn very low-key; the parallel avenue des Druides, a couple of blocks inland, is much busier, with shops and restaurants.

Further west, nearer the yacht club, the small **plage Légenèse** is reputed to be the beach on which the ill-fated *Chouan* Royalists landed in 1795. The two most attractive beaches, usually counted together as one of the five, are **plages Men Dû** and **Beaumer**, which lie to the east towards La Trinité beyond Pointe Churchill.

Accommodation and eating

Hotels in Carnac are at a premium in July and August, when you can expect higher prices and intense pressure to take half-board (*demi-pension*). Carnac-Ville is marginally cheaper than Carnac-Plage, although the distinction is blurred where the two merge.

Hôtel Chez Nous, at 5 place de la Chapelle in **Carnac-Ville** (☎02.97.52.07.28; closed mid-Nov to mid-April; ③), is central and convenient, with a nice garden, but no restaurant; the old stone, ivy-clad *Hôtel le Ratelier*, at 4 chemin de Douët (☎02.97.52.05.04; closed Tues pm, plus Wed Oct–March; ③), has menus from 90F.

In **Carnac-Plage**, the *Hôtel-Restaurant Ho-Ty*, 15 av de Kermario (☎02.97.52.11.12; ②), is the best value. The more expensive *Hôtel Le Bateau Ivre*, 70 bd de la Plage (☎02.97.52.19.55; ⑤), is set in large gardens that were formerly owned by Antoine de St-Exupèry (author of *Le Petit Prince*) and Sydney Churchill, a relative of Sir Winston Churchill. Hence the adjacent headland, at the eastern end of Grande Plage, is called Pointe Churchill, and hence, too, the name of the hotel's restaurant, *Le Churchill*, comfortably alongside a heated swimming pool.

Most of the **restaurants** worth recommending are in hotels, such as the bright and cheerful *Hôtel Lann-Roz* at 36 av de la Poste (☎02.97.52.10.48; closed Jan to mid-Feb; ⑤). *Chez Marie*, facing St-Cornély church in the main town square (☎02.97.52.83.05), is a worthwhile *crêperie*.

There's a **market** in Carnac on Wednesday and Sunday mornings; in the surrounding area, Locmariaquer holds them on Tuesday and Saturday, La Trinité on Tuesday and Friday, and Auray on Monday.

As befits such a family-oriented place, there are as many as seventeen **campsites** in and around Carnac. Among the best are the *Men Dû* (mid-April to Sept; ☎02.97.52.04.23) near the sea, inland from the plage du Men Dû, and the more expensive *Grande Metairie* (April to mid-Sept; ☎02.97.52.24.01), near the Kercado tumulus, with tennis, horse-riding and a swimming pool.

La Trinité

An alternative base to Carnac proper is **LA TRINITÉ**, 3km or 4km along the coast to the east, around the sweep of Beaumer bay. The town itself is uninteresting –

just an upmarket yacht harbour without a proper beach – but has achieved fame as the former home of yachtsman Eric Tabarley, twice winner of the single-handed transatlantic race in 1964 (*Pen Duick I*) and 1976 (*Pen Duick VI*), who was lost at sea off Wales in 1998, and as the birthplace of Jean-Marie Le Pen, founder of the ultra-right National Front. The *Hôtel du Commerce* (☎02.97.55.72.36; closed Oct–March; ②) here is good value.

Locmariaquer

LOCMARIAQUER, easily accessible from Auray or Carnac, stands right at the mouth of the Gulf of Morbihan – its cape separated by only a few hundred metres from the tip of the Rhuys peninsula. On the ocean side, it has a long sandy beach, popular not only with swimmers but also with beachcombers and shellfish-scavengers; on the Gulf side, it has a small tidal port.

Menhirs and dolmens
The **Grand Menhir Brise** at Locmariaquer (daily: June–Sept 10am–6pm; April & May 10am–1pm & 2–6pm; 25F) is supposed to have been the crucial central point of the megalithic observatory of the Morbihan (see Contexts). Before being floored by an earthquake in 1722, it was by far the largest known menhir – 20m high and weighing rather more than a full jumbo jet, at 347 tonnes. It now lies on the ground in four pieces (a possible fifth is missing). Archeologists have established that the stone itself was quarried at Kerdaniel, 4km north, and estimate that the job of moving it required a workforce of between two thousand and four thousand people.

Alongside the Grand Menhir, the **Table des Marchands** is a dolmen which was once exposed but has now been reburied for its protection under a tumulus. You can, however, go inside, along a narrow passage, and stand beneath its huge roof. Carvings overhead seem to depict ploughing, which may well have been a recent innovation when they were made. It has recently been discovered that this roof is part of the same stone as that on the tumulus at Gavrinis and on another local dolmen – the carvings match like a jigsaw. This is another mystery for the archeologists, possibly suggesting that the builders did not revere the stones in themselves, as most theories had previously implied. In addition, the stone at the end of the central chamber was originally erected as a stand-alone menhir, so the "table" must have been built around an earlier monument.

The rest of the megaliths of Locmariaquer are open at all times – open to the weather as well, so watch out for muddy and waterlogged underground passages, and be sure to take a torch if you want to explore them thoroughly. The most interesting are the **Dolmen des Pierres Plates**, at the end of the town beach, with what looks like an octopus divinity deep in its long chamber, and the **Dolmen de Mané-Rethual**, a long covered tunnel leading to a burial chamber capped with a huge rock, reached along a narrow footpath that starts behind the phone boxes next to the Mairie/tourist office. At a third dolmen, the **Mané-Lud**, a horse's skull was found on top of each stone during excavations.

Practicalities
There are a couple of reasonable small **hotels** in Locmariaquer, both with good restaurants. *L'Escale* (☎02.97.57.32.51; closed Oct–March; ③) is right on the waterfront, so you get a great view from its terrace, while the *Lautram* is set

slightly back from the sea, facing the church on place de l'Église
(☎02.97.57.31.32; closed Oct–March; ②).

Campsites include the excellent *La Ferme Fleurie* (mid-Feb to Nov;
☎02.97.57.34.06), 1km towards Kerinis and open all year, and the summer-only
Lann Brick (June to mid-Sept; ☎02.97.57.32.79), 1.5km further on, nearer the
beach.

Boats from Locmariaquer

Boat trips run in all directions, for which tickets are bought in the town centre
or at the port, although the boats themselves leave from further down towards
the narrow straits. As well as trips around the gulf and up the River Auray, there
is an intermittent ferry service to the island of Gavrinis (see p.343), which is more
usually (and more easily) reached from Larmor-Baden. For full details, contact
Navix (☎02.97.57.36.78) or Compagnie des Îles (☎02.97.46.18.19).

In summer, the Vedette Lez-V (daily 10am–7pm; ☎02.97.53.99.25), which carries bikes but not cars, leaves hourly on the hour for the three-kilometre crossing
to Port Navalo on the Rhuys peninsula (see p.345).

Auray

Some people find **AURAY**, with its over-restored ancient quarter, slightly dull –
but it is a lot less crowded than Vannes, a lot cheaper than Quiberon town, and
usefully placed for exploring Carnac, the Quiberon peninsula and the Gulf of
Morbihan.

The natural centre of the town today is the **place de la République**, with its
eighteenth-century Hôtel de Ville. In a neighbouring square, linked to the place
de la République by rue du Lait, is the seventeenth-century **church of St-Gildas**,
with its fine Renaissance porch. A **covered market** adjoins the Hôtel de Ville, but
on Mondays an open-air market fills the surrounding streets with colour – and
stops all traffic for a considerable radius.

However, Auray's showpiece is undoubtedly the ancient quarter of **St-
Goustan**, with its delightful fifteenth- and sixteenth-century houses, albeit
restored. The bend in the River Loch, an early defended site, was a natural setting
for a town – and, with its easy access to the gulf, it soon became one of the busiest
ports of Brittany. Today, as you look at it from the Promenade du Loch on the
opposite bank, with the diminutive seventeenth-century stone bridge still spanning the river, it is not difficult to imagine it in its heyday. In 1776, Benjamin
Franklin landed here on his way to seek the help of Louis XVI in the American
War of Independence; Auray is also said to have been the last place Julius Caesar
reached in his conquest of Gaul.

Practicalities

Auray's **tourist office** is up in town at 20 rue du Lait, very near the Hôtel de Ville
on place de la République (Mon–Sat 9.30am–noon & 2–6pm; ☎02.97.24.09.75). A
small annexe is maintained in July and August at the gare SNCF, twenty minutes'
walk from the centre, from where buses run through the centre of Auray and on
to La Trinité, Carnac and the gare SNCF at Quiberon. If you're making for the
islands, you can pick up comprehensive details at the Îles du Ponant Promotional
Association at 11 place du Joffre.

The most appealing place to **stay** in Auray is down by the port in the St-Goustan quarter, where the *Hôtel du Marin*, 1 place du Rolland (☎02.97.24.14.58; ②), offers simple accommodation over a bar. Up in town, *Hôtel de la Mairie*, place de la Mairie (☎02.97.24.04.65; ②), is also pleasant, and the *Olympic Bar*, 19 rue Clémenceau (☎02.97.24.06.69), is a friendly restaurant-cum-bar with menus at 47F and 75F. There are also a couple of hotels out near the station, including the *Hôtel Terminus*, place de la Gare (☎02.97.24.00.09; ①), which has a snack bar and *crêperie*.

North of Auray

A short way north of Auray's train station – and thus quite a long way out from the town, on the B768 towards Baud – is the imposing and evocative **Abbaye de Chartreuse** (daily 10am–noon & 2–5.30pm). This houses a David d'Angers mausoleum of black and white marble, commemorating the failed *Chouan* landing at Quiberon in 1795 (see p.323), and viewable, bones and all, 10am until noon and 2pm to 5.30pm. For Bretons the event was something more than an attempt at a Royalist restoration, with strong undertones of a struggle for independence. Another gloomy piece of counter-Revolutionary history is recalled by the nearby **Champ des Martyrs**, where 350 of the *chouans* were executed. It's located on the right of the D120, going out of town.

Two kilometres further along the D120, towards Brech, you come to the **Eco-Musée St-Degan** (July to mid-Sept daily 2–6pm; 25F), a group of reconstructed farm buildings, representing local peasant life at the beginning of this century. It's a bit determinedly rustic and charming, but at least it does attempt to escape the glass cases and wax models of most folk museums.

In **BRECH** itself there's a fine parish church with a weather-beaten and faded calvary in its yard; a nice café, *des Bretons*; and a **gîte d'étape** – not a very eventful place to stay, perhaps, but a peaceful one.

Ste-Anne d'Auray

Should you be in the area of Auray around July 26, one of the largest of the Breton *pardons* takes place on that day at **STE-ANNE D'AURAY**. Some 25,000 pilgrims gather for the occasion to hear Mass in the church, mount the *scala sancta* on their knees and buy trinkets and snacks from the street stalls.

The origin of this **pardon**, typical of many, was the discovery in 1623 of a statue of Ste Anne (the mother of Mary) by a local peasant, one Nicolazic. He claimed that the saint directed him to the spot where the statue had been buried for over nine hundred years and instructed him to build a church. Twenty years later, on his deathbed, Nicolazic was still being interrogated by the ecclesiastical authorities as to the truth of his story, but the church had been constructed and had already become a place of pilgrimage. Nicolazic was an illiterate peasant who spoke no French; it is a testimony to his obduracy that his claims were eventually accepted against the opposition of sceptical clergy and nobility. The continuing campaign for his canonization is polarized along similar lines today. Nicolazic's supporters see him as a representative of the downtrodden classes, and as a symbol of Breton independence – the wealthy Church establishment continue to oppose him.

As a major centre for pilgrimage – Pope John Paul II visited as recently as September 1996 – Ste-Anne was chosen as the site for the vast **Monument aux**

Morts erected by public subscription as a memorial to the 250,000 Breton dead of the Great War. One in fourteen of the population died, the highest proportion of losses of any region involved. The monument, a crypt topped by a dome with a granite altar, is surrounded by a wall that must be 200m long, covered with inscriptions to the dead; and yet even that huge and sombre wall does not contain room to list them all by name, often just cataloguing the horrific death tallies of tiny and obscure villages.

A short distance north on the D102 is a **National Necropolis**, with dead from all wars since 1870.

Practicalities

Ste-Anne is a sad and solemn place. The town, away from the spacious promenades for the pilgrims, is small, low and drab; not really a place for a long stay, although there is no particular shortage of **hotels**. Among the best value in the centre are *le Moderne*, 8 rue de Vannes (☎02.97.57.66.55; closed mid-Dec to mid-Jan; ②), which has a good restaurant, and the slightly more expensive *Croix Blanche*, nearby at 25 rue de Vannes (☎02.97.57.64.44, closed mid-Jan to mid-Feb, plus Sun pm & Mon out of season; ②).

Vannes

It was from **VANNES** that the great Breton hero Nominoë set out to unify Brittany at the start of the ninth century; he beat the hell out of the Franks, and pushed the borders past Nantes and Rennes to where they were to remain up until the French Revolution nearly a millennium later. Here too, the Breton *États* assembled in 1532 to ratify the Act of Union with France, in the building known as La Cohue; and here, also, 22 of the Royalists captured at Quiberon (see p.323) were executed in the Jardins de la Garrène in 1795. Parisian soldiers fired the shots because local regiments refused.

Vieux Vannes, the old centre of chaotic streets crammed around the cathedral and enclosed by ramparts and gardens and a tiny stream, is still there, though now bordered by a new administrative centre. In refreshing contrast to the somewhat insane road system around the modern parts of the city, most of the inner area is pedestrianized.

Arrival and information

Vannes's tourist office, which has a well-restored seventeenth-century frontage, is at 1 rue Thiers (July & Aug Mon–Sat 9am–7pm, Sun 10am–1pm & 3–7pm; Sept–June Mon–Sat 9am–noon & 2–6pm; ☎02.97.47.24.34), on the corner of rue du Drézen and rue Thiers and near place Gambetta.

The **gare SNCF** (☎02.97.42.50.50) is 25 minutes' walk north of the town centre. Buses to Auray, Carnac, Quiberon and other destinations leave from the **gare routière** alongside; the one to Nantes, run by Societé Transports Tourisme de l'Ouest (☎02.97.47.29.64), avoids the rail journey via Redon, and allows a stop-over in La Roche-Bernard. **Parking** can be a problem unless you head straight for the west side of the port, south of town. **Mountain bikes** are available for rent from a stand on rue du Féty, just east of place Gambetta near the port (daily 9am–7.30pm; ☎02.97.47.64.88).

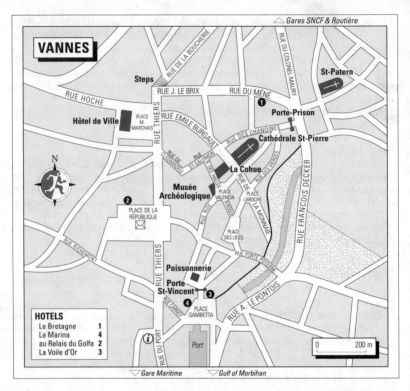

Boats around the gulf are operated from the **gare maritime**, a little way south of the centre on the parc du Golfe, by Navix (☎02.97.46.60.00) and Compagnies des Îles (☎02.97.46.60.00), among others; see p.344. Pick up all the latest brochures and schedules in the tourist office.

Accommodation

In peak season Vannes can become quite claustrophobic, but it still offers a better choice of **hotels** than anywhere else around the Golfe de Morbihan. Much the nicest place to stay, if you can get a room, is **place Gambetta** overlooking the port. This is the one part of Vannes that stays busy well into the evening throughout the year, but the traffic noise is not too bad at all.

Vannes has finally acquired its own **youth hostel**, 4km southeast of the town center in Séné (☎02.97.66.94.25; dorm bed 87F), on bus route #4 from place de la République. The nearest **campsite** is *Camping Conleau* at the far end of avenue du Maréchal-Juin, beyond the Aquarium, and alongside the gulf (April–Sept; ☎02.97.63.13.88).

Hôtel le Bretagne, 36 rue du Méné (☎02.97.47.20.21). Just outside the walls, around the corner from the Porte-Prison. Simple rooms – one is utterly basic, several have showers or bath – above the *Taverne de Maître* brasserie, which specializes in *choucroute* and has a wide assortment of draught lagers. ①–②.

Hôtel le Marina, 4 place Gambetta (☎02.97.47.22.81, fax 02.97.47.00.34). Fourteen pleasantly refurbished rooms, right in the thick of the things by the port, with sea views and bright sun in the morning. Downstairs there's a bar rather than a restaurant. ②.

Hôtel au Relais du Golfe, 10 place du Général-du-Gaulle (☎02.97.47.14.74, fax 02.97.42.52.28). Small cheap rooms, rather crudely converted, above a bar near the post office. ①.

Hôtel-Restaurant la Voile d'Or, 1 place Gambetta (☎02.97.42.71.81). Extremely central, taking up half of the grand crescent at the head of the port, but the actual rooms are neither especially grand nor expensive. Standard menus in the restaurant that spreads out into the square below start at either 105F indoors, or 120F on the terrace, with the usual *soupe de poissons* and *steak-frites*. ②.

The Town

The new town centre of Vannes is **place de la République**; the focus was shifted outside the medieval city in the nineteenth-century craze for urbanization. The grandest of the public buildings here, guarded by a pair of sleek and dignified bronze lions, is the **Hôtel de Ville** at the top of rue Thiers.

By day, however, the cobbled streets of the old city, especially in the area around the cathedral, are the chief source of pleasure, as well as being where most of Vannes's busy commercial life takes place. With their skew-windowed and half-timbered houses – most overhanging and witch-hatted, some tumbling down, some newly propped-up and painted – they amply repay time spent wandering.

Place Henri-IV in particular, with its charming fifteenth- and sixteenth-century gabled houses, is stunning, as are the views from it down the narrow side streets. The ramparts can be followed for quite a length, above what what used to be the moat but now consists for much of the way of neat and colourful flowerbeds. Near the **Poste Poterne**, the "back gate", an old slate-roofed wash house survives.

La Cohue, which fills a block between rue des Halles and place du Cathédrale, is currently the **Musée de Vannes** (June–Sept daily 10am–6pm; Oct–May Mon & Wed–Sat 10am–noon & 2–6pm, Sun 2–6pm; 25F), having served at various times over the past 750 years as High Court and assembly room, prison, Revolutionary tribunal, theatre and marketplace. Upstairs it still houses the collection of what was the local Beaux-Arts museum, while the main gallery downstairs is the venue for different temporary exhibitions.

The **Cathédrale St-Pierre** is a rather forbidding place, with its stern main altar almost imprisoned by four solemn grey pillars. The light, purple through the new stained glass, spears in to illuminate the finger of the Blessed Pierre Rogue, who was guillotined in the main square on March 3, 1796. Opposite this desiccated digit is the black-lidded sarcophagus that marks the current site of the tomb of fifteenth-century Spanish Dominican preacher St Vincent Ferrier (which has meandered around the cathedral for centuries). For a small fee, you can in summer examine the assorted **treasure** in the chapterhouse, which includes a twelfth-century wedding chest, brightly decorated with enigmatic scenes of romantic chivalry.

Housed in the sombre fifteenth-century Château Gaillard on rue Noé, the **Musée Archéologique** is said to have one of the world's finest collections of prehistoric artefacts (July & Aug Mon–Sat 9.30am–6pm; Sept–June Mon–Sat 2–6pm; 20F). But, much like the displays at Carnac, it's all pretty lifeless – some elegant stone axes, more recent Oceanic exhibits by way of context, but nothing very illuminating. Further collections of fossils, shells and stuffed birds, equally traditional in their display, are on show around the corner in the **Hôtel de Roscannec** at 19 rue des Halles (same hours as museum).

There's a bit more life about the city's excellent **fish market**, active in the covered hall on place de la Poissonnerie every morning between Tuesday and Saturday. A general market spreads slightly higher up on the streets towards the cathedral on Wednesday and Saturday.

The huge **Aquarium**, in the parc du Golfe on the right bank of the port from place Gambetta, claims the best collection of tropical fish in Europe, 400-odd electric eels and a crocodile "discovered in the Paris sewers" (daily: June–Aug 9am–7pm; Sept–May 9am–noon & 1.30–6.30pm; 50F).

Eating and nightlife

Dining out in old Vannes can be an expensive experience, whether you eat in the intimate little restaurants along the rue des Halles, or down by the port. If you're just looking for a snack, try the area outside the walls in the northeast, extending from the Porte-Prison towards the gare SNCF.

The leading venues for **live music** are *Le Studio*, on place Bir-Hakeim, which puts on jazz, blues and African bands when they come to town, and *Le Contretemps*, at 22 rue Hoche (☎02.97.42.40.11; closed Sun), which is more a jazz buffs' hangout. During the first week of August, the open-air concerts of the **Vannes Jazz Festival** take place in the Théâtre de Verdure.

Breizh Caffe, 13 rue des Halles (☎02.97.54.37.41). One of the less pricey options on this attractive cobbled street, but every bit as good as its rivals, with a strong emphasis on Breton dishes and ingredients. Weekday lunches for 66F, traditional evening menus from 90F. Closed Sun, & Mon lunchtime in low season.

Le Commodore, 3 rue Pasteur (☎02.97.46.42.62). Unassuming marine-themed local restaurant, tucked away around the back of the post office, which offers plenty of fishy treats on menus that start at little over 50F at lunchtime, more like 70F in the evening. Closed Sun, & Mon lunchtime.

Crêperie La Cave St-Gwenaël, 23 rue St-Gwenaël (☎02.97.47.47.94). Atmospheric, good-value *crêperie* in the cellar of a lovely old house, facing the cathedral. Closed Sun, Mon lunchtime & all Jan.

La Jonquière, 9 rue des Halles (☎02.97.54.08.34). Very central option, part of a popular Brest-based chain with a modern approach and efficient multilingual staff. Despite the road being very narrow, it manages to squeeze a few tables onto the cobbles. For 66F you can take your pick from the buffets of hors d'oeuvres and desserts; set menus start at a little more, with the 138F option offering a full *assiette*, plus, perhaps, pan-fried angler fish with scallops.

Le Lys, 51 rue Maréchal-Leclerc (☎02.97.42.29.30). Gourmet restaurant, a short way east of the walled city. The *nouvelle*-tinged seafood concoctions get progressivly more inventive as the menus rise from 120F, but the portions are never less than reasonable. Closed Sun pm, & Mon in low season.

East of Vannes

Though Gavrinis and the Morbihan islands are the most exciting excursions from Vannes, various sights inland, to the east of the city, can fill a day's round-trip. Vannes's **traffic system** will do its damnedest to prevent you leaving the city in any direction, however, so you can't be too choosy about where you end up.

The Château de Largoët

If you follow the **N166** 10km towards Elven, and then turn off to the left about 4km short, you come to the ruins of the **Château de Largoët**, perched on an eminence in the small forest (July & Aug daily 10.30am–6.30pm; mid-March to June & Sept–Oct Sat & Sun 2–6.30pm; 20F). It's still guarded by its old gatehouse, carved all over with granite bunnies.

The castle consists mainly of two stark towers, inside which the wooden flooring has long since rotted away to leave the shafts open to the sky. The donjon proper is topped by a finger-like watchtower, one of the highest in the country at over 45m, where from 1474 until 1476 the Breton Duke Francis imprisoned the future English king, Henry VII. At that time simply Henry Tudor, Duke of Richmond – a title traditionally awarded to royal bastards or English nobility with Breton connections – he had fled to Brittany after the Battle of Tewkesbury, in which Lancastrian ambitions in the Wars of the Roses were defeated. François welcomed Henry as a guest, then realized his value and held him for ransom.

Under its alternative name of *Elven Towers*, the castle also puts on *son et lumière* costume spectacles of unsurpassed tackiness, combining Henry's drama with the site's spurious claim to Arthurian authenticity as the home of Sir Lancelot of the Lake. The show takes place on Fridays and Saturdays between mid-June and the end of August, starting at 11pm – far too late at night to be much use to most holiday-makers, certainly those with families.

Le Gorvello and Questembert

There's little point going to **ELVEN** itself, though if you've always wondered where René Descartes grew up you can find the answer en route at the manor house of Kerleau. More rewarding is to head south, to the beautiful village of **LE GORVELLO**, at a crossroads with the D7. Bedecked with potted geraniums and huge azaleas, it has at its centre a perfect roadside cross.

Beyond Le Gorvello, the D7 leads on into **QUESTEMBERT**, where the low-roofed wooden market hall from 1675 makes a classy cycle park. Purely as a **hotel**, the ivy-coated *Hôtel du Bretagne* at 13 rue St-Michel (☎02.97.26.11.12; ⑧) is very appealing, with lavish fittings to merit its astronomical room rates. As a **restaurant**, it's a strange place. Chef Georges Paineau is regarded, not least by himself, as one of the finest chefs in France, and prepares unarguably sumptuous menus starting at 180F for lunch and 295F for dinner; specialities include steamed parcels of oysters wrapped in spinach and cabbage stuffed with lobster. However, the air of formality in the oak-panelled and often all-but-empty dining room can be very intimidating – which is especially ludicrous because M Paineau also fancies himself as a painter, and his truly dreadful pop-art acrylics adorn every spare centimetre of wall space.

If you can't take that sort of pressure, the *Hôtel de la Gare* (☎02.97.26.11.47; ②), in rather nondescript surroundings well north of town near the gare SNCF, is a *logis* with a good restaurant.

If you continue east or north from Questembert, you come to the **Nantes–Brest canal** at Malestroit (see p.305) or Redon (see p.307).

The Golfe de Morbihan

By popular tradition, the **Golfe de Morbihan** ("little sea" in Breton) holds 365 scattered islands – one for every day of the year. For centuries, though, the waters have been rising, and the figure now is more like one per week. Of these, some thirty are owned by film stars and the like, while two – the **Île-aux-Moines** and **Île d'Arz** – have regular ferry services and permanent populations, and end up

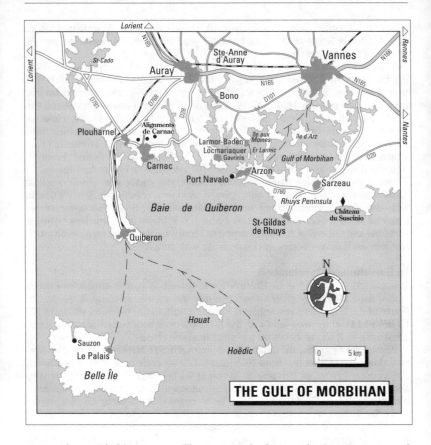

THE GULF OF MORBIHAN

extremely crowded in summer. The rest are the best, and a **boat tour** around them, or at least a trip out to **Gavrinis**, near the mouth of the gulf, is one of the most compelling attractions of southern Brittany.

As the boats thread their way through the baffling muddle of channels you lose track of which is island and which is mainland; and everywhere there are mega-lithic ruins, stone circles disappearing beneath the water and solitary menhirs on small hillocks. At the time when they were built, the sea level is thought to have been around 5m lower than it is today, and the islands may have been mounds amid the marshlands. Flaubert evocatively described Celtic mercenaries far off in Carthage pining for the Morbihan – "*Les Celtes regrettaient trois pierres brutes, sous un ciel plouvieux, dans un golfe remplie d'îlots*" – not that the Celts actually set up the stones in the first place.

Larmor-Baden and Le Bono

Making your own way to Larmor-Baden, the best route is along the main road down the Auray estuary, the D17. This crosses the River Bono on a high bridge;

visible way below it to the left is a beautiful iron bridge. A side turning before the river leads across that bridge into **LE BONO**, a harbour village that looks almost ludicrously idyllic seen from one of the *vedettes* out in the gulf. Simple rooms are available at the *Vieux-Pont*, a *crêperie* in the heart of the village at 23 rue Pasteur (☎02.97.57.87.71; closed Mon in low season; ①), but for most visitors Le Bono is simply a tempting stopover for a meal or picnic. *Au Matefaim*, 9 rue du Port (☎02.97.57.84.16), is another good *crêperie*, known for its gorgeous flambéed *crêpes*.

LARMOR-BADEN itself is a subdued little town lying at the bottom of a long slope of fields of dazzling sunflowers. The port looks out on the tangle of islands in the Gulf of Morbihan, which at this point is so narrow that Arzon on the Rhuys peninsula (see p.345) appears to be on just another nearby island. It is not really an inspiring place to stay – not properly a resort or town – but there's a functional **campsite**, the *Ker Eden* (April–Sept; ☎02.97.57.05.23), and a fair number of hotels including the *Hôtel des Îles*, 32 rue Berder (☎02.97.57.03.31; ②), and the *du Centre*, 3 rte de Vannes (☎02.97.57.04.68; closed Jan & Feb; ②).

Gavrinis

The reason to visit the island of **Gavrinis** is its megalithic site. The most impressive and remarkable in Brittany, it would be memorable just for its location. But it really is extraordinary as a structure, standing comparison with Newgrange in Ireland and – in shape as well as size and age – with the earliest pyramids of Egypt.

It is essentially a **tumulus**, an earth mound covering a stone cairn and "passage grave". However, in 1981 half of the mound was peeled back and, using the original stones around the entrance as a basis, the side of the cairn that faces the water was reconstructed to make a facade resembling a step-pyramid. Inside, every stone of the passageway and chamber is covered in carvings, with a restricted "alphabet" of fingerprint whorls, axe-heads and other conventional signs, including the spirals familiar in Ireland but seen only here in Brittany. It has been thought for a long time that the stones were brought at least the few kilometres from Locmariaquer; and this view received dramatic confirmation when in 1984 the roof was shown to be made from the self-same piece of carved stone as covers the Table des Marchands there (see p.334).

One mystery has consistently eluded explanation: the purpose of the three holes leading to a recessed niche in one of the walls of the chamber. Some medieval monks were buried in the mound, but the cairn itself seems never to have been a grave.

Erosion since the site was opened has so rapidly damaged the tumulus that it may well soon be barred to visitors altogether; it is no longer possible to climb on the mound itself, and conceivably a replica will be built.

From Gavrinis, you can look across to the half-submerged stone circle on the tiny island of **Er Lanic**, which rests on its skirt of mud like an abandoned hovercraft. It has been identified as a major centre for the manufacture of ceremonial axes, using stone brought from Port Navalo.

Getting to Gavrinis

The island of Gavrinis is a fifteen-minute **ferry** ride from Larmor-Baden; in summer, the boat trips include guided tours of the cairn (April–Oct daily every 30min

---

GULF TOURS

In season, dozens of boats leave for **gulf tours** each day from Vannes, Port Navalo, La Trinité, Locmariaquer, Auray and Larmor-Baden. These are among the options:

NAVIX (☎02.97.46.60.00), who are based in **Vannes**, run deluxe *vedettes* around the gulf, including half-day (95F) and full-day (115F) tours, excursions to the Île-aux-Moines and the Île d'Arz, and gastronomic cruises for lunch (July & Aug daily except Mon, departs noon) and dinner (July & Aug Tues, Fri & Sat, departs 8pm). Other Navix sailings depart from **Port Navalo** and **Locmariaquer** (95–150F, plus expensive dinner cruises) and, to no fixed schedule, from Auray, Le Bono and La Trinité. In July and August, they also go to **Belle-Île** (140F) and **Houat** (130F)

from **Vannes** and **Port Navalo**.

COMPAGNIE DES ÎLES (☎02.97.46.18.19) run gulf tours (95–150F) and excursions to the Île-aux-Moines (75F) from **Vannes**. They also operate a more limited programme of similar cruises from **Port Navalo** (115F) and Port Haliguen in **Quiberon** (115–135F).

IZENAH CROISIÈRES (☎02.97.57.23.24 or 02.97.26.31.45) run gulf tours in summer (60–85F) and a year-round ferry service, with departures every half-hour, to the Île-aux-Moines (20F return) from **Port Blanc** at **Baden**.

9.30–11.30am & 1.30–5pm; ☎02.97.42.63.44; 55F). Most gulf cruises sail close enough to the island to give a view of the cairn, but do not land.

Southern Morbihan: the Rhuys peninsula

Though the tip of the **Presqu'île de Rhuys** is just a few hundred metres across the mouth of the Gulf of Morbihan from Locmariaquer, it somehow seems to mark a distinctly southwards shift in climate. The Côte Sauvage is lost and in its wake appear pomegranates, fig trees, camellias, even vineyards (Rhuys produces the only Breton wine), along with cultivated oysters down below in the mud.

There are, unfortunately, fierce currents in the gulf – which, all the way along here, is very unsafe for swimming. The **ocean beaches**, however, have potential. They break out intermittently to either side of **St-Gildas-de-Rhuys**, amid the glittering gold- and silver-coloured rocks. For details on the whole peninsula, call in at the new **information centre** (☎02.97.26.45.26), just off the main road as you come into **Sarzeau**.

Sarzeau and the Château de Suscinio

The D780 runs through the heart of the Rhuys peninsula, with no sea views to speak of. As it starts an extravagant curve to the south of the central town of **SARZEAU**, a short detour to the left, south along the D198, will bring you to the impressive fourteenth-century **Château de Suscinio**. This completely moated castle, once a hunting lodge of the dukes of Brittany, is set in marshland at the edge of a tiny village, and contains a sagging but vivid mosaic floor. You can take a precarious stroll around its high ramparts (July & Aug daily 10am–7pm; April–June & Sept daily 10am–noon & 2–7pm; Oct–March Mon–Wed & Fri 2–5pm, Thurs, Sat & Sun 10am–5pm; 20F), and it also reopens on summer evenings for musical or theatrical performances.

All the rooms at the *Hôtel Bar du Port* in Sarzeau (☎02.97.41.93.51; ④) have balconies that look out across the port to the gulf.

St-Gildas-de-Rhuys

At **ST-GILDAS-DE-RHUYS**, Pierre Abélard, the theologian/lover of Héloïse, was abbot for a period from 1126, having been exiled from Paris. "I live in a wild country where every day brings new perils," he wrote to Héloïse, eventually fleeing after his brother monks – hedonists unimpressed by his stern scholasticism – attempted to poison him.

By the beaches around the village are a handful of **campsites**, among them *Le Menhir* (May to mid-Sept; ☎02.97.45.22.88); there's also a **hotel**, the *Giquel* (☎02.97.45.23.12; ③).

Arzon and Port Navalo

If you're spending any length of time on the peninsula, the most appealing places to stay are congregated at its far western end, around the village of **ARZON**. Immediately before the centre, however, the **Port du Crouesty** is a desperately unattractive modern marina, dominated by the hideous crab-like *Hôtel Miramar* (☎02.97.67.68.00; closed Dec; ⑨), where the cheapest single room costs well over 1000F.

On first glance, **Port Navalo** at the very tip has little more character, but there's a cute little beach tucked into the headland, and the *Hôtel de la Plage* (☎02.97.53.75.92; closed Dec–March; ②) offers some cosy little rooms above its busy bar. The *Grand Largue* (☎02.97.53.71.58; closed mid-Nov to mid-Dec; ④) is a considerably more luxurious option, with dinner menus from 140F. Vedettes Thalassa (☎02.97.53.70.25) run **ferries** to the islands and across the gulf from the jetty nearby.

Stay at either of Arzon's two big **campsites**, *Port Sable* (April to mid-Oct; ☎02.97.53.71.98) in Port Navalo or *Le Tindio* (April–Oct; ☎02.97.53.75.59) north of town, and you're well poised for the less-crowded beaches east of St-Gildas.

The Tumulus de Thumiac

Not far from the end of the peninsula, clearly visible to the north of the main road, the **Tumulus de Thumiac** is also known as the Butte de César, or "Caesar's Mount". From its summit, Julius Caesar is supposed to have watched the sea battle in which the Romans defeated the Veneti (see p.358) – the only naval victory they ever won away from the Mediterranean, and out on the ocean. In fact, excavations in the nineteenth century revealed a 5000-year-old burial, complete with 32 stone axes and a pearl necklace.

Today, it's easy enough to walk to the top of the tumulus, but there's nothing to see apart from the view over the gulf. A short way north, the ivy-covered twelfth-century **Moulin du Pen Castel** is no longer run as a restaurant, but still makes an attractive spot for a picnic.

The Grande-Brière

South of the **River Vilaine** at La Roche-Bernard you leave the Morbihan – and technically you leave Brittany as well, entering the *département* of Loire Atlantique. The roads veer firmly east and west – to Nantes and La Baule respectively. Inland between them, as you approach the wide Loire estuary, are the otherworldly marshes of the **Grande-Brière**.

These 20,000 acres of peat bog have for centuries been deemed to be the common property of all who live in them. The scattered population, the *Brièroise*, made and make their living by fishing for eels in the streams, gathering reeds, and – on the nine days permitted each year – cutting the peat. The few villages are known as *îles*, being hard granite outcrops in the boggy wastes. Most of them consist of a circular road around the inside of a ring of thatched cottages, slightly raised above the waters onto which they back. For easy access to the watery flatlands, filled with lilies and irises and browsed by Shetland ponies, each village is encircled by its own canal, or *curée*. The houses themselves typically consist of two rooms and a stable, with a door on the north side and windows on the south. A few crops are grown in the adjacent ring of fields, which always remain above high water.

This can be quite a captivating region for unhurried exploration – though, if you're simply passing through, the waterways are not very visible from the road unless you pause on one of the occasional humpback bridges. Instead, the widely touted attraction is **renting a punt**, known as a *chaland* or a *blain*. This activity seems to be promoted with the unstated intention of getting you lost for a few hours with your pole tangled in the rushes.

Much of the Grande-Brière has been designated as a **bird sanctuary**, obviously mostly for waterfowl. The headquarters of the sanctuary (☎02.40.88.42.72) is in the most authentic surviving village, the **ÎLE DE FEDRUN**, which is filled with traditional dwellings, and also has a small but expensive **hotel**, the *Auberge du Parc* (☎02.40.88.53.01; closed Jan & Feb; ④), where dinner menus start at 150F.

The Coast at the Mouth of the Loire

There is something very surreal about emerging from the Brière to the coast at **La Baule**. For this is by far Brittany's most upmarket pocket – an imposing, moneyed landscape where the dunes are bonded together no longer with scrub and pines but with massive apartment blocks and luxury hotels. However, in the vicinity of La Baule, **Guérande** is a superb medieval walled town, while **Piriac-sur-mer**, and to a lesser extent **Le Croisic**, are less frenetic alternatives to the giant resort.

Guérande

On the edge of the marshes of the Grande-Brière, just before you come to the sea, is the absolutely gorgeous walled town of **GUÉRANDE**, which no visitor to the region should miss. Guérande gave its name to this peninsula, and derived its fortune from controlling the salt pans that form a chequerboard across the surrounding inlets. This "white country" is composed of bizarre-looking *oeillets*, each 70 to 80 square metres in extent, in which sea water, since Roman times, has been collected and evaporated.

Guérande today, a tiny little place, is still entirely enclosed by its stout fifteenth-century **ramparts**. Although you can't walk along them, a spacious promenade leads right the way around the outside, passing four fortified gateways; for half its length the broad old moat remains filled with water. Historically, the main entrance was the **Porte St-Michel** on the east side of town, which now holds a small museum of local history (April–Sept daily 10am–12.30pm & 2.30–7pm; Oct daily 10am–noon & 2–6pm; 10F).

Within the walls, pedestrians share the narrow cobbled streets with the odd car, the old houses are bright with windowboxes, and there's a market in the centre next to the **church of St-Aubin**. Another, smaller church stands just to the south; this is Notre Dame La Blanche, where the second Treaty of Guérande was signed in 1381.

Practicalities

Guérande's **tourist office** is just outside the Porte St-Michel at 1 place du Marché au Bois (July & Aug Mon–Sat 9.30am–7pm, Sun 10am–1pm; Sept–June Mon–Sat 9.30am–12.30pm & 1.30–6pm; ☎02.40.24.96.71).

Near St-Aubin church, but tucked out of sight behind the market, the pretty *Roc-Maria*, 1 rue des Halles (☎02.40.24.90.51; closed mid-Nov to mid-Dec, plus Wed & Thurs in low season; ③), is a lovely little village **hotel** that offers cosy rooms above a *crêperie* in a fifteenth-century town house. Opposite the porte Vannetoise and the most impressive stretch of ramparts, to the north, the *Hôtel de Voyageurs*, 1 place du 8-Mai-1945 (☎02.40.24.90.13; hotel closed Sun pm & Mon in low season, restaurant closed Oct–March; ③), is a *logis* serving good menus from 90F, featuring dishes such as braised salmon.

At the wooden tables of the *Restaurant de la Pêcherie*, facing the main church doors in place de la Psalette (☎02.40.24.91.18), you can enjoy a 65F menu with a fine *soupe de poissons*, or kick off with scallops on the four-course 105F menu.

Piriac-sur-mer

If you prefer your seaside resorts quiet and peaceful, head west from Guérande to **PIRIAC-SUR-MER**, 13km distant, instead of continuing to La Baule. Although the adjacent headland offers some fine sandy beaches within a couple of minutes' walk from the centre, the pleasant little village itself turns its back on the Atlantic, preferring to face the protective jetty that curls back into the little bay to shield its small fishing fleet.

Practicalities

Piriac's twisting narrow lanes see enough tourists in summer to keep half a dozen *crêperies* in business, of which the nicest is the *St-Michel*, whose courtyard tables take up most of the place de la Chope, between the old granite church and the beach.

There are also a handful of **hotels**, with the *Hôtel-Restaurant de la Pointe* (☎02.40.23.50.04; closed Nov to mid-March, plus Wed in low season; ②) looking out over the port, and the *Hôtel de la Poste*, in a large house at 26 rue de la Plage (☎02.40.23.50.90; closed Dec–March; ③), a few streets in from the sea. The shady

Parc du Guibel (April–Sept; ☎02.40.23.52.67), further on towards Mesquer, is among the best of several local **campsites**.

La Baule

LA BAULE certainly is a place apart from its rival Breton resorts, almost any of which can seem appealingly rustic and shambolic by comparison. Sited on the long stretch of dunes that link the former island of Le Croisic to the mainland, it owes its existence to a violent storm in 1779 that engulfed the old town of Escoublac in silt from the Loire, and thereby created a wonderful crescent of sandy beach that's sometimes claimed to be the largest in Europe. That has survived, albeit now lined for several kilometres with a Riviera-style spread of palm-tree-fronted hotels and residences.

Neither La Baule's permanence nor its affluence seems in any doubt these days; it's hard to imagine the England football team staying anywhere else in homely Brittany than La Baule, which was their base during the ill-fated World Cup campaign of 1998. This is a resort that very firmly imagines itself in the south of France: around the crab-shaped bay, bronzed nymphettes and would-be Clint Eastwoods ride across the sands into the sunset against a backdrop of cruising lifeguards, horse-dung removers and fantastically priced cocktails. It can be fun if you feel like a break from the more subdued Breton attractions – and the beach is undeniably impressive. It's not a place to imagine you're going to enjoy strolling around in search of hidden charms; the backstreets have an oddly rural feel, but hold nothing of any interest.

Practicalities

Full details on staying in La Baule can be had from the **tourist office**, away from the seafront in a new postmodern office at 8 place de la Victoire (mid-May to mid-Sept daily 9am–7.30pm; mid-Sept to mid-May Mon–Sat 9.30am–noon & 2–6pm; ☎02.40.24.34.44). La Baule has two **gares SNCF**, the barely used La-Baule-les-Pins, and the main La-Baule-Escoublac near the tourist office on place Rhin-et-Danube (☎02.40.66.50.50), where the TGVs from Paris arrive. The **gare routière** is at 4 place de la Victoire (☎02.40.60.25.58).

Few of the **hotels** are cheap, particularly in high season, and in low season more than half of them are closed. The cheapest options are near the main gare SNCF, less than 1km from the beach; these include the *Hôtel-Restaurant la Coquille*, 10 av Clémenceau (☎02.40.60.38.47; ①), and the classier *Marini*, 22 av Clémenceau (☎02.40.60.23.29; closed mid-Nov to mid-March; ③). The best of the many local **campsites**, 2km back from the beach, is *La Roseraie*, 20 av Sohier (April–Sept; ☎02.40.60.46.66).

Right in the centre, set back less than 50m from the sea and not far from the tourist office, is the *Lutetia* at 13 av des Evens (☎02.40.60.25.81; ④), where the *Rossini* restaurant (closed Sun pm & Mon) offers magnificent fish cookery on menus that start at 115F.

Le Croisic and beyond

The small port of **LE CROISIC**, sheltering from the ocean around the corner of the headland, is probably a more realistic (and to many perceptions, more attractive) place to stay than La Baule.

These days Le Croisic is basically a pleasure port, but fishing boats do still sail from its harbour, near the very slender mouth of the bay, and there's a modern **fish market** near the long Tréhic jetty, where you can go to see the day's catch auctioned. Incidentally, the hills on either side of the harbour, Mont Lénigo and Mont Esprit, are not natural; they are formed from the ballast left by the ships of the salt trade.

Practicalities

If you are staying in Le Croisic, choose between the **hotels** *Les Nids*, 15 rue Pasteur (☎02.40.23.00.63; closed Jan–March; ③), or the purple and white *Estacade*, near the end of the port at 4 quai de Lénigo (☎02.40.23.03.77; ③), where the 85F menu includes *soupe de poissons* and fish of the day.

Close by, all around the rocky sea coast known as the **Grande Côte**, are a whole range of **campsites**. Just outside Le Croisic itself is the *Océan* (April–Sept; ☎02.40.23.07.69); and at Batz, another former island, is the *Govelle* (April–Sept; ☎02.40.23. 91.63).

For equally good beaches and a chance of cheaper **hotel** accommodation, you could alternatively go east from La Baule to **PORNICHET** (though preferably keeping away from the plush marina) or to the tiny **ST-MARC**, where in 1953 Jacques Tati filmed *Monsieur Hulot's Holiday*.

St-Nazaire

The best sandy coves in the region, bizarrely enough, are to be found on the outskirts of **ST-NAZAIRE**: just off to the west, they are linked by wooded paths and almost deserted. But it's a gloomy city, distinguishable from afar by the black silhouettes of its mighty cranes and the soaring arch of the Loire bridge. Bombed to extinction in the last war, its shipyards, in more or less continuous operation since they built Julius Caesar's fleet, are closing all around it.

Practicalities

The one reason you might want to stay in St-Nazaire is the relative ease of finding inexpensive **hotel** space – so elusive in this area in summer. Options include the *St Louis*, 48 rue des Halles (☎02.40.22.40.34; ①), and the new *Korali*, opposite the station on place de la Gare (☎02.40.01.89.89; ③). There's also a **hostel**, the *Foyer du Jeune Travailleur*, at 30 rue Soleil-Levant (☎02.40.00.94.10).

South of the Loire

From St-Nazaire you can cross the mouth of the Loire via an inspired piece of engineering, the **Pont St-Nazaire**. This is a great elongated S-curve of a suspension bridge, its lines only visible at an acute angle at either end. A hefty toll is demanded for the privilege of driving across its three-kilometre length, but bikes go for free.

From this high viewpoint (up to 131m), you can see that the **Loire** is a definite climatic dividing line (a point regularly confirmed by French television weather bulletins). To the north of the river, the houses have steep grey-slate roofs against the storms; to the south, in the Pays de Retz, the roofs are flat and red-tiled. Nonetheless the vast deposits of Loire silt have affected both banks of the huge estuary – they buried the ancient town of Montoise on the southern side just as they did Escoublac to the north.

As you continue **south** along the coast, Brittany begins to slip away. Dolmens stand above the ocean, and the rocky coast is interspersed with bathing beaches, but the climate, the architecture, the countryside and, most obvious of all, the vineyards make it clear that this is the start of the south.

Pornic

The **Pays de Retz** coast is developed for most of its length – an almost unbroken line of holiday flats, *Pepsi*, *frites* and *crêpes* stands. **PORNIC** is the nicest of the resorts, with a functional fishing port and one of "Bluebeard" Gilles de Rais's many castles. It is a small place: you can walk beyond the harbour and along the cliffs to a tiny beach where the rock walls glitter from phosphorescent sea water.

The **hotels** in town are not cheap, though better value than those of La Baule. The *Relais St Gilles*, 7 rue Fernand de Mun (☎02.40.82.02.25; closed mid-Nov to mid-March; ③), just down the road from the post office, is the most reasonable, with a menu to match.

Inland towards Nantes

As you head away from the coast, towards the metropolis of Nantes, the countryside is once more marshy, although richer than that of the Brière, with some scenic lakes and waterways. The largest of the lakes, the **Grand-Lieu**, contains two drowned villages, Murin and Langon. Along the **estuary** itself, the towns are depressed and depressing, their traditional industries struck hard by unemployment.

For **NANTES** itself, see Chapter 6.

travel details

Trains

Redon–Quimper/Brest 4 times daily TGV, stopping at Vannes (25min), Auray (40min) and Lorient (1hr), plus 5 slower services, stopping at Questembert (25min), Vannes (45min), Auray (1hr) and Lorient (1hr 30min).

Auray–Quiberon The Tire Bouchon runs 3 times daily between mid-June and mid-Sept (40min), stopping at Plouharnel (20min) with connecting buses to Carnac and La Trinité.

Le Croisic–Paris (3hr 10min), 5 express TGV services daily, via **La Baule** (10min), **St-Nazaire** (20min) and Nantes (1hr 10min); also 5 normal services daily from Le Croisic to **Nantes** (1hr 20min), for connecting trains to Paris and elsewhere.

Buses

From Vannes to Rennes (8 daily; 2hr) via Josselin (1hr); to Nantes via La Roche Bernard (1hr 30min);

to Quiberon (1hr 45min) via Auray and Carnac (1hr 15min); and to Larmor-Baden via Arradon: all run by TTO (☎02.97.47.29.64).

From Vannes to Arzon; to Pontivy; and to Elven, Malestroit and Ploërmel: operated by CTM from the place de la Gare (☎02.97.01.22.10).

From Vannes to Port-Blanc (for the Île-aux-Moines), Transport Cautru, 26 rue Hoche (☎02.97.47.22.86).

From Auray From the SNCF: 4 daily to Quiberon (1hr) via Carnac (30min); 4 daily to Vannes (30min); both services operated by Transports Le Bayon (☎02.97.57.31.31).

From Lorient From the SNCF: 4 daily to Pontivy (1hr); 2 daily to Carnac (1hr).

Ferries

Groix For details of ferries to Groix from **Lorient**, see p.321.

Lorient Shuttle service to Port-Louis, 20 per day (☎02.97.33.40.55).

Belle Île For details of ferries to Belle-Île from **Quiberon**, **Lorient**, **Vannes**, **La Trinité**, **Port-Navalo**, **Locmariaquer**, **Auray** and **Le Bono**, see p.322.

Gulf of Morbihan For details of gulf tours and trips to the islands, from **Vannes**, **Locmariaquer**, **Auray**, **Port-Navalo**, **La Trinité** and **Le Bono**, see p.344 or contact Navix (☎02.97.46.60.00) or Compagnie des Îles (☎02.97.46.18.19).

Houat and Hoëdic For details of ferries to Houat and Hoëdic from **Quiberon**, **Vannes** and **Port-Navalo**, see p.328.

Air

From Lorient direct flights to **Paris**, 2 daily from Easter–Oct. Contact Lorient (☎02.97.82.32.93) or Vannes (☎02.97.60.78.79). To Belle-Île, by arrangement with Insul'Air (☎02.97.31.41.14).

From Quiberon Aérodrome (☎02.97.31.83.09 or 97.30.40.00), Easter–Oct, trips around Gulf of Morbihan, over Carnac, and to Belle-Île.

PART FOUR

THE
CONTEXTS

A BRIEF HISTORY OF BRITTANY AND NORMANDY

Although Brittany and Normandy – the western provinces – have belonged to the French State for over 450 years, they have been distinct entities throughout recorded history and their traditions and interests remain separate.

Brittany, for most of the five millennia during which its past can be traced, drew its cultural links and influences not inland, from the rest of France, but from the Atlantic seaboard. Isolated both by the difficulty of its marsh and moorland terrain, and its sheer distance from the heartland of Europe, it was nonetheless at the centre of a sophisticated prehistoric culture that was intimately connected with those of Britain and Ireland. It is populated today by the descendants of the Celtic immigrants who arrived from Britain and Ireland at around the time that the Romans were leaving Gaul. The "golden age" of Brittany came in the fifteenth century, when it was ruled as an independent duchy – but it was eventually absorbed into France after centuries of military and dynastic struggles with the English.

The economic decline of the province in recent centuries is attributed by Breton nationalists wholly to the union with France. Other factors, inevitably, were also at play, but it's certainly true to say that the rulers of France often ignored or oppressed their westernmost region, and even now the current revival of Brittany's fortunes is largely due to the conscious attempt to revive the old pan-Celtic trading routes.

Normandy has no equivalent prehistoric remains, and only very briefly did it possess the identity of an independent nation. Its founders were Scandinavian, the Vikings who raided along the Seine in the ninth century. These Northmen gave the region its name, and were the warriors who brought it military glory in the great Norman age of the eleventh century, when William conquered England and his nobles controlled swaths of land as far afield as Sicily and the Near East. They were also responsible for the cathedrals, castles and monasteries that still stand as the most enduring monuments of Normandy's past.

The Normans blended into the general mass of the population, both in France and in England, and Normandy itself was formally surrendered to Louis IX by Henry III of England in 1259. After the fluctuations of the Hundred Years' War, the province was firmly integrated into France, and all but disappears from history until the Allied invasion of 1944. Supposedly, a handful of Normans still regard Queen Elizabeth II as the true duchess of Normandy – which is one of the many titles she still bears. The majority of contemporary Normans, however, put their faith in the industrial and agricultural wealth of the province, and take pride in their individualism and conservatism.

THE MEGALITHS OF BRITTANY

Megalithic sites can be found all around the Mediterranean, most notably in Malta and Sardinia, and along the Atlantic seaboard from Spain to Scandinavia. Among the most significant are Newgrange in Ireland, Stonehenge in England, and the Ring of Brodgar in the Orkneys. However, it is by no means certain that the megalith-building culture originated in the Mediterranean and spread out to the "barbarian" outposts of Europe. In fact, the tumuli, alignments and single standing stones of Brittany are of pre-eminent importance. The very words used for the megaliths are Breton: *menhir* (long stone), *dolmen* (flat stone), *cromlech* (stone circle).

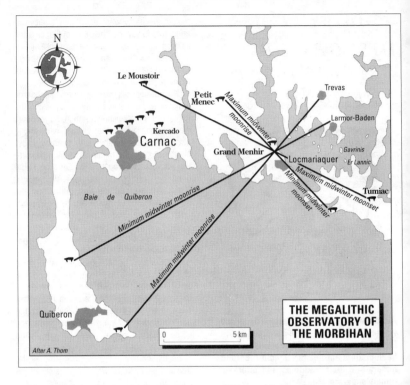

N

Le Moustoir

Petit Menec

Trevas

Maximum midwinter moonrise

Kercado

Carnac

Larmor-Baden

Grand Menhir

Gavrinis

Locmariaquer

Er Lannic

Baie de Quiberon

Minimum midwinter moonrise

Maximum midwinter moonset

Minimum midwinter moonset

Tumiac

Maximum midwinter moonrise

Quiberon

0   5 km

THE MEGALITHIC OBSERVATORY OF THE MORBIHAN

After A. Thom

Archeological evidence suggests that late Stone Age settlements had been established at various points along the Breton coast by around 6000 BC. Soon afterwards, the culture responsible either evolved to become the megalith builders, or was displaced by megalith-building newcomers. Dated at 5700 BC, the tumulus of Kercado at **Carnac**, in southern Brittany, appears to be the earliest stone construction in Europe, predating the palace of Knossos on Crete and even the Egyptian pyramids.

Each megalithic centre seems to have had its own distinct styles and traditions. Brittany has relatively few stone circles, and a greater proportion of free-standing stones; fewer burials, and more evidence of ritual fires; different styles of carving; and, uniquely, the sheer complexity of the Carnac alignments, which may be an astronomical observatory. (The fact that so many megalithic remains are on bleak seaside heathland sites may just be because these were the most likely to survive; for example those at

Rétiers and Fougères do not fit the stereotype.)

Little is known of the **people** who erected the megaliths. Only rarely have skeletons been found in the graves, but what few there have been seem to indicate a short, dark, hairy race with a life expectancy of no more than the mid-30s. Legends speak of shambling subhuman giants who served as their slaves, assisting Merlin, for example, in bringing the slabs of Stonehenge from Wales, and building the Giant's Causeway on the coast of Antrim in Northern Ireland. What is certain is that the civilization was a long-lasting one; the earliest and the latest constructions at Carnac are over five thousand years apart.

As for the actual **purpose of the stones**, there are numerous theories and few definite conclusions. Flaubert commented: "those who like mythology see them as the Pillars of Hercules; those who like natural history see here a symbol of the Python . . . lovers of astronomy see a zodiac". In the eighteenth century, for example, enthusiasts managed to see snakes in everything, and declared the megalithic sites to be remnants of some Druidic serpent cult. In fact, the stones were already ancient before the Druids appeared. Innumerable theses have wandered off into considerations of "Lost Atlantis", water divining, mysterious psychic energies and extraterrestrial assistance.

The **theories** that have become most fashionable with the general public these days see the megaliths as part of a vast system of **astronomical measurement**, record-keeping, and prediction. Precise measurements of sites all over Europe suggest that they share a standard measure of length, the "megalithic yard" – equivalent to 83 modern centimetres. In Brittany, the argument goes, the now fallen Grand Menhir of Locmariaquer was erected, using this prehistoric calibration, as a "universal lunar foresight". Its alignments with eight other sites are said to correspond to the eight extreme points of the rising and setting of the moon during its 18.61-year cycle. The Golfe de Morbihan made an ideal location for such a marking stone – set on a lagoon surrounded by low peninsulas, the menhir was visible from all directions. Once the need for the Grand Menhir was decided upon, it would then have taken hundreds of years of careful observation of the moon to fix the exact spot for it. It is thought that this was done by lighting fires on the top of high poles at trial points on the crucial nights every nine years. The alignments of Carnac are thus explained as the graph paper, as it were, on which the lunar movements were plotted.

This "megalithic observatory" explanation, researched in great detail by Professor Thom – despite being hindered by occasional "encounters with irate peasants" – and most clearly expounded in his *Megalithic Remains in Britain and Brittany* (1978), is certainly appealing. However, **rival experts** have come up with damning counterevidence. To quote from Aubrey Burl's authoritative *Megalithic Brittany* (1985): "of the eight proposed backsights, three do not exist, and of the five others the Carnac mound at Tumiac is not accurately placed, the Goulvarch menhir, the stone at Kerran, the Carnac mound of Le Moustoir with its menhir, and the passage grave of Petit-Mont, are too dissimilar in architecture and date to be convincing purpose-built Neolithic viewing-stations." Controversy rages as to whether the

Grand Menhir ever stood or, if it did, whether it fell or was broken up before the eight supposedly associated sites came into being, and the measurements are accused of ignoring the fact that the sea level in southern Brittany 6600 years ago was 10m lower than it is today.

In any case, the stones at Carnac have been so greatly eroded that perhaps it is little more than wishful thinking to imagine that their original size, shape and orientation can be accurately determined. They have been knocked down and pulled out by farmers seeking to cultivate the land; they have been quarried for use in making roads; they have been removed by landowners angry at the trespass of tourists and scientists; nineteenth-century pseudo-scientists have tampered with them, re-erecting some and shifting others; and what may have gone on in much earlier periods is anyone's guess.

An alternative approach, more favoured by conventional archeologists, places much greater emphasis on sociological factors. This argues that the stones date from the great period of transition when humankind was changing from a predatory role to a productive one, and that they can only have been erected by the coordinated efforts of a large and stable **community**. It's possible that the megaliths were erected by Neolithic settlers, who generation by generation advanced across Europe from the east bringing advances in agriculture. As they came into conflict with existing Stone Age groups, they may have set up menhirs as territorial markers. The ability to construct large monuments – which probably required the acquisition of a large agricultural surplus – would also have demonstrated that the group in question was "favoured" by the gods, and thus of "pure" or "noble" lineage.

In 1979 an experiment was carried out which demonstrated that 260 people, using rollers, were required to set up a 32,000-kilogramme stone, together with a large number of auxiliaries to provide food and shelter. The united physical exertion created very much a festival atmosphere, and the participants described the event as a "bonding" experience. Those who originally and perhaps unwillingly dragged the Carnac stones into place might feel that to be a trifle sentimental. Even so, it does make some sense to imagine the act of setting up a menhir as serving a valuable social purpose, both as an achievement in its own right and as a celebration of some other event. The annual or occasional setting-up of a new stone is easier to envisage than the vast effort required to erect them all at once – in which case the social significance of constructing these lines, mounds and circles could have been of greater importance than any physical characteristics of the arrangements themselves.

For all the pervasive legends, the megaliths cannot be attributed to the Celts. Even so, theological parallels have been drawn between ancient and modern **Breton beliefs**. It is argued that there is a uniquely Breton attitude to death, dating back thousands of years, in which the living are in everyday communication with the dead. The phenomenon of the "parish close" is said to mirror the design of the ancient passage graves, with the Christian ossuary serving the same function as the buried passageways of the old tombs – a link between the place of the dead and the place of the living.

True or false, the popular significance of the prehistoric sites was something about which later Christian authorities were somewhat ambivalent. They felt it necessary to place crosses on the top of many menhirs, or even to destroy them altogether. There are reports of the "Indecent Stone" at Reguiny being "cut down and made harmless" in 1825, and of steps being taken to stop naked couples sliding down the Grand Menhir on May Day as a fertility rite, or rubbing against the "protuberances" of the Kerloas menhir.

CELTS AND ROMANS

While Brittany in particular prospered during the **Bronze Age** and was a major manufacturer of bronze axes that were distributed throughout Atlantic Europe, its peoples were left behind by the technological advances of the **Iron Age**, and became increasingly peripheral from around 700 BC onwards. The economy turned instead towards supplying raw materials to the more developed cultures of Germany and southern France, and it is as traders in **tin and copper** that both the Bretons and the Normans make their first appearance in recorded history. Small trading ports emerged all along the Atlantic coast, and the routes went up the rivers Loire and Seine. The tin itself was mined in both Brittany and Cornwall, and the Seine became important as the "Tin Road", the most direct means for the metals to be transported towards the heart of Europe. Iron Age forts, traces of one of which remain in the forest of Huelgoat, show evidence of large-scale, stable communities even far inland.

That was why the **Romans**' top priority, when they came to Gaul centuries later, was to secure control of the Seine valley and tie the province firmly into the network of empire. Brittany, less accessible to the invading armies, was able to put up a more spirited resistance, although sadly there was no such last-ditch rebel stronghold as Astérix's fictional village. The **Breton Gauls**, descendants of a first influx of Celts, were divided into five major tribes, each of which controlled an area roughly corresponding to the modern *départements*.

The most powerful of these tribes were the **Veneti**, based in the Morbihan with what is now Vannes as their capital. The decisive sea battle in which they were defeated in 56 BC took place around the Golfe de Morbihan, and was the only major naval battle the Romans ever won outside the Mediterranean. Seafaring was not one of the Romans' strong points – hence their predilection for roads and foot-slogging – but on this occasion their galleys, built somewhere near St-Nazaire, had far superior mobility to the leather-sailed ships of the Veneti. The cost of defeat for the tribes was severe; those who were not killed were sold into slavery, and their children mutilated. Julius Caesar was there to see the battle; he went no further than Auray, but the whole Breton peninsula was swiftly conquered, and incorporated with much of Normandy into the province of Armorica.

Roman Armorica experienced five hundred years of peace, though without the benefit of any great prosperity. While the Roman-built roads were the first efficient means of land communication, they served mainly to channel wealth away towards the centre of their empire. Walled cities were founded, such as Rennes, Vannes, Rouen and Caen, but little was done to change, let alone improve, the lives of the native population. During the fourth century, a couple of Bretons, Magnence and Maximus, managed to become emperors of Rome, but by then pirate incursions had made fortifications essential along the coast.

What civilizing effect the Romans had had disappeared in any case during the **barbarian**

invasions as the Empire disintegrated at the start of the fifth century. The one thread of continuity was provided by the **Christian** Church. The first Christians had already arrived in Normandy during Roman rule, and at Rouen the bishopric had been established by St Mellon as early as 300 AD. They were followed in the fifth and sixth centuries by waves of Celtic immigrants crossing from Britain to Brittany. Traditional history considered these to be the "Dark Ages" of terror and chaos throughout Europe, with the immigrants as no more than panic-stricken refugees. However, recent evidence of stable diplomatic and trading contact across the Channel suggests that there was a much more ordered process of movement and interchange.

The vigorous Welsh and Irish missionaries named their new lands **Little Britain**, and their Christianity supplanted the old Celtic and Roman gods. The era is characterized by great legendary confrontations of elemental forces – the Devil grappling with the Archangel Michael from Dol to Mont St-Michel, St Pol driving out the "laidley worm" from the Île de Batz – symbolizing the forcible expulsion of paganism. Often the changes were little more than superficial: crosses were erected on top of menhirs, mystical springs and wells became the sites of churches, Christian processions such as *pardons* traced circuits of megalithic sites, and ancient tales of magic and witchcraft were retold as stories of Jesus and the saints. The names of innumerable Celtic religious leaders – Malo, Brieuc, Pol – have survived in place names, even if the Church has never officially recognized them as saints.

The cultural links with Britain and Ireland meant that Brittany played an important role in many of the **Arthurian legends**. Breton minstrels, like their Welsh counterparts, did much to popularize the tales in the Middle Ages. None of the local claimants to Arthur's Camelot carry much conviction, although Tristan who loved Iseult came from Brittany (the lovers may have hidden at Trémazan castle in Finistère), as did King Ban and his son Lancelot. Sir Galahad found the Holy Grail somewhere in Brocéliande Forest, said also to be the home of such diverse residents as Merlin, Morgan le Fay, and the Fisher King.

Such legends reflect the fact that, for all this time, central Brittany was an almost impenetrable wilderness, and the region as a whole was split into two separate petty monarchies, Dumnonia in the north and Cornubia (the basis of Cornouaille) in the south. Charlemagne amalgamated the two by force under **Frankish control** in 799, after they had consistently failed to pay tribute. When the Frankish Empire began to fall apart, their appointee as governor, **Nominoë**, seized the opportunity to become the first leader of an independent Brittany, by defeating Charles the Bald in the Battle of Redon (near modern La Bataille) in 845. He has taken on the status of a prototype independent leader in Breton history.

Without Celtic immigration on anything like the same scale, it took longer for **Normandy** to become fully Christianized. It was only when it too came under the control of Charlemagne's **Merovingian** dynasty that the newly founded monasteries of Jumièges and St-Wandrille became pre-eminent.

As the Franks' authority weakened over the succeeding centuries, there were repeated Viking raids along the Seine, while raids on the Breton coast drove many monks into exile across the Channel. Major Viking incursions took place in the second half of the ninth century, interspersed with attempts to conquer England. They came more often and for longer, until in 911 King Charles the Simple acknowledged the inevitable and granted their leader **Rollo** formal title to the **Duchy of Normandy**. A few years later, in 932 AD, the Breton prince known as Alain Barbetorte returned from England to re-establish control over Brittany, and many of its monasteries were subsequently rebuilt in the new Romanesque style.

THE NORMANS

In the eleventh century **the Normans** became one of the most significant forces in Europe. Not only did the Dukes of Normandy invade and conquer England, but Norman mercenaries and adventurers fought to gain lands for themselves wherever they found the opportunity. They insinuated themselves into the wars of Italy, individually acquiring control of Aversa, Apulia and Calabria, and most of Sicily, their greatest prize. They took part in the church's wars, too, fighting in campaigns in Greece against Byzantium, and in the First Crusade – which in 1098 saw the Norman leader Bohemond take Antioch.

In their adopted French homeland, the pagan Scandinavians had so rapidly acquired the culture, language and religion of their new subjects that spoken Norse had died out in Rouen by the time of Rollo's grandson, Duke Richard I. Yet they were still seen as a race apart – and not a very pleasant one at that. One authority describes them as without exception physically repellent, cruel and unscrupulous.

Duke William's **invasion of England** is portrayed by the Bayeux Tapestry as a just struggle: the result solely of William's conviction that he was the rightful heir to Edward the Confessor, a succession acknowledged under oath by Harold. Be that as it may, the sheer speed of what proved to be such a permanent conquest indicates the extent of Norman power at the time. Having crossed the Channel to defeat the usurper Harold in September 1066, the Conqueror was crowned king in Westminster Abbey on Christmas Day, and by the next Easter was secure enough to be able to return to Normandy. The Battle of Hastings was a decisive moment in the balance of Europe. Almost paradoxically, the Norsemen from France finally freed England from the threat of invasion from Scandinavia, which had persisted for centuries up until 1070. English attention was thus reorientated towards the mainland of Europe – a shift that was to have a major impact on history.

The Norman capacity for **organization** was primarily responsible not just for the military triumphs, but also for the consolidation of power and wealth that followed. The Domesday Book, which catalogued the riches of England, was paralleled by a similar undertaking in Sicily, the *Catalogus Baronum*. William's son Henry introduced trial by jury in the king's Courts – justice that had to be paid for. Henry II established the Exchequer to collect royal revenue.

Intellectually, too, the Normans were dominant; the Abbey of Bec-Hellouin, for example, was a renowned centre of learning, inspired first by Lanfranc and then by the theologian Anselm, each of whom moved on to become archbishop of Canterbury. And **architecturally**, the wealth and technical expertise of the Normans made possible the construction of such lasting monuments as the cathedrals of Bayeux, Coutances and Durham, and the monasteries of Mont St-Michel, Jumièges and Caen.

The twelfth-century "**Anglo-Normans**" who invaded Ireland were recognizably descended from the army of the Conqueror, and Norman

French remained the legal and administrative language of England until 1400. Elsewhere the mark of the conquerors was less distinct. The Norman kings of Sicily did not style themselves Normans, and ruled over a cosmopolitan society dependent largely on the skills of Moslem craftsmen. Their architecture barely resembles what is thought of today as "Norman", and the Norman bloodline soon vanished into the general population of Sicily.

However, for the duchy and the kingdom on either side of the Channel, the shared rulers made close connections inevitable. The Norman lords in England required luxury items to be imported. Flemish weavers were encouraged to settle in London and East Anglia, and gradually the centre of affluence and importance shifted away from Normandy. By the time Henry II, great-grandson of William the Conqueror, inherited the throne, England was a major power and the seeds of the Hundred Years' War had been sown. Fifteen years later Château Gaillard on the Seine was taken by **Philippe Auguste**, and Normandy for the first time became part of France.

THE HUNDRED YEARS' WAR

While Normandy was at the height of its power, the Bretons lived in constant fear of invasion by their belligerent neighbours. Although their own leaders had managed to prevent a parallel Viking takeover of **Brittany**, it was at the price of numerous **warlords** setting up their own private strongholds. Their emergence seriously weakened the authority of Nominoë's successors, and the resultant anarchy devastated the Breton economy. Frequent power bids by the Norman English and the kings of France – the Hundred Years' War – hardly helped the situation.

Bertrand du Guesclin, born in 1321 in the unprepossessing town of Broons, south of Dinan, was the outstanding military genius of the Middle Ages. After an ignominious start, when his father disowned him because of his ugliness, he practised his novel tactics as an outlaw chief in the heart of Brittany. With little truck for chivalric conventions, he simplified the chaotic feudal map, and in a bewildering succession of French and Spanish campaigns earned the command of the French army. Eschewing prearranged battles in favour of ambush and general guerrilla tactics, he taught the French to fight dirty – in medieval terms. Nobles were forced to dismount and fight on foot, while the fact that his soldiers were paid ensured that they did not alienate the peasantry by plundering. This formidable man was also responsible for the development of the use of gunpowder, combined with new assault techniques capable of devastating the strongest fortresses.

The net result of du Guesclin's strategies was that by 1377 the English had been driven almost completely out of France. Virtually every town and castle in Brittany and Normandy seems to have some du Guesclin connection; not only did he live, besiege or fight almost everywhere, but after his death in 1380 parts of his body were buried in no fewer than four different cities. Yet, despite all his myriad intrigues and battles, Brittany benefited very little from his activities.

The **Hundred Years' War** resurfaced after du Guesclin's death, with much of the fighting taking place in Normandy. Henry V of England recaptured the province step by step, until by 1420 he was in a position to demand recognition of his claim to the French throne. Eight years later, the French were defending their last significant stronghold, Orléans on the Loire. It was here that the extraordinary figure of **Joan of Arc** appeared on the scene and relieved the siege of the city. In a very different way to du Guesclin she ensured that the mass of ordinary, miserable peasants, not to mention the demoralized soldiers of the French army, made the enemy occupation untenable. Within two astonishing years, the Dauphin, not Henry, had been crowned, to become King Charles VII of France. Jeanne herself was captured by the Burgundian allies of the occupiers, tried by a French bishop and an English commander, and burned at the stake as a witch in Rouen – for a full account, see p.86. Nonetheless, in 1449, Charles VII was able to make a triumphal entry into the regional capital. Within twelve months this latest 32-year English occupation of Normandy was at an end.

THE DUCHY OF BRITTANY

Breton involvement in the opening stages of the second phase of the Hundred Years' War was minimal and from 1399 to 1442 **Duc Jean V** took a neutral stand, allowing the economy of the province to prosper. Fishing, shipbuilding

and sail manufacture developed, accompanied by a flowering of the arts. It was in this period that the Kreisker chapel and the church of Folgoët were built.

Although involvement in the Anglo-French conflict was inevitable, Jean's heirs for a time continued to rule over a successful and **independent duchy**. Arthur III, duke in the mid-fifteenth century, had fought alongside Jeanne d'Arc but used his connections with the French army to protect Breton autonomy. His successor, however, Duc François II, was less astute. Brittany, the last large region of present-day France to resist agglomeration, was a very desirable prize for King Louis XI. To resist encroachment, François needed allies beyond France; and in looking for those allies he antagonized and alarmed the French. A pretext was eventually found for the royal army to invade Brittany, where the Breton army was defeated at the battle of St-Aubin-du-Cormier in 1488. Duc François was forced to concede to the French king the right to determine his own daughter's marriage, and died of shame (so the story goes) within a few weeks.

François's heiress, **Duchess Anne**, was to be the last ruler of an independent Brittany. Having once been engaged to the Prince of Wales, she then married Maximilian of Austria by proxy in December 1490, in the hope of a strong alliance against the French. Charles VIII of France (who was himself in theory married to Maximilian's daughter) demanded adherence to the treaty of 1488, captured Nantes, advanced north and west and proposed to Anne.

By and large the population preferred a royal wedding to death by starvation or massacre, and it duly took place on September 16, 1491. Anne bemoaned "Must I thus be so unfortunate and friendless as to have to enter into marriage with a man who has so ill-treated me?" – and then, to the amazement of all, the couple actually fell in love with each other. Despite the marriage, the duchy remained independent, but Anne was contractually obliged to marry Charles's successor should he die before they produced an heir. When Charles duly bumped his head and died in 1498, his successor, Louis XII, divorced his wife and married Anne. This time Anne's position was considerably stronger, and in the contract she laid down certain conditions that were to be a source of Breton pride and frustration for many centuries. The three main clauses stipulated that no taxes could be imposed without the consent of the Breton *États*; conscripts were only to fight for the defence of Brittany; and Bretons could only be tried in their own courts. When Anne died, Bretons mourned – all records show that she was a genuinely loved leader.

In 1514, the still independent duchy passed to Anne's daughter Claude, whom the future François I of France married with every intention of incorporating Brittany into his kingdom. This he did, and the permanent **union of Brittany and France** was endorsed by the Breton *États* at Vannes in 1532. In theory, the act confirmed Anne's stipulations that all the rights and privileges of Brittany would be observed and safeguarded as inviolable. But it was rarely honoured and their subsequent violation by successive French kings and governments has been the source of conflict ever since.

THE ANCIEN RÉGIME

As the French Crown gradually consolidated its power and began to centralize its economy, the ports of the two western provinces developed, serving the **colonial interests** of the State. In fact as early as 1364 sailors from Dieppe had established the city of Petit Dieppe in what is now Sierra Leone. Le Havre was founded in 1517 to be France's premier Atlantic port and, between intermittent attacks and takeovers by the English, became a centre for the coffee and cotton markets. Sailors from Granville, Dieppe and Cherbourg set up colonies in Brazil, Canada, Florida and Louisiana.

In Brittany, St-Malo and Lorient were the two top trading ports, with the latter benefiting every time the English decided to harass Channel ports and shipping. **Jacques Cartier** of St-Malo sailed up the St Lawrence River and added Canada to the possession of the French Crown. Nantes too was an important base for trade with the Americas, India and the Middle East, with **slaves** one of the most profitable "commodities". Though the business of exploitation and battles with rival foreign ships was motivated by private profit, the net result was very much to the advantage of the State.

The early contact with England, and the cosmopolitan nature of its Channel ports, meant that Normandy became one of the main **Protestant** centres of France, with Caen and its university having very active Huguenot popula-

tions. The region was therefore in the front line when the **Wars of Religion** flared up in 1561–63, and again in 1574–76. When the Edict of Nantes with its Protestant privileges and immunities was revoked, large-scale Huguenot emigration took place, seriously damaging the local textile industry.

Brittany on the other hand was an area of minimal Protestant presence, and the Wars of Religion were only significant as a cover for a brief attempt to win back independence. Breton linen manufacture had taken advantage of the lack of French tolls and customs dues, and only declined much later – when England, post-Industrial Revolution, was flooding the market with mass-produced textiles.

Although the power of the French kings increased over the centuries, practical considerations meant that outlying regions were not always completely under royal control. The rural nobles were persistently lawless, and intermittent **peasant revolts** took place, such as that of the dispossessed *nu-pieds* in 1639. In 1675 came the most serious rebellion against the Crown, when Louis XIV's finance minister put a tax on tobacco, pewter and all legal documents to raise money for the war with Holland. This "Stamped Paper" revolt, which started with riots in Nantes, Rennes and Guingamp, soon spread to the country, with the peasants making demands very similar in their content to those of the revolutionaries a hundred years later. The aristocracy took great delight in brutally crushing the uprising, pillaging several towns and stringing up insurgents and bystanders from every tree.

The reign of **Louis XIV** saw numerous infringements of Breton liberties, including the uprooting of vines throughout the province on the royal grounds that the people were all drunkards. If the Bretons could not get revenge they could at least be entertained by court scandals. In 1650 Louis's Superintendent of Finance, **Nicolas Fouquet**, bought the entire island of Belle-Île and fortified it as his own private kingdom. The alarmed king had to send D'Artagnan and the three musketeers to arrest him before his ambitious plans went any further.

While taxes on Brittany increased in the early eighteenth century, Normandy found new prosperity from the proximity of Paris for its edible produce. Lacemaking became a major regional industry, and several abbeys that had been closed during the Wars of Religion were now revitalized. However, by 1763 France had lost Canada and given up all pretensions to India. The ports declined and trade fell off as England became the workshop of the world.

THE REVOLUTION

The people of both Brittany and Normandy at first welcomed the **Revolution**. Breton representatives at the *États Généraux* in Paris seized the opportunity to air all Brittany's grievances, and the "Club Breton" they formed was the basis of the **Jacobins**. Caen, meanwhile, became the centre of the bourgeois **Girondist** faction. In August of 1789 it was a Breton *député* who proposed the abolition of privileges. However, under the Convention it became clear that the price to be paid for the elimination of the *ancien régime* was further reductions in local autonomy and the suppression of the Breton language.

Neither province was sympathetic to the execution of the king – in Rouen 30,000 people took to the streets to express their opposition. The Girondins came out worst in the factional infighting at the Convention, having opposed the abolition of the monarchy and supported the disastrous war in the Netherlands. Some Girondist deputies managed to flee the edict of June 2, 1793 which ordered their arrest, but the army they organized to march on Paris was defeated at Pacy-sur-Eure. The final major Norman contribution to Revolutionary history was provided on that same day by **Charlotte Corday** of Caen, when she stabbed Jean-Paul Marat in his bath.

The concerted attack on religion and the clergy was not happily received, particularly in Brittany where the Church was closely bound up with the region's independent identity. The attempt to conscript an army of 300,000 Bretons was deeply resented as an infringement of the Act of Union. The popular image of the Revolution in Brittany, where the riots and disturbances of 1787 had been crucial, was now further damaged by the brief **Reign of Terror** in 1793 of Carrier, the Convention's representative in Nantes. Under the slogan "all the rich, all the merchants are counter-revolutionaries", he killed perhaps 13,000 people in three months, by such methods as throwing prisoners into the Loire tied together in pairs. This was done without Tribunal sanction or approval, and Carrier

was himself guillotined before the end of the year.

All this made Brittany an inevitable focal point for the Royalist **counter-revolution** known as the *Chouannerie*, which also had adherents in a few outlying areas of Normandy. A vast invasion force of exiled and foreign nobility, backed by the English, was supposed to sweep through France, rallying all dissenters to the Royalist flag. In the event only 8000 landed at Quiberon in 1795, and were not even capable of escaping from the self-imposed trap of the peninsula. They devastated what little they could before themselves being brutally massacred. Much of the local support was motivated by the age-old desire to win back independence, but the Breton *Chouans* ("screech owls") fighting elsewhere ended up being tarred with the same aristocratic brush and then abandoned to years of quixotic and doomed guerrilla warfare.

A rebel army continued to fight sporadically in the Cotentin and the Bocage until 1800, while in Brittany another **royalist revolt** in 1799 was easily crushed. In 1804, Cadoudal, "the last *Chouan*", was captured and executed in Paris, where he had gone to kidnap Napoléon – having refused the emperor's offer of a generalship if he surrendered.

The rebel movement lingered on until 1832, when the duchess of Berry failed to engage anyone's interest in the restoration of the *ancien régime*.

THE NINETEENTH CENTURY

Normandy, at the beginning of the nineteenth century, remained a wealthy region despite the crippling of its ports by the blockade imposed by the European coalition against Napoléon. It had proportionally five times as many people eligible, as property owners, to vote as the impoverished mountain areas of the south. Its agriculture accounted for eleven percent of France's produce on six percent of its land, while industry remained relatively unadvanced.

When protectionist tariffs were removed from grain in 1828, and Normandy was forced to compete with other producers, widespread **rural arson and tax riots** ensued. But, when the revolution of 1848 offered the prospect of socialism, the deeply conservative Catholic peasantry showed little enthusiasm for change. Even the re-emergence of a rural textile industry in the 1840s, relying on outworkers brutally exploited by the capitalists of Rouen, added no radical impetus.

The advent of the **railways** and the patronage of the imperial court encouraged the development of Normandy's resorts, while along the Seine watermills provided the power for the major spinning centres at Louviers, Évreux and Elbeuf. Serious decline did not come until the 1880s, when **rural depopulation** was brought on by emigration combined with a low birth rate – and a high death rate in which excessive drinking played a part.

Nineteenth-century Brittany was no longer an official entity, save as five *départements* of France. The railways were of negative benefit, submitting the province to competition from more heavily industrialized regions, while the Nantes–Brest canal did not achieve the expected success, and **emigration** increased. Culturally, the century witnessed a revival of Breton language, customs and folklore, but the initiative came from intellectuals, not the mainly illiterate masses.

Around the turn of the **twentieth century** both provinces experienced a surge of artistic creativity, with painters such as Gauguin in Pont-Aven and Monet in Giverny, and such writers as Proust in Normandy and Pierre Loti in Brittany.

As everywhere in Europe, this idyll was shattered by the **Great War** – although removed from the actual battlefields, both Brittany and Normandy were dramatically affected. Brittany, for its size, suffered the heaviest death toll of anywhere in the world. The vast memorial at Ste-Anne-d'Auray is testimony to the extent of the loss, while a parallel spiritual grief can be seen in the dramatic growth in Normandy of the cult of the recently dead Thérèse of Lisieux. Symbols of a changing world are embodied in the two leading aristocratic families of the regions; the heir to the Rohans of Josselin was killed on the Somme, while Prince Louis de Broglie became the first physicist to question the solidity of matter.

WORLD WAR II AND THE BATTLE OF NORMANDY

That the **beaches of Normandy** were chosen as the site of the Allied invasion of Europe in June 1944 was by no means inevitable. Far from the major disputed areas and communication routes of Europe, Normandy had seen almost no military activity since the Hundred Years' War. But in that blazing summer six armies and millions of men fought bloody battles across the placid Norman countryside. A whole swath of the province was laid in ruins before Hitler's defensive line was broken and the road to Paris cleared.

France, under **Marshal Pétain**, had surrendered to the Germans in 1940. A year later, the Fascist armies turned east to invade the Soviet Union – America and Britain declaring full support for the Soviets but resisting Stalin's demand for a second front. In 1942 the two western powers promised a landing in northern France, but all that ensued was an abortive commando raid on Dieppe. By the time the second front materialized, the tide of the war had already been turned at Stalingrad.

The Germans had meanwhile fortified the whole northwest seaboard of Europe. They expected the attack to come, however, at the Channel's narrowest point, across the Straits of Dover. The **D-Day invasion** of June 6, 1944, was presaged by months of intensive aerial bombardment across Europe, without concentrating too obviously on the chosen landing sites. In the event, the Nazis vastly overestimated Allied resources – two weeks after D-Day Rommel still thought the Normandy landings might be no more than a preliminary diversion to a larger-scale assault around Calais.

A photographic survey of the whole Norman coast had been prepared in Britain, using every possible source, including prewar holiday snaps. In the absence of any easily capturable ports, the landing forces actually took their own "Mulberry" harbours with them (see p.123). The basic plan was for the British and Commonwealth forces under Montgomery to strike for Caen, the pivot around which the Americans (whose General Eisenhower was in overall command) were to swing following their own landings further west.

Not everything went smoothly. There are appalling stories of armoured cars full of men plunging straight to the bottom of the sea as they rolled off landing craft unable to get near enough to the shore. Many of the early objectives took much longer to capture than was originally envisaged – the British took weeks rather than hours to reach Caen, while American hopes of a rapid seizure of the deep-water port at Cherbourg were thwarted. Most notorious of all, the opportunity to capture the bulk of the German army, which was all but surrounded in the "Falaise pocket", was lost.

Military historians say that man for man the German army was the more effective fighting force; but with their sheer weight of resources the Allies achieved a fairly rapid victory. Crucially, the concentration of German air power on the eastern front meant that there was never a significant German air presence over Normandy. Parachutists, reconnaissance flights and air support for ground troops were all able to operate virtually unimpeded, as too were the bombing raids on Norman towns and on every bridge across the Seine west of Paris. Furthermore, the muddled enemy command, in which generals at the front were obliged to follow broad directives from Berlin, caused an American general to comment, "one's imagination boggled at what the German army might have done to us without Hitler working so effectively for our side".

Within a few days of D-Day, **de Gaulle** was able to return to Free France, making an emotional first speech at Bayeux (see p.129), while a seasick Winston Churchill sailed up to Deauville in a destroyer and "took a plug at the Hun". At the end of July, General Patton's Third Army broke out across Brittany from Avranches with the aid of 30,000 **French Resistance** fighters, and on August 25 Allied divisions entered Paris, where the German garrison had already been routed by the Resistance. In the east the Red Army were sweeping back the Axis powers.

Though the war in Europe still had several bloody months to run, with Hitler coming very close to smashing the western front in December 1944, the road to Berlin was finally opening up.

POSTWAR: THE BRETON RESURGENCE

The war left most of **Normandy** in ruins: while it remained a relatively prosperous area in terms of its produce, decades of reconstruction were required. The development of private transport also meant that Normandy became ever more filled with the second homes of the rich. This has often been resented – the film actor Jean Gabin, for example, was literally besieged in his new country house by hundreds

of peasants insisting that he had "too much land", and was obliged to sell some of it off.

Meanwhile, there was very little happening in **postwar Brittany** save ever-increasing migration from the countryside to the main towns and from there, often, out of the province altogether. By the 1950s some 300,000 Bretons lived in Paris, industry was almost exclusively limited to the Loire estuary, and agriculture was dogged by archaic marketing and distribution.

However, since the late 1960s Brittany has experienced considerable economic advance, due in part to the initiatives of **Alexis Gourvennec**. He first came to prominence at the age of 24, in 1961, when he led a group of fellow farmers into Morlaix to occupy the government's regional offices in an effective (if violent) protest at exploitation by middlemen. The act set the pace for his lifetime's concern – to obtain the best possible price for Breton agricultural produce. To this end he lobbied Paris for a deep-water port at Roscoff, and once that was built his farmers' cooperative set up Brittany Ferries to carry Breton artichokes and cabbages to English markets. The company was an explicit move to re-establish the old trading links of the Atlantic seaboard, independent of Paris and central French authority.

Brittany Ferries has prospered, thanks to the British and Irish entry to the EC upon which Gourvennec had gambled. And it has proved that Brittany's future economic fortunes are more closely linked to its old Celtic connections than to the French state. Yet, despite Gourvennec's enthusiasm for his Celtic cousins, there have been several instances of ugly right-wing **protectionism** – attacking British lorries importing meat, violently breaking up strikes in Brittany, and forcibly preventing Townsend Thoresen from starting a rival ferry service to St-Malo.

In 1973 a semi-decentralized **regional administration** was set up to provide an intermediate level between the *départements* and the State. Normandy, being rich, became two regions – *Basse* and *Haute* – while Brittany was a single entity, but lost the Loire-Atlantique *département*, which included what was traditionally its principal city, **Nantes**. The new boundaries had no impact on people's perception of the provinces, though they did start to have some practical consequence when the Socialist government increased regional powers in 1981.

The traditional industrial centres on the Loire estuary, such as the shipbuilding town of St-Nazaire, no longer come under Breton planning – perhaps just as well, given the recession. Fishing and agriculture are still the mainstay of the Breton economy, though the former has never benefited from an equivalent to Gourvennec. The socialist policy of **decentralization** brought certain industries to the region – such as a Citroën plant at Rennes, and a Renault one in Lorient – but it is still industrially backward compared to most of France.

Something over a decade ago, hopes of new riches were raised by drilling for offshore oil in Finistère. If oil is discovered, it would create interesting parallels with the experience in Scotland. As yet, however, these remain pipe dreams and Brittany's experience of oil has been at the receiving end of major disasters – the *Torrey Canyon* in March 1967 and the *Amoco Cadiz* in 1978 both polluting hundreds of kilometres of coastline.

At the end of the 1980s, leading Breton economic figures began to prepare themselves for a future in which the province would not be able to depend so heavily on its agriculture. They earmarked the development of the city of Brest as being the best way forward. The **Brest Charter**, approved by the French government in February 1988, planned for large-scale investment in the city area, partly in higher education and research facilities, and partly in upgrading the harbour and airport to cope with international traffic. The ultra-fast Paris–Brest TGV rail link in particular, inaugurated in 1989, has made a considerable difference.

Politically, Bretons have consistently provided an above-average proportion of the conservative vote, with the most traditional, rural, areas being the most conservative of all. Perhaps for that reason the **separatist movement**, as a positive celebration of the Breton nation rather than a reactionary throwback, has never been all that powerful. In 1932 a bomb in Rennes destroyed the monument to Franco-Breton unity, and since 1966 the Front de Libération de Bretagne has intermittently attacked such targets as the nuclear power station in the Monts d'Arrée, and the Hall of Mirrors at the palace of Versailles in 1978. The emphasis for most Breton activists these days, however, is on cultural pride rather than militancy. The idea is to establish a clear and vital sense of national identity – to create, as one leader put it, "the spiritual basis for a new political thrust". Although overall use of the Breton language may be declining, great stress has been placed on its historical and artistic significance, and notable victories have been won on the question of its official status.

Recent years have also been characterized by increasingly bitter inter-European disputes over **agriculture** and **fishing** rights. The economic survival of Breton fishermen in particular has been seriously threatened by a flood of cheap imports from the factory-fishing trawlers of the former Soviet Union. In February 1994, the streets of Rennes were turned into a battlefield when five thousand fishermen rioted during a visit by Prime Minister Édouard Balladur, and a stray flare set light to the roof of the ancient Breton Parliament. The next month, the GATT talks on world trade were briefly derailed by a French blockade on fish flown in from the US; American threats to retaliate by banning imports of Camembert and other French cheeses soon forced a climb-down.

Thirty percent of fish caught by British vessels are exported to Europe through French ports, and there have been repeated instances of the blockading of various Channel ports, with hypermarkets being ransacked and Scottish fish landed at Roscoff destroyed by angry mobs. In response to a threat by trawlermen wishing to fish for scallops and spider crabs to blockade the Channel Islands, the French government reduced the tax burden on self-employed fishermen, and set minimum prices for cod, haddock, coley and monkfish.

The most recent controversy to hit the headlines has centred on Cogema's UP3 nuclear reprocessing plant at **Cap de la Hague**, near Cherbourg in Normandy. The state-owned facility "reprocesses" spent nuclear fuel from power stations all over the world, and in doing so discharges 230 million litres of nuclear waste each year into the Atlantic. Analysis of the ocean floor in the vicinity has shown it to be so contaminated that legally the stones on the sea bed should themselves be classified as controlled nuclear waste. Researchers from the environmental group **Greenpeace** have labelled the La Hague plant as being "the single largest source of radioactive contamination in the European Union", and also "the single largest source of aerial radioactivity in the world". Campaigners have focused in particular on the demonstrable contamination of the beach at the Plage des Moulinets, nearby, where a waste pipe from the plant is exposed at low tide, and also on the independently verified high incidence of leukemia in the local population. Traditionally, the French authorities have stonewalled on the issue, proud of the fact that 75 percent of the country's electricity is produced by nuclear power stations. However, with the advent of left-wing governments – not only in France itself, but also in Germany, which has long been Cogema's single largest customer – it finally seems as if the French espousal of nuclear power may be coming to an end.

AN HISTORICAL CHRONOLOGY

BC

c450,000 Evidence of Paleolithic activity at St Columban

c5700 Earliest megalithic site – tumulus of Kercado

c4600 Tomb containing antlers and shells, Hoëdic island

up to 1800 Megalithic age; construction of Carnac alignments

2500 on Seine becomes the "Tin Road"

6th C First wave of Celts arrive, the Gauls

56 Julius Caesar's fleet defeats Veneti

AD

up to 476 Roman occupation of Armorica

497 Franks arrive in Normandy; Clovis occupies Rouen

5th–6th C Celts fleeing from Britain rename Brittany

6th C First monasteries founded in Brittany and Normandy

St Pol kills "laidley worm" on island of Batz

709 Mont-St-Michel consecrated by bishop of Avranches

799 Charlemagne controls all Brittany

8th–9th C Forest of Scissy drowns to form Mont-St-Michel Bay

Viking expeditions against Normandy

845 Battle of Redon, Nominoë first duke of Brittany

911 Rollo becomes first duke of Normandy, capital Rouen

9th–10th C Repeated Norman invasions of Brittany

1035 Birth of William "The Bastard" at Falaise

1064 Harold and William together at Battle of Brittany (Dol)

1066 William invades and conquers England

1067 Abbey of Jumièges consecrated

1077 Bishop Odo dedicates Bayeux cathedral, complete with Tapestry

1087 William dies, making William Rufus king of England and leaving Normandy to his eldest son Robert

11th C Golden age of Abbey of Bec – Lanfranc and Anselm

1120 William, heir to the English throne, drowns at Barfleur

1136 Pierre Abelard abbot of St Gildas

1162 Eleanor of Aquitaine born at Domfront

12th C Romanesque cloister of Abbey of Daoulas

1160 Robert Wace visits Brocéliande forest "like a fool"

1171 Henry II, in Argentan, hears news of Becket's murder

1172 Henry does public penance at Avranches

1195 Richard the Lionheart builds Château Gaillard

1204 Normandy reunited with French throne

1211–28 Building of *La Merveille* at Mont-St-Michel

1218 Construction of cathedral at Coutances

1303 St Yves dies, Tréguier

1351 "Combat of the Thirty" between Josselin and Ploermel

1359 Du Guesclin fights single combat at Dinan

1375 Building of Kreisker belfry at St-Pol

1420	Henry V of England king of France, after Agincourt
1431	Joan of Arc's trial and execution (May 30) at Rouen
1437	John the Baptist's finger arrives at St-Jean-du-Doigt
1440	"Bluebeard" burned at stake in Nantes
1450	Normandy finally recovered by France
1450	Frescoes at Kermaria-an-Isquit
1469	Locronan starts its ascendancy in the linen trade
1474–6	Henry Tudor, England's future king, prisoner at Elven
1491	Duchess Anne of Brittany becomes queen of France
1499	Duchess Anne becomes queen of France again
1510	Monk, Vincelli, invents Benedictine liqueur
1517	Construction of Le Havre
1526	Aître de St-Maclou, charnel house, built at Rouen
1532	Vannes parliament ratifies Brittany–France union
1548	Mary Queen of Scots at Morlaix
1550–1750	Rival Breton towns build the "parish closes"
1562	Rouen sacked by Protestants
1598	Henry IV signs Edict of Nantes
1608	Champlain sails from Honfleur to found Quebec
1661	Three musketeers end Fouquet's ownership of Belle-Île
1668	10,000 die of plague in Dieppe
1675	"Stamped Paper" peasant revolt in Brittany
1693	English "infernal machine" devastates St-Malo
1698	Gouin de Beauchère of St-Malo colonizes the Falklands
1722	Dec 22; Drunken carpenter burns down most of Rennes
1745	Bonnie Prince Charlie sails from Nantes
1758	Duke of Marlborough attacks St-Malo with 15,000 men
1776	Benjamin Franklin lands at Auray (by mistake)
1789	Revolution makes no concessions to Breton autonomy
1793	Carrier kills thousands in "marriages" at Nantes
1794	Soldiers play *boules* with heads from Guéhenno calvary
1795	Royalist and exile *Chouans* land at Quiberon
1801	Robert Fulton tests first submarine at Camaret
1808	Napoleon arrives by barge for his ball at Nantes
c1810	Marie Herel invents Camembert
1821	Flaubert born at Rouen
1836	Opening of the Nantes–Brest canal
1843	Victor Hugo's daughter drowns in Seine
1852	First major Icelandic fishery expedition from Paimpol
1866	Composer Érik Satie born in Honfleur
1873	Thérèse Martin born, Lisieux; died 1897, sainted 1925
1881	Young Marcel Proust pays his first visit to Combourg
1883–1926	Monet paints waterlilies in his garden at Giverny
1888	Gauguin at Pont-Aven
1896	*Drummond Castle* goes down off Ouessant
1899	Second trial of Dreyfus at Rennes
1905	France secularized, although Brittany votes against
1927	Nungesser and Coli disappear over Étretat attempting first transatlantic flight

1928 Amundsen's air-rescue flight from Caudebec disappears

1932 Bomb destroys Rennes monument to Franco-Breton unity

1930s Nauseous Jean-Paul Sartre teaches philosophy in Le Havre

1940 All the men of Sein join de Gaulle in England

1942 March 28; British commando raid on St-Nazaire

August; 1000 Canadians die in commando raid on Dieppe

1944 June 6; D-Day – Battle of Normandy

1954 Consecration of Basilica of St Thérèse at Lisieux

1962 First Telstar transatlantic signals at Pleumeur-Bodou

1966 Tidal power dam built across the Rance estuary

1967 *Torrey Canyon* disaster; oil slicks hit Brittany

1972 Loire-Atlantique no longer officially in Brittany

1980 *Rainbow Warrior* pursues nuclear-dumping vessel into Cherbourg; anti-nuclear riots at Plogoff

1987 Oct 15; hurricane causes extensive damage in Finistère

1988 Brest Charter on Brittany's economic future approved by French government.

1994 World leaders attend commemorations of fiftieth anniversary of D-Day.

Burning of Breton Parliament in Rennes during protests by fishermen

1995 Opening of the Pont de Normandie

BOOKS

Where separate editions exist in the UK and US, publishers are detailed below with the British publisher first, followed by the American publisher. Where books are published in one country only, this follows the publisher's name. O/p signifies an out-of-print, but still recommended, book. University Press has been abbreviated to UP.

PREHISTORY AND MEGALITHS

Aubrey Burl *Megalithic Brittany* (Thames & Hudson, o/p). Detailed guide to the prehistoric sites of Brittany, area by area. Very precise on how to find each site, and what you see when you get there, but little historical or theoretical overview. It is not intended as a practical guidebook for anything other than ancient stones.

John Michell *Megalithomania* (Thames & Hudson/Cornell UP). General popularizing work about megaliths everywhere, with a lot of entertaining descriptions of how modern visitors have reacted to them.

Mark Patton *Statements in Stone* (Routledge). Sober, scientific account of Brittany's megalithic heritage, reappraised in the light of recent archeological discoveries.

A. Thom and A. S. Thom *Megalithic Remains in Britain and Brittany* (OUP, UK, o/p). A scientific rather than anecdotal account of the Thoms' extensive analysis. The mathematics and astronomy can be a bit overpowering without necessarily convincing you of anything.

Uderzo and Goscinny *Astérix the Gaul* (Hodder). Breton history mixed together in a magic cauldron.

HISTORY AND POLITICS

Patrick Galliou and Michael Jones *The Bretons* (Basil Blackwell). Accessible and illuminating hardback account of Breton history from the megaliths, through the Romans, as far as the union with France.

David C. Douglas *The Norman Achievement 1050–1100* (Fontana, o/p/University of California Press, o/p). Comprehensive and readable assessment of the Norman conquerors.

Barbara Tuchman *Distant Mirror* (Papermac/Ballantine). A history of the fourteenth century as experienced by a French nobleman. Makes sense of the human complexities of the Hundred Years' War.

Marina Warner *Joan of Arc* (Vintage). Stimulating examination of the symbolism and mythology of the Maid of Orléans.

Mark Twain *Joan of Arc* (Ignatius US). Little-known fictionalized biography of Joan by America's greatest nineteenth-century writer; quite extraordinarily hagiographic considering his normal scorn for religion.

Theodore Zeldin *France 1845–1945* (OUP). Five thematic volumes on French history.

Alfred Cobban *A History of Modern France* (Penguin, three vols). Very complete political history from Louis XIV to de Gaulle.

John Ardagh *France Today* (Penguin). Detailed journalistic survey of modern France, with an interesting and relevant section on "Brittany's revival".

Morvan Lebesque *Comment Peut-on Être Breton?* (Éditions du Seuil). A classic of Breton separatism, taking a psychological and sociological approach rather than a political one. He argues that awareness of one's cultural identity is vital for participation in the international community.

Kendalc'h *Breiz Hor Bro* (Éditions Breiz). Produced by a Breton youth association in French, this militant pamphlet covers history, language, literature and folklore, without ever losing an opportunity to take a swipe at the age-old oppressors of Brittany.

THE NORMANDY LANDINGS

Max Hastings *Overlord* (Papermac/Simon & Schuster). Detailed history of D-Day and its aftermath. Balanced and objective; Hastings distances himself thoroughly from propaganda and myth-making.

Donald Horne *The Great Museum: the Representation of History* (Pluto/Westview). A stimulating analysis of how history is presented to the tourist. Particularly interesting for its treatment of the D-Day landing sites.

John Keegan *Six Armies in Normandy* (Pimlico/Penguin). A fascinating military history, which combines the personal and the public to original effect. Each of the participating armies in the Battle of Normandy is followed during the most crucial phase of its involvement; some of the lesser details of the conflict are missed, but the overall sweep is compelling.

Anthony Kemp *D-Day; The Normandy Landings and the Liberation of Europe* (Thames & Hudson/Abrams). Full-colour pocketbook guide to the D-Day story, with a wealth of fascinating information. Published to mark the fiftieth anniversary of the invasion.

Studs Terkel *The Good War* (New Press, US). Excellent collection of interviews with participants of every rank and nation, including civilians, in World War II.

ART AND ARCHITECTURE

Henry Adams *Mont St-Michel and Chartres* (Princeton UP, US). Extraordinary, idiosyncratic account of the two medieval masterpieces, attempting through prayer, song and sheer imagination to understand the society and the people that created them. A tribute to Norman wisdom.

John Ardagh *Writers' France* (Hamish Hamilton, o/p). Entertaining anecdotes about most of the writers mentioned in this book, with colour photos.

Christina Björk *Linnea in Monet's Garden* (Raben & Sjogern/Farrar, Straus & Giroux). A Swedish book for children, which tells the story of a young girl achieving her unlikely lifetime's dream of visiting Monet's home in Giverny. A well-illustrated introduction to the Impressionists.

Sophie Bowness and others *The Dieppe Connection* (Herbert Press/New Amsterdam Books). Companion volume to a fascinating exhibition in Brighton, exploring Dieppe's

nineteenth-century role as a meeting place for artists. Colour reproductions of Dieppe scenes by Turner, Whistler, Gauguin and Renoir, among others.

Alfonso Castelao *Les Croix de Pierre en Bretagne* (available by post for 59F from the Comité Bretagne-Galice, BP66A, 35031 Rennes). A real collector's item; a pocket-sized collection of sketches of Breton calvaries made by the Gallego writer and illustrator during a visit in the 1920s. Includes an obsessive series of studies of Christ's ribcage. For more on Castelao, see the *Rough Guide to Spain*.

Claire Joyes *Monet at Giverny* (Matthews Millar Dunbar). Large-format account of Monet's years at Giverny, combining biography with good reproductions of the famous waterlilies.

BRITTANY IN FICTION

Honoré de Balzac *The Chouans* (Penguin). A hectic and crazily romantic story of the royalist *Chouan* rebellion shortly after the Revolution, set mainly in Fougères.

Alexandre Dumas *The Three Musketeers* (OUP/Penguin). Brilliant swashbuckling romance with peripheral Breton scenes on Belle-Île and elsewhere.

Victor Hugo *Ninety-Three* (Carroll & Graf, US). Rather more restrained, but still compelling, *chouan* novel.

Jack Kerouac *Satori in Paris* (Flamingo/Grove) . . . and in Brittany. Inconsequential anecdotes.

Pierre Loti *Pêcheur d'Islande* (Livre de Poche). Much-acclaimed novel (on which the film was based) which focuses on the whaling fleets that sailed from Paimpol. Not available in translation.

NORMANDY IN FICTION

Julian Barnes *Flaubert's Parrot* (Picador/Random House). A lightweight novel which rambles around the life of Flaubert, with much of the action taking place in Rouen and along the Seine.

Peter Benson *Odo's Hanging* (Sceptre, UK). Delicate but dramatic fictionalized account of the human stories behind the creation of the Bayeux Tapestry.

Gustave Flaubert *Bouvard and Pécuchet* (Viking, US). Two petits-bourgeois retire to a village between Caen and Falaise and attempt to practise every science of the time. Very funny or dead boring, according to taste.

Gustave Flaubert *Madame Bovary* (Wordsworth/Bantam Books). "The first modern novel", by the Rouennais writer. Drawn from a real-life story from Ry – see p.96 – it contains little that is specifically Norman, however.

Marcel Proust *In Remembrance of Things Past* (Penguin/Random House). Dense autobiographical trilogy evocative of almost everything except the places in Normandy and Brittany that his memories take him back to.

Julian Rathbone *The Last English King* (Abacus, UK). Lyrical and extremely readable fictionalized version of the Norman Conquest, as told by King Harold's one surviving bodyguard. The Normans themselves are depicted as heartless villains.

Jean-Paul Sartre *Nausea* (Norton, US). Sartre's relentlessly gloomy description of just how unpleasant it was to drag out one's existence in Le Havre (or "Bouville") in the 1930s.

BRETON MYTH AND FOLKTALES

Pierre-Jakez Hélias *The Horse of Pride* (Yale UP). A deeply reactionary and sentimental account of a Breton childhood in the Bigouden district earlier this century, which has sold over two million copies in France.

Professor Anatole Le Braz *La Legende du Mort* (Éditions Jeanne Laffitte). The definitive French text on Breton myths centred on Ankou and the prescience of death.

F. M. Luzel *Celtic Folk-Tales from Armorica* (Llanerch Enterprises, Lampeter, Wales). A collection of timeless Breton fairy stories, in English, and complete with commentaries.

W. Y. Evans Wentz *The Fairy Faith in Celtic Countries* (Citadel Press/Carol Publishing). Bizarre survey of similarities and differences in folk beliefs and religion between Celtic nations, with extensive details about Brittany.

BRETON MUSIC

Breton music, which draws richly in its themes, style and instrumentation on the common Celtic heritage of the Atlantic seaboard, has remained for centuries a unifying and inspiring part of the culture of the province. Despite the intermittent efforts of a reactionary clergy to stifle its popularity, it survived the union with France and the general suppression of indigenous art and language.

However, attempting to pin even an approximate date on the origins of traditional Breton music is a haphazard business. No literature survives in the native tongue from any period prior to the fifteenth century, although we do know that wandering Breton minstrels, known as *conteurs*, had enjoyed great popularity abroad long before this. Many of the songs they wrote were translated into French, being otherwise unintelligible to audiences outside Brittany, but unfortunately both versions have vanished with time. Only a number of Norse and English translations, probably dating from the twelfth century, escaped destruction. These works tell of romances won and lost, acrimonious relationships between fathers and their sons, and the testing of potential lovers.

The historical record of Breton music really begins with the publication of **Barzaz-Breizh**, a major collection of traditional songs and poems, in 1839. It was compiled by a nobleman, Hersart de la Villemarqué, from his discussions with fishermen, farmers and oyster-and-pancake women, and in view of the scarcity of other literature in the native language has come to be acknowledged as a treasure of Breton folk culture. Though serious doubts have frequently been raised as to its authenticity – many sceptics believe Villemarqué doctored those parts of the material he found distasteful, and even composed portions of it himself – it is unquestionably a work of linguistic brilliance and great beauty, and its appearance triggered the serious study of popular Breton culture.

INSTRUMENTATION

As for the traditional **instruments** on which the music is played, perhaps the most important is the **bombard** – an extremely old and shortened version of the oboe which, depending on the condition of your brain on any given day, sounds either like a hypnotic trance-inducing paean to the gods, or a sackful of weasels being yanked through a mincer. The **biniou**, the Breton bagpipe, dates in its current form from the nineteenth century, although several types are still in use, distinguished by the length of the chanter.

The harp, **telenn**, was also a native instrument long ago. Its influence had declined to a barely peripheral level until **Alan Stivell**'s appearance on the scene in the 1960s inspired a resurgence. His international hit *Renaissance of the Celtic Harp* introduced Breton as well as Irish, Welsh and Scottish, traditional music to a worldwide audience, and subsequently stimulated interest in less accessible material.

FESTOU-NOZ

The most rewarding setting in which to witness traditional Breton music is undoubtedly a **Fest-Noz** ("Night Feast") – a night of serious eating, drinking and dancing which can sometimes verge on the orgiastic. During the summer months, such events are very common, attracting hordes of revellers from kilometres around. Though they are often held in barns and halls in the more isolated parts of the region, discovering their whereabouts shouldn't present any problems, as an avalanche of posters advertising them appears absolutely everywhere. Once the evening gets underway, the dancers, often in their hundreds, whirl around in vast dizzy circles, hour after hour, sometimes frenzied and leaping, sometimes slow and graceful with their

DISCOGRAPHY

A few Breton discs – mainly of the rock-crossover variety – find their way into international sections of record stores abroad. For the real roots stuff, however, you'll need to go to Brittany itself, and in particular to **Ar Bed Keltiek**, a record store with branches in Rennes, Quimper and Brest (and a useful Web site at *www.arbedkeltiek.com/e0.htm*), or, best of all, to **Chant de l'Alouette** (4 rue des États, 35600 Redon, Brittany; ☎99.72.44.94), run by musician Jakez le Soueff – a living Breton encyclopedia on all matters musical, who will track down any recording that exists. These shops are also good for information about forthcoming gigs and events.

Compilations

Various *Celtic La Compile* (Le Cine Jaune, France). An eclectic eighteen-track compilation of Breton music of just about every style: sentimental balladeers, marching bands, loud rockers, quirky accordions and bagpipes – it's all here.

Various *Dans* (Iguane, France). Traditional dance tunes given new life with superb new arrangements and restrained electrification.

Various *Gwerziou et Chants de Haute-Voix* (Keltia Musique, France). Unaccompanied Breton songs by the region's top artists; the best example of the genre.

Artists/Bands

Dan Ar Braz *Septembre Bleu* and *Borders of Salt* (Keltia Musique, France). Recent releases from the ex-Stivell, Malicorne and Fairport guitarist.

Barzaz *An den Kozh dall* (Keltia Musique, France). A classic 1992 release of mellow, intense acoustic music, with some lovely flute-playing.

The Chieftains *Celtic Wedding* (RCA, UK). The Irish band turn their hand to traditional Breton dance tunes. A fresh, and highly accessible, perspective.

Gwerz *Live* (Gwerz, France). Electric and acoustic material from perhaps the best Breton musicians of the last decade, now pursuing individual projects.

Kornog *Première: Music from Brittany* (Green Linnet, US). An excellent live album from this adventurous Breton (and Scots) band, formed by ex-Gwerz guitarist Soïg Siberil.

Patrick Molard, Jack Molard and Jacques Pellen *Triptyque* (Gwerz, France). An innovative release of jazzy interpretations of Breton traditions.

Pennou Skoulm *Pennou Skoulm* (Slog, France). Traditional dance music from a group who regularly appear on the *fest-noz* circuit. Cassette only.

Les Soeurs Goadeg *Moueziou Brudez à Vreiz* (Keltia Musique, France). Alan Stivell produced this disc of old-time Breton singing in 1975. Goadeg, a trio of sisters, were into their seventies at the time, and the album showcases their highly traditional *gwerziou* (ballads) and *kan ha diskan* singing.

Alan Stivell *Journée à la Maison* (Rounder, US). A good compilation of Stivell's Breton Celtic harp folkrockery – more accessible than the recent esoteric output.

LIVE MUSIC VENUES AND FESTIVALS

Visitors to Brittany get the chance to enjoy Breton music at several annual **festivals**. The most famous of these is the pan-Celtic Lorient festival (see p.320); others include Quimper's Festival de Cornouaille (mid-late July), Rennes's Tombées de la Nuit (early July), and the intimate Printemps de Chateauneuf-du-Faou (Easter Sunday), when Breton singers and musicians take over a small town near Carhaix.

In addition, most Breton towns and villages, even in the middle of nowhere, have **pubs** that offer live music, often of the spontaneous boot-tappin' booze-swillin' variety. Among the best of these are:

Brest: *Café de la Plage*, *Café le Triskel* and the *Bar Écossais*.

Douarnenez: *Le Pourquois Pas* promotes larger bands in the mainstream mould.

Gouarec, near Gourin: *Bar de Daoulas*.

Gwern, near Pontivy: The *Korn Ar Pont* is a highly regarded venue which promotes mostly rock music and attracts punters from kilometres around for a weekend's bopping and bevvying. Own transport essential.

Île de Bréhat: *La Mary Morgan*.

Lorient: The *Galway Inn* – run by an Irishman – puts on touring bands of an acoustic nature, and has regular Irish folk sessions too.

Plouha: The *Ti Elise*, owned by a Welshman from Merthyr, is the local of Yann Skoarnek, a venerable old character who'll sing you songs about horse-thieving in Breton.

Plouhinec, near Lorient: *Café de la Barre*.

Quimper: The *Ceili Bar* specializes in folk music. Very small, very cramped and very drunk.

Quimperlé: The superb hosts at the *OK Pub* arrange occasional summer gigs of a folksy sort – and it serves Murphy's into the bargain.

Redon: Ask at *Le Chant de l'Allouette* music shop just off the main street for info. They sometimes promote events at a nearby farm.

Rennes: *Barantic* puts on semi-regular gigs in the folk-rock vein as well as less-organized affairs at the weekend. Friendly bar staff, relaxed atmosphere.

little fingers intertwined. It can be a bizarre and exhilarating spectacle – and a very affordable one too, with admission fees rarely amounting to more than a few pounds.

Traditionally, the most common form of *festou-noz* music is that of a **couple de sonneurs**, a pair of musicians playing *bombard* and *biniou*. They play the same melody line, with a drone from the *biniou*, and keep up a fast tempo – one player covering for the other when he or she pauses for breath. This is defiantly dance music, with no vocals and no titles for the tunes, although there are countless varieties of rhythms, often highly localized and generally known by the name of the dance. There is a purely vocal counterpart to this, known as **kan ha diskan**. Once again dance music, this is performed by a pair of unaccompanied "call-and-response" singers. In its basic form the two singers – the *kader* and *diskader* – alternate verses, joining each other at the end of each phrase. As dances were in the past unamplified, the parts were (and are) often doubled up, creating a startling rhythmic sound. The best singers might also give the dancers the odd break with a *gwerz*, or ballad, again sung unaccompanied. Over the past couple of decades, these traditional accompaniments have been supplanted more and more by four- or five-piece **bands**, who add fiddle and accordion, and sometimes electric bass and drums, to the *bombard*, and less often the *biniou*. The tunes have been updated with more of a rock sound, while the balladeers have given way to folk-style singer-songwriters, with guitar backing. Purists might regret the changes, but they have probably ensured the survival of *festou-noz*, with the enthusiastic participation of musicians and dancers of pretty much all ages. They have also nurtured successive generations of Breton musicians who move onto the festival and concert circuit.

BARDS AND BANDS

The godfather of the modern Breton music scene, **Alan Stivell**, started the ball rolling in the mid-1960s with one of the first folk-rock bands in Europe. He played harp, bagpipes and Irish flute, alongside **Dan Ar Braz** on electric and acoustic guitar, on a repertoire that drew on wider Celtic traditions. Both artists are still performing and recording, individually. Stivell's efforts are increasingly esoteric, while Ar Brasz,

who played with Fairport Convention in 1976, is a fixture at that band's Cropredy reunions, and produces mellow acoustic solo albums. The other key figure from Stivell's band was **Gabriel Yucoub,** who led **Malicorne,** the best-known Breton band of the 1970s and 1980s, through a series of experiments with folk-rock and electronic music, often using archaic instruments. Latterly, he has played as an acoustic duo, with his wife Marie Matheson.

Folk-rock, however, has been just one direction for Breton music in the 1990s. On the concert circuit, the biggest Breton names tend to be the singers, among whom the most famous is **Andrea Ar Gouilh**. Her recent output includes a return to Breton roots with a recording of old songs taken from the *Barzaz-Breizh*, though her concert repertoire is as likely to include a rendition of Bob Dylan's *Blowin' in the Wind*, which sounds rather marvellous sung in Breton.

Youenn Gwernig, a druid and singer, is another name to look out for at festivals. He lived for many years in New York and delivers his own ballads in a deep booming voice, sometimes accompanied by his two daughters, who sing Brooklyn English translations.

Equally weird is **Kristen Nikolas**, a wandering poet who makes his own idiosyncratic records, in Breton, in foreign studios, while the most compelling name has to be that of the duo **Bastard Hag e Vab** (Bastard and Son), who have been stalwarts of the live circuit for years.

Other notable Breton singers include **Bernez Tangi**, who for a while fronted a fine band called Storlok; **Yann Fanch Kemener**, well-known among Bretons but somewhat inaccessible to others with his unbelievably long traditional *gwerziou;* the singer-songwriter **Gilles Servat**, who sings in both Breton and French, mixing his own protest songs with renderings of Breton poems; and a trio of younger *fest-noz* performers, **Jean Do Robin, Claude An Intanv and Anni Ebrel**, who are slowly gaining recognition and who write some of their own material.

Fest-noz singers are sometimes accompanied by harpists, among whom the best contemporary players are **Ar Breudeur Keffelean**, virtuoso twin brothers who also have a **group, Triskell.** The more mystic 1960s side of the tradition is encapsulated by the suitably bearded and misty Merlin-type, **Myrzhin**, harper of the mysterious.

If you have a more casual interest in Breton sounds, though, you're likely to find some of the bands rather more rewarding. A fine *fest-noz* act to look out for is **Strobinell,** who have a lineup of *bombard*, *biniou*, violin, flute and guitar, and make occasional forays into a looser, jazzier groove. Another, always visually entertaining group is the mega-ensemble **Klik Ha Farz,** whose members wander around the hall as they play. They use a bass drum in conjunction with traditional instruments, rather in the manner of Gallego and Portuguese groups.

For the electric *fest-noz* sound, complete with full rock-drum kit, the best exponents are **Bleizi Ruz** (Red Wolves) and **Sonerien Du** (Black Musicians). Bleizi Ruz, who started out some 25 years ago playing traditional songs, play less at *fest-noz* these days and more on concert stages. Musically, the most adventurous band of the last decade has been **Gwerz**, who made several records of traditional songs and ethereal instrumentals, using *bombard*, *biniou*, uilleann pipes, and guitars. Their singer, **Erie Marchand**, has also collaborated with Indian musicians to interesting effect. Also

making crossovers from a Breton base are **Les Pires**, a zany instrumental quintet comprising violin, accordion, clarinet, double bass and piano, who play essentially middle European dance music. Strangely enough, while these musicians are looking out, some of the most interesting new "Breton" sounds have been emerging from bands of mixed nationality. **Étre-Vroadel** (EV), Brittany's most popular rock band, are a mix of Finnish and Breton musicians who use the *bombard* and cover traditional material. More folk-oriented, and purely acoustic, are **Kornog**, who feature Scots singer, mandolin and bouzouki player Jamie McMenemy, alongside three Breton instrumentalists, among them Soïg Siberil, who played guitar in Gwerz. They have rearranged Breton material quite radically for guitar, fiddle and bouzouki, slowing down the tempo to highlight solo playing and adding the occasional Scots ballad.

Raymond Travers
Another version of this piece appears in
The Rough Guide to World Music

BRETON LANGUAGE

Although Breton does remain a living language, in both Brittany and Normandy every encounter you are likely to have with the local people will be conducted in French. This is of course a lot more familiar than Breton, sharing numerous words with English, but it's not a particularly easy language to pick up.

The bare essentials of French, though, are not difficult, and make all the difference. Even just saying "Bonjour Madame/Monsieur" when you go into a shop, and then pointing, will usually get you a smile and helpful service. People working in hotels, restaurants, and tourist offices almost always speak some English, and tend to use it even if you're trying in French – be grateful, not insulted.

Breton is one of the Celtic family of languages, with an especially strong oral tradition ranging from medieval minstrels to modern singers and musicians. If you have a familiarity with Welsh or Gaelic, you should find yourself understanding, and being understood, in it.

Current estimates put the number of people who understand spoken Breton at between 400,000 and 800,000. However, only perhaps a third of those actually speak the language with any fluency or frequency, and you are only likely to find it spoken as a first, day-to-day language either among the old, or in the more remote parts of Finistère. For centuries it was discouraged by the State; its use was forbidden for official and legal purposes, and even Breton-speaking parents would seek to enhance their children's prospects by bringing them up to speak French. Although it is now taught in schools once again, learning Breton is not really a viable prospect for visitors who do not already have a grounding in another Celtic language. However, as you travel through the province it's interesting to note the roots of Breton place names, many of which have a simple meaning in the language. The box below lists some of the most common.

A GLOSSARY OF BRETON PLACE NAMES

Aber	estuary	*Lann*	heath
Avel	wind	*Lech*	flat stone
Bihan	little	*Men*	stone
Bran	hill	*Menz*	mountain
Braz	big	*Mario*	dead
Creach	height	*Menhir*	long stone
Cromlech	stone circle	*Meur*	big
Dol	table	*Mor*	sea
Du	black	*Nevez*	new
Gavre	goat	*Parc*	field
Goat	forest	*Penn*	end, head
Goaz	stream	*Plou*	parish
Guen	white	*Pors*	port, farmyard
Hen	old	*Roch*	stone
Heol	sun	*Ster*	river
Hir	long	*Stivel*	fountain, spring
Inis	island	*Trez*	sand, beach
Ker	town or house	*Trou*	valley
Koz	old	*Ty*	house
Lan	church	*Wrach*	witch

GLOSSARY OF FRENCH TERMS

ABBAYE abbey

ABER estuary

ACCUEIL reception

ARRÊT D'AUTOBUS bus stop

ASSEMBLÉE NATIONALE the French Parliament

AUBERGE DE JEUNESSE (AJ) youth hostel

AUTOBUS city bus

BANQUE bank

BASSIN harbour basin

BEAUX-ARTS Fine Arts school (and often museum)

BIBLIOTHÈQUE library

BISTRO small restaurant or bar

BOIS wood

BOULANGERIE baker

BRASSERIE café/restaurant

BUREAU DE CHANGE money exchange

CAR coach, bus

CAVE (wine) cellar

CHARCUTERIE delicatessen

CHASSE, CHASSE GARDÉE hunting grounds (beware)

CHÂTEAU castle or mansion

CIMETIÈRE cemetery

CITADELLE fortified city

CLOÎTRE cloister

CODENE French CND

CONSIGNE left luggage

COUVENT monastery

CRÊPERIE pancake restaurant

DÉGUSTATION tasting

DÉPARTEMENT county equivalent

DOLMEN megalithic stone "table"

DONJON castle keep

ÉGLISE church

ENCLOS group of church buildings

ENTRÉE entrance

FERMETURE closing time/period

FORÊT forest

FOUILLES archeological excavations

GARE ROUTIÈRE bus station

GARE SNCF train station

GÎTE D'ÉTAPE countryside hostel

GROTTE cave

HALLES covered market

HLM publicly subsidized housing

HÔPITAL hospital

HÔTEL hotel – but also used for an aristocratic town house or mansion

HÔTEL DE VILLE town hall

ÎLE island

JOURS FÉRIÉS public holidays

MAIRIE town hall

MAISON literally a house – can also be an office or base of an organization

MARCHÉ market

MENHIR single megalithic stone

OFFICE DU TOURISME (OT) tourist office

OUVERTURE opening time/period

PÂTISSERIE pastry shop

PHARMACIE chemist

PLACE square

PLAGE beach

PORTE gate

POSTE post office

PRESQU'ÎLE peninsula

PRIVÉ private

PTT post office

QUARTIER quarter of a town

RELAIS ROUTIER truck-stop restaurant

REZ-DE-CHAUSSÉE ground floor (UK), first floor (US)

RN route nationale (main road)

SALON DE THÉ tearoom

SI tourist office (see syndicat d'initiative below)

SNCF French railways

SYNDICAT D'INITIATIVE (SI) tourist office

TABAC bar or shop selling stamps, cigarettes, etc

TOUR tower

VAUBAN seventeenth-century military architect

ZONE BLEUE parking zone

ZONE PIÉTONNIÈRE pedestrian zone

A BRIEF GUIDE TO SPEAKING FRENCH

PRONUNCIATION

One easy rule to remember is that **consonants** at the ends of words are usually silent. *Pas plus tard* (not later) is thus pronounced "pa-plu-tarr". But when the following word begins with a vowel, you run the two together: *pas après* (not after) becomes "pazapre".

Vowels are the hardest sounds to get right. Roughly:

a	as in h**a**t		*i*	as in mach**i**ne
e	as in g**e**t		*o*	as in h**o**t
é	between g**e**t and g**a**te		*o, au*	as in **o**ver
è	between g**e**t and g**u**t		*ou*	as in f**oo**d
eu	like the **u** in h**u**rt		*u*	as in a pursed-lip version of **u**se

More awkward are the **combinations** *in/im, en/em, an/am, on/om, un/um* at the ends of words, or followed by consonants other than n or m. Again, roughly:

in/im	like the **an** in **an**xious	*on/om*	like the d**on** in D**on**caster said
an/am, en/em	like the d**on** in D**on**caster when		by someone with a heavy cold
	said with a nasal accent	*un/um*	like the **u** in **u**nderstand

Consonants are much as in English, except that: *ch* is always "sh", *h* is silent, *th* is the same as "t," *ll* is like the "y" in yes, *w* is "v," and *r* is growled (or rolled).

BASIC WORDS AND PHRASES

French nouns are divided into masculine and feminine. This causes difficulties with adjectives, whose endings have to change to suit the gender of the nouns they qualify. If you know some grammar, you will know what to do. If not, stick to the masculine form, which is the simplest – that's what we have done below.

today	*aujourd'hui*	that one	*celà*
yesterday	*hier*	open	*ouvert*
tomorrow	*demain*	closed	*fermé*
in the morning	*le matin*	big	*grand*
in the afternoon	*l'après-midi*	small	*petit*
in the evening	*le soir*	more	*plus*
now	*maintenant*	less	*moins*
later	*plus tard*	a little	*un peu*
at one o'clock	*à une heure*	a lot	*beaucoup*
at three o'clock	*à trois heures*	cheap	*bon marché*
at ten-thirty	*à dix heures et demie*	expensive	*cher*
at noon	*à midi*	good	*bon*
man	*un homme*	bad	*mauvais*
woman	*une femme*	hot	*chaud*
here	*ici*	cold	*froid*
there	*là*	with	*avec*
this one	*ceci*	without	*sans*

TALKING TO PEOPLE

When addressing people you should always use *Monsieur* for a man, *Madame* for a woman, *Mademoiselle* for a girl. Plain *bonjour* by itself is not enough. This isn't as formal as it seems, and it has its uses when you've forgotten someone's name or want to attract someone's attention.

Excuse me	*Pardon*	please	*s'il vous plaît*
Do you speak English?	*Vous parlez anglais?*	thank you	*merci*
		hello	*bonjour*
How do you say it in French?	*Comment ça se dit en Français?*	goodbye	*au revoir*
What's your name?	*Comment vous appelez-vous?*	good morning/ afternoon	*bonjour*
My name is . . .	*Je m'appelle . . .*	good evening	*bonsoir*
I'm English/	*Je suis anglais[e]/*	good night	*bonne nuit*
Irish/Scottish	*irlandais[e]/écossais[e]/*	How are you?	*Comment allez-vous? Ça va?*
Welsh/American/	*gallois[e]/américain[e]/*		
Australian/	*australien[ne]/*	Fine, thanks	*Très bien, merci*
Canadian/	*canadien[ne]/*	I don't know	*Je ne sais pas*
a New Zealander	*néo-zélandais[e]*	Let's go	*Allons-y*
yes	*oui*	See you tomorrow	*À demain*
no	*non*	See you soon	*À bientôt*
I understand	*Je comprends*	Sorry	*Pardon, Madame/ Je m'excuse*
I don't understand	*Je ne comprends pas*		
Can you speak slower?	*S'il vous plaît, parlez moins vite*	Leave me alone (aggressive)	*Fichez-moi la paix!*
OK/agreed	*d'accord*	Please help me	*Aidez-moi, s'il vous plaît*

FINDING THE WAY

bus	*autobus/bus/car*	on foot	*à pied*
bus station	*gare routière*	Where are you going?	*Vous allez où?*
bus stop	*arrêt d'autobus*		
car	*voiture*	I'm going to . . .	*Je vais à . . .*
train/taxi/ferry	*train/taxi/ferry*	I want to get off at . . .	*Je voudrais descendre à . . .*
boat	*bâteau*		
plane	*avion*	the road to . . .	*la route pour . . .*
train station	*gare*	near	*près/pas loin*
platform	*quai*	far	*loin*
What time does it leave?	*Il part à quelle heure?*	left	*à gauche*
		right	*à droite*
What time does it arrive?	*Il arrive à quelle heure?*	straight on	*tout droit*
		on the other side of	*à l'autre côté de*
a ticket to . . .	*un billet pour . . .*	on the corner of	*à l'angle de*
single ticket	*aller simple*	next to	*à côté de*
return ticket	*aller retour*	behind	*derrière*
validate your ticket	*compostez votre billet*	in front of	*devant*
valid for . . .	*valable pour . . .*	before	*avant*
ticket office	*vente de billets*	after	*après*
how many kilometres?	*combien de kilomètres?*	under	*sous*
		to cross	*traverser*
how many hours?	*combien d'heures?*	bridge	*pont*
hitch-hiking	*autostop*		

QUESTIONS AND REQUESTS

The simplest way of asking a question is to start with *s'il vous plaît* (please), then name the thing you want in an interrogative tone of voice. For example:

Where is there a bakery, please?	*S'il vous plaît, la boulangerie?*
Which way is it to Caen, please?	*S'il vous plaît, la route pour Caen?*

Similarly with **requests**:

We'd like a room for two	*S'il vous plaît, une chambre pour deux*
Can I have a kilo of oranges	*S'il vous plaît, un kilo d'oranges*

Question words

where?	*où?*	why?	*pourquoi?*
how?	*comment?*	at what time?	*à quelle heure?*
how many/how much?	*combien?*	what is/which is?	*quel est?*
when?	*quand?*		

ACCOMMODATION

a room for one/two people	*une chambre pour une/deux personnes*	do laundry	*faire la lessive*
a double bed	*un lit double*	sheets	*draps*
a room with a shower	*une chambre avec douche*	blankets	*couvertures*
		quiet	*calme*
a room with a bath	*une chambre avec salle de bain*	noisy	*bruyant*
		hot water	*eau chaude*
For one/two/three nights	*Pour une/deux/trois nuits*	cold water	*eau froide*
Can I see it?	*Je peux la voir?*	Is breakfast included?	*Est-ce que le petit déjeuner est compris?*
a room on the courtyard	*une chambre sur la cour*	I would like breakfast	*Je voudrais prendre le petit déjeuner*
a room over the street	*une chambre sur la rue*	I don't want breakfast	*Je ne veux pas le petit déjeuner*
first floor	*premier étage*	Can we camp here?	*On peut camper ici?*
second floor	*deuxième étage*	campsite	*un camping/ terrain de camping*
with a view	*avec vue*	tent	*une tente*
key	*clef*	tent space	*un emplacement*
to iron	*repasser*	youth hostel	*auberge de jeunesse*

NUMBERS

1	*un*	12	*douze*	30	*trente*	100	*cent*
2	*deux*	13	*treize*	40	*quarante*	101	*cent-et-un*
3	*trois*	14	*quatorze*	50	*cinquante*	200	*deux cents*
4	*quatre*	15	*quinze*	60	*soixante*	300	*trois cents*
5	*cinq*	16	*seize*	70	*soixante-dix*	500	*cinq cents*
6	*six*	17	*dix-sept*	75	*soixante-quinze*	1000	*mille*
7	*sept*	18	*dix-huit*	80	*quatre-vingts*	2000	*deux milles*
8	*huit*	19	*dix-neuf*	90	*quatre-vingt-dix*		
9	*neuf*	20	*vingt*			5000	*cinq milles*
10	*dix*	21	*vingt-et-un*	95	*quatre-vingt-quinze*	1,000,000	*un million*
11	*onze*	22	*vingt-deux*				

HEALTH MATTERS

doctor	*médecin*	stomachache	*mal à l'estomac*
I don't feel well	*Je ne me sens pas bien*	period	*règles*
medicines	*médicaments*	pain	*douleur*
prescription	*ordonnance*	it hurts	*ça fait mal*
I feel sick	*Je suis malade*	chemist	*pharmacie*
headache	*J'ai mal à la tête*	hospital	*hôpital*

OTHER NEEDS

bakery	*boulangerie*	bank	*banque*
food shop	*alimentation*	money	*argent*
supermarket	*supermarché*	toilets	*toilettes*
to eat	*manger*	police	*police*
to drink	*boire*	telephone	*téléphone*
camping gas	*camping gaz*	cinema	*cinéma*
tobacconist	*tabac*	theatre	*théâtre*
stamps	*timbres*	to reserve/book	*réserver*

DAYS AND DATES

January	*janvier*	Tuesday	*mardi*
February	*février*	Wednesday	*mercredi*
March	*mars*	Thursday	*jeudi*
April	*avril*	Friday	*vendredi*
May	*mai*	Saturday	*samedi*
June	*juin*	August 1	*le premier août*
July	*juillet*	September 6	*le six septembre*
August	*août*	July 14	*le quatorze juillet*
September	*septembre*	November 23	*le vingt-trois novembre*
October	*octobre*	1999	*dix-neuf-cent-quatre-*
November	*novembre*		*vingt-dix-neuf*
December	*décembre*	2000	*deux milles*
Sunday	*dimanche*		
Monday	*lundi*		

DICTIONARIES AND PHRASE BOOKS

Rough Guide French Phrase Book (Rough Guides). Mini dictionary-style phrase book with both English–French and French–English sections, along with cultural tips for tricky situations and a menu reader.

Mini French Dictionary (Harrap-Chambers). French–English and English–French, plus a brief grammar and pronunciation guide.

Breakthrough French (Pan; book and two cassettes). Excellent teach-yourself course.

French and English Slang Dictionary (Harrap); *Dictionary of Modern Colloquial French* (Routledge). Both volumes are a bit large to carry, but they are the key to all you ever wanted to understand.

À Vous La France; Franc Extra; Franc-Parler (BBC Publications; each has a book and two cassettes). BBC radio courses, which can take you right the way through from beginners' to fairly advanced language.

INDEX

Stay in touch with us!

ROUGH*NEWS* is Rough Guides' free newsletter. In three issues a year we give you news, travel issues, music reviews, readers' letters and the latest dispatches from authors on the road.

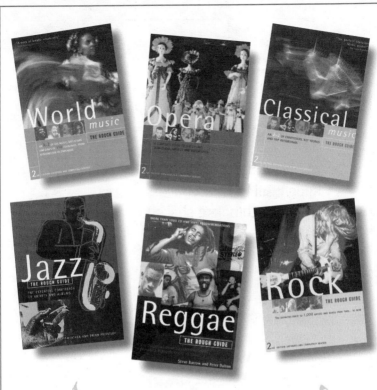